Library of America, a nonprofit organization,
champions our nation's cultural heritage
by publishing America's greatest writing in
authoritative new editions and providing resources
for readers to explore this rich, living legacy.

GARY SNYDER

Gary Snyder
ESSENTIAL PROSE

Jack Shoemaker, *editor*

With an Introduction by Kim Stanley Robinson

THE LIBRARY OF AMERICA

GARY SNYDER: ESSENTIAL PROSE
Volume compilation and backmatter copyright © 2025 by
Literary Classics of the United States, Inc., New York, N.Y.
All rights reserved.
No part of this book may be reproduced in any manner whatsoever without
the permission of the publisher, except in the case of brief
quotations embodied in critical articles and reviews.

Published in the United States by Library of America.
14 East 60th Street, New York, NY 10022, U.S.A.
Visit our website at www.loa.org.

*Earth House Hold: Technical Notes & Queries to Fellow Dharma
Revolutionaries* copyright © 1957, 1963, 1967, 1968, 1969 by Gary Snyder.
The Real Work: Interviews and Talks copyright © 1977 by Gary Snyder and
Peter Barry Chowka. All texts reprinted by arrangement with
New Directions Publishing Corporation.
He Who Hunted Birds in His Father's Village copyright © 1979, 2007
by Gary Snyder. *Passage Through India* copyright © 1972, 1983, 2014
by Gary Snyder. *A Place in Space* copyright © 1995 by Gary Snyder.
The Great Clod copyright © 2016 by Gary Snyder.
All texts reprinted by arrangement with Counterpoint Press.
"Gary Snyder, The Art of Poetry No. 74" interview by Eliot Weinberger
copyright © 1996 by *The Paris Review*. Published by arrangement with
The Wylie Agency LLC.

This paper exceeds the requirements of
ANSI/NISO Z39.48–1992 (Permanence of Paper).

Distributed to the trade in the United States
by Penguin Random House Inc.
and in Canada by Penguin Random House Canada Ltd.

Library of Congress Control Number: 2024943688
ISBN 978-1-59853-810-6

The authorized representative in the EU for product safety
and compliance is eucomply OÜ,
Pärnu mnt 139b-14, 11317 Tallinn, Estonia.
hello@eucompliancepartner.com

First Printing
The Library of America—391

Manufactured in the United States of America

Contents

Introduction by Kim Stanley Robinson xi

From EARTH HOUSE HOLD 1
   Lookout's Journal 3
   Japan First Time Around 24
   Spring Sesshin at Shokoku-ji 35
   Buddhism and the Coming Revolution 44
   Passage to More Than India 48
   Poetry and the Primitive 57
   Suwa-no-se Island and the Banyan Ashram 69

From HE WHO HUNTED BIRDS IN HIS FATHER'S
      VILLAGE 77
   The Myth 79
   Function of the Myth 84

From THE REAL WORK 101
   The Real Work 103
   The East West Interview 131
   Poetry, Community & Climax 176

From PASSAGE THROUGH INDIA 191
   The *Cambodge* 193
   Pondicherry 199
   Khajuraho 204
   Dharamshala 206
   Dalai Lama 209

From THE PRACTICE OF THE WILD 213
   The Etiquette of Freedom 215
   The Place, the Region, and the Commons 235
   Tawny Grammar 255
   Good, Wild, Sacred 281
   Blue Mountains Constantly Walking 297
   Ancient Forests of the Far West 313
   On the Path, Off the Trail 338
   Grace 348

From A PLACE IN SPACE 353
Smokey the Bear Sutra............................. 355
Four Changes, with a Postscript 360
"Energy Is Eternal Delight" 371
Unnatural Writing................................. 374
The Porous World 381
Coming into the Watershed........................ 386
Kitkitdizze: A Node in the Net 398

THE PARIS REVIEW INTERVIEW................... 407
The Art of Poetry LXXIV........................... 409

From BACK ON THE FIRE 439
The Ark of the Sierra............................... 441
Ecology, Literature and the New World Disorder 448
Writers and the War Against Nature 463
Entering the Fiftieth Millennium 473
Lifetimes with Fire 480
Regarding "Smokey the Bear Sutra" 491

From TAMALPAIS WALKING 497
Underfoot Earth Turns 499

THE GREAT CLOD 515
Summer in Hokkaido 517
All He Sees Is Blue: Basic Far East.................... 521
The Great Clod: China and Nature 526
"Wild" in China 539
Ink and Charcoal................................. 550
Walls Within Walls 556
Beyond Cathay: The Hill Tribes of China 577
Wolf-Hair Brush 582

UNCOLLECTED ESSAYS........................... 591
Walking the Great Ridge Ōmine on the Womb-
Diamond Trail................................. 593
Turn Off the Calculating Mind! 607

Chronology 611
Note on the Texts................................... 633
Notes 639
Index... 663

Introduction

KIM STANLEY ROBINSON

Gary Snyder's prose consists of various philosophical, historical, and personal essays that accompany his poetry, which was recently collected by Library of America in 2022 as *Collected Poems* and he has had a significant presence in American literature from 1955 to the present.

In supplementing his poetry with prose, he is not at all unusual among twentieth-century American poets. From Whitman's *Specimen Days* on, American poets have often published prose pieces that shed light on their poetry and their lives. Sometimes these prose pieces have been fiction, as in some fine work by William Carlos Williams and W. S. Merwin, or nonfiction, as seen in the literary and historical works of Adrienne Rich, Ezra Pound, T. S. Eliot, and Kenneth Rexroth, among many others. Occasionally the poet's prose focus has been on aesthetics and philosophy, as in Wallace Stevens, or on anthropology, as in the wonderful travel essays of William Bronk. Snyder's prose began in anthropology with his undergraduate thesis, later published as *He Who Hunted Birds in His Father's Village*, and it has retained many anthropological aspects throughout his career, as can be seen in the many essays that explore his lifelong interests in religion, indigenous peoples, East Asia, communal forms of living, and the deep history of humanity.

All these interests have always been syncretic in Snyder, forming part of a whole vision that connects his body of work, no matter the form or genre. Form matters to him, and there is a clear formal distinction between his poetry and his prose, but his poetry is often expository, while his prose is often poetic in its concision and musicality. The poem he made out of a prose paragraph of John Muir's (Part 8 of *Myths and Texts*), demonstrates Snyder's feeling that poetry and prose are not greatly differentiated and that both forms benefit from clarity and rhythm. His own easy shifts from one to the other show signs of his early immersion in the East Asian practice of alternations between the two, as in Han Shan, Wang Wei, Dōgen, and Bashō. As in their work, Snyder's prose and poetry take turns, as appropriate to the task at hand. His poetry darts, suggests, sings; the words on the page look like riprap, which is an interlocking style of stone trail building and the title of one of his first poetry chapbooks. In his prose he is more linear, the sentences like a trail's stone staircase, uplifting and sharply articulated. There isn't a single sentence in this book that doesn't convey its meaning immediately.

Many of the earliest essays in this volume were collected in *Earth House Hold*, a slim book that looked like the rest of Snyder's volumes from New Directions. That was good marketing, and effective; Gary Snyder looked like a brand, and in fact he was. These volumes taken together were major interventions in the creation of the American counterculture of that time, especially in its West Coast or Californian manifestation. They stood on brick-and-board bookshelves mixed with titles from Ram Dass and D. T. Suzuki, Alan Watts and Aldous Huxley and Carlos Castaneda, along with the many do-it-yourself manuals associated with *The Whole Earth Catalog*, such as *Small Is Beautiful* or *Appropriate Technology* or *The Integral Urban House*. As the 1960s morphed into the '70s, and the Beat and hippie youths had children and began to try to figure out ways of living that would continue to resist capitalist consumerism, and to enact the fiery values of their youth, Snyder's books were primary texts. Before he was the "poet laureate of deep ecology," he was the practical, down-to-earth Zen teacher of the counterculture, suggesting various ways of "becoming native to this place," as Wes Jackson's contribution to this literature has put it. What to do, how to live? This was a painfully gripping question in those years, when many options remained open—or so we hoped. On the one hand, as American society stalled and curdled in the late '70s, it would have been all too easy to declare the revolutionary '60s a fever dream, and fall back into the American nightmare. On the other hand, new ways still seemed possible.

Snyder's poems and essays had a certain calmness at their heart, a kind of William James pragmatism, and a deep-time long view anchored in the Paleolithic. Live well, Snyder suggested; it's not that hard, and it feels better. From "Why Tribe," an essay in *Earth House Hold*: "The man of wide international experience, much learning and leisure—luxurious product of our long and sophisticated history—may with good reason wish to live simply, with few tools and minimal clothes, close to nature."

Why? Because we evolved to live that way, so it fits us and feels right. Pay attention to where you live, and to the people you live with, your family, friends, and neighbors.

So, Snyder in those years was really bringing the news—and with tremendous gusto and wild humor. I well remember my own youth, trying to figure out how to be a California writer, and even just a young man in the world, with examples out of American literature that mostly struck me as appalling: alcoholism, casual sexism, cars and urban life, New York, Europe—it all seemed so ugly, so pointless. Even the supposed paleface/Red Indian split in American literature was unhelpful to me, although I knew immediately that I was in the Red Indian camp. But was it really true you could go from lumberjacking or deep-sea fishing straight to a quart of whisky, and therefore write a masterpiece? Maybe not! Gary had done some lumberjacking, in fact, but he also had a degree in anthropology and was a scholar. It was important to do both, as he showed by example. Here was a fellow Californian, articulating a way of life that was compelling in its logic and magnetic in its sense of joyous freedom. I saw him first at the University of California, San Diego, in 1972, and this was no ordinary reading; this was an event, a revelation. O California! Forget about the East Coast and its sad self-imposed literary dilemmas!

Of course California is a wild mélange, filled with the craziness of its Three Fates: the Gold Rush, Hollywood, and Silicon Valley. No one person can be credited or blamed for such a maelstrom as California has been since Europeans stumbled into it, intent on plunder and "the American dream." But now, after all that has happened this way and that, there at the heart of our Golden State stands Gary Snyder, saying with his life, Pay attention—stay calm—get real—have some fun—live life in the here and now.

In *Earth House Hold*, one of the crucial essays is "Buddhism and the Coming Revolution." Boldly syncretic, it is a call for action that yokes together Western Marxist attention to social justice with Buddhist regard for individual enlightenment. These two angles of approach were at that time seen as a kind of either/or; my left comrades, when we were using Marcuse's *One-Dimensional Man* to teach freshmen how to write, fell on my distributed copies of Snyder's essay with an eager hostility. Buddhism? Could I be serious? It was my pleasure to point out sentence after sentence in the essay rebutting their critiques. Snyder had anticipated objections and dealt with them in advance. It's a great example of rhetoric as persuasion, which by admitting historical complexity as the permanent social ecology that we must work in, can then make a cogent case for action in spite of all that. Because the prose of the essay is so informal, even seemingly casual, its critics among my comrades were taken aback when they were asked to read it closely. Eventually, grudgingly or not, they had to agree that the essay made an undeniable point: we are individuals in society. Both these aspects of reality matter, and both need action.

And there, near the end of the essay, stood the great Wobbly IWW slogan, "building the new society in the shell of the old." This phrase calls to Gary's own upbringing in the New Deal Pacific Northwest, and it remained in the '70s, and remains even now, the great slogan of Snyder's life, eternally suggestive of what we all can do to shape our projects.

Snyder's Buddhism has informed his life, it is fundamental to his thinking, and he is both a scholar and practitioner of it. His essays keep coming back to it, because he has never left it. He brought it back to California from years of study and practice in Japan, and subsequent strands of "California Zen" have been hugely influenced by him. Snyder's and California's are not precisely the same Zen; there is a more formal, rigorous, and dare I say pretentious Zen practice in California that Snyder does not manifest. I've seen the brutally espaliered gardens and rote chanting on display in certain Zen centers in California, and Snyder is not like that: he studies Buddhism, there is a zendo on his property, and his own practice seems to derive from the intently straightforward Japanese school of Zen that mainly insists on paying attention to the moment, giving regard to all sentient beings, and to chopping wood and carrying water. Life as devotion. His writing on the topic is always more scholarly and exploratory than exhortatory.

Earth House Hold changed people, in part because it included vivid journal accounts of Snyder's years at sea and as a fire lookout. The personal accounts mattered in making that book influential.

Then, one of his later volumes of prose made an equally powerful contribution to our culture, not just in California or the United States, but all over the world. Published in 1990, *The Practice of the Wild* is the mature and full expression of Snyder's ecological praxis. It contains his most sustained and elaborated thinking about humanity in relation to the biosphere. *Earth House Hold* was a youthful book, written in snatches and at speed, sometimes on request, and over many years; it was gathered into a book after its parts were written, and it's a tribute to Snyder's persistence of vision that it holds together as well as it does. *The Practice of the Wild* was written after two more decades of busy experience and study, all based at his home in the Sierra foothills. It is a coherent, intentional project, written while Snyder was teaching at the University of California at Davis, helping to lead the Nature and Culture major there, and associating with a large actor network of fellow thinkers and practitioners, as revealed in the book's acknowledgments. Its chapters systematically take on all the aspects of contemporary life that Snyder felt were most important. In these same years he was also assembling and writing new sections of his epic poem *Mountains and Rivers Without End*, teaching poetry and ecology, and engaging in an active routine of lectures and travel. These were the years when he came into his prime as a theorist and public intellectual, and this book remains his fullest statement as "poet laureate of deep ecology." Among many other significant features, it takes on the supposed dilemma of the concept of "wilderness" being defined as places without people in them; Snyder demolishes that false dichotomy (which is mostly a straw-man argument concocted by certain recent academics) by demonstrating repeatedly that humans and the rest of the Earth's living creatures can and should coexist on the same land, in a beautiful symbiotic community. This is also the book in which Snyder is exploring and enjoying the art of the essay as never before, weaving narrative and exposition, observation and aphorism, into a worldview expressed through storytelling.

This vibrant living philosophy was extended in Snyder's next volume, *A Place in Space*, which appeared in 1995. Here the personal account, equivalent to the journal extracts included in *Earth House Hold*, is called "Kitkitdizze: A Node in the Net," which gathers and relates some of the accumulated experiences that brought the mature wisdom of this period into being.

A perpetual interest of Snyder's that feels very contemporary now is precisely this: deep time. Now some call this topic Big History or Deep History, and the more confused we become in the Great Acceleration of everything that has been well documented since World War II, the more pressing this topic becomes: What made us what we are? What remains constant in us over the life of our species, in all this flux of rapid change?

Early on, perhaps starting with the final essay in *Earth House Hold*, "Suwa-no-se Island and the Banyan Ashram," Snyder's deep-time dating system makes its first appearance. The postscript of that essay reads, "Eighth Moon, 40067," with an explanatory note: "(reckoning roughly from the earliest cave paintings)." For many decades after that, Snyder marked his essays and letters with this dating, which tacked 37,000 years onto our "common era," to give us a better sense of our history as a species. This particular date came from the "creative explosion" idea that was hypothesized out of material traces by some archaeologists of the '60s, who thought they saw signs of some kind of shift in human consciousness around 40,000 years ago. It was a powerful gesture on Snyder's part to foreground that thought, and being the good anthropologist that he is, I'm sure he would agree that now the date should be adjusted even further back, since the evidence seems clear that human cognition and art arrived coterminously with the evolution of our species out of earlier hominids. We should therefore date our present as 100,000 years old, or even 200,000 years old, and then contemplate what that means. We have the same DNA as those ancestors, we are genetically the same as they were, inventing new technologies as always, then dealing with the consequences: this is important to know, as Snyder has always reminded us.

Two other elements in this volume are worth noting. The interviews included here were well chosen from the many Snyder has given through the years; these are particularly articulate and expressive. Then the essays included from the recent book *The Great Clod* reveal Snyder's lifelong interest in Chinese history. Here the scholarly poet is studying earlier scholar poets, in a way that brings to mind the proverb Snyder referenced in "Axe Handles": "When making an axe handle, the pattern is never far off."

"How we go on." This is the last line of that poem, and Snyder's enduring topic.

Poet, helpful neighbor, political leader, public intellectual, spiritual figure: Do all these activities make Snyder a shaman? With his respect for anthropological accuracy, I think he would say no. The term is historical and specific in what it designates. It's true that we find examples of Paleolithic shamanic figures all over the world; it is probably the first religion or devotional practice, invented in Africa and carried with us as we walked out into all the rest of the world. Some of these first cultures persist into modern times, even to the extent of having shamans, but for us, living in civilization now, I think it's better just to say that Gary Snyder is an exemplary Californian and world citizen.

As such, he has been influential. Of course, we still live in capitalism, and of course we are now engaged in a wicked political battle for the fate of the biosphere. We tremble on the brink of causing a mass extinction event that will cause a collapse of civilization, creating a war of all against all. It's very clear what we must continue to fight against. But what are we fighting for, what would we like to get to? There it isn't so clear. When you look back at California culture in the mid-twentieth century (Eurocentric, provincial, exploitative, alcoholic, racist, urban, factory-agricultural) and then compare that with California culture now (transpacific, worldly, progressive, multicultural, ecological), it's startling to note how closely these changes map to Snyder's interests and to the example he's provided. He has been a central node in a network of people, ideas, and practices that have changed California—and therefore the world. His essays have been crucial in that. And his poems are gold. Read them back and forth, and feel the world get bigger.

From
EARTH HOUSE HOLD
TECHNICAL NOTES & QUERIES
TO FELLOW DHARMA REVOLUTIONARIES

Lookout's Journal

A. CRATER MOUNTAIN

22 June 52 Marblemount Ranger Station
  Skagit District, Mt. Baker National Forest

Hitchhiked here, long valley of the Skagit. Old cars parked in the weeds, little houses in fields of bracken. A few cows, in stumpland.

Ate at the "parkway café" real lemon in the pie
  "—why don't you get a jukebox in here"
   "—the man said we weren't important enough"

---

28 June

   Blackie Burns:
"28 years ago you could find a good place to fish.
GREEDY & SELFISH   NO RESPECT FOR THE
  LAND
  tin cans, beer bottles, dirty dishes
  a shit within a foot of the bed
one sonuvabitch out of fifty
fishguts in the creek
the door left open for the bear.
If you're takin forestry fellas keep away
from the recreation side of it:
first couple months you see the women you say
  'there's a cute little number'
the next three months it's only another woman
after that you see one coming out of the can
   & wonder if she's just shit on the floor

ought to use pit toilets"

Granite creek Guard station   9 July

   the boulder in the creek never moves
           the water is always falling
    together!

A ramshackle little cabin built by Frank Beebe the miner.
Two days walk to here from roadhead.
         arts of the Japanese: moon-watching
                   insect-hearing
Reading the sutra of Hui Nêng.

   one does not need universities and libraries
   one need be alive to what is about

saying "I don't care"

---

11 July

cut fresh rhubarb by the bank
the creek is going down
last night caught a trout
today climbed to the summit of Crater Mountain and back
high and barren: flowers I don't recognize
ptarmigan and chicks, feigning the broken wing.

   Baxter: "Men are funny, once I loved a girl
   so bad it hurt, but I drove her away. She was
   throwing herself at me—and four months later she
   married another fellow."

A doe in the trail, unafraid.
A strange man walking south
A boy from Marblemount with buckteeth, learning machine shop.

LOOKOUT'S JOURNAL

—

Crater Mountain   Elevation: 8049 feet   23 July

Really wretched weather for three days now—wind, hail, sleet, snow; the FM transmitter is broken / rather the receiver is / what can be done?

 Even here, cold foggy rocky place, there's life—4 ptarmigan by the A-frame, cony by the trail to the snowbank.

 hit my head on the lamp,
 the shutters fall, the radio quits,
 the kerosene stove won't stop, the wood stove
 won't start, my fingers are too numb to write.

& this is mid-July. At least I have energy enough to read science-fiction. One has to go to bed fully clothed.

—

The stove burning wet wood—windows misted over giving the blank white light of shoji. Outside wind blows, no visibility. I'm filthy with no prospect of cleaning up. (Must learn yoga-system of Patanjali—)

—

Crater Shan   28 July

 Down for a new radio, to Ross Lake, and back up. Three days walking. Strange how unmoved this place leaves one; neither articulate nor worshipful; rather the pressing need to look within and adjust the mechanism of perception.

A dead sharp-shinned hawk, blown by the wind against the lookout. Fierce compact little bird with a square head.

—If one wished to write poetry of nature, where an audience? Must come from the very conflict of an attempt to articulate the vision poetry & nature in our time.

> (reject the human; but the tension of
> human events, brutal and tragic, against
> a nonhuman background? like Jeffers?)

———

Pair of eagles soaring over Devil's Creek canyon

———

31 July

This morning:
> floating face down in the water bucket
> a drowned mouse.

"Were it not for Kuan Chung, we should be wearing our hair unbound and our clothes buttoning on the left side"

> A man should stir himself with poetry
> Stand firm in ritual
> Complete himself in music
> > Lun Yü

———

Comparing the panoramic Lookout View photo dated 8 August 1935: with the present view. Same snowpatches; same shapes. Year after year; snow piling up and melting.

> "By God" quod he, "for pleynly, at a word
> Thy drasty ryming is not worth a tord."

———

LOOKOUT'S JOURNAL

Crater Shan   3 August

How pleasant to squat in the sun
Jockstrap & zoris

form—leaving things out at the right spot
ellipse, is emptiness
      these ice-scoured valleys
      swarming with plants
 "I am the Queen Bee!
      Follow Me!"

———

Or having a wife and baby,
 living close to the ocean, with skills for
 gathering food.

QUEBEC DELTA 04 BLACK

Higgins to Pugh (over)
 "the wind comes out of the east
 or northeast,
 the chimney smokes all over the room.
 the wind comes out of the west;
 the fire burns clean."

Higgins L.O. reads the news:
 "flying saucer with a revolving black band
 drouth in the south.
Are other worlds watching us?"
The rock alive, not barren.
 flowers lichen *pinus albicaulis* chipmunks
mice even grass.

—first I turn on the radio
—then make tea & eat breakfast
—study Chinese until eleven

—make lunch, go chop snow to melt for water,

read Chaucer in the early afternoon.
   "Is this real
   Is this real
   This life I am living?"
            —Tlingit or Haida song

"Hidden Lake to Sourdough"
—"This is Sourdough"
—"Whatcha doing over there?"
—"Readin some old magazines
         they had over here."

6 August

Clouds above and below, but I can see Kulshan, Mt. Terror, Shuksan; they blow over the ridge between here and Three-Fingered Jack, fill up the valleys. The Buckner Boston Peak ridge is clear.

What happens all winter; the wind driving snow; clouds—wind, and mountains—repeating

   this is what always happens here,

and the photograph of a young female torso hung in the lookout window, in the foreground. Natural against natural, beauty.

         two butterflies
      a chilly clump of mountain
            flowers.

zazen   non-life.   An art: mountain-watching.

      leaning in the doorway whistling
         a chipmunk popped out
            listening

9 August

Sourdough: Jack, do you know if a fly is an electrical conductor? (over)
Desolation: A fly? Are you still trying to electrocute flies? (over)
Sourdough: Yeah   I can make em twitch a little. I got five number six batteries on it (over)
Desolation: I don't know, Shubert, keep trying. Desolation clear.

---

10 August

First wrote a haiku and painted a haiga for it; then repaired the Om Mani Padme Hum prayer flag, then constructed a stone platform, then shaved down a shake and painted a zenga on it, then studied the lesson.

>   a butterfly
>   scared up from its flower
>   caught by the wind and swept over the cliffs
>   SCREE

Vaux Swifts: in great numbers, flying before the storm, arcing so close that the sharp wing-whistle is heard.

>   "The śrāvaka
> disciplined in Tao, enlightened, but on the wrong path."
> summer,
>   on the west slopes creek beds are brushy
>   north-faces of ridges, steep and
>   covered late with snow
>
>   slides and old burns on dry hills.

(In San Francisco: I live on the Montgomery Street drainage—
at the top of a long scree slope just below a cliff.)

―

sitting in the sun in the doorway
picking my teeth with a broomstraw
listening to the buzz of the flies.

―

12 August

   A visit all day, to the sheep camp, across the glacier and into Devil's park. A tent under a clump of Alpine fir; horses, sheep in the meadow.

   take up solitary occupations.

Horses stand patiently, rump to the wind.
   —gave me one of his last two cigars.

Designs, under the shut lids, glowing in sun

  (experience! that drug.)
Then the poor lonely lookouts, radioing forth and back.

After a long day's travel, reached the ridge,
followed a deer trail down
   to five small lakes.
in this yuga, the moral imperative is to COMMUNICATE.
Making tea.

fewer the artifacts, less the words,
   slowly the life of it
a knack for nonattachment.

Sourdough radioing to the smoke-chaser crew

"you're practically there
 you gotta go up the cliff
 you gotta cross the rock slide
 look for a big blaze on a big tree"
       [two climbers killed by lightning
        on Mt. Stuart]
"are you on the timber stand
 or are you on the side of the cliff?
 Say, Bluebell, where are you?
 A patch of salmonberry and tag-alder to the right"
       —must take a look.

Cratershan   15 August

When the mind is exhausted of images, it invents its own.

    orange juice is what she asked for
        bright chrome restaurant, 2 A.M.
    the rest of us drinking coffee
    but the man brought orange pop.   haw!

late at night, the eyes tired, the teapot empty, the tobacco damp.

Almost had it last night: *no identity.* One thinks, "I emerged from some general, nondifferentiated thing, I return to it." One has in reality never left it; there is no return.
        my language fades.   Images of erosion.

"That which includes all change never changes; without change time is meaningless;   without time, space is destroyed.   Thus we arrive at the void."

"If a Bodhisattva retains the thought of an ego, a person, a being, or a soul, he is no more a Bodhisattva."

You be Bosatsu,
I'll be the taxi-driver
Driving you home.

The curious multistratified metamorphic rock. Blue and white, clouds reaching out. To survive a winter here learn to browse and live in holes in the rocks under snow.
Sabi: One does not have a great deal to give. That which one does give has been polished and perfected into a spontaneous emptiness; sterility made creative, it has no pretensions, and encompasses everything.

              Zen view, OK?

―

21 August

 Oiling and stowing the tools. (artifact / tools: now there's a topic.)
When a storm blows in, covering the south wall with rain and blotting out the mountains. Ridges look new in every light. Still discovering new conformations—every cony has an ancestry but the rocks were just here.
 Structure in the lithosphere / cycles of change in rock / only the smallest percentage sanded and powdered and mixed with life-derived elements.

Is chemical reaction a type of perception??—Running through all things motion and reacting, object against object / there is more than enough time for all things to happen: swallowing its own tail.

―

Diablo Dam 24 August

 Back down off Crater in a snowstorm, after closing up the lookout. With Baxter from Granite Creek all the way to the dam for more supplies. Clouds on the rocks; rain falls and falls. Tomorrow we shall fill the packs with food and return to Granite Creek.

―

In San Francisco: September 13.

Boys on bicycles in the asphalt playground wheeling and circling aimlessly like playful gulls or swallows. Smell of a fresh-parked car.

B. SOURDOUGH

Marblemount Ranger Station   27 June 53

The antique car managed it to Marblemount last week, and then to Koma Kulshan for a week of gnats, rain, & noise.
 The Philosophy of the Forest Service: Optimistic view of nature—democratic, utilitarian. "Nature is rational." Equals, treat it right and it will make a billion board feet a year. Paradox suppressed. What wd an Aristocratic F.S. be like? Man traps?

Forest equals crop / Scenery equals recreation / Public equals money. :: The shopkeeper's view of nature.

> Hail Mr. Pulaski, after whom the Pulaski
> Tool is named.

—the iron stove, the windows, and the trees. "It is, and is not, I am sane enough." Get so you don't have to think about what you're doing because you *know* what you're doing.
J. Francis: Should I marry? It would mean a house; and the next thirty years teaching school."   LOOKOUT!
 Old McGuire and the fire of 1926: 40,000 acres on the upper Skagit, a three-mile swathe.   Going to scrub my clothes & go down to Sedro-Woolley now with Jack.

―

28 June

A day off—went to Bellingham and out to Gooseberry Bay, the Lummi reservation. Past a shed with three long cedar canoes in it. Finally to where the Lummi Island ferry stops, and this was about the end of the road, but we could drive a little farther on, and it was there we went through the Kitchen Midden. Through it, because the road cut right through shells and oysters and all. While looking at this a lady in a house shouted out to us; then came closer, & said if you're interested in the kitchen midden "as such" come out in back and "look where we had it bulldozed." And I said how do you like living on somebody's old kitchen heap, and she said it made her feel kind of funny sometimes. Then I said, well it's got about 3000 years in it vertical, but that might be dead wrong. It was 10 feet high, 45 feet wide, and 325 feet long, with one cedar stump on it about 110 years old, to show when (at least) it was finished with. Full of oyster, butter clam, cockle, mussel, snail and assorted shells.

We went back by the same road and at the outskirts of Bellingham Jack pointed out a ratty-looking place called Coconut Grove where he said he had spent time drinking with a "rough crowd." They drank beer out of steins and called the place the Cat's Eye instead.

Outskirts of Bellingham, something of clear sky to the west over the waters of Puget Sound, the San Juan islands; and very black clouds up the Skagit, toward the vast mountain wilderness of the North Cascades. We turned off 99 to go into that black, wet hole, and it did start raining pretty quick after we went up that road. Coffee in Sedro-Woolley, a sign "No Drinks Served to Indians" and there are many Indians, being strawberry-picking season, and Loggerodeo is next week. Marblemount Ranger Station about 8.30 & in the bunkhouse found a magazine with an article about an eighteen-year-old girl who could dance and paint and compose and sew and was good looking, too, with lots of pictures.

―

Story: a Tarheel at Darrington had this nice dog. One day he was out dynamiting fish—threw a stick of powder into the

water, all lit and ready to go. The dog jumped in, retrieved it, and ran back with it in his mouth. The logger took off up a tree shouting
—Git back, Dog! Then it blasted. Tarheel still limps.
—Blackie.

—And then there was this young married couple, who stay locked in their room four weeks—when friends finally break in all they find is two assholes, jumping back and forth through each other.

—

Ruby Creek Guard Station   30 June

The foamy wake behind the boat *does* look like the water of Hokusai. Water in motion is precise and sharp, clearly formed, holding specific postures for infinitely small frozen moments.
Four mules: Tex, Barney Oldfield, Myrtle, Bluejay. Four horses: Willy, Skeezix, Blaze, Mabel.

—

Sourdough Mountain Lookout Elevation: 5977 feet 17 July 53

"GREENEST Goddam kid I EVER saw. Told him he couldn't boil beans at that altitude, he'd have to fry them. When I left I said, now, be careful, this is something you gotta watch out about, don't flog your dummy too much! And he says real serious, Oh no, I won't. Hawww—"

"And then he was trying to fry an egg and he missed the pan and he missed the stove and landed the egg on both feet, he didn't know whether to run, shit, or go blind!"

Just managed to get through to Phil Whalen, on the radio, him up on Sauk Lookout now.

Rode up here on Willy the Paint, a pleasant white-eyed little horse that took great caution on rock and snow. Had to lead him across the whitewater at Sourdough Creek. Horses look noble from the side, but they sure are silly creatures when seen from the front. Mules just naturally silly—Whenever we stopped, Myrtle would commence kicking Bluejay & Bluejay would kick Barney, all with great WHACKS on the forkies, but Tex behaved, being neither kicked nor kicking. Shoeing Willy required the twitch, anvil, nails, three of us, and great sweating groaning and swearing. Blackie whacks him with a hammer while Roy twists his nose to make him be good.

This is the place to observe clouds and the gradual dissolution of snow. Chipmunk got himself locked in here and when I tried to shoo him out he'd just duck in a corner. Finally when I was sorting screws he came out and climbed up on the waterbucket looking I guess for a drink—hung on, face down, with his hind legs only to the edge of the pail, inside, for a long time, and finally fell in. Helped him out, splashing about—nobody been there he'd have drunned.

Keep looking across to Crater Mountain and get the funny feeling I am up there looking out, right now, "because there are no calendars in the mountains" —shifting of light & cloud, perfection of chaos, magnificent *jiji mu-ge* / interlacing interaction.

Sourdough Mountain Lookout   19 July

Up at a quarter to six, wind still blowing the mist through the trees and over the snow. Rins'd my face in the waterhole at the edge of the snowfield—ringed with white rock and around that, heather. Put up the SX aerial on a long pole made by some lookout of years past, sticks & limbs & trunks all wired and tied together. Made a shelf for papers out of half an old orange crate, and turned the radio receiver off. Walked down the ridge, over the snow that follows so evenly the very crest—snow on the north slope, meadows and trees on the south. Small ponds, lying in meadows just off the big snowfields, snags, clumps of mountain hemlock, Alpine fir, a small amount of Alaska cedar.

Got back, built a fire and took the weather. About six, two bucks came, one three-point, one four-point, very warily, to nibble at huckleberries and oats and to eat the scraps of mouldy bacon I threw out. Shaggy and slender, right in the stiff wind blowing mist over the edge of the ridge, or out onto the snowfield, standing out clear and dark against the white. Clouds keep shifting—totally closed in; a moment later across to Pyramid Peak or up Thunder Creek it's clear. But the wind stays.

Now I've eaten dinner and stuffed the stove with twisted pitchy Alpine fir limbs. Clumps of trees fading into a darker and darker gray. White quartz veins on the rocks out the south window look like a sprinkling of snow. Cones on the top boughs of the Alpine fir at the foot of the rocks a DARK PURPLE, stand perfectly erect, aromatic clusters of LINGAMS fleshy and hard.

Lookout free talk time on the radio band: Sauk called Koma Kulshan, Church called Sauk, Higgins is talking to Miner's Ridge. Time to light the lamp.

—

23 July

Days mostly cloudy—clouds breaking up to let peaks through once in a while. Logan, Buckner, Boston, Sahale, Snowpeak, Pyramid, Névé, Despair, Terror, Fury, Challenger. And the more distant Redoubt and Glacier Peak. As well as Hozomeen and Three-Fingered Jack. Right now looking down on the Skagit—pink clouds—pale rose-water pink, with soft shadings of gray and lavender, other combinations of pastel reds and blues, hanging over Pyramid Peak.

Fretting with the Huang Po doctrine of Universal Mind. What a thorny one.

—

25 July

Last night: thunderstorm. A soft piling of cumulus over the Little Beaver in late afternoon—a gradual thickening and darkening. A brief shower of hail that passed over & went up Thunder Creek valley: long gray shreds of it slowly falling and bent in the wind—while directly above Ruby Creek sunlight is streaming through. Velvety navy blue over Hozomeen, with the sun going down behind Mt. Terror and brilliant reds and pinks on the under-clouds, another red streak behind black Hozomeen framed in dark clouds. Lightning moving from Hozomeen slowly west into red clouds turning gray, then black; rising wind. Sheet lightning pacing over Little Beaver, fork lightning striking Beaver Pass.

This morning a sudden heavy shower of rain and a thick fog. A buck scared: ran off with stiff springy jumps down the snowfield. Throwing sprays of snow with every leap: head held stiffly high.

—

9 August

Sourdough radio relay to Burns:

to: Ray Patterson, District Assistant, Early Winters
      Ranger Station.
from: Jud Longmoor.
   "Kit, Ted and Lucky went out over Deception Pass
   probably headed for airport. Belled but not
   hobbled. Horse took out in night, August 3, above
   Fish Camp. The Shull Creek trail is not passable now.
   Mt. Baker string will pack us to Skypilot Pass
   Thursday August 5. Have Ken Thompson meet us
   there with pack string and saddle horse for Loring. We
   will have pack gear and riding saddle."

Lightning storm again: first in twilight the long jagged ones back of Terror & Fury, later moving down Thunder Creek, and then two fires: right after the strikes, red blooms in the night. Clouds drifting in & obscuring them.

—

Discipline of self-restraint is an easy one; being clear-cut, negative, and usually based on some accepted cultural values.

Discipline of following desires, *always* doing what you want to do, is hardest. It presupposes self-knowledge of motives, a careful balance of free action and sense of where the cultural taboos lay—knowing whether a particular "desire" is instinctive, cultural, personal, a product of thought, contemplation, or the unconscious. Blake: if the doors of perception were cleansed, everything would appear to man as it is, infinite. For man has closed himself up, 'til all he sees is through narrow chinks of his caverns. Ah.

>   the frustrate bumblebee turns over
>   clambers the flower's center upside down
>   furious hidden buzzing
>   near the cold sweet stem.

In a culture where the aesthetic experience is denied and atrophied, genuine religious ecstasy rare, intellectual pleasure scorned—it is only natural that sex should become the only personal epiphany of most people & the culture's interest in romantic love take on staggering size.

The usefulness of hair on the legs: mosquitoes and deerflies have to agitate it in drawing nigh the skin—by that time warned—Death to Bugs.

(an empty water glass is no less empty than a universe full of nothing)—the desk is under the pencil.

Sourdough Mountain Lookout   12 August

3:55 P.M.	Desolation calls in his weather.
4:00	Sourdough starts calling Marblemount.
4:00	Sam Barker asks for the air: "Dolly, call the doctor at Concrete and have him go up to Rockport. There's a man got hurt up here."
4:01	Marblemount: "Up where?"
4:01	Barker: "Up here on Sky Creek. A fellow from Stoddard's logging outfit."

4:01	Marblemount: "Okay Sam. Marblemount clear."
4:10	Sourdough calls his weather in to Marblemount.
4:11	Barker: "Dolly, did you make that call through?"
4:11	Marblemount: "You mean for the doctor?"
4:12	Barker: "Yeah. Well the man's dead."
4:12	Marblemount: "Who was he?"
4:12	Barker: "I don't know, the one they call the Preacher."
4:13	Somebody I couldn't hear, calling Marblemount.
4:13	Marblemount: "The Sky Creek trail. I don't know. Somebody they call the Preacher." Marblemount clear.

―

14 August

11:30 Hidden Lake spots a smoke; he hardly gets an azimuth in to Marblemount but I've got it too & send my reading in. Then all the other Lookouts in the North Cascades catch it—a big column in the Baker River District, between Noisy and Hidden Creeks.

So Phil on Sauk Mountain is busy calling Darrington and Marblemount for the suppression crews, and then the patrol plane comes to look at it and says it's about six acres of alpine timber. And the trucks are off, and Willey the cook has to go too, and the plane flies over to drop supplies at a fire-fighter's camp.

―

Don't be a mountaineer, be a mountain.
    And shrug off a few with avalanches.

Sourdough Mountain at the hub of six valleys: Skagit, Thunder, Ruby, Upper Skagit, Pierce Creek, Stetattle creek.

―

20 August

> Skirt blown against her hips, thighs, knees
> > hair over her ears
> > climbing the steep hill in high-heeled shoes

(the Deer come for salt, not affection)

—Government Confucianism, as in the *Hsiao-ching* / Filial Piety—a devilish sort of liberalism. Allowing you should give enough justice and food to prevent a revolution, yet surely keeping the people under the thumb. "If you keep the taxes just low enough, the people will not revolt, and you'll get rich." Movements against this psychology—the Legalistic rule of Ch'in; Wang An-shih perhaps?
This is Chinese; plus Blake's collected, *Walden* and sumi painting, pass the time.

———

Nature a vast set of conventions, totally arbitrary, patterns and stresses that come into being each instant; could disappear totally anytime; and continues only as a form of play: the cosmic / comic   delight.
"For in this period the Poet's work is done and all the great events of time start forth and are conceived in such a period, within a moment, a Pulsation of the artery."
—True insight a love-making hovering between the void & the immense worlds of creation. To symbolically represent Prajñā as female is right. The Prajñā girl statue from Java.

———

22 August

Old Roy Raymond hike up and see me. About noon I'm chopping wood. We spend the afternoon playing horseshoes with mule-shoes; this morning playing poker.

"My Missus died a few years ago so I sold the house
and the furniture 'til I got it down now to where I can get
everything into a footlocker. My friends'd ask me
What you sell that for, & hell, what use did I have for it?
I'll never marry again."

So he spends his time in the mountains—construction jobs, forestry, mining. Winters in Aberdeen.

Kim on Desolation radios over (evenings) to read bits of picturesque speech and patter from antique *Reader's Digests* he's found chez Lookout.

—

Ross Lake Guard Station   31 August

Friday morning with snow coming in and storms all across the North Cascades, straight down from Canada, Blackie radios to come down. Work all morning with inventory; put the shutters down & had to pack an enormous load of crap off the mountain. About 85 pounds.

Forest Service float on Ross Lake: all on a big raft; corrugated walls and roofing. Porch with woodpile. A floating dock with crosscuts, falling saws, spikes, wood, in't. At one end the green landing barge moored alongside. The main raft, with a boat-size wood door; inside a tangle of tools, beds, groceries. A vast Diesel marine engine-block in the middle of the deck with a chainsaw beside it. Kim on a cot next to that. Shelves on the unpainted wall with rice, coffee, pancake syrup. Cords, vises, wires on the workbench. A screen cooler full of bacon and ham. And this enters, under the same roof, into another dockroom in which the patrol boat floats, full of green light from the water. Around the edge bales of hay and drums of Diesel. Moored alongside outside, the horse raft. Covered with straw and manure. A sunny windy day, lapping the logs.

—

Trail crew work up Big Beaver Creek   4 September

Crosscutting a very large down cedar across the trail and then wedging, Kim gets below Andy bellers out

"Get your goddamn ass out of there you fuckin squarehead you wanna get killed?"

We make an extra big pot of chocolate pudding at the shelter that night, make Kim feel better.

Surge Milkers: "This man had a good little brown heifer that gave lots of milk, and one morning he put the milker on her and went back inside and fell asleep and slept an hour. And that little heifer had mastitis in two days."

———

Hitching south   ca. 21 Sept

> Down from Skykomish, evening light,
> back of a convertible wind whipping the blanket
> clear sky darkening, the road winding along the river
> willow and alder on the bank, a flat stretch of
> green field; fir-covered hills beyond, dark
> new barns and old barns—silvery shake barns—
> the new barns with tall round roofs.

———

In Berkeley: 1 October 53

> "I am here to handle some of the preliminary
>   arrangements for the Apocalypse.
> Sand in pockets, sand in hair,
> Cigarettes that fell in seawater
> Set out to dry in the sun.
> Swimming in out of the way places
> In very cold water, creek or surf
> Is a great pleasure."

Under the Canary Island Pine
zazen and eating lunch.   We are all immortals
        & the ground is damp.

Japan First Time Around

"Arita Maru"   at sea   7: V: 56

Red ooze of the North Pacific—only sharks' teeth and the earbones of whales.   An endless mist of skeletons, settling to the ocean floor.
Marine limestone in the Himalaya at 20,000 feet
breadfruit, laurel, cinnamon and figtree grew in Greenland—cretaceous. "Length of fetch" the distance a batch of waves has run without obstruction.
salts—diatoms—copepods—herring—fishermen—us. eating.

―

A sudden picture of Warm Springs Camp A loggers making flower arrangements in the yellow-pine tokonomas of their plank camp cabins. I'd work hard all day for that.
    any single thing or complex of things *literally* as great as the whole.
  wild lilac and lizards / blowing seafog down the hill.
A square is: because the world is round.

―

At sea   16: V: 56

Moon in the first quarter sinking a path of light on the sea; Jupiter by the sickle of Leo in the west, Cygnus and Lyra in the east, Delphinus just over the haze of the night horizon. The tail of Scorpio in the water.
    POETRY is to give access to persons— cutting away the fear and reserve and camping of social life: thus for Chinese poetry. Nature poetry too: "this is what I've

seen." Playing with the tools—language, myth, symbolism, intellect—fair enough but childish to abuse.
 just where am I in this food-chain?

Red-tailed Tropic birds, and fields of plankton. Lawrence, in *Aaron's Rod:* "The American races—and the South Sea islanders—the Marquesans, the Maori blood. That was the true blood. It wasn't frightened."

". . . Why don't you be more like the Japanese you talk about? Quiet, aloof little devils. They don't bother about being loved. They keep themselves taut in their own selves—there, at the bottom of the spine, the devil's own power they've got there."

 Lawrence and his fantastic, accurate, lopsided intuitions. The American Indians and Polynesians developed great cultures and almost deliberately kept their populations down. and again,
 "Love is a process of the incomprehensible human soul: love also incomprehensible but still only a process. The process should work to a completion, not to some horror of intensification and extremity wherein the soul and body ultimately perish. The completion of the process of love is the arrival at a state of simple, pure self-possession, for man and woman. Only that."

At sea   21: V   and into Kobe

 Coasting along Wakayama: the sharp cut steep green haze hills, boats about, high-prowed dip slop in wave wash and new white-bellied birds following wave-lick over, then, morning passing—sitting under a lifeboat watching land slip by. Beyond Awaji Isle—jokes about Genji. Into the long smoggy Osaka Bay leading finally up to Kobe—ship upon ship—rusty Korean tiny freighters—and to the pier.
 A truckload of Seals on the road by Customs snaking their small heads about. And train, and thousands of crowded tile-roof houses along the track, patches of tended ground; O man—poorness and small houses.

Kyoto   23: V: 56

. . . some Americans here make reference to short hours of sleep and simple food—good Xrist you'd think Zen was just a roundabout way for the rich to live like the workingman—there are friends in America who are humble about their interest in the Dharma and ashamed of their profligacy while living on salvaged vegetables and broken rice—sleep six hours a night so as to study books and think, and so to work, to keep the wife and kids: what foppery is this—and it turns out you got to spend $30 for a special meditation cushion. The center in this world is quietly moving to San Francisco where it's most alive—these Japanese folks may be left behind and they won't (in the words of Fêng Kuan) recognize it when they see it.

25: V

Today up Hiei-zan. Jodo-in, young bonze named Somon; the tomb of Dengyo Daishi. Vast cool wooden temple in the mountain shade—it smells good. A monk in white came with lunch on trays: pickles and rice and peas. Then W. and I went to the main room and picture of Dengyo Daishi, and a small shrine room to Kwannon that looked like a peyote dream.
(the only superstitions that are really dangerous to peasant Buddhist types are the superstitions of nationalism and the state)

Then: in fog-rain and frog-croak climbed up and along by a Cryptomeria sawmill (they fell trees same method we do judging by the butt cuts) to another temple; finally below that an even larger temple recently repainted—went in and lit candles. Uguisu don't sing, they shout.

7: VI

. . . one begins to see the connecting truths hidden in Zen, Avatamsaka and Tantra. The giving of a love relationship is a Bodhisattva relaxation of personal fearful defenses and self-interest strivings—which communicates unverbal to the other and leaves *them* do the same. "Enlightenment" is this interior ease and freedom carried not only to persons but to all the universe, such-such-and void—which is in essence and always, freely changing and interacting. The emptiness of "both self and things"—only a Bodhisattva has no Buddha-nature. (*Lankavatara-sōtra.*)

So, Zen being founded on Avatamsaka, and the net-network of things; and Tantra being the application of the "interaction with no obstacles" vision on a personal-human level—the "other" becomes the lover, through whom the various links in the net can be perceived. As Zen goes to *anything* direct—rocks or bushes or people—the Zen Master's presence is to help one keep attention undivided, to always look one step farther along, to simplify the mind: like a blade which sharpens to nothing.

Tantra, Avatamsaka and Zen really closely historically related: and these aspects of philosophy and practice were done all at once, years ago, up on Hiei-zan.   Knit old dharma-trails.

———

An ant is dragging a near-dead fly through the mosswoods by the tongue.

   —dreamed of a new industrial-age dark ages: filthy narrow streets and dirty buildings with rickety walks over the streets from building to building—unwashed illiterate brutal cops—a motorcycle cop and sidecar drove up and over a fat workingman who got knocked down in a fight—tin cans and garbage and drooping electric wires everywhere—

———

15: VI

Leaving the temple this morning walked by a small fox shrine where a Zen monk was chanting: there I heard the subtle steady single-beat of oldest American-Asian shamanism. The basic song. "Buddhist lectures on Shoshone texts" or *Shastra* / commentaries on Navajo creation myth.

―

Koen-ji   28: VI

Key to evolution adaptability: the organism alters itself rather than continue fruitless competition.
            . . . logging camp morning, high clouds moving east, birds, morning light on the pine and sugi; everyone getting up to go to work. Chao-chou: "Wal I been trainin horses for thirty yars and now I git kicked by a dunkey."
—the brain and nervous system all infolded ectoderm: thought but a kind of skin perception.
And now there are too many human beings. Let's be animals or buddhas instead.

―

The altar figure is Manjusri, in gold-lacquered wood. Not only can you tell "enlightenment" from the face, but you can tell how it was achieved. The old Zen Master statues in the meditation hall show them as human beings who made it through will, effort, years of struggle and intensity. Manjusri has the face of a man who did it with cool intellect and comprehension, cynicism and long historical views. Another made it by poverty, wandering, and simple-minded self-sufficient detachment.
Poking about in the abandoned monks' rooms—smell of an old unused mining cabin or logging shanty—a cupboard of bindles the boys left behind, a drawer full of letters, notebooks, seals; like magazines and coffee cups full of dust and mouseshit. The old dark smoky kitchen where Han Shan might have worked. Now making udon noodles out of wheat flour batter with a pressing-and-cutting machine you crank by hand.

Kyoto   30: IX

Nō-play Yang Kuei Fei/Yōkihi–the episode of the Shaman's visit to Hōrai (Jade nowhere Island place)—he receives a hairpin, then she dances. The headdress gold-jewelled triangles and floral danglers: quiver although the dancer is immobile. A seismograph of imperceptible within. American Nō stage: background painting a desert and distant mountains? chorus on a long low bench. Maybe one large real boulder.

Eternal crouching ancient women in dark smoky temple kitchens, fanning the thornwood fire and dusting the hard black dirt floor—once the virgin of what ritual? And gold glittering temple hall?—
    self-discipline is bad for the character.
THY HAND, GREAT ANARCH

"wisdom and berries grow on the same bush, but only one could ever be plucked at one time"—Emerson's Journals   (but I knew a packer could chew copenhagen snoose while eating huckleberries on opposite sides of the mouth and never did mix em up). "The profoundly secret pass that leads from fate to freedom."

6: X

W. the tender secret sensitive square artist, all in himself, a tiny smile, walks out and makes a clean bow, his head all curly blond, and sits down at black piano, him in black. Against the gold zigzag screen: and plays Haydn—as I could hear him for weeks on, practicing in his corner of Rinko temple; bluejeans and coffee in his double-sized cup through hot days and between naps. Decorous passionate music of Old Europe out his Zen fingers, to the hall full of culture-thirsty student boys and girls in blackwhite uniform, fierce-eyed and full of orderly resentment, making their heart's Europe out of thousandfold paperback translations, Aesop to Sartre—digging this lush music. All in a land of rice paddy and green hills and rains where still deep-hatted Dharma-hobos try to roam.

24: X

Leaves begin very gradually to fall—what crazy communion of the birds wheeling and circling back and forth in calling flock, above the pine and against sunset cold white-and-blue clouds—a bunch of birds being one—

Breaking the aspected realms into names—the "Three Realms" or the Trikaya or the "Three Worlds"—done a step farther, as mythology, and seeing the powers and aspects in terms of personalities and relationships archetypally expressed. As the three worlds are one, but seen as three from different angles, so the Goddess is mother, daughter, and wife at the same time. Indra's net is not merely two-dimensional. The movements of the triad of mother, father and child can be made to express any device of mythological or metaphysical thought.

(Beware of anything that promises freedom or enlightenment—traps for eager and clever fools—a dog has a keener nose—every creature in a cave can justify himself. Three-fourths of philosophy and literature is the talk of people trying to convince themselves that they really like the cage they were tricked into entering.)

> My love thoughts these days
> Come thick like the summer grass
> Which soon as cut and raked
> Grows wild again
> Yakamochi

—two days contemplating ecology, food chains and sex. Looking at girls as mothers or daughters or sisters for a change of view. Curious switch.

13: XI

And dreamed that the Egyptian god Set appeared to me & delivered a long prophetic poem, which I forgot.

O Muse who comes in a fiery cart wearing a skirt of revolving swords, trumpeting and insistent; O Muse who comes through the hedge wearing a gray coat, to stand under the ash-tree beckoning . . .

Comes a time when the poet must choose: either to step deep in the stream of his people, history, tradition, folding and folding himself in wealth of persons and pasts; philosophy, humanity, to become richly foundationed and great and sane and ordered. Or, to step beyond the bound onto the way out, into horrors and angels, possible madness or silly Faustian doom, possible utter transcendence, possible enlightened return, possible ignominious wormish perishing.

22: XI   Founder's day at Daitoku-ji

A ringing bell starts it all—a few "cloud and water" monks in traveling clothes, in a cluster, chatting under the pines at the corner of the Dharma Hall.   Colored banners.   Priests in purple and gold and Chinese high-toed slippers with raven-beak hats on.

A black-and-white dragon splashed across the ceiling glaring down, body a circle in cloud and lightning—six burning two-foot candles, and two four-foot pine boughs.   Priests walk in file scuffing the boat shoes.   Sunshine comes in through tree-beams; inside the hall here it's like a grove of Redwood, or under a mountain. Oda Rōshi made eighteen bows.

26: XI   Rinko-in

Barefoot down cold halls.
Maple red now glows, the high limbs first. Venus the morning star—at daybreak and evening, sparrows hurtle in thousands. Five men in jikatabi work shoes slouching across the baseball diamond by the Kamo river. A woman under the bridge nursing her baby at noon hour, shovel and rake parked by. Faint windy mists in the hills north—smoke and charcoal and straw—at night hot soup "kasujiru" made of saké squeezings. Little girls in long tan cotton stockings, red garters, still the skimpy skirts. College boys cynically amble around in their worn-flat geta clogs and shiny black uniforms looking raw, cold and helpless. Big man on a motorcycle with a load of noodles.

"It is unspeakably wonderful to see a large volume of water falling with a thunderous noise."

"Sparrows entertained me singing and dancing, I've never had such a good time as today."

Japanese lesson.

21: I: 57   Daikan, period of Great Cold

Thick frost and a few flakes of dry cold snow; ice thick in the stone hole water bowl boulder where the doves drink, frost keen lines on all the twigs of the naked plum and each small leaf of a tree.

EROTICISM of China and Japan a dark shadowy thing—a perfumed cunt in a cave of brocades; Greek eroticism is nakedness in full blast of sunlight; fucking on high sunny hills. India is hips and breasts, agile limbs on stone floors with intricate design.

Depth is the body. How does one perceive internal physical states—yoga systems I guess—well well.   soil conservation / reforestation / birth control / spelling reform: "love the body."

15: II: 57   Rinko-in

Fine clear morning sun melts frost—plum trees soon bloom—Dove early to the stone water bowl (froze hard, so it walked and pecked on it, no drink). Full moon last night—home from zazen—flying eaves of the Dharma Hall silvery slate tile against Orion—icy air slamming into the mouth. Stupid self dragging its feet while I sit fooling with recall and fantasy—where the sound or sight HITS and is transformed by the mental, at THAT razoredge is the gate. MU is the wedge to chock it up with, that very crack.

―

12: III: 57   Tōdai-ji's "Water-gathering" ceremony

Tōdai-ji's enormous Chinese-Indian Gate of Power. Mangy saw-horn bucks walking around. Mizutori, "water-gathering" at Second Month temple. Grandaddy of all sugi trees in front. Complex beaming and gabling—iron lanterns hanging, ornate, faintly glowing. Far off dream lamps of former birth, exotic and familiar. At seven P.M. monks run up the long stairway with twenty-foot torches and wave and shake them at the crowd, which delights to have the luck of standing under falling clouds of sparks. Inside the hall, priests run clack-clack around and around the central shrine in white wood shoes; stop, sit, and blow conch-shells. They recite the names of all the Gods of Japan, and all the thousands of Buddhas and Bodhisattvas. It takes most of the night. Finally a group comes out and goes down the steps to the well, makes two trips with decked-and-garlanded buckets of water to be blessed by Kwannon. Last, a bit more chanting and then the biggest torch of all is lit and danced INSIDE the hall by masked and head-dressed man—like a raven-beak—the bell bonging. Three A.M.

Later had breakfast with priests at a branch temple—came back on the early train to Kyoto watching the fresh snow-powdered hills and rising chill March sun, the last morning of the spring to wake up snowy. All those little houses, some smoking faint wispy blue in the long blue valley, and pure air.

21: III

Kyoto City Hospital: Nurse girls in starch white scud through the halls in flocks—teal over the mountains—Nurse girls play ball in the yard, patients watching. In the next walled yard puppies on chains wait queer medical fates; a dead one belly up, strange tubes in his throat and intestines, beside two dull cowering dogs in filth.

14: IV

Cherries, cherries—and over the hills from Pete's school—up past Hideyoshi's tomb and down and through a tunnel, out by a lake—on—air dry and dusty wind blowing—just rambling—drank saké on top of Higashiyama under a white petal-scattering tree. Down, almost trapped by the Miyako Hotel, on along the canal past drunk dancing grandmothers, and over brush hills, blue wild bushes blooming—again canal—to Pete's friend's house, a mycologist who does Nō and writes haiku and paints—days gone thus, spring rambles and flowers; beyond there lies—

9: V: 57

In the monastery sesshin / intensive meditation week: from May Day on. One night I dreamt I was with Miura Rōshi, or maybe an unheard-of Polish revolutionary poet with a bald head—looking at Berkeley. But a new Berkeley—of the future—the Bay beach clean and white, the bay blue and pure; white buildings and a lovely boulevard of tall Monterey pines that stretched way back to the hills. We saw a girl from some ways off walking toward us, long-legged, her hair bound loosely in back.

Spring Sesshin at Shokoku-ji

SHOKOKU TEMPLE is in northern Kyoto, on level ground, with a Christian college just south of it and many blocks of crowded little houses and stone-edged dirt roads north. It is the mother-temple of many branch temples scattered throughout Japan, and one of the several great temple-systems of the Rinzai Sect of Zen. Shokoku-ji is actually a compound: behind the big wood gate and tile-topped crumbling old mud walls are a number of temples each with its own gate and walls, gardens, and acres of wild bamboo grove. In the center of the compound is the soaring double-gabled Lecture Hall, silent and airy, an enormous dragon painted on the high ceiling, his eye burning down on the very center of the cut-slate floor. Except at infrequent rituals the hall is unused, and the gold-gilt Buddha sits on its high platform at the rear untroubled by drums and chanting. In front of the Lecture Hall is a long grove of fine young pines and a large square lotus-pond. To the east is a wooden bell tower and the unpretentious gate of the Sodo, the training school for Zen monks, or unsui.[1] They will become priests of Shokoku-ji temples. A few, after years of zazen (meditation), koan study,[2]

---

[1]*Unsui*. The term is literally "cloud, water"—taken from a line of an old Chinese poem, "To drift like clouds and flow like water." It is strictly a Zen term. The Japanese word for Buddhist monks and priests of all sects is *bozu* (bonze). One takes no formal vows upon becoming an unsui, although the head is shaved and a long Chinese-style robe called koromo is worn within Sodo walls. Unsui are free to quit the Zen community at any time. During the six months of the year in which the Sodo is in session (spring and fall) they eat no meat, but during the summer and winter off-periods they eat, drink and wear what they will. After becoming temple priests (Osho, Chinese Ho-shang), the great majority of Zen monks marry and raise families. The present generation of young unsui is largely from temple families.

[2]Koans are usually short anecdotes concerning the incomprehensible and illogical behavior and language of certain key Chinese Zen Masters of the T'ang Dynasty. The koan assigned to the student is the subject of his meditation, and his understanding of it is the subject of sanzen, an interview with the Zen Master. Very advanced students are also required to relate koan-understanding to the intellectual concepts of Buddhist philosophy.

and final mastery of the Avatamsaka (Kegon) philosophy, become roshi[3] (Zen Masters), qualified to head Sodos, teach lay groups, or do what they will. Laymen are also permitted to join the Unsui in evening Zendo (meditation hall) sessions, and some, like the Unsui, are given a koan by the Roshi and receive regular sanzen—the fierce face-to-face moment where you spit forth truth or perish—from him. Thus being driven, through time and much zazen, to the very end of the problem.

In the routine of Sodo life, there are special weeks during the year in which gardening, carpentry, reading and such are suspended, and the time given over almost entirely to zazen. During these weeks, called *sesshin*, "concentrating the mind"— sanzen is received two to four times a day, and hours of zazen in the Zendo are much extended. Laymen who will observe the customs of Sodo life and are able to sit still are allowed to join in the sesshin. At Shokoku-ji, the spring sesshin is held the first week of May.

The sesshin starts in the evening. The participants circle in single file into the mat-floored Central Hall of the Sodo and sit in a double row in dim light. The roshi silently enters, sits at the head, and everyone drinks tea, each fishing his own teacup out of the deep-sleeved black robe. Then the Jikijitsu—head unsui of the Zendo (a position which revolves among the older men, changing every six months)—reads in formal voice the rules of Zendo and sesshin, written in Sung Dynasty Sino-Japanese. The roshi says you all must work very hard; all bow and go out, returning to the Zendo for short meditation and early sleep.

At three A.M. the Fusu (another older zenbo who is in charge of finances and meeting people) appears in the Zendo ringing a hand-bell. Lights go on—ten-watt things tacked under the beams of a building lit for centuries by oil lamps—and everyone wordlessly and swiftly rolls up his single quilt and

---

[3]Roshi. Literally, "old master"—Chinese Lao-shih. A roshi is not simply a person who "understands" Zen, but specifically a person who has received the seal of approval from his own Zen Master and is his "Dharma heir." A person may comprehend Zen to the point that his roshi will say he has no more to teach him, but if the roshi does not feel the student is intellectually and scholastically equipped to transmit Zen as well, he will not permit him to be his heir. Most roshi are Zen monks, but laymen and -women have also achieved this title.

stuffs it in a small cupboard at the rear of his mat, leaps off the raised platform that rings the hall, to the stone floor, and scuffs out in straw sandals to dash icy water on the face from a stone bowl. They come back quickly and sit crosslegged on their zazen cushions, on the same mat used for sleeping. The Jikijitsu stalks in and sits at his place, lighting a stick of incense and beginning the day with the rifleshot crack of a pair of hardwood blocks whacked together and a ding on a small bronze bell. Several minutes of silence, and another whack is heard from the Central Hall. Standing up and slipping on the sandals, the group files out of the Zendo, trailing the Jikijitsu—who hits his bell as he walks—and goes down the roofed stone path, fifty yards long, that joins the Zendo and the Central Hall. Forming two lines and sitting on the mats, they begin to chant sutras. The choppy Sino-Japanese words follow the rhythm of a fish-shaped wooden drum and a deep-throated bell. They roar loud and chant fast. The roshi enters and between the two lines makes deep bows to the Buddha-image before him, lights incense, and retires. The hard-thumping drum and sutra-songs last an hour, then suddenly stop and all return to the Zendo. Each man standing before his place, they chant the *Prajña-paramita-hridaya Sutra*, the Jikijitsu going so fast now no one can follow him. Then hoisting themselves onto the mats, they meditate. After half an hour a harsh bell-clang is heard from the roshi's quarters. The Jikijitsu bellows "Getout!" and the zenbos dash out racing, feet slapping the cold stones and robes flying, to kneel in line whatever order they make it before the sanzen room. A ring of the bell marks each new entrance before the roshi. All one hears from outside is an occasional growl and sometimes the whack of a stick. The men return singly and subdued from sanzen to their places.

Not all return. Some go to the kitchen, to light brushwood fires in the brick stoves and cook rice in giant black pots. When they are ready they signal with a clack of wood blocks, and those in the Zendo answer by a ring on the bell. Carrying little nested sets of bowls and extra-large chopsticks, they come down the covered walk. It is getting light, and at this time of year the azalea are blooming. The moss-floored garden on both sides of the walk is thick with them, banks under pine and maple, white flowers glowing through mist. Even the meal, nothing but salty radish pickles and thin rice gruel, is begun and ended by whacks of wood and chanting of short verses. After breakfast the zenbos scatter: some to wash pots, others to mop the long wood verandas of the central hall and sweep and mop the roshi's rooms or rake leaves and paths in the garden. The younger unsui and the outsiders dust, sweep, and mop the Zendo.

The Shokoku-ji Zendo is one of the largest and finest in Japan. It is on a raised terrace of stone and encircled by a stone walk. Outside a long overhang roof and dark unpainted wood—inside round log posts set on granite footings—it is always cool and dark and very still. The floor is square slate laid diagonal. The raised wood platform that runs around the edge has mats for forty men. Sitting in a three-walled box that hangs from the center of the ceiling, like an overhead-crane operator, is a life-size wood statue of the Buddha's disciple Kasyapa, his eyes real and piercing anyone who enters the main door. In an attached room to the rear of the Zendo is a shrine to the founder of Shokoku-ji, his statue in wood, eyes peering out of a dark alcove.

By seven A.M. the routine chores are done and the Jikijitsu invites those cleaning up the Zendo into his room for tea. The Jikijitsu and the Fusu both have private quarters, the Fusu lodging in the Central Hall and the Jikijitsu in a small building adjoining the Zendo. The chill is leaving the air, and he slides open the paper screens, opening a wall of his room to the outside. Sitting on mats and drinking tea they relax and smoke and quietly kid a little, and the Jikijitsu—a tigerish terror during the zazen sessions—is very gentle. "You'll be a roshi one of these days" a medical student staying the week said to him. "Not me, I can't grasp koans," he laughs, rubbing his shaved head where the roshi has knocked him recently. Then they talk of work to be done around the Sodo. During sesshin periods work is kept to a minimum, but some must be done. Taking off robes and putting on ragged old dungarees everyone spreads out, some to the endless task of weeding grass from the moss garden, others to the vegetable plots. The Jikijitsu takes a big mattock and heads for the bamboo-grove to chop out a few bamboo shoots for the kitchen. Nobody works very hard, and several times during the morning they find a warm place in the sun and smoke.

At ten-thirty they quit work and straggle to the kitchen for lunch, the main meal. Miso soup full of vegetables, plenty of rice, and several sorts of pickles. The crunch of bicycles and shouts of children playing around the bell tower can be heard just beyond the wall. After lunch the laymen and younger unsui return to the Zendo. More experienced men have the greater responsibilities of running the Sodo, and they keep busy at accounts, shopping and looking after the needs of the roshi. Afternoon sitting in the Zendo is informal—newcomers take plenty of time getting comfortable, and occasionally go out to walk and smoke a bit. Conversation is not actually forbidden, but no one wants to talk.

Shortly before three, things tighten up and the Jikijitsu comes in. When everyone is gathered, and a bell heard from the Central Hall, they march out for afternoon sutra-chanting. The sutras recited vary from day to day, and as the leader announces new titles some men produce books from their sleeves to read by, for not all have yet memorized them completely. Returning to the Zendo, they again recite the *Prajña-paramita-hridaya Sutra*, and the Jikijitsu chants a piece alone, his voice filling the hall, head tilted up to the statue of Kasyapa, hand cupped to his mouth as though calling across miles.

After they sit a few minutes the signal is heard for evening meal, and all file into the kitchen, stand, chant, sit, and lay out their bowls. No one speaks. Food is served with a gesture of "giving," and one stops the server with a gesture of "enough." At the end of the meal—rice and pickles—a pot of hot water is passed and each man pours some into his bowls, swashes it around and drinks it, wipes out his bowls with a little cloth. Then they are nested again, wrapped in their cover, and everyone stands and leaves.

It is dusk and the Zendo is getting dark inside. All the zenbos begin to assemble now, some with their cushions tucked under arm, each bowing before Kasyapa as he enters. Each man, right hand held up before the chest flat like a knife and cutting the air, walks straight to his place, bows toward the center of the room, arranges the cushions, and assumes the cross-legged "half-lotus" posture. Other arrive too—teachers, several college professors and half a dozen university students wearing the black uniforms that serve for classrooms, bars and temples equally well—being all they own. Some enter uncertainly and bow with hesitation, afraid of making mistakes, curious to try zazen and overwhelmed by the historical weight of Zen, something very "Japanese" and very "high class." One student, most threadbare of all, had a head shaved like an unsui and entered with knowledge and precision every night, sitting perfectly still on his cushions and acknowledging no one. By seven-thirty the hall is half full—a sizable number of people for present-day Zen sessions—and the great bell in the bell tower booms. As it booms, the man ringing it, swinging a long wood-beam ram, sings out a sutra over the shops and homes of the neighborhood. When he has finished, the faint lights in the Zendo go on and evening zazen has begun.

The Jikijitsu sits at the head of the hall, marking the half-hour periods with wood clackers and bell. He keeps a stick of incense burning beside him, atop a small wood box that says "not yet" on it in Chinese. At the end of the first half-hour he claps the blocks once and grunts "kinhin." This is "walking zazen," and the group stands—the Unsui tying up sleeves and tucking up robes—and at another signal they start marching single file around the inside of the hall. They walk fast and unconsciously in step, the Jikijitsu leading with a long samurai stride. They circle and circle, through shadow and under the light, ducking below Kasyapa's roost, until suddenly the Jikijitsu claps his blocks and yells "Getout!"—the circle broken and everyone dashing for the door. Night sanzen. Through the next twenty minutes they return to resume meditation—not preparing an answer now, but considering the roshi's response.

Zazen is a very tight thing. The whole room feels it. The Jikijitsu gets up, grasps a long flat stick and begins to slowly prowl the hall, stick on shoulder, walking before the rows of sitting men, each motionless with eyes half-closed and looking straight ahead downward. An inexperienced man sitting out of balance will be lightly tapped and prodded into easier posture. An unsui sitting poorly will be without warning roughly knocked off his cushions. He gets up and sits down again. Nothing is said. Anyone showing signs of drowsiness will feel a light tap of the stick on the shoulder. He and the Jikijitsu then bow to each other, and the man leans forward to receive four blows on each side of his back. These are not particularly painful—though the loud whack of them can be terrifying to a newcomer—and serve to wake one well. One's legs may hurt during long sitting, but there is no relief until the Jikijitsu rings his bell. The mind must simply be placed elsewhere. At the end of an hour the bell does ring and the second kinhin begins—a welcome twenty minutes of silent rhythmic walking. The walking ends abruptly and anyone not seated and settled when the Jikijitsu whips around the hall is knocked off his cushion. Zen aims at freedom but its practice is disciplined.

Several unsui slip out during kinhin. At ten they return—they can be heard coming, running full speed down the walk. They enter carrying big trays of hot noodles, udon, in large lacquer bowls. They bow to the Jikijitsu and circle the room setting a bowl before each man; giving two or even three bowls to those who want them. Each man bows, takes up chopsticks, and eats the noodles as fast as he can. Zenbos are famous for fast noodle-eating and no one wants to be last done. As the empty bowls are set down they are gathered up and one server follows, wiping the beam that fronts the mats with a rag, at a run. At the door the servers stop and bow to the group. It bows in return. Then one server announces the person—usually a friend or patron of the Sodo—who footed the bill for the sesshin noodles that night. The group bows again. Meditation is resumed. At ten-thirty there is another rest period and men gather to smoke and chat a little in back. "Are there really some Americans interested in Zen?" they ask with astonishment—for their own countrymen pay them scant attention.

At eleven bells ring and wood clacks, and final sutras are chanted. The hall is suddenly filled with huge voices. The evening visitors take their cushions and leave, each bowing to the Jikijitsu and Kasyapa as he goes. The others flip themselves into their sleeping quilts immediately and lie dead still. The Jikijitsu pads once around, says, "Take counsel of your pillow," and walks out. The hall goes black. But this is not the end, for as soon as the lights go out, everyone gets up again and takes his sitting cushion, slips outside, and practices zazen alone wherever he likes for another two hours. The next day begins at three A.M.

This is the daily schedule of the sesshin. On several mornings during the week, the roshi gives a lecture (*teisho*) based on some anecdote in the Zen textbooks—usually from *Mumonkan* or *Hekiganroku*. As the group sits in the Central Hall awaiting his entrance, one zenbo stands twirling a stick around the edge-tacks of a big drum, filling the air with a deep reverberation. The roshi sits cross-legged on a very high chair, receives a cup of tea, and delivers lectures that might drive some mad—for he tells these poor souls beating their brains out night after night that "the Perfect Way is without difficulty" and he means it and they know he's right.

In the middle of the week everyone gets a bath and a new head-shave. There is a Zen saying that "while studying koans you should not relax even in the bath," but this one is never heeded. The bathhouse contains two deep iron tubs, heated by brushwood fires stoked below from outside. The blue smoke and sweet smell of crackling hinoki and sugi twigs, stuffed in by a fire-tender, and the men taking a long time and getting really clean. Even in the bathhouse you bow—to a small shrine high on the wall—both before and after bathing. The Jikijitsu whets up his razor and shaves heads, but shaves his own alone and without mirror. He never nicks himself anymore.

On the day after bath they go begging (*takuhatsu*). It rained this day, but putting on oiled-paper slickers over their robes and wearing straw sandals they splashed out. The face of the begging zenbo can scarcely be seen, for he wears a deep bowl-shaped woven straw hat. They walk slowly, paced far apart, making a weird wailing sound as they go, never stopping. Sometimes they walk for miles, crisscrossing the little lanes and streets of Kyoto. They came back soaked, chanting a sutra as they entered the Sodo gate, and added up a meager take. The rain sluiced down all that afternoon, making a green twilight inside the Zendo and a rush of sound.

The next morning during tea with the Jikijitsu, a college professor who rents rooms in one of the Sodo buildings came in and talked of koans. "When you understand Zen, you know that the tree is really *there*."—The only time anyone said anything of Zen philosophy or experience the whole week. Zenbos never discuss koans or sanzen experience with each other.

The sesshin ends at dawn on the eighth day. All who have participated gather in the Jikijitsu's room and drink powdered green tea and eat cakes. They talk easily, it's over. The Jikijitsu, who has whacked or knocked them all during the week, is their great friend now—compassion takes many forms.

Buddhism and the Coming Revolution

BUDDHISM HOLDS that the universe and all creatures in it are intrinsically in a state of complete wisdom, love, and compassion, acting in natural response and mutual interdependence. The personal realization of this from-the-beginning state cannot be had for and by one-"self,"——because it is not fully realized unless one has given the self up and away.

In the Buddhist view, what obstructs the effortless manifestation of this realization is ignorance, which projects into fear and needless craving. Historically, Buddhist philosophers have failed to analyze out the degree to which ignorance and suffering are caused or encouraged by social factors, considering fear and desire to be given facts of the human condition. Consequently the major concern of Buddhist philosophy is epistemology and "psychology," with no attention paid to historical or sociological problems. Although Mahayana Buddhism has a grand vision of universal salvation, the actual achievement of Buddhism has been the development of practical systems of meditation toward the end of liberating a few dedicated individuals from psychological hang-ups and cultural conditionings. Institutional Buddhism has been conspicuously ready to accept or ignore the inequalities and tyrannies of whatever political system it found itself under. This can be death to Buddhism, because it is death to any meaningful function of compassion. Wisdom without compassion feels no pain.

No one today can afford to be innocent, or to indulge themselves in ignorance of the nature of contemporary governments, politics, and social orders. The national polities of the modern world are "states" that maintain their existence by deliberately fostered craving and fear: monstrous protection rackets. The "free world" has become economically dependent on a fantastic system of stimulation of greed that cannot be fulfilled, sexual desire that cannot be satiated, and hatred that has no outlet except against oneself, the persons one is supposed to love, or the revolutionary aspirations of pitiful, poverty-stricken marginal societies. The conditions of the Cold War have turned most modern societies—both communist and capitalist—into vicious distorters of true human potential. They try to create populations of "preta"—hungry ghosts, with giant appetites and throats no bigger than needles. The soil, the forests, and all animal life are being consumed by these cancerous collectivities; the air and water of the planet are being fouled by them.

There is nothing in human nature or the requirements of human social organization that requires a society to be contradictory, repressive, and productive of violent and frustrated personalities. Findings in anthropology and psychology make this more and more evident. One can prove it for oneself by taking a good look at Original Nature through meditation. Once a person has this much faith and insight, one will be led to a deep concern for the need for radical social change through a variety of nonviolent means.

The joyous and voluntary poverty of Buddhism becomes a positive force. The traditional harmlessness and avoidance of taking life in any form has nation-shaking implications. The practice of meditation, for which one needs only "the ground beneath one's feet," wipes out mountains of junk being pumped into the mind by the mass media and supermarket universities. The belief in a serene and generous fulfillment of natural loving desires destroys ideologies that blind, maim, and repress—and points the way to a kind of community which would amaze "moralists" and transform armies of men who are fighters because they cannot be lovers.

Avatamsaka (Kegon or *Hua-yen)* Buddhist philosophy sees the world as a vast, interrelated network in which all objects and creatures are necessary and illuminated. From one standpoint, governments, wars, or all that we consider "evil" are uncompromisingly contained in this totalistic realm. The hawk, the swoop, and the hare are one. From the "human" standpoint we cannot live in those terms unless all beings see with the same enlightened eye. The Bodhisattva lives by the sufferer's standard, and must be effective in aiding those who suffer.

The mercy of the West has been social revolution; the mercy of the East has been individual insight into the basic self/void. We need both. They are both contained in the traditional three aspects of the Dharma path: wisdom *(prajñā),* meditation *(dhyana)*, and morality *(shila)*. Wisdom is intuitive knowledge of the mind of love and clarity that lies beneath one's ego-driven anxieties and aggressions. Meditation is going into the mind to see this for yourself—over and over again, until it becomes the mind you live in. Morality is bringing it back out in the way you live, through personal example and responsible action, ultimately toward the true community *(sangha)* of "all beings." This last aspect means, for me, supporting any cultural and economic revolution that moves clearly toward a truly free world. It means using such means as civil disobedience, outspoken criticism, protest, pacifism, voluntary poverty, and even gentle violence if it comes to a matter of restraining some impetuous crazy. It means affirming the widest possible spectrum of nonharmful individual behavior—defending the right of individuals to smoke hemp, eat peyote, be polygamous, polyandrous, or homosexual. Worlds of behavior and custom long banned by the Judaeo-Capitalist-Christian-Marxist West. It means respecting intelligence and learning, but not as greed or means to personal power. Working on one's own responsibility, but willing to work with a group. "Forming the new society within the shell of the old"—the I.W.W. slogan of seventy years ago.

The traditional, vernacular, primitive, and village cultures may appear to be doomed. We must defend and support them as we would the diversity of ecosystems; they are all manifestations of Mind. Some of the elder societies accomplished a condition of Sangha, with not a little of Buddha and Dharma as well. We touch base with the deep mind of peoples of all times and places in our meditation practice, and this is an amazing revolutionary aspect of the Buddhadharma. By a "planetary culture" I mean the kind of societies that would follow on a new understanding of that relatively recent institution, the national state, an understanding that might enable us to leave it behind. The state is greed made legal, with a monopoly on violence; a natural society is familial and cautionary. A natural society is one that "follows the way," imperfectly but authentically.

Such an understanding will close the circle and link us in many ways with the most creative aspects of our archaic past. If we are lucky, we may eventually arrive at a world of relatively mutually tolerant small societies attuned to their local natural region and united overall by a profound respect and love for the mind and nature of the universe.

I can imagine further virtues in a world sponsoring societies with matrilineal descent, free-form marriage, "natural credit" economics, far less population, and much more wilderness.

Passage to More Than India

*"It will be a revival, in higher form, of the liberty,
equality, and fraternity of the ancient gentes."*
LEWIS HENRY MORGAN

THE TRIBE

THE CELEBRATED human Be-In in San Francisco, January of 1967, was called "A Gathering of the Tribes." The two posters: one based on a photograph of a Shaivite sadhu with his long matted hair, ashes, and beard; the other based on an old etching of a Plains Indian approaching a powwow on his horse—the carbine that had been cradled in his left arm replaced by a guitar. The Indians, and the Indian. The tribes were Berkeley, North Beach, Big Sur, Marin County, Los Angeles, and the host, Haight-Ashbury. Outriders were present from New York, London, and Amsterdam. Out on the polo field that day the splendidly clad ab/originals often fell into clusters, with children, a few even under banners. These were the clans.

Large old houses are rented communally by a group, occupied by couples and singles (or whatever combinations) and their children. In some cases, especially in the rock-and-roll business and with light-show groups, they are all working together on the same creative job. They might even be a legal corporation. Some are subsistence farmers out in the country, some are contractors and carpenters in small coast towns. One woman can stay home and look after all the children while the other women hold jobs. They will all be cooking and eating together and they may well be brown-rice vegetarians. There might not be much alcohol or tobacco around the house, but there will certainly be a stash of marijuana and probably some LSD. If the group has been together for some time it may be known by some informal name, magical and natural. These households provide centers in the city and also out in the country for loners and rangers; gathering places for the scattered smaller hip families and havens for the questing adolescent children of the neighborhood. The clan sachems will sometimes gather to talk about larger issues—police or sheriff department harassments, busts, anti-Vietnam projects, dances, and gatherings.

All this is known fact. The number of committed total tribesmen is not so great, but there is a large population of crypto-members who move through many walks of life undetected and only put on their beads and feathers for special occasions. Some are in the academies, others in the legal or psychiatric professions—useful friends indeed. The number of people who use marijuana regularly and have experienced LSD is (considering it's all illegal) staggering. The impact of all this on the cultural and imaginative life of the nation—even the politics—is enormous.

And yet, there's nothing very new about it, in spite of young hippies just in from the suburbs for whom the "beat generation" is a kalpa away. For several centuries now Western Man has been ponderously preparing himself for a new look at the inner world and the spiritual realms. Even in the centers of nineteenth-century materialism there were dedicated seekers— some within Christianity, some in the arts, some within the occult circles. Witness William Butler Yeats. My own opinion is that we are now experiencing a surfacing (in a specifically "American" incarnation) of the Great Subculture which goes back as far perhaps as the late Paleolithic.

This subculture of illuminati has been a powerful undercurrent in all higher civilizations. In China it manifested as Taoism—not only Lao-tzu but the later Yellow Turban revolt and medieval Taoist secret societies—and the Zen Buddhists up till early Sung. Within Islam the Sufis. In India the various threads converged to produce Tantrism. In the West it has been represented largely by a string of heresies starting with the Gnostics, and on the folk level by "witchcraft."

Buddhist Tantrism, or *Vajrayana* as it's also known, is probably the finest and most modern statement of this ancient shamanistic-yogic-gnostic-socioeconomic view: that mankind's mother is Nature and Nature should be tenderly respected; that man's life and destiny are growth and enlightenment in self-disciplined freedom; that the divine has been made flesh and that flesh is divine; that we not only should but *do* love one another. This view has been harshly suppressed in the past as threatening to both Church and State. Today, on the contrary, these values seem almost biologically essential to the survival of humanity.

THE FAMILY

Lewis Henry Morgan (d. 1881) was a New York lawyer. He was asked by his club to reorganize it "after the pattern of the Iroquois confederacy." His research converted him into a defender of tribal rights and started him on his career as an amateur anthropologist. His major contribution was a broad theory of social evolution which is still useful. Morgan's *Ancient Society* inspired Engels to write *Origins of the Family, Private Property and the State* (1884, and still in print in both Russia and China), in which the relations between the rights of women, sexuality and the family, and attitudes toward property and power are tentatively explored. The pivot is the revolutionary implications of the custom of matrilineal descent, which Engels learned from Morgan; the Iroquois are matrilineal.

A schematic history of the family:

Hunters and gatherers—a loose monogamy within communal clans usually reckoning descent in the female line (matrilineal).

Early agriculturalists—a tendency toward group and polyandrous marriage, continued matrilineal descent and smaller-sized clans.

Pastoral nomads—a tendency toward stricter monogamy and patrilineal descent; but much premarital sexual freedom.

Iron-Age agriculturalists—property begins to accumulate and the family system changes to monogamy or polygyny with patrilineal descent. Concern with the legitimacy of heirs.

Civilization so far has implied a patriarchal, patrilineal family. Any other system allows too much creative sexual energy to be released into channels that are "unproductive." In the West, the clan, or gens, disappeared gradually, and social organization was ultimately replaced by political organization, within which separate male-oriented families compete: the modern state.

Engels' Marxian classic implies that the revolution cannot be completely achieved in merely political terms. Monogamy and patrilineal descent may well be great obstructions to the inner changes required for a people to truly live by "communism." Marxists after Engels let these questions lie. Russia and China today are among the world's staunchest supporters of monogamous, sexually turned-off families. Yet Engels' insights were not entirely ignored. The Anarcho-Syndicalists showed a sense for experimental social reorganization. American anarchists and the I.W.W. lived a kind of communalism, with some lovely stories handed down of free love—their slogan was more than just words: "Forming the new society within the shell of the old." San Francisco poets and gurus were attending meetings of the "Anarchist Circle"—old Italians and Finns—in the 1940s.

THE REDSKINS

In many American Indian cultures it is obligatory for every member to get out of the society, out of the human nexus, and "out of his head," at least once in his life. He returns from his solitary vision quest with a secret name, a protective animal spirit, a secret song. It is his "power." The culture honors the man who has visited other realms.

Peyote, the mushroom, morning glory seeds, and jimsonweed are some of the best-known herbal aids used by Indian cultures to assist in the quest. Most tribes apparently achieved these results simply through yogic-type disciplines: including sweat-baths, hours of dancing, fasting, and total isolation. After the decline of the apocalyptic fervor of Wovoka's Ghost Dance religion (a pan-Indian movement of the 1880s and 1890s that believed that if all the Indians would dance the Ghost Dance with their Ghost shirts on, the Buffalo would rise from the ground, trample the white men to death in their dreams, and all the dead game would return; America would be restored to the Indians), the peyote cult spread and established itself in most of the western American tribes. Although the peyote religion conflicts with preexisting tribal religions in a few cases (notably with the Pueblo), there is no doubt that the cult has been a positive force, helping the Indians maintain a reverence for their traditions and land through their period of greatest weakness—which is now over. European scholars were investigating peyote in the twenties. It is rumored that Dr. Carl Jung was experimenting with peyote then. A small band of white peyote users emerged, and peyote was easily available in San Francisco by the late 1940s. In Europe some researchers on these alkaloid compounds were beginning to synthesize them. There is a karmic connection between the peyote cult of the Indians and the discovery of lysergic acid in Switzerland.

Peyote and acid have a curious way of tuning some people in to the local soil. The strains and stresses deep beneath one in the rock, the flow and fabric of wildlife around, the human history of Indians on this continent. Older powers become evident: west of the Rockies, the ancient creator-trickster, Coyote. Jaime de Angulo, a now-legendary departed Spanish shaman and anthropologist, was an authentic Coyote-medium. One of the most relevant poetry magazines is called *Coyote's Journal.* For many, the invisible presence of the Indian, and the heartbreaking beauty of America work without fasting or herbs. We make these contacts simply by walking the Sierra or Mohave, learning the old edibles, singing and watching.

THE JEWEL IN THE LOTUS

At the Congress of World Religions in Chicago in the 1890s, two of the most striking figures were Swami Vivekananda (Shri Ramakrishna's disciple) and Shaku Soyen, the Zen Master and Abbot of Engaku-ji, representing Japanese Rinzai Zen. Shaku Soyen's interpreter was a college student named Teitaro Suzuki. The Ramakrishna-Vivekananda line produced scores of books and established Vedanta centers all through the Western world. A small band of Zen monks under Shaku Sokatsu (disciple of Shaku Soyen) was raising strawberries in Hayward, California, in 1907. Shigetsu Sasaki, later to be known as the Zen Master Sokei-an, was roaming the timberlands of the Pacific Northwest just before World War I, and living on a Puget Sound Island with Indians for neighbors. D. T. Suzuki's books are to be found today in the libraries of biochemists and on stone ledges under laurel trees in the open-air camps of Big Sur gypsies.

A Californian named Walter Y. Evans-Wentz, who sensed that the mountains on his family's vast grazing lands really did have spirits in them, went to Oxford to study the Celtic belief in fairies and then to Sikkim to study Vajrayana under a lama. His best-known book is *The Tibetan Book of the Dead*.

Those who do not have the money or time to go to India or Japan, but who think a great deal about the wisdom traditions, have remarkable results when they take LSD. The *Bhagavad-Gita*, the Hindu mythologies, *The Serpent Power*, the *Lankavatara-sōtra*, the *Upanishads*, the *Hevajra-tantra*, the *Mahanirvana-tantra*—to name a few texts—become, they say, finally clear to them. They often feel they must radically reorganize their lives to harmonize with such insights.

In several American cities traditional meditation halls of both Rinzai and Soto Zen are flourishing. Many of the newcomers turned to traditional meditation after initial acid experience. The two types of experience seem to inform each other.

THE HERETICS

"When Adam delved and Eve span,
Who was then a gentleman?"

The memories of a Golden Age—the Garden of Eden—the Age of the Yellow Ancestor—were genuine expressions of civilization and its discontents. Harking back to societies where women and men were more free with each other; where there was more singing and dancing; where there were no serfs and priests and kings.

Projected into future time in Christian culture, this dream of the Millennium became the soil of many heresies. It is a dream handed down right to our own time—of ecological balance, classless society, social and economic freedom. It is actually one of the possible futures open to us. To those who stubbornly argue "it's against human nature," we can only patiently reply that you must know your own nature before you can say this. Those who have gone into their own natures deeply have, for several thousand years now, been reporting that we have nothing to fear if we are willing to train ourselves, to open up, explore and grow.

One of the most significant medieval heresies was the Brotherhood of the Free Spirit, of which Hieronymus Bosch was probably a member. The Brotherhood believed that God was immanent in everything, and that once one had experienced this God-presence in himself he became a Free Spirit; he was again living in the Garden of Eden. The brothers and sisters held their meetings naked, and practiced much sharing. They "confounded clerics with the subtlety of their arguments." It was complained that "they have no uniform . . . sometimes they dress in a costly and dissolute fashion, sometimes most miserably, all according to time and place." The Free Spirits had communal houses in secret all through Germany and the Lowlands, and wandered freely among them. Their main supporters were the well-organized and affluent weavers.

When brought before the Inquisition they were not charged with witchcraft, but with believing that man was divine, and with making love too freely, with orgies. Thousands were burned. There are some who have as much hostility to the adepts of the subculture today. This may be caused not so much by the outlandish clothes and dope, as by the nutty insistence on "love." The West and Christian culture on one level deeply wants love to win—and having decided (after several sad tries) that love can't, people who still say it will are like ghosts from an old dream.

Love begins with the family and its network of erotic and responsible relationships. A slight alteration of family structure will project a different love-and-property outlook through a whole culture . . . thus the communism and free love of the Christian heresies. This is a real razor's edge. Shall the lion lie down with the lamb? And make love even? The Garden of Eden.

WHITE INDIANS

The modern American family is the smallest and most barren family that has ever existed. Each newly married couple moves to a new house or apartment—no uncles or grandmothers come to live with them. There are seldom more than two or three children. The children live with their peers and leave home early. Many have never had the least sense of family.

I remember sitting down to Christmas dinner eighteen years ago in a communal house in Portland, Oregon, with about twelve others my own age, all of whom had no place they wished to go home to. That house was my first discovery of harmony and community with fellow beings. This has been the experience of hundreds of thousands of men and women all over America since the end of World War II. Hence the talk about the growth of a "new society." But more; these gatherings have been people spending time with each other—talking, delving, making love. Because of the sheer amount of time "wasted" together (without TV) they know each other better than most Americans know their own family. Add to this the mind-opening and personality-revealing effects of grass and acid, and it becomes possible to predict the emergence of groups who live by mutual illumination—have seen themselves as of one mind and one flesh—the "single eye" of the heretical English Ranters; the meaning of sahajiya, "born together"—the name of the latest flower of the Tantric community tradition in Bengal.

Industrial society indeed appears to be finished. Many of us are, again, hunters and gatherers. Poets, musicians, nomadic engineers, and scholars; fact-diggers, searchers, and re-searchers scoring in rich foundation territory. Horse-traders in lore and magic. The super hunting-bands of mercenaries like RAND or CIA may in some ways belong to the future, if they can be transformed by the ecological conscience, or acid, to which they are very vulnerable. A few of us are literally hunters and gatherers, playfully studying the old techniques of acorn flour, seaweed-gathering, yucca-fiber, rabbit snaring, and bow hunting. The densest Indian population in pre-Columbian America north of Mexico was in Marin, Sonoma, and Napa Counties, California.

And finally, to go back to Morgan and Engels, sexual mores and the family are changing in the same direction. Rather than the "breakdown of the family" we should see this as the transition to a new form of family. In the near future, I think it likely that the freedom of women and the tribal spirit will make it possible for us to formalize our marriage relationships in any way we please—as groups, or polygynously or polyandrously, as well as monogamously. I use the word "formalize" only in the sense of make public and open the relationships, and to sacramentalize them; to see family as part of the divine ecology. Because it is simpler, more natural, and breaks up tendencies toward property accumulation by individual families, matrilineal descent seems ultimately indicated. Such families already exist. Their children are different in personality structure and outlook from anybody in the history of Western culture since the destruction of Knossos.

The American Indian is the vengeful ghost lurking in the back of the troubled American mind. Which is why we lash out with such ferocity and passion, so muddied a heart, at the black-haired young peasants and soldiers who are the "Viet Cong." That ghost will claim the next generation as its own. When this has happened, citizens of the USA will at last begin to be Americans, truly at home on the continent, in love with their land. The chorus of a Cheyenne Indian Ghost dance song—*hi-niswa' vita'ki'ni*—"We shall live again."

> "Passage to more than India!
> Are thy wings plumed indeed for such far flights?
> O soul, voyagest thou indeed on voyages like those?"

Poetry and the Primitive

NOTES ON POETRY AS AN ECOLOGICAL
SURVIVAL TECHNIQUE

BILATERAL SYMMETRY

"POETRY" as the skilled and inspired use of the voice and language to embody rare and powerful states of mind that are in immediate origin personal to the singer, but at deep levels common to all who listen. "Primitive" as those societies that have remained nonliterate and nonpolitical while necessarily exploring and developing in directions that civilized societies have tended to ignore. Having fewer tools, no concern with history, a living oral tradition rather than an accumulated library, no overriding social goals, and considerable freedom of sexual and inner life, such people live vastly in the present. Their daily reality is a fabric of friends and family, the field of feeling and energy that one's own body is, the earth they stand on and the wind that wraps around it; and various areas of consciousness.

At this point some might be tempted to say that the primitive's real life is no different from anybody else's. I think this is not so. To live in the "mythological present" in close relation to nature and in basic but disciplined body/mind states suggests a wider-ranging imagination and a closer subjective knowledge of one's own physical properties than is usually available to men living (as they themselves describe it) impotently and inadequately in "history"—their mind-content programmed, and their caressing of nature complicated by the extensions and abstractions which elaborate tools are. A hand pushing a button may wield great power, but that hand will never learn what a hand can do. Unused capacities go sour.

Poetry must sing or speak from authentic experience. Of all the streams of civilized tradition with roots in the paleolithic, poetry is one of the few that can realistically claim an unchanged function and a relevance which will outlast most of the activities that surround us today. Poets, as few others, must live close to the world that primitive men are in: the world, in its nakedness, that is fundamental for all of us—birth, love, death; the sheer fact of being alive.

Music, dance, religion, and philosophy of course have archaic roots—a shared origin with poetry. Religion has tended to become the social justifier, a lackey to power, instead of the vehicle of hair-raising liberating and healing realizations. Dance has mostly lost its connection with ritual drama, the miming of animals, or tracing the maze of the spiritual journey. Most music takes too many tools. The poet can make it on his own voice and mother tongue, while steering a course between crystal clouds of utterly incommunicable nonverbal states—and the gleaming daggers and glittering nets of language.

In one school of Mahayana Buddhism, they talk about the "Three Mysteries." These are Body, Voice, and Mind. The things that are what living *is* for us, in life. Poetry is the vehicle of the mystery of voice. The universe, as they sometimes say, is a vast breathing body.

With artists, certain kinds of scientists, yogins, and poets, a kind of mind-sense is not only surviving but modestly flourishing in the twentieth century. Claude Lévi-Strauss (*The Savage Mind*) sees no problem in the continuity: "It is neither the mind of savages nor that of primitive or archaic humanity, but rather mind in its untamed state as distinct from mind cultivated or domesticated for yielding a return. . . . We are better able to understand today that it is possible for the two to coexist and interpenetrate in the same way that (in theory at least) it is possible for natural species, of which some are in their savage state and others transformed by agriculture and domestication, to coexist and cross . . . whether one deplores or rejoices in the fact, there are still zones in which savage thought, like savage species, is relatively protected. This is the case of art, to which our civilization accords the status of a national park."

MAKING LOVE WITH ANIMALS

By civilized times, hunting was a sport of kings. The early Chinese emperors had vast fenced hunting reserves; peasants were not allowed to shoot deer. Millennia of experience, the proud knowledges of hunting magic—animal habits—and the skills of wild plant and herb gathering were all but scrubbed away. Much has been said about the frontier in American history, but overlooking perhaps some key points: the American confrontation with a vast wild ecology, an earthly paradise of grass, water, and game—was mind-shaking. Americans lived next to vigorous primitives whom they could not help but respect and even envy, for three hundred years. Finally, as ordinary men supporting their families, they often hunted for food. Although marginal peasants in Europe and Asia did remain part-time hunters at the bottom of the social scale, these Americans were the vanguard of an expanding culture. For Americans, *nature* means wilderness, the untamed realm of total freedom—not brutish and nasty, but beautiful and terrible. Something is always eating at the American heart like acid: it is the knowledge of what we have done to our continent, and to the American Indian.

Other civilizations have done the same, but at a pace too slow to be remembered. One finds evidence in T'ang and Sung poetry that the barren hills of central and northern China were once richly forested. The Far Eastern love of nature has become fear of nature: gardens and pine trees are tormented and controlled. Chinese nature poets were too often retired bureaucrats living on two or three acres of trees trimmed by hired gardeners. The professional nature-aesthetes of modern Japan, tea-teachers and flower-arrangers, are amazed to hear that only a century ago dozens of species of birds passed through Kyoto where today only swallows and sparrows can be seen; and the aesthetes can scarcely distinguish those. "Wild" in the Far East means uncontrollable, objectionable, crude, sexually unrestrained, violent; actually ritually polluting. China cast off mythology, which means its own dreams, with hairy cocks and gaping pudenda, millennia ago; and modern Japanese families participating in an "economic miracle" can have daughters in college who are not sure which hole babies come out of. One of the most remarkable intuitions in Western thought was Rousseau's Noble Savage: the idea that perhaps civilization has something to learn from the primitive.

Man is a beautiful animal. We know this because other animals admire us and love us. Almost all animals are beautiful and paleolithic hunters were deeply moved by it. To hunt means to use your body and senses to the fullest: to strain your consciousness to feel what the deer are thinking today, this moment; to sit still and let your self go into the birds and wind while waiting by a game trail. Hunting magic is designed to bring the game to you—the creature who has heard your song, witnessed your sincerity, and out of compassion comes within your range. Hunting magic is not only aimed at bringing beasts to their death, but to assist in their birth—to promote their fertility. Thus the great Iberian cave paintings are not of hunting alone—but of animals mating and giving birth. A Spanish farmer who saw some reproductions from Altamira is reported to have said, "How beautifully this cow gives birth to a calf!" Breuil has said, "The religion of those days did *not* elevate the animal to the position of a god . . . but it was *humbly entreated* to be fertile." A Haida incantation goes:

> The Great One coming up against the current
> > begins thinking of it.
> The Great One coming putting gravel in his mouth
> > thinks of it
> You look at it with white stone eyes—
> > Great Eater begins thinking of it.

People of primitive cultures appreciate animals as other people off on various trips. Snakes move without limbs, and are like free penises. Birds fly, sing, and dance; they gather food for their babies; they disappear for months and then come back. Fish can breathe water and are brilliant colors. Mammals are like us, they fuck and give birth to babies while panting and purring; their young suck their mothers' breasts; they know terror and delight, they play.

Lévi-Strauss quotes Swanton's report on the Chickasaw, the tribe's own amusing game of seeing the different clans as acting out the lives of their totemic emblems: "The Raccoon people were said to live on fish and wild fruit, those of the Puma lived in the mountains, avoided water of which they were very frightened and lived principally on game. The Wild Cat clan slept in the daytime and hunted at night, for they had keen eyes; they were indifferent to women. Members of the Bird clan were up before daybreak: 'They were like real birds in that they would not bother anybody . . . the people of this clan have different sorts of minds, just as there are different species of birds.' They were said to live well, to be polygamous, disinclined to work, and prolific . . . the inhabitants of the 'bending-post-oak' house group lived in the woods . . . the High Corncrib house people were respected in spite of their arrogance: they were good gardeners, very industrious but poor hunters; they bartered their maize for game. They were said to be truthful and stubborn, and skilled at forecasting the weather. As for the Redskunk house group: they lived in dugouts underground."

We all know what primitive cultures don't have. What they *do* have is this knowledge of connection and responsibility that amounts to a spiritual ascesis for the whole community. Monks of Christianity or Buddhism, "leaving the world" (which means the games of society), are trying, in a decadent way, to achieve what whole primitive communities—men, women, and children—live by daily; and with more wholeness. The shaman-poet is simply the man whose mind reaches easily out into all manners of shapes and other lives, and gives song to dreams. Poets have carried this function forward all through civilized times: poets don't sing about society, they sing about nature—even if the closest they ever get to nature is their lady's queynt. Class-structured civilized society is a kind of mass ego. To transcend the ego is to go beyond society as well. "Beyond" there lies, inwardly, the unconscious. Outwardly, the equivalent of the unconscious is the wilderness: both of these terms meet, one step even farther on, as *one*.

One religious tradition of this communion with nature which has survived into historic Western times is what has been called witchcraft. The antlered and pelted figure painted on the cave wall of Trois Frères, a shaman-dancer-poet, is a prototype of both Shiva and the Devil.

Animal marriages (and supernatural marriages) are a common motif of folklore the world around. A recent article by Lynn White puts the blame for the present ecological crisis on the Judaeo-Christian tradition—animals don't have souls and can't be saved; nature is merely a ground for us to exploit while working out our drama of free will and salvation under the watch of Jehovah. The Devil? "The Deivill apeired vnto her in the liknes of ane prettie boy in grein clothes . . . and at that tyme the Deivil gaive hir his markis; and went away from her in the liknes of ane blak dowg." "He wold haw carnall dealling with ws in the shap of a deir, or in any vther shap, now and then, somtyme he vold be lyk a stirk, a bull, a deir, a rae, or a dowg, etc, and haw dealling with us."

The archaic and primitive ritual dramas, which acknowledged all the sides of human nature, including the destructive, demonic, and ambivalent, were liberating and harmonizing. Freud said *he* didn't discover the unconscious, poets had centuries before. The purpose of California shamanism was "to heal disease and resist death, with a power acquired from dreams." An Arapaho dancer of the Ghost Dance came back from his trance to sing:

> "I circle around, I circle around
>
> The boundaries of the earth,
> The boundaries of the earth
>
> Wearing the long wing feathers as I fly
> Wearing the long wing feathers as I fly."

THE VOICE AS A WOMAN

"Everything was alive—the trees, grasses, and winds were dancing with me, talking with me; I could understand the songs of the birds." This ancient experience is not so much—in spite of later commentators—"religious" as it is a pure perception of beauty. The phenomenal world experienced at certain pitches is totally living, exciting, mysterious, filling one with a trembling awe, leaving one grateful and humble. The wonder of the mystery returns direct to one's own senses and consciousness: inside and outside; the voice breathes, "Ah!"

Breath is the outer world coming into one's body. With pulse—the two always harmonizing—the source of our inward sense of rhythm. Breath is spirit, "inspiration." Expiration, "voiced," makes the signals by which the species connects. Certain emotions and states occasionally seize the body; one becomes a whole tube of air vibrating—all voice. In mantra chanting, the magic utterances, built of seed-syllables such as

OM and AYNG and AH, repeated over and over, fold and curl on the breath until—when most weary and bored—a new voice enters, a voice speaks through you clearer and stronger than what you know of yourself; with a sureness and melody of its own, singing out the inner song of the self, and of the planet.

Poetry, it should not have to be said, is not writing or books. Nonliterate cultures with their traditional training methods of hearing and reciting, carry thousands of poems—death, war, love, dream, work, and spirit-power songs—through time. The voice of inspiration as an "other" has long been known in the West as the Muse. Widely speaking, the muse is anything other that touches you and moves you. Be it a mountain range, a band of people, the morning star, or a diesel generator. Breaks through the ego-barrier. But this touching-deep is as a mirror, and man in his sexual nature has found the clearest mirror to be his human lover. As the West moved into increasing complexities and hierarchies with civilization, Woman as nature, beauty, and the Other came to be an all-dominating symbol; secretly striving through the last three millennia with the Jehovah or Imperator God-figure, a projection of the gathered power of anti-nature social forces. Thus in the Western tradition the Muse and Romantic Love became part of the same energy, and woman as nature the field for experiencing the universe as sacramental. The lovers' bed was the sole place to enact the dances and ritual dramas that link primitive people to their geology and the Milky Way. The contemporary decline of the cult of romance is linked to the rise of the sense of the primitive, and the knowledge of the variety of spiritual practices and paths to beauty that cultural anthropology has brought us. We begin to move away now, in this interesting historical spiral, from monogamy and monotheism.

Yet the muse remains a woman. Poetry is voice, and according to Indian tradition, voice, vāk (vox)—is a Goddess. Vāk is also called Sarasvati, she is the lover of Brahma and his actual creative energy; she rides a peacock, wears white, carries a book-scroll and a vina. The name Sarasvati means "the flowing one." "She is again the Divine in the aspect of wisdom and learning, for she is the Mother of Veda; that is of all knowledge touching Brahman and the universe. She is the Word of which it was born and She is that which is the issue of her great womb, Mahāyoni. Not therefore idly have men worshipped Vāk, or Sarasvati, as the Supreme Power."

As Vāk is wife to Brahma ("wife" means "wave" means "vibrator" in Indo-European etymology) so the voice, in everyone, is a mirror of his own deepest self. The voice rises to answer an inner need; or as BusTon says, "The voice of the Buddha arises, being called forth by the thought of the living beings." In esoteric Buddhism this becomes the basis of a mandala meditation practice: "In their midst is Nayika, the essence of *Ali*, the vowel series—she possesses the true nature of Vajrasattva, and is Queen of the Vajra-realm. She is known as the Lady, as Suchness, as Void, as Perfection of Wisdom, as limit of Reality, as Absence of Self."

The conch shell is an ancient symbol of the sense of hearing, and of the female; the vulva and the fruitful womb. At Koptos there is a bas-relief of a four-point buck, on the statue of the god Min, licking his tongue out toward two conches. There are many Magdalenian bone and horn engravings of bear, bison, and deer licking abstract penises and vulvas. At this point (and from our most archaic past transmitted) the mystery of voice becomes one with the mystery of body.

How does this work among primitive peoples in practice? James Mooney, discussing the Ghost Dance religion, says, "There is no limit to the number of these [Ghost Dance] songs, as every trance at every dance produces a new one, the trance subject after regaining consciousness embodying his experience in the spirit world in the form of a song, which is sung at the next dance and succeeding performances until superseded by other songs originating in the same way. Thus a single dance may easily result in twenty or thirty new songs. While songs are thus born and die, certain ones which appeal especially to the Indian heart, on account of their mythology, pathos, or peculiar sweetness, live and are perpetuated."

Modern poets in America, Europe, and Japan are discovering the breath, the voice, and trance. It is also for some a discovery to realize that the universe is not a dead thing but a continual creation, the song of Sarasvati springing from the trance of Brahma. "Reverence to Her who is eternal, Raudrī, Gaurī, Dhātri, reverence and again reverence, to Her who is

the Consciousness in all beings, reverence and again reverence.
... Candī says."

HOPSCOTCH AND CATS CRADLES

> *The clouds are "Shining Heaven" with his*
> *different bird-blankets on*
> —Haida

The human race, as it immediately concerns us, has a vertical axis of about 40,000 years and as of A.D. 1900 a horizontal spread of roughly 3000 different languages and 1000 different cultures. Every living culture and language is the result of countless cross-fertilizations—not a "rise and fall" of civilizations, but more like a flowerlike periodic absorbing—blooming—bursting and scattering of seed. Today we are aware as never before of the plurality of human life-styles and possibilities, while at the same time we are tied, like in an old silent movie, to a runaway locomotive rushing headlong toward a singular catastrophe. Science, as far as it is capable of looking "on beauty bare," is on our side. Part of our being modern is the fact of our awareness that we are one with our beginnings—contemporary with all periods—members of all cultures. The seeds of every social structure or custom are in the mind.

The anthropologist Stanley Diamond has said, "The sickness of civilization consists in its failure to incorporate (and only then) to move beyond the limits of the primitive." Civilization is so to speak a lack of faith, a human laziness, a willingness to accept the perceptions and decisions of others in place of one's own—to be less than a full man. Plus, perhaps, a primate inheritance of excessive socializing; and surviving submission/dominance traits (as can be observed in monkey or baboon bands) closely related to exploitative sexuality. If evolution has any meaning at all we must hope to slowly move away from such biological limitations, just as it is within our power to move away from the self-imposed limitations of small-minded social systems. We all live within skin, ego, society, and species boundaries. Consciousness has boundaries of a different order—"the mind is free." College students trying something different because "they do it in New Guinea" are part of the real work of modern man: to uncover the inner structure and actual boundaries of the mind. The third Mystery. The charts and maps of this realm are called mandalas in Sanskrit. (A poem by the Sixth Dalai Lama runs "Drawing diagrams I measured / Movement of the stars / Though her tender flesh is near / Her mind I cannot measure.") Buddhist and Hindu philosophers have gone deeper into this than almost anyone else but the work is just beginning. We are now gathering all the threads of history together and linking modern science to the primitive and archaic sources.

The stability of certain folklore motifs and themes, while showing evidences of linguistic borrowing and offering examples of the deeper meaning of linguistic drift, finally prove that the laws which styles and structures (art-forms and grammars, songs and ways of courting) attend all relate and reflect each other as mirrors of the self. Even the uses of the word *nature,* as in the seventeenth-century witch Isobel Gowdie's testimony about what it was like to make love to the Devil—"I found his nature cold within me as spring-well-water"—throw light on human nature.

Thus nature leads into nature—the wilderness—and the reciprocities and balances by which man lives on earth. Ecology: "eco" (*oikos*) meaning "house" (cf. "ecumenical"): Housekeeping on Earth. Economics, which is merely the housekeeping of various social orders—taking out more than it puts back—must learn the rules of the greater realm. Ancient and primitive cultures had this knowledge more surely and with almost as much empirical precision (see H. C. Conklin's work on Hanunoo plant-knowledge, for example) as the most concerned biologist today. Inner and outer: the *Brihadāranyaka Upanishad* says, "Now this Self is the state of being of all contingent beings. In so far as a man pours libations and offers sacrifice, he is in the sphere of the gods; in so far as he recites the Veda he is in the sphere of the seers; in so far as he offers cakes and water to the ancestors, in so far as he gives food and lodging to men, he is of the sphere of men. In so far as he finds grass and water for domestic animals, he is in the sphere of domestic animals; in so far as wild beasts and birds, even down to ants, find something to live on in his house, he is of their sphere."

The primitive world view, far-out scientific knowledge, and the poetic imagination are related forces which may help if not to save the world or humanity, at least to save the Redwoods. The goal of Revolution is Transformation. Mystical traditions within the great religions of civilized times have taught a doctrine of Great Effort for the achievement of Transcendence. This must have been their necessary compromise with civilization, which needed for its period to turn man's vision away from nature, to nourish the growth of the social energy. The archaic, the esoteric, and the primitive traditions alike all teach that beyond transcendence is Great Play, and Transformation. After the mind-breaking Void, the emptiness of a million universes appearing and disappearing, all created things rushing into Krishna's devouring mouth; beyond the enlightenment that can say "these beings are dead already; go ahead and kill them, Arjuna" is a loving, simple awareness of the absolute beauty and preciousness of mice and weeds.

Tsong-kha-pa tells us of a transformed universe:

"1. This is a Buddha-realm of infinite beauty
2. All men are divine, are subjects
3. Whatever we use or own are vehicles of worship
4. All acts are authentic, not escapes."

Such authenticity is at the heart of many a primitive world view. For the Anaguta of the Jos plateau, Northern Nigeria, North is called "up"; South is called "down." East is called "morning" and West is called "evening." Hence (according to Dr. Stanley Diamond in his *Anaguta Cosmography*), "Time flows past the permanent central position . . . they live at a place called noon, at the center of the world, the only place where space and time intersect." The Australian aborigines live in a world of ongoing recurrence—comradeship with the landscape and continual exchanges of being and form and position; every person, animals, forces, all are related via a web of reincarnation—or rather, they are "interborn." It may well be that rebirth (or interbirth, for we are actually mutually creating each other and all things while living) is the objective fact of existence which we have not yet brought into conscious knowledge and practice.

It is clear that the empirically observable interconnectedness of nature is but a corner of the vast "jewelled net" that moves from without to within. The spiral (think of nebulae) and spiral conch (vulva/womb) is a symbol of the Great Goddess. It is charming to note that physical properties of spiral conches approximate the Indian notion of the world-creating dance, "expanding form"—"We see that the successive chambers of a spiral Nautilus or of a straight Orthoceras, each whorl or part of a whorl of a periwinkle or other gastropod, each additional increment of an elephant's tusk, or each new chamber of a spiral foraminifer, has its leading characteristic at once described and its form so far described by the simple statement that it constitutes a *gnomon* to the whole previously existing structure" (D'Arcy Thompson).

The maze dances, spiral processions, cats cradles, Micronesian string star-charts, mandalas, and symbolic journeys of the old wild world are with us still in the universally distributed children's game. Let poetry and Bushmen lead the way in a great hop forward:

> In the following game of long hopscotch, the part marked H is for Heaven: it is played in the usual way except that when you are finishing the first part, on the way up, you throw your tor into Heaven. Then you hop to 11, pick up your tor, jump to the very spot where your tor landed in Heaven, and say, as fast as you can, the alphabet forwards and backwards, your name, address and telephone number (if you have one), your age, and the name of your boy-friend or girl-friend (if you have one of those).
>
> Patricia Evans, *Hopscotch*

XII. '67

Suwa-no-se Island and the Banyan Ashram

SEVERAL years ago Nanao Sakaki, the wanderer and poet, was traveling on a small interisland freighter between Kyushu and Amami Oshima and got into a conversation with a fellow passenger, an islander, who casually invited Nanao to come visit his island. Nanao did, another year, and just when a typhoon came; so he was holed up for over a week in a farmhouse waiting for the storm to blow over.

The island has only eight households—forty people—and, though the major part of the island is volcano and lavaflow, there is plenty of unoccupied land that is livable. Hence the islanders told Nanao that if he or his friends wished to come camp or live there, they'd be welcome.

Nanao's old circle of friends in Tokyo, the "Emerald Breeze" branch of the "Harijan" (formerly known as the Bum Academy), had already started a farm in the highlands of Nagano prefecture. They decided to add Suwa-no-se Island to their plans: In May, Nanao, Miko, and Shinkai went down; Pon in June with several others; Franco, Naga, Masa, and me in July. You have to go to Kagoshima, the southernmost town of size in Kyushu. A boat leaves for the "Ten Islands" once a week. Unpredictably. So that we were hung up for five days in Kagoshima, a cheap waterfront inn, while the ship waited out a typhoon scare. Did our grocery shopping and walked out to the ends of breakwaters waiting.

The *Toshima Maru* left at six in the evening. A little diesel freighter of 250 tons. At daybreak coming in on Kuchi-no-erabu Island—silvery rainsqualls, green cliffs, flashings of seabirds. The ship called at three islands through the day—anchoring beyond the edge of the coral reef, loading and unloading from tossing little unpainted island boats.

Late in the afternoon the ship was approaching Suwa-no-se, a violet mountain from afar, with cloudcaps and banners of mist. (The fishermen who come down from Miyazaki on Kyushu in their seaworthy little 3 ton fishing boats call it "Yake-jima"—Burning Island. Because much of the time the volcano is smoking.)

Anchoring offshore, the *Toshima Maru* blows its whistle and finally, down a steep trail through bamboo, a few men running. After half an hour a small boat puts out from behind a big boulder and cement breakwater at the base of the cliffs — steers through a path in the coral reef and comes alongside the freighter. The islanders bring out watermelons and wild goats. The goats go down to Amami Oshima where people like to eat them. Then, us, with our rucksacks and provisions, aboard the little boat, ashore through rough waves and getting wet, up on the rocky beach. Stepping over and through the lines and cables of several small fishing boats, nets, cables of the winch system for handling the boats in and out. Everybody waiting for us, almost black from being always in the sun. Packed all our groceries and rucksacks up the switchbacks and across a mile or so of trail through semijungle to the abandoned house and clearing they were using. Nanao and Shinkai had just finished a small extra shelter of bamboo; dome-shaped, with a thatch roof—so there was sleeping space for everyone. Fourteen people, almost half of them women.

Suwa-no-se is latitude 29° 36', which puts it on a level roughly with the Canary Islands, Cairo, Chihuahua, Persepolis, and Lhasa. Almost halfway from Kyushu to Amami Oshima. The Amami group of islands continue into the Ryukyus and the culture is quite similar to the Okinawan but there are dialect differences. From Yoron Island you can see Okinawa they say. Yoron is part of Japan. Suwa-no-se was probably populated off and on for several thousand years, depending on the activity of the volcano. The "Ten Islands" are part of a steppingstone system of islands all the way from Taiwan to Kyushu, by which paleolithic voyagers worked their way up to Japan. So they must have stopped off. Suwa-no-se was abandoned after the great eruption of the fifteenth century, and nobody returned until a century ago when some settlers came up from Amami to try again. Our villagers are thus of the Amami line, and speak Amami dialect; play the snake-head "jabisen" instead of the catskin-head "shamisen." They keep pigs, which is also an Amami custom. Mainland Japanese have never much taken to pigs. Also, they drink distilled sweet-potato liquor instead of sake; and sweet potatoes make a main part of the year's food—cheaper and easier to raise on the windy islands than rice.

The main part of the island is mountainous and uninhabited, but there is a kind of plateau about 400 feet above sea level that makes a southern extension, with several good streams running through it—an arable plateau maybe two miles by three miles, and covered for the most part by bamboo and grasses. A great pasture of fifty or so acres toward the east, and some pine and *Tabu* forests on the flanks of the mountain. Banyan trees and other large subtropical plants follow in the watercourses.

Sweet-potato and watermelon fields are cut-out squares in the bamboo here and there. The houses are clustered toward the west, which is closest to the little harbor; each house separate and enclosed in a wall of bamboo. Even the trails are shadowy corridors through the bamboo jungle and under the limbs of the banyan.

In the open pasture twenty-three head of black beef cattle at large, and on the edge of the pasture the abandoned farmhouse that became our headquarters. Up the meadow a way toward the mountain is a magnificent banyan on the edge of a ravine—we cleared out a meditation ground within its hanging roots—finally called our whole place "Banyan Ashram," or Pon calls it "Banyan Dream."

Daily work was clearing a new field for sweet-potato planting. We had to get all the bamboo root runners out, turning it over with hoes and grubbing the roots. Backbreaking work, and very slow. Because of midday heat it could only be done before ten-thirty or after four. In midday we napped in the shade of the banyan, or in the Bamboo House. Other work was fuel-gathering (dead pine underbranches; dead bamboo; or driftwood from the beaches loaded in a carrying basket and toted with a tumpline on the forehead) and cooking; done by turn in pairs in an open kitchen-shed with a thatch roof on an old brick campfire stove. Chinese style. (Our diet was basically brown rice and miso soup with potatoes and sweet potatoes and occasional watermelons or local bananas.) Also a lot of carpentry and construction work was continually going on, and a few hands every few days down to the village to join in on a village project, community trail-repair, or helping gut and flay an extra-large flying fish catch before it could spoil.

The ocean: every day except when the wind was too strong (fringe of a typhoon somewhere) most of us made it to the beach. There are three places to go: the eastern beach, forty minutes by trail, is wide and rough, with a good view of the volcano. The waves are very heavy. It looks across the Pacific toward Mexico. The coral reef goes out a long way, so it's not suitable for skindiving except when the weather is exceptionally calm. The beach has splendid driftwood and drift-lumber, and lots of seashells to gather. There's a cave toward one end within which thirty-six cows can stand in a rainstorm without getting wet. The southern beach is reached by a brushy trail also forty minutes—steep descent down the cliff but possible no-hands; it has a shorter coral ledge and a lovely natural cove within the coral which is deep and affords a passage into deep water under the breakers (you swim out to the gate and dive and glide underwater for thirty or forty feet and surface beyond the heavy pounding). There are strong tidal currents here, and we decided it was dangerous for anyone not an excellent swimmer and diver.

The western beach is the most sheltered and the best for fishing. We had vague ideas about spearfishing from the beginning and I brought a pocketful of steel harpoon heads (the smallest ones) with me—but it wasn't until Arikawa-san, the youngest family man of the islanders, showed us how to make a long bamboo spear with an iron rod in the end on which the spearhead sockets (attached to the main bamboo by leader) that we seriously began to think about adding fish to our diet. The spear is powered by inner-tube rubber, and is about nine feet long. Ito and I made three of these. With flippers and goggles, spent two fruitless days in the water till we began to understand the habits and feelings of the different species. Then we began to take them regularly. It became noticeably easier to do heavy work with more protein in the diet.

Most of us would be vegetarians by choice, but this was a real case of necessity and ecology. The volcanic soil of the island (and the volcanic ash fallout) makes it hard to raise many vegetables there; but the waters are rich in fish. We offered our respects and gratitude to the fish and the Sea Gods daily, and ate them with real love, admiring their extraordinarily beautiful, perfect little bodies.

Hundreds of varieties and thousands of individuals, all edible. Cobalt blue, shades of yellow and orange seemed the most common. None of the fish are really "tropical" and strange—but they are clearly subtropical with more variety than you'd find in colder waters. I became absorbed in the life of the sea. Without a fish book I came to recognize dozens of species and gradually came to know their habits and peculiarities and territories and emotions.

There is a great truth in the relationship established by hunting: as in love or art, you must become one with the other. (Which is why Paleolithic hunting magic is so important historically: the necessities of identity, intuition, stillness, that go with hunting make it seem as though shamanism and yoga and meditation may have their roots in the requirements of the hunter—where a man learns to be motionless for a day, putting his mind in an open state so that his consciousness won't spook creatures that he knows will soon be approaching.)

In spearfishing we learned you must never choose a specific fish for a quarry: you must let the fish choose you, and be prepared to shoot the fish that will come into range. For some fish you must be one with the sea and consider yourself a fish among fish. But there was one large and unpredictable variety (cobalt with a crescent-shaped tail) that digs the strange. When one of those was around I would change my mind and consider myself a freak and be out of place; in which case he will come to look at you out of curiosity.

When you go down with the fishes minus your spear they treat you differently too. I got so I could go down to twenty-five or thirty feet fairly comfortably. An old man originally from Okinawa, Uaji-san, dives sixty feet. He's seventy years old, and has a wise, tough, beautiful young wife. He caught a sea turtle and gave most of it to the Ashram once.

Sometimes the islanders had special catches on their little boats; once we had all the shark meat we could eat; another time a giant feast of raw sawara; once a whole bucket of flying-fish eggs. A few times went on shellfish-gathering expeditions together. By next summer the Ashram plans to have a small boat, which will make fishing a regular and efficient operation.

The weather is breezy, the sun hot. The ocean sends up great squalls and sudden rainstorms which dry up in twenty minutes. The volcano goes grummmmmmmm and lots of purple smoke comes up, into the sky, to 15,000 feet.

Meals were served on the mat-floor of the farmhouse, everybody crosslegged, with Taku-chan the Gotos' two-year-old boy wandering stark naked through it all. After supper at night we generally sat almost totally silent around our two or three candles, sometimes humming mantras or folksongs; or went out in the cow pasture with a bottle of shochu and played the jew's-harp (which the Harijan all call a bigigi, the New Guinea name for it) and the Kenya drum (a present from Ginzap four years ago) to our patron star, Antares.

Those who rose very early went to meditate under the banyan—a lovely thing especially because of the song of the Akahige ("Redbeard" Temminck's Robin) which sings in the early-morning canyons with a remarkable trilling, falling song that drops three octaves and echoes across hills and meadows. Also the songs of the Hototo-gisu (Himalayan Cuckoo) and Blue Doves—filling up the whole morning world with song. While morning mists blow and curl around and the grass is all dewy and the Rising Sun of Japan comes up through the ocean and the fog like a big red rising sun flag.

After breakfast every morning there would be a quiet, natural discussion of the day's work; people would volunteer for various tasks—never any pressuring—somebody might say, "Let's be sure and put the tools back where we got them, I couldn't find the file yesterday" or something—but without acrimony; Westerners have much to learn from this easy cooperativeness and sense of getting the work done without fuss. The Banyan people had less ego-friction (none!) and difficulty over chores than any group I've ever seen.

Masa Uehara and I were married on the island on August 6, the new moon. The whole ashram stayed up late the night before, packing a breakfast for the morrow—and broiling a splendid pink tai that was a present from the village. (No marriage is complete if you don't eat tai afterwards, the noble, calm AUSPICIOUS FISH of Japan.) We got up at 4:30 and started up the brush trail in the dark. First dipping into a ravine and then winding up a jungly knife-edge ridge. By five we were out of the jungle and onto a bare lava slope. Following the long ridge to an older, extinct crater, and on to the crest of the main crater and the summit shortly after sunrise. The lip of the crater drops off into cloud; and out of the cloud comes a roaring like an airport full of jets: a billowing of steam upwards. The cloud and mist broke, and we could see 800 feet or so down into the crater—at least a mile across—and fumaroles and steam-jets; at the very center red molten lava in a little bubbly pond. The noise, according to the switch of the wind, sometimes deafening.

Standing on the edge of the crater, blowing the conch horn and chanting a mantra; offering shochu to the gods of the volcano, the ocean, and the sky; then Masa and I exchanged the traditional three sips—Pon and Nanao said a few words; Masa and I spoke; we recited the Four Vows together, and ended with three blasts on the conch. Got out of the wind and opened the rucksacks to eat the food made the night before, and drink the rest of the shochu. We descended from the summit and were down to the Banyan tree by eleven—went direct on out to the ocean and into the water; so that within one morning we passed from the windy volcanic summit to the warm coral waters. At four in the afternoon all the villagers came to the Ashram—we served sake and shochu—pretty soon everyone was singing Amami folksongs and doing traditional dances.

The sweet-potato field got cleared and planted; Franco left a bit early to be in San Luis Obispo by mid-September; we started clearing another patch of land and built a big outdoor table of driftwood; went around to the north side of the island in a small boat to investigate other possibilities of settlements and fishing.

Masa and I caught the *Toshima Maru* heading on south at the end of August and visited Cho in Koniya; with Shinkai checked on boatbuilders' prices; took another ship up to Kagoshima (all night on the deck sitting on matting watching the full moon).

And hitchhiked to Miyazaki for a three-day Harijan gathering and a look at the neolithic tumuli in the region; and back to Kyoto. Miko and Akibananda and others will be on the island all year; Pon and Nanao are back up in Nagano at the mountain Ashram now.

It is possible at last for Masa and me to imagine a little of what the ancient—archaic—mind and life of Japan were. And to see what could be restored to the life today. A lot of it is simply in being aware of clouds and wind.

Eighth Moon, 40067
(reckoning roughly from the earliest cave paintings)

From
HE WHO HUNTED BIRDS IN HIS FATHER'S VILLAGE
THE DIMENSIONS OF A HAIDA MYTH

The Myth

HE WHO HUNTED BIRDS IN HIS FATHER'S VILLAGE
(Told by Walter McGregor of the Sealion-town people)

He was a chief's son. He wore two marten-skin blankets, one over the other. After he had shot birds for some time he went along among some bull pines, which stood in an open space behind the town, and presently heard geese calling. Then he went thither. Two women were bathing in a lake. On the shore opposite two goose skins hung over a stick. The roots of their tails were spotted with white.

After he had looked a while he ran quickly (to them). He sat down on the two skins. Then they asked him for their (skins). He asked the best looking to marry him. The other said to him: "Do not marry my younger sister. I am smarter. Marry me." "No; I am going to marry your younger sister." Now she agreed. "Even so, marry my younger sister. You caught us swimming in the lake our father owns. Come, give me my skin." Then he gave it to her. She put her head into it as she swam in the lake. Lo, a goose swam about in the lake. It swam about in it making a noise.

Then she flew. She was unwilling to fly away from her younger sister. After she had flown about above her for a while, she flew up. She vanished through the sky. Then he gave her (the other) one marten-skin blanket and went home with her. He put his wife's skin between two heads of a cedar standing at one end of the town. He entered his father's house with her.

The chief's son had a wife. So his father called the people together for the marriage feast. They gave her food. Instead (of eating it) she merely smelled it. She ate no kind of human food.

By and by her mother-in-law steamed some *tcal*. But she liked that. While her mother-in-law was yet cooking them she told her husband to tell her to hurry. They put some before her. She ate it all. Then they began giving her that only to eat.

One day, when he was asleep, he was surprised to find that his wife's skin, after she came in and lay down, was cold. And, when the same thing happened again, he began watching her. He lay as if asleep. He felt her get up quietly. Then she went out, and he also went out just after her. She passed in front of the town. She went to the place where her skin was kept. Thence she flew away. She alighted on the farther side of a point at one end of the town.

Then he went thither quickly. She was eating the stalks of the sea grass that grew there. As the waves broke in they moved her shoreward. He saw it. Then she flew up to the place where her (feather) skin had been kept. And he entered the house before her. Then he lay down where they had their bed, after which his wife lay down cold beside him.

They became nearly starved in the town. One day the woman said to him from the place where she was sitting: "Now my father has sent down food to me." Behind the town geese were coming down making a great noise, and she went thither. They went with her. All kinds of good food lay there such as *tcal* and wild clover roots. They brought them away. For this her father-in-law called in the people.

When this was gone she said the same thing again: "Now my father is bringing food down to me." Geese again made a great noise coming down behind the town and she went thither. Again heaps of food of all kinds lay around, and they carried that also out. For that, too, her father-in-law called together the people.

At that time someone in the town said: "They think a great deal of goose food." The woman heard it. Immediately she went off. Her husband in vain tried to stop her. She went off as one of a strange family would. In the same way he tried to stop her in front of the town. She went to the place where her skin was. She flew up. She flew around above the town for a while. Her heart was not strong to fly away from her husband. By and by she vanished through the sky.

Then her husband began to walk about the town wailing. By and by he entered the house of an old man at one end of the town and asked him: "Do you know the trail that leads to my wife?" "Why, brave man, you married the daughter of a supernatural being too great for people even to think of." At once he began bringing over all sorts of things to him. After he had given him twisted cedar limbs, a gimlet, and bones, he said to him: "Now, brave man, take oil. Take two wooden wedges also. Take as well, a comb, thongs, boxes of salmon eggs, the skin of a silver salmon, the point of a salmon spear." After he had got all these he came to him. "Old man, here are all the things you told me to take." "Now, brave man, go on. The trail runs inland behind my house."

Then he started in on it. After he had gone on for a while he came to someone who was looking upon himself for lice. Every time he turned around the lice fell off from him. After he had looked at him unobserved for a while he said to him: "Now brave man, do not tickle me by looking at me. It was in my mind that you were coming." Then he came out to him and combed his head. He also put oil on it. He cleared him of lice. He gave the comb and the hair oil to him. Then he said to him: "This trail leads to the place where your wife is."

He started along the trail. After he had gone on for a while (he saw) a mouse with cranberries in its mouth going along before him. She came to a fallen tree. She could not get over it. Then he took her by the back with his fingers and put her across. Her tail was bent up between her ears (for joy), and she went on before him. Presently she went among the stalks of a clump of ferns.

Now he rested himself there. Something said to him: "The chief-woman asks you to come in." Then he raised the ferns. He stood in front of a big house. He entered. The chief-woman was steaming cranberries. She talked as she did so. Her voice sounded sharp. And, after she had given him something to eat, Mouse Woman said to him: "You helped me when I went to get some poor cranberries from a patch I own. I will lend you what I wore when I went hunting when I was young."

Then she brought out a box. After she had opened a nest of five boxes, she took out of the inmost a mouse skin with small, bent claws. And she said to him: "Practice wearing this." And, although it was so small, he entered it. It went on easily. Then he climbed around upon the roof of the house inside. And Mouse Woman said to him again: "You know how to use it. Now go on."

Again he set out upon the trail. After he had gone along for a while he heard someone grunting under a heavy burden. Then he came to the place. A woman was trying to carry off a pile of large, flat stones upon her back. The twisted cedar limbs she had kept breaking. After he had looked at her for a while he went out to her. "Say, what are you doing?" Then the woman said: "They got me to carry the mountains of the Haida Island. I am doing it."

Then he took out his thongs and said to her: "Let me fix it." And he bound the thongs around it. He said to her, "Now carry it on your back," and she carried it. It did not break. Then the woman said to him, "Now brave man, thank you for helping me. The trail to your wife's place runs here."

Then he set out upon it. After he had gone on for a while he came to a hill in an open place on top of which rose something red. Then he went to it. Around the bottom of this something lay human bones. There was no way in which one could go up. Then he entered the mouse skin and rubbed salmon eggs before him (on the pole). He went up after it. When he stood on top of this he clambered up on the sky.

There, too, there ran a trail, and he started off upon it. After he had gone on for a while he heard the noise of laughter and singing. After he had gone on a while longer (he came to where) a big stream flowed down. Near it sat Eagle. On the other side also sat Heron. Above sat Kingfisher. On the other side sat Black Bear. He (Black Bear) had no claws. He said to Eagle: "Grandfather, lend me some claws." Then he lent him some. At that time he came to have claws.

After he had sat there for a while a half-man came vaulting along. He had only one leg and one arm. He had but half a head. He speared silver salmon in the river and pulled them in. Then he entered his silver salmon skin and swam up to meet him. When he speared him he could not pull him down. Then he cut his string. And the half-man said: "What did it is like a human being."

Now he came to him. "Say, did something pull off your spearpoint?" "Yes," he said to him. Then he gave him the one he had. That was Master Hopper, they say. After he had gone up (he came upon) two large old men who had come after firewood. They were cutting at the trunks of rotten trees and throwing the chips into the water, when silver salmon went down in a shoal.

He went behind and put stones in from behind, and their wedges were broken off. Then he (one) said: "Alas, they will make trouble for us." Then he went and gave them his two wedges. They were glad and said to him: "This house is your wife's."

Then he went out (to it). He went and stood in front of the house. His wife came out to him. Then he went in with her. She was glad to see her husband. And all the things they gathered he, too, gathered along with them.

After he had been there for some time he came to dislike the place. And his wife told her father. Then his father-in-law called the people. In the house he asked them: "Who will take my son-in-law down?" And Loon said: "I will put him near my tail, dive into the water right in front with him, come up at the end of his father's village, and let him off." Then they thought he was not strong enough for it.

Then he asked again. Grebe said the same thing. Him, too, they thought not strong enough to do it. Then Raven said that he would take him down. And they asked him: "How are you going to do it?" "I will put him into my armpit and fly down with him from the end of the town. When I get tired I will fall over and over with him." Then they thought he could do it.

They stood in a crowd at the end of the town looking at him. He did with him as he had said. When he became very tired and was nearly down he threw him off upon a reef which lay there. "Yuwaiya, what a heavy thing I am taking down." Shortly he (the man) was making a noise there as a seagull.

Function of the Myth

1. INTRODUCTORY

CONTEMPORARY theory of the function of mythology almost inevitably involves theory of the function of language, ritual, religion, and art—either as similar but separate modes of psychocultural activity, or as ultimately identical aspects of the same thing, sometimes termed "Myth" in the broader sense of all symbolic cognition. The philosophical substructures implied in most of these theories include everything from metaphysics to theory of knowledge. In utilizing concepts from them it will be impossible to take into account the possible criticisms of their basic assumptions. My intention is to present the possible extent of the cultural function of the Haida Swan-Maiden myth, through a description and discussion of general statements by individuals of philosophical, literary, psychological, and anthropological persuasions. In doing so it may be argued that I am misinterpreting a theory or ignoring some underlying assumptions. I can only answer that the total view achieved by this method is my own doing, created by the selection of relevant concepts and implying no criticism of or assent to, any one point of view. It may appear, through my manner of presentation, that the scholars quoted are all in essential agreement. This is, to the best of my knowledge, only occasionally true, and under the peaceful surface of this discussion rage a number of minor controversies with which I am but superficially acquainted.

Anthropological studies dealing with oral literature as a functional element in culture are rare; and they are, with few exceptions, restricted to generalizing on the subject of mythology. Functionally oriented ethnology has never been practiced on the Haida. The concluding definition of the Haida Swan-Maiden myth will be the product of the most speculative approach in this thesis. Its verification would require residence in the culture, which for me is not possible.

The basic assumption of this chapter is that mythology has a function in culture. This may seem too obvious a fact to require statement, but many past theories of mythology have operated as if myths were irrational diseases from which savage minds suffered, or the result of idle, mistaken savage speculation in which elaborate stories were constructed to describe the phases of the moon or processes of sunrise and sunset. Much of the modern interest in mythology stems from the recognition of its social function, as does the even more recent attitude of some scholars and poets that the function mythology serves in primitive culture is desperately needed by contemporary society. The progress-minded nineteenth-century anthropologists, for whom mythology seemed curious, irrational, and "wrong," could never have discovered the world-shaking significance in irrational and (to Andrew Lang's continual dismay) sometimes bestial little stories which today are seen as descriptions of man's inmost needs. For example, take the modern associations attached to the Oedipus myth.

This chapter will first present statements of the function and nature of mythology, then clarify the sociopsychological processes as studied by Abram Kardiner, link together a number of other views on the function of mythology in his terms, and conclude with a summary of the entire thesis and the dimensions of mythology as indicated by this study.

2. DESCRIPTION OF THE FUNCTION

Recognition of the social function of mythology may be traced, in terms of the first influential, articulate public statement on the subject, to Bronislaw Malinowski's "Myth in Primitive Psychology," published in 1926. His essay was based on field observation among the Trobriand Islanders. He wrote:

> Myth as it exists in a savage community, that is, in its living primitive form, is not merely a story told but a reality lived. It is not of the nature of fiction, such as we read today in a novel, but it is a living reality, believed to have once happened in primeval times, and continuing ever since to influence the world and human destinies. This myth is to the savage what, to a fully believing Christian, is the Biblical story of Creation, of

the Fall, of the Redemption by Christ's Sacrifice on the Cross. As our sacred story lives in our ritual, in our morality, as it governs our faith and controls our conduct, even so does his myth for the savage.

... Myth fulfills in primitive culture an indispensable function: it expresses, enhances, and codifies belief; it safeguards and enforces morality; it vouches for the efficiency of ritual and contains practical rules for the guidance of man. Myth is thus a vital ingredient of human civilization; it is not an idle tale, but a hard-worked active force; it is not an intellectual explanation or an artistic imagery, but a pragmatic character of primitive faith and moral wisdom.

Although Malinowski's essay, which was limited to primitive culture, emphasized the necessity of studying mythology in the cultural context, he has been cited by later writers with divergent and much more inclusive views of myth. Mark Schorer, for example:

Myths are the instruments by which we continually struggle to make our experience intelligible to ourselves. A myth is a large, controlling image that gives philosophical meaning to the facts of ordinary life; that is, which has organizing value for experience.

... Literature ceases to be perceptual and tends to degenerate into mere description without adequate myth; for, to cite Malinowski, myth, continually modified and renewed by the modification of history, is in some form an "indispensable ingredient of all culture."

On the same page Schorer quotes Jung, and shows indebtedness to Jung's view of myth by the statement "Myth is fundamental, the dramatic representation of our deepest instinctual life."

The same essay provoked an objection from Robert Lowie:

... What if myth is "not merely a story but a reality lived?" We cannot relive the reality, but we can study that textual rendering which Malinowski disdains as merely the "intellectual" aspect of the tales divorced from their mystic aura.

C. Kerenyi made the complete marriage of Malinowski's view and Jungian theory, while setting out to show that we *can* relive the reality. He quotes the entire "reality lived" passage and writes:

> The myth, he (Malinowski) says, is not an explanation put forward to satisfy scientific curiosity; it is the re-arising of a primordial reality in narrative form.

> Mythology gives a ground, lays a foundation. It does not answer the question "why," but "whence?" In Greek we can put this difference very nicely. Mythology does not actually indicate "causes," *aitia*. It does this (is "aetiological") only to the extent that ... the *aitia* are *archai* or first principles ... (happenings in mythology) are the *archai* to which everything individual and particular goes back and out of which it is made, whilst they remain ageless, inexhaustible, invincible in timeless primordiality, in a past that proves imperishable because of its eternally repeated rebirths.

Kerenyi suggests the possibility of the archetypal "mythologems" being present—literally—in the physical beginnings of man:

> He experiences it (the mythologem) as his own absolute *archai*, a beginning since when he was a unity fusing in itself all the contradictions of his nature and life to be. To this origin, understood as the beginning of a new world-unity, the mythologem of the *divine child* points. The mythologem of the *maiden goddess* points to yet another *archai*, also experienced as one's own origin but which is at the same time the *archai* of countless beings before and after oneself, and by virtue of which the individual is endowed with infinity already in the germ.

Another scholar who is well aware of Malinowski's work is I. A. Richards. He wrote of the "greater and saner mythologies"—

> They are no amusement or diversion to be sought as a relaxation and an escape from the hard realities of life. They are these hard realities in projection, their symbolic recognition, coordination and acceptance. Through such mythologies our will is collected, our powers unified, our growth controlled....

> Without his mythologies man is only a cruel animal without a soul—for a soul is a central part of his governing mythology—he is a congeries of possibilities without order and without aim.

Kerenyi's theory remains so problematical as to render no heuristic service. Of Schorer's and Richards' views—if they are to prove of value—we must ask: how and why are hard realities projected, and how, once projected, do they serve as "controlling images"—and what do they control? The two key words "projection" and "control" have been used before in this essay in connection with the cultural content of mythology, and the operation of magic and ritual. The investigation of these words will show them to mean essentially the same thing in the various contexts cited, and demonstrate what Malinowski probably had in mind when he said that a myth is a reality lived.

3. KARDINER'S USE OF THE TERM "PROJECTION"

Abram Kardiner uses the term "projection" in a fairly specific sense, and in doing so describes what he conceives the process to be psychologically—and how values get into myths. His psychology is a socially-oriented neo-Freudianism. In *The Individual and His Society* and *The Psychological Frontiers of Society* he has presented a method of study and interpretation of culture that he believes will enable the student to determine the formative institutions (those institutions which regulate the formative experiences of childhood) and the influences of these institutions on the individual personality and total cultural configuration. The analysis of the mythology of the culture under observation plays an important part in Kardiner's analysis:

> We have had up to this point a series of inferences about the probable effects of certain formative institutions. How can this guess be substantiated or contradicted? If your hypothesis is correct, namely that these conditions in childhood become consolidated and form a basis for subsequent projective use, then we can expect to find some evidence of it in all projective systems ... religious, folklore, and perhaps

other institutions. In other words, if we know how the basic personality is established, we can make certain predictions about the institutions this personality is likely to invent. If we follow the particular personality created by the above mentioned conditions (sporadic minimal parental care, teasing of and deliberate misrepresentation to, children by parents) we expect to find folk tales dealing with parental hatred, with desertion by parents. . . .

Kardiner's assumption is that as the individual personality is shaped by the primary institutions, the oral prose-narrative, possessed and transmitted by the group, will mirror a group-personality derived from childhood experience. In reversing the process, he believes the culture's basic personality will reflect the psychologically relevant elements to be found in the tales. Kardiner's technique in both books is to cite ethnographic material on a culture, including a selection of abstracted tales, then to analyze the culture on the basis of the ethnographer's report and his own psychological assumptions, and finally, to cite the folktales as corroborative evidence of the truth of his analysis. In doing so, he avoids any discussion of the world distribution of types and motifs involved. The primary institutions center in the family structure—maternal care, induction of affectivity, maternal attitudes, early disciplines, sexual disciplines and institutionalized sibling attitudes. He lists these and a number of other institutions as the "Key Integrative Systems," which he ranks in terms of their manifestation in the basic personality structure as follows:

1. Projective systems based on experience with the aid of rationalizations, generalizations, systematization and elaboration. To this category belong the security system of the individual and the superego systems, that is, those dealing with conscience and ideals.
2. Learned systems connected with drives.
3. Learned systems in which no drives are involved but ideas associated with activities. Groups 2 and 3 lay the basis for specific psychosomatic tension release routes.
4. Taboo systems, all learned as part of reality.
5. Pure empirical reality systems, subject to demonstrations.

6. Value systems and ideologies (which cut across all previous systems).

Projective systems are schematically represented by Kardiner as being created in the following manner:

> Nuclear experiences which define apperceptions and emotionally directed interests, e.g., punishments for delinquency.

(resulting in:)

> Abstraction and generalization: e.g., "If I am obedient I will suffer no pain."

(resulting in:)

> Projection and systematization: e.g., "I am ill, therefore I have wronged."

(resulting in:)

> Rationalization (equals) ideology (equals) a system to overcome tensions:
> "There is a supreme being who observes my behavior. He has the attributes of omnipotence and omniscience, etc. If I do wrong I will be punished. If I suffer I will be reinstated." Once this system is accepted as reality, any number of rational systems can be devised to "prove" it, to modify it, or to render it workable.

By the same process a body of mythology is created, although the projected attitudes are contained in narrative form. In his analysis of Comanche folklore, for instance, Kardiner finds these underlying projections:

> The story of the faithless wife who sides with the Ute against her husband and is punished by him is another evidence of the underlying distrust of women, undoubtedly a projection of their (the Comanches') own anxiety about loss of power for war and sex alike.

A magic-flight story of children (Hansel and Gretel type):

It belittles the importance of parental care, and in sour-grapes fashion indicates that they (the children) don't need the parents anyway, they can look after themselves. This seems very like a protest against the unusual burdens placed on the child to emulate the parents and to become prematurely independent.

Kardiner divides the integrational systems into the major categories of "reality" and "projective" systems. He writes:

> In every society studied we found evidence of these two systems. The empirical reality systems were found in the manipulation and making of tools, the knowledge of planting, and so forth; the projective systems in religion, folklore, and many other systems.
> These two types of mental process depend upon different orders of experience.... Both have emotional components ... the experiential base of a projective system is generally forgotten; its only remains in the personality are to be found in the conditioned perceptions.... Projective systems are ... excrescences developed from nuclear traumatic experiences within the growth pattern of the individual.

He terms the latter system the "projective screen"—and in his discussion of its operation, becomes so annoyed with it as to ignore its functional value:

> The fantasy or projective screen hides social realities, and one cannot come to grips with them because the fantasy screen itself becomes the chief object of preoccupation and is mistaken for the reality to be dealt with.

In the same chapter, he admits "there is no difference between the actual logical or ratiocinative processes in the two (reality and projective) systems." The projective screen appears to be identical with what writers term "myth" in its broadest sense: the myth that reflects projected values, and in doing so reinforces the social fabric individual by individual, making it possible for the culture to survive. In admitting the identity of mental processes in the two systems, Kardiner lays himself open to the charge of projecting Western values in assuming that there are any "social realities" actually masked by the projective screen. For the culture in question, mythological and social realities are identical, and the function of mythology is to enforce this fusion—even though, to use Richards' term, the projections are of "hard realities." An even more extreme attack on Kardiner's dichotomy between projective and reality systems could be made from the philosophical stand denying the dualism of subject and object: the whole world is a projection, and mythology a particularly ordered projection that enables the more chaotic aspects of the world to be classified and comprehended.

Whether one agrees with Kardiner's projective-reality dichotomy or not, the careful scholarship and documented arguments of the two books, particularly the later one, are extremely convincing. Kardiner's description of the nature of projection undoubtedly covers a number of its most basic aspects and provides, if one accepts the Freudian tenets, a very workable theory of the interrelations of culture, personality, and mythology.

4. PROJECTION AND CONTROL

The ideas, attitudes, or situations projected into a myth—those derived from everyday experience as well as the less obvious ones based on childhood experience—have a peculiar relationship with the symbolic units representing them in narrative. The social value and the values expressed in myth are somehow connected, and in the myth's function, the projected unit appears to control and shape the experiences it was derived from, rather than remaining a subsidiary reflection of experience. Wherever mythology functions as a living part of culture, this may generally be said to be true. It is a fact of great significance about the human mind, and it has puzzled and annoyed rational-minded thinkers from the beginnings of Western philosophy right up to Kardiner. The myth unit does not control by any physical means, however, but by a metaphorical similarity to experience: by a process of sympathetic magic.

The identification of the operation of mythical narrative for the group with the principles of sympathetic magic—through the association of images with acts, causing the culture to take the image as primary to the act, and then to organize the acts in accordance with the myth, seems less farfetched when the close relationships between ritual and myths are recalled. Ritual is a conscious, community-enacted drama—often based on mythical plots and portraying characters from mythology—designed to control certain natural forces by enacting metaphorically similar situations in which the desired results are symbolically attained. Ritual unites the group and individual consciousness in a sense of community that not only breaks down the distinction between the two psychologically, but enforces the identity of projective and physical reality so as to make the whole universe become an aspect of the human community. Individual acts of magic operate in a similar fashion, taking place within the larger framework of belief. The whole "religious control of the universe" derives its potency from sympathetic, not physical actions on things. Sympathetic magic is, as Frazer points out, based on "mistaken" associations, and never actually shapes physical events. Functionally, however, it is a real force, and literally controls human affairs. It never controls them according to principles that run counter to physical fact in nature—part of the efficacy of the projective screen is its close integration with physical laws which concern the economic survival of the group. On the basis of this fact, Campbell writes,

> It has been customary to describe the seasonal festivals of so-called native peoples as efforts to control nature. This is a misrepresentation. There is much of the will to control in every act of man . . . (but) . . . the dominant motive in all truly religious (as opposed to black-magical) ceremonial is that of submission to the inevitables of destiny—and in the seasonal festivals this motive is particularly apparent.
>
> No tribal rite has yet been recorded which attempts to keep winter from descending; on the contrary, all rites prepare the community to endure, together with the rest of nature, the season of the terrible cold. And in the spring, the rites do not seek to compel nature to pour forth immediately corn, beans, and squash for the lean community; on the contrary: the rites dedicate the whole people to the work of nature's season.

Myth is, functionally, the verbal equivalent of ritual, magically operating with words, images, and situations in narrative form as ritual operates with symbolic acts.

Each of the narrative levels in a myth is capable of working as sympathetic magic, so that the complex of symbol-referent equivalences that may be found in any one myth in principle is a hierarchy (proceeding from particulars to wholes) of symbolic modes which is, at its farthest extent, culture itself. To clarify this, Frazer's description of the magical function of words must be recalled:

> Unable to discriminate clearly between words and things, the savage commonly fancies that the link between a name and the person or thing denominated by it is not a mere arbitrary and ideal association, but a real and substantial bond which unites the two in such a way that magic may be wrought on a man just as easily through his name as through his hair, his nails, or any other material part of his person.

This is elaborated by Malinowski, who based his discussion on field observation:

> . . . we are made to realize how deeply rooted is the belief that a word has some power over a thing, that it is akin or even identical in its contained "meaning" with the thing or with its prototype. . . . The word gives power, allows one to exercise an influence over an object or an action. . . . The word acts on the thing and the thing releases the word in the human mind. This indeed is nothing more or less than the essence of the theory which underlies the use of verbal magic.

Language and myth both derive from these principles, and although they become divergent at later "stages," the underlying relationship may always be seen, according to Ernst Cassirer:

> . . . for, no matter how widely the contents of myth and language may differ, yet the same form of mental conception is operative in both. It is the form which one may denote as *metaphorical thinking*.

Metaphorical thinking is the subjective identification of symbols and referents—on the basis of the control of symbol over referent—in Cassirer's view; another way of saying sympathetic magic.

Language, it is sometimes argued, is a fundamental prerequisite of ideation. Although this point cannot be adequately proved or refuted, it is certain A. L. Kroeber is right in assuming the necessity of language for the existence of culture:

> Cultural activity, even of the simplest kind, inevitably rests on ideas or generalizations; and such or any ideas, in turn, human minds seem to be able to formulate and operate with and transmit only through speech. Nature consists of an endless array of particular phenomena. To combine these particulars into a generalization or an abstraction, such as passing from potential awareness of the thousands of stones along a river bed into the idea of stone as a distinctive material—this synthesis appears to require production of some kind of symbol, perhaps as a sort of psychological catalyzing agent: a symbol such as the sounds that make up the word *stone*. In short, culture can probably function only on the basis of abstractions, and these in turn seem to be possible only through speech.

As the single word abstracts and controls for the user the essence of its referent; the image, metaphor, and myth abstract, organize, and symbolically represent larger blocks of experience—patterns of experience—which can be psychologically controlled by the individual because of their essential compact form. Actual experience is too disorganized and chaotic to allow the individual or group any feeling of security and order without the myth mechanism. In culture, language is a learned function that almost always communicates over any length of time within patterns of verbal significance larger than particular words. Mythology is the central patterning force of that verbal organization which survives through generations, containing the cosmology and value-system of the group. Even if the mythology is, as Kardiner says, ultimately the product of certain human institutions—the survival of the institutions in culture depends on the continuation of the mythological function. Myth is a "reality lived" because for every individual it contains, at the moment of telling, the projected content of both his unarticulated and conscious values: simultaneously ordering, organizing, and making comprehensible the world within which the values exist. One might even reformulate the statement to say "Reality is a myth lived."

The mythological symbolizing of experience, and the subsequent control of experience, has been seen by some writers as the principle of any organization of value and knowledge. A comparatively early statement of this view was that of George Santayana:

> Mythology and theology are the most striking illustrations of this human method of incorporating much diffuse experience into graphic and picturesque ideas; but steady reflection will hardly allow us to see anything else in the theories of science and philosophy.

This attitude toward the projective screen of "Myth" is common today among literary critics and a few philosophers. Susanne Langer's *Philosophy in a New Key* relates the nature and function of mythology and ritual to a fundamental symbol-making activity of man, basic to his nature. She states the relation of this theory to modern science:

> The problem of observation is all but eclipsed by the problem of *meaning*. And the truth of empiricism in science is jeopardized by the surprising truth that our sense-data are primarily symbols.

Individuals create their private symbolisms, and as the private symbolisms become articulately expressed in some cultures—particularly those with writing—complicated interactions of individual and group mythologies

> ... in a never ending interplay of symbolic gestures, built up the pyramided structure called civilization. In this structure very few bricks touch the ground.

The function of mythology may then be summarized: it provides a symbolic representation of projected values and empirical knowledge within a framework of belief which relates individual, group, and physical environment, to the end of integration and survival. The implication of this function for modern literary theory has been seized by many critics. In *Theory of Literature,* René Wellek and Austin Warren say:

Our view ... sees the meaning and function of literature as centrally present in metaphor and myth.

Or T. S. Eliot's discussion of the use of the *Odyssey* by James Joyce as an ordering framework for his novel *Ulysses:*

> In using the myth, in manipulating a continuous parallel between contemporaneity and antiquity, Mr. Joyce is pursuing a method which others must pursue after him. They will not be imitators, any more than the scientist who uses the discoveries of an Einstein in pursuing his own, independent, further investigations. It is simply a way of controlling, of ordering, of giving a shape and a significance to the immense panorama of futility and anarchy which is contemporary history.... Psychology (such as it is, and whether our reaction to it be comic or serious), ethnology, and *The Golden Bough* have concurred to make what was impossible even a few years ago. Instead of narrative method, we may now use the mythical method.

One of the most extreme statements by a contemporary literary critic is that of Philip Wheelwright, who sees the community myth-consciousness as essential for good literature—

> The poetry of our time doesn't matter much, it is a last echo of something important that was alive long ago. What matters is the myth-consciousness of the next generations, the spiritual seed that we plant in our children; their loves and insights and incubating sense of significant community. On that depend the possibilities of future greatness—in poetry and everything else.

A number of contemporary poets are not giving up yet, however. Some, like Robert Graves and Peter Viereck, have taken to speaking of the "magical" nature of poetry. Viereck sees no contradiction in his insistence on both "classicism" in poetry and its "holy dread"—the two formulate a

> ... dualism of what Nietzsche called the Dionysian and Apollonian; also the "dark gods" of the unconscious and the more rational, civilized conscious mind. The creative tension of these antitheses is in the shiver of holy dread, the tragic exaltation

which makes the hair stand on end and is the difference between poetry and verse.

He refers to the "all-important night-side of art, its magic" much as Graves claims,

> Poetry began in the matriarchal age, and derives its magic from the moon, not from the sun. No poet can hope to understand the nature of poetry unless he has had a vision of the Naked King crucified to the lopped oak, and watched the dancers, red-eyed from the acrid smoke of the sacrificial fires, stamping out the measure of the dance, their bodies bent uncouthly forward, with a monotonous chant of: "Kill! kill! kill!" and "Blood! blood! blood!"

The literary interest in magic derives from three sources: Frazer's *The Golden Bough*, Malinowski's *Myth in Primitive Psychology*, and Jung's *Psychology of the Unconscious*. Frazer presented the theory of magic and the concrete symbols attached to the strangely memorable myths of the dying god; Malinowski described the function of myth, and Jung suggested the possibility that it might be possible to write literature using symbols from Frazer which would function in modern civilization—for individuals—as myth functions in primitive culture for the group. In doing so, the poet would not only be creating workable private mythologies for his readers, but moving toward the formation of a new social mythology. This is the duty of the modern artist, according to Campbell, who believes that only in the "storehouse of recorded values"—literature—can this be accomplished:

> It is not society that is to guide and save the creative hero, but precisely the reverse. And so every one of us shares the supreme ordeal—carries the cross of the redeemer—not in the bright moments of his tribe's great victories, but in the silences of his personal despair.

It is impossible to test the function of the Haida Swan-Maiden myth against such inclusive theorizing. It is important to repeat, nonetheless, that the Swan-Maiden story was a myth, not a tale, among the Haida. An element of belief was present. The myth undoubtedly had some function—not very important, perhaps, since it is merely a very short myth and not the whole mythology. It played an inconspicuous role among the longer, more important myths of the Raven cycle, probably serving as entertainment during potlatches and the long winter ceremonials. It must be remembered that this is no mean role: the potlatch, as described in chapter two, was one of the key institutions of the Haida, enabling the prestige and class system to reassert itself periodically, and providing a social situation in which the reciting of myths was required. As one of these myths, the Swan-Maiden story was at the center of Haida life. It reinforced the Haida conception of the universe, of the nature of supernatural beings and animals, and of the nature of human intercourse with the supernatural sphere. Many large, important works of literature in the Western canon do proportionately less in relation to the values of their culture.

5. CONCLUSION

The dimensions of the myth: The myth has been seen as social document, as the product of historical diffusion and compounded from motifs distributed all over the world, as metaphysical and psychological truth in symbolic form, as literature, and as a vital functioning aspect of a culture. The fact that a myth is many things at once is obvious, but the specialists in each of the many realms of knowledge I have drawn from do not communicate much with each other. For that reason, in almost any single-approach study of mythology it is always possible to find statements which a specialist from another field could easily refute.

The dimensions of the approaches: The problems of mythology cut across the boundaries of scholarly disciplines—and no one approach can hope to do justice to the many ways in which any myth is related to (1) its culture, (2) the body of world mythology, (3) culture as an abstract universal, (4) the working of the human mind and the values it sets up. In its totality the study of a myth is the study of "man and his works."

The thorough investigation: such inclusiveness is neither possible nor desirable in the work of individual scholars. One can ask which aspect of the study of mythology should the student concerned with oral literature consider central to an investigation which would take into account the many factors suggested in this thesis, yet not lose itself in theoretical ramifications which do not illuminate oral literature itself. The answer, I believe, must be the individual version. Working with a single version, complete with language and culture attached, will keep one continually referring back to the social existence of the myth or tale, even while pursuing the fascinating but occasionally fanciful possibilities it may possess. Within any single version, as this study has suggested, there is a richness of process and significance that remains important—no matter how slight the version and how marginal the culture—to all human activity. Concrete insights derived from the study of individual versions, rare as they are in present-day studies, will surely prove useful to the understanding of the imaginative and social life of man. I have not unearthed any particular insights of this order, but perhaps I have shown why one may validly point to even "He Who Hunted Birds in His Father's Village" and say, "There digge!"

From
THE REAL WORK
INTERVIEWS & TALKS 1964–1979

The Real Work

Paul Geneson drove from his home in Boulder, Colorado, to California in the summer of 1976 to interview Snyder. The interview first appeared in the Ohio Review *(Fall 1977).*

GENESON: For you personally, what is the attraction of the rural life?

SNYDER: Well, apart from arguments about poetry, and *city* or *country*, it's obvious that city life has become difficult. It's *quite* obvious. And it's only natural that people should look for other ways to live. There is an implicit satisfaction in rural life, and in backcountry life—at least for some people. The pleasures are numerous and the work is hard, and one is literally less alienated from one's water, one's fuel, one's vegetables, and so forth. Those are fundamentals, those are ancient human fundamentals.

And it wouldn't be going too far to say that human creativity and all of the arts will begin to wither if they are pulled too far away from fundamentals of how people really should and have had to live, over millennia. We are, after all, an animal that was brought into being on this biosphere by these processes of sun and water and leaf. And if we depart too far from them, we're departing too far from the mother, from our own heritage.

The problem is, where do you put your feet down, where do you raise your children, what do you do with your hands. Now, working in a tanker with my body and with my hands in the engine room of a ship is in some ways less alienated than it would be to sit and look at this beautiful view, talking constantly on a telephone and typing on a typewriter and never *touching* it. It's the use of the *body* and the involvement of all the senses that is important at that point.

GENESON: What poets did you read when you were young that have influenced you?

SNYDER: A main progression of interests and influences would be: Carl Sandburg in early teens, and Edgar Lee Masters and some of the other Middle American poets, especially Sandburg, who's very beautiful for a kid, going directly into the poetry of D. H. Lawrence, which was a very powerful discovery for me when I was about seventeen.

[Sandburg's poems] are in a populist style, they're in a big spirit. They're in the sense of the city as the marketplace for the agriculture of the Plains. That's something real.

And Whitman, at the age, too. Then D. H. Lawrence. And from Lawrence into, on the one hand, Robinson Jeffers, whom I saw as a twentieth-century reverse image of Walt Whitman. And on the other hand into Eliot, Wallace Stevens, and Williams.

GENESON: How is Jeffers a "reverse image" of Whitman?

SNYDER: Well, Whitman was optimistic and Jeffers is pessimistic and they're talking about the same thing.

GENESON: About the land?

SNYDER: About the prophecy of America. They are the prophets of America, each in their own century.

GENESON: You mentioned Eliot—don't you find Eliot more of a *heady* poet?

SNYDER: What's really fun about Eliot is his intelligence and his highly selective and charming use of Occidental symbols which point you in a certain direction. I read *From Ritual to Romance,* and went on to read *Prolegomena to the Study of Greek Religion,* Jane Ellen Harrison, and it just kept pushing me back. It takes you all the way back to the cave at Trois Frères in France, ultimately. If you follow anything that has any meat to it it'll take you back there. And so Eliot, without maybe even consciously being aware of it, points us some profound directions. *Four Quartets* is my favorite Eliot work, and I think that it is a major work.

GENESON: Do you think that maybe Eliot, unknowingly, was Whitmanesque even as he was denying Whitman? I'm thinking of the sense of place in the *Quartets*—East Coker, the river?

SNYDER: But the way he uses that, it seems to me, is as symbol rather than for the *Ding an sich*. He uses it with irony and almost with contempt—not for itself but for what it means in his system of things. Which is all right. But it's a different use.

Now, Eliot is a ritualist, a very elegant ritualist of key Occidental myth-symbols with *considerable* grasp of what they were about: like Joyce was, in another way—they're working from slightly different positions. And I think that's what he was. With "The Dry Salvages" there's an almost pedantic voice of the ritualist coming through.

GENESON: How did Eliot influence your poetry?

SNYDER: Precision. I went from *From Ritual to Romance* to *The Mabinogion*—the ways that take you back to the archaic roots. He had the sense of the roots. He had the sense of the roots more deeply than Pound did, actually. Pound was never able to get back earlier than the Early Bronze Age. Olson at least gets to the Pleistocene.

GENESON: What do you mean when you say a modern poet can get back to the Pleistocene?

SNYDER: I mean their imagination is able to encompass it, that they feel that it's part of their lives, that they feel comradeship in connection with it, that they feel that there is humanity in that that speaks to them. This is part of our history.

GENESON: T. S. Eliot, the Anglo-Catholic?

SNYDER: Yes. As Anglo-Catholic, it's all right. The Catholic Church is full of people who did that—not *full*, but there were a number of them. The latest being Teilhard de Chardin, the best example, actually. I mean Catholic does mean catholic in the best sense, if they do it right.

GENESON: Some of the other poets who influenced you?

SNYDER: Okay, I was continuing my beginnings: Stevens, Eliot, Pound, Williams, and Yeats.

GENESON: Stevens's abstraction?

SNYDER: I just looked at it, that's all. I looked at it and I proceeded to toy with it. I'm not describing that as an influence, actually.

GENESON: Just people that you read?

SNYDER: People that I read and listened to closely. I listened to Gerard Manley Hopkins very closely.

GENESON: Because of his ear?

SNYDER: Because of the good sense he had of English and of the accentual line. And Yeats for his sense of symbol and imagery. And Pound for his peculiar ear. And after that I'm just out reading everything. But those are the ones I see as critical in my reading.

And then Chinese poetry—in translation, to begin with. And later Chinese poetry in Chinese.

Another body of material I ran onto that was extremely important to me was translations of American Indian song and myth in the Bureau of American Ethnology, Memoirs and Reports Series, which I started reading when I was around nineteen. Haida songs, Kwakiutl mythology—all of those things.

GENESON: Would you say that the study of anthropology per se is a little too dry?

SNYDER: If I were recommending anybody to study anything in the university over anything else, I would either recommend biology or anthropology. Anthropology is probably the most intellectually exciting field in the universities. The most *intellectually* exciting, the one where something's happening in *humanistic terms.* If you want to get exciting science, you go into biochemistry or something like that. But if you want to get interesting ideas you go into anthropology.

GENESON: In the genesis of the poem as you write it: do you take notes, or do these things just come to you? How does it arrive and what do you do first?

SNYDER: I listen to my own interior mind-music closely, and most of the time there's nothing particularly interesting happening. But once in a while I hear something which I recognize as belonging to the sphere of poetry. I listen very closely to that.

GENESON: Inside?

SNYDER: Inside. But it's coming from outside if you like.

GENESON: Are you talking about voices or ideas that are being directed at you? For example, your son might mention something about the creek that might trigger something—

SNYDER: I might hear that too, that's true. Prior to the writing of the poems I tend to have a sense of key areas that I'm watching that are beginning to evolve as points I must know about, that are beginning to evolve in my life. And poems will flow out of those in time. Now here's the list of things I want to watch right now. (*He opens a file drawer and takes out several cards.*) These three cards. That's how I identify things, by those little phrases. Part of my psychological and spiritual evolution is tied up with that. Out of that more precise language and symbol ultimately will come—more precise *music* will come.

GENESON: Do you have a special attachment to California?

SNYDER: My sense of place is the whole West Coast. No, not the whole West Coast, Northern California, Oregon and Washington are where I feel most at home. On the west slope. Plus the mountains. So this is a good place to live for me.

GENESON: And your advice to someone who grew up, say, in Cincinnati would be?

SNYDER: Learn about Cincinnati. It could be beautiful, Cincinnati could. This is what I tried to teach for two months: how to get to know Cincinnati. Which means, first of all, you have to get rid of the name *Cincinnati*.

GENESON: You suggested that?

SNYDER: Oh yes, of course, because after all it's the Ohio River Valley, really, that you're looking at. And *Ohio* means *beautiful* in Shawnee. And there you go, you start going back and connecting with all those loops.

GENESON: Did you feel people found that rather surprising? Or did they little by little come to accept that idea?

SNYDER: I think that they began to get a handle on why I was doing it after a while. It didn't seem quite right to them at first, though.

GENESON: Can you conceive of a person being a good teacher of poetry?

SNYDER: I like the apprentice relation as a way to go for that. I think that young people who want to have a teacher should not look at a university as a university, but look for the teacher. If the teacher happens to be a professor in the university, that's all right. But if not, not. In either case you go to that person directly, not to the administration building, and you say, "I want to be your student. What do I have to do?" And in doing that you expand the relationship into something more *personal,* more *menial,* more *direct.*

The model for that, for me, is the Japanese potters who take apprentices. And the thing that the apprentice first learns how to do is mix clay. Or Japanese carpentry apprentices who will spend months learning how to sharpen chisels and planes before they ever touch the tools to do work. You could learn as much from a good mechanic and how parts go together, and how you move and what goes in what order—

GENESON: Are you talking about poetry?

SNYDER: I'm talking about poetry. You learn how to use your mind in the act of handling parts and working. You learn how to work. You learn how things go together.

GENESON: You're making an analogy here.

SNYDER: But it's a *true* analogy. A master is a master. If you saw a man who was a master mechanic you'd do better—say you wanted to be a poet, and you saw a man that you recognized as a master mechanic or a great cook. You would do better, for yourself as a poet, to study under that man than to study under another poet who was not a master, that you didn't recognize as a master.

GENESON: Who was not a true poet?

SNYDER: Not only a true poet but a master—a *real* craftsman. There are true poets who can't teach because they're hooked onto inspiration, spontaneity, voice, language—they do it but they're not grounded in details. They don't *really* know the materials. A carpenter, a builder knows what Ponderosa pine can do, what Douglas fir can do, what incense cedar can do and builds accordingly. You can build some very elegant houses without knowing that, but some of them aren't going to work, ultimately.

And so, I'm saying that behind the scenes there is the structural and the fundamental knowledge of materials in poetry, and learning from a master mechanic would give you some of those fundamentals as well as studying from an academician, say.

GENESON: It sounds as if you're talking more about an Oriental or an Eastern kind of mechanic, someone who is more sensitive, or *sensitized*.

SNYDER: No. I use the term master mechanic because I know a master mechanic, Rod Coburn. Whenever I spend any time with him, I learn something from him.

GENESON: About?

SNYDER: About *everything*. But I see it in terms of my craft as a poet. I learn about my craft as a poet. I learn about what it really takes to be a craftsman, what it really means to be committed, what it really means to work. What it means to be *serious* about your craft and no bullshit. Not backing off any of the challenges that are offered to you. You know, like not being willing to read books, for Christ's sake. You run into people who want to write poetry who don't want to read anything in the tradition. That's like wanting to be a builder but not finding out what different kinds of wood you use.

GENESON: When a person teaches poetry, ought he to talk about inspiration?

SNYDER: Inspiration is something that can be talked about, but can't be taught in the university context. What you *can* point out is that inspire has the word *spirit* in it, and is related to expire, respire, and conspire. And point out a few other connections like that. I would say, offhand, if you want inspiration the two simplest and best ways to get it are to go on a long walking trip by yourself, or take a sweatbath. This will inspire you for poetry. Sweatbaths, especially.

GENESON: And did you tell your students this? Did you do any of this together?

SNYDER: Well, you see, the facilities aren't there. Now if I were teaching a poetry course at the university and I had everything I needed, there would have to be a sauna right there, and a quarter of an acre of garden plot, and a good kitchen, and some musical instruments and God knows what-all. That was what Philip Whalen said years ago when they asked him to teach a poetry workshop at Berkeley. Philip stated his demands: it would have to have a pump-organ and a kitchen—in the classroom. Because how can you teach poetry without at least those things? (*Spontaneous laughter.*) So, we're in harmony, Phil and I are, on that one.

GENESON: Kerouac talks a lot about the idea of spontaneity: the "spontaneous get with it," the "spontaneous recall of the unconscious." Do you also feel that way about composing poetry?

SNYDER: It's only part of it. The spontaneity is beautiful, and Jack's haiku, in *Mexico City Blues*, are some of the prettiest poems in the English language. But to complete the work of poetry as I see it in our time, here, I'd like to see some instantly-apprehended because so-well-digested larger loopings of lore. Now, if you haven't digested it and it hasn't become part of you, then you are looking things up in your library books. Or, as Philip Whalen says, in your Handbook of Comparative Mythology to look for the symbols to put in. That, of course, is wrong. But if you've absorbed and apprehended and digested it, why your apprehensive, pre-hensive mass that you can draw on is very large and very beautiful. This is part of the training you come in there with. Your spontaneity, in other words, can be very rich.

GENESON: But it's a prior experience that makes it rich?

SNYDER: That's right. That's really what we mean by learning and by being cultured—that the time process really does enrich and deepen what you have at hand at any time. And there's a point where you have enough at hand at any time and you're so comfortable with it that you can really turn some very rich thing out. That's what a great potter is.

GENESON: Do you feel the university has a function beyond what Allen Ginsberg feels is its importance—cataloguing?

SNYDER: Well, that's a great value of it. But in fact the university also has the function of reassessing our tradition, our body of lore, every generation. And in the process sometimes discovering things that were missed before and bringing them back to our attention—like Blake was brought to us, or like Melville's poetry was brought to us—that might have been lost otherwise. So the English department is a cardboard box that everybody throws every poetry magazine that comes in the mail into and says, "Well, we'll look at that later. I haven't got time to read it now." It's a backward function in time. Like some kinds of academic and intellectual pursuits are forward-looking—most of the sciences are looking for new breakthroughs, new discoveries. An English department is looking backward in time, trying to understand what happened as they go—you know, looping backward as they go, and trying to connect.

So they're establishing the tradition and that is their value. And I respect that. I have great respect for that. I don't think that they *understand* their function enough to have enough pride or enough pleasure in their work, though. And that's what makes me sad. They don't have a *tribal* sense of their own work, and it is a truly tribal work.

GENESON: What would you suggest to them?

SNYDER: I suggest that they get an anthropological and a prehistoric perspective on these things and then they'll see where what they're doing fits into the picture. And how the professors in the English department are like kiva priests, priests of the kiva that we have to go to from time to time to say, "Now why was it that there are three lines painted at the top of this eagle feather, with a little bit of red fluff on it. Now what was the reason for doing that?" Somebody who keeps that in mind for us.

It doesn't mean that they have to care a lot about it. But they do have to care about their role, about their function. And their function is maybe to tell some young guy who's going to be a beautiful poet or a beautiful dancer, to give him that one little extra bit of information to deepen what he's doing.

Because, you know, they carry the lore, they bear it. And they bear it for the benefit of the dancers who get inspired out there in the plaza.

In earlier times the English professor would have also been the raconteur, the storyteller who would, to a small select audience of students after the storytelling was over and the audience had gone home, tell them some of the *inner* meanings, some of the *background,* some of the *professional secrets* of what he had just recited. He doesn't have to be the poet who made it up necessarily, see?

GENESON: What has been your own relationship with the academy?

SNYDER: I went to Reed College in Oregon, I had some marvelous teachers, I learned how to use a library, I was in an atmosphere that challenged me and pushed me to the utmost, which was just what I needed. They wouldn't tolerate bullshit, made me clean up my prose style, exposed me to all varieties of intellectual positions and gave me a territory in which I could speak out my radical politics and get arguments and augmentations on it. It was an intensive, useful experience.

And also it was an intense enough education that I perceived that I would have to de-educate myself later. An education is only valuable if you're willing to give as much time to de-educating yourself as you gave to educating yourself. So, you go to college for four years, you have to figure you're going to do four years of coming off of it, too.

GENESON: When you say "de-educate yourself," you mean what?

SNYDER: I mean get back in touch with people, with ordinary things: with your body, with the dirt, with the dust, with anything you like, you know—the streets. The streets or the farm, whatever it is. Get away from books and from the elite sense of being bearers of Western culture, and all that crap. But also, ultimately, into your mind, into *original mind* before any books were put into it, or before any language was invented.

GENESON: You just mentioned that the professors were the bearers of the lore—

SNYDER: And the *best* professors, the best priests of the kiva are the ones who are able to show you the path out the door where there isn't any lore.

GENESON: And this is what you call the postuniversity experience?

SNYDER: It's what you call higher education. (*He laughs.*)

GENESON: Some people would say to a young poet, "Poetry is self-expression. Sit down and write what you can whenever you can." Would you say that?

SNYDER: No, I wouldn't say that. I don't think that's true. I think that poetry is a social and traditional art that is linked to its past and particularly its language, that *loops* and draws on its past and that serves as a vehicle for contact with the depths of our own unconscious—and that it gets better by practicing. And that the expression of self, although it's a nice kind of energy to start with, would not make any expression of poetry per se.

We all know that the power of a great poem is not that we felt that person expressed himself well. We don't think that. What we think is, "How deeply *I* am touched." That's our level of response. And so a great poet does not express his or her self, he expresses *all* of our selves. And to express *all* of ourselves you have to go beyond your own self. Like Dōgen, the Zen master, said, "We study the self to forget the self. And when you forget the self, you become *one* with all things." And that's why poetry's not self-expression in those small self terms.

GENESON: Japan plays a considerable role in your poetry. Would you say to a young poet, "Go to Japan"?

SNYDER: Good heavens no. What Japan as advice implies is: if there's a spiritual path that you feel is important to you, go out and study it, no matter where it leads. And the other thing that implies is: if you have the will and the energy and the opportunity, go live in an alien culture for a while. It really does, as they say, "broaden" you. (*He laughs.*)

I like the way Jack Spicer saw it where all pure and true poetry is ultimately inspired in origin. It comes to us as a voice from outside. To even say that it comes from within is to mislead yourself. So we are the vehicle of that voice. However, if we are people who can hear that voice, then we should strive to be the best possible vehicle of that voice we can. Which means to learn other languages, to become as broadly human and as well-informed and aware as we can because that will give strength to our handling and expressing the power of the voice.

GENESON: Including translations?

SNYDER: Including translations. Reading. Learning how to *do* translations.

GENESON: Wallace Stevens said that the translator is a parasite. Do you agree with that?

SNYDER: We need everyone who can do it. Any good translator is a great help to all of us. A translator's no more a parasite than an interpreter standing at the edge of the creek helping a group of Crow and a group of Hunkpapa Sioux do some trading is a parasite—it's a valuable function. A translator is a valuable switch in an energy exchange flow.

GENESON: Apart from Oriental poets, what other poets have you read? Have you read many Spanish poets?

SNYDER: In translation.

GENESON: Neruda?

SNYDER: Vallejo.

GENESON: Which of these non-English poets that you've read in translation are especially interesting to you?

SNYDER: I'm not overwhelmingly moved by any one given poet in Spanish. I look at them. But I don't make fine distinctions. The only poets outside the English tradition that I make fine distinctions in my choices about are in Chinese, Japanese, and to some extent in the East Indian languages. The rest I just read.

GENESON: Do you think more people ought to study Chinese and Japanese? Do we need more translations of these poets?

SNYDER: I don't know if we *need* them. Yes, they'd be nice. There's a tremendous amount of poetry in Chinese that hasn't even been translated—I'm not sure it's all that good. Good translations of Tu Fu, whom the Chinese themselves consider their greatest poet and who undoubtedly must be one of the greatest poets of the world, are yet to come. Understanding the aesthetics of Japanese poetry is a marvelous exercise, also.

I quote to you one of Bashō's disciples who took down something Bashō once said to a group of students. He said, "To learn about the pine, go to the pine. To learn about bamboo, go to the bamboo. But this *learn* is not just what you think learn is. You only learn by becoming totally absorbed in that which you wish to learn. There are many people who think that they have learned something and willfully construct a poem which is artifice and does not flow from their delicate entrance into the life of another object."

GENESON: So when Sartre, the Western philosopher, goes to the tree, touches the tree trunk and says, "I feel in an absurd position—I cannot break through my skin to get in touch with this bark, which is outside me," the Japanese poet would say what?

SNYDER: Sartre is confessing the sickness of the West. At least he's honest.

The Oriental will say, "But there are ways to do it, my friend. It's no big deal." It's no big deal, especially if you get attuned to that possibility from early in life. There's something where, say, the American Indians and the Japanese are right on the same spot. They both know that that's possible, and that it is a major mode of knowledge—to learn about the pine from the pine rather than from a botany textbook. They know that that's right. They also know that you can look at the botany textbook and learn a few things, too.

GENESON: You mention in *Turtle Island* the idea of being in touch with the land, and the Indian myths of the land. In other places you use the Oriental teachings that you've personally experienced. How do you link these two?

SNYDER: Oh, it's all one teaching. There is an ancient teaching, which we have American Indian expressions of, and Chinese,

Tibetan, Japanese, Indian, Buddhist expressions of. And other expressions in the world. Each of us, according to our own needs and nature, can draw up the criteria for what expression suits us best, and what *practice* suits us best out of that. We will prefer some to others. There may be some lines of teaching which are really a little wrongheaded. So I would not argue that all paths necessarily lead to the same goal—I think some paths go to other places. But there is a body of paths which do come to the same goal—some with a more earthly stress, some with a more spiritual stress. But what they share in common is the exploration of consciousness itself: self-understanding, transcendence of self.

Native American people have many paths, many varieties in their paths, so you can't even speak of all of that as one. But they have, throughout Turtle Island, an ancient and clarified sense of what a right path is. And some of those societies, not all of them maybe, were actually living like a Zen monastery—a whole society *on the way*. Which is preferable to a fragmented, monastic transmission. A whole social transmission is more to be desired than a monastic and esoteric transmission.

GENESON: Do you still feel that a certain tribalism is implicit, or latent, in the culture?

SNYDER: Whatever we mean by that. Tribalism is I guess what we mean in suggesting that there's an alternative to the fragmented and alienated kind of social fabric we have now which lacks community and lacks communication. So yes, that's one of the things we hope for—still.

GENESON: So the subculture which had its roots in the sixties is not something you're pessimistic about even today?

SNYDER: No, because the subculture had its roots 40,000 years ago.

GENESON: We're not talking about fads then?

SNYDER: We're *not* talking about fads. To the contrary—the subculture is the main line and what we see around us is the anomaly.

GENESON: In *Turtle Island*: when you talk about the subculture, are you talking about myths of the land? A rediscovery of Indian lore? Or just a rediscovery of one's own humanity and a new set of myths?

SNYDER: Well, what's implied in the title is, first of all, not even a rediscovery but a *dis*covery of North America—we haven't discovered North America yet. People live on it without knowing what it is or where they are. They live on it literally like invaders. You know whether or not a person knows where he is by whether or not he knows the plants. By whether or not he knows what the soils and waters do. Now that is so fundamental and basic, and so true that it's easy to overlook. There it is, it's not even arguable.

But we live in a nation of fossil fuel junkies, very sweet people and the best hearts in the world. But nonetheless fossil fuel junkies of tremendous mobility zapping back and forth, who are still caught on the myth of the frontier, the myth of boundless resources and a vision of perpetual materialistic growth. Now that is all very bad metaphysics, a metaphysics that is leading us to ruin. Turtle Island is *good* metaphysics because it points in the direction of real seeing. And the first step in real seeing is to throw out a European name and take a creative native name. And the second step is to erase arbitrary and nonexistent political boundaries from your mind and look at what the land really is, with mountain ridges, and rivers and tree zones and rain zones, and just keep going from there, you know, following those implications.

GENESON: And the cities?

SNYDER: And the cities are periodic tribal marketplaces.

GENESON: That people will be leaving or—

SNYDER: Well, they do all the time—they're coming and going all the time. Coming and going, coming and going. You know what cities really are? They're at the mouths of rivers, or at fords on rivers—hence *Oxford* University. They're at access to trails which are passes over mountain ranges, they are transportation and exchange nodes, essentially, that have become stable and permanent. Or, the only other variety of city that counts, really, is a religious pilgrimage center, a city that evolves out of access to a sacred spot. Like Benares in India. Or like Jerusalem.

GENESON: As you see it, what is the function of poetry?

SNYDER: You ask me what is the function of poetry so I think, "What is the function of poetry since 40,000 years ago?" In all cultures of the world—total planetary overview. And in that sense the function of poetry is not only the intensification and clarification of the implicit potentials of the language, which means a sharpening, a bringing of more delight to the normal functions of language and making maybe language even work better since communication is what it's about. But on another level poetry is intimately linked to any culture's fundamental worldview, body of lore, which is its myth base, its symbol base, and the source of much of its values—that myth-lore foundation that underlies any society. That foundation is most commonly expressed and transmitted in the culture by poems, which is to say *by songs*. By songs that are linked to a dramatic or ritual performance much of the time. The oral tradition almost always puts its transmission into a form of measured language, which is easier to remember and can be chanted. Much of the world's lore has been transmitted, in one form or another, via poetic forms, measured language or sung language.

GENESON: One might argue that the world is just too large, that in order to have a campfire you'd have to have a *media* campfire. Would that be feasible?

SNYDER: Well, Marshall McLuhan tried to make the media into a tribal campfire. Since I'm not a person who has watched media much in my lifetime, I can't really speak with accuracy on that. I do think, though, that as we move, *of necessity,* toward some more decentralized and labor-intensive ways of working and living with each other, there will be a reemergence of community and neighborhood. And out of that, either in the city or in the country, a campfire circle, so to speak, reevolves. Any time any group of people in New York get together in somebody's apartment and read poems to each other, it's happening. Or get together to put on a play together, or make up a skit together, it's happening. It's the face-to-face working-it-out of the forms of the art with human beings that is real.

GENESON: W. H. Auden said about poetry that it won't change anything. Is that how you see poetry?

SNYDER: Ezra Pound said, to quote an oft-quoted line, that artists are the antennae of the race. How that probably functions in practice is that some people's sensibilities, as well as maybe their lifestyles, are out at the very edge of the unraveling cause-and-effect network of a society in time. And also are, by virtue of the nature of their sensibilities, tuned into other voices than simply the social or human voice. So they are like an early warning system that hears the trees and the air and the clouds and the watersheds beginning to groan and complain a little bit. And so they try to send a little bit of a warning back, although they themselves may not know what it is they're hearing. They also can hear the stresses and the fault block slippage creaking in the social batholith and also begin to give out warnings.

What proceeds on that is, for the poet in particular, a sense of the need to look at the key archetype image and symbol blocks and see if the blocks are working. Poetry effects change by fiddling with the archetypes and getting at people's dreams about a century before it actually effects historical change. A poet would be, in terms of the ecology of symbols, noting the main structural connections and seeing which parts of the symbol system are no longer useful or applicable, though everyone is giving them credence. And out of his own vision and hearing of voices he seeks for new paths for the mind-energy to flow, which would be literally more creative directions, but directions which change politics. Poets are more like mushrooms, or fungus—they can digest the symbol-detritus.

Thus, you proceed from an animistic idea that you can hear voices from trees. And a few decades later a lawyer, like Christopher Stone, writes a *legalistic* argument—"Should Trees Have Standing?"—arguing that trees should be involved in the democratic process. Now, where does it go from there? That is a myth-block idea in which a kind of language which is known to our whole culture—the rights of things, the potentiality of salvation of things—the idea is being turned around just a trifle. And it *catches* it a little. And you push it toward a generation or two in the future that can actually feel on a gut level that nonhuman nature has rights. And that will be the work of the poet, to set that direction.

GENESON: Some of the things you were writing in the fifties and sixties are just beginning to be talked about today: the preservation of the forests, and the whole general ecology, which seems to have reached near crisis—

SNYDER: Yes. But that's only one side of it. The work of poetry is really not the work of prophecy. Nor is it, ultimately, the work of social change. That's just part of it. The other part of it is in the eternity of the present, and doesn't have to do with evolutionary processes at all, but has to do with bringing us back to our original, true natures from whatever habit-molds that our perceptions, that our thinking and feeling get formed into. And bringing us back to original true mind, seeing the universe freshly in eternity, yet any moment.

GENESON: You would like to see poetry "grounded" essentially, rather than off in some metaphysical flight?

SNYDER: I would like to see *people* "grounded."

GENESON: In touch with their environment?

SNYDER: In touch with their own lives.

GENESON: With their bodies?

SNYDER: Yes. And let the poetry do what it wants from that. Get the people grounded and the poetry'll take care of itself.

GENESON: A problem that might be suggested is that, in terms of the popular mind, few people read Pound, few people read Bly. How does one propagate these ideas, then?

SNYDER: Few people read Pound, that's true. But Pound's power is in his role as an influence, for sure. More people read Bly, considerably more. And he also is an influence. The game is not to be measured in terms of popularity or readibility anyway. It has its effect several steps down the line—. The kind of poetry that we're talking about now has indirect effects, not direct effects if you want to talk about "masses," although I don't know if at this point we are talking about the "masses."

GENESON: Well, the popular sense of the value of poetry to a society.

SNYDER: I'm not sure that *value* is the same word as *function*. The *value* of poetry and the *function* of poetry in a society are two different things.

The value and function of poetry can be said in very few words. One side of it is *in-time*, the other is *out-of-time*. The in-time side of it is to tune us in to *mother* nature and *human* nature so that we live *in time*, in our societies in a way and on a path in which all things can come to fruition equally, and together in harmony. A path of beauty. And the out-of-time function of poetry is to return us to our own true original nature at this instant forever. And those two things happen, sometimes together, sometimes not, here and there and all over the world, and always have.

Now whether or not that particular pattern of processes has had any great or small effects on the major flow of human social evolution is not something I can say. And yet if you look at a society that *sings* and that *dances* as a regular thing, it's not that it has an effect on their life—it *is* their life. It is their life: the lore of the culture is carried in the songs. And so poetry *is* our life. It's not that poetry has an effect on it, or a function in it, or a value for it. It *is* our life as much as eating and speaking is our life. It's like asking, "Well, what's the function of eating? What's the value of speaking?"

GENESON: Walt Whitman says we need a more democratic America, a mythology of America. Some people today say that consensus is gone in America, and there can be no mythology of America. How can these ideas be reconciled?

SNYDER: There's a poem that Tu Fu wrote after the capital of China, Chang-an, fell to An Lu-shan, who was a rebel, and it looked as though the whole dynasty had been overthrown. He wrote, "Though the nation is lost, the mountains and rivers remain." The mountains and rivers remain. That's the real country.

GENESON: Do you think Whitman was talking about that?

SNYDER: I don't know if he was talking about it or not. When he says there should be more democracy, I go along with that. We all see what more democracy means, too. It means that the Navajo should get their own nation, that Rosebud and Pine Ridge maybe should be a separate nation, that the Indians of Puget Sound have fishing rights, that trees and rocks should be able to vote in Congress, that whales should be able to vote—that's democracy.

GENESON: But who votes for them? How do they vote?

SNYDER: Well, Christopher Stone, in his essay "Should Trees Have Standing?" said legalistically it's very simple—the court appoints someone to be their representative. Like someone to be the spokesman for the yellow pine–black oak communities of Northern California and Southern Oregon. That's a possibility. Legally, this is not out of line: it would be analogous to the court appointing someone, a lawyer, to speak for a minor, or for the interests of a mentally retarded person, something like that.

Actually, that's not so interesting. We can see it has been one of the jobs of poetry to speak for these things, to carry their voice into the human realm. That it *is* in poetry and in song and in ritual and in certain kinds of dance drama that the nonhuman realms have been able to speak to the human society. There are large numbers of people who don't have an ear for that anymore, although once we all had an ear for it. So yes, the democracy can be extended and if it is it'll be a great employment for poets. I mean they'll be talking about CETA, and the federal government will be appointing poets to be spokesmen for the short grass prairies of Montana, and we'll all have seats in Congress. (*He laughs.*)

GENESON: But shouldn't the poet represent with his pen, and not be present in any center of power?

SNYDER: Oh, he has to get his poetry reading down there, that's all. They say, you know, when the time comes for speeches, they're going to be voting on whether or not to adopt laws which will prohibit tuna fishermen from catching porpoises in their nets. Everyone has been consulted except the porpoises.

At that point we call on the poet from the marine mammals. What do the porpoises feel about that? So he gets up and does his dance. (*Sustained laughter.*)

GENESON: Do you actually foresee this?

SNYDER: Well, I'm saying that that's what Whitman foresaw when he said we should be more democratic. If he was a true poet he couldn't have foreseen anything less than that.

GENESON: Do you read Whitman for this kind of message?

SNYDER: What I read Whitman for is for inspiration. He's inspiring. I love to read "The Song of the Open Road," or "By Blue Ontario's Shores," or "Passage to India"—I love to read 'em aloud, to a small audience. He's a good *communal* poet in that way. I don't know if you could read *The Four Quartets* in a social atmosphere that is quite so delightful. You could create an atmosphere in which there was a great expression of respect. But not that goofy *expansion* of things that Whitman accomplishes, with funny lines like "tender and junior Buddha."

GENESON: Ought all poetry be able to be read aloud? Or should some poetry be contemplative?

SNYDER: Even contemplative poetry can be read aloud. Witness Gregorian chants. Or Japanese or Chinese sutra chanting. That's contemplative poetry read aloud.

GENESON: You mentioned Whitman as a communal poet: Can a true communal poetry be possible?

SNYDER: It has been. It's been practiced much through time and is probably more the case rather than the exception. But it seems very hard to do now, right now. And it hasn't been customary in any literate, civilized tradition, as far as I can see, although it certainly is there in all of the oral traditions. An oral tradition *is* virtually a communal poetry.

GENESON: Why is it difficult now?

SNYDER: Because of the stress on individual names. And because the emphasis is on keeping a text pure.

GENESON: I'm thinking of poetry in the Communist world—they obviously have a didactic poetry, a poetry which speaks to the masses and which glorifies the masses. Is that poetry?

SNYDER: Could be. I mean, it's got a good subject matter to start with. Excellent subject matter.

GENESON: I was thinking of those people who would say that, by definition, a mass poetry cannot be good or great poetry.

SNYDER: You know, if I can write a poem in praise of planet earth, or in praise of the Douglas fir forests in Northern Washington, I don't see why I can't write a poem in praise of the masses of China. (*He laughs.*) Obviously it's possible.

GENESON: But don't you, as an individual poet, envision certain problems living in China?

SNYDER: Sure. I can also envision a lot of pleasure. I like getting together with other people and working. Wailing away on a job.

GENESON: But are you talking now about work, or about poetry?

SNYDER: I'm talking about *work*. I *love* getting together with a bunch of people and wailing away, building an earth dam, or peeling poles, or trucking gravel. (*Laughter.*)

GENESON: That I can see. But when it comes to poetic expression?

SNYDER: Well, that comes at night when you have a little saké to pass around and a little bonfire, and then you start singing. And that's where you make up a song about how many beautiful wheelbarrows we wheeled around today, and put in a few jokes about somebody.

GENESON: On a personal level: is the individual poet important? Does he need recognition?

SNYDER: Some do, some don't. I think for a lot of poets recognition from their peers is essentially what they need. You know, architects seldom get recognition from the public—the public doesn't see what's going on. An architect is pleased to have a fellow architect say, "I saw what you did there—that's really something." That's what you need, for the most part. People who crave recognition beyond that I tend to suspect a little bit as wanting some food for their ego, which won't do them any good. Excessive recognition—it does no harm to have lots of money, to be sure. That's not entirely true. But maybe it doesn't do much harm to have lots of money. But *recognition* can really be detrimental to somebody who's interested in getting their work done and not in collecting their Karma Cookies at testimonial dinners.

GENESON: So things like poetry prizes and awards are—

SNYDER: They don't do any harm as long as they don't make you come to New York and have a dinner to get the prize. That's what's nice about the Pulitzer—they send a check in the mail. (*He laughs.*)

I'll tell you what I get off on. I get off on getting an occasional letter from somebody I've never met that says, "I know what you're doing in that poem"; that tells me that I've got it across. That's the only thing that really—that's what I call recognition. Those little signs that what I am trying to do in my craft on its more subtle levels is occasionally working.

GENESON: Do you like the idea of gatherings of poets? What Allen Ginsberg has in Boulder? Do you think it's valuable to either the students or the poets who are there?

SNYDER: I'm not against it in principle. But I don't like to go to things in the summertime because I have work to do here. I appreciate those gatherings in the right atmosphere, which is not too hectic or too disorderly. I would like to be able to go to gatherings like that where we all participated in the cooking and in the washing of the dishes, and were not served things cafeteria style: plastic, with little old ladies who cleaned up after us. I don't like to live that way. I like to be involved in the cooking and the cleanup, too. Ginsberg once put his finger on it really nicely after staying three days at Kent State. He said, "This is like an Old Folks Home here where everything is done for you. Except everybody's young." Now, I'm not knocking the academies now, I'm knocking the style of life on campuses. So, in other words, I don't like gatherings of poets on campuses. They're crummy. And I don't like staying up too many nights in a row, drinking too much and just talking.

GENESON: You mention drinking: I wanted to ask you if a person can get poetic material from either drinking or from drugs.

SNYDER: Sure you can. Anything that starts your head going, or releases a flow of feeling from within. Maybe that happens accidentally and naturally sometimes when you're a little stoned, or you've been drinking. But you would be getting into trouble if you had to go back to the booze or the grass—if you got to think that that was the way to do it. We'll say it may have been really the way to do it for several poets who have killed themselves with booze—it's also self-destructive.

—Like Lew [Welch]. Or like Jack Spicer. Alcohol did 'em in, finally. Alcohol did 'em in, and I don't believe that was the only way they could have been inspired. Even though they do call alcohol *spirits*.

GENESON: But does one actually write while on these?

SNYDER: I don't. I've had probably more than my share of psilocybin, peyote, et cetera. And I don't recall having ever written anything that was particularly useful to me while under the influence of any of those. Just think it through, feel it through. As a matter of fact, some experiences like that, triggered by psychedelics or via meditation or long walks in the mountains or sweat-baths or whatever, are a little bit too precious and too pure to just run off and write about right away. You do yourself and them a disservice if you try to put them in print. In other words, you're being a poetic journalist, you want to get the news *right now*. Which is equivalent to picking up the first beads you find scattered inside the entrance to the cave and running out with them, rather than having the patience to go in deeper and deeper into the cave and ignore those little gewgaws at the entrance. So this is something that some poets see and some poets don't see.

I'm saying that *certain* states of mind are too special even to put into poetry. And that you mess yourself up if you try to do that, if you try to exploit them for poetry.

GENESON: Related to the idea of the poet as either individually important or as anonymous: you at one point have written that the poet should not say, "I did it," but instead there should be a sense of "cool water." Does that tie in with the idea of whether you want to be remembered after your death—with anonymity?

SNYDER: I don't think we have any choice whether we're going to be remembered or not remembered. I think that's what happens.

GENESON: Yes. But Borges, for example, told me he doesn't want to be remembered, that it's just important that poetry goes on, that the pool of literature is increased, and that it doesn't matter who did the increasing.

SNYDER: As Nanao Sakaki, the great Japanese wandering poet, once said to me, "No need to survive." "*No need* to survive." (*The repetition is spoken as a hoary old man in robes would speak it.*) And that sums it all up. Absolutely. Not just poetry. Not the race. The whole universe. "No need to survive." It doesn't matter. To speak to anonymity: you can't really claim the poem is your own, so you'd feel dishonest if you took too much credit for it.

GENESON: Not your own because inspired?

SNYDER: Because inspired. Because from a place that your day-to-day mind isn't making happen. It's your original mind, which isn't mirrors—it belongs to everybody.

GENESON: *The* original mind?

SNYDER: *The* original mind. Original Mind is doing it, like it's doing everything else, too. And so you can't look at a poem—I mean literally you get a good poem and you don't know where it came from. "Did I say that?" And so all you feel is: you feel humility and you feel gratitude. And you'd feel a little uncomfortable, I think, if you capitalized too much on that without admitting at some point that you got it from the Muse, or whoever, wherever, or however. Which is just simply a confession that we're all part of everything. And if one individual seems to stand out, that's okay for that individual to stand out but that individual should remember, and we should all remember, that his standing out is only part of the dance, too.

GENESON: In your Introduction to *Selected Poems of Lew Welch* you mention that poets are the "sons of witches." Are you referring here specifically to the feminine self of the poet? Is this just a metaphor that you're using?

SNYDER: Well, it's an attempt to try to clarify what the language of Muses means, and also what is involved in the psychology of male poets. I don't know *what* applies in the psychology of female poets. I think that there is quite obviously an intense and deep connection between mother and son, and that the son relationship to the complex tooth-mother ecstatic-mother type is apt to produce environmentally, psychologically, genetically, by whatever means, the line of magic that produces poetry.

Let me expand on that. To be a poet you have to be tuned into some of the darkest and scariest sides of your own nature. And for a male, the darkest and scariest is the destructive side of the female.

GENESON: That's what you mean by the "tooth-mother"?

SNYDER: Right. As an infant in your dependence you trust, and in a sense *crave,* the female to be beneficent, because of the helplessness. The mother is, in general, the nourisher. But the female, as well as the male, also has a negative side. To a male child the negative side of the mother is the darkest, scariest thing he can perceive. What could be scarier than that? A bunch of scary warriors coming through would be rationally acceptable—they're not your mother, at least.

So a woman who, of her own nature, has a dark side—she will also be creative. Something is triggered by being a witness to that most paradoxical of human situations, witnessing the dark and the light side of the mother simultaneously. Most people only witness the light side of the mother. Literally. They only see the bright side of the mother, in one way or another. But some people see the *dark* side of the mother. If you only see the dark side you probably go crazy. The poet holds the dark and the light in mind, together. Which, by extension, means birth and death in its totality. We worship not only the positive forces, the life-giving forces—not just that. We can all say, "Ah, planet earth biosphere, mother earth, mother wonderful—all these green plants." But there's also death, there's also the unknown, there's also the demonic. And that's the womb and the tomb, that's samsara, that's birth and death, that's where the Buddhists go in. And that's where poetry goes in: That's where poetry gets its hands on something real. And it is triggered, I think—in many people I know it is triggered by seeing *that* in their infancy as a condition of the universe in the psychology of their own life.

GENESON: You suggest that just *poets* see that. Wouldn't there be people who, for example, would see the same thing as the poet and yet never write a line of poetry?

SNYDER: Sure.

GENESON: And is this related to the idea of the Muse as woman, unifying the dark and light?

SNYDER: The *paradox* is there. That which is born must die. The womb is the gate to the tomb—to put it in the sense that the ancients saw it. A very ancient perception.

GENESON: In your poem, "The Real Work," you mention that the "real work" is

> washing and sighing,
> sliding by.

What exactly is "the real work"?

SNYDER: I've used that phrase, "the real work," a few times before. I used that term, "the real work," and then I asked myself a lot: what is the real work? I think it's important, first of all, because it's good to work—I love work, work and play are one. And that all of us will come back again to hoe in the ground, or gather wild potato bulbs with digging sticks, or hand-adze a beam, or skin a pole, or scrape a hive—we're never going to get away from that. We've been living a dream that we're going to get away from it, that we won't have to do it again. Put that out of our minds. We'll always do that work. That work is always going to be there. It might be stapling papers, it might be typing in the office. But we're never going to get away from that work, on one level or another. So that's real. The real work is what we really do. And what our lives are. And if we can live the work we have to do, knowing that we are real, and it's real, and that the world is real, then it becomes right. And that's the *real work*: to make the world as real as it is, and to find ourselves as real as we are within it.

I used that phrase again at the end of the poem "I Went into the Maverick Bar," where we go back out of that bar in Farmington, New Mexico, out onto the highway

> under the tough old stars—
> . . .
> To the real work, to
> "What is to be done."

To take the struggle on without the *least* hope of doing any good. To check the destruction of the interesting and necessary diversity of life on the planet so that the dance can go on a little better for a little longer. The other part of it is that it is always here,

> washing and sighing,
> sliding by.

That was the wash of the waves on the island out in San Francisco Bay with the seabirds, and the feeding and schooling of the little fish—that's going on. The *real work* is eating each other, I suppose.

GENESON: This is beginning to sound like the Auden quote—that poetry changes nothing.

SNYDER: Yes. Well, in that sense poetry does no more than woodchopping, or automobile repair, or anything else does because they're all equally real.

GENESON: Poetry does as much as?

SNYDER: As much as and no more than anything else. It's all real.

The East West Interview

Peter Barry Chowka interviewed Snyder in New York City over a five-day period in April of 1977. The interview was conducted in Allen Ginsberg's apartment, on the subway, while walking the New York City streets. Snyder was in New York to give a series of readings and to participate in a conference sponsored by the American Academy of Poets on "Chinese Poetry and the American Imagination."

Chowka is a free-lance writer and researcher whose detailed, in-depth studies of subjects ranging from fast-food chains to the politics of cancer have been widely published. The interview first appeared in the summer, 1977, issues of East West Journal.

CHOWKA: You have said that you left graduate school "to pursue the Dharma which had become more interesting to me." In some detail, could you recount the context—influences, people, books—of those years which led you to Buddhism?

SNYDER: When I was young, I had an immediate, intuitive, deep sympathy with the natural world which was not taught me by anyone. In that sense, nature is my "guru" and life is my sadhana. That sense of the authenticity, completeness, and reality of the natural world itself made me aware even as a child of the contradictions that I could see going on around me in the state of Washington, in the way of exploitation, logging, development, pollution. I lived on the edge of logging country, and the trees were rolling by on the tops of trucks, just as they are still. My father was born and raised on the Kitsap County farm that my grandfather had homesteaded; he was a smart man, a very handy man, but he only knew about fifteen different trees and after that he was lost. I wanted more precision; I wanted to look deeper into the underbrush.

I perceived, also without it being taught to me, that there were such things as native people who were still around. In particular, one of them was an old man who came by about once a month to our little farm north of Seattle selling salmon that his people had smoked. They were Salish people who lived in a little Indian settlement on the shores of Puget Sound a few miles from us. My childhood perception of the world was white people, a few old Salish Indians, and this whole natural world that was half-intact and half-destroyed before my eyes.

At that age I had no idea of European culture or of politics. The realities were my mind, my self, and my place. My sympathies were entirely with my place—being able to see Mount Rainier far off to the east on a clear day or to climb the bluff of the hill to the west and look out over Puget Sound and the islands and see the Olympic Mountains. That was far more real to me than the city of Seattle, about ten miles south, which seemed like a ghost on the landscape.

(*Peter Orlovsky joins us at this point.*)

ORLOVSKY: What kind of a farm did your father have?

SNYDER: It was a little dairy farm, only two acres in pasture, surrounded by woods. As early as I was allowed, at age nine or ten, I went off and slept in the woods at night alone. I had a secret camp back in the woods that nobody knew about; I had hidden the trail to it. As soon as my father figured I knew how to put out a campfire, he let me go off and cook for myself and stay a day or two.

CHOWKA: This interest was mainly self-taught?

SNYDER: Very much self-taught. As soon as I was permitted, from the time I was thirteen, I went into the Cascade Mountains, the high country, and got into real wilderness. At that age I found very little in the civilized human realm that interested me. When I was eleven or twelve, I went into the Chinese room at the Seattle art museum and saw Chinese landscape paintings; they blew my mind. My shock of recognition was very simple: "It looks just like the Cascades." The waterfalls, the pines, the clouds, the mist looked a lot like the northwest United States. The Chinese had an eye for the world that I saw as real. In the next room were the English and European landscapes, and they meant nothing. It was no great lesson except for an instantaneous, deep respect for something in Chinese culture that always stuck in my mind and that I would come back to again years later.

When I went into college I was bedeviled already by the question of these contradictions of living in and supposedly being a member of a society that was destroying its own ground. I felt the split between two realms that seemed equally real, leading me into a long process of political thought, analysis, and study, and—of course—the discovery of Marxist thought. For a long time I thought it was only capitalism that went wrong. Then I got into American Indian studies and at school majored predominantly in anthropology and got close to some American Indian elders. I began to perceive that maybe it was all of Western culture that was off the track and not just capitalism—that there were certain self-destructive tendencies in our cultural tradition. To simplify a long tale, I also saw that American Indian spiritual practice is very remote and extremely difficult to enter, even though in one sense right next door, because it is a practice one has to be born into. Its intent is not cosmopolitan. Its content, perhaps, is universal, but you must be a Hopi to follow the Hopi way.

By this time I was also studying Far Eastern culture at Reed College. I read Ezra Pound's and Arthur Waley's translations of Chinese poetry, a translation of the *Tao Te Ching*, and some texts of Confucius. Within a year or so I went through the *Upanishads, Vedas, Bhagavad-Gita*, and most of the classics of Chinese and Indian Buddhist literature. The convergence that I found really exciting was the Mahayana Buddhist wisdom-oriented line as it developed in China and assimilated the older Taoist tradition. It was that very precise cultural meeting that also coincided with the highest period of Chinese poetry—the early and middle T'ang Dynasty Zen masters and the poets who were their contemporaries and in many cases friends— that was fascinating. Then I learned that this tradition is still alive and well in Japan. That convinced me that I should go and study in Japan.

CHOWKA: How did you discover that it was still alive?

SNYDER: By reading books and also by writing letters. It's obvious that Buddhism presents itself as cosmopolitan and open to everyone, at least if male. I knew that Zen monasteries in Japan would be more open to me than the old Paiute or Shoshone Indians in eastern Oregon, because they *have* to be open—that's what Mahayana Buddhism is all about. At that point, spring 1952, I quit graduate school in linguistics and anthropology at Indiana University and hitchhiked back to Berkeley to enroll in the Oriental languages department at the University of California so I could prepare myself to go to Asia. I spent my summers working in the Northwest in lookouts and trail crews and logging and forest service jobs, like a migratory bird going north in summer and returning south in winter.

CHOWKA: You have said that you taught yourself zazen from books although you then decided a teacher was necessary.

SNYDER: I decided that quite clearly when I was twenty-one or twenty-two.

CHOWKA: And after that, then, you grounded yourself in the languages and philosophy to prepare to go to Japan?

SNYDER: Right, although sitting, you know, isn't that hard a thing to learn, if you understand what posture is.

ORLOVSKY: In what year did you first sit in meditation?

SNYDER: It must have been in '49 that I taught myself to sit.

CHOWKA: Is there a particular book which gave you the direction?

SNYDER: Several translations of various texts from India and China told how to sit. And looking at a good statue and seeing that it has good posture and how the legs are crossed—it's not hard. I soon corrected my errors because you cannot sustain sitting for very long if your posture is off; it becomes painful, breath doesn't feel right, et cetera.

ORLOVSKY: Did you sit regularly from '51 on?

SNYDER: Pretty much. Not a whole lot—though maybe a half an hour every morning when I was going to graduate school. When I was working in the mountains in the summers, I was able to sit a lot.

ORLOVSKY: By '55 was your sitting practice different from when you began?

SNYDER: I didn't feel self-conscious about it anymore. When I first sat, I recall how very strange, how very un-Western, it felt. I remember at Indiana University I was doing zazen in the apartment that I shared with the anthropologist Dell Hymes. Somebody walked in and caught me sitting there and I felt strange, they felt strange, and then it got all around the university: "That graduate student from Oregon does weird things." But that's the way it was, twenty years ago! It's nice now that people can sit cross-legged and nobody pays much attention.

ORLOVSKY: When did you first sit ten hours a day?

SNYDER: I never started sitting like that until I went to Japan and was forced to. I still wouldn't sit ten hours a day unless somebody forced me, because there's too much other work in the world to be done. Somebody's got to grow the tomatoes. There's not going to be that much meditation in the world if we're going to have a democratic world that isn't fueled with nuclear energy, because there isn't that much spare energy. We damn well better learn that our meditation is primarily going to be our work with our hands. We can't have twenty-five percent of the population going off and becoming monks at the expense of the rest, like in Tibet; that's a class structure thing, a by-product of exploitation—sitting an hour a day is not. Sitting ten hours a day means that somebody else is growing your food for you; for special shots, okay, but people can't do it for a whole lifetime without somebody else having to give up their meditation so that *you* can meditate.

CHOWKA: When you first began sitting, how did it change your life? Did it immediately affect the poetry you were writing, or was the effect more gradual?

SNYDER: It was gradual.

CHOWKA: But you knew when you began sitting that you liked it and wanted to continue it.

SNYDER: I had a pretty fair grasp of what the basic value of meditation is—an intellectual grasp, at least—even then. It wasn't alien to my respect for primitive people and animals, all of whom/which are capable of simply just *being* for long hours of time. I saw it in that light as a completely natural act. To the contrary, it's odd that we don't do it more, that we don't, simply like a cat, *be* there for a while, experiencing ourselves as whatever we are, without any extra thing added to that. I approached meditation on that level; I wasn't expecting anything to happen. I wasn't expecting instantaneous satori to hit me just because I got my legs right. I found it a good way to be. There are other ways to be taught about that state of mind than reading philosophical texts: the underlying tone in good Chinese poetry, or what is glimmering behind the surface in a Chinese Sung Dynasty landscape painting, or what's behind a haiku, is that same message about a way to *be,* that is not explicatable by philosophy. Zen meditation—zazen—is simply, literally, a way to be, and when you get up, you see if you can't be that way even when you're not sitting: just *be,* while you're doing other things. I got that much sense of sitting to make me feel that it was right and natural even though it seemed unnatural for a while.

CHOWKA: Could you tell us about your teacher, Oda Sesso?

SNYDER: I spent my first year in Japan living in Shokoku-ji, learning Japanese and serving as personal attendant to Miura Isshu Roshi. As my first teacher, he instructed me to continue my studies with Oda Sesso Roshi, who was the head abbot of Daitoku-ji at that time. So I went up to Daitoku-ji, was accepted as a disciple by Oda Sesso, and started going to sesshins and living periodically in the monastery.

I still think a lot about Oda Sesso Roshi. You know, we have an image of Zen masters: Rinzai masters are supposed to shout and hit you; Soto Zen masters are supposed to do something else—I'm not sure what. In actual fact, they're all very human and very different from one another. Oda Roshi was an especially gentle and quiet man—an extremely subtle man, by far the subtlest mind I've ever been in contact with, and a marvelous teacher whose teaching capacity I would never have recognized if I hadn't stayed with it, because it was only after five or six years that I began to realize that he had been teaching me all along. I guess that's what all the roshis are doing: teaching even when they're not "teaching." One of the reasons that you have to be very patient and very committed is that the way the transmission works is that you don't *see* how it works for a long time. It begins to come clear later. Oda Roshi delivered *teisho* lectures in so soft a voice nobody could hear him. Year after year, we would sit at lectures—lectures that only roshis can give, spontaneous commentaries on classical texts—and not hear what he was saying. Several years after Oda Roshi had died one of the head monks, with whom I became very close, said to me, "You know those lectures that Oda Roshi gave that we couldn't hear? I'm beginning to hear them now."

CHOWKA: How did you come to choose Rinzai over Soto Zen, or was it a function of the contacts you had made?

SNYDER: It was partly a function of contacts. But if I'd had a choice I would have chosen Rinzai Zen. As William Butler Yeats says, "The fascination of what's difficult / has dried the sap out of my veins. . . ." The challenge of koan study—the warrior's path, almost—and maybe some inner need to do battle ("Dharma combat") were what drew me to it. By the time I went to Japan, I had the language capacity to handle the texts enough to be able to do it. Another reason: the koans are a mine of Chinese cultural information. Not only do they deal with fundamental riddles and knots of the psyche and ways of unraveling the Dharma, it's done in the elegant and pithy language of Chinese at its best, in which poetry (a couplet, a line, or even an entire poem) is employed often as part of the koan.

CHOWKA: You wrote in *Earth House Hold*: "Zen aims at freedom through practice of discipline," and the hardest discipline is "always following your own desires." Within that context, how is the "original mind" or "no mind" of Zen different from the so-called unenlightened normal consciousness of a non-Buddhist?

SNYDER: Unenlightened consciousness is very complicated—it's not simple. It's already overlaid with many washes of conditioning and opinion, likes and dislikes. In that sense, enlightened, original mind is just simpler, like the old image of the mirror without any dust on it, which in some ways is useful. My own personal discovery in the Zen monastery in Kyoto was that even with the extraordinary uniformity of behavior, practice, dress, gesture, every movement from dawn till dark, in a Zen monastery everybody was really quite different. In America everybody dresses and looks as though they are all different, but maybe inside they're all really the same. In the Far East, everybody dresses and looks the same, but I suspect inside they're all different. The dialectic of Rinzai Zen practice is that you live a totally ruled life, but when you go into the sanzen room, you have absolute freedom. The roshi wouldn't say this, but if you forced him to, he might say, "You think our life is too rigid? You have complete freedom here. Express yourself. What have you got to show me? Show me your freedom!" This really puts you on the line—"Okay, I've *got* my freedom; what do I want to do with it?" That's part of how koan practice works.

CHOWKA: Why did you not take formal vows of a monk?

SNYDER: Well, I actually did at one time; my hair is long now simply because I haven't shaved it lately. There is no role for a monk in the U.S.

CHOWKA: While you were studying in Japan for most of ten years, you always knew that you'd return to the U.S.?

SNYDER: Oh, yes.

CHOWKA: Was your return hastened by the death of your teacher?

SNYDER: Probably. At a certain point I realized that, for the time, I'd been in Japan enough. I began to feel the need to put my shoulder to the wheel on this continent. It wasn't just returning—the next step of my own practice was to be here.

CHOWKA: When you were interviewed in 1967 for *Conversations: Christian and Buddhist* you were studying at Daitoku-ji but not actually living in the monastery.

SNYDER: I was living in a small house that was ten minutes' walk from the monastery. It was really necessary to spend most of the time at the house, because in a monastery you have no access to texts or dictionaries. All of the other monks had already memorized everything, literally. As an outsider-novice-foreigner, you are continually wrestling with problems of translation and terminology—you have to go look things up.

ORLOVSKY: Was there a library at the monastery?

SNYDER: No. There are no books and no reading at a monastery. There was also the economic consideration of having to make a living. So part-time I taught conversational English to the engineers of various electronics companies to make enough money to rent a little house, buy my food, ride a bicycle.

CHOWKA: A decade ago, or even earlier, you prophesied a great development of interest in Buddhism in the West. In 1967 you said, "The 'truth' in Buddhism is not dependent in any sense on Indian or Chinese culture." Could you comment on your view now that ten years have passed?

SNYDER: What I felt at the time and what I think all of us feel is that we're talking about the Dharma without any particular cultural trapping. If a teaching comes from a given place, it's a matter of courtesy and also necessity to accept it in the form that it's brought. Things take forms of their own; we don't *know* what's going to happen in the future. The Buddhadharma, which is the Dharma as taught by a line of enlightened human beings (rather than the Dharma as received from deities via trance, revelation, or *bhakta,* which is what Hinduism is) is *nirmanakaya*-oriented—it goes by changeable bodies. Right now it goes primarily through human bodies. Already it is all over the globe, and it has no name and needs no name.

CHOWKA: In a 1961 essay, "Buddhist Anarchism," revised in *Earth House Hold* as "Buddhism and the Coming Revolution," you criticize institutional Buddhism in the East as "conspicuously ready to accept or ignore the inequalities/tyrannies of whatever political system it found itself under." In your 1967 conversation with Aelred Graham in Kyoto, you spoke of the other organized faiths as "degenerations that come with complex civilized social systems," although you added that "In the Christian world there is much more serious thought about the modern age and what to do with it than in the Buddhist world." Now, ten years later, Buddhism, especially the Tibetan and Zen varieties, is much more widely available in North

America. Has the coming of the Buddhadharma to the West altered your view about its complicity with degenerate, oppressive political systems?

SNYDER: Not particularly. It has to be understood that in Asia—India, China, and Japan—the overwhelming fact of life for three millennia has been the existence of large, centralized, powerful states. Much as in Europe until the Renaissance, it was assumed that the government was a reflection of natural order and that if there were inequalities or tyrannies that came from the government, although one might dislike them, there was no more use in complaining about them than there would be use in complaining about a typhoon. The better part was to *accept.* One of the most interesting things that has ever happened in the world was the Western discovery that history is arbitrary and that societies are human, and not divine, or natural, creations—that we actually have the capacity of making choices in regard to our social systems. This is a discovery that came to Asia only in this century. We in the West have an older history of dealing with it.

The organizations of Buddhism, Taoism, and Hinduism made the essential compromises they had to make to be tolerated by something that was far more powerful than themselves, especially in the imperial state of China. One of those compromises was to not criticize the state. You can't blame them for it, because they had no sense of there being an alternative. Even so, an interesting set of historical moves occurred in Chinese Buddhism. During the early period of Zen an essay was written that said Buddhist monks do not have to bow to the emperor since they are outside the concerns of the state. Later, in the thirteenth century, in Zen monasteries, sutras were chanted on behalf of the long life of the emperor; the monasteries supported and aided the regime. What it came to most strikingly was the almost complete cooperation of the Buddhist establishment in Japan (with some notable exceptions) with the military effort of World War II.

We don't have to go into how passionately nationalistic the Hindu Party of India is. The fact is that all of the world religions—Hindu, Buddhist, Islamic, Christian—share certain characteristics because they are all underneath the umbrella of civilization. As it turns out, one of the "World Religions'" main functions is to more or less support or reinforce the societies they are within. Even those who define their mission as liberating human beings from illusion have found it necessary to make compromises so that their little subculture wouldn't lose its tax-free buildings and landholdings and would be permitted to have a corner of existence in the society. This is also why monastic institutions are celibate. If they gave birth to their own children, they would become a tribe; as a tribe, they would have a deeper investment in the transformation of society and would *really* be a thorn in the flesh. As it is, if they simply are replenished by getting, in every generation, individuals from outside, they will never have that much investment in social transformation. If it's not a celibate *sangha*, then it's an alternative to society, an alternative that might be too threatening.

CHOWKA: You wrote in *Earth House Hold*: "Beware of anything that promises freedom or enlightenment—traps for eager and clever fools—three-quarters of philosophy and literature is the talk of people trying to convince themselves that they really like the cage they were tricked into entering." In an interview in the August *East West Journal*, Robert Bly agrees with Gurdjieff, who said it is important that true teachings be somewhat hard to find—there is only so much "knowledge" available at any one time and one's psyche can be changed only if a lot of knowledge comes at once; if offered to too many people via mass movements, the knowledge is dissipated. Bly goes on to say that there has been an infantilization of humanity, citing a book on the subject by Kline and Jonas, whose thesis is that each generation following the Industrial Revolution is more infantile than the previous, thus, for example, needing many more supportive devices merely to survive.

Would you comment on these observations in terms of your own view of the spiritual movements which have proliferated during this decade?

SNYDER: There is a very fine spiritual line that has to be walked between being unquestioning/passive on the one hand and obnoxiously individualistic/ultimately-trusting-no-one's-ideas-but-your-own on the other. I don't think it's uniquely

American; I think that all people have these problems on one level or another. Maybe that's one meaning of the Middle Way: to walk right down the center of that. In one of the Theravada scriptures the Buddha says, "Be a light unto yourself. In this six-foot-long body is birth and death and the key to the liberation from birth and death." There is one side of Buddhism that clearly throws it back on the individual—each person's own work, practice, and life. Nobody else can do it for you; the Buddha is only the teacher.

Americans have a supermarket of adulterated ideas available to them, thinned out and sweetened, just like their food. They don't have the apparatus for critical discernment either. So that the term "infantilization" is something I can relate to. I think there's a lot of truth in it. The primary quality of that truth is the lack of self-reliance, personal hardiness—self-sufficiency. This lack can also be described as the alienation people experience in their lives and work. If there is any one thing that's unhealthy in America, it's that it is a whole civilization trying to get out of work—the young, especially, get caught in that. There is a triple alienation when you try to avoid work: first, you're trying to get outside energy sources/resources to do it for you; second, you no longer know what your own body can do, where your food or water come from; third, you lose the capacity to discover the unity of mind and body via your work.

The overwhelming problem of Americans following the spiritual path is that they are doing it with their heads and not with their bodies. Even if they're doing it with their heads *and* bodies, their heads and bodies are in a nice supportive situation where the food is brought in on a tray. The next step, doing their own janitorial work and growing their own food, is missing, except in a few places.

CHOWKA: Would you like to comment on those few places where people are provided with teaching which requires work, too?

SNYDER: The San Francisco Zen Center is a good example. In both the mountain and city centers they are striving conscientiously to find meaningful work for everybody—work that, in the city center, is not foppish or artificial but is relevant to the immediate needs of that neighborhood, which is predominantly black, with lots of crime. Zen Center opened a grocery store and a bakery; they sell vegetables from their garden in Green Gulch in the grocery store. It's an effort in the right direction—that which is "spiritual" and that which is sweeping the floor are not so separated. This is one of the legacies of Zen, Soto or Rinzai—to steadily pursue the unity of daily life and spiritual practice.

CHOWKA: Does that relate to a difference between the Chinese and Indian legacies as they've been applied to North American spiritual disciplines?

SNYDER: The spiritual legacy of Chinese culture is essentially Zen or Ch'an Buddhism. The secondary spiritual legacy of China is in the aesthetics—the poetry and painting (Confucius, Lao-tzu, and Chuang-tzu are included in that; also Mencius, whose work will be appreciated more in time for its great human sanity, although it's deliberately modest in its spiritual claims). Ch'an Buddhism added to Indian Buddhism the requirement that everybody work: "a day without work, a day without food." The cultural attitude toward begging in China was totally different from that in India; the Chinese public wouldn't stand for beggars. Long before, in India, giving money to beggars was considered praiseworthy and merit-creating, which created an ecological reinforcing niche for people to live by begging. You can see it in the strictly yogic or sadhu approach, which separates lay society from people who follow a religious path. When the society is so strictly split, lay people have no access to spirituality except to gain merit by giving money to those who follow a spiritual path. This is true today in Theravadin countries like Thailand and Ceylon.

In India, although the word bhikkhu means beggar, it also meant that these people were aristocrats; they wouldn't pick up a hoe, they certainly wouldn't touch shit, they wouldn't even touch money, because that's demeaning and low-caste. This is a tendency that possibly is imbibed from Brahminism and caste structure. So although Buddhism starts out with no caste, with the concept of bhikkhu, nonetheless, the bhikkhu becomes rated so highly socially that, in a certain way, he's like a Brahmin—he's "pure" and shouldn't become defiled in any way. This lays the groundwork for the later extraordinary hierarchization of the Buddhist orders of India and Tibet. The Chinese culture wouldn't tolerate that. Po-chang, in his monastic rules written during the T'ang Dynasty, makes clear that begging is not a main part of our way of self-support. Our way of self-support is to grow our own food, build our own buildings, and make everybody, including the teacher, work. As long as he's physically able, the teacher must go out and labor with his hands along with his students. For all of the later elegance and elitism that crept into Ch'an and Zen, this is a custom that has not broken down. Roshis in Japan do physical work alongside their monks, still. That has been for them a source of abiding health.

There are other things within the Ch'an administrative structures, within the monasteries, which are quite amazingly democratic when it comes to certain kinds of choices. All of the monks—whether novices or elders—have an equal vote. That is a Chinese quality in that spiritual legacy. Another development that is Chinese, as far as I can tell, is group meditation. In India and Tibet, meditation is practiced primarily in a solitary form. The Chinese and Japanese made group sitting a major part of their practice. There is a communalization of practice in China, a de-emphasis of individual, goofy, yogic wandering around. For the Chinese monk there is a phase of wandering, but it's after many years of group practice/labor. I love both India and China; I love the contradictions. I can identify with both—see the beauty of both ways of going at it.

CHOWKA: Buddhism as practiced in the East is criticized often for being dominated by males. Is this situation improving?

SNYDER: The single most revolutionary aspect of Buddhist practice in the United States is the fact that women are participating in it. This is the one vast sociological shift in the entire history of Buddhism. From the beginning, women essentially had been excluded. But in America, fully fifty percent of the followers everywhere are women. What that will do to some of these inherited teaching methods and attitudes is going to be quite interesting.

One of the things I learned from being in Japan and have come to understand with age is the importance of a healthy family. The family is the Practice Hall. I have a certain resistance to artificially created territories to do practice in, when we don't realize how much territory for practice we have right at hand always.

CHOWKA: In the later draft of your essay "Buddhist Anarchism" you added the qualifier "gentle" to the "violence" you felt was occasionally permissible in dealing with the system. I'm curious if this word change means your view was tempered during the eight years that separated the two versions; perhaps oddly, too, the adjective "gentle" appeared at the end of the sixties, when talking about "violence," at least, had become quite acceptable.

SNYDER: If I were to write it now, I would use far greater caution. I probably wouldn't use the word "violence" at all. I would say now that the time comes when you set yourself against something, rather than flow with it; that's also called for. The very use of the word "violence" has implications—we know what they are. I was trying to say that, to be true to Mahayana, you have to act in the world. To act responsibly in the world doesn't mean that you always stand back and let things happen: you play an active part, which means making choices, running risks, and karmically dirtying your hands to some extent. That's what the Bodhisattva ideal is all about.

CHOWKA: You once mentioned an intuitive feeling that hunting might be the origin of zazen or samadhi.

SNYDER: I understand even more clearly now than when I wrote that, that our earlier ways of self-support, our earlier traditions of life prior to agriculture, required literally thousands of years of great attention and awareness, and long hours of stillness. An anthropologist, William Laughlin, has written a useful article on hunting as education for children. His first point is to ask why primitive hunters didn't have better tools than they did. The bow of the American Indians didn't draw more than forty pounds; it looked like a toy. The technology was really very simple—piddling! They did lots of other things extremely well, like building houses forty feet in diameter, raising big totem poles, making very fine boats. Why, then, does there seem to be a weakness in their hunting technology? The answer is simple: they didn't hunt with tools, they hunted with their minds. They did things—learning an animal's behavior—that rendered elaborate tools unnecessary.

You learn animal behavior by becoming an acute observer—by entering the mind—of animals. That's why in rituals and ceremonies that are found throughout the world from ancient times, the key component of the ceremony is animal *miming*. The miming is a spontaneous expression of the capacity of becoming physically and psychically one with the animal, showing the people know just what the animal does. (*Snyder mimics a lizard.*) Even more interesting: in a hunting and gathering society you learn the landscape as a field, multidimensionally, rather than as a straight line. We Americans go everywhere on a road; we have points A and B to get from here to there. Whenever we want something, we define it as being at the end of this or that line. In Neolithic village society, that was already becoming the case, with villages linked by lines. In a society in which everything comes from the field, however, the landscape with all its wrinkles and dimensions is memorized. You know that over there is milkweed from which come glue and string, over the hill beyond that is where the antelopes water. . . . That's a field sensing of the world. All of it partakes of the quality of samadhi.

More precisely, certain kinds of hunting are an entering into the movement-consciousness-mind-presence of animals. As the Indians say, "Hunt for the animal that comes to you." When I was a boy I saw old Wishram Indians spearing salmon on the Columbia River, standing on a little plank out over a rushing waterfall. They could stand motionless for twenty to thirty minutes with a spear in their hands and suddenly—they'd have a salmon. That kind of patience!

I am speculating simply on what are the biophysical, evolutionary roots of meditation and of spiritual practice. We know a lot more about it than people think. We know that the practices of fasting and going off into solitude—stillness—as part of the shaman's training are universal. All of these possibilities undoubtedly have been exploited for tens of thousands of years—have been a part of the way people learned what they are doing.

CHOWKA: In a 1975 interview you said, "The danger *and* hope politically is that Western civilization has reached the end of its ecological rope. Right now there is the potential for the growth of a real people's consciousness." In *Turtle Island* you identify the "nub of the problem" as "how to flip over, as in jujitsu, the magnificent growth-energy of modern civilization into a nonacquisitive search for deeper knowledge of self and nature." You hint that "the 'revolution of consciousness' [can] be won not by guns but by seizing key images, myths, archetypes . . . so that life won't seem worth living unless one is on the transforming energy's side." What specific suggestions and encouragement can you offer today so that this "jujitsu flip" can be hastened, practically, by individuals?

SNYDER: It cannot even be begun without the first of the steps on the Eightfold Path, namely Right View. I'll tell you how I came to hold Right View in this regard, in a really useful way. I'm a fairly practical and handy person; I was brought up on a farm where we learned how to figure things out and fix them. During the first year or two that I was at Daitoku-ji Sodo, out back working in the garden, helping put in a little firewood, or firing up the bath, I noticed a number of times little improvements that could be made. Ultimately I ventured to suggest to the head monks some labor- and time-saving techniques. They were tolerant of me for a while. Finally, one day one of them took me aside and said, "We don't want to do things any better or any faster, because that's not the point—the point is that you live the whole life. If we speed up the work in the garden, you'll just have to spend that much more time sitting in the zendo, and your legs will hurt more." It's all one meditation. The importance is in the right balance, and not how to save time in one place or another. I've turned that insight over and over ever since.

What it comes down to simply is this: If what the Hindus, the Buddhists, the Shoshone, the Hopi, the Christians are suggesting is true, then all of industrial/technological civilization is really on the wrong track, because its drive and energy are purely mechanical and self-serving—*real* values are someplace else. The real values are within nature, family, mind, and into liberation. Implicit are the possibilities of a way of living and being which is dialectically harmonious and complexly simple, because that's the Way. Right Practice, then, is doing the details. And how do we make the choices in our national economic policy that take into account *that* kind of cost accounting—that ask, "What is the natural-spiritual price we pay for this particular piece of affluence, comfort, pleasure, or labor saving?" "Spiritual price" means the time at home, time with your family, time that you can meditate, the difference between what comes to your body and mind by walking a mile as against driving (plus the cost of the gas). There's an accounting that no one has figured out how to do.

The only hope for a society ultimately hell-bent on self-destructive growth is not to deny growth as a mode of being, but to translate it to another level, another dimension. The literalness of that other dimension is indeed going to have to be taught to us by some of these other ways. There are these wonderfully pure, straightforward, simple, Amish, won't-have-anything-to-do-with-the-government, plain folk schools of spiritual practice that are already in our own background.

The change can be hastened, but there are preconditions to doing that which I recognize more clearly now. Nobody can move from Right View to Right Occupation in a vacuum as a solitary individual with any ease at all. The three treasures are Buddha, Dharma, and Sangha. In a way the one that we pay least attention to and have least understanding of is Sangha—community. What have to be built are community networks—not necessarily communes or anything fancy. When people, in a very modest way, are able to define a certain unity of being together, a commitment to staying together for a while, they can begin to correct their use of energy and find a way to be mutually employed. And this, of course, brings a commitment to the place, which means right relation to nature.

CHOWKA: In a letter to the editor in a recent issue of *East West Journal*, a reader wondered if the editor and other people who share so-called "new consciousness" occupations (jobs that might be more independent and rewarding, or less alienating than the norm), in interacting primarily with other like-minded or similarly engaged people, tend to become isolated from ordinary mainstream humanity. In talking with Aelred Graham ten years ago, you touched on this: "I almost can't escape from a society of turned-on people, which amounts to ten or fifteen thousand. . . . This is my drawback . . . I never meet those people (bourgeois, puritanical) in America." In his *Southern Review* article on your work in 1968, Thomas Parkinson notes (although he does not agree with) one criticism of your writing, thus: "Snyder does not face problems of modern life. . . . His poetry doesn't answer to the tensions of modern life and depends on a life no longer accessible or even desirable for man." There is also the danger that Herbert Marcuse sees in *One Dimensional Man*, that "the peculiar strength of the technological culture [is] to be able to make tame commodities out of potentially revolutionary states of consciousness." Would you comment on these points—isolation, irrelevance, and cooptation?

SNYDER: Taking the first point: At the time I talked to Graham, I was living in Kyoto and I hadn't lived in America in any serious way for many years; that was a very special statement I made to Graham at that point. In actual fact, I've lived more in the flux of society on more levels than practically anybody I know. I've held employment on all levels of society. I can pride myself on the fact that I worked nine months on a tanker at sea and nobody once ever guessed I had been to college.

I grew up with a sense of identification with the working class. I have lots of experience with this society—always have had and still do. I realize the danger of getting locked into a self-justifying group, which we see all around us. Since I've come back to the U.S.—and for the last seven years I've lived in rural California—I've been able to live and move with all kinds of people, which has been very good for me. A lot of my friends are doing the same. The whole "back to the land" movement, at least in California, at first had the quality of people going off into little enclaves. But the enclaves broke down rapidly as people discovered not only that they would *have to* but that they would *enjoy* interacting with their backwoods neighbors. A wonderful exchange of information and pleasure came out of what originally was hostile; each side discovered that they had something to learn from the other. Certain things that at first were taboo have become understood and acceptable.

The interesting point is the criticism of my poetry as invoking essentially outmoded values or situations that are not relevant or desirable. It's complicated to try to defend that. The answer lies in a critique of contemporary society and the clarification of lots of misunderstandings people have about what "primitive" constitutes, and even simpler clarifications about what your grandmother's life was like. It isn't really a main thrust in my argument or anyone else's I know that we should go backward. Whenever you get into this kind of discussion, one of the first things you are charged with from some corner is that "Well, you want to go backwards." So you have to answer it over and over again, but still people keep raising it. I remember a journalist once told David Brower of Friends of the Earth, "You want us to go back to the Stone Age!" and David replied, "Well, I'd be quite content to go back to the twenties, when the population was half of what it is now." Jerry Brown asked me the same question in a discussion about three weeks ago; he said, "You're going against the grain of things all the time, aren't you?" I said, "It's only a temporary turbulence I'm setting myself against. I'm in line with the big flow." (*Snyder laughs.*)

When we talk about a "norm" or a "Dharma," we're talking about the grain of things in the larger picture. Living close to earth, living more simply, living more responsibly, are all quite literally in the grain of things. It's coming back to us one way or another, like it or not—when the excessive energy supplies are gone. I will stress, and keep stressing, these things, because one of the messages I feel I have to convey—not as a preaching but as a demonstration hidden within poetry—is of deeper harmonies and deeper simplicities, which are essentially sanities, even though they appear irrelevant, impossible, behind us, ahead of us, or right now. "Right now" is an illusion, too.

The point by Marcuse that you raised is a real danger. I'm conscious enough of it, but I'm not sure about how one handles it except by being really careful and wary; that's one of the reasons why I stay out of the media pretty much—maybe a simpleminded way of keeping myself from being preempted or made into a commodity.

CHOWKA: You studied anthropology in school and it's remained one of your main interests. Some time ago you said, "We won't be white men 1,000 years from now . . . or fifty years from now. Our whole culture is going someplace else." More recently, you told a Montana newspaper, "We may be the slight degeneration of what was really a fine form," as you cited a recent study of a Stone Age habitation in southern France which showed the people to have had larger brains, much leisure time, and an aesthetic or religious orientation. Would you give your anthropologically grounded innate/intuitive assessment in this larger "Dharma" view of where we're at now?

SNYDER: We have to develop a much larger perspective on the historical human experience. Much of that perspective is simply knowing the facts—facts that are available but simply haven't entered into people's thinking. This is the new, larger humanism, and it helps us to understand our spiritual strivings, too. On the average, the human brain was larger 40,000 years ago than it is now. Even the Neanderthal had a brain larger than modern man. This information is from a study of skull casts. Whether or not it's terribly relevant, we don't know, but it's a very interesting point. Marshall Sahlins, an economic anthropologist at the University of Chicago, in *Stone Age Economics*, offers the research, methodology, and conclusion that upper Paleolithic people worked about fifteen hours a week and devoted the rest of their time to cultural activities. That period and shortly thereafter coincides with the emergence of the great cave art—for example, in the Pyrenees in southern France. We can only speculate about who those people were; however, we do know that they were fully intelligent, that their physical appearance was no different from people you see today (except their stature—at least that of the Cro-Magnon—was a little larger), and that they ate extremely well.

Not only are there thousands of caves and thousands of paintings in the caves, but paintings occur in caves two miles deep where you have to crawl through pools of cold water and traverse narrow passages in the dark, which open up on chambers that have great paintings in them. This is one of our primary koans: What have human beings been up to? The cave tradition of painting, which runs from 35,000 to 10,000 years ago, is the world's longest single art tradition. It completely overwhelms anything else. In that perspective, civilization is like a tiny thing that occurs very late.

The point that many contemporary anthropologists, like Sahlins and Stanley Diamond, are making is that our human experience and all our cultures have not been formed within a context of civilization in cities or large numbers of people. Our self—biophysically, biopsychically, as an animal of great complexity—was already well formed and shaped by the experience of bands of people living in relatively small populations in a world in which there was lots of company: other life forms, such as whales, birds, animals. We can judge from the paintings, from the beauty and accuracy of the drawings, and also from the little Magdalenian stone carvings, the existence of a tremendous interest, exchange, and sympathy between people and animals. The most accurate animal drawings that have been done until modern scientific animal drawings are these cave drawings: right perspective, right attention.

To come a step farther: in certain areas of the world, the Neolithic period was long a stable part of human experience. It represented 8,000 to 10,000 years of relative affluence, stability, a high degree of democracy, equality of men and women—a period during which all of our vegetables and animals were domesticated, and weaving and ceramics came into being. Most of the arts that civilization is founded on, the crafts and skills, are the legacy of the Neolithic. You might say that the groundwork for all the contemporary spiritual disciplines was well done by then. The world body of myth and folklore—the motifs of folklore and the main myths and myth themes distributed universally around the globe—is evidence of the depth of the tradition. So, in that perspective, civilization is new, writing is even newer, and writing as something that has an influence on many people's lives came only during the last three or four centuries. Libraries and academies are very recent developments, and world religions—Buddhism among them—are quite new. Behind them are millennia of human beings sharpening, developing, and getting to know themselves.

The last eighty years have been like an explosion. Several billion barrels of oil have been burned up. The rate of population growth, resource extraction, destruction of species, is unparalleled. We live in a totally anomalous time. It's actually quite impossible to make any generalizations about history, the past or the future, human nature, or anything else, on the basis of our present experience. It stands outside of the mainstream. It's an anomaly. People say, "We've got to be realistic, we have to talk about the way things *are*." But the way things for now *are* aren't real. It's a temporary situation.

CHOWKA: In *Earth House Hold* you wrote of Native Americans, "Their period of greatest weakness is over."

SNYDER: I hope that wasn't wishful thinking.

CHOWKA: You're not sure now?

SNYDER: Ah, it's touch and go. In a sense, they're in the same boat with all of us. Maybe a few of the peoples can hold something together because they have a population of sufficient size. But it's going to be very tricky. Diamond says the major theme of civilization is the slow but steady destruction or absorption of local, kin-based, or tribal populations by the Metropole. That process is still at work. The other side of it is the amazing resistance that some cultures show to being worn away, like the Hopi and the other Pueblos. They're incredibly strong and may well survive.

I've often wondered what makes these societies so tough. And it may well be that they are close to an original source of integrity and health. Erasing all negative associations for the word "primitive," it means *primus* or "first," like "original mind," original human society, original way of being. Another curious thing about the relationship between "primitive" and "civilized" is that no primitive society ever became civilized of its own free will; if it had the choice, it stayed itself.

In India today, three or four miles as the crow flies away from a 3,000-year-old agricultural civilization using Sanskrit, having temples and Brahmins—three miles up into the hills are original tribal societies that have lived that close to civilization for 3,000 years, and still they are the same people; they just can't be bothered. There is a reason why some of them are really strong; it's a systems/ecology reason, which I hit on finally after reading Margalef's book *Perspectives in Ecological Theory* and Eugene Odum.

Every given natural region has a potential top situation where all of the plants that will grow there have grown up now and all of those that will push out something else have pushed out something else, and it reaches a point of stability. If you cut all the forests and you wait many hundreds of years, it'll come to something again.

CHOWKA: It's an optimum condition.

SNYDER: This condition, called "climax," is an optimum condition of diversity—optimum stability. When a system reaches climax, it levels out for centuries or millennia. By virtue of its diversity it has the capacity to absorb all sorts of impacts. Insects, fungi, weather conditions come and go; it's the opposite of monoculture. If you plant a forest back into all white pine, one of these days the white pine blister rust comes along and kills all the white pine. If you have a natural mixed forest, the white pine will be hit a little by blister rust but they won't be in a solid stand, they'll be broken up. Another aspect of a climax situation is that almost half of the energy that flows in the system does not come from annual growth, it comes from the recycling of dead growth. In a brand-new system—for instance, after a piece of ground has been scraped with a bulldozer, when weeds and grass come up—the annual energy production is all new growth production; there is very little to be recycled. But with a forty percent recycling situation, there is a rich population of fungi, and beetles, and birds that feed on bugs, and predators that feed on birds that feed on bugs that eat the rotten wood; you've then achieved the maximum optimal biomass (actual quantity of living beings) in one place. This is also what is called "maturity." By some oddity in the language it's also what we call a virgin forest, although it's actually very experienced, wise, and mature. Margalef, a Spanish ecologist, theoretician, genius, has suggested that the evolution of species flows in line with the tendency of systems to reach climax. Many species exist in relation to the possibility of climax and to its reinforcement.

Certain human societies have demonstrated the capacity to become mature in the same way. Once they have achieved maturity, they are almost indestructible. But this kind of maturity has nothing to do with the maturity of civilization. (The only societies that are mature are primitive societies—they actually are that old, too: 30,000 years here, 10,000 years there.) "Civilization" is analogous to a piece of scraped-back ground that is kept perpetually scraped back so that you always get a lot of grass quickly every year—monoculture, rapid production, a few species, lots of energy produced, but no recycling to fall back on. So, civilization is a new kind of system rather than an old or mature one.

CHOWKA: An essay in *Turtle Island* tells us to "Find your place on the planet and dig in." Could you speak about your attempt to "dig in" in northern California, and the local political action you have found to be necessary?

SNYDER: To say "we must dig in" or "here we must draw our line" is a far more universal application than growing your own food or living in the country. One of the key problems in American society now, it seems to me, is people's lack of commitment to any given place—which, again, is totally unnatural and outside of history.

Neighborhoods are allowed to deteriorate, landscapes are allowed to be strip-mined, because there is nobody who will live there and take responsibility; they'll just move on. The reconstruction of a people and of a life in the United States depends in part on people, neighborhood by neighborhood, county by county, deciding to stick it out and make it work where they are, rather than flee. Zen Center has certainly demonstrated this with their tenacity in San Francisco, where, instead of being overwhelmed by the deterioration processes at work around them, they've reversed the flow by refusing to leave and by, against all odds, putting in a park—turning things around just by being there. Any group of people (not just Zen Center) who have that consciousness can do that. A corollary to that is my own experience in rural California: I have never learned so much about politics or been so involved in day-to-day social problems. I've spent years arguing the dialectic, but it's another thing to go to supervisors' meetings and deal with the establishment, to be right in the middle of whatever is happening right here, rather than waiting for a theoretical alternative government to come along.

I'll say this real clearly, because it seems that it has to be said over and over again: There is no place to flee to in the U.S. There is no "country" that you can go and lay back in. There is no quiet place in the woods where you can take it easy and be a stoned-out hippie. The surveyors are there with their orange plastic tape, the bulldozers are down the road warming up their engines, the real estate developers have got it all on the wall with pins on it, the county supervisors are in the back room drinking coffee with the real estate subdividers, the sheriff's department is figuring to get a new deputy for your area soon, and the forest service is just about to let out a big logging contract to some company. That's the way it is everywhere, right up to the north slope of Alaska, all through Canada, too. It's the final gold rush mentality. The rush right now is on for the last of the resources that are left standing. And that means that the impact is hitting the so-called country and wilderness. In that sense, we're on the front lines. I perceived that when I wrote the poem; that's why I called it "Front Lines." I also figured that we were going to have to stay and hold the line for our place.

A friend of mine came to where I live five years ago, and he could see what was going to come down. He said, "I'm not going to settle here, I'm going to British Columbia." So with his wife and baby he drove two hundred and fifty miles north of Vancouver, B.C., and then seventy miles on a dirt road to the end of the road, and then walked two miles to a cabin that they knew about, and bought a piece of land only a few miles south of the St. Elias range. That summer there they discovered they were surrounded by chain saws that were clear-cutting the forest, and that there were giant off-the-road logging trucks running up and down the seventy miles of dirt road, so that it was to take your life in your hands to try to go into town to get something. "Town" was a cluster of laundromats, discarded oil drums, and mobile homes that had been flown in. That's the world. My friends came back down to California; it was too industrial up there.

I would take this all the way back down to what it means to get inside your belly and cross your legs and sit—to sit down on the ground of your mind, of your original nature, your place, your people's history. Right Action, then, means sweeping the garden. To quote my teacher, Oda Sesso: "In Zen there are only two things: you sit, and you sweep the garden. It doesn't matter how big the garden is." That is not a new discovery; it's what people have been trying to do for a long time. That's why there are such beautiful little farms in the hills of Italy, people did that.

CHOWKA: Could you give examples of some issues that have arisen in your county and that you've addressed—the kinds of action required and support you received?

SNYDER: One issue was building codes: housing and toilets. A number of people had their houses tagged as illegal, because they hadn't gotten a building permit, the construction used did not conform to the code, or they substituted outhouses for septic tanks.

CHOWKA: This happened where you live. What is it like there?

SNYDER: Genuinely rural and remote. A lot of time and work on the part of hundreds of people all over California, ultimately, went into fighting a tactic whose purpose was to try to get them out as an undesirable minority population who had moved in and lowered real estate values. Such things were reversed by intelligence and research, and the very clear argument that it's obviously unfair to impose suburban housing development standards in a rural area. Now some changes have been made in the code of California to permit rural people to build their homes in a simpler way. A small victory—to have an outhouse! Some other changes have been made in the code to make it legal not to have electricity and legal to have a wood stove. The codes were actually getting to the point where you *had* to have electricity to be legal. It's a small issue but one in which people's lives and homes are at stake.

More interesting is the question of schools, school boards, and the degree of autonomy you can practice with education if you have a school board with some kind of vision and a unity of purpose behind it. We went through quite a number building a public school locally—it was clearly the will of the people to build it in a beautiful, careful, and craftly way, not making it into an interchangeable-pod schoolhouse. Because the architects, Zach Stewart and Dan Osborne, who were hired by the school board also were visionary men with great patience, it was possible, at the cost of two extra years of work, to get the state to approve it. It was also possible because hundreds of people donated thousands of hours of free time to the building of it; it became a work of art. That's what a community can do for its children. It's also possible to keep on top of the local forest service and their timber policies in a way that the conservationists in the big city can't. They can do a lot—they have lobbyists with a lot of clout in Washington. But there are certain things that are effectively accomplished when local people say, "We don't like the way this is being handled here on public land." If you have both local people and people with a lobbyist in Washington coming with the same message, then you have something working on these public land managers, who tend to be rather arrogant.

Where I live, the greater proportion of the land in the county is public land; we find ourselves in the position of being the only ombudsman for the use of that land. Nobody else is watching but us. At the same time we can't be too unrealistic or idealistic about it, because we know what those jobs mean to our neighbors. If you want to say that there should be no more logging in this section, you also have to ask what the alternative employment will be. Many people where I live are interested in developing crafts, skills, industries, co-ops that give the whole population a long-range economic viability. So throughout California—which is my main area of experience—I know of both rural and urban enclaves that are trying to develop, on every level, appropriate technologies, both material and spiritual. And I guess it's going on all over the country.

CHOWKA: I wonder about the value given to poetry in our society. *Turtle Island*, which won for you a Pulitzer Prize and is by contemporary standards a successful poetry book (selling almost 70,000 copies), when compared to mass market novels, for example, has sold very little.

SNYDER: For a book of formal poetry, *Turtle Island* sold quite a bit. But it's only one kind of poetry. Actually, Americans love poetry, pay huge sums of money for it, and listen to it constantly. Of course, I'm talking about song, because poetry is really song. Rock 'n' roll, ballad, and all other forms of song are really part of the sphere that, since ancient times, has been what poetry is. If you accept poetry as song, then there are plenty of songs already which are doing most of the work that poetry is supposed to do for people.

CHOWKA: You're using song a lot more now in your own poetry, as in "California Water Plan."

SNYDER: Yes, I'm using literal song-voice, singing voice or chanting voice, in poetry and probably will be doing it more. But even the way I read the other poems has the element of song in it, because the intensification of language and the compression of the already existing sound-system musicality of the spoken language itself is manifested by the reading of the poem. Part of the work of the poet is to intensify and clarify the existing musical sound-possibilities in the spoken language.

CHOWKA: You speak a lot about the "old ways" and the fact that song comes from a prehistoric tradition. Is the fact that song is so popular today, in poetry and popular song, proof that these "old ways" cannot be lost, that they are with us still?

SNYDER: One of the things that little children do first is to sing and chant to themselves. People spontaneously sing out of themselves—a different use of voice. By "song" we don't have to limit ourselves to the idea of lyric and melody, but should understand it as a joyous, rhythmic, outpouring voice, the voice *as* voice, which is the Sanskrit goddess Vak—goddess of speech, music, language, and intelligence. Voice itself is a manifestation of our inner being.

CHOWKA: We know that poetry shares its roots with religion, music, dance. Why isn't poetry as compromised or diluted as you've said these other things—religion, music, et cetera—tend to be?

SNYDER: None of them is functioning with the wholeness that we can guess that they had once. That wholeness, in part, was a function of the fact that they all worked together: poetry didn't exist apart from song, song didn't exist apart from dance, dance didn't exist apart from ritual, ritual didn't exist apart from vision and meditation. Nonetheless, all of these forms have their own intrinsic validity. I wouldn't say that poetry today is any more valid than dance or drama.

CHOWKA: But you did say that in *Earth House Hold*.

SNYDER: Okay, I did say that, didn't I? What I meant was that poetry has maintained itself with more of its original simplicity perhaps than some of these other forms—it has taken on less technology in support of it. But then I would have to qualify that as to allow how the music which is popular song—which I think is a fascinating phenomenon apart from the fact that it's being used as a commodity—as it stands now is backed by a very complex technology; however, you can remove most of that technology and go back to an acoustic situation and it still has the power in a live setting.

CHOWKA: In *Earth House Hold* you write that "there comes a time when the poet must choose" between the "traditional-great-sane-ordered stream" and one that's "beyond the bound onto the way out, into . . . possible madness . . . possible enlightened return." Did you have yourself in mind when writing that? It's not completely clear if you've chosen one way or the other—I can see elements of both in your work.

SNYDER: I wrote that a long time ago, and I was able to say it because I could see both sides in myself and say, maybe somewhat artificially, that you have to be one way or the other. I'll rephrase it in terms of how I see it now: We have a sense that great artists and geniuses have to be crazy, or that genius and creativity are functions somehow of a certain kind of brilliant craziness, alienation, disorder, disassociation.

CHOWKA: Like Baudelaire, Rimbaud.

SNYDER: The model of a romantic, self-destructive, crazy genius that they and others provide us is understandable as part of the alienation of people from the cancerous and explosive growth of Western nations during the last one hundred and fifty years. Zen and Chinese poetry demonstrate that a truly creative person is more truly sane; that this romantic view of crazy genius is just another reflection of the craziness of our times. In a utopian, hoped-for, postrevolutionary world, obviously, poets are not going to have to be crazy and everybody, if they like, can get along with their parents; that would be the way it is. So I aspire to and admire a sanity from which, as in a climax ecosystem, one has spare energy to go on to even more challenging—which is to say more spiritual and more deeply physical—things. Which is not to disallow the fact that crazy, goofy, clowning, backwards behavior isn't fun and useful. In mature primitive societies the irrational goofy element is there and well accounted for.

CHOWKA: I want to return to this idea later in discussing the fifties. But first, who are some of the people you feel personify the "beyond the bound onto the way out" tradition today?

SNYDER: I don't know if I want to say anybody personifies it.

CHOWKA: You didn't have individuals in mind when you wrote it?

SNYDER: I can think of parts of individuals. I would say that maybe we can discriminate between poets who have fed on a certain kind of destructiveness for their creative glow (and some of those are no longer with us, consequently) as against those who have "composted" themselves and turned part of themselves back in on themselves to become richer and stronger, like Wendell Berry, whose poetry lacks glamour but is really full of nutrients.

CHOWKA: You mention Berry frequently; I gather he's one of your favorite poets. Could you talk about some other contemporary poets whom you read and enjoy?

SNYDER: I have a special regard for Robert Duncan because of his composting techniques and also because of his care, scholarship, acquaintance with the Western tradition and its lore, knowledge, and wisdom (which I have neglected)—I'm glad that he's doing it and I can learn from him. I'm glad that Robert Bly is looking at the Western tradition. I'm also a close reader of Michael McClure's poetry, for his long, careful, intense dedication to developing a specific biological/wild/unconscious/fairytale/new/scientific/imagination form. Maybe he's closer to Blake than anybody else writing. I can think of poets who are little known—like Robert Sund, who has only one book out—who have cultivated a fine observation and ear and tuned it to daily life, work, people, scenes of the West or wherever they are, who are unpretentious in the presentation of themselves, but who have very high-quality work. Wendell Berry is a man who does very high-quality work and is also a working farmer and a working thinker, who draws on the best of American roots and traditional mindfulness, like his Kentucky farming forebears, to teach us something that we're not going to learn by studying Oriental texts.

CHOWKA: He's grounded himself in this country.

SNYDER: He's grounded here, but at the same time opening it out so that we can say, "There was something like the Oriental wisdom here all along, wasn't there?"

CHOWKA: That wisdom tradition is universal.

SNYDER: It is universal, as good farming, and attention to how to treat things, are universal.

CHOWKA: The poets you've mentioned so far are all personal acquaintances to some degree. How much does knowing a poet personally, knowing how he/she writes, affect your appreciation of the poet's work?

SNYDER: I've run into poems by poets I haven't known in the least that have excited me instantaneously, like Lillian Robinson, who lives in upstate New York, whose work (a poem called "In the Night Kitchen") I saw in a little magazine. (I got her address and asked her to send me a couple more poems.) I watch for those things—for the growth of people who are our peers and contemporaries—and hopefully, too, I try to see something of what's coming in from other places.

I've been responding to your question about who I read and what I think of poets; I've been answering in a conventional modern American poet mold. I'd like to explain how I *really* do things, because it's part of my view and my practice. I no longer feel the necessity to identify myself as a member of the whole society.

CHOWKA: North American society?

SNYDER: Yes. It's too large and too populous to have any reasonable hope of keeping your fingers on it, except by the obviously artificial mode of mass media television, which I don't see anyway, and which presents only a very highly specialized surface from that society. What I realistically aspire to do is to keep up with and stimulate what I think is really strong and creative in my own viable region, my actual nation: northern California/southern Oregon, which we might call Kuksu country, subdivision of Turtle Island continent. Within that, I do know what's happening and I do read and follow and go to readings with and read poems with the poets who are beginning to develop a depth and a grounding out of it. We also have our own way of keeping touch in terms of our local drainage (which is the North Pacific) across the North Pacific rim, with companion poets in Japan, like Nanao Sakaki and his circle—great Japanese bioregional poets who, analogously to us calling North America "Turtle Island," call Japan "Jomonia" and have an island-Pacific-bioregion sense of it. I don't see anything provincial or parochial in it because it implies a stimulus to others to locate themselves equally well. Having done so, we will see a mosaic of natural regions which then can talk across the boundaries and share specifics with each other. Southwest specifics, like I get from the rancher-writer Drummond Hadley, teach me ecosystems and mind-understandings that are different from ours in the sense of how you relate to the blue sky and to turquoise. I can talk about how we relate to heavy winter rains and large conifers.

CHOWKA: But you retain still a global consciousness to the extent that you've identified nuclear power as the greatest danger to the planet, which is not purely a local issue.

SNYDER: There are two kinds of earth consciousness: one is called global, the other we call planetary. The two are 180 degrees apart from each other, although on the surface they appear similar. "Global consciousness" is world-engineering-technocratic-utopian-centralization men in business suits who play world games in systems theory; they include the environmentalists who are employed at the backdoor of the Trilateral Commission. "Planetary thinking" is decentralist, seeks biological rather than technological solutions, and finds its teachers for its alternative possibilities as much in the transmitted skills of natural peoples of Papua and the headwaters of the Amazon as in the libraries of the high Occidental civilizations. It's useful to make this distinction between a planetary and a global mind.

"Planetary mind" is old-ways internationalism which recognizes the possibility of one earth with all of its diversity; "global consciousness" ultimately would impose a not-so-benevolent technocracy on everything via a centralized system.

CHOWKA: I'd like to return the discussion to your career, and how you began to have your work published. At one point you said that very early you decided, in effect, that "there was nothing more to be done vis-à-vis seeking a poetic career." Did publishing your first poems and books require some exertion or did it literally all fall into place without any effort?

SNYDER: I had sent poems around a little bit for a while. I think maybe only one or two things were published. It was partly a Buddhist decision. I was working for the forest, fixing trails up in the high country of Yosemite, I was getting more into meditation—walking or mountain meditation—by myself. I finished off the trail crew season and went on a long mountain meditation walk for ten days across some wilderness. During that process—thinking about things and my life—I just dropped poetry. I don't want to sound precious, but in some sense I did drop it. Then I started writing poems that were better. From that time forward I always looked on the poems I wrote as gifts that were not essential to my life; if I never wrote another one, it wouldn't be a great tragedy. Ever since, every poem I've written has been like a surprise. I've never expected or counted on writing another one. What I really got to work on at that time was studying Chinese and preparing myself to go to Japan and study. But I guess I really didn't give up poetry enough because while I was in Japan I was always what is described as the lowest type of Zen student—the type who concerns himself once in a while with literature. So, I confess I did go on writing poems from time to time, which is inexcusable! I couldn't help myself.

CHOWKA: You mentioned China positively in *Turtle Island* ("I lost my remaining doubts about China") and in a letter about Suwa-no-se Island ("People's China has many inspiring examples"). You also published a poem in *The Back Country* titled "To the Chinese Comrades." What are your feelings about China now?

SNYDER: I guess I probably spoke too soon in saying I've lost my remaining doubts; I still have doubts about China—certainly doubts about China as a model for the rest of the industrial world. Many lessons, though, can be learned but they cannot be applied wholesale—people wouldn't stand for it. But, yes, China is filled with inspiring examples of cooperation, reforestation, and less inspiring examples like the campaign to kill sparrows some years ago.

CHOWKA: What about their disaffiliation with their spiritual lineage?

SNYDER: That doesn't trouble me too much. I believe the Chinese had been pretty well disaffiliated from that already for some time. But, in a sense, the primary values already had sunk in so deeply that they didn't have to articulate them much anymore. Also, as a student of Chinese history, I perceive a little about the cycles that it moves in. If the rest of the world holds together, I would bet that a century and a half from now China again will be deeply back into meditation, as part of the pendulum swing of things. In a way, People's China is a manifestation of wonderful qualities of cooperation and selfless endeavor toward a common goal that were there all along. The negative side, though, is that China has been the most centralized, bureaucratic, civilized culture on earth for the longest time; unquestionably because of that, much was lost within and without. Much diversity was lost. The Chinese in the past, and probably still, don't have an appreciation for the ethnic or the primitive. For centuries, they have been looking down on their own border people or on the small aboriginal enclaves—tiny cultures in the hills of which there are still hundreds within China. So I feel ambivalent about China. Without doubt one can recognize the greatness of its achievement on all levels and think of it as a model of what a civilization can be; but then I can just as soon say, "But I wish there *weren't* any civilization!"

Sir Joseph Needham is very impressed by the Chinese revolution; in his book *Science and Civilization in China* he says that Taoism foreshadows the Revolution, and that's true. Taoism is a Neolithic world view and a matrilineal, if not matriarchal, Chinese world view that somehow went through the sound barrier of early civilization and came out the other side halfway intact, and continued to be the underlying theme of Chinese culture all through history up until modern times—antifeudalistic; appreciative of the female principle, women's powers, intuition, nature, spontaneity, and freedom. So Needham says that Taoism through history has been a 2,000-year-long holding action for China to arrive at socialism. That's how positively *he* looks at it. The contemporary Chinese look back on Taoism as a heritage in their past that as socialists they can respond to. Buddhism is a foreign religion—it came from India! But the Taoist component in Chinese culture will surely return again to the surface.

(*Peter Orlovsky enters the conversation.*)

ORLOVSKY: Are there any tribes in China still that have been left alone?

SNYDER: There are some. You can't communalize certain kinds of production in certain areas—you can't improve on what they're doing already. If a group has a good communal village agriculture—a hill situation not susceptible to use of tractors—it might as well be left alone.

The present Chinese regime, like every regime in the world, has been guilty of some very harsh and ethnocentric treatment of people, especially the Tibetans, which is inexcusable. At the same time they hold out a certain measure of hope, especially to people of the Third World underdeveloped countries, who are offered only two models of what to do. One model is to plug into the nearest fossil fuel source and become a satellite country of the United States or some other industrial nation; the other option is the Chinese: get the landlords off your back, straighten out the tax structure, and then do better agriculture with the tools you have available. The Chinese are perhaps on the verge of becoming more industrialized, and this good opinion of them may soon evaporate; as a strategy for what they consider to be their own survival, they may go the same route we have. The other point I want to make is that although it's true that China is the world's most centralized and bureaucratic, the oldest, and in some ways the most autocratic civilization, at the same time it has been filled with a rich mix of humanity from north to south, east to west: dialects, subcultures, of all sorts, of great vigor—many of them in one way or another amazingly still around. But it isn't something we would want to be, we would never want to be as populated as China.

CHOWKA: One of the more interesting points to arise during the "Chinese Poetry and the American Imagination" conference this week is a question that you raised. We had assumed that there was a tone of intimacy, of cooperation, of communality in a lot of the Chinese poetry that was discussed. You wondered if the new, wider, Occidental interest in classical Chinese poetry presaged the development of similar qualities here.

SNYDER: I think it's inevitable that American society move farther and farther away from certain kinds of extreme individualism, for no reason other than that the frontier is gone and the population has grown; partially, it may be the social dynamics of crowding. (Although, of course, many societies that are not crowded are nonetheless highly cooperative.) But I didn't raise this point as a prophecy, but as a question. The negative side of the spirit of individualism—the "everybody get their own" exploitative side—certainly is no longer appropriate. It can be said to have been in some ways productive when there were enormous quantities of resources available; but it's counterproductive in a postfrontier society. It's counterproductive when the important insight for everyone is how to interact appropriately and understand the reciprocity of things, which is the actual model of life on earth—a reciprocal, rather than a competitive, network. The ecological and anthropological sciences are in the forefront of making models for our new value systems and philosophies. We are moving away from social Darwinism. As the evolutionary model dominated nineteenth- and early twentieth-century thinking, henceforth the ecological model will dominate our model of how the world is—reciprocal and interacting rather than competitive.

CHOWKA: Many of the ideas you've expressed are certainly as radical as those of Allen Ginsberg and the other writers who were part of the Beat literary group. You share a similar, unequivocal vision of where and how society went wrong, which unsettles many people. Compared to Allen and the others, however, relatively little has been written about you in a negative way. Why the difference?

SNYDER: Allen became extremely famous! He got a lot of negative criticism, but he also got an enormous amount of positive criticism. The proof of the pudding is in the eating: he sold hundreds of thousands of copies of *Howl*. It's great not to have had much negative criticism, but there are some people who never have had a negative word said about them, and nobody's read their books either. The point is to enter the dialogue of the times. Certainly, some of the things I have to say strike at the root. Until recently, most people, including Marxists, have been unable to bring themselves to think of the natural world as part of the dialectic of exploitation; they have been human-centered—drawing the line at exploitation of the working class. My small contribution to radical dialectic is to extend it to animals, plants: indeed, to the whole of life.

CHOWKA: I'd like to talk about your work in Governor Jerry Brown's administration as a member of the Arts Council. What does that job entail?

SNYDER: As a member of the Arts Council, I attend monthly meetings and committee meetings, answer a lot of mail, talk to many people and check things out, so to speak, all of which is connected with some policies and ideas that we as a council of nine members are beginning to formulate on the thorny question of how to use the people's money—how to feed it back to the people for the support of art and culture.

CHOWKA: Are the members of the Council working artists?

SNYDER: With one exception they are all working artists, which was Brown's idea.

CHOWKA: The Council is new under his administration?

SNYDER: Yes. It's a departure from the usual arts commission being peopled by essentially wealthy patrons of the arts for whom being on a state's arts council is a social plum—perpetuating the idea that there are "good people" who have made a lot of money and also love the arts who then decide how to give money to artists. It was Brown's idea to change that, which has made a small ripple across the country; it demonstrates that artists can read, write, administer, and do things that a lot of people said they couldn't. (It takes me away from my own work, though.)

CHOWKA: When I met Robert Bly this week he told me he has strong objections to your being on the Arts Council; he sees a danger in the state trying to deal with and fund the arts in a centralized way.

SNYDER: This is a dialogue that goes on now across the U.S., in England, and in other places where the state uses public money to support art. When Governor Brown first took office, he had strong reservations about whether there should be a state arts council at all, from several standpoints, ranging from the question of "Is this a proper use of tax money?" to whether government involvement in the arts would result in implicit censorship or ultimately thought or aesthetic control. Those of us he talked to at that time shared those fears and worries, and were ourselves ambivalent about being on an arts council. But, it was with a strong experimental hope that there might be a way to use people's money to benefit creativity, avoiding these pitfalls, that we got involved.

There is no question that art meets real needs of the people. For artists—whether full-time professionals or part-time amateurs—ecologically, economically, their niche is there. But within the complexities of our present industrialized, civilized world, you have to come to grips with the problem in a new way. An economic subsidy of a very special order accounts for so much of the energy, affluence, craziness, and speed of the last eighty years. Fossil fuel subsidy is underwriting mass production. Fossil fuel energy is a subsidy from nature; we do not have to pay for the BTUs in oil what we would have to pay if it were not already concentrated and available in an easily usable form in the ground. Put simply, the arts—with the exception of certain modern media arts—are labor-intensive. Labor-intensive activities of any sort cannot compete with fossil-fueled ones—hand-thrown as against mass-produced pots, for example. As it happens, art cannot mass produce. To produce an opera requires hours of rehearsal; there is no way of automating that.

CHOWKA: And study, too—the preparation of an individual artist.

SNYDER: Yes. If we value art and higher cultural forms (and they should be valued, because they are preserves of the human spirit—as Lévi-Strauss says, "national parks of the mind"), then the people themselves are going to have to keep them going, until the time when the fossil fuel subsidy is withdrawn and the arts can compete in the free market economy like the family farm (when labor-intensive agriculture can be economically competitive once again). My view is that public support is necessary to carry the arts through, in the same way that we are trying to carry endangered species through.

Since we have taken on this task, we in California have been considered populists, because we have tried to adjust the balances of where money goes and what deserves support. We've put a stress on thinking of art in terms of creativity and process rather than commodity and product. We look on creativity as a birthright of everybody; we're trying to play down the sense of artist as special genius or talent, and be more sensitive to the community roles and possibilities of artists working on many levels of professionalism.

The local craftsperson or artist down the street is as valuable in being the yeast of social change and direction as anyone else. In terms of quality, we in California are concerned with recognizing and rewarding excellence, but we don't want to impose standards of excellence that derive simply from the Western European high cultural tradition. So our Arts Council is a very diverse group.

You raised the question of centralization. Actually, the Arts Council is less centralized than it would appear. The actual selection of who gets grants is decided by panelists—other artists or teachers—chosen from around the state who donate time to read applications. We translate their opinions into actions. Further, the state is divided demographically into five areas of racial, cultural, and economic spread, so that without compromising quality we make a point of affirmative action.

We make sure that folks from the back country and the inner city know what's happening so that they can participate.

CHOWKA: You don't see any conflict between having a state job administering money to artists and writers and being a poet and writer yourself?

SNYDER: Arts Council members don't get paid. The time I give to it is public service time; and it takes a lot of my time. You have to trust that the people whom the governor appoints are going to be fair. The fact that we're artists should be seen as a plus, because we're in a position to know from inside with our own hearts how things can and should be. The knowledge of what kind of work it takes to be an artist is also one of our strengths. Concerning other conflicts of interest, we members of the Arts Council are the only artists in the state who cannot apply for grants!

CHOWKA: Can you say more about your own evolving practice?

SNYDER: You're asking me what is my Buddhist practice? I'll ask you, "What do you mean by 'practice'?"

CHOWKA: The realization that there is something to be done.

SNYDER: What about the realization that there is nothing to be done?

CHOWKA: Then why would one go to Japan to study?

SNYDER: But what is "practice"?

CHOWKA: Sitting, for one thing.

SNYDER: Sitting—okay. So you're defining "practice" essentially as a concrete, periodic activity.

CHOWKA: Partially.

SNYDER: It might be mantra chanting, too; it might be doing a certain number of prostrations every day.

Periodic, repetitive behavior, to create, recreate, enforce, reinforce certain tendencies, certain potentialities, in the biopsyche. There is another kind of practice which also is habitual and periodic, but not necessarily as easily or clearly directed by the will: that's the practice of necessity. We are six-foot-long vertebrates, standing on our hind legs, who have to breathe so many breaths per minute, eat so many BTUs of plant-transformed solar energy per hour, et cetera. I wouldn't like to separate our mindfulness into two categories, one of which is your forty-minute daily ritual, which is "practice," and the other not practice. Practice simply is one intensification of what is natural and around us all of the time. Practice is to life as poetry is to spoken language. So as poetry is the practice of language, "practice" is the practice of life. But from the enlightened standpoint, all of language is poetry, all of life is practice. At any time when the attention is there fully, then all of the Bodhisattva's acts are being done.

I've had many teachers who have taught me good practices, good habits. One of the first practices I learned is that when you're working with another person on a two-person crosscut saw, you never push, you only pull; my father taught me that when I was eight. Another practice I learned early was safety: where to put your feet when you split wood so that the ax won't glance off and hurt your feet. We all have to learn to change oil on time or we burn out our engines. We all have to learn how to cook. By trial and error, but also by attention, it gets better. Another great teaching that I had came from some older men, all of whom were practitioners of a little-known esoteric indigenous Occidental school of mystical practice called mountaineering. It has its own rituals and initiations, which can be very severe. The intention of mountaineering is very detached—it's not necessarily to get to the top of a mountain or to be a solitary star. Mountaineering is done with team work. Part of its joy and delight is in working with two other people on a rope, maybe several ropes together, in great harmony and with great care for each other, your motions related to what everyone else has to do and can do to the point of ascending. The real mysticism of mountaineering is the body/mind practice of moving on a vertical plane in a realm that is totally inhospitable to human beings.

From many people I learned the practice of how to handle your tools, clean them, put them back; how to work together with other men and women; how to work as hard as you can when it's time for you to work, and how to play together afterwards. I learned this from the people to whom I dedicated my first book, *Riprap*. I came also to a specific spiritual practice, Buddhism, which has some extraordinary teachings within it. The whole world is practicing together; it is not rare or uncommon for people who are living their lives in the world, doing the things they must do, if they have not been degraded or oppressed, to be fully conscious of the dignity and pride of their life and their work. It's largely the fellaheen oppression and alienation that is laid down on people by certain civilized societies throughout history that breaks up people's original mind, original wisdom, the sense and sanity of their work and life. From that standpoint Buddhism, like Christianity, is responding to the alienation of a fragmented society. In doing this, Buddhism developed a *sangha*, which is celibate as a strategy to maintain a certain kind of teaching that in a sense goes against the grain of the contemporary civilization, but will not go *too* much against the grain because it's a survival matter.

The larger picture is the possibility that humanity has more original mind from the beginning than we think. Part of our practice is not just sitting down and forming useful little groups within the society but, in a real Mahayana way, expanding our sense of what has happened to us all into a realization that natural societies are in themselves communities of practice. The community of practice that is right at the center of Buddhism, and Hinduism also, is the Neolithic cattle-herding proto-Brahmin family that sang the Vedas together, morning and night. The singing of the Vedas by a group of people, in the family/household, is what lies behind all of the mantras, chants, sutras, and ceremonies that go on all over the Hindu-Buddhist world today. It all goes back to nine thousand years ago, when families sat down and sang together. The yogic practices and meditation come through a line of teaching concerned with life, death, and healing.

To me, the natural unit of practice is the family. The natural unit of the play of practice is the community. A *sangha* should mean the community, just as the real Mahayana includes all living beings. There is cause and consequence. On one level, Theravadin Buddhism says, "Life is suffering, and we must get out of the Wheel"—that's position of cause. But from position of consequence we can say, "The life cycle of creation is endless. We watch the seasons come and go, life into life forever.

The child becomes parent, who then becomes our respected elder. Life, so sacred; it is good to be a part of it all." That's an American Indian statement that also happens to be the most illuminated statement from the far end of Buddhism, which does not see an alienated world that we must strive to get out of, but a realized world, in which we know that all plays a part.

Still, so far I've been making my points on practice and original mind from the standpoint of culture and history. That must be done as a corrective, because almost no one understands what civilization is, what it has done, and what the alternatives could be. But I'm not saying an "ideal society" would mean no more work, no more practice, all enlightened play. We still have to get at something called the *kleshas*—obstacles, poisons, mixed-up feelings, mean notions, angriness, sneaky exploitations. Buddhism evolved to deal with these. We're born with them; I guess they come with the large brain super-survival ego sense this primate climaxes with. Maybe all that ego-survival savvy was evolutionary once; now it's counter-revolutionary. But whether we say "Meditate and follow the Buddhadharma" or "Work well and have gratitude to Mother Earth," we're getting at these poisons; that's what the shaman's healing song is all about.

CHOWKA: The place where you've settled—your home in the northern California Sierras—is important to your practice.

SNYDER: Where I live, there is a friendly number of people, diverse as they are, who have a lot of the same spirit. Because we are together in the same part of the world and expect to be together there for the next two or three thousand years, we hope to coevolve our strengths and help each other learn. That cooperation and commitment is in itself practice. In addition, many of the people there have a background in one or another school of Buddhism or Hinduism (although the constellation by which we playfully describe the possibilities is Zen/Hopi/Jew).

Some people in the world don't have to do a hundred thousand prostrations, because they do them day by day in work with their hands and bodies. All over the world there are people who are doing their sitting while they fix the machinery, while they plant the grain, or while they tend the horses. And they *know* it; it's not unconscious. Everybody is equally smart and equally alive.

Where I am, we love occasions to come together. We have a little more time now that we've gotten some of our main water system, fence building, and house building done; we now have the chance to sit together, dance together, and sing together more often.

Poetry, Community & Climax

The following text is based on talks given at Oberlin College and Brown University in the fall of 1978. It was first published in Field 20 *(Spring, 1979).*

I

I WROTE a small piece ten years ago called "Poetry and the Primitive." It was subtitled "Notes on Poetry as an Ecological Survival Technique." In a brisk and simple way, I was trying to indicate what modern people might want to learn and use from the way poetry/song works in a strong, self-contained preliterate society. I have also spoken of poetry's function as an occasional voice for the nonhuman rising within the human realm, and the value of that. Survival.

But it's clear now, 1979, that survival is not exactly the problem. Not for human beings, who will survive come hell or high water—and both may—to find themselves sole operators of the equipment on a planet where vertebrate evolution has come to an end. Clouds of waterfowl, herds of bison, great whales in the ocean, will be—almost are—myths from the dreamtime, as is, already, "the primitive" in any virgin sense of the term. Biological diversity, and the integrity of organic evolution on this planet, is where I take my stand: not a large pretentious stand, but a straightforward feet-on-the-ground stand, like my grandmother nursing her snapdragons and trying at grafting apples. It's also inevitably the stand of the poet, child of the Muse, singer of saneness, and weaver of rich fabric to delight the mind with possibilities opening both inward and outward.

There is a huge investment in this nation: bridges, railway tracks, freeways, downtown office buildings, airports, aircraft carriers, miles of subdivisions, docks, ore-carriers, factories. All that belongs to somebody, and they don't want to see it become useless, unprofitable, obsolete. In strict terms of cash flow and energy flow it still works, but the hidden costs are enormous and those who pay that cost are not the owners. I'm speaking of course not only of human alienation but air and water, stands of trees, and all the larger, more specialized, rarer birds and animals of the world who pay the cost of "America" with their bodies—as mentioned above. To keep this investment working, the several thousand individuals who own it have about convinced the rest of us that we are equal owners with them of it; using language like "don't turn out the lights," "let's not go back to the Stone Age," and "you've worked hard for what you got, don't lose it now." Their investment requires continual growth, or it falters. A "steady state economy" and "small is beautiful" are terrifying concepts for them because without growth, the gross inequalities in the distribution of wealth in this land would become starkly clear. From this it's evident that the future of capitalism and perhaps all industrial society is intimately staked on the question of nuclear energy—no other way to keep up growth. This leads to the disastrous fast breeder reactor (which is not dead yet by a long shot), and the fast breeder leads to a police state. But food shortages may bring it down even before energy shortages—the loss of soils and the growing inefficiencies of chemical fertilizers.

I repeat this well-known information to remind us, then, that monoculture—heavy industry, television, automobile culture—is not an ongoing accident; it is deliberately fostered. Any remnant city neighborhood of good cheer and old friendships, or farming community that "wants to stay the way it is" are threats to the investment. Without knowing it, little old ladies in tennis shoes who work to save whooping cranes are enemies of the state, along with other more flamboyant figures. I guess there are revolutionaries who still hope for their own kind of monocultural industrial utopia, however. And there are some for whom alienation is a way of life, an end in itself. It's helpful to remember that what we'd hope for on the planet is creativity and sanity, conviviality, the real work of our hands and minds: those apples and snapdragons. Existential *angst* won't go away nohow, if that's how you get your energy.

Although it's clear that we cannot again have seamless primitive cultures, or the purity of the archaic, we can have neighborhood and community. Communities strong in their sense of place, proud and aware of local and special qualities, creating to some extent their own cultural forms, not humble or subservient in the face of some "high cultural" over-funded art form or set of values, are in fact what one healthy side of the original American vision was about. They are also, now, critical to "ecological survival." No amount of well-meaning environmental legislation will halt the biological holocaust without people who live where they are and work with their neighbors, taking responsibility for their place, and *seeing to it*: to be inhabitants, and to not retreat. We feel this to be starting in America: a mosaic of city neighborhoods, small towns, and rural places where people are digging in and saying "if not now, when? if not here, where?" This trend includes many sorts of persons, some of whom are simply looking out for themselves and finding a better place to live. The process becomes educational, and even revolutionary, when one becomes aware of the responsibility that goes with "rootedness" and the way the cards are stacked against it; we live in a system that rewards those who leap for the quick profit and penalizes those who would do things carefully with an eye to quality. Decentralization could start with food production. Old/new-style biologically sophisticated farming doesn't imply total local self-sufficiency, but at least the capacity to provide food and fiber needs within a framework of two or three hundred miles. Then come new definitions of territory and region, and fresh ways to see local government limits—watershed politics, bioregion consciousness. Sense of community begins to include woodpeckers and cottontails. Decentralization includes the decentralization of "culture," of poetry.

II

Now to speak of twenty-five years of poetry readings in the U.S. When I was working on the docks in San Francisco and occasionally taking night courses in conversational Japanese around '52 or '53, writing poems and sending them off to magazines, *Kenyon Review,* and *Hudson Review* and *Partisan*, and getting them back, we had no sense of a community of poets and even less of an audience. Kenneth Rexroth held open house in his apartment on Friday evenings, and four or five or sometimes ten people might drop by; some out of an old Italian anarchist group, some from the filmmakers' and artists' circles of the Bay

Area. In 1954 I knew virtually every poet, filmmaker, and artist in the region. I hardly know who works in Berkeley anymore, let alone the rest.

In 1955, because Allen Ginsberg and Philip Whalen, Michael McClure, Philip Lamantia and several others, and myself, found ourselves with large numbers of unpublished poems on our hands, it occurred to us to give a poetry reading. It was like holding a sale. In those days all we ever thought of doing with poetry was to get it published; we didn't know who saw it, and didn't think to offer it up publicly. But we went ahead and organized a poetry reading. We did have a model or two; Dylan Thomas had passed through a year before; Ted Roethke had come down from Seattle and read; the San Francisco Poetry Center had organized a few readings in five or six years. Still, poetry readings were definitely not a part of the cultural and social landscape. That reading held in November, 1955, in a space borrowed from an art gallery, was a curious kind of turning point in American poetry. It succeeded beyond our wildest thoughts. In fact, we weren't even thinking of success; we were just trying to invite some friends and potential friends, and we borrowed a mailing list from the art gallery and sent out maybe two hundred postcards. Poetry suddenly seemed useful in 1955 San Francisco. From that day to this, there has never been a week without a reading in the Bay Area—actually more like three a night, counting all the coffee shops, plus schools, the art museum, the aquarium, and the zoo. Those early readings led to publication for some. *Howl* became the second book in Ferlinghetti's Pocket Poets series, and Ginsberg's extensive early readings all over the United States began to draw audiences of a size not seen before. Kerouac's novels were published, and the "beat generation" was launched. Allen was to a great extent responsible for generating the excitement, but a number of other poets (myself not among them because I had gone to Japan) traveled widely over the United States landing like crows first in coffee houses and later becoming gradually accepted more and more into the network of universities.

One thing that was clearly an error in the mentality of the early fifties literary world was the idea that poetry cannot have an audience, and indeed that it was a little shameful if a poem was too popular. There are people who still believe that, incidentally. There was also the defeatist attitude that "we live in a philistine culture" and "no one is interested in art anyway, so we'll just write to each other." My generation found that boldly, to put it bluntly, having something to say helped with audiences. It also should be apparent that one is not *owed* an audience by the culture; but one can indeed go out and try to build an audience. Building that audience is done in part by going on the road and using your voice and your body to put the poems out there; and to speak to the people's condition, as the Quakers would say, to speak to the conditions of your own times, and not worry about posterity. If you speak to the condition of your times with some accuracy and intention, then it may speak to the future, too. If it doesn't, fine, we live in the present. So poetry readings as a new cultural form enhanced and strengthened poetry itself, and the role of the poet. They also taught us that poetry really is an oral art. It would be fascinating to undertake an examination of how poetry of the last twenty years has been shaped by the feedback that comes with reading in front of people. Poems go through revisions, adaptations and enhancements following on the sense of how audiences have been hearing you. So there is a communal aspect to the evolution of the art. Does this mean that poets, knowing that they were writing for an audience, might have catered to that possibility? Sure. But it also means that audiences have come up to the possibility of hearing better over the years. My experience is that the latter tends to be the case and that audiences have grown in maturity and the poetry with them. With a skilled audience, such as you often find in New York or San Francisco (and recently in Midwestern cities like Minneapolis), the poet knows that he/she can try for more, and really push it to the difficult, the complex, the outrageous, and see where the mind of the people will go.

This practice of poetry reading has had an effect on the poets who were quite content to regard poetry as a written art that sits on a printed page and belongs in libraries, too. They have been forced to actually learn how to read poetry aloud better out of sheer competition if nothing else. There are economic rewards involved.

Poetry belongs to everybody, but there are always a few skilled raconteurs or creators or singers, and we live in a time in which the individual actor or creator is particularly valued. The art wouldn't die out if we lost track of the name of the fellow who made it up, though, and the fact that we don't know the names of the men or women who made the songs in the past doesn't really matter.

All of this goes one more step, then, to a conscious concern and interest on the part of some poets in the actual performance skills of preliterate people. My own studies in anthropology, linguistics, and oral literature brought me to the realization that the performance, in a group context, is the pinnacle of poetic activity and precision, and we have yet to develop the possibilities of that circle with music, dance, and drama in their original archaic poetic relationship. The Ainu singers of Hokkaido chant their long epic stories to a beat. The güslars of southern Yugoslavia use a little dulcimer-like stringed instrument. No wonder we say "lyric poetry"—they used to sing with a lyre. Most of the songs that you hear on the country and western hit parade are in good old English ballad meter, showing that the ballad is the backbone of English-language poetics and will be for a long time to come. Other examples, simple examples: Robert Bly knows almost all his poems by heart and Roethke knew his. Reciting from memory (which I can't do) liberates your hands and mind for the performance—liberates your eyes. Noh drama, with its aristocratic spareness and simplicity, could be another model. Percussive, almost nonmelodic music is very strong; a bare stage is all you need.

In this era of light shows, huge movie screens, and quadraphonic sound systems, it is striking that an audience will still come to hear a plain, ordinary, unaugmented human being using nothing but voice and language. That tells us that people do appreciate the compression, the elegance, and the myriad imageries that come out of this art of distilling language and giving it measure which is called poetry.

III

The next step then is to ask what has a more public poetry done for the possibility of community? The modern poetry audience has a certain kind of network associated with it. Everywhere I go I meet people I know—from one corner of the United States to the other I never give a reading anymore but at least one person comes out of the audience, an old friend. A dozen other people that I haven't met before step up to tell me about how they are riding their horses or growing sunflowers somewhere, or are in the middle of making a zendo inside an old building downtown. It's a fine exchange of news and information, and also the reaffirmation of a certain set of interests to which I (among others) speak. The community that is called together by such events is not just literary. It's interesting to see, then, that the universities have served as community halls, public space, that draw out people from beyond the immediate academic world. In other times and places such public spaces have been riverbeds—which is no-man's land—where the gypsies and the traveling drama companies are allowed to put up their tents, or where the homeless samurai are allowed to act out their final duels with each other and nobody cares—it might be riverbeds, it might be the streets, or temples and churches— or in the tantric tradition of late medieval north India, some groups met in cemeteries.

What is this network of interests and old friends I speak of? None other than that branch of the stalwart counterculture that has consistently found value and inspiration in poetry, and intellectual excitement in watching the unfolding of twentieth-century poetics. Also certain sets of values have been—in recent decades—more clearly stated in poetry than any other medium. (Other post–World War II cultural branches are primarily affiliated to music; some to more specific and intellectually formulated political or religious ideologies; a few go directly to crafts, or to gardening.) Anyway: the people who found each other via poetry readings in the late fifties and sixties produced another generation of poets who were committed to an oral poetics and a nonelite vision of communicating to larger and more diverse audiences. There are roughly three shoots from that root. I'll call them the dealers, the homegrowers, and the ethnobotanists.

The "dealers" came in part with the growth of a certain academic and social acceptance of new poets and their readings, which led to the poetry policies of the NEA; the founding of the little magazines and small presses support organizations, the poets-in-the-schools programs, and on the academic side, several MFA-in-writing programs at several universities; workshops in poetry. At this point, via the poets-in-the-schools programs in particular, twentieth-century poetry began to find its way into ordinary American communities. The programs employed people who had gotten their MFA or a little book published (through a small press, with federal aid often)—and put them into high schools or grade schools, doing creative work, creative word playfulness, image playfulness; generating imagination and spontaneity among school children whose usual teachers couldn't. I consider this quite valid as a mode of poetic imagination and practice, in its broadest sense, filtering down through the population. The school districts themselves, after some resistance, began to accept the possibilities of poets and other artists doing local residencies. For every horror story of a brought-in poet reading a poem to the sixth grade with the word "penis" in it, there are countless unadvertised little openings of voice and eye as children got that quick view of playfulness, of the flexibility and power of their own mind and mother tongue. I've watched this at work in my own school district, which is rural and short on money, but has backed the artists in schools as far as it could. In fact this school district (and many others) has chosen to keep arts programs going even after state or federal funding is withdrawn. One local poet found that what the children needed first was an introduction to the basic sense of story and of lore. He became the master of lore, myth, and word-hoard for the whole district. By much research and imagination, he provided, following the calendar and seasons, the true information—as story—about what Easter, May Day, Christmas, Hanukkah, Halloween, and Lammas are about. Neither the parents nor the school teachers in most cases could provide this fundamental lore of their own culture to the children. The poet was Steve Sanfield, doing the work of mythographer to the community in the ancient way.

The "home-growers" (and the above folks often overlap with this) are those poets who themselves live in a place with some intention of staying there—and begin to find their poetry playing a useful role in the daily life of the neighborhood. Poetry as a tool, a net or trap to catch and present; a sharp edge; a medicine, or the little awl that unties knots. Who are these poets? I haven't heard of most of them, neither have you; perhaps we never will. The mandarins of empire-culture arts organizations in the U.S. might worry about little-known poets working in the schools, because they are afraid of a decline in "standards of quality." I think I am second to none in my devotion to Quality; I throw myself at the lotus feet of Quality and shiver at the least tremor of her crescent moon eyebrow. What they really fear is losing control over the setting of standards. But there is room for many singers, and not everyone need aspire to national level publication, national reputation. The United States is, bioregionally speaking, too large to ever be a comprehensible social entity except as maintained at great expense and effort via the media and bureaucracy. The price people pay for living in the production called American society is that they are condemned to continually watch television and read newspapers to know "what's happening," and thus they have no time to play with their own children or get to know the neighbors or birds or plants or seasons. What a dreadful cost! This explains why I do not even try to keep up with what's going on in nationwide poetry publishing. We are talking about real culture now, the culture that things *grow* in, and not the laboratory strains of seeds that lead to national reputation. Poetry is written and read for real people: it should be part of the gatherings where we make decisions about what to do about uncontrolled growth, or local power plants, and who's going to be observer at the next county supervisors' meeting. A little bit of music is played by the guitarists and five-string banjo players, and some poems come down from five or six people who are really good—speaking to what is happening *here*. They shine a little ray of myth on things; memory turning to legend.

It's also useful to raise a sum of money for a local need with a benefit poetry reading, and it's good to know this can be done successfully maybe twice a year. It works, a paying audience comes, because it's known that it will be a strong event. Sooner or later, if a poet keeps on living in one place, he is going to have to admit to everyone in town and on the backroads that he writes poetry. To then appear locally is to put your own work to the real test—the lady who delivers the mail might be there, and the head sawyer of the local mill. What a delight to mix all levels of poems together, and to see the pleasure in the eyes of the audience when a local tree, a local river or mountain, comes swirling forth as part of proto-epic or myth. (Michael McClure once said his two favorite provincial literary periodicals were *Kuksu,* "Journal of Backcountry Writing," and *The New York Review of Books.* Two poetry reading invitations that I count as great honors were to the Library of Congress, and the North San Juan Fire Hall.) It is a commitment to place, and to your neighbors, that—with no loss of quality—accomplishes the decentralization of poetry. The decentralization of "culture" is as important to our long-range ecological and social health as the decentralization of agriculture, production, energy, and government.

By the "ethnobotanist" shoot from that sixties root I mean the roving specialists and thinkers in poetics, politics, anthropology, and biology who are pursuing the study of what it would mean to be citizens of natural nations; to be part of stable communities; participants in a sane society. We do this with the point in mind that the goal of structural political change is not a crazy society, but a sane one. These are in a sense studies in postrevolutionary possibilities, and in the possibilities of making small gains now; "forming the new society within the shell of the old." Such are (and though I list them here it doesn't mean they necessarily agree with all or anything I say) Bob Callahan and associates at Turtle Island Foundation; Peter Berg and the Planet Drum group; Joe Meeker, Vine Deloria, Jr., and others working on the "new natural philosophy"; the Farallones Institute; Jerome Rothenberg and the *New Wilderness Newsletter*; Dennis Tedlock and *Alcheringa* magazine; Stewart Brand's *CoEvolution Quarterly*; the long list of useful publications from Richard Grossinger and Lindy Hough; the Lindisfarne Association; New Alchemy; and in another more technical dimension, Stanley Diamond's work and his journal *Dialectical Anthropology. Organic Gardening* and other Rodale Press publications, with their consistent emphasis on *health* as the basic measure, might also belong on this list. There are others; I'm not even mentioning poetry magazines in this context. As a sort of ethnobotanist myself, I make the following offering:

IV

Poetry as song is there from birth to death. There are songs to ease birth, good luck songs to untie knots to get babies born better; there are lullabies that you sing to put the babies to sleep—Lilith Abye—("get away negative mother image!"); there are songs that children sing on the playground that are beginning poetries—

> baby baby suck your toe
> all the way to Mexico
>
> kindergarten baby
> wash your face in gravy

(I get these from my kids) or

> Going down the highway, 1954,
> Batman let a big one, blew me out the door—
> wheels wouldn't take it,
> engine fell apart,
> all because of Batman's supersonic fart.

  (If you start poetry teaching on the grade school level, use rhyme, they love it. Go with the flow, don't go against it. Children love word play, music of language; it really sobered me up to realize that not only is rhyme going to be with us but it's a good thing.) And as we get older, about eleven or twelve years, we go into the work force and start picking strawberries or drying apples; and work songs come out of that. Individually consciously created poetry begins when you start making up love songs to a sweetie, which are called courting songs. Then, some individuals are sent out in adolescence to see if they can get a power vision song all by themselves. They go out and come back with a song which is their own, which gives them a name, and power; some begin to feel like a "singer." There are those who use songs for hunting, and those who use a song for keeping themselves awake at night when they are riding around slow in circles taking care of the cows; people who use songs when they haul up the nets on the beach. And when we get together we have drinking songs and all kinds of communal pleasure gathering group music. There are war songs, and particular specialized powerful healing songs that are brought back by those individuals (shamans) who make a special point of going back into solitude for more songs: which will enable them to heal. There are also some who master and transmit the complex of songs and chants that contain creation-myth lore and whatever ancient or cosmic gossip that a whole People sees itself through. In the Occident we have such a line, starting with Homer and going through Virgil, Dante, Milton, Blake, Goethe, and Joyce. They were workers who took on the ambitious chore of trying to absorb all the myth/history lore of their times, and of their own past traditions, and put it into order as a new piece of writing and let it be a map or model of world and mind for everyone to steer by.

It's also clear that in all the households of nonliterate ordinary farming and working people for the past fifty thousand years the context of poetry and literature has been around the fire at night—with the children and grandparents curled up together and somebody singing or telling. Poetry is thus an intimate part of the power and health of sane people. What then? What of the danger of becoming provincial, encapsulated, self-righteous, divisive—all those things that we can recognize as being sources of mischief and difficulty in the past?

That specialized variety of poetry which is the most sophisticated, and is the type which most modern poetry would aspire to be, is the "healing songs" type. This is the kind of healing that makes whole, heals by making whole, that kind of doctoring. The poet as healer is asserting several layers of larger realms of wholeness. The first larger realm is identity with the natural world, demonstrating that the social system, a little human enclave, does not stand by itself apart from the plants and the animals and winds and rains and rivers that surround it. Here the poet is a voice for the nonhuman, for the natural world, actually a vehicle for another voice, to send it into the human world, saying there is a larger sphere out there; that the humans are indeed children of, sons and daughters of, and eternally in relationship with, the earth. Human beings buffer themselves against seeing the natural world directly. Language, custom, ego, and personal advantage strategies all work against clear seeing. So the first wholeness is wholeness with nature.

The poet as myth-handler-healer is also speaking as a voice for another place, the deep unconscious, and working toward integration of interior unknown realms of mind with present moment immediate self-interest consciousness. The outer world of nature and the inner world of the unconscious are brought to a single focus occasionally by the work of the dramatist-ritualist artist-poet. That's another layer. Great tales and myths can give one tiny isolated society the breadth of mind and heart to be *not* provincial and to know itself as a piece of the cosmos.

The next layer, when it works, is harder: that's the layer that asserts a level of humanity with other people outside your own group. It's harder actually because we are in clear economic dependence and interrelationship with our immediate environment; if you are gathering milkweed, fishing, picking berries, raising apples, and tending a garden it shouldn't be too difficult to realize that you have some relationship with nature. It's less obvious what to do with the folks that live on the other side of the mountain range, speaking another language; they're beyond the pass, and you can faintly feel them as potential competitors. We must go beyond just feeling at one with nature, and feel at one with each other, with ourselves. That's where all natures intersect. Too much to ask for? Only specialists, mystics, either through training or good luck, arrive at that. Yet it's the good luck of poetry that it sometimes presents us with the accomplished fact of a moment of true nature, of total thusness:

> Peach blossoms are by nature pink
> Pear blossoms are by nature white.

This level of healing is a kind of poetic work that is forever "just begun." When we bring together our awareness of the worldwide network of folktale and myth imagery that has been the "classical tradition"—the lore-bearer—of everyone for ten thousand and more years, and the new (but always there) knowledge of the worldwide interdependence of natural systems, we have the biopoetic beginning of a new level of world poetry and myth. That's the beginning for this age, the age of knowing the planet as one ecosystem, our own little watershed, a community of people and beings, a place to sing and meditate, a place to pick berries, a place to be picked in.

The communities of creatures in forests, ponds, oceans, or grasslands seem to tend toward a condition called climax, "virgin forest"—many species, old bones, lots of rotten leaves, complex energy pathways, woodpeckers living in snags, and conies harvesting tiny piles of grass. This condition has considerable stability and holds much energy in its web—energy that in simpler systems (a field of weeds just after a bulldozer) is lost back into the sky or down the drain. All of evolution may have been as much shaped by this pull toward climax as it has by simple competition between individuals or species. If human beings have any place in this scheme it might well have to do with their most striking characteristic—a large brain, and language. And a consciousness of a peculiarly self-conscious order. Our human awareness and eager poking, probing, and studying is our beginning contribution to planet-system energy-conserving; another level of climax!

In a climax situation a high percentage of the energy is derived not from grazing off the annual production of biomass, but from recycling dead biomass, the duff on the forest floor, the trees that have fallen, the bodies of dead animals. Recycled. Detritus cycle energy is liberated by fungi and lots of insects. I would then suggest: as climax forest is to biome, and fungus is to the recycling of energy, so "enlightened mind" is to daily ego mind, and art to the recycling of neglected inner potential. When we deepen or enrich ourselves, looking within, understanding ourselves, we come closer to being like a climax system. Turning away from grazing on the "immediate biomass" of perception, sensation, and thrill; and re-viewing memory, internalized perception, blocks of inner energies, dreams, the leaf-fall of day-to-day consciousness, liberates the energy of our own sense-detritus. Art is an assimilator of unfelt experience, perception, sensation, and memory for the whole society. When all that compost of feeling and thinking comes back to us then, it comes not as a flower, but—to complete the metaphor—as a mushroom: the fruiting body of the buried threads of mycelia that run widely through the soil, and are intricately married to the root hairs of all the trees. "Fruiting"—at that point—is the completion of the work of the poet, and the point where the artist or mystic reenters the cycle: gives what she or he has done as nourishment, and as spore or seed spreads the "thought of enlightenment," reaching into personal depths for nutrients hidden there, back to the community. The community and its poetry are not two.

From
PASSAGE THROUGH INDIA

The Cambodge

We left Kyoto on a cold frosty morning—tenth of December 1961, I think it was—just two days after the end of the big Rohatsu Sesshin at the Daitoku-ji monastery, clear and blue sky—with our rucksacks, but Joanne in high heels because we were going on one of the classier express trains, and she still didn't believe me when I said travel in India would be like camping out. In Tokyo we stayed two days with a young couple I'd known only by correspondence—Clayton Eshleman, a new poet, and his new wife. On the twelfth we took the interurban electric from Tokyo down to Yokohama, cleared through immigration and customs, and walked down this long dock to the *Cambodge* where it was moored alongside—a pretty big ship, all painted white. Up the gangplank, and immediately were transported into a new non-Japanese world. Here was a sudden warm perfumy smell, and perfumy stewards, all talking French, and women stewards with sharp permanent hairdos and thin eyebrow lines like older French women seem to go for. I recollect Joanne getting kind of tangled up with her rucksack and the narrow doors and passageways and becoming sort of rattled—I was immediately uncomfortable because of the warmth of the heated ship when we had just come from unheated Japan, and were wearing heavy winter underwear, and sweaters. A steward led us to our cabins, way forward into cabin class. The change is abrupt, because in tourist class they have wooden doors and trim, and a few carpets, but in cabin class it's all steel doors and steel lockers and steel bunks and rubbertile flooring. But nice and clean. Showed us the dining room, which is all bright yellow and red, recently redone, with bright red plastic-covered chairs and couches along the wall, very cheery and happy, with portholes to look out and a music system playing popular music constantly. We unpacked and put our stuff in our lockers—at the last minute in Kyoto I decided to buy a camera and be sure of getting good photos in India, so I bought an Asahi Pentax single-lens reflex 35 mm with f2 lens, and was paranoid about it, hiding it in the back of the locker and putting padlocks where I could and locking the cabin. We were given the freedom of the forward deck so there we stood in the late afternoon as the ship pulled away from the dock and we saw the last of the low glare of Yokohama neon (it's a real port town) turning on as it got dark and we sailed away—not really knowing if we'd ever get back to Japan again, India seeming so remote and scary still.

The first few days on the ship were chilly and rough, lots of people stayed in their cabins. A young couple we knew from Kyoto was also on board. Jack Craig had come originally from Cupertino, California, to study Zen, then through a friend of Al Klyce (who is probably back in San Francisco now with his Japanese wife) met a girl working in a bar, whom he fell for, and after several months of tedious hassling they got married and six months later or so left Japan bound for Hong Kong, and thence India by plane, Europe, and New York, where they are now. Jack's lovely wife Ginko was so miserably seasick she thought she'd perish.

Just before Hong Kong the weather cleared and the water smoothed, and we got a chance to talk to some of our fellow cabin-class tween-deck passengers. One was Helmut Kugl, a German who had gone off to Australia and worked as a carpenter, then went to Japan for four months, and was now off to India to "find Krishnamurti" because he had picked up a book by Krishnamurti and decided this was what he wanted. Anti-German, and totally against any kind of discipline or authority, but he was only about twenty-four, red-haired and freckly—a perpetual frown of doubt on his brow and constant deep and contradictory philosophical questions—he claimed not to have even finished high school. Hilda Hunt was about sixty, divorcée, dressed up in lavender, always having her drink before dinner and always talking about her days on the New Orleans *Times-Picayune* (she "knew Hemingway" when he was living in New Orleans)—wrote verse—and had numerous fantastic stories to tell, but was withal quite sweet—had been visiting some younger relatives who were with the armed services in Japan, and was now on the long trip round to Europe, to visit some more young relatives stationed in Germany.

An Australian named Neale Hunter had done French, Chinese, and Japanese literature at the University of Melbourne, then went to work in the bush for a year or so, took the money and went to Japan, Tokyo—lived for about four months in Shinjuku, Tokyo (a kind of bar and underworld hangout zone of enormous dimensions) then took off for India—fellow who knows about literature, wild life, and for some reason became a converted Catholic and is now trying to reconcile Catholicism and Buddhism to suit himself. Among others were a French couple, early-middle-aged anarchists who live in New Caledonia; a pair of nineteen-year-old American boys from Los Angeles off on a world tour, and a couple of gentle Ceylonese school teachers who played chess all the time and argued their respective religions, Catholic and Buddhist.

Hong Kong: we first off headed for the Japanese Consul and presented our papers, applying for a new visa to Japan. Then walked around on the hillside back of town—Joanne went shopping for a raincoat, and Neale and I went into an old-style wineshop and talked to the old men in broken Chinese, sampling from various crocks and getting a little drunk—wandered up and down through the crowded alleys, people hanging all their laundry out the apartment balcony windows, old stained concrete and plaster. New buildings don't seem to last long. Hong Kong so crowded—and barbed wire machine-gun emplacements set up all around. Lively, shopping is a major activity, stores are filled with every conceivable thing, especially luxury. Joanne got a French raincoat—we met back at the ship. The next day Joanne, Neale, and I took a bus out to the border—about a thirty-mile ride. This is on the mainland side. We got up on a hill and gazed out through pine trees at the Chinese People's Republic—spread out before us, a watery plain with houses here and there—a barbed-wire fence along a river at the foot of the hill showing where the actual line is. We could see men far off in China loading a little boat on the river, and hear the geese and chickens and water buffaloes from far away. It was warmish, gray cloudy, soft. Went back on the train to Kowloon (nine dragons) where our ship was—the seamen out handling rigging, sheaves, and cables. Joanne is wearing her fine yellow raincoat. The villages in mainland Hong Kong have a very different feeling from those in Japan. The rows in the gardens aren't so straight, the buildings not so neat—and the building material is brick instead of wood (though roofs are thatch); the people all wear the wide trousers and jackets, men and women alike, and the coolie hats in the field. But Hong Kong has food in a way no Japanese town could. The Japanese simply don't have the Chinese sense for cooking and eating (and a Japanese meal out, dinner party, say, is always a drag until people are finally drunk enough on sake to loosen up; whereas the Chinese have glorious multi-course banquets as a matter of course). In Hong Kong it's like walking along the market sections of Grant Avenue, Chinatown, only better, the wineshops and herb shops in between. That evening to an Australian-run bar for a while, then back to the end of the pier, looking across to the Victoria (Island) side, the celebrated lights going up the steep hill, drinking beer in the dark—a freighter comes in, blotting out the neon, the bridge decks alight, and a junk in full sail, batwing taut membrane over bones—goes out darkly and silent, a single yellow kerosene lamp dim in the stern.

The houses on the New Territory are all thatched, dry brown colors as the parched winter brown of the long plain stretching north—fallow paddies, with water buffalo, cows, pigs, and flocks of geese here and there browsing.

> The dried out winter ricefields
> men far off loading junks in the river
> bales of rice on their shoulders
> a little boat poles out
>   —roosters and geese—
>   —looking at China

Bought $347 worth of rupees in Hong Kong at 7 RS to $1 US, where official rate in India is 4.75 to $1. Ship sailed at midnight and we were bound for Saigon.

Out of Hong Kong they moved Joanne and me from our cabin-class cabins and put us together in one tiny two-man cabin in the tourist-class section. Food was still to be taken deck-class, but our living quarters had been altered. I never understood why except they did get a large number of additional cabin-class passengers, Indians and Chinese, and perhaps were overcrowded. So now in the messhall, besides our previous friends, there were women in saris and pigtailed old Chinese women in silk trousers—and the waters were warm, we were sunbathing on deck. At night took up the star map and a flashlight, and identified the southern stars, Canopus and Achernar, and the Southern Cross, until one of the seamen came down from the bridge and said our little flashing of the flashlight was hard on the bridge lookout, so we stopped. Always in motion.

Coasting South Vietnam—come into muddy waters, the smell from ashore—go in a bay and up the river. Both banks jungle swamps, a bird or a fishing canoe now and then. A thick almost-comfortable warmth over it all. Turns and twists in the river. A freighter comes sailing over the jungle. One P.M. land in Saigon—surrounded by shaggy ricefield delta plains, a few thatched houses in clumps of palm. Long bridge and double-spire church visible . . . Saigon is really French. They sell French bread everywhere, right along with funny-looking broiled animal innards, fruits, and kinds of fish and vegetables, which knowing the name wouldn't help you. The women are all beautiful and wear silk pajamas with a silk tunic and long loose hair, and apparently brassieres that make them all come to sharp points in front. Walked a bit in the afternoon, and then out in the night street stalls—fruit juices, caged birds, crushed sugarcane with ice and lime. Next day went to the botanical gardens and zoo and museum compound, dug most of all the gibbon, which has no tail and a maniac laugh while running on the ground with his arms, which are longer than his whole body, sort of crossed behind his neck up. Tall trees, shuttered, colored houses, white or yellow walls. The architecture seems to be colonial Franco-Spanish. We fed the elephant's trunk nose finger some apples from the ship. Then she curtseyed.

Vietnam women fluttering and trailing high-collared, tight-waisted, loose floppy ankles and thin silk swish legs—high small sharp breasts, waves of black heavy clean hair. Always a gold ring in the right ear. Sidewalk cafes and cheap beer, so later in the day we sit and watch, eat ham sandwich and French pastries. Sail back down the river at 1:30 in the afternoon. You'd never guess there was any kind of war going on around here, but for a very rare truck going through with soldiers in jungle outfits, but no weapons visible, no guards with submachine guns on the corners or guys in tanks parked at intersections. Yet we read in the newspapers of ambushes and kidnappings just 15 miles out of town. Government of South Vietnam is bunch of Catholic elite westernized prudes anyhow, completely out of touch with "the people."

Next was Singapore. As we approached it the weather became muggy and the ocean surface heavy and oily, the water changed from blue to green. Also I got dysentery about then, terrible cramps. So I went ashore for only five hours in Singapore, feeling miserable, and remember little from that time. Our new passengers included a lot of adolescent Sikh boys with their fuzzed young faces and girlish wisps of hair sticking out from under their turbans. Indian women and children all over the deck, squabbling—and a tall white-haired fine-featured Swiss lady with her Chinese husband. They had just recently left mainland China—had been traders in Shanghai for many many years. With them was their son who looked in his mid-twenties. They were on their way to Switzerland. They claimed no good had come out of communism in China; the peasants were worse off than before on account of bad agricultural practices, everyone miserable and resigned—no bars or lights at night, everybody the same dull clothes, blue suit; but they were freely allowed to leave China and were never in any way molested. I think they just found life getting dull there, and they had no love for Chiang Kai-shek.

Now we were crossing the Bay of Bengal, bound for Ceylon. The Indians out on the deck all day listening to Indian radio on their Singapore or Hong Kong transistors. Saris blowing and swirling about the deck—several hours spent reexamining our loads and lightening our packs—give away the long underwear (which was scratchy old army surplus stuff full of holes anyhow)—and Joanne planning to leave her heavy coat and high heels behind in Colombo to pick up later—even so we have about forty pounds each, with sleeping bags, cooking pots, etc. We knew the jig was up when I went up on deck and saw our two Ceylonese teacher friends had mysteriously changed from Western dress and were now in Ceylonese sarongs—and weren't bothering to speak much English anymore—they were in their own waters. That night we passed the light on the southern end of Ceylon, and at dawn we were in Colombo harbor, to be thrust off the security of the ship and into the "world."

Pondicherry

THAT EVENING caught a third-class sleeping car on northbound for Pondicherry. Third-class sleeping means cars with huge ledges overhead, and a ledge that folds up and hooks on chains where the back was, above the usual bench seat, making in all a triple-tiered bunk arrangement for each seat. Luggage goes under the bottom seat or just on the aisle between the two facing benches (compartment style). We got into one of these and slept in our board bunks, like Chinamen being sent back to China to die, until early morning, transferred to another train, and by 7 A.M. were nearing the coast.

Train we transferred to was a small, deserted local engine, and when we climbed into the third-class car it looked like the compartment I got into was empty. Actually a couple of people were huddled across from us, under a big handspun shawl. I started to put my rucksack under the seat, and found a man sleeping there, so put it on the seat beside me. Joanne huddled up and slept some more, while I watched the pair across from us. They stirred and moved around some; it was a man with long hair, earrings, and a girl about twelve . . . when they threw back the shawl I saw both were dressed only in skimpy loincloths under the single shawl . . . she had large gold hoops in her ears, bangles on her wrists and ankles, and wild brownish hair down over her shoulders, looked as if it had never been combed . . . both were barefoot, and covered with dust, looked at Joanne and me with kind of vague wild curiosity . . . at the next stop they both got off on the wrong side of the train and walked off across the tracks and into a grove . . . They had been riding free, and were (as I came to know later) probably "tribal people," still thinking of themselves as members of a certain tribe, not necessarily Hindus, in fact still living rather primitive lives . . . they both had lovely faces.

Pondicherry was formerly a French enclave and when we got there, sure enough the policemen and train officials were speaking French. We took a bicycle rickshaw to the head office of the

Sri Aurobindo Ashram where we planned to stay. An ashram is a unique Indian institution, it is a religious community based around some teacher and branch of Hinduism; the person of the teacher being very important. Not all ashrams are actually religious—the Gandhi ashrams and Vinoba Bhave ashrams are primarily aimed at combining a kind of spiritual communism with community service and social work. The Aurobindo ashram was founded sometime after World War I (I think) by Sri Aurobindo Ghose, a Bengali who had been educated from childhood on in England, returned to India and became a rabid nationalist, and then switched to yoga. He claimed to have founded a new type of yoga, "Integral Yoga," and heralded a new "Divine Life" on earth. From the mid-twenties on he was assisted in his work by a woman known only as the Mother. I have been told she was a French lady to begin with, who left her husband to live in Pondicherry. She came gradually to be the person actually running the ashram, and Sri Aurobindo spent the last years of his life in virtual seclusion. He died in 1950. The Mother runs it all now. I had heard of Aurobindo some years ago around the Academy of Asian Studies. Frederick Spiegelberg was an Aurobindo fan, and they had a few copies of Aurobindo's huge book, *The Life Divine,* around. I don't want to go into his philosophy here, but it is a rather eclectic spirit-oriented system, which has affinities with neo-Platonism, Gnosticism, as well as Vedanta, and it is not truly monistic, as Vedanta is, but rather belongs, it seems to me, in the class with antimatter dualisms like Manichaeism, Nestorian Xtianity, some sorts of Gnosticism, and Catharites. I rather doubt that it is a truly Indian philosophy. Maybe if I read more on it I'll change my mind.

The ashram is considered to be the best organized in India. It has supposedly 1300 members, all under the direct control of the Mother. They live in various buildings and houses owned by the ashram (i.e., owned by the Mother) scattered through the old French section of Pondicherry. ". . . a few things are strictly forbidden: they are—(1) politics, (2) smoking, (3) alcoholic drink and (4) sex enjoyment"—this applies only to actual inmates of the ashram, not guests (thank god!).

Now the funny thing is, to digress, that this absurd list of prohibitions, once you are within India, seems less and less outrageous. The prohibition of politics is probably the one that would hurt most Indians most. But the rest of us might give up politics. As for smoking, Indian tobacco was so bad I quit smoking in India anyway, and haven't taken it up again yet. Alcohol is almost impossible to buy in India, rather expensive if you find it, and absolutely foul to drink. Actually illegal in many states. As for "sex enjoyment" (and they mean this to apply to married inmates of the ashram along with everyone else), practically all Indian semireligious or religious traditional thought is in agreement on the notion that sexual activity of any sort is deleterious to Spiritual Progress. Brahmacharya is considered a very Good Thing. One who practices continence, usually a married man who has taken a vow of continence, is called a Brahmacharin. Gandhi was a Brahmacharin, from something like 1914 on never slept with his wife, and urged all his followers to adopt similar practice. Somebody once taxed Gandhi with this saying, "you became a Brahmacharin after you were all dried up anyway"—to which he replied, "my wife never looked so attractive to me, nor was my sexual potency ever as strong, as when I took the vow." Of course, a family man isn't supposed to do this until he's at least had a son.

The only exception to this view in religious circles is amongst the Shaivite-Shakti-Tantric circles (which people say still flourish in Orissa and Bengal) where sexual intercourse is practiced as a ritual designed, after long preparation, to hook everyday orgasm into the Cosmic Orgasm. But nobody (except the millions of peasants and untouchables) takes sex simply as sex, and leaves it at that. Anyway, anything that Gandhi urged is tantamount to an *order* to the semi-intelligentsia (except get along with Muslims).

To get back to Pondicherry, it is a lovely French-looking town, deserted almost—really dead but for the ashram, facing on a long white beach, with warm gentle surf. On side alleys you notice the bristly long-snouted black pigs rooting about, eating horrible garbage, and the hovels of the Scheduled Castes (untouchables) that make up a major portion of the population of South India.

Two little girls squatting on the cement rim of a canal, stark naked, taking craps, talking to each other all the while, the yellow shit sort of dribbling down the edge of the cement, then up they jump and run off playing.

Secretary at the ashram headquarters sent us in a bike rick to a place called Parc-a-charbon, right by the sea, where we were to stay a few nights. We got a little room with two wooden cots, actually sort of boxes with drawers underneath to put your gear in, and hasps for padlocking, a thin mattress on top, and a wood frame over it with a mosquito netting. A table, a chair, a big earthenware waterpot in the corner, damp all over, the water inside cool from the constant evaporation.

We were the only people living here but for a Cambodian Buddhist monk, some lay Yogins, and the man who was caretaker for the building (a converted godown from French merchant days) who was a large goodnatured fellow with elephantiasis of one leg and hence had smelly wet bandages wrapped around it all the time and couldn't go far because it was so hard to walk. His room was covered with pictures of the Mother.

We got to see the Mother the next morning early, at her *darshan*. Darshan is another big Indian thing, it simply means appearance, or presence. Underlying it is a belief that you don't need to be instructed or led by a holy person, just by proximity or seeing them you are immeasurably benefited. So the Mother appears every morning about 6:15 A.M. on the balcony of her house, and three or four hundred people gather on the street below. She comes out, looks at everybody slowly in big circles, then looks up and out and goes into "a meditative trance"—eyes open, body shifting from time to time. Then, smiling a bit, she looks at everybody once more, and backs off the balcony. She has a gauzy silk scarf over her head and brow, and a kind of twenties-ish elegance. A real production. And she must be close to her eighties. Her age doesn't seem to worry the ashram people, though.

A woman from Canada named Beverly Siegerman, who has been at the ashram three years, told us that the Mother would never die, and that by a gradual process of physical-spiritual transformation some of the other people around the ashram would live forever too. The goal is that mankind becomes, in time, entirely transmuted, lives immortally and sexlessly.

Some of the people there are quite intelligent, but for their acceptance of some of these doctrines. That's India for you. There is a staggering amount of Aurobindo literature in

English, all published right in Pondicherry by ashram workers. The POINT is, though, from my standpoint, that there was no practice of any kind—study, meditation, etc., to be seen. And this is what I am always looking for. No matter how ridiculous a theory or doctrine may be, it may have associated meditation exercises that are pragmatically quite good. Aurobindo ashramites seem to exist entirely on a devotion-and-faith basis, "open yourself to the influence of the Mother." This also can be a valid path (devotion and submission) but it requires a very critical study of doctrine.

Khajuraho

NEXT DAY, February 17, left Banaras on the Kashi Express, 1:15 P.M., bound for the little town of Satna. At Satna detrained 11:30 P.M. No retiring room here, so prepared to sleep in the waiting rooms. I went into the men's waiting room, spread my sleeping-bag cover out on a couch and washed up. Joanne came in and said she had gone into the women's waiting room and went right on into the washroom and started cleaning up, wearing her slacks. An old woman in there started talking to her in some language but Joanne couldn't understand so didn't pay much attention. Finally the old lady left and came back a few minutes later leading some RR stationmen. One asked Joanne in English, "Are you a woman?" She said, "Last time I looked I was," and the men laughed nervously and told the old lady Joanne was a woman all right, and then scolded her for being such a stupid old country lady, and left laughing.

Railway station life—going to the refreshment stand and getting cupfuls of boiled tea in our tin cups; buying *pera* (a kind of candy made of boiled down milk) or *puri* from venders.

Following morning caught a 6 A.M. bus, bound cross country for the ancient erotic temple, Khajuraho. A fine rolling drive through a flat landscape of occasional twisty deciduous trees, boulders, distant New Mexico-type bluffs. This is in the state of Madhya Pradesh, a somewhat backward area, with the aboriginal Bhil and Gond tribes still around, and center of Thuggee activities in the eighteenth–nineteenth centuries. Indian highways are pretty good. At 11 A.M. were at Khajuraho and marched off with our packs to the circuit house, where we got a room. Circuit houses were originally built to accommodate civil servants and traveling British parties—there is a network of them all over India. Now some of them, as at Khajuraho, have been cleaned up, enlarged, and developed into government-run tourist hostels, at very reasonable prices. We spent the afternoon of the eighteenth and all day the nineteenth closely studying the ten or so temples, set a mile apart in two groups.

These also were built in the eleventh–twelfth centuries, during the high period of Tantric Hinduism, when at the courts of several rulers, as in Madhya Pradesh and Orissa both, the people in control became adepts at sexual yoga and devotees of the Goddess. Hence this great flowering of incredibly elegant soaring stone buildings, carved in intricate detail both inside and out with the forms of beautiful women and men, often embracing and frequently making love in a variety of postures. They are so moving, and true, that under their spell one wonders what's wrong with the world that everyone simply doesn't make love with everyone else, it seems the naturalest and most beautiful thing to do. I took as many photographs as I could, actually cliff-climbing the temple walls. These are Archeological Survey controlled, hence you are allowed to make rubbings and take photographs without hindrance; kept up beautifully with grass- and flower-lined lawns.

The great Shiva temple is a model of Mt. Kailash, where Shiva is supposed to live; hence it is a model of a mountain, hollow, with Shiva inside—and the structure of the towers reproduces a feeling of ridges, gendarmes, subpeaks; the horizontal molding lines reproduced from the base of the plinth up in a variety of variations are a kind of geological-paleontological system of strata, moving up through animal friezes to the "human" level—fossils of dancers, lovers, fighters with leogriffs—temple wall like a human paleontology laid bare—rising; to the Divine Couples seated in shrines on sub-pinnacles—vegetable, mineral, and animal universes—complete—to the mountain summit, spire of pure geometry, a rock crown like the sun. And also, the lingam—inside, in the center of the hill in a small dark room—the main figure of it all; damp gloom—holding it all, lovers and animals, in history, vertically, to the brilliant light and heat of the outside sun. The north walls of temples mossier, darker, with lichen.

Dharamshala

After an all-night ride, we arrived at Pathankot, in northwest Punjab, at five in the morning March 28. This is the jumping-off point for the two-day bus trip to Kashmir. It is not far from the Pakistan border. We turned east, however, toward the mountains. There is a valley system about a hundred and fifty miles deep into the Punjab Himalaya. The first section is the Manali and the second the Kulu valley. They are very beautiful. We wanted to go to the Kulu and walk over a 14,000-foot pass to visit the Tibetan-culture, barren, and mountainous Lahoul valley, but didn't have time. So we went up the hillside in the Manali valley, to the 6,000-foot town of Dharamshala, where the Dalai Lama has his permanent headquarters (courtesy of the Indian government) and a sizeable settlement of Tibetan refugees. Lodged in a tourist bungalow. A long gentle slope below us, of green wheatfields, orchards, running water creeks, and cascades everywhere. The richest-feeling, cleanest, and airiest region we'd seen in India. Above Dharamshala white-capped ridges rise to 14,000 feet and there are fine deodar forests around. We had dinner at the Lhasa Hotel—a meal of Tibetan noodles with meat in it. (First meat in months, as we had gone all-out vegetarian for a while.) In the evening we all smoked opium, since Allen and Peter had picked some up in Delhi and gotten a pipe as well. It was a funny kind of opium, mixed with charcoal in a little ball to make it burn better. Usual opium is a sticky ball you have to warm in a spoon over a candle or stove and then lay a burning coal next to it in the bowl to make it smoke when you inhale. It tasted OK, and after a few balls Joanne and I retired. An interesting feeling—all night a sensation of being not awake and not asleep, just sort of floating, with pleasant thoughts but nothing of consequence— quite different from the heavy content of peyote with all its visual kicks and bad-take possibilities. In the morning we were all nauseated, another effect of opium. Next morning tried to reach the Dalai Lama's ashram, two miles farther up the hill, but the phone was out of order. So we make arrangements to stay a night in the Triund Forest bungalow, which is a seven-mile hike up the hill at 10,000 feet, and go off at the invitation of a young Sikh to a local fair. Walked about two miles along the hillside, through little tributary valleys full of thundering creeks, and above wheatfields with neat channels and ditches leading the clear running water. It was a beautiful day, with just a few banner clouds above us on the snowpeaks.

It was a fair of the local hillpeople, called Gaddis, who are big sheepherders. The men wore robelike tan wool coats hitched up in the belt so that they only hung down to midthigh. The belt is a coil of woven wool rope, which they can unwind and use if they need it. The men wear small gold earrings and little woven caps. The women have a complicated costume and pounds of jewelry, at least on fair days. It was held on a wide, high, grassy plateau. Hand-run ferris wheels, goat carcasses hung in trees being skinned out; a bank of drums and drummers, long-haired sheep standing on top of boulders. "Shakespearean," Allen said—it was indeed anciently and idyllically pastoral.

A series of amateur wrestling matches: an older-looking man, light of build, with one weak polio-affected leg, matched against a heavier, more muscular, younger man. Gurdip the Sikh said the old man would win, but we couldn't see how. They wore tiny jockstraps, and fought in a dirt pit in the middle of the grass. The old man was underneath all the time, but he couldn't seem to be put on his back. At one point he was on his hands and knees, and the big fellow was on his back. The old man reached up and caught him back of the neck, and threw him clean over his shoulder and laid him out flat, then got up and did a limpy little victory dance while the other man got up rubbing his neck and looking sheepish and bewildered—the old guy joined with a little orchestra band marching around the perimeter of the wrestling ground, dancing and hopping along.

Morning of March 30 we set out climbing with our ruck-sacks. Passing the Dalai Lama's ashram we made arrangements to meet him the following afternoon, then went on climbing up the trail. A long steady climb. Eat lunch by a snowbank. Behind us finally comes the *chowkidar* (caretaker) of the bungalow, who doesn't live in it full time. He could speak no English, and was kind of a problem for us. The Triund house is on a ridge that climbs up higher toward the main mountains, and drops off steeply on both sides. Spectacular view. This house is really for the Forest Service, but non-civil-servants can use it if it's not officially occupied. We have a terrible time getting firewood, water (by melting snow), and kerosene lamps. This chowkidar is the most useless creature, just sort of hanging around watching us, and doing nothing himself. Part of the trouble was that it was well before the usual season when people use the place. In the logbook, we noticed that the Dalai Lama had come, with two or three others, seven times up here, often for three or four days at a time. He is always referred to in English as "His Holiness."

In the evening we built a cozy fire in the fireplace. Next morning I got up quite early and left the others sleeping, and pushed up the ridge. It was blowing mist, and pretty soon started to snow lightly. I climbed to timberline and a little beyond, until finally I was on a great snowfield leading up toward the actual peak of the mountain, Dhaulagiri. Instead of an iceaxe I was using a steel-tipped cane I had got at the village below. The wind became extremely strong and I was getting covered with snow on one side, and there was no view whatsoever. So I turned reluctantly back, from my highest elevation in the Himalayas, about 12,500 feet. That wouldn't even get you to the base of Everest. On the way down, in a little nook at the base of two cliffs, I saw a stone platform with splashes of faded orange color on it, and some rusty steel tridents stuck in the boulders beside it. The meditation-platform and living quarters of a Shiva-ascetic, at some time. Back at the Forest House the smoke was coming out the chimney and there was a hot breakfast. Around noon we started down.

Dalai Lama

THE DALAI LAMA's ashram has fences around it, and a few armed Indian army guards. Between the tops of the deodars are strung long ribbons of prayer flags. After getting cleared through the guardhouse (and washing up at a pump, right in front of the guards) we were led to a group of low wooden buildings and given a waiting room to wait in. I guess the Indians are afraid the Chinese might come and kidnap the Dalai if they're not careful. A few minutes later the Dalai Lama's interpreter came in, a neatly Western-dressed man in his thirties with a Tibetan cast, who spoke perfect English. His name is Sonam Topgay. He immediately started to ask me about Zen Buddhism. It seems he had found a book on Zen (if I understood him right) in a public toilet in Calcutta, and was immediately struck by its resemblance to the school of Tibetan Buddhism he followed. After that we didn't talk about Zen much, but he told me about the Zok-chen branch of Rnin ma-pa (Red Hat), which is a Tantric meditation school. He said it was by far the highest and greatest of all schools of Buddhism, including the Yellow Hat (which happens to be the sect his employer, the Dalai Lama, is head of). (Don't tell the Dalai Lama I said this.) He is originally from Sikkim, went to college in Delhi majoring in psychology. Got fits of depression and figured out a method of "introspection" to see what was the mind that felt depressed. Then he went to Lhasa and met a saintly old woman age 122 who told him to go see Dudjon Rimpoche of the Rnin ma-pa, which he did, becoming that man's disciple. He also married a girl in Lhasa. He said that one of the good things about his school of Buddhism was that you could marry, and you and your wife could meditate together while making love. Then they came out, when the Chinese moved in, with their baby girl. (A book by Evans-Wentz called *The Tibetan Book of Liberation*, I believe, is of this sect. *Book of the Dead*, also.) They also say, perfect total enlightenment can come: 1) at the moment of dying, 2) by eating proper sacramental food, 3) through dance and drama, and 4) at the moment of orgasm.

Then he told us the Dalai Lama was busy talking to the Maharajah of Sikkim, who had just dropped in, and that's why it had been such a long wait. So we went into the Dalai Lama's chamber. It has colorful *tankas* hanging all around and some big couches in a semicircle. We shake hands with him except that I do a proper Buddhist deep bow. The Dalai Lama is big and rather handsome. He looks like he needs more exercise. Although he understands a lot of English, always keeps an interpreter by when talking to guests. Allen and Peter asked him at some length about drugs and drug experiences, and their relationship to the spiritual states of meditation. The Dalai Lama gave the same answer everyone else did: drug states are real psychic states, but they aren't ultimately useful to you because you didn't get them on your own will and effort. For a few glimpses into the unconscious mind and other realms, they may be of use in loosening you up. After that, you can too easily come to rely on them, rather than undertaking such a discipline as will actually alter the structure of the personality in line with these insights. It isn't much help to just glimpse them with no ultimate basic alteration in the ego that is the source of lots of the psychic-spiritual ignorance that troubles one. But he said he'd be interested in trying psilocybin, the mushroom derivative, just to see what Westerners are so excited about. Allen promised to try and put Harvard onto it, and have this professor Dr. Tim Leary send him some.

Then the Dalai Lama and I talked about Zen sect meditation, him asking "how do you sit? how do you put your hands? how do you put your tongue? where do you look?"—as I told or showed him. Then he said, yes, that's just how we do it. Joanne asked him if there couldn't be another posture of meditation for Westerners, rather than crosslegged. He said, "It's not a matter of national custom," which I think is about as good an answer as you could get.

The Dalai doesn't spend all his time in his ashram; in fact he had just returned from a tour of south India, Mysore, where a few Tibetan refugee resettlements are. And last thing I've heard (since I got back to Japan) is that he's going to set out and do some real Buddhist preaching over India, and maybe Europe and America eventually, spinning the wheel of the Dharma. He is at the least a very keen-minded well-read man, and probably lots more than that. Also, he himself is still in training—there are the "Senior Gurus of the Dalai Lama," the most learned of Tibetans, who keep him on a hard study schedule and are constantly testing and debating with him.

Walked back down the hill, two miles in the dark, illuminated by occasional lightning flash, to our bungalow. To sleep late, some Englishman shouting under our windows.

On April 1, two in the afternoon, we took the bus back out of Dharamshala, our last look at the mountains; hardly had the bus got started and I said "my God I've forgot the cameras!" Joanne turned white and Allen and Peter looked serious. So I said April Fools. Little Tibetan kids running down the street in the black-and-red boots, little robes flying, long braided hair. By evening we were in Pathankot, and took a railway retiring room. I went out and bought some eggs, some bananas, and some orange gin (the Punjab isn't dry). It was hotter than it had been up at Dharamshala. We got one of the sweepers to promise to wake us at 4:30 A.M., because we were going to catch the Pathankot Express, which leaves at 5:00, the next morning.

From
THE PRACTICE OF THE WILD

The Etiquette of Freedom

THE COMPACT

ONE JUNE afternoon in the early seventies I walked through the crackly gold grasses to a neat but unpainted cabin at the back end of a ranch near the drainage of the South Yuba in northern California. It had no glass in the windows, no door. It was shaded by a huge Black Oak. The house looked abandoned and my friend, a student of native California literature and languages, walked right in. Off to the side, at a bare wooden table, with a mug of coffee, sat a solid old gray-haired Indian man. He acknowledged us, greeted my friend, and gravely offered us instant coffee and canned milk. He was fine, he said, but he would never go back to a VA hospital again. From now on if he got sick he would stay where he was. He liked being home. We spoke for some time of people and places along the western slope of the northern Sierra Nevada, the territories of Concow and Nisenan people. Finally my friend broke his good news: "Louie, I have found another person who speaks Nisenan." There were perhaps no more than three people alive speaking Nisenan at that time, and Louie was one of them. "Who?" Louie asked. He told her name. "She lives back of Oroville. I can bring her here, and you two can speak." "I know her from way back," Louie said. "She wouldn't want to come over here. I don't think I should see her. Besides, her family and mine never did get along."

That took my breath away. Here was a man who would not let the mere threat of cultural extinction stand in the way of his (and her) values. To well-meaning sympathetic white people this response is almost incomprehensible. In the world of his people, never overpopulated, rich in acorn, deer, salmon, and flicker feathers, to cleave to such purity, to be perfectionists about matters of family or clan, were affordable luxuries. Louie and his fellow Nisenan had more important business with each other than conversations. I think he saw it as a matter of keeping their dignity, their pride, and their own ways—regardless of what straits they had fallen upon—until the end.

Coyote and Ground Squirrel do not break the compact they have with each other that one must play predator and the other play game. In the wild a baby Black-tailed Hare gets maybe one free chance to run across a meadow without looking up. There won't be a second. The sharper the knife, the cleaner the line of the carving. We can appreciate the elegance of the forces that shape life and the world, that have shaped every line of our bodies—teeth and nails, nipples and eyebrows. We also see that we must try to live without causing unnecessary harm, not just to fellow humans but to all beings. We must try not to be stingy, or to exploit others. There will be enough pain in the world as it is.

Such are the lessons of the wild. The school where these lessons can be learned, the realms of caribou and elk, elephant and rhinoceros, orca and walrus, are shrinking day by day. Creatures who have traveled with us through the ages are now apparently doomed, as their habitat—and the old, old habitat of humans—falls before the slow-motion explosion of expanding world economies. If the lad or lass is among us who knows where the secret heart of this Growth-Monster is hidden, let them please tell us where to shoot the arrow that will slow it down. And if the secret heart stays secret and our work is made no easier, I for one will keep working for wildness day by day.

"Wild and free." An American dream-phrase loosing images: a long-maned stallion racing across the grasslands, a V of Canada Geese high and honking, a squirrel chattering and leaping limb to limb overhead in an oak. It also sounds like an ad for a Harley-Davidson. Both words, profoundly political and sensitive as they are, have become consumer baubles. I hope to investigate the meaning of *wild* and how it connects with *free* and what one would want to do with these meanings. To be truly free one must take on the basic conditions as they are—painful, impermanent, open, imperfect—and then be grateful for impermanence and the freedom it grants us. For in a fixed universe there would be no freedom. With that freedom we improve the campsite, teach children, oust tyrants. The world is nature, and in the long run inevitably wild, because the wild, as the process and essence of nature, is also an ordering of impermanence.

Although *nature* is a term that is not of itself threatening, the idea of the "wild" in civilized societies—both European and Asian—is often associated with unruliness, disorder, and violence. The Chinese word for nature, *zi-ran* (Japanese *shizen*) means "self-thus." It is a bland and general word. The word for wild in Chinese, *ye* (Japanese *ya*), which basically means "open country," has a wide set of meanings: in various combinations the term becomes illicit connection, desert country, an illegitimate child (open-country child), prostitute (open-country flower), and such. In an interesting case, *ye-man zi-yu* ("open-country southern-tribal-person-freedom") means "wild license." In another context "open-country story" becomes "fiction and fictitious romance." Other associations are usually with the rustic and uncouth. In a way *ye* is taken to mean "nature at its worst." Although the Chinese and Japanese have long given lip service to nature, only the early Daoists might have thought that wisdom could come of wildness.

Thoreau says "give me a wildness no civilization can endure." That's clearly not difficult to find. It is harder to imagine a civilization that wildness can endure, yet this is just what we must try to do. Wildness is not just the "preservation of the world," it *is* the world. Civilizations east and west have long been on a collision course with wild nature, and now the developed nations in particular have the witless power to destroy not only individual creatures but whole species, whole processes, of the earth. We need a civilization that can live fully and creatively together with wildness. We must start growing it right here, in the New World.

When we think of wilderness in America today, we think of remote and perhaps designated regions that are commonly alpine, desert, or swamp. Just a few centuries ago, when virtually *all* was wild in North America, wilderness was not something exceptionally severe. Pronghorn and bison trailed through the grasslands, creeks ran full of salmon, there were acres of clams, and grizzlies, cougar, and bighorn sheep were common in the lowlands. There were human beings, too: North America was *all populated*. One might say yes, but thinly—which raises the question of according to whom. The fact is, people were everywhere. When the Spanish foot soldier Alvar Núñez Cabeza de Vaca and his two companions (one of whom was African) were wrecked on the beach of what is now Galveston, and walked to the Rio Grande valley and then south back into Mexico between 1528 and 1536, there were few times in the whole eight years that they were not staying at a native settlement or camp. They were always on trails.

It has always been part of basic human experience to live in a culture of wilderness. There has been no wilderness without some kind of human presence for several hundred thousand years. Nature is not a place to visit, it is *home*—and within that home territory there are more familiar and less familiar places. Often there are areas that are difficult and remote, but all are *known* and even named. One August I was at a pass in the Brooks Range of northern Alaska at the headwaters of the Koyukuk River, a green three-thousand-foot tundra pass between the broad ranges, open and gentle, dividing the waters that flow to the Arctic Sea from the Yukon. It is as remote a place as you could be in North America, no roads, and the trails are those made by migrating caribou. Yet this pass has been steadily used by Inupiaq people of the north slope and Athapaskan people of the Yukon as a steadily north-south trade route for at least seven thousand years.

All of the hills and lakes of Alaska have been named in one or another of the dozen or so languages spoken by the native people, as the researches of Jim Kari (1982; 1985) and others have shown. Euro-American mapmakers name these places after transient exploiters, or their own girlfriends, or home towns in the Lower 48. The point is: it's all in the native story, yet only the tiniest trace of human presence through all that time shows. The place-based stories the people tell, and the naming they've done, is their archaeology, architecture, and *title* to the land. Talk about living lightly.

Cultures of wilderness live by the life and death lessons of subsistence economies. But what can we now mean by the words *wild* and for that matter *nature*? Languages meander like great rivers leaving oxbow traces over forgotten beds, to be seen only from the air or by scholars. Language is like some kind of infinitely interfertile family of species spreading or mysteriously declining over time, shamelessly and endlessly hybridizing, changing its own rules as it goes. Words are used as signs, as stand-ins, arbitrary and temporary, even as language reflects (and informs) the shifting values of the peoples whose minds it inhabits and glides through. We have faith in "meaning" the way we might believe in wolverines—putting trust in the occasional reports of others or on the authority of once seeing a pelt. But it is sometimes worth tracking these tricksters back.

THE WORDS *NATURE*, *WILD*, AND *WILDERNESS*

Take *nature* first. The word *nature* is from Latin *natura*, "birth, constitution, character, course of things"—ultimately from *nasci*, to be born. So we have *nation, natal, native, pregnant*. The probable Indo-European root (via Greek *gna*—hence cognate, agnate) is *gen* (Sanskrit *jan*), which provides *generate* and *genus*, as well as *kin* and *kind*.

The word gets two slightly different meanings. One is "the outdoors"—the physical world, including all living things. Nature by this definition is a norm of the world that is apart from the features or products of civilization and human will. The machine, the artifact, the devised, or the extraordinary (like a two-headed calf) is spoken of as "unnatural." The other meaning, which is broader, is "the material world or its collective objects and phenomena," including the products of human action and intention. As an agency nature is defined as "the creative and regulative physical power which is conceived of as operating in the material world and as the immediate cause of all its phenomena." Science and some sorts of mysticism rightly propose that *everything* is natural. By these lights there is nothing unnatural about New York City, or toxic wastes, or atomic energy, and nothing—by definition—that we do or experience in life is "unnatural."

(The "supernatural"? One way to deal with it is to say that "the supernatural" is a name for phenomena that are reported by so few people as to leave their reality in doubt. Nonetheless these events—ghosts, gods, magical transformations, and such—are described often enough to make them continue to be intriguing and, for some, credible.)

The physical universe and all its properties—I would prefer to use the word *nature* in this sense. But it will come up meaning "the outdoors" or "other-than-human" sometimes even here.

The word *wild* is like a gray fox trotting off through the forest, ducking behind bushes, going in and out of sight. Up close, first glance, it is "wild"—then farther into the woods next glance it's "wyld" and it recedes via Old Norse *villr* and Old Teutonic *wilthijaz* into a faint pre-Teutonic *ghweltijos* which means, still, wild and maybe wooded (*wald*) and lurks back there with possible connections to *will*, to Latin *silva* (forest, sauvage), and to the Indo-European root *ghwer*, base of Latin *ferus* (feral, fierce), which swings us around to Thoreau's "awful ferity" shared by virtuous people and lovers. The Oxford English Dictionary has it this way:

Of animals—not tame, undomesticated, unruly.

Of plants—not cultivated.

Of land—uninhabited, uncultivated.

Of foodcrops—produced or yielded without cultivation.

Of societies—uncivilized, rude, resisting constituted government.

Of individuals—unrestrained, insubordinate, licentious, dissolute, loose. "Wild and wanton widowes"—1614.

Of behavior—violent, destructive, cruel, unruly.

Of behavior—artless, free, spontaneous. "Warble his native wood-notes wild"—John Milton.

Wild is largely defined in our dictionaries by what—from a human standpoint—it is not. It cannot be seen by this approach for what it *is*. Turn it the other way:

Of animals—free agents, each with its own endowments, living within natural systems.

Of plants—self-propagating, self-maintaining, flourishing in accord with innate qualities.

Of land—a place where the original and potential vegetation and fauna are intact and in full interaction and the landforms are entirely the result of nonhuman forces. Pristine.

Of foodcrops—food supplies made available and sustainable by the natural excess and exuberance of wild plants in their growth and in the production of quantities of fruit or seeds.

Of societies—societies whose order has grown from within and is maintained by the force of consensus and custom rather than explicit legislation. Primary cultures, which consider themselves the original and eternal inhabitants of their territory. Societies which resist economic and political domination by civilization. Societies whose economic system is in a close and sustainable relation to the local ecosystem.

Of individuals—following local custom, style, and etiquette without concern for the standards of the metropolis or nearest trading post. Unintimidated, self-reliant, independent. "Proud and free."

Of behavior—fiercely resisting any oppression, confinement, or exploitation. Far-out, outrageous, "bad," admirable.

Of behavior—artless, free, spontaneous, unconditioned. Expressive, physical, openly sexual, ecstatic.

Most of the senses in this second set of definitions come very close to being how the Chinese define the term *Dao*, the *way* of Great Nature: eluding analysis, beyond categories, self-organizing, self-informing, playful, surprising, impermanent, insubstantial, independent, complete, orderly, unmediated, freely manifesting, self-authenticating, self-willed, complex, quite simple. Both empty and real at the same time. In some cases we might call it sacred. It is not far from the Buddhist term *Dharma* with its original senses of forming and firming.

The word *wilderness*, earlier *wyldernesse*, Old English *wildeornes*, possibly from "wild-deer-ness" (*deor*, deer and other forest animals) but more likely "wildern-ness," has the meanings:

A large area of wild land, with original vegetation and wildlife, ranging from dense jungle or rainforest to arctic or alpine "white wilderness."

A wasteland, as an area unused or useless for agriculture or pasture.

A space of sea or air, as in Shakespeare, "I stand as one upon a Rock, environ'd with a Wilderness of Sea" (*Titus Andronicus*). The oceans.

A place of danger and difficulty: where you take your own chances, depend on your own skills, and do not count on rescue.

This world as contrasted with heaven. "I walked through the wildernesse of this world" (*Pilgrim's Progress*).

A place of abundance, as in John Milton, "a wildernesse of sweets."

Milton's usage of wilderness catches the very real condition of energy and richness that is so often found in wild systems. "A wildernesse of sweets" is like the billions of herring or mackerel babies in the ocean, the cubic miles of krill, wild prairie grass seed (leading to the bread of this day, made from the germs of grasses)—all the incredible fecundity of small animals and plants, feeding the web. But from another side, wilderness has implied chaos, eros, the unknown, realms of taboo, the habitat of both the ecstatic and the demonic. In both senses it is a place of archetypal power, teaching, and challenge.

WILDNESS

So we can say that New York City and Tokyo are "natural" but not "wild." They do not deviate from the laws of nature, but they are habitat so exclusive in the matter of who and what they give shelter to, and so intolerant of other creatures, as to be truly odd. Wilderness is a *place* where the wild potential is fully expressed, a diversity of living and nonliving beings flourishing according to their own sorts of order. In ecology we speak of "wild systems." When an ecosystem is fully functioning, all the members are present at the assembly. To speak of wilderness is to speak of wholeness. Human beings came out of that wholeness, and to consider the possibility of reactivating membership in the Assembly of All Beings is in no way regressive.

By the sixteenth century the lands of the Occident, the countries of Asia, and all the civilizations and cities from the Indian subcontinent to the coast of North Africa were becoming ecologically impoverished. The people were rapidly becoming nature-illiterate. Much of the original vegetation had been destroyed by the expansion of grazing or agriculture, and the remaining land was of no great human economic use, "waste," mountain regions and deserts. The lingering larger animals—big cats, desert sheep, serows, and such—managed to survive by retreating to the harsher habitats. The leaders of these civilizations grew up with less and less personal knowledge of animal behavior and were no longer taught the intimate wide-ranging plant knowledge that had once been universal. By way of trade-off they learned "human management," administration, rhetorical skills. Only the most marginal of the *paysan*, people of the land, kept up practical plant and animal lore and memories of the old ways. People who grew up in towns or cities, or on large estates, had less chance to learn how wild systems work. Then major blocks of citified mythology (Medieval Christianity and then the "Rise of Science") denied first soul, then consciousness, and finally even sentience to the natural world. Huge numbers of Europeans, in the climate of a nature-denying mechanistic ideology, were losing the opportunity for direct experience of nature.

A new sort of nature-traveler came into existence: men who went out as resource scouts, financed by companies or aristocratic families, penetrating the lightly populated lands of people who lived in and with the wilderness. Conquistadores and priests. Europe had killed off the wolves and bears, deforested vast areas, and overgrazed the hills. The search for slaves, fish, sugar, and precious metals ran over the edge of the horizon and into Asia, Africa, and the New World. These overrefined and warlike states once more came up against wild nature and natural societies: people who lived without Church or State. In return for gold or raw sugar, the white men had to give up something of themselves: they had to look into their own sense of what it meant to be a human being, wonder about the nature of hierarchy, ask if life was worth the honor of a king, or worth gold. (A lost and starving man stands and examines the nicked edge of his sword and his frayed Spanish cape in a Florida swamp.)

Some, like Nuño de Guzmán, became crazed and sadistic. "When he began to govern this province, it contained 25,000 Indians, subjugated and peaceful. Of these he has sold 10,000 as slaves, and the others, fearing the same fate, have abandoned their villages" (Todorov, 1985, 134). Cortés, the conqueror of Mexico, ended up a beaten, depressed beggar-to-the-throne. Alvar Núñez, who for eight years walked naked across Texas and New Mexico, came out transformed into a person of the New World. He had rejoined the old ways and was never the same again. He gained a compassionate heart, a taste for self-sufficiency and simplicity, and a knack for healing. The types of both Guzmán and Núñez are still among us. Another person has also walked onto the Noh stage of Turtle Island history to hold hands with Alvar Núñez at the far end of the process—Ishi the Yahi, who walked into civilization with as much desperation as Núñez walked out of it. Núñez was the first European to encounter North America and its native myth-mind, and Ishi was the last Native American to fully know that mind—and he had to leave it behind. What lies between those two brackets is not dead and gone. It is perennially within us, dormant as a hard-shelled seed, awaiting the fire or flood that awakes it again.

In those intervening centuries, tens of millions of North and South American Indians died early and violent deaths (as did countless Europeans), the world's largest mammal herd was extinguished (the bison), and fifteen million Pronghorn disappeared. The grasslands and their soils are largely gone, and only remnants survive from the original old-growth eastern hardwood and western conifer forests. We all know more items for this list.

It is often said that the frontier gave a special turn to American history. A frontier is a burning edge, a frazzle, a strange market zone between two utterly different worlds. It is a strip where there are pelts and tongues and tits for the taking. There is an almost visible line that a person of the invading culture could walk across: out of history and into a perpetual present, a way of life attuned to the slower and steadier processes of nature. The possibility of passage into that myth-time world had been all but forgotten in Europe. Its rediscovery—the unsettling vision of a natural self—has haunted the Euro-American peoples as they continually cleared and roaded the many wild corners of the North American continent.

Wilderness is now—for much of North America—places that are formally set aside on public lands—Forest Service or Bureau of Land Management holdings or state and federal parks. Some tiny but critical tracts are held by private nonprofit groups like The Nature Conservancy or the Trust for Public Land. These are the shrines saved from all the land that was once known and lived on by the original people, the little bits left as they were, the last little places where intrinsic nature totally wails, blooms, nests, glints away. They make up only 2 percent of the land of the United States.

But wildness is not limited to the 2 percent formal wilderness areas. Shifting scales, it is everywhere: ineradicable populations of fungi, moss, mold, yeasts, and such that surround and inhabit us. Deer mice on the back porch, deer bounding across the freeway, pigeons in the park, spiders in the corners. There were crickets in the paint locker of the *Sappa Creek* oil tanker, as I worked as a wiper in the engine room out in mid-Pacific, cleaning brushes. Exquisite complex beings in their energy webs inhabiting the fertile corners of the urban world in accord with the rules of wild systems, the visible hardy stalks and stems of vacant lots and railroads, the persistent raccoon squads, bacteria in the loam and in our yogurt. The term *culture*, in its meaning of "a deliberately maintained aesthetic and intellectual life" and in its other meaning of "the totality of socially transmitted behavior patterns," is never far from a biological root meaning as in "yogurt culture"—a nourishing habitat. Civilization is permeable, and could be as inhabited as the wild is.

Wilderness may temporarily dwindle, but wildness won't go away. A ghost wilderness hovers around the entire planet: the millions of tiny seeds of the original vegetation are hiding in the mud on the foot of an arctic tern, in the dry desert sands, or in the wind. These seeds are each uniquely adapted to a specific soil or circumstance, each with its own little form and fluff, ready to float, freeze, or be swallowed, always preserving the germ. Wilderness will inevitably return, but it will not be as fine a world as the one that was glistening in the early morning of the Holocene. Much life will be lost in the wake of human agency on earth, that of the twentieth and twenty-first centuries. Much is already lost—the soils and waters unravel:

"What's that dark thing in the water?
Is it not an oil-soaked otter?"

Where do we start to resolve the dichotomy of the civilized and the wild?

Do you really believe you are an animal? We are now taught this in school. It is a wonderful piece of information: I have been enjoying it all my life and I come back to it over and over again, as something to investigate and test. I grew up on a small farm with cows and chickens, and with a second-growth forest right at the back fence, so I had the good fortune of seeing the human and animal as in the same realm. But many people who have been hearing this since childhood have not absorbed the implications of it, perhaps feel remote from the nonhuman world, are not *sure* they are animals. They would like to feel they might be something better than animals. That's understandable: other animals might feel they are something different than "just animals" too. But we must contemplate the shared ground of our common biological being before emphasizing the differences.

Our bodies are wild. The involuntary quick turn of the head at a shout, the vertigo at looking off a precipice, the heart-in-the-throat in a moment of danger, the catch of the breath, the quiet moments relaxing, staring, reflecting—all universal responses of this mammal body. They can be seen throughout the class. The body does not require the intercession of some conscious intellect to make it breathe, to keep the heart beating. It is to a great extent self-regulating, it is a life of its own. Sensation and perception do not exactly come from outside, and the unremitting thought and image-flow are not exactly inside. The world is our consciousness, and it surrounds us. There are more things in mind, in the imagination, than "you" can keep track of—thoughts, memories, images, angers, delights, rise unbidden. The depths of mind, the unconscious, are our inner wilderness areas, and that is where a bobcat is *right now*. I do not mean personal bobcats in personal psyches, but the bobcat that roams from dream to dream. The conscious agenda-planning ego occupies a very tiny territory, a little cubicle somewhere near the gate, keeping track of some of what goes in and out (and sometimes making expansionistic plots), and the rest takes care of itself. The body is, so to speak, in the mind. They are both wild.

Some will say, so far so good. "We are mammal primates. But we have language, and the animals don't." By some definitions perhaps they don't. But they do communicate extensively, and by call systems we are just beginning to grasp.

It would be a mistake to think that human beings got "smarter" at some point and invented first language and then society. Language and culture emerge from our biological-social natural existence, animals that we were/are. Language is a mind-body system that coevolved with our needs and nerves. Like imagination and the body, language rises unbidden. It is of a complexity that eludes our rational intellectual capacities. All attempts at scientific description of natural languages have fallen short of completeness, as the descriptive linguists readily confess, yet the child learns the mother tongue early and has virtually mastered it by six.

Language is learned in the house and in the fields, not at school. Without having ever been taught formal grammar we utter syntactically correct sentences, one after another, for all the waking hours of the years of our life. Without conscious device we constantly reach into the vast word-hoards in the depths of the wild unconscious. We cannot as individuals or even as a species take credit for this power. It came from someplace else: from the way clouds divide and mingle (and the arms of energy that coil first back and then forward), from the way the many flowerlets of a composite blossom divide and redivide, from the gleaming calligraphy of the ancient riverbeds under present riverbeds of the Yukon River streaming out the Yukon flats, from the wind in the pine needles, from the chuckles of grouse in the ceanothus bushes.

Language teaching in schools is a matter of corralling off a little of the language-behavior territory and cultivating a few favorite features—culturally defined elite forms that will help you apply for a job or give you social credibility at a party. One might even learn how to produce the byzantine artifact known as the professional paper. There are many excellent reasons to master these things, but the power, the *virtu*, remains on the side of the wild.

Social order is found throughout nature—long before the age of books and legal codes. It is inherently part of what we are, and its patterns follow the same foldings, checks and balances, as flesh or stone. What we call social organization and order in government is a set of forms that have been appropriated by the calculating mind from the operating principles in nature.

THE WORLD IS WATCHING

The world is as sharp as the edge of a knife—a Northwest Coast saying. Now how does it look from the standpoint of peoples for whom there is no great dichotomy between their culture and nature, those who live in societies whose economies draw on uncultivated systems? The pathless world of wild nature is a surpassing school and those who have lived through her can be tough and funny teachers. Out here one is in constant engagement with countless plants and animals. To be well educated is to have learned the songs, proverbs, stories, sayings, myths (and technologies) that come with this experiencing of the nonhuman members of the local ecological community. Practice in the field, "open country," is foremost. Walking is the great adventure, the first meditation, a practice of heartiness and soul primary to humankind. Walking is the exact balance of spirit and humility. Out walking, one notices where there is food. And there are firsthand true stories of "Your ass is somebody else's meal"—a blunt way of saying interdependence, interconnection, "ecology," on the level where it counts, also a teaching of mindfulness and preparedness. There is an extraordinary teaching of specific plants and animals and their uses, empirical and impeccable, that never reduces them to objects and commodities.

It seems that a short way back in the history of occidental ideas there was a fork in the trail. The line of thought that is signified by the names of Descartes, Newton, and Hobbes (saying that life in a primary society is "nasty, brutish, and short"—all of them city-dwellers) was a profound rejection of the organic world. For a reproductive universe they substituted a model of sterile mechanism and an economy of "production." These thinkers were as hysterical about "chaos" as their predecessors, the witch-hunt prosecutors of only a century before, were about "witches." They not only didn't enjoy the possibility that the world is as sharp as the edge of a knife, they wanted to take that edge away from nature. Instead of making the world safer for humankind, the foolish tinkering with the powers of life and death by the occidental scientist-engineer-ruler puts the whole planet on the brink of degradation. Most of humanity—foragers, peasants, or artisans—has always taken the other fork. That is to say, they have understood the play of the real world, with all its suffering, not in simple terms of "nature red in tooth and claw" but through the celebration of the gift-exchange quality of our give-and-take. "What a big potlatch we are all members of!" To acknowledge that each of us at the table will eventually be part of the meal is not just being "realistic." It is allowing the sacred to enter and accepting the sacramental aspect of our shaky temporary personal being.

The world is watching: one cannot walk through a meadow or forest without a ripple of report spreading out from one's passage. The thrush darts back, the jay squalls, a beetle scuttles under the grasses, and the signal is passed along. Every creature knows when a hawk is cruising or a human strolling. The information passed through the system is intelligence.

In Hindu and Buddhist iconography an animal trace is registered on the images of the Deities or Buddhas and Bodhisattvas. Manjusri the Bodhisattva of Discriminating Wisdom rides a lion, Samantabhadra the Bodhisattva of Kindness rides an elephant, Sarasvati the Goddess of Music and Learning rides a peacock, Shiva relaxes in the company of a snake and a bull. Some wear tiny animals in their crowns or hair. In this ecumenical spiritual ecology it is suggested that the other animals occupy spiritual as well as "thermodynamic" niches. Whether or not their consciousness is identical with that of the humans is a moot point. Why should the peculiarities of human consciousness be the narrow standard by which other creatures are judged? "Whoever told people that 'Mind' means thoughts, opinions, ideas, and concepts? Mind means trees, fence posts, tiles, and grasses," says Dōgen (the philosopher and founder of the Sōtō school of Japanese Zen) in his funny cryptic way.

We are all capable of extraordinary transformations. In myth and story these changes are animal-to-human, human-to-animal, animal-to-animal, or even farther leaps. The essential nature remains clear and steady through these changes. So the animal icons of the Inupiaq people ("Eskimos") of the Bering Sea (here's the reverse!) have a tiny human face sewn into the fur, or under the feathers, or carved on the back or breast or even inside the eye, peeping out. This is the *inua*, which is often called "spirit" but could just as well be termed the "essential nature" of that creature. It remains the same face regardless of the playful temporary changes. Just as Buddhism has chosen to represent our condition by presenting an image of a steady, solid, gentle, meditating human figure seated in the midst of the world of phenomena, the Inupiaq would present a panoply of different creatures, each with a little hidden human face. This is not the same as anthropocentrism or human arrogance. It is a way of saying that each creature is a spirit with an intelligence as brilliant as our own. The Buddhist iconographers hide a little animal face in the hair of the human to remind us that we see with archetypal wilderness eyes as well.

The world is not only watching, it is listening too. A rude and thoughtless comment about a Ground Squirrel or a Flicker or a Porcupine will not go unnoticed. Other beings (the instructors from the old ways tell us) do not mind being killed and eaten as food, but they expect us to say please, and thank you, and they hate to see themselves wasted. The precept against needlessly taking life is inevitably the first and most difficult of commandments. In their practice of killing and eating with gentleness and thanks, the primary peoples are our teachers: the attitude toward animals, and their treatment, in twentieth-century American industrial meat production is literally sickening, unethical, and a source of boundless bad luck for this society.

An ethical life is one that is mindful, mannerly, and has style. Of all moral failings and flaws of character, the worst is stinginess of thought, which includes meanness in all its forms. Rudeness in thought or deed toward others, toward nature, reduces the chances of conviviality and interspecies communication, which are essential to physical and spiritual survival. Richard Nelson, a student of Indian ways, has said that an Athapaskan mother might tell her little girl, "Don't point at the mountain! It's rude!" One must not waste, or be careless, with the bodies or the parts of any creature one has hunted or gathered. One must not boast, or show much pride in accomplishment, and one must not take one's skill for granted. Wastefulness and carelessness are caused by stinginess of spirit, an ungracious unwillingness to complete the gift-exchange transaction. (These rules are also particularly true for healers, artists, and gamblers.)

Perhaps one should not talk (or write) too much about the wild world: it may be that it embarrasses other animals to have attention called to them. A sensibility of this sort might help explain why there is so little "landscape poetry" from the cultures of the old ways. Nature description is a kind of writing that comes with civilization and its habits of collection and classification. Chinese landscape poetry begins around the fifth century A.D. with the work of Xie Lingyun. There were fifteen hundred years of Chinese song and poetry before him (allowing as the *Shi-jing*—China's first collection of poems and songs, "The Book of Songs"—might register some five centuries of folksong prior to the writing down) and there is much nature, but no broad landscapes: it is about mulberry trees, wild edible greens, threshing, the forager and farmer's world up close. By Hsieh's time the Chinese had become removed enough from their own mountains and rivers to aestheticize them. This doesn't mean that people of the old ways don't appreciate the view, but they have a different point of view.

The same kind of cautions apply to the stories or songs one might tell about oneself. Malcolm Margolin, publisher of *News from Native California*, points out that the original people of California did not easily recount an "autobiography." The details of their individual lives, they said, were unexceptional: the only events that bore recounting were descriptions of a few of their outstanding dreams and their moments of encounter with the spirit world and its transformations. The telling of their life stories, then, was very brief. They told of dream, insight, and healing.

BACK HOME

The etiquette of the wild world requires not only generosity but a good-humored toughness that cheerfully tolerates discomfort, an appreciation of everyone's fragility, and a certain modesty. Good quick blueberry picking, the knack of tracking, getting to where the fishing's good ("an angry man cannot catch a fish"), reading the surface of the sea or sky—these are achievements not to be gained by mere effort. Mountaineering has the same quality. These moves take practice, which calls for a certain amount of self-abnegation, and intuition, which takes emptying of yourself. Great insights have come to some people only after they reached the point where they had nothing left. Alvar Núñez Cabeza de Vaca became unaccountably deepened after losing his way and spending several winter nights sleeping naked in a pit in the Texas desert under a north wind. He truly had reached the point where he had nothing. ("To have nothing, you must *have nothing*!" Lord Buckley says of this moment.) After that he found himself able to heal sick native people he met on his way westward. His fame spread ahead of him. Once he had made his way back to Mexico and was again a civilized Spaniard he found he had lost his power of healing—not just the ability to heal, but the *will* to heal, which is the will to be whole: for as he said, there were "real doctors" in the city, and he began to doubt his powers. To resolve the dichotomy of the civilized and the wild, we must first resolve to be whole.

One may reach such a place as Alvar Núñez by literally losing everything. Painful and dangerous experiences often transform the people who survive them. Human beings are audacious. They set out to have adventures and try to do more than perhaps they should. So by practicing yogic austerities or monastic disciplines, some people make a structured attempt at having nothing. Some of us have learned much from traveling day after day on foot over snowfields, rockslides, passes, torrents, and valley floor forests, by "putting ourselves out there." Another—and most sophisticated—way is that of Vimalakirti, the legendary Buddhist layman, who taught that by directly intuiting our condition in the actually existing world we realize that we have had nothing from the beginning. A Tibetan saying has it: "The experience of emptiness engenders compassion."

For those who would seek directly, by entering the primary temple, the wilderness can be a ferocious teacher, rapidly stripping down the inexperienced or the careless. It is easy to make the mistakes that will bring one to an extremity. Practically speaking, a life that is vowed to simplicity, appropriate boldness, good humor, gratitude, unstinting work and play, and lots of walking brings us close to the actually existing world and its wholeness.

People of wilderness cultures rarely seek out adventures. If they deliberately risk themselves, it is for spiritual rather than economic reasons. Ultimately all such journeys are done for the sake of the whole, not as some private quest. The quiet dignity that characterizes so many so-called primitives is a reflection of that. Florence Edenshaw, a contemporary Haida elder who has lived a long life of work and family, was asked by the young woman anthropologist who interviewed her and was impressed by her coherence, presence, and dignity, "What can I do for self-respect?" Mrs. Edenshaw said, "Dress up and stay home." The "home," of course, is as large as you make it.

The lessons we learn from the wild become the etiquette of freedom. We can enjoy our humanity with its flashy brains and sexual buzz, its social cravings and stubborn tantrums, and take ourselves as no more and no less than another being in the Big Watershed. We can accept each other all as barefoot equals sleeping on the same ground. We can give up hoping to be eternal and quit fighting dirt. We can chase off mosquitoes and fence out varmints without hating them. No expectations, alert and sufficient, grateful and careful, generous and direct. A calm and clarity attend us in the moment we are wiping the grease off our hands between tasks and glancing up at the passing clouds. Another joy is finally sitting down to have coffee with a friend. The wild requires that we learn the terrain, nod to all the plants and animals and birds, ford the streams and cross the ridges, and tell a good story when we get back home.

And when the children are safe in bed, at one of the great holidays like the Fourth of July, New Year's, or Halloween, we can bring out some spirits and turn on the music, and the men and the women who are still among the living can get loose and really wild. So that's the final meaning of "wild"—the esoteric meaning, the deepest and most scary. Those who are ready for it will come to it. Please do not repeat this to the uninitiated.

The Place, the Region, and the Commons

"When you find your place where you are, practice occurs."   DŌGEN

THE WORLD IS PLACES

WE EXPERIENCE SLUMS, prairies, and wetlands all equally as "places." Like a mirror, a place can hold anything, on any scale. I want to talk about place as an experience and propose a model of what it meant to "live in place" for most of human time, presenting it initially in terms of the steps that a child takes growing into a natural community. (We have the terms *enculturation* and *acculturation*, but nothing to describe the process of becoming placed or re-placed.) In doing so we might get one more angle on what a "civilization of wildness" might require.

For most Americans, to reflect on "home place" would be an unfamiliar exercise. Few today can announce themselves as someone *from* somewhere. Almost nobody spends a lifetime in the same valley, working alongside the people they knew as children. Native people everywhere (the very term means "someone born there") and Old World farmers and city people share this experience of living in place. Still—and this is very important to remember—being inhabitory, being place-based, has never meant that one didn't travel from time to time, going on trading ventures or taking livestock to summer grazing. Such working wanderers have always known they had a home-base on earth, and could prove it at any campfire or party by singing their own songs.

The heart of a place is the home, and the heart of the home is the firepit, the hearth. All tentative explorations go outward from there, and it is back to the fireside that elders return. You grow up speaking a home language, a local vernacular. Your own household may have some specifics of phrase, of pronunciation, that are different from the *domus*, the *jia* or *ie* or *kum*, down the lane. You hear histories of the people who are your neighbors and tales involving rocks, streams, mountains, and trees that are all within your sight. The myths of world-creation tell you how *that mountain* was created and how *that peninsula* came to be there. As you grow bolder you explore your world outward from the firepit (which is the center of each universe) in little trips. The childhood landscape is learned on foot, and a map is inscribed in the mind—trails and pathways and groves—the mean dog, the cranky old man's house, the pasture with a bull in it—going out wider and farther. All of us carry within us a picture of the terrain that was learned roughly between the ages of six and nine. (It could as easily be an urban neighborhood as some rural scene.) You can almost totally recall the place you walked, played, biked, swam. Revisualizing that place with its smells and textures, walking through it again in your imagination, has a grounding and settling effect. As a contemporary thought we might also wonder how it is for those whose childhood landscape was being ripped up by bulldozers, or whose family moving about made it all a blur. I have a friend who still gets emotional when he recalls how the avocado orchards of his southern California youth landscape were transformed into hillside after hillside of suburbs.

Our place is part of what we are. Yet even a "place" has a kind of fluidity: it passes through space and time—"ceremonial time" in John Hanson Mitchell's phrase. A place will have been grasslands, then conifers, then beech and elm. It will have been half riverbed, it will have been scratched and plowed by ice. And then it will be cultivated, paved, sprayed, dammed, graded, built up. But each is only for a while, and that will be just another set of lines on the palimpsest. The whole earth is a great tablet holding the multiple overlaid new and ancient traces of the swirl of forces. Each place is its own place, forever (eventually) wild. A place on earth is a mosaic within larger mosaics—the land is all small places, all precise tiny realms replicating larger and smaller patterns. Children start out learning place by learning those little realms around the house, the settlement, and outward.

One's sense of the scale of a place expands as one learns the *region*. The young hear further stories and go for explorations which are also subsistence forays—firewood gathering, fishing, to fairs or to market. The outlines of the larger region become part of their awareness. (Thoreau says in "Walking" that an area twenty miles in diameter will be enough to occupy a lifetime of close exploration on foot—you will never exhaust its details.)

The total size of the region a group calls home depends on the land type. Every group is territorial, each moves within a given zone, even nomads stay within boundaries. A people living in a desert or grassland with great visible spaces that invite you to step forward and walk as far as you can see will range across tens of thousands of square miles. A deep old-growth forest may rarely be traveled at all. Foragers in gallery forests and grasslands will regularly move broadly, whereas people in a deep-soiled valley ideal for gardens might not go far beyond the top of the nearest ridge. The regional boundaries were roughly drawn by climate, which is what sets the plant-type zones—plus soil type and landforms. Desert wastes, mountain ridges, or big rivers set a broad edge to a region. We walk across or wade through the larger and smaller boundaries. Like children first learning our homeland we can stand at the edge of a big river, or on the crest of a major ridge, and observe that the other side is a different soil, a change of plants and animals, a new shape of barn roof, maybe less or more rain. The lines between natural regions are never simple or clear, but vary according to such criteria as biota, watersheds, landforms, elevation. (See Jim Dodge, 1981.) Still, we all know—at some point—that we are no longer in the Midwest, say, but in the West. Regions seen according to natural criteria are sometimes called bioregions.

(In pre-conquest America people covered great distances. It is said that the Mojave of the lower Colorado felt that everyone at least once in their lives should make foot journeys to the Hopi mesas to the east, the Gulf of California to the south, and to the Pacific.)

Every region has its wilderness. There is the fire in the kitchen, and there is the place less traveled. In most settled regions there used to be some combination of prime agricultural land, orchard and vine land, rough pasturage, woodlot, forest, and desert or mountain "waste." The de facto wilderness was the extreme backcountry part of all that. The parts less visited are "where the bears are." The wilderness is within walking distance—it may be three days or it may be ten. It is at the far high rough end, or the deep forest and swamp end, of the territory where most of you all live and work. People will go there for mountain herbs, for the trapline, or for solitude. They live between the poles of home and their own wild places.

Recollecting that we once lived in places is part of our contemporary self-rediscovery. It grounds what it means to be "human" (etymologically something like "earthling"). I have a friend who feels sometimes that the world is hostile to human life—he says it chills us and kills us. But how could we *be* were it not for this planet that provided our very shape? Two conditions—gravity and a livable temperature range between freezing and boiling—have given us fluids and flesh. The trees we climb and the ground we walk on have given us five fingers and toes. The "place" (from the root *plat*, broad, spreading, flat) gave us far-seeing eyes, the streams and breezes gave us versatile tongues and whorly ears. The land gave us a stride, and the lake a dive. The amazement gave us our kind of mind. We should be thankful for that, and take nature's stricter lessons with some grace.

UNDERSTANDING THE COMMONS

I stood with my climbing partner (Allen Ginsberg) on the summit of Glacier Peak looking all ways round, ridge after ridge and peak after peak, as far as we could see. To the west across Puget Sound were the farther peaks of the Olympic Mountains. He said: "You mean there's a senator for all this?" As in the Great Basin, crossing desert after desert, range after range, it is easy to think there are vast spaces on earth yet unadministered, perhaps forgotten, or unknown (the endless sweep of spruce forest in Alaska and Canada)—but it is all mapped and placed in some domain. In North America there is a lot that is in public domain, which has its problems, but at least they are problems we are all enfranchised to work on. David Foreman, founder of the Earth First! movement, once stated his radical provenance. Not out of Social Justice, Left Politics, or Feminism did I come—says David—but from the Public Lands Conservation movement—the solid stodgy movement that goes back to the thirties and before. Yet these land and wildlife issues were what politicized John Muir, John Wesley Powell, and Aldo Leopold—the abuses of public land.

American public lands are the twentieth-century incarnation of a much older institution known across Eurasia—in English called the "commons"—which was the ancient mode of both protecting and managing the wilds of the self-governing regions. It worked well enough until the age of market economies, colonialism, and imperialism. Let me give you a kind of model of how the commons worked.

Between the extremes of deep wilderness and the private plots of the farmstead lies a territory which is not suitable for crops. In earlier times it was used jointly by the members of a given tribe or village. This area, embracing both the wild and the semi-wild, is of critical importance. It is necessary for the health of the wilderness because it adds big habitat, overflow territory, and room for wildlife to fly and run. It is essential even to an agricultural village economy because its natural diversity provides the many necessities and amenities that the privately held plots cannot. It enriches the agrarian diet with game and fish. The shared land supplies firewood, poles and stone for building, clay for the kiln, herbs, dye plants, and much else, just as in a foraging economy. It is especially important as seasonal or full-time open range for cattle, horses, goats, pigs, and sheep.

In the abstract the sharing of a natural area might be thought of as a matter of access to "common pool resources" with no limits or controls on individual exploitation. The fact is that such sharing developed over millennia and always within territorial and social contexts. In the peasant societies of both Asia and Europe there were customary forms that gave direction to the joint use of land. They did not grant free access to outsiders, and there were controls over entry and use by member households. The commons has been defined as "the undivided land belonging to the members of a local community as a whole." This definition fails to make the point that the commons is both specific land *and* the traditional community institution that determines the carrying capacity for its various subunits and defines the rights and obligations of those who use it, with penalties for lapses. Because it is traditional and *local*, it is not identical with today's "public domain," which is land held and managed by a central government. Under a national state such management may be destructive (as it is becoming in Canada and the United States) or benign (as it often has been in the past)—but in no case is it locally managed. One of the ideas in the current debate on how to reform our public lands is that of returning them to regional control.

An example of traditional management: what would keep one household from bringing in more and more stock and tempting everyone toward overgrazing? In earlier England and in some contemporary Swiss villages (Netting, 1976), the commoner could only turn out to common range as many head of cattle as he could feed over the winter in his own corrals. This meant that no one was allowed to increase his herd from outside with a cattle drive just for summer grazing. (This was known in Norman legal language as the rule of *levancy and couchancy*: you could only run the stock that you actually had "standing and sleeping" within winter quarters.)

The commons is the contract a people make with their local natural system. The word has an instructive history: it is formed of *ko*, "together," with (Greek) *moin*, "held in common." But the Indo-European root *mei* means basically to "move, to go, to change." This had an archaic special meaning of "exchange of goods and services within a society as regulated by custom or law." I think it might well refer back to the principle of gift economies: "the gift must always move." The root comes into Latin as *munus*, "service performed for the community" and hence "municipality."

There is a well-documented history of the commons in relation to the village economies of Europe and England. In England from the time of the Norman Conquest the enfeoffed knights and overlords began to gain control over the many local commons. Legislation (the Statute of Merton, 1235) came to their support. From the fifteenth century on the landlord class, working with urban mercantile guilds and government offices, increasingly fenced off village-held land and turned it over to private interests. The enclosure movement was backed by the big wool corporations who found profit from sheep to be much greater than that from farming. The wool business, with its exports to the Continent, was an early agribusiness that had a destructive effect on the soils and dislodged peasants. The arguments for enclosure in England—efficiency, higher production—ignored social and ecological effects and served to cripple the sustainable agriculture of some districts. The enclosure movement was stepped up again in the eighteenth century: between 1709 and 1869 almost five million acres were transferred to private ownership, one acre in every seven. After 1869 there was a sudden reversal of sentiment called the "open space movement" which ultimately halted enclosures and managed to preserve, via a spectacular lawsuit against the lords of fourteen manors, the Epping Forest.

Karl Polanyi (1975) says that the enclosures of the eighteenth century created a population of rural homeless who were forced in their desperation to become the world's first industrial working class. The enclosures were tragic both for the human community and for natural ecosystems. The fact that England now has the least forest and wildlife of all the nations of Europe has much to do with the enclosures. The takeover of commons land on the European plain also began about five hundred years ago, but one-third of Europe is still not privatized. A survival of commons practices in Swedish law allows anyone to enter private farmland to pick berries or mushrooms, to cross on foot, and to camp out of sight of the house. Most of the former commons land is now under the administration of government land agencies.

A commons model can still be seen in Japan, where there are farm villages tucked in shoestring valleys, rice growing in the *tanbo* on the bottoms, and the vegetable plots and horticulture located on the slightly higher ground. The forested hills rising high above the valleys are the commons—in Japanese called *iriai*, "joint entry." The boundary between one village and the next is often the very crests of the ridges. On the slopes of Mt. Hiei in Kyoto prefecture, north of the remote Tendai Buddhist training temples of Yokkawa, I came on men and women of Ohara village bundling up slender brush-cuttings for firewood. They were within the village land. In the innermost mountains of Japan there are forests that are beyond the reach of the use of any village. In early feudal times they were still occupied by remnant hunting peoples, perhaps Japanese-Ainu mixed-blood survivors. Later some of these wildlands were appropriated by the government and declared "Imperial Forests." Bears became extinct in England by the thirteenth century, but they are still found throughout the more remote Japanese mountains, even occasionally just north of Kyoto.

In China the management of mountain lands was left largely to the village councils—all the central government wanted was taxes. Taxes were collected in kind, and local specialties were highly prized. The demands of the capital drew down Kingfisher feathers, Musk Deer glands, Rhinoceros hides, and other exotic products of the mountains and streams, as well as rice, timber, and silk. The village councils may have resisted overexploitation of their resources, but when the edge of spreading deforestation reached their zone (the fourteenth century seems to be a turning point for the forests of heartland China), village land management crumbled. Historically, the seizure of the commons—east or west—by either the central government or entrepreneurs from the central economy has resulted in degradation of wild lands and agricultural soils. There is sometimes good reason to kill the Golden Goose: the quick profits can be reinvested elsewhere at a higher return.

In the United States, as fast as the Euro-American invaders forcefully displaced the native inhabitants from their own sorts of traditional commons, the land was opened to the new settlers. In the arid West, however, much land was never even homesteaded, let alone patented. The native people who had known and loved the white deserts and blue mountains were now scattered or enclosed on reservations, and the new inhabitants (miners and a few ranchers) had neither the values nor the knowledge to take care of the land. An enormous area was de facto public domain, and the Forest Service, the Park Service, and the Bureau of Land Management were formed to manage it. (The same sorts of land in Canada and Australia are called "Crown Lands," a reflection of the history of English rulers trying to wrest the commons from the people.)

In the contemporary American West the people who talk about a "sagebrush rebellion" might sound as though they were working for a return of commons land to local control. The truth is the sagebrush rebels have a lot yet to learn about the place—they are still relative newcomers, and their motives are not stewardship but development. Some westerners are beginning to think in long-range terms, and these don't argue for privatization but for better range management and more wilderness preservation.

The environmental history of Europe and Asia seems to indicate that the best management of commons land was that which was locally based. The ancient severe and often irreversible deforestation of the Mediterranean Basin was an extreme case of the misuse of the commons by the forces that had taken its management away from regional villages (Thirgood, 1981). The situation in America in the nineteenth and early twentieth centuries was the reverse. The truly local people, the Native Americans, were decimated and demoralized, and the new population was composed of adventurers and entrepreneurs. Without some federal presence the poachers, cattle grazers, and timber barons would have had a field day. Since about 1960 the situation has turned again: the agencies that were once charged with conservation are increasingly perceived as accomplices of the extractive industries, and local people—who are beginning to be actually local—seek help from environmental organizations and join in defense of the public lands.

Destruction extends worldwide and "encloses" local commons, local peoples. The village and tribal people who live in the tropical forests are literally bulldozed out of their homes by international logging interests in league with national governments. A well-worn fiction used in dispossessing inhabitory people is the declaration that the commonly owned tribal forests are either (1) private property or (2) public domain. When the commons are closed and the villagers must buy energy, lumber, and medicine at the company store, they are pauperized. This is one effect of what Ivan Illich calls "the 500-year war against subsistence."

So what about the so-called tragedy of the commons? This theory, as now popularly understood, seems to state that when there are open access rights to a resource, say pasturage, everyone will seek to maximize his take, and overgrazing will inevitably ensue. What Garrett Hardin and his associates are talking about should be called "the dilemma of common-pool resources." This is the problem of overexploitation of "unowned" resources by individuals or corporations that are caught in the bind of "If I don't do it the other guy will" (Hardin and Baden, 1977). Oceanic fisheries, global water cycles, the air, soil fertility—all fall into this class. When Hardin et al. try to apply their model to the historic commons it doesn't work, because they fail to note that the commons was a social institution which, historically, was never without rules and did not allow unlimited access (Cox, 1985).

In Asia and parts of Europe, villages that in some cases date back to neolithic times still oversee the commons with some sort of council. Each commons is an entity with limits, and the effects of overuse will be clear to those who depend on it. There are three possible contemporary fates for common pool resources. One is privatization, one is administration by government authority, and the third is that—when possible—they become part of a true commons, of reasonable size, managed by local inhabitory people. The third choice may no longer be possible as stated here. Locally based community or tribal (as in Alaska) landholding corporations or cooperatives seem to be surviving here and there. But operating as it seems they must in the world marketplace, they are wrestling with how to balance tradition and sustainability against financial success. The Sealaska Corporation of the Tlingit people of southeast Alaska has been severely criticized (even from within) for some of the old-growth logging it let happen.

We need to make a world-scale "Natural Contract" with the oceans, the air, the birds in the sky. The challenge is to bring the whole victimized world of "common pool resources" into the Mind of the Commons. As it stands now, any resource on earth that is not nailed down will be seen as fair game to the timber buyers or petroleum geologists from Osaka, Rotterdam, or Boston. The pressures of growing populations and the powers of entrenched (but fragile, confused, and essentially leaderless) economic systems warp the likelihood of any of us seeing clearly. Our perception of how entrenched they are may also be something of a delusion.

Sometimes it seems unlikely that a society as a whole can make wise choices. Yet there is no choice but to call for the "recovery of the commons"—and this in a modern world which doesn't quite realize what it has lost. Take back, like the night, that which is shared by all of us, that which is our larger being. There will be no "tragedy of the commons" greater than this: if we do not recover the commons—regain personal, local, community, and peoples' direct involvement in sharing (in *being*) the web of the wild world—that world will keep slipping away. Eventually our complicated industrial capitalist / socialist mixes will bring down much of the living system that supports us. And, it is clear, the loss of a local commons heralds the end of self-sufficiency and signals the doom of the vernacular culture of the region. This is still happening in the far corners of the world.

The commons is a curious and elegant social institution within which human beings once lived free political lives while weaving through natural systems. The commons is a level of organization of human society that includes the nonhuman. The level above the local commons is the bioregion. Understanding the commons and its role within the larger regional culture is one more step toward integrating ecology with economy.

BIOREGIONAL PERSPECTIVES

The Region is the elsewhere of civilization.   MAX CAFARD

The little nations of the past lived within territories that conformed to some set of natural criteria. The culture areas of the major native groups of North America overlapped, as one would expect, almost exactly with broadly defined major bioregions (Kroeber, 1947). That older human experience of a fluid, indistinct, but genuine home region was gradually replaced—across Eurasia—by the arbitrary and often violently imposed boundaries of emerging national states. These imposed borders sometimes cut across biotic areas and ethnic zones alike. Inhabitants lost ecological knowledge and community solidarity. In the old ways, the flora and fauna and landforms are *part of the culture*. The world of culture and nature, which is actual, is almost a shadow world now, and the insubstantial world of political jurisdictions and rarefied economies is what passes for reality. We live in a backwards time. We can regain some small sense of that old membership by discovering the original lineaments of our land and steering—at least in the home territory and in the mind—by those rather than the borders of arbitrary nations, states, and counties.

Regions are "interpenetrating bodies in semi-simultaneous spaces" (Cafard, 1989). Biota, watersheds, landforms, and elevations are just a few of the facets that define a region. Culture areas, in the same way, have subsets such as dialects, religions, sorts of arrow-release, types of tools, myth motifs, musical scales, art styles. One sort of regional outline would be floristic. The coastal Douglas Fir, as the definitive tree of the Pacific Northwest, is an example. (I knew it intimately as a boy growing up on a farm between Lake Washington and Puget Sound. The local people, the Snohomish, called it *lukta tciyats*, "wide needles.") Its northern limit is around the Skeena River in British Columbia. It is found west of the crest through Washington, Oregon, and northern California. The southern coastal limit of Douglas Fir is about the same as that of salmon, which do not run south of the Big Sur River. Inland it grows down the west slope of the Sierra as far south as the north fork of the San Joaquin River. That outline describes the boundary of a larger natural region that runs across three states and one international border.

The presence of this tree signifies a rainfall and a temperature range and will indicate what your agriculture might be, how steep the pitch of your roof, what raincoats you'd need. You don't have to know such details to get by in the modern cities of Portland and Bellingham. But if you do know what is taught by plants and weather, you are in on the gossip and can truly feel more at home. The sum of a field's forces becomes what we call very loosely the "spirit of the place." To know the spirit of a place is to realize that you are a part of a part and that the whole is made of parts, each of which is whole. You start with the part you are whole in.

As quixotic as these ideas may seem, they have a reservoir of strength and possibility behind them. The spring of 1984, a month after equinox, Gary Holthaus and I drove down from

Anchorage to Haines, Alaska. We went around the upper edge of the basin of the Copper River, skirted some tributaries of the Yukon, and went over Haines Summit. It was White and Black Spruce taiga all the way, still frozen up. Dropping down from the pass to saltwater at Chilkat inlet we were immediately in forests of large Sitka Spruce, Skunk Cabbage poking out in the swamps, it was spring. That's a bioregional border leap. I was honored the next day by an invitation to Raven House to have coffee with Austin Hammond and a circle of other Tlingit elders and to hear some long and deeply entwined discourses on the responsibilities of people to their places. As we looked out his front window to hanging glaciers on the peaks beyond the saltwater, Hammond spoke of empires and civilizations in metaphors of glaciers. He described how great alien forces—industrial civilization in this case—advance and retreat, and how settled people can wait it out.

Sometime in the mid-seventies at a conference of Native American leaders and activists in Bozeman, Montana, I heard a Crow elder say something similar: "You know, I think if people stay somewhere long enough—even white people—the spirits will begin to speak to them. It's the power of the spirits coming up from the land. The spirits and the old powers aren't lost, they just need people to be around long enough and the spirits will begin to influence them."

Bioregional awareness teaches us in *specific* ways. It is not enough just to "love nature" or to want to "be in harmony with Gaia." Our relation to the natural world takes place in a *place*, and it must be grounded in information and experience. For example: "real people" have an easy familiarity with the local plants. This is so unexceptional a kind of knowledge that everyone in Europe, Asia, and Africa used to take it for granted. Many contemporary Americans don't even *know* that they don't "know the plants," which is indeed a measure of alienation. Knowing a bit about the flora we could enjoy questions like: where do Alaska and Mexico meet? It would be somewhere on the north coast of California, where Canada Jay and Sitka Spruce lace together with manzanita and Blue Oak.

But instead of "northern California" let's call it Shasta Bioregion. The present state of California (the old Alta California territory) falls into at least three natural divisions, and the northern third looks, as the Douglas Fir example shows, well to the north. The boundaries of this northern third would roughly run from the Klamath/Rogue River divide south to San Francisco Bay and up the delta where the Sacramento and San Joaquin rivers join. The line would then go east to the Sierra Crest and, taking that as a distinct border, follow it north to Susanville. The watershed divide then angles broadly northeastward along the edge of the Modoc Plateau to the Warner Range and Goose Lake.

East of the divide is the Great Basin, north of Shasta is the Cascadia/Columbia region, and then farther north is what we call Ish River country, the drainages of Puget Sound and the Straits of Georgia. Why should we do this kind of visualization? Again I will say: it prepares us to begin to be at home in this landscape. There are tens of millions of people in North America who were physically born here but who are not actually living here intellectually, imaginatively, or morally. Native Americans to be sure have a prior claim to the term native. But as they love this land they will welcome the conversion of the millions of immigrant psyches into fellow "Native Americans." For the non-Native American to become at home on this continent, he or she must be *born again* in this hemisphere, on this continent, properly called Turtle Island.

That is to say, we must consciously fully accept and recognize that this is where we live and grasp the fact that our descendants will be here for millennia to come. Then we must honor this land's great antiquity—its wildness—learn it—defend it—and work to hand it on to the children (of all beings) of the future with its biodiversity and health intact. Europe or Africa or Asia will then be seen as the place our ancestors came from, places we might want to know about and to visit, but not "home." Home—deeply, spiritually—must be here. Calling this place "America" is to name it after a stranger. "Turtle Island" is the name given this continent by Native Americans based on creation mythology (Snyder, 1974). The United States, Canada, Mexico, are passing political entities; they have their legitimacies, to be sure, but they will lose their mandate if they continue to abuse the land. "The State is destroyed, but the mountains and rivers remain."

But this work is not just for the newcomers of the Western Hemisphere, Australia, Africa, or Siberia. A worldwide purification of mind is called for: the exercise of seeing the surface of the planet for what it is—by nature. With this kind of consciousness people turn up at hearings and in front of trucks and bulldozers to defend the land or trees. Showing solidarity with a region! What an odd idea at first. Bioregionalism is the entry of place into the dialectic of history. Also we might say that there are "classes" which have so far been overlooked—the animals, rivers, rocks, and grasses—now entering history.

These ideas provoke predictable and usually uninformed reactions. People fear the small society and the critique of the State. It is difficult to see, when one has been raised under it, that it is the State itself which is inherently greedy, destabilizing, entropic, disorderly, and illegitimate. They cite parochialism, regional strife, "unacceptable" expressions of cultural diversity, and so forth. Our philosophies, world religions, and histories are biased toward uniformity, universality, and centralization—in a word, the ideology of monotheism. Certainly under specific conditions neighboring groups have wrangled for centuries—interminable memories and hostilities cooking away like radioactive waste. It's still at work in the Middle East. The ongoing ethnic and political miseries of parts of Europe and the Middle East sometimes go back as far as the Roman Empire. This is not something that can be attributed to the combativeness of "human nature" per se. Before the expansion of early empires the occasional strife of tribes and natural nations was almost familial. With the rise of the State, the scale of the destructiveness and malevolence of warfare makes a huge leap.

In the times when people did not have much accumulated surplus, there was no big temptation to move in on other regions. I'll give an example from my own part of the world. (I describe my location as: on the western slope of the northern Sierra Nevada, in the Yuba River watershed, north of the south fork at the three-thousand-foot elevation, in a community of Black Oak, Incense Cedar, Madrone, Douglas Fir, and Ponderosa Pine.) The western slope of the Sierra Nevada has winter rain and snowfall and a different set of plants from the dry eastern slope. In pre-white times, the native people living across the range had little temptation to venture over, because their skills were specific to their own area, and they could go hungry in an unfamiliar biome. It takes a long education to know the edible plants, where to find them, and how to prepare them. So the Washo of the Sierra east side traded their pine nuts and obsidian for the acorns, yew bows, and abalone shells of the Miwok and Maidu to the west. The two sides met and camped together for weeks in the summer Sierra meadows, their joint commons. (Dedicated raiding cultures, "barbarians," evolve as a response to nearby civilizations and their riches. Genghis Khan, at an audience in his yurt near Lake Baikal, was reported to have said: "Heaven is exasperated with the decadence and luxury of China.")

There are numerous examples of relatively peaceful small-culture coexistence all over the world. There have always been multilingual persons peacefully trading and traveling across large areas. Differences were often eased by shared spiritual perspectives or ceremonial institutions and by the multitude of myths and tales that cross language barriers. What about the deep divisions caused by religion? It must be said that most religious exclusiveness is the odd specialty of the Judeo/Christian/Islamic faith, which is a recent and (overall) minority development in the world. Asian religion, and the whole world of folk religion, animism, and shamanism, appreciates or at least tolerates diversity. (It seems that the really serious cultural disputes are caused by different tastes in food. When I was chokersetting in eastern Oregon, one of my crew was a Wasco man whose wife was a Chehalis woman from the west side. He told me that when they got in fights she would call him a "goddamn grasshopper eater" and he'd shout back "fish eater"!)

Cultural pluralism and multilingualism are the planetary norm. We seek the balance between cosmopolitan pluralism and deep local consciousness. We are asking how the whole human race can regain self-determination in place after centuries of having been disenfranchised by hierarchy and/or centralized power. Do not confuse this exercise with "nationalism," which is exactly the opposite, the impostor, the puppet of the State, the grinning ghost of the lost community.

So this is one sort of start. The bioregional movement is not just a rural program: it is as much for the restoration of urban neighborhood life and the greening of the cities. All of us are fluently moving in multiple realms that include irrigation districts, solid-waste management jurisdictions, long-distance area code zones, and such. Planet Drum Foundation, based in the San Francisco Bay Area, works with many other local groups for the regeneration of the city as a living place, with projects like the identification and restoration of urban creeks (Berg and others, 1989). There are groups worldwide working with Third and Fourth World people revisualizing territories and playfully finding appropriate names for their newly realized old regions (*Raise the Stakes*, 1987). Many bioregional congresses have since been held on Turtle Island.

As sure as impermanence, the nations of the world will eventually be more sensitively defined and the lineaments of the blue earth will begin to reshape the politics. The requirements of sustainable economies, ecologically sensitive agriculture, strong and vivid community life, wild habitat—and the second law of thermodynamics—all lead this way. I also realize that right now this is a kind of theater as much as it is ecological politics. Not just street theater, but visionary mountain, field, and stream theater. As Jim Dodge says: "The chances of bioregionalism succeeding . . . are beside the point. If one person, or a few, or a community of people, live more fulfilling lives from bioregional practice, then it's successful." May it all speed the further deconstruction of the superpowers. As "The Surre(gion)alist Manifesto" says:

> Regional politics do not take place in Washington, Moscow, and other "seats of power." Regional power does not "sit"; it flows everywhere. Through watersheds and bloodstreams. Through nervous systems and food chains. The regions are everywhere & nowhere. We are all illegals. We are natives and we are restless. We have no country; we live in the country. We are off the Inter-State. The Region is against the Regime—any Regime. Regions are anarchic. (Cafard, 1989)

FINDING "NISENAN COUNTY"

Burt Hybart retired from driving dump truck, backhoe, grader, and Cat after many years. Roads, ponds, and pads were his sculpture, shapes that will be left on the land long after the houses have vanished. (How long for a pond to silt up?) Burt still witched wells, though. The last time I saw him he was complaining about his lungs: "Dust boiling up behind the Cat you couldn't see from here to there, those days. When I worked on the Coast. And the diesel fumes."

Some of us went for a walk in the Warner Range. It's in the far northeast corner of California, the real watershed boundary between the headwaters of the Pit River and the *nors* of the Great Basin. From the nine-thousand-foot scarp's high points you can see into Oregon, Goose Lake, and up the west side of the Warners to the north end of Surprise Valley. Dry desert hills to the east.

Desert mountain range. A touch of Rocky Montain flora here that leapfrogs over desert basins via the Steens Mountains of southeastern Oregon, the Blue Mountains, and maybe the Wallowas. Cattle are brought up from Eagleville on the east side, a town out of the 1880s. The proprietor of the Eagleville Bar told how the sheepherders move their flocks from Lovelock, Nevada, in early March, heading toward the Warners, the ewes lambing as they go. In late June they arrive at the foot of the range and move the sheep up to the eight-thousand-foot meadows on the west side. In September the flocks go down to Madeline—the lambs right onto the meat trucks. Then the ewes' long truck ride back to Lovelock for the winter. We find the flock in the miles-long meadow heavens of Mule-ear flowers. The sheep business is Basque-run on all levels. Old aspen grove along the trail with sheepherder inscriptions and designs in the bark, some dated from the 1890s.

Patterson Lake is the gem of the Warners, filling an old cirque below the cliffs of the highest peak. The many little ledges of the cliffs are home to hawks. Young raptors sit solemnly by their nests. Mt. Shasta dominates the western view, a hub to these vast miles of Lodgepole and Jeffrey Pine, lava rock, hayfield ribbons, rivers that sink underground. Ha! This is the highest end of what we call "upriver"—and close to where it drains both ways, one side of the plateau tipping toward the Klamath River, the other to the Pit and the Sacramento.

Mt. Shasta visible for so far—from the Coast Range, from Sierra Buttes down by Downieville—it gleams across the headwaters of all of northern California.

Old John Hold used to walk up a streambed talking to it: "So that's what you've been up to!" Reading the geology, the wash and lay of the heavy metal that sinks below the sand, never tarnishing or rusting—gold. The new-style miners come and go here, too. For a while St. Joseph Minerals was exploring the "diggings," the tertiary gravels. The county supervisors finally approved the EIR and the exploratory drilling began, and they said they'd come back in eighteen months with their big proposal. For a while there was a little tower and a trailer lost in the gravel canyons and ridges that were left from the days of hydraulicking. The diggings returned to being the playground of quads and off-road motorcycles, and then another outfit, Siskon Gold, came and fenced along the single gravel road. Siskon went bankrupt, and again the diggings sit there, manzanita, natural bonsai pine, and gravel in the moonlight: waiting whatever fate comes next.

Two old gents in the Sacramento Greyhound station. I'm next to an elder who swings his cane back and forth, lightly, the tip pivoting on the ground—and he looks about the room, back and forth, without much focus. He has egg on his chin. A smell of old urine comes from him, blows my way, time to time. Another elder walks past and out. He's very neat: a plastic-wrapped waterproof blanket-roll slung on his shoulder, a felt hat, a white chin beard like an Amish. Red bandanna tied round his neck, bib overalls. Under the overall bottoms peep out more trousers, maybe suit pants. So that's how he keeps warm, and keeps some clothes clean! Back in my traveling days men said, "Yeah, spend the winter in Sac."

I caught the bus on down to Oakland. In Berkeley, on the wall of the Lucas Books building, is a mural that shows a cross section of Alta California from the Northwest Coast to the Mojave Desert. I walked backward through the parking lot to get a look at it whole, sea lions, coyote, redtail hawk, creosote bush. Then noticed a man at one corner of it, touching it up.

Talked to him, he is Lou Silva, who did the painting. He was redoing a mouse, and he said he comes back from time to time to put in more tiny fauna.

San Juan Ridge lies between the middle and south forks of the Yuba River in a political entity called Nevada County. New settlers have been coming in here since the late sixties. The Sierra counties are a mess: a string of them lap over the mountain crest, and the roads between the two sides are often closed in winter. A sensible redrawing of lines here would put eastern Sierra, eastern Nevada, and eastern Placer counties together in a new "Truckee River County" and the seat could be in Truckee. Western Placer and western Nevada counties south of the south fork of the Yuba would make a good new county. Western Sierra County plus a bit of Yuba County and northern Nevada County put together would fit into the watershed of the three forks of the Yuba. I would call it "Nisenan County" after the native people who lived here. Most of them were killed or driven away by the gold rush miners.

People live on the ridges because the valleys are rocky or brushy and have no level bottoms. In the Sierra Nevada a good human habitat is not a valley bottom, but a wide gentle *ridge* between canyons.

Tawny Grammar

THE SAME OLD SONG AND DANCE

I WAS standing outside the wood-frame community hall of the newly built St. Johns Woods housing project in Portland, Oregon, on a Saturday summer eve, 1943. It pulsed, glowed, and wailed like a huge jellyfish—there was a dance going on. Most of the people who had come to live in St. Johns Woods were working in the shipyards, but there were a few servicemen home on leave, and a lot of teenagers from the high school. Most of them were from the Midwest or the South. I was from farther north, up by Puget Sound, and had never heard people speak southern before. I hung around and finally got up my nerve to go in and listen to the live band play swing and jitterbug. At some point they were playing the Andrews Sisters song "Drinking Rum and Coca Cola." A girl from St. Johns high school saw me. I was a smallish thirteen-year-old freshman and she was a large gentle woman of a girl who (for what reason I'll never know) relentlessly drew me out on the floor and got me to dance with her.

I had no social confidence or experience. My usual pastimes were watching the migratory waterfowl in the sloughs along the Columbia River or sewing moccasins. The war and its new jobs had brought my family off the farm and into the city. I was first exhilarated and then terrified: as I reached around this half-known girl—taller than I—I could feel her full breasts against my ribs. My hand settled into the unfamiliar triangle at the base of her broad back and I smelled her sweet and physical odor. I was almost overpowered by the intuition of sexuality, womanliness, the differences of bodies. I had never danced before, never held a woman. I could barely get my breath. She simply kept me moving, swinging, swaying, with infinite patience, and as I got my breath back I knew I was, now, dancing. I exulted then, knowing I could do it. It was "our era, our dance, our song." I didn't dance with her again, she was soon gone with an older boy. But she had given me entry to the dance, and I had with astonishing luck passed a barrier of fear and trembling before the warmth of a grown woman. I had been in on adult society and its moment.

Each dance and its music belong to a time and place. It can be borrowed elsewhere, or later in time, but it will never be in its moment again. When these little cultural blooms are past, they become ethnic or nostalgic, but never quite fully present—manifesting the web of their original connections and meanings—again.

Maize, rice, reindeer, sweet potato—these indicate places and cultures. As plants they stand for the soil and rainfall, and as food sources they reflect society and its productive arrangements. Another indicator is the local "song and dance." The occasion of singers, musicians, storytellers, mask makers, and dancers joining together is the flower of daily life. Not only the human is danced, but raven, deer, cow, and rainstorm make their appearance. The dance enables us to present our many human and nonhuman selves to each other, and to the place. The place is offered to itself. Art and economics are both matters of gift-exchange and the dance-offering in particular has been a proper sort of trade for the taking of fruits, grain, or game. Such giving also helps us overcome our tendencies toward stinginess and arrogance.

Every traditional culture has its dance. The young people who come to the study of dance bring their peerless perennial grace and power. They must learn to count rhythm, memorize the chants, identify certain plants, observe the seasons, absorb the gestures of animals, and to move as timely as a falcon on a stoop. Thus they are borne by their culture to become culture-bearers. The yoga of dance (as the great Bharat Natyam performer and teacher Balasaraswati called it) can be one of the paths to self-realization.

But that's only the spiritual side of it. The middle or main part is the perpetual reincarnation of a sacramental sense of the world, and dance carries that forward. It's true that many people today do not quite have their own song and dance. Current music is too much a commodity, too much in flux, it cannot dye us. We are not quite sure what our home music is. When men drink together in Japan, at a certain point in the evening they begin to take turns singing the folksongs of their home provinces. When the American in the group is called on, he has a hard time knowing what to sing. (I used to sing the quintessential ballad of Puget Sound, "Acres of Clams.")

Because dance clearly has such cultural and religious significance it often comes under attack from the administrators for imperialist powers—or fundamentalist preachers or ayatollahs. When missionaries went into Inupiaq Eskimo territory—on the Alaskan coast of the Bering and Chukchi seas, and the northern coast of Alaska—in the last years of the nineteenth century, one of the first things they banned was dance. People there today still hunt, fish, sew mukluks, make birchbark containers, but there is no dance. A bit farther south on the Bering Sea coast is Yu'pik Eskimo territory. Some of the Yu'pik villages were missioned by the Russian Orthodox church, which did not ban dance. A dance revival has been going on in those villages—an invigorating cultural renaissance which is taking them away from TV sets and back to the community hall to rehearse and perform.

In Hawai'i the political renaissance of native culture has two strong cultural poles: a renewal of interest in the traditional techniques of taro-growing and ancient or "*kahiku*" hula. The hula teachers with their schools, called *halau*, accept students of all races but they insist that the students master Hawai'ian-language dance terminology. Students must memorize the oral epics in Hawai'ian, make their own costumes, and learn how to make offerings to Laka, Goddess of Dance. Its multicultural openness makes it possible for newcomers to have an entry into the traditional Hawai'ian sense of the islands.

Bharat Natyam, the dance of South India, is a confluence of archaic folk tradition, court patronage, northern-derived religious devotionalism, professional temple dance-offering, and twentieth-century cultural revival. The tradition has exceptionally high standards—the music alone is a lifetime study, the categories and qualities of gesture and expression are another study, and the accompanying drumming is a specialty of its own. The myth-derived narratives chanted to accompany certain dances evoke a vast and timeless cosmos. I didn't know all this when I first saw Padma Bhushan Shrimati Balasaraswati in a Bharat Natyam performance in Jaipur, India, in March of 1962. It was storming. We sat on the ground under a circus tent shaking in the wind, and then it began to rain in warm torrents and half the people left. The performance went on. I saw Bala act out, dance out, that moment when Krishna's mother—trying to remove the clod of dirt he's teething on from his baby mouth—looks in and sees not dirt but the depths of the whole universe and all its stars. She straightens up, backs away, in divine awe. To music. (This was Krishna's mischief on his mother.) My hair stood up.

I followed Bala to Bombay to watch her again, and was invited to a private late-night concert in an apartment. I asked Bala, "When you move in your dance to the point where you look into Krishna's mouth, are you already visualizing stars?" She laughed sardonically and said: "Of course not. I must start with dirt. It must become stars. Sometimes all I see is dirt, and the dance fails. That night it was stars."

Back on the west coast of North America ten years later we discovered that Balasaraswati—"Baby Saraswati" (Saraswati the goddess is the partner of Brahma and patron of poetry, music, and learning)—would be teaching classes in Berkeley. We connected with her, and I learned more about her tradition. Under English rule Bharat Natyam had been made virtually illegal because some of the dancers had served as Devadasis, "Servants of the God." These were young women who had been apprenticed to the Hindu temples in childhood to learn the dance. Their main role was in the presentation of daily dance-offerings in the inner shrine. An occasional part of the service to Shiva was to make love with very wealthy temple patrons. It is said that when they left temple service they made good marriages. The new laws totally forbade women to dance in Hindu temples.

Balasaraswati and her circle struggled to return Bharat Natyam to a position of respect within Indian society. The puritanized South Indian conservatives feared the erotic component, which Bala defended, purified, and resanctified. She was a yogini of dance. After a precocious start as a seventeen-year-old performer, she had a dark time for several years. It became her deep wish to dance before Shiva, known in the south as Murugan, in the temple of Tiruttani. She bribed the watchman, entered the inner chamber late at night, and danced alone in the shrine-room. She says she offered herself and her art to Shiva and to the world that night. Bala made a name for herself first in India and then in Europe and America. She traced the upturn in her fortunes to that dance within the shrine.

In Bala's repertoire was a folk dance that completed the loop from cosmic myth to village life. In South India the adolescents are charged with keeping parrots out of the ripening crops. The bird-chasing work is known as an occasion for trysting. The dancer sings and strolls forward and back through the gardens, waving a stick, startling up flocks of birds, to an old Telugu folksong chorus. The crops, the soil, the parrots, the work, the dance, and young love all come together. Much of the vernacular culture of South India is compressed into this one little performance.

THE KUUVANGMIUT AND THE HUMANITIES

The Safeway store in Fairbanks, Alaska, stays open twenty-four hours a day, summer or winter. Virtually all the food in the stores of Alaska is flown in. We were shopping at 2 A.M., the second week of April, buying pineapples, mangoes, broccoli, and kiwi to take as gifts to friends in the Inupiaq villages of Shungnak and Kobuk. Next morning early Steve Grubis and I helped Tom George fuel his Cessna 182 and back it out and across the dirt road and onto the airstrip across from his place at China Marina. We flew north across the Yukon River and then west, along the southern edge of the Brooks Range and down the broad basin of the Kobuk River, which drains into the Chukchi Sea. It was all under snow. I had been reading about the archaeological site at "Onion Portage," so our scholarly pilot flew an extra twenty miles downstream to swing over a big oxbow in the river. As the plane turned on its side, looking straight down I got a glimpse of this 15,000-year-old campsite and homesite that possibly hosted people who had come walking the land bridge from Siberia. The Kobuk River valley has never been under glacier ice. There's a pre-Pleistocene sagebrush, *Artemisia borealis*, and a legume, *Oxytropis kobukensis*, that grow here and nowhere else in the world.

The plane turned back upriver and glided over a solitary moose. We landed on the snowy strip at Kobuk on wheels, not skis. I was there to meet some schoolteachers and native leaders to exchange thoughts on what the role of occidental myth, folklore, poetry, and philosophy might be for the rising generation in the villages. Steve Grubis and I had worked over these questions before. He is with the cross-cultural orientation program at the University of Alaska, and he had old connections along the Kobuk River too. Some twenty years earlier he had been running the river on a log raft which was destroyed in a rapids, and with great travail over several weeks he had made his way downstream to Kobuk village where he was generously fed, clothed, and rested. Steve was also friends with Hans and Bonnie Boenish, who taught the school in Kobuk and were going to put us up. It was a few hundred yards' walk to the village. A snowmobile pulling the mail sled accompanied us. The sun was bright on the red and yellow kids' clothes hanging on the clotheslines, frozen stiff. The tethered sled dogs set up a happy racket, and some children were just going back up the steps of the modular metal classroom from an outdoor play recess. The school thermometer said ten below zero. The modular classroom, up on piers, looked a world apart from the low log cabins each with its log meat-cache on stilts and a woodsmoke plume rising straight up from each chimney.

As remote as the upper Kobuk River is, accessible only by plane or dogsled in winter and barely accessible by boat coming upriver in the brief summer, there is a mine nearby. The area is called Bornite and it is supposed to contain some of the largest copper deposits in the world. Roads and railroads have been surveyed, and company research on logistics has been going on for many years. The Kobuk people, "Kuuvangmiut" in Inupiaq, are still very much involved in the subsistence economy. Many get government aid, but they all depend on fishing (dog salmon, whitefish, blackfish, grayling, shee) and the essential caribou hunt. In season there is duck soup. Some run traplines. Everyone picks quantities of blueberries in the fall—lots of tricks to picking, preparing, and keeping the blueberries, *asriaviich.*

Mining, when and if it comes, will bring great changes to their economic and social life and they know it. So Hans, Bonnie, Steve, and I were soon engaged in the perennial discussion of what a useful schooling would be. Hans and Bonnie have been there for several years and Hans has his own sleds and team. They have a deep respect and concern for their Kuuvangmiut neighbors and employers.

We were speaking as outsiders, of course. We could agree that it might be wise to schedule school so that the students could be released at crucial times in the cycle of the year and learn subsistence skills from their parents and elders. This might enable them to maintain a sustainable and relatively autonomous economy into the twenty-first century. The village people I talked to were divided: some wanted traditional skills to be maintained while others felt that it was too late and their children should be getting an education that would work for them as well in Los Angeles as in Alaska. "Traditional skills" does not simply mean staying with pre-contact technology, of course—modern tools and machines are very practical and are at work in the service of native peoples all over the north, helping them to live in place. An updated subsistence economy in the circumpolar arctic is quite feasible. But there is also a strong likelihood that tastes and appetites for commercial goods and the need for more cash would tempt the next generation to choose the role of wage-earners in a mining economy.

So these children should prepare to be mining engineers? The company will bring its own experts with it. Heavy equipment operator? Maybe. Computers? Computers are in all the schools of the Far North, along with video cameras. There may be more computer literacy in the schools of northwest Alaska than in those of Los Angeles. Even so, there is no guarantee that any school anywhere in the whole world can give a child an education which will be of practical use in twenty years. So much is changing so fast—except, perhaps, caribou migrations and the berry ripening.

The native people of northwest Alaska have been intent on clarifying their own value system in recent years. This effort is called the "Inupiaq spirit movement"—the revival of Inupiaq spirit. On the wall of the classroom of the Kobuk school was a poster-sized list of "Inupiaq values":

                    HUMOR
                    SHARING
                    HUMILITY
                   HARD WORK
                  SPIRITUALITY
                  COOPERATION
                  FAMILY ROLES
                 AVOID CONFLICT
                 HUNTER SUCCESS
                 DOMESTIC SKILLS
                LOVE FOR CHILDREN
                RESPECT FOR NATURE
                RESPECT FOR OTHERS
                RESPECT FOR ELDERS
              RESPONSIBILITY FOR TRIBE
              KNOWLEDGE OF LANGUAGE
              KNOWLEDGE OF FAMILY TREE

These warm and workable values are full of "grandmother wisdom," the fundamental all-time values of our species. Given a little stretching here and there, they'd work anywhere. What's lacking maybe is a clear articulation of what values apply to difficult or different neighbors—the concern is for conditions within the Inupiaq family, not for how to get along with outsiders.

People today are caught between the remnants of the ongoing "grandmother wisdom" of the peoples of the world (within which I include several of the Ten Commandments and the first five of the Ten Great Buddhist Precepts) and the codes that serve centralization and hierarchy. Children grow up hearing contradictory teachings: one for getting what's yours, another for being decent. The classroom teacher, who must keep state and church separate, can only present the middle ground, the liberal humanistic philosophy that comes out of "the university." It's a kind of thinking that starts (for the Occident) with the Greek effort to probe the literal truth of myth by testing stories and theories against experience. The early philosophers were making people aware of the faculty of reason and the possibility of objectivity. The philosopher is required to conduct the discussion with both hands on the table, and cannot require that you ingest a drug, eat a special diet, or follow any out-of-the-way regimen (other than intelligent reflection) to follow the argument. I'd say this was a needed corrective in some cases. A kind of intellectual clarity could thus be accomplished without necessarily discarding myth. Keeping myth alive requires a lively appreciation of the depths of metaphor, of ceremony, and the need for stories. Allegorizing and rationalizing myth kills it. That's what happened later in Greek history.

Still, the fifth-century Greeks did not invent the critical attitude. Myth, drama, *and* community discussion and intellectual argument are virtually universal. What the Greeks did do was exteriorize their intellectual life, make it convivial and explicit, define consistency in thinking, and publicly enjoy it. They saw an active and articulate intellectual stance as both modish and practical, sharpening and refining their ability to fulfill the obligations of citizenship in a society where clear and convincing argument counted for much. The give and take of their friendships and schools laid the groundwork for a continuing attitude of study that became in time textual and archival. But a practical and analytical intelligence does not necessarily require formal dialectics. Early pottery and the kiln, early metallurgy, the elegantly designed kayak and umiak, the navigation of the Melanesians, are all the end products of accurate and practical thinking.

People who already have all the answers argue that the humanistic stance lacks moral decisiveness. There are always some who think that judgments must come down hard. In the thought of India, the world is said to be a matter of many viewpoints—*darshan* (view)—each of which appears convincingly complete and self-contained to the one who is within it. One Buddhist system resolved to have "no particular view" and to practice a sublimely detached objectivity. Even so this school of thought—Madhyamika—did not swerve from accepting the first precept, *ahimsa*, nonharming. (This precept is implied in the Inupiaq list under the headings of humility, cooperation, sharing, and respect for nature.) There is no place in the philosopher's enterprise where greed and hatred are given any kind of support or approval. It's also clear that the humanist is not necessarily an agnostic. Socrates' last act was to ask that his promised offering to the spirit realm be carried out: "I owe a cock to Asclepius." The philosopher might despise mystification, but will respect the mysteries.

By April the arctic days are already pretty long. It was still a kind of twilight at 11 P.M. when the conversation wound down, with the sun just under the northern horizon. The next morning Steve and I borrowed a sno-go and went off over snowdrifts and crust through the open White Spruce tundra and muskeg toward the mountains and the mines at Bornite. There's a low pass and just over that we came on the shut-up wooden tower and sheds of an old copper mine. Cables, rope, and chain drooped from spikes on the board walls, the Schwatka Range mountains hovered to the north in an ice crystal haze. We walked around the mine buildings in the snow, then returned back down the sno-go trail with a great view across the wide basin and its frozen clusters of trees. Sub-boreal taiga: White Spruce, Black Spruce and treeless bogs, willow and birch. In two more weeks, one of the men had said, the ducks might be back.

When Steve Grubis stumbled half-dead into Kobuk twenty years before, he was taken in and befriended by the postmaster, Guy Moyers. We walked over to visit Guy, who would be in his eighties. He was still the postmaster and the post office was the front room of his little house. Linoleum floor, new iron wood-burning range, a desk of shelves, and scales for mail. A black-haired infant in a springy toddler swing was hanging and jouncing by the stove. "My granddaughter," he said. A teenager entered behind us, just out of school, and he introduced Wanda, another granddaughter. Wanda went into a tiny room screened by a blanket and turned on a tape of the music that young people play from the tropics to Greenland. Guy's wife was working kneeling on the floor by the stove. She was fleshing a piece of hide with a scraper made from sharpened steel pipe. She smiled and introduced herself as Faith. One wall was lined with shelves of stitched, bent, folded, birchbark baskets, a craft of this region.

Guy only vaguely remembered Steve, but that did not slow our conversation as we drank coffee. Guy said he came here by accident: he was let off at the wrong lake by a plane fifty years ago. He found his way to Kobuk and has been here ever since. A photo on the wall of Guy and his wife when they were newly married: her fine strong-boned features, a beautiful smiling young Inupiaq woman, and Guy a handsome young man with all his hair. "I was born here seventy-two years ago," she said. "I've stayed here."

Suppose I was a teacher at Kobuk or Shungnak, I thought, and had to teach the culture and history of this civilization that is moving in on them. Maybe we would read Shakespeare, some Homer, one of Plato's dialogues. (They are already well versed in Protestant Christianity.) "This is what they valued century after century," I'd have to say. And then they would live to see a mining operation open up nearby. The day-by-day procedures and attitudes of businessmen and engineers reflect little of anybody's supposed Western Culture. The experience of contradictions, like taking little doses of poison, would prepare them to survive in a tricky pluralistic society. Could they keep alive a glimmer of respect for the Greek accounts of long after-dinner debates between articulate friends? And also remember their own tales of god-animals forming relationships with human men and women? And should not the teachers uncover the greed and corruption of successive empires, veiled behind art and philosophy? Sitting through such conversations in log cabins in Alaska helped me understand what my own boys and the sons and daughters of my neighbors on San Juan Ridge in California are up against. It seems as though everything except mathematics and linguistics—and myth—will become obsolete.

American society (like any other) has its own set of unquestioned assumptions. It still maintains a largely uncritical faith in the notion of continually unfolding progress. It cleaves to the idea that there can be unblemished scientific objectivity. And most fundamentally it operates under the delusion that we are each a kind of "solitary knower"—that we exist as rootless intelligences without layers of localized contexts. Just a "self" and the "world." In this there is no real recognition that grandparents, place, grammar, pets, friends, lovers, children, tools, the poems and songs we remember, are what we *think with*. Such a solitary mind—if it could exist—would be a boring prisoner of abstractions. *With no surroundings there can be no path, and with no path one cannot become free.* No wonder the parents of the Eskimo children of the whole Kotzebue Basin posted the "Inupiaq Values" in their schools.

The poor literati, I was thinking. Have philosophers and writers and such always been ineffectual bystanders while the energetic power-players of church, state, and market run the show? In the shorter time scale, this is true. Measured in centuries and millennia, it can be seen that philosophy is always entwined with myth as both explicator and critic and that the fundamental myth to which a people subscribe moves at glacial speed but is almost implacable. Deep myths change on something like the order of linguistic drift: the social forces of any given time can attempt to manipulate and shape language usages for a while, as the French Academy does for French, trying to stave off English loanwords. Eventually languages return to their own inexplicable directions.

The same is true of the larger outline of world philosophies. We (who stand aside) stand on the lateral moraine of the glacier eased along by Newton and Descartes. The revivified Goddess Gaia glacier is coming down another valley, from our distant pagan past, and another arm of ice is sliding in from another angle: the no-nonsense meditation view of Buddhism with its emphasis on compassion and insight in an empty universe. Someday they will probably all converge, and yet carry (like the magnificent Baltoro glacier in the Karakoram) streaks on each section that testify to their place of origin. Some historians would say that "thinkers" are behind the ideas and mythologies that people live by. I think it also goes back to maize, reindeer, squash, sweet potatoes, and rice. And their songs.

It is appropriate to feel loyalty to a given glacier; it is advisable to investigate the whole water cycle; and it is rare and marvelous to know that glaciers do not always flow and that mountains are constantly walking.

My own grandparents certainly didn't tell us stories around the campfire before we went to sleep. Their house had an oil furnace instead, and a small library. (My grandfather did once say to me: "Read Marx!") So the people of civilization read books. For some centuries the "library" and the "university" have been our repository of lore. In this huge old occidental culture our teaching elders are books. *Books are our grandparents!* This charming thought came to me while riding John Cooper's dogsled from Kobuk to Shungnak down the Kobuk River ice and up the banks and bluffs, cutting across the portages. My nose, toes, and fingers were numb. The creaking of the rawhide thongs that bind the sled and give it flex, the gamelan-like complex pattering of dog feet running out of step, and the swish of snow. The dogs panting, happy, bright-eyed, breath steaming, we were coasting on the energy of the wolf-dog joy to run in packs—to run and run.

The library looks a little more interesting in this light. Useful, demanding, and friendly elders are available to us—I think of Bartolomé de las Casas, Baruch Spinoza, Henry David Thoreau. I always liked libraries: they were warm and stayed open late.

Arriving at Shungnak, crossing the river ice, we were greeted by boys who shouted the names of each of John's dogs—he had raced in the Iditarod the previous year and was a local hero. Hans and Bonnie Boenish came up behind us with another sled and team. We took the dogs out of their traces and chained them each to their own little house, then boiled up frozen whitefish to a stew in a 55-gallon oil drum cookpot outside over a spruce fire. (I there recalled watching Hawai'ians boiling drums of taro to feed the pigs.) Serving a dollop of fish stew to each dog in his or her own metal bowl, I found myself chanting the Zen hall meal verses to myself. I was the server. It was like being back home at Ring of Bone Zendo at mealtime—

> Fish Stew is effective in ten ways
> To aid the dogs that pull sleds
> No limit to the good results
> Consummating eternal frolicking!

The sled dogs sung along to the *gatha* in an unstructured chorus of sweet mournful howls.

We walked over to our hosts—the teachers, Bob and Cora McGuire, in their little house below the bluff and on the beach of the frozen Kobuk River. It must have been about zero degrees, but the McGuire girls, Jennifer and Arlene, were playing in the thin sunshine.

Inside the house the oil-burning cook range was kept on low and the wood stove was always going. With long underwear, and wool halibut shirts over our sweaters, we all stayed warm enough. Red plastic containers full of water had been carried down the hill from the school. They were kept in the kitchen so they wouldn't freeze. Over coffee the stories went on—Bob has been teaching for many years. A while back he left the north for a year to study remote schools around the world. Cora is also a teacher and her people are Athapaskan. Bob and Cora met at the university.

"If we actually tried to teach the values of western civilization, we'd just be peddling the ideology of individualism, of human uniqueness, special human dignity, the boundless potential of Man, and the glory of success," I said, giving it another look. Isn't that finally the Oil Pipeline philosophy? ("Jewish Inwardness—Greek Narcissism—Christian Domination" is how Doug Peacock the Grizzly Bear scholar puts it.) After Protestantism, capitalism, and world conquest, maybe that's still what occidental culture comes to.

But it wasn't that way when Greek learning made its way back into history. From the standpoint of the lively Italian minds of the fifteenth and sixteenth centuries the message of the Greek texts was that human beings are freely intelligent, imaginative, physical, bold, and beautiful. "Pagan." "Poetic." Maybe not so great an inflation of the human race (except in the eyes of the church) but a rediscovery of secular culture and of human beings as natural beings in a natural world. At any rate, an excited and deep study of antiquity—as occidental thinkers have gone through several times over—is akin to an apprenticeship with traditional elders. The freshness of the Renaissance slid into the stuffy Latin, Language, and Culture curriculum of the European middle classes. The fascination with personality and possibility got lost in authoritarianism and smugness.

For the children's teachers—native or white—the opportunity to teach a little history, philosophy, or literature is welcome, whatever culture it comes from. The rural school teachers that I have met in the north willingly arrange for tribal elders to come to classes and strongly support the teaching of traditional culture. Some village leaders said they have come to sense that we are all in the same boat—occidental culture, with its punky advanced capitalism and conky socialism, as well as the ragtag remnants of the great paleolithic hunting and gathering dignities.

Maybe the humanists of Europe were not exactly on the side of the power elites. Superficially they served urban masters, but their "project," whether they clearly knew it or not, was at bottom a defense of the vernacular—because to think clearly we must avoid narrow interests or entrenched opinions, and village values are in implicit opposition to the special interests of corporations or capital or traders or centralized religious bureaucracies and other such institutions. Being regional, being in place, has its own sort of bias, but it cannot be too inflated because it is rooted in the inviolable processes of the natural world.

Philosophy is thus a place-based exercise. It comes from the body and the heart and is checked against shared experience. (Grandmother wisdom suspects the men who stay too long talking in the longhouse when they should be mending nets or something. They are up to trouble—inventing the State, most likely.) We make a full circle in acknowledging that it is necessary to pay attention to the village elders and also to the wise elders of the Occident who have been miraculously preserved through the somewhat fragile institution of the library.

I gave a poetry reading at the Kobuk school one night. That's when John Cooper first turned up. He had driven his dogs forty miles south from his cabin on the Ambler River to hear some poems. The word was out on the two-way radio. It set all the dogs in the world barking when his team glided in. I had met John at Colorado State in the early seventies when he was studying Range Management and becoming a wilderness defender. The audience was local native people and a few white teachers—many of whom had never heard poetry read aloud before. Later that evening we talked of the singer-drummers who accompanied the dancers and the similarity of their role to the work of poets. An Inupiaq couple who had also come in from outside the village for the reading commented on the antiquity of myth. Our ancestors, they said, told the same stories as the Greeks, and the people in India, and the rest of Native America. *We all had a classical culture.*

There were questions about the civilizations of the Far East, and I loaned a copy of Lao-zi's *Dao De Jing* to a thoughtful woman leader who was active in both native culture and the church. Two days later over coffee she returned it saying, "Old. That book's really wise and old. I didn't know the Chinese went back so far." I asked her about her involvement with the church, because I knew her also to be very strong on Inupiaq spirit revival. "It's nice to be part of something international too," she said. "I didn't know in those days about China or India and their thought. But because I'm in the church I have friends all over, and people I see when I go to Seattle."

Steve and I left Shungnak very early one morning. We rode on a couple of sno-gos to the strip, two ravens hopped around a dog sleeping on the snow, frosty air swept back to Old Man Mountain and even farther to the notch in the hills where the track goes to Bornite. There had been a basketball game at the school the previous night, and the girls of the village had come up to see the out-of-town team off. Two hung on the wings of the Ambler Airlines plane, crying and sobbing for their new boyfriends, as some slightly older girls scolded them for being uncool. Aboard the plane there was another team, headed for a game in Fairbanks, all girls—the "Ambler Grizzlyettes." As long as the price of oil stayed up in Alaska, the bush airlines could cover their nut on high school basketball.

> "Prudhoe Bay," John Cooper said—"I used to work summers there. Guys at Prudhoe Bay working 'seven-twelve'—seven days a week, twelve hours a day. Blow it on cocaine."

NATURE'S WRITING

One of the formal criteria of humanistic scholarship is that it be concerned with the scrutiny of texts. A text is information stored through time. The stratigraphy of rocks, layers of pollen in a swamp, the outward expanding circles in the trunk of a tree, can be seen as texts. The calligraphy of rivers winding back and forth over the land leaving layer upon layer of traces of previous riverbeds is text. The layers of history in language become a text of language itself. In Paul Friedrich's book *Proto-Indo-European Trees* he identifies the "semantic primitives" of the

Indo-European tribe of languages through a group of words that have not changed much through twelve thousand years—and those are tree names: especially birch, willow, alder, elm, ash, apple, and beech (*bher, wyt, alysos, ulmo, os, abul, bhago*) (Friedrich, 1970). Seed syllables, *bija,* of the life of the west.

In very early China diviners heated tortoise shell over flame till it cracked and then read meanings from the design of the cracks. It's a Chinese idea that writing started from copying these cracks. Every kind of writing relates to natural materials. The current form of Chinese characters with their little hooks and right angles came about when the Han Chinese shifted from incising signs with a stylus on shaved bamboo staves to writing with a rabbit-hair brush dipped in a pine soot ink on absorbent mulberry-fiber paper. The Chinese character forms are entirely a function of the way a brush tip turns when it lifts off the page. Lifting a brush, a burin, a pen, or a stylus is like releasing a bite or lifting a claw.

Light planes like kites, wobbling in the winds. In the long days of the arctic spring, people fly any hour of the day or night. Cutting south of Bettles and then taxiing down and skidding in the snow. In Fairbanks, I went to visit Erik Granquist, a Finnish paleotaxidermist, to take a look at his finished reconstruction of the body of an earlier sort of bison that had died thirty-six thousand years ago. At that time it was still in the lab at the university. It was a smallish, beautifully tight, and filled-out animal whose hide now has a bluish cast. Erik's previous project had been a Wooly Mammoth in Poland that had been found where it fell into a salt deposit.

He showed me how to read the story of the Pleistocene bison: "It's on its four legs, crumpled straight down, because when a bison is killed it doesn't fall over on its side like a moose, it drops straight down. These scratches on the hide were done by the lion that attacked it from the rear. The lion was no different from a contemporary African Lion. You can see the claw marks, then the fang punctures. They are exactly the width of the teeth of the modern lion. There are also the marks on the nose and the claw marks under the jaw and on the neck that show a second lion held it by the nose and held the head down. Next, the way the hide was opened up shows that they ate it from the rear, taking the backstrap along the tail and spine, and then left it. They didn't eat the neck or head, so it stayed collapsed in place with just one line of hide torn open right along the backbone. Shortly after the lions were finished with it, the weather turned cold and it froze. It was fall. In the following spring (and it was on the north side of the slope), mud melting at the top of the slope avalanched over and covered the frozen bison, still on its four legs, and carried it into the permafrost and sealed it anaerobically where it stayed frozen until it was washed out by hydraulic mining a few years back."

Erik also told me how on his birthday and at the end of the reconstruction, he had sacramentally eaten a tiny bit of the flesh that had been frozen for millennia and then helicoptered to a freezer. This bison body, a lyric salvaged from a very ancient manuscript, can now be seen in a University of Alaska museum display, where it is called "Babe."

Western culture is very brief when measured against one time-transcending bison corpse, or the wandering calligraphy of a river down the Yukon flats, or the archaic circumpolar cosmopolitanism of the traditions that connect with the Kuuvangmiut people. Euro-American humanism has been a story of writers and scholars who were deeply moved and transformed by their immersion in earlier histories and literatures. Their writings have provided useful cultural—rather than theological or biological—perspectives on the human situation. The Periclean Greeks digested the Homeric lore, which went back to the Bronze Age and before. The Romans enlarged themselves by their study of Greece. Renaissance seekers nourished themselves on Greece and Rome. Today a new breed of posthumanists is investigating and experiencing the diverse little nations of the planet, coming to appreciate the "primitive," and finding prehistory to be an ever-expanding field of richness. We get a glimmering of the depth of our ultimately single human root. Wild nature is inextricably in the weave of self and culture. The "post" in the term *posthumanism* is on account of the word *human*. The dialogue to open next would be among all beings, toward a rhetoric of ecological relationships. This is not to put down the human: the "proper study of mankind" *is* what it means to be human. It's not enough to be shown in school that we are kin to all the rest: we have to feel it all the way through. Then we can also be uniquely "human" with no sense of special privilege. Water is the koan of water, as Dōgen says, and human beings are their own koan. The Grizzlies or Whales or Rhesus Monkeys, or *Rattus*, would infinitely prefer that humans (especially Euro-Americans) got to know *themselves* thoroughly before presuming to do Ursine or Cetacean research.

When humans know themselves, the rest of nature is right there. This is part of what the Buddhists call the Dharma.

MOTHER LEOPARDS

The word *grammar* is used by language scholars to mean the description of the structure of a language and the system of rules that govern it. A grammar is like a basket that can hold sentences in that language which would all work. In earlier times language scholars confused writing with speech. This is evident in the word *grammar* itself—the Greek *gramma* means "letter" with the root *gerebh* or *grebh* "to scratch" (hence kerf, graph, carve). Grammar comes from *gramma techne*, "woven scratches." But it is quite clear that the primary existence of language ("tongue") is in the event, the utterance. Language is not a carving, it's a curl of breath, a breeze in the pines.

Metaphors of "nature as books" are not only inaccurate, they are pernicious. The world may be replete with signs, but it's not a fixed text with archives of variora. The overattachment to the bookish model travels along with the assumption that nothing of much interest happened before the beginning of written history. Writing systems do confer an advantage. Those with writing have taken themselves to be superior to people without it, and people with a Sacred Book have put themselves above those with vernacular religion, regardless of how rich the myth and ceremony.

From Fairbanks I went back south to Anchorage. One night Ron Scollon and I were in the Pioneer Bar in Anchorage: I was telling of our trip out the Kobuk River and he was bringing me up to date on what had been happening in the field of linguistics. Ron and Suzanne Scollon are professional linguists who have worked for years with the Athapaskan family of languages and have published papers based on the observation of language-learning by both Athapaskan and Caucasian infants in the subarctic villages. So I took up my idea with him—that language belongs to our biological nature and writing is just moose-tracks in the snow. "Ron," I said, "does language not in some sense belong to biology?"

Ron's response was basically the following lecture: "Wilhelm von Humboldt—probably with some influence from his brother Alexander—started the 'speciation' metaphor for both organic phenomena and language. Ever since, languages have been viewed as though each was a different species, and the earlier historical linguists used to talk about a kind of Darwinian competition among them. But in biology species never converge, they only diverge. All languages belong to the same species and can interbreed, hence they can converge. Interlanguage dynamics will not just be competitive, but also familial and ecological. There is no sort of evolutionary improvement to be inferred from language history either: all languages work equally well and each has its own elegances. There's no such thing as the 'fittest' among languages. English became an international language only by virtue of British and American adventurism. (English is a rich midden-heap of semi-composted vocabularies further confused by the defeat at the hands of the Normans—a genuine creolized tongue that lucked out in becoming the second language to the world.) The fact is that changes in language, vowel shifts, consonant shifts, tendencies toward simpler or more complex grammars, do not seem to be in response to any practical needs."

"Well—so evolutionary principles don't apply. What about ecological forces? Human beings are still a wild species (our breeding has never been controlled for the purpose of any specific yield), and would you agree that language is also wild? The basic structures are not domesticated or cultivated. They belong to the wild side of the mind." "Sure," he said. "But if language is just one species there must be some other creatures in your mind-wilderness it interacts with, because a wilderness is a system. If language is a Pleistocene bison, what's the lion?"

"Ha! If language is an herbivore," said I, "it's not at the top of the chain. One might say 'poetry' is the lion because poetry clearly eats and intensifies natural speech. But given that almost all of our thinking is colored by language, and poetry is a subset of language use, that can't be it. I'd say it was the unconditioned mind-in-the-moment that eats, transforms, goes beyond, language. Art, or creative play, sometimes does this by going directly to the freshness and uniqueness of the moment, and to direct unmediated experience."

Ron tested me with a Whorfian challenge: "Is there *any* experience whatsoever that is not mediated by language?" I banged my heavy beer mug sharply on the table and half a dozen people jumped and looked at us. We had to give up and laugh at this point, since it always seems to come back to an ordinary mystery. Our table was under the branching head of a caribou.

All of my acquaintances in the Alaskan intelligentsia, both native and white, have been involved in trying to keep the native languages alive. Michael Krauss, James Kari, Gary Holthaus, the Scollons, Katherine Peters, Richard and Nora Dauenhauer, Elsie Mather, Steve Grubis, teachers like the Boenishes, the ecologist-anthropologist Richard Nelson, have all taken the language-survival question to heart. Krauss, who is head of the Alaska Native Languages Center, is not optimistic—the youngest speakers of the native tongues grow older and older every year. The village of Kobuk is one of the strongest, but even there I was told the youngest speakers were in their late teens, and the kids on the schoolground played in English. Though there's a statewide program supporting bilingual education and there are excellent bilingual texts and teaching texts for all the native languages, they seem to be fading. Most of the native families seem to perceive English as the wave of the future and the source of potential economic success for their children, so they don't make an effort to speak Language at home. (In Australia I always heard whatever local tongue was under discussion referred to as "Language." "Does she speak Language?")

This may be a passing phase. The native languages might regain their strength. It would help if teachers and administrators who were educated in the United States, which is (outside of a few areas) massively monolingual, would understand that bilingualism is neither rare nor difficult. An administrator who dreaded high school Spanish when young cannot believe that a little Eskimo girl can easily be bilingual. In the past, the cosmopolitanism of the worldwide mosaics of small bioregionally based nations was guaranteed by virtually universal multilingualism. An elderly Yu'pik man who died on a caribou hunt several years ago—he drowned while crossing a river—was reported to have been one of the last of the multilingual older generation. He was known to speak Yu'pik, Dena'ina (an Athapaskan language), Russian, English, and some Inupiaq.

To speak of an "ecology of language" might start with recognizing the common coexistence of levels, codes, slangs, dialects, whole languages, and languages even of different families—in one speaker. John Gumperz (1964) describes the situation of a village in North India where "local dialects serve as vernaculars for most villagers. There may also be some untouchable groups with distinct vernaculars of their own. In addition to the vernaculars there will be several argots. One form of the subregional dialect is used with traders from nearby bazaar towns. Other different forms may be employed with wandering performers or religious ascetics . . . wandering ascetics of the Krishna cult might use Braj Bhasa while worshipers of Ram would use Avadhi. Standard Hindi is the norm for intercourse with educated outsiders. . . . In business transactions or when talking to educated Muslims, Urdu is called for. Furthermore the educated people know English and there are others who have at least some knowledge of Sanskrit" (p. 420).

So we are back in the villages. The local mix of dialects and standard languages is unique to the place. All are rooted in nature; but their vines and creepers reach worldwide. (But tonight the people out in the Alaskan bush, in McGrath, Kobuk, or Kiana, are watching TV off the satellite, maybe the same program that's playing down at the end of the bar.)

That's where the classics might come in. The Classic provides a kind of norm. Not the statistical norm of behaviorism but a norm that is proved by staying power and informed consensus. Staying power through history is related to the degree of intentionality, intensity, mindfulness, playfulness, and incorporation of previous strategies and standards within the medium—plus creative reuse or reinterpretation of the received forms, plus intellectual coherence, time-transcending long-term human relevance, plus resonances with the deep images of the unconscious. To achieve this status a text or tale must be enacted across many nations and a few millennia and must have received multiple translations.

The immediate time frame of human experience is the climates and ecologies of the Holocene—the "present moment," the ten or eleven thousand years since the latest ice age. Within the traditional literatures there are probably a few complete tales that are *that* old, as well as a huge quantity of later literature composed of elements borrowed from the oldest tradition. For most of this time, human populations were relatively small and travel took place on foot, by horse, or by sail. Whether Greece, Germania, or Han China, there were always nearby areas of forest, and wild animals, migratory waterfowl, seas full of fish and whales, and these were part of the experience of every active person. Animals as characters in literature and as universal presences in the imagination and in the archetypes of religion are there because they were *there*. Ideas and images of wastelands, tempests, wildernesses, and mountains are born not of abstraction but of experience: cisalpine, hyperboreal, circumpolar, transpacific, or beyond the pale. This is the world people lived in up until the late nineteenth century. (When was worldwide population one-half of what it is today? The 1950s.)

The condition of life in the Far North still approaches the experience of the hunter-gatherer world, the kind of world that was not just the cradle but the young adulthood of humanity. The north still has a wild community, in most of its numbers, intact. There is a relatively small group of hardy individuals who live as hunters and foragers and who have learned to move with the mindful intensity that is basic to elder human experience. It is not the "frontier" but the last of the Pleistocene in all its glory of salmon, bear, caribou, deer, ducks and geese, whales and walruses, and moose. It will not, of course, last much longer. The Arctic Wildlife Refuge will be drilled for oil, and the Tongass Forest of southeastern Alaska has been roaded and logged beyond belief.

The New World north is a window into the European past: where do the sacred salmon of the Celts, the Bjorns and Brauns and Brun-(hilde) [*bhar*-bear]-s of northern European literature, the dolphins of the Mediterranean, the bear dances of

Artemis, the lion-skin of Herakles come from but the wild systems that the humans lived near? The persistence of these marvelous creatures in literature and imagination tells us how important they are to the health of our souls.

Ron and I turned our conversation then to China. He and I share this double focus: we appreciate Alaska as the most open and wildest place in the north—and one of the wildest places left on earth—and China as the most thoroughly literary of civilizations. They are not so far from each other across the globe. Both look like they are each nearing the end of their own case. But China, destructive as its recent environmental history may be, is a great civilization that will perhaps stay vital by virtue of its tiny thread of surviving wildness (call it Miao songs and Chan poems), and something of Alaska may survive by converting its newly arrived Euro-American population into postindustrial wilderness lovers by the magic of its casual danger, all-day darkness, all-night light, emptiness, uselessness, facelessness, frozen breath, smoked fish. The Anchorage newspaper reported that two moose had been walking around in the shopping mall parking lots again—malls that are right up against the spruce forest that leads to the Chugach Mountains.

A young white woman asked me (this was another time): "If we have made such good use of animals, eating them, singing about them, drawing them, riding them, and dreaming about them, what do they get back from us?" An excellent question, directly on the point of etiquette and propriety, and putting it from the animals' side. The Ainu say that the deer, salmon, and bear like our music and are fascinated by our languages. So we sing to the fish or the game, speak words to them, say grace. Periodically we dance for them. A song for your supper: performance is currency in the deep world's gift economy. The other creatures probably do find us a bit frivolous: we keep changing our outfits, and we eat too many different things. Nonhuman nature, I cannot help feeling, is well inclined toward humanity and only wishes modern people were more reciprocal, not so bloody.

Gary Holthaus, a long-time Alaskan and director of the Alaska Humanities Forum, and I walked down to the basement of the Captain Cook Hotel for breakfast. I had attended their annual meeting the day before to make a report on my time among the Kuuvangmiut. (Back in the seventies when he and I traveled to the southeast Alaskan Yu'pik village of Aleknagik I saw him packing his copy of Marcus Aurelius.) We were still discussing some of the ideas from the previous day's meeting, and we weren't in a mood to be so kind to the humanistic project. We were saying that it had not really been all that concerned for the real life of myth, poetry, and value. The Greek thinkers *started* with an oral repository of amazingly lively songs and stories—the Homeric poems and Hesiod. But their humanistic studies turned into an oddly formalistic and cramped concern for language.

A niche had opened up in the spaces between shaman, priest, poet, and mythographer. That niche was the city, the small city-state. Thought in the city reflected a kind of contest: the poetic and mythic way of seeing that was common to the villages versus the daily argumentation and *reportage* that dominated town life. At bottom it was a contest between subsistence economies and surplus—the centralized merchants. So the philosophers—the Sophists—were instructors to the rich young men on how to argue effectively in public. They did a fine job. They are the Founding Teachers of the whole occidental intellectual lineage. Ninety percent of what all so-called humanists have done throughout history has been to fiddle with language: grammar and rhetoric and then philology. For two and a half thousand years they believed not only in the Word but in a correct format for it. And if some of the French are trying to take the Word apart right now, it's because they are in the same tradition with the same obsession. But there were some fine people in the tradition: Hypatia with her mathematical intellectual paganism and Petrarch, the first modern mountaineer and the first vernacular lyric poet, to mention only two.

There's nothing wrong with clear speaking and honest argumentation. "Nothing specially occidental or high class or educated about speaking well," Holthaus said. "I've been to hundreds of meetings, and a lot of them were in the bush. Yu'pik or Inupiaq or Gwi'chin people—they all talk freely and to the point. The women are powerful speakers too. They didn't learn that from reading Cicero in school."

Thoreau wrote of "this vast, savage, howling mother of ours, Nature, lying all around, with such beauty, and such affection for her children, as the leopard; and yet we are so early weaned from her breast to society." Is it possible that a society as a whole might stay on better terms with nature, and not simply by being foragers? Thoreau replies: "The Spaniards have a good term to express this wild and dusky knowledge, *Gramatica parda*, tawny grammar, a kind of mother-wit derived from that same leopard to which I have referred." The grammar not only of language, but of culture and civilization itself, is of the same order as this mossy little forest creek, this desert cobble.

In one of his talks Dōgen said: "To carry yourself forward and experience myriad things is delusion. But myriad things coming forth and experiencing *themselves* is awakening." Applying this to language theory, I think it suggests that when occidental logos-oriented philosophers uncritically advance language as a unique human gift which serves as the organizer of the chaotic universe—it is a delusion. The subtle and many-layered cosms of the universe have found their own way into symbolic structure and have given us thousands of tawny human-language grammars.

Good, Wild, Sacred

WEEDING OUT THE WILD

MY FAMILY and I have been living since the nineteen-seventies on land in the Sierra Nevada range of northern California. These ridges and slopes are somewhat "wild" and not particularly "good." The original people here, the Nisenan (or Southern Maidu) were almost entirely displaced or destroyed during the first few decades of the gold rush. It seems there is no one left to teach us which places in this landscape were once felt to be "sacred"—though with time and attention, I think we will be able to feel and find them again.

Wild land, good land, sacred land. At home working on our mountain farmstead, in town at political meetings, and farther afield studying the problems of indigenous peoples, I hear such terms emerging. By examining these three categories perhaps we can get some insights into the problems of rural habitation, subsistence living, wilderness preservation, and Third and Fourth World resistance to the appetites of industrial civilization.

Our idea of Good Land comes from agriculture. Here "good" (as in good soil) is narrowed to mean land productive of a small range of favored cultivars, and thus it favors the opposite of "wild": the cultivated. To raise a crop you fight the bugs, shoo the birds, and pull the weeds. The wild that keeps flying, creeping, burrowing in—is sheer frustration. Yet wild nature cannot be called unproductive, and no plant in the almost endless mosaics of micro and macro communities is ever out of place. For hunting and gathering peoples for whom that whole spread of richness, the wild natural system, is also their economy, a cultivated patch of land might seem bizarre and definitely not good, at least at first. Gathering people draw on the whole field, ranging widely daily. Agricultural people live by a map constructed of highly productive nodes (cleared fields) connected by lines (trails through the scary forest)—a beginning of "linear."

For preagricultural people the sites considered sacred and given special care were of course wild. In early agrarian civilizations, ritually cultivated land or special temple fields were sometimes considered sacred. The fertility religions of those times were not necessarily rejoicing in the fertility of all nature, but were focusing on their own harvest. The idea of cultivation was conceptually extended to describe a kind of training in social forms that guarantees membership in an elite class. By the metaphor of "spiritual cultivation" a holy man has weeded out the wild from his nature. This is agrarian theology. But weeding out the wild from the natures of members of the *Bos* and *Sus* clans—cattle and pigs—gradually changed animals which are intelligent and alert in the wild into sluggish meat-making machines.

Certain groves from the original forest lingered on into classical times as "shrines." They were viewed with much ambivalence by the rulers from the metropole. They survived because the people who worked the land still half-heard the call of the old ways, and lore that predated agriculture was still whispered around. The kings of Israel began to cut down the sacred groves, and the Christians finished the job. The idea that "wild" might also be "sacred" returned to the Occident only with the Romantic movement. This nineteenth-century rediscovery of wild nature is a complex European phenomenon—a reaction against formalistic rationalism and enlightened despotism that invoked feeling, instinct, new nationalisms, and a sentimentalized folk culture. It is only from very old place-centered cultures that we hear of sacred groves, sacred land, in a context of genuine belief and practice. Part of that context is the tradition of the commons: "good" land becomes private property; the wild and the sacred are shared.

Throughout the world the original inhabitants of desert, jungle, and forest are facing relentless waves of incursions into their remotest territories. These lands, whether by treaty or by default, were left in their use because the dominant society thought the arctic tundra or arid desert or jungle forest "no good." Native people everywhere are now conducting an underprivileged and underfunded fight against unimaginably wealthy corporations to resist logging or oil exploration or uranium mining on their own land. They persist in these struggles not just because it has always been their home, but also because some places in it are sacred to them. This last aspect makes them struggle desperately to resist the powerful temptation to sell out—to take the cash and accept relocation. And sometimes the temptations and confusion are too great, and they do surrender and leave.

Thus some very cogent and current political questions surround the traditional religious use of certain spots. I was at the University of Montana in the spring of 1982 on a program with Russell Means, the American Indian Movement founder and activist, who was trying to get support for the Yellow Thunder Camp of Lakota and other Indian people of the Black Hills. Thunder Camp was on traditional tribal land that was under Forest Service jurisdiction at the time. These people wanted to block further expansion of mining into the Black Hills. Their argument was that the particular place they were reoccupying is not only ancestral but sacred.

During his term in office California Governor Jerry Brown created the Native American Heritage Commission specifically for California Indians, and a number of elders were charged with the task of locating and protecting sacred sites and native graves in California. This was done partly to head off confrontations between native people versus landowners or public land managers who start developments on what is now considered their property. The trouble often involves traditional grave sites. It was a sensitive move, and though barely comprehensible to the white voters, it sent a ripple of appreciation through all the native communities. Although the white Christian founders of the United States were probably not considering American Indian beliefs when they guaranteed freedom of religion, some court decisions over the years have given support to certain Native American churches. The connection of religion to *land*, however, has been resisted by the dominant culture and the courts. This ancient aspect of religious worship remains virtually incomprehensible to Euro-Americans. Indeed it might: if even some small bits of land are considered sacred, then they are forever not for sale and *not for taxing*. This is a deep threat to the assumptions of an endlessly expansive materialist economy.

WATERHOLES

In the hunting and gathering way of life, the whole territory of a given group is fairly equally experienced by everyone. Those wild and sacred spots have many uses. There are places where women go for seclusion, places where the bodies of the dead are taken, and spots where young men and women are called for special instruction. Such places are numinous, loaded with meaning and power. The memories of such spots are very long. Nanao Sakaki, John Stokes, and I were in Australia in the fall of 1981 at the invitation of the Aboriginal Arts Board doing some teaching, poetry readings, and workshops with both aboriginal leaders and children. Much of the time we were in the central Australian desert south and west of Alice Springs, first into Pitjantjara tribal territory and then three hundred miles northwest into Pintubi lands. The aboriginal people in the central desert all still speak their languages. Their religion is fairly intact, and most young men are still initiated at fourteen, even the ones who go to high school at Alice Springs. They leave the high school for a year and are taken into the bush to learn bush ways on foot, to master the lore of landscapes and plants and animals, and finally to undergo initiation.

We were traveling by truck over dirt track west from Alice Springs in the company of a Pintubi elder named Jimmy Tjungurrayi. As we rolled along the dusty road, sitting back in the bed of a pickup, he began to speak very rapidly to me. He was talking about a mountain over there, telling me a story about some wallabies that came to that mountain in the dreamtime and got into some kind of mischief with some lizard girls. He had hardly finished that and he started in on another story about another hill over here and another story over there. I couldn't keep up. I realized after about half an hour of this that these were tales to be told while *walking*, and that I was experiencing a speeded-up version of what might be leisurely told over several days of foot travel. Mr. Tjungurrayi felt graciously compelled to share a body of lore with me by virtue of the simple fact that I was there.

So remember a time when you journeyed on foot over hundreds of miles, walking fast and often traveling at night, traveling nightlong and napping in the acacia shade during the day, and these stories were told to you as you went. In your travels with an older person you were given a map you could memorize, full of lore and song, and also practical information. Off by yourself you could sing those songs to bring yourself back. And you could maybe travel to a place that you'd never been, steering only by songs you had learned.

We made camp at a waterhole called Ilpili and rendezvoused with a number of Pintubi people from the surrounding desert country. The Ilpili waterhole is about a yard across, six inches deep, in a little swale of bush full of finch. People camp a quarter mile away. It's the only waterhole that stays full through drought years in tens of thousands of square miles. A place kept by custom open to all. Until late at night Jimmy and the other old men sat around a small thornbrush fire and sang a cycle of journey songs, walking through a space of desert in imagination and music. They kept a steady rhythmic beat to the song by clapping two boomerangs together. They stopped between songs and would hum a phrase or two and then argue a bit about the words and then start again. One would defer to another and let him start. Jimmy explained to me that they have so many cycles of journey songs they can't quite remember them all, and they have to be constantly rehearsing.

Each night they'd start the evening saying, "What will we sing?" and get a reply like "Let's sing the walk up to Darwin." They'd start out and argue and sing and clap their way along through it. It was during the full moon period: a few clouds would sail and trail in the cool light and mild desert wind. I had learned that the elders liked black tea, and several times a night I'd make a pot right at the fire, with lots of white sugar, the way they wanted it. The singers would stop when they felt like it. I'd ask Jimmy, "How far did you get tonight?" He'd say, "Well, we got two-thirds of the way to Darwin." This can be seen as one example of the many ways landscape, myth, and information were braided together in preliterate societies.

One day driving near Ilpili we stopped the truck and Jimmy and the three other elderly gentlemen got out and he said, "We'll take you to see a sacred place here. I guess you're old enough." They turned to the boys and told them to stay behind. As we climbed the bedrock hill these ordinarily cheery and loud-talking aboriginal men began to drop their voices.

As we got higher up they were speaking whispers and their whole manner changed. One said almost inaudibly, "Now we are coming close." Then they got on their hands and knees and crawled. We crawled up the last two hundred feet, then over a little rise into a small basin of broken and oddly shaped rocks. They whispered to us with respect and awe of what was there. Then we all backed away. We got back down the hill and at a certain point stood and walked. At another point voices rose. Back at the truck, everybody was talking loud again and no more mention was made of the sacred place.

Very powerful. Very much in mind. We learned later that it was indeed a place where young men were taken for ceremony.

I traveled by pickup truck along hundreds of miles of rough dirt tracks and hiked into the mountainous and rocky country where the roads stopped. I was being led to special places. There were large unique boulders, each face and facet a surprise. There was the sudden opening out of a hidden steep defile where two cliffs meet with just a little sandbed between, and some green bushes, some parrots calling. We dropped down cliffs off a mesa into a waterhole you wouldn't guess was there, where a thirty-foot blade of rock stands on end, balancing. Each of these spots was out of the ordinary, fantastic even, and sometimes rich with life. Often there were pictographs in the vicinity. They were described as teaching spots and some were "dreaming spots" for certain totem ancestors, well established in song and story over tens of thousands of square miles.

"Dreaming" or "dreamtime" refers to a time of fluidity, shape-shifting, interspecies conversation and intersexuality, radically creative moves, whole landscapes being altered. It is often taken to be a "mythical past," but it is not really in *any* time. We might as well say it is *right now*. It is the mode of the eternal moment of creating, of being, as contrasted with the mode of cause and effect in time. Time is the realm where people mainly live and within which history, evolution, and progress are imagined to take place. Dōgen gave a difficult and playful talk on the resolution of these two modes early in the winter of 1240. It is called "Time/Being."

In Australian lore the totem dreaming place is first of all special to the people of that totem, who sometimes make pilgrimages there. Second, it is sacred (say) to the honey-ants which actually live there—there are hundreds of thousands of them. Third, it's like a little Platonic cave of ideal honey-antness, maybe the creation spot for all honey-ants. It mysteriously connects the essence of honey-antness with the archetypes of the human psyche and makes bridges between humanity, the ants, and the desert. The honey-ant place is in stories, dances, songs, and it is a real place which also happens to be optimum habitat for a world of ants. Or take a green parrot dreaming place: the stories will tell of the tracks of the ancestors going across the landscape and stopping at that dreaming place, and it is truly a perfect place for parrots. All this is a radically different way of expressing what science says, as well as another set of metaphors for the teachings of the Hua-yen or the Avatamsaka Sutra.

This sacredness implies a sense of optimal habitat for certain kinfolk that we have out there—the wallabies, red kangaroo, bush turkeys, lizards. Geoffrey Blainey (1976, 202) says, "The land itself was their chapel and their shrines were hills and creeks and their religious relics were animals, plants, and birds. Thus the migrations of aboriginals, though spurred by economic need, were also always pilgrimages." Good (productive of much life), wild (naturally), and sacred were one.

This way of life, frail and battered as it is, still exists. Now it is threatened by Japanese and other uranium mining projects, large-scale copper mining, and petroleum exploration. The issue of sacredness has become very political—so much so that the Australian Bureau of Aboriginal Affairs has hired some bilingual anthropologists and bush people to work with elders of the different tribes to try and identify sacred sites and map them. There has been much hope that the Australian government would act in good faith and declare certain areas off-limits before any exploratory team even gets near them. This effort is spurred by the fact that there have already been some confrontations in the Kimberly region over oil exploration, as at Nincoomba. The local native people stood their ground, making human lines in front of bulldozers and drilling rigs, and the media coverage of this resistance won over some of the Australian public. Since in Australia a landowner's mineral rights are always reserved to "The Crown," even somebody's ranch might be subject to mining. So to consider sacred land a special category, even in theory, is an advanced move. But it's shaky. A "registered site" near Alice Springs was bulldozed supposedly on the instructions of a government land minister, and this was in the relatively benign federal jurisdiction!

SHRINES

The original inhabitants of Japan, the Ainu, had a way of speaking of the sacredness and specialness of a whole ecosystem. Their term *iworu* means "field" with implications of watershed region, plant and animal communities, and spirit force—the powers behind the masks or armor, *hayakpe*, of the various beings. The *iworu* of the Great Brown Bear would be the mountain habitat—and connected lowland valley system—in which the bear is dominant, and it would mean the myth and spirit world of the bear as well. The *iworu* of salmon would be the lower watersheds with all their tributaries (and the associated plant communities), and on out to sea, extending into oceanic realms only guessed at, where the salmon do their weaving. The bear field, the deer field, the salmon field, the Orca field.

In the Ainu world a few human houses are in a valley by a little river. The doorways all face east. In the center of each house is the firepit. The sunshine streams through the eastern door each morning to touch the fire, and they say the sun goddess is visiting her sister the fire goddess in the firepit. One should not walk through sunbeams that shine on the fire—that would be breaking their contact. Food is often foraged in the local area, but some of the creatures come down from the inner mountains and up from the deeps of the sea. The animal or fish (or plant) that allows itself to be killed or gathered, and then enters the house to be consumed, is called a "visitor," *marapto*.

The master of the sea is Orca, the Killer Whale; the master of the inner mountains is Bear. Bear sends his friends the deer down to visit humans. Orca sends his friends the salmon up the streams. When they arrive their "armor is broken"—they are killed—enabling them to shake off their fur or scale coats and step out as invisible spirit beings. They are then delighted by witnessing the human entertainments—saké and music.

(They love music.) The people sing songs to them and eat their flesh. Having enjoyed their visit they return to the deep sea or to the inner mountains and report: "We had a wonderful time with the human beings." The others are then prompted themselves to go on visits. Thus if the humans do not neglect proper hospitality—music and manners—when entertaining their deer or salmon or wild plant *marapto*, the beings will be reborn and return over and over. This is a sort of spiritual game management.

Modern Japan is another sort of example: a successful industrialized country with remnants of sacred landscape consciousness still intact. There are Shinto shrines throughout the Japanese islands. Shinto is "the way of the spirits." *Kami* are a formless "power" present in everything to some degree but intensified in strength and presence in certain outstanding objects such as large curiously twisted boulders, very old trees, or thundering misty waterfalls. Anomalies and curiosities of the landscape are all signs of *kami*—spirit-power, presence, shape of mind, energy. The greatest of *kami* centers is Mt. Fuji. The name Fuji is now thought to derive from that of the Ainu Fire Goddess, the only one who stands above and can scold and correct the *kimun kamui*, mountain deity, Bear. All of Mt. Fuji is a Shinto shrine, the largest in the nation, from well below timberline all the way to the summit. (Many place names left behind by the displaced Ainu are still current in Japan.)

Shinto got a bad name during the 1930s and World War II because the Japanese had created an artificial "State Shinto" in the service of militarism and nationalism. It and folk Shinto became confused in the minds of many Euro-Americans. Long before the rise of any state, the islands of Japan were studded with little shrines—*jinja* and *omiya*—that were part of neolithic village culture. Even in the midst of the onrushing industrial energy of the current system, shrine lands still remain untouchable. It would make your hair stand up to see how a Japanese developer will take bulldozers to a nice slope of old pines and level it for a new town. When the New Island was created in Kobe harbor to make Kobe the second busiest port in the world (after Rotterdam), it was raised from the bay bottom with dirt obtained by shaving down a whole range of hills ten miles south of the city. This was barged to the site for twelve years—a steady stream of barges carrying dirt off giant conveyor belts that totally removed soil two rows of hills back from the coast. The newly leveled area became a housing development. In industrial Japan it's not that "nothing is sacred," it's that the *sacred* is sacred and that's *all* that's sacred.

We are grateful for these microscopic traces of salvaged land in Japan because the rule in shrines is that (away from the buildings and paths) you never cut anything, never maintain anything, never clear or thin anything. No hunting, no fishing, no thinning, no burning, no stopping of burning: leaving us a very few stands of ancient forests right inside the cities. One can walk into a little *jinja* and be in the presence of an 800-year-old Cryptomeria (*Sugi*) tree. Without the shrines we wouldn't know so well what the original Japanese forest might have been. But such compartmentalization is not healthy: in this patriarchal model some land is saved, like a virgin priestess, some is overworked endlessly, like a wife, and some is brutally publicly reshaped, like an exuberant girl declared promiscuous and punished. Good, wild, and sacred couldn't be farther apart.

Europe and the Middle East were once studded with similar shrines. They were even spoken of as "sacred groves." It may be that in the remote past the most sacred spot in all of Europe was under the Pyrenees, where the great cave paintings are. I suspect they were part of a religious center thirty thousand years ago, where animals were "conceived" underground. Perhaps a dreaming place. Maybe a thought that the animals' secret hearts were thereby hidden under the earth, a way of keeping them from becoming extinct. But many species did become extinct, some even before the era of cave paintings was over. Many more have become so during the last two thousand years, victims of civilization. Occidental expansion brought an acceleration of habitat degradation to the whole globe, but it is interesting to note that even before that expansion such political and economic processes were already well under way. The destruction of species, the impoverishment and enslavement of rural people, and the persecution of nature-worship traditions have long been part of Europe.

So the French and English explorers of North America, the early fur traders, had no teachings from the societies they left behind that would urge them to look on wild nature with reverence. They did find much that was awe-inspiring, and some expressed it well. Some even joined the Indians and became people of the New World. These few almost forgotten exceptions were overwhelmed by trading entrepreneurs and, later, settlers. Yet all through American history there were some who kept joining the Indians in fact or in style—and some, even in the eighteenth century, who realized that the world they saw would shrink away. In the Far East, or Europe, the notion of an ancient forest or original prairie and all the splendid creatures that might live there is now a tale told from the neolithic. In the western United States it was the world of our grandmothers. For many of us today this loss is a source of grief. For Native Americans this was a loss of land, traditional life, and the sources of their culture.

TRUE NATURE

Thoreau set out to "make the soil say beans" while living by his pond. To cause land to be productive according to our own notion is not evil. But we must also ask: what does mother nature do best when left to her own long strategies? This comes to asking what the full potential vegetation of a spot would be. For all land, however wasted and exploited, if left to nature (*zi-ran*, the self-so), will arrive at a point of balance between biological productivity and stability. A sophisticated post-industrial "future primitive" agriculture will be asking: is there any way we can go *with* rather than against nature's tendency? Go toward, say, in New England, deciduous hardwoods—or, as where I live, a mix of pine and oak with kitkitdizze ground cover? Doing horticulture, agriculture, or forestry with the grain rather than against it would be in the human interest and not just for the long run.

Wes Jackson's research suggests that a diverse and perennial-plant-based agriculture holds real promise for sustaining the locally appropriate communities of the future. This is acknowledging that the source of fertility ultimately is the "wild." It has been said that "good soil is good because of the wildness in it."

How could *this* be granted by a victorious king dividing up his spoils? The fatuity of "Spanish land grants" and "Real Estate." The power that gives us good land is none other than Gaia herself, the whole network. It might be that almost all civilized agriculture has been on the wrong path from the beginning, relying as it does on the monoculture of annuals. In *New Roots for Agriculture* Wes Jackson develops this argument. I concur with his view, knowing that it raises even larger questions about civilization itself, a critique I have worked at elsewhere. Suffice it to say that the sorts of economic and social organization we invoke when we say "civilization" can no longer be automatically accepted as useful models. To scrutinize civilization is not, however, to negate all the meanings of cultivation.

The word *cultivation*, harking to etymologies of *till* and *wheel about*, generally implies a movement away from natural process. In agriculture it is a matter of "arresting succession, establishing monoculture." Applied on the spiritual plane this has meant austerities, obedience to religious authority, long bookish scholarship, or in some traditions a dualistic devotionalism (sharply distinguishing "creature" and "creator") and an overriding image of divinity being "centralized," a distant and singular point of perfection to aim at. The efforts entailed in such a spiritual practice are sometimes a sort of war against nature—placing the human over the animal and the spiritual over the human. The most sophisticated modern variety of hierarchical spirituality is the work of Father Teilhard de Chardin, who claims a special evolutionary spiritual destiny for humanity under the name of higher consciousness. Some of the most extreme of these Spiritual Darwinists would willingly leave the rest of earthbound animal and plant life behind to enter an off-the-planet realm transcending biology. The anthropocentrism of some new age thinkers is countered by the radical critique of the Deep Ecology movement.

On the social level cultivation has meant the absorption of language, lore, and manners that guarantee membership in the elite class and is to be contrasted with "vernacular manners." The truth is, of course, that the etiquette of villagers or nomads (Charles Doughty having black coffee with his Bedouin hosts in Arabia Deserta) can be as elaborate, complex, and arbitrary as that of any city-dweller.

Yet there is such a thing as training. The world moves by complementaries of young and old, foolish and wise, ripe or green, raw or cooked. Animals too learn self-discipline and caution in the face of desire and availability. There is learning and training that goes *with* the grain of things as well as against it. In early Chinese Daoism, "training" did not mean to cultivate the wildness out of oneself, but to do away with arbitrary and delusive conditioning. Zhuang-zi seems to be saying that all social values are false and generate self-serving ego. Buddhism takes a middle path—allowing that greed, hatred, and ignorance are intrinsic to ego, but that ego itself is a reflex of ignorance and delusion that comes from not seeing who we "truly" are. Organized society can inflame, pander to, or exploit these weaknesses, or it can encourage generosity, kindness, trust. There is reason, therefore, to be engaged in a politics of virtue. Still it is a matter of individual character as to whether or not one makes a little private vow to work for compassion and insight or overlooks this possibility. The day-to-day actualization of the vow calls for practice: for a training that helps us realize our own true nature, and nature.

Greed exposes the foolish person or the foolish chicken alike to the ever-watchful hawk of the food-web and to early impermanence. Preliterate hunting and gathering cultures were highly trained and lived well by virtue of keen observation and good manners; as noted earlier, stinginess was the worst of vices. We also know that early economies often were more manipulative of the environment than is commonly realized. The people of mesolithic Britain selectively cleared or burned in the valley of the Thames as a way to encourage the growth of hazel. An almost invisible system of nut and fruit tree growing was once practiced in the jungles of Guatemala. A certain kind of training and culture can be grounded in the wild.

We can all agree: there is a problem with the self-seeking human ego. Is it a mirror of the wild and of nature? I think not: for civilization itself is ego gone to seed and institutionalized in the form of the State, both Eastern and Western. It is not nature-as-chaos which threatens us, but the State's presumption that *it* has created order. Also there is an almost self-congratulatory *ignorance* of the natural world that is pervasive in Euro-American business, political, and religious circles.

Nature is orderly. That which appears to be chaotic in nature is only a more complex kind of order.

Now we can rethink what sacred land might be. For a people of an old culture, *all* their mutually owned territory holds numinous life and spirit. Certain places are perceived to be of high spiritual density because of plant or animal habitat intensities, or associations with legend, or connections with human totemic ancestry, or because of geomorphological anomaly, or some combination of qualities. These places are gates through which one can—it would be said—more easily be touched by a larger-than-human, larger-than-personal, view.

Concern for the environment and the fate of the earth is spreading over the world. In Asia environmentalism is perceived foremost as a movement concerned with health—and seeing the condition of their air and water, this is to be expected. In the Western Hemisphere we have similar problems. But here we are blessed with a bit of remaining wilderness, a heritage to be preserved for all the people of the world. In the Western Hemisphere we have only the tiniest number of buildings that can be called temples or shrines. The temples of our hemisphere will be some of the planet's remaining wilderness areas. When we enter them on foot we can sense that the *kami* or (Maidu) *kukini* are still in force here. They have become the refuge of the Mountain Lions, Mountain Sheep, and Grizzlies—three North American animals which were found throughout the lower hills and plains in prewhite times. The rocky icy grandeur of the high country—and the rich shadowy bird and fish-streaked southern swamps—remind us of the overarching wild systems that nourish us all and underwrite the industrial economy. In the sterile beauty of mountain snowfields and glaciers begin the little streams that water the agribusiness fields of the great Central Valley of California. The wilderness pilgrim's step-by-step breath-by-breath walk up a trail, into those snowfields, carrying all on the back, is so ancient a set of gestures as to bring a profound sense of body-mind joy.

Not just backpackers, of course. The same happens to those who sail in the ocean, kayak fjords or rivers, tend a garden, peel garlic, even sit on a meditation cushion. The point is to make intimate contact with the real world, real self. *Sacred* refers to that which helps take us (not only human beings) out of our little selves into the whole mountains-and-rivers mandala universe. Inspiration, exaltation, and insight do not end when one steps outside the doors of the church. The wilderness as a temple is only a beginning. One should not dwell in the specialness of the extraordinary experience nor hope to leave the political quag behind to enter a perpetual state of heightened insight. The best purpose of such studies and hikes is to be able to come back to the lowlands and see all the land about us, agricultural, suburban, urban, as part of the same territory—never totally ruined, never completely unnatural. It can be restored, and humans could live in considerable numbers on much of it. Great Brown Bear is walking with us, Salmon swimming upstream with us, as we stroll a city street.

To return to my own situation: the land my family and I live on in the Sierra Nevada of California is "barely good" from an economic standpoint. With soil amendments, much labor, and the development of ponds for holding water through the dry season, it is producing a few vegetables and some good apples. It is better as forest: through the millennia it has excelled at growing oak and pine. I guess I should admit that it's better left wild. Most of it is being "managed for wild" right now—the pines are getting large and some of the oaks were growing here before a Euro-American set foot anywhere in California. The deer and all the other animals move through with the exception of Grizzly Bear and wolf; they are temporarily not in residence in California. We will someday bring them back.

These foothill ridges are not striking in any special way, no postcard scenery, but the deer are so at home here I think it might be a "deer field." And the fact that my neighbors and I and all of our children have learned so much by taking our place in these Sierra foothills—logged-over land now come back, burned-over land recovering, considered worthless for decades—begins to make this land a teacher to us. It is the place on earth we work with, struggle with, and where we stick out the summers and winters. It has shown us a little of its beauty.

And sacred? One could indulge in a bit of woo-woo and say, yes, there are newly discovered sacred places in our reinhabited landscape. I know my children (like kids everywhere) have some secret spots in the woods. There is a local hill where many people walk for the view, the broad night sky, moon-viewing, and to blow a conch at dawn on Bodhi Day. There are miles of mined-over gravels where we have held ceremonies to apologize for the stripping of trees and soil and to help speed the plant-succession recovery. There are some deep groves where people got married.

Even this much connection with the place is enough to inspire the local community to hold on: renewed gold mining and stepped-up logging press in on us. People volunteer to be on committees to study the mining proposals, critique the environmental impact reports, challenge the sloppy assumptions of the corporations, and stand up to certain county officials who would sell out the inhabitants and hand over the whole area to any glamorous project. It is hard, unpaid, frustrating work for people who already have to work full time to support their families. The same work goes on with forestry issues—exposing the scandalous favoritism shown the timber industry by our nearby national forest, as its managers try to pacify the public with sweet words and frivolous statistics. Any lightly populated area with "resources" is exploited like a Third World country, even within the United States. We are defending our own space, and we are trying to protect the commons. More than the logic of self-interest inspires this: a true and selfless love of the land is the source of the undaunted spirit of my neighbors.

There's no rush about calling things sacred. I think we should be patient, and give the land a lot of time to tell us or the people of the future. The cry of a Flicker, the funny urgent chatter of a Gray Squirrel, the acorn whack on a barn roof—are signs enough.

Blue Mountains Constantly Walking

FUDŌ AND KANNON

> The mountains and rivers of this moment are the actualization of the way of the ancient Buddhas. Each, abiding in its own phenomenal expression, realizes completeness. Because mountains and waters have been active since before the eon of emptiness, they are alive at this moment. Because they have been the self since before form arose, they are liberated and realized.

This is the opening paragraph of Dōgen Kigen's astonishing essay *Sansuikyo*, "Mountains and Waters Sutra," written in the autumn of 1240, thirteen years after he returned from his visit to Song-dynasty China. At the age of twelve he had left home in Kyoto to climb the well-worn trails through the dark hinoki and sugi (cedar-and-sequoia-like) forests of Mt. Hiei. This three-thousand-foot range at the northeast corner of the Kamo River basin, the broad valley now occupied by the huge city of Kyoto, was the Japanese headquarters mountain of the Tendai sect of Buddhism. He became a novice monk in one of the red-painted shadowy wooden temples along the ridges.

"The blue mountains are constantly walking."

In those days travelers walked. The head monk at the Daitoku-ji Zen monks' hall in Kyoto once showed me the monastery's handwritten "Yearly Tasks" book from the nineteenth century. (It had been replaced by another handwritten volume with a few minor updates for the twentieth century.) These are the records that the leaders refer to through the year in keeping track of ceremonies, meditation sessions, and recipes. It listed the temples that were affiliated with this training school in order of the traveling time it took to get to them: from one day to four weeks' walk. Student monks from even those distant temples usually made a round trip home at least once a year.

Virtually all of Japan is steep hills and mountains dissected by fast shallow streams that open into shoestring valleys and a few wider river plains toward the sea. The hills are generally covered with small conifers and shrubs. Once they were densely forested with a cover of large hardwoods as well as the irregular pines and the tall straight hinoki and sugi. Traces of a vast network of well-marked trails are still found throughout the land. They were tramped down by musicians, monks, merchants, porters, pilgrims, and periodic armies.

We learn a place and how to visualize spatial relationships, as children, on foot and with imagination. Place and the scale of space must be measured against our bodies and their capabilities. A "mile" was originally a Roman measure of one thousand paces. Automobile and airplane travel teaches us little that we can easily translate into a perception of space. To know that it takes six months to walk across Turtle Island/North America walking steadily but comfortably all day every day is to get some grasp of the distance. The Chinese spoke of the "four dignities"— Standing, Lying, Sitting, and Walking. They are "dignities" in that they are ways of being fully ourselves, at home in our bodies, in their fundamental modes. I think many of us would consider it quite marvelous if we could set out on foot again, with a little inn or a clean camp available every ten or so miles and no threat from traffic, to travel across a large landscape—all of China, all of Europe. That's the way to see the world: in our own bodies.

Sacred mountains and pilgrimage to them is a deeply established feature of the popular religions of Asia. When Dōgen speaks of mountains he is well aware of these prior traditions. There are hundreds of famous Daoist and Buddhist peaks in China and similar Buddhist and Shinto-associated mountains in Japan. There are several sorts of sacred mountains in Asia: a "sacred site" that is the residence of a spirit or deity is the simplest and possibly oldest. Then there are "sacred areas"— perhaps many dozens of square miles—that are special to the mythology and practice of a sect with its own set of Daoist or Buddhist deities—miles of paths—and dozens or hundreds of little temples and shrines. Pilgrims might climb thousands of feet, sleep in the plain board guesthouses, eat rice gruel and a few pickles, and circumambulate set routes burning incense and bowing at site after site.

Finally there are a few highly formalized sacred areas that have been deliberately modeled on a symbolic diagram (mandala) or a holy text. They too can be quite large. It is thought that to walk within the designated landscape is to enact specific moves on the spiritual plane (Grapard, 1982). Some friends and I once walked the ancient pilgrimage route of the Ōmine Yamabushi (mountain ascetics) in Nara prefecture from Yoshino to Kumano. In doing so we crossed the traditional center of the "Diamond-Realm Mandala" at the summit of Mt. Ōmine (close to six thousand feet) and four hiking days later descended to the center of the "Womb-Realm Mandala" at the Kumano ("Bear Field") Shrine, deep in a valley. It was the late-June rainy season, flowery and misty. There were little stone shrines the whole distance—miles of ridges—to which we sincerely bowed each time we came on them. This projection of complex teaching diagrams onto the landscape comes from the Japanese variety of Vajrayana Buddhism, the Shingon sect, in its interaction with the shamanistic tradition of the mountain brotherhood.

The regular pilgrimage up Mt. Ōmine from the Yoshino side is flourishing—hundreds of colorful Yamabushi in medieval mountain-gear scale cliffs, climb the peak, and blow conches while others chant sutras in the smoky dirt-floored temple on the summit. The long-distance practice has been abandoned in recent years, so the trail was so overgrown it was almost impossible to find. This four-thousand-foot-high direct ridge route makes excellent sense, and I suspect it was the regular way of traveling from the coast to the interior in paleolithic and neolithic times. It was the only place I ever came on wild deer and monkeys in Japan.

In East Asia "mountains" are often synonymous with wilderness. The agrarian states have long since drained, irrigated, and terraced the lowlands. Forest and wild habitat start at the very place the farming stops. The lowlands, with their villages, markets, cities, palaces, and wineshops, are thought of as the place of greed, lust, competition, commerce, and intoxication—the "dusty world." Those who would flee such a world and seek purity find caves or build hermitages in the hills—and take up the practices which will bring realization or at least a long healthy life. These hermitages in time became the centers of temple complexes and ultimately religious sects. Dōgen says:

> Many rulers have visited mountains to pay homage to wise people or ask for instructions from great sages. . . . At such time these rulers treat the sages as teachers, disregarding the protocol of the usual world. The imperial power has no authority over the wise people in the mountains.

So "mountains" are not only spiritually deepening but also (it is hoped) independent of the control of the central government. Joining the hermits and priests in the hills are people fleeing jail, taxes, or conscription. (Deeper into the ranges of southwestern China are the surviving hill tribes who worship dogs and tigers and have much equality between the sexes, but that belongs to another story.) Mountains (or wilderness) have served as a haven of spiritual and political freedom all over.

Mountains also have mythic associations of verticality, spirit, height, transcendence, hardness, resistance, and masculinity. For the Chinese they are exemplars of the "yang": dry, hard, male, and bright. Waters are feminine: wet, soft, dark "yin" with associations of fluid-but-strong, seeking (and carving) the lowest, soulful, life-giving, shape-shifting. Folk (and Vajrayana) Buddhist iconography personifies "mountains and waters" in the *rupas*—"images" of Fudō Myō-ō (Immovable Wisdom King) and Kannon Bosatsu (The Bodhisattva Who Watches the Waves). Fudō is almost comically ferocious-looking with a blind eye and a fang, seated or standing on a slab of rock and enveloped in flames. He is known as an ally of mountain ascetics. Kannon (Kuan-yin, Avalokitesvara) gracefully leans forward with her lotus and vase of water, a figure of compassion. The two are seen as buddha-work partners: ascetic discipline and relentless spirituality balanced by compassionate tolerance and detached forgiveness. Mountains and Waters are a dyad that together make wholeness possible: wisdom and compassion are the two components of realization. Dōgen says:

> Wenzi said, "The path of water is such that when it rises to the sky, it becomes raindrops; when it falls to the ground, it becomes rivers." . . . The path of water is not noticed by water, but is realized by water.

There is the obvious fact of the water-cycle and the fact that mountains and rivers indeed form each other: waters are precipitated by heights, carve or deposit landforms in their flowing descent, and weight the offshore continental shelves with sediment to ultimately tilt more uplifts. In common usage the compound "mountains and waters"—*shan-shui* in Chinese—is the straightforward term for landscape. Landscape painting is "mountains and waters pictures." (A mountain range is sometimes also termed *mai*, a "pulse" or "vein"—as a network of veins on the back of a hand.) One does not need to be a specialist to observe that landforms are a play of stream-cutting and ridge-resistance and that waters and hills interpenetrate in endlessly branching rhythms. The Chinese feel for land has always incorporated this sense of a dialectic of rock and water, of downward flow and rocky uplift, and of the dynamism and "slow flowing" of earth-forms. There are several surviving large Chinese horizontal handscrolls from premodern eras titled something like "Mountains and Rivers Without End." Some of them move through the four seasons and seem to picture the whole world.

"Mountains and waters" is a way to refer to the totality of the process of nature. As such it goes well beyond dichotomies of purity and pollution, natural and artificial. The whole, with its rivers and valleys, obviously includes farms, fields, villages, cities, and the (once comparatively small) dusty world of human affairs.

THIS

"The blue mountains are constantly walking."

Dōgen is quoting the Chan master Furong. Dōgen was probably envisioning those mountains of Asia whose trails he had walked over the years—peaks in the three- to nine-thousand-foot range, hazy blue or blue-green, mostly tree-covered, maybe the steep jumbled mountains of coastal South China where he had lived and practiced thirteen years earlier. (Timberline at these latitudes is close to nine thousand feet—none of these are alpine mountains.) He had walked thousands of miles. ("The Mind studies the way running barefoot.")

If you doubt mountains walking you do not know your own walking.

Dōgen is not concerned with "sacred mountains"—or pilgrimages, or spirit allies, or wilderness as some special quality. His mountains and streams are the processes of this earth, all of existence, process, essence, action, absence; they roll being and nonbeing together. They are what we are, we are what they are. For those who would see directly into essential nature, the idea of the sacred is a delusion and an obstruction: it diverts us from seeing what is before our eyes: plain thusness. Roots, stems, and branches are all equally scratchy. No hierarchy, no equality. No occult and exoteric, no gifted kids and slow achievers. No wild and tame, no bound or free, no natural and artificial. Each totally its own frail self. Even though connected all which ways; even *because* connected all which ways.

This, *thusness*, is the nature of the nature of nature. The wild in wild.

So the blue mountains walk to the kitchen and back to the shop, to the desk, to the stove. We sit on the park bench and let the wind and rain drench us. The blue mountains walk out to put another coin in the parking meter, and go on down to the 7-Eleven. The blue mountains march out of the sea, shoulder the sky for a while, and slip back into the waters.

HOMELESS

The Buddhists say "homeless" to mean a monk or priest. (In Japanese, *shukke*—literally "out of the house.") It refers to a person who has supposedly left the householder's life and the temptations and obligations of the secular world behind. Another phrase, "leaving the world," means getting away from the imperfections of human behavior—particularly as reinforced by urban life. It does not mean distancing yourself from the natural world. For some it has meant living as mountain hermits or members of religious communities. The "house" has been set against "mountains" or "purity." Enlarging the scale of the homeless world the fifth-century poet Zhiang-yan said the proper hermit should "take the purple heavens to be his hut, the encircling sea to be his pond, roaring with laughter in his nakedness, walking along singing with his hair hanging down" (Watson, 1971, 82). The early Tang poet Han-shan is taken as the veritable model of a recluse—his spacious home reaches to the end of the universe:

> I settled at Cold Mountain long ago,
> Already it seems like years and years.
> Freely drifting, I prowl the woods and streams
> And linger watching things themselves.
> Men don't get this far into the mountains,
> White clouds gather and billow.
> Thin grass does for a mattress,
> The blue sky makes a good quilt.
> Happy with a stone underhead
> Let heaven and earth go about their changes.

"Homeless" is here coming to mean "being at home in the whole universe." In a similar way, self-determining people who have not lost the wholeness of their place can see their households and their regional mountains or woods as within the same sphere.

I attended the ceremonies at the shrine for the volcanic mountain of Suwa-nō-se Island, in the East China Sea, one year. The path through the jungle needed brushing, so rarely did people go there. Two of us from the Banyan Ashram went as helpers to three elders. We spent the morning cutting overgrowth back, sweeping the ground, opening and wiping the unpainted wood altar-structure (about the size of a pigeon coop), and then placing some offerings of sweet potatoes, fruit, and *shochu* on the shelf before the blank space that in fact framed the mountain itself. One elder then faced the peak (which had been belching out ash clouds lately) and made a direct, perfunctory personal speech or prayer in dialect. We sat on the ground sweating and cut open watermelon with a sickle and drank some of the strong *shochu* then, while the old guys told stories of other days in the islands. Tall thick glossy green trees arched over us, roaring with cicada. It was not trivial. The domestic parallel is accomplished in each household with its photos of ancestors, offerings of rice and alcohol, and a vase with a few twigs of wild evergreen leaves. The house itself, with its funky tiny kitchen, bath, well, and entranceway altars, becomes a little shrine.

And then the literal "house," when seen as just another piece of the world, is itself impermanent and composite, a poor "homeless" thing in its own right. Houses are made up, heaped together, of pine boards, clay tiles, cedar battens, river boulder piers, windows scrounged from wrecking yards, knobs from K-Mart, mats from Cost Plus, kitchen floor of sandstone from some mountain ridge, doormat from Longs—made up of the same world as you and me and mice.

> Blue mountains are neither sentient nor insentient. You are neither sentient nor insentient. At this moment, you cannot doubt the blue mountains walking.

Not only plum blossoms and clouds, or Lecturers and Rōshis, but chisels, bent nails, wheelbarrows, and squeaky doors are all teaching the truth of the way things are. The condition of true "homelessness" is the maturity of relying on nothing and responding to whatever turns up on the doorstep. Dōgen encourages us with "A mountain always practices in every place."

LARGER THAN A WOLF, SMALLER THAN AN ELK

All my life I have been in and around wild nature, working, exploring, studying, even while living in cities. Yet I realized a few years ago that I had never made myself into as good a botanist or zoologist or ornithologist as so many of the outdoor people I admire have done. Recalling where I had put my intellectual energies over the years it came to me that I had made my fellow human beings my study—that I had been a naturalist of my own species. I had been my own object-of-study too. I enjoy learning how different societies work out the details of subsistence and celebration in their different landscapes. Science, technology, and the economic uses of nature need not be antithetical to celebration. The line between use and misuse, between objectification and celebration, is fine indeed.

The line is in the details. I once attended the dedication of a Japanese temple building that had been broken down and transported across the Pacific to be resurrected on the West Coast. The dedication ceremony was in the Shinto style and included offerings of flowers and plants. The difficulty was that they were the plants that would have been used in a traditional Japanese dedication and had been sent from Japan—they were not plants of the new place. The ritualists had the forms right but clearly didn't grasp the substance. After everyone had gone home I tried to make brief introductions myself: "Japanese building of hinoki wood, meet manzanita and Ponderosa Pine . . . please take care of yourself in this dry climate. Manzanita, this building is used to damp air and lots of people. Please accept it in place of your dusty slopes." Humans provide their own sort of access to understanding nature and the wild.

The human diverseness of style and costume, and the constant transformations of popular culture, are a kind of symbolic speciation—as though humans chose to mimic the colors and patterns of birds. People from the high civilizations in particular have elaborate notions of separateness and difference and dozens of ways to declare themselves "out of nature." As a kind of game this might be harmless. (One could imagine the phylum Chordata declaring, "We are a qualitative leap in evolution representing something entirely transcendent entering what has hitherto been merely biology.") But at the very minimum this call to a special destiny on the part of human beings can be seen as a case of needlessly multiplying theories (Occam's razor). And the results—in the human treatment of the rest of nature—have been pernicious.

There is a large landscape handscroll called "Interminable Mountains and Streams" (attributed to Lu Yuan of the Ching dynasty; now in the Freer). We see, within this larger scope of rocks, trees, ridges, mountains, and watercourses, people and their works. There are peasants and thatched huts, priests and complexes of temples, scholars at their little windows, fishermen in their boats, traveling merchants with their loads, matrons, children. While the Buddhist tradition of North India and Tibet made the mandala—painted or drawn charts of the positions of consciousness and cause-and-effect chains—their visual teaching aids, the Chan tradition of China (especially the Southern Song) did something similar (I will venture to suggest) with landscape painting. If a scroll is taken as a kind of Chinese mandala, then all the characters in it are our various little selves, and the cliffs, trees, waterfalls, and clouds are our own changes and stations. (Swampy reedy thicket along a stream—what does *that* say?) Each type of ecological system is a different mandala, a different imagination. Again the Ainu term *iworu*, field-of-beings, comes to mind.

> All beings do not see mountains and waters in the same way. . . . Some see water as wondrous blossoms, hungry ghosts see water as raging fire or pus and blood. Dragons see water as a palace or a pavilion. . . . Some beings see water as a forest or a wall. Human beings see water as water. . . . Water's freedom depends only on water.

One July walking down from the headwaters of the Koyukuk River in the Brooks Range of Alaska I found myself able to look into the realm of Dall (mountain) Sheep. The green cloudy tundra summer alps—in which I was a frail visitor—were the most hospitable they would ever be to a hairless primate. The long dark winters do not daunt the Dall Sheep, though—they do not even migrate down. The winds blow the scant loose snow, and the dried forbs and grasses of arctic summer are nibbled through the year. The dozens of summer sheep stood out white against green: playing, napping, eating, butting, circling, sitting, dozing in their high smoothed out beds on ledges at the "cliff-edge of life and death." Dall Sheep (in Athapaskan called *dibee*) see mountains—Dōgen might say—"as a palace or pavilion." But that provisional phrase "palace or pavilion" is too high-class, urban, and human to really show how totally and uniquely *at home* each life-form must be in its own unique "buddha-field."

> Green mountain walls in blowing cloud
> white dots on far slopes, constellations,
> slowly changing, not stars, not rocks
> "by the midnight breezes strewn"
> cloud tatters, lavender arctic light
> on sedate wild sheep grazing
> tundra greens, held in the web of clan
> and kin by bleats and smells to the slow

> rotation of their Order living
> half in the sky—damp wind up from the
> whole North Slope and a taste of the icepack,
> the primus roaring now,
> here, have some tea.

And down in the little arctic river below the slopes the Grayling with their iridescent bodies are in their own (to us) icy paradise. Dōgen again:

> Now when dragons and fish see water as a palace, it is just like human beings seeing a palace. They do not think it flows. If an outsider tells them, "What you see as a palace is running water," the dragons and fish will be astonished, just as we are when we hear the words, "Mountains flow."

We can begin to imagine, to visualize, the nested hierarchies and webs of the actual nondualistic world. Systems theory provides equations but few metaphors. In the "Mountains and Waters Sutra" we find:

> It is not only that there is water in the world, but there is a world in water. It is not just in water. There is a world of sentient beings in clouds. There is a world of sentient beings in the air. There is a world of sentient beings in fire. . . . There is a world of sentient beings in a blade of grass.

It would appear that the common conception of evolution is that of competing species running a sort of race through time on planet earth, all on the same running field, some dropping out, some flagging, some victoriously in front. If the background and foreground are reversed, and we look at it from the side of the "conditions" and their creative possibilities, we can see these multitudes of interactions through hundreds of other eyes. We could say a food brings a form into existence. Huckleberries and salmon call for bears, the clouds of plankton of the North Pacific call for salmon, and salmon call for seals and thus orcas. The Sperm Whale is sucked into existence by the pulsing, fluctuating pastures of squid, and the open niches of the Galápagos Islands sucked a diversity of bird forms and functions out of one line of finch.

Conservation biologists speak of "indicator species"—animals or birds that are so typical of a natural area and its system that their condition is an indicator of the condition of the whole. The old conifer forests can be measured by "Spotted Owl," and the Great Plains once said (and would say it again) "bison." So the question I have been asking myself is: what says "humans"? What sucks *our* lineage into form? It is surely the "mountains and rivers without end"—the whole of this earth on which we find ourselves more or less competently at home. Berries, acorns, grass-seeds, apples, and yams call for dextrous creatures something like us to come forward. Larger than a wolf, smaller than an elk, human beings are not such huge figures in the landscape. From the air, the works of humanity are scratches and grids and ponds, and in fact most of the earth seems, from afar, to be open land. (We know now that our impact is far greater than it appears.)

As for towns and cities—they are (to those who can see) old tree trunks, riverbed gravels, oil seeps, landslide scrapes, blowdowns and burns, the leavings after floods, coral colonies, paper-wasp nests, beehives, rotting logs, watercourses, rock-cleavage lines, ledge strata layers, guano heaps, feeding frenzies, courting and strutting bowers, lookout rocks, and ground-squirrel apartments. And for a few people they are also palaces.

DECOMPOSED

"Hungry ghosts see water as raging fire or pus and blood . . ."

Life in the wild is not just eating berries in the sunlight. I like to imagine a "depth ecology" that would go to the dark side of nature—the ball of crunched bones in a scat, the feathers in the snow, the tales of insatiable appetite. Wild systems are in one elevated sense above criticism, but they can also be seen as irrational, moldy, cruel, parasitic. Jim Dodge told me how he had watched—with fascinated horror—Orcas methodically batter a Gray Whale to death in the Chukchi Sea. Life is not just a diurnal property of large interesting vertebrates; it is also nocturnal, anaerobic, cannibalistic, microscopic, digestive, fermentative: cooking away in the warm dark. Life is well maintained at a four-mile ocean depth, is waiting and sustained on a frozen rock wall, is clinging and nourished in hundred-degree desert temperatures. And there is a world of nature on the decay side, a world of beings who do rot and decay in the shade. Human beings have made much of purity and are repelled by blood, pollution, putrefaction. The other side of the "sacred" is the sight of your beloved in the underworld, dripping with maggots. Coyote, Orpheus, and Izanagi cannot help but look, and they lose her. Shame, grief, embarrassment, and fear are the anaerobic fuels of the dark imagination. The less familiar energies of the wild world, and their analogs in the imagination, have given us ecologies of the mind.

Here we encounter the peculiar habitat needs of the gods. They settle on the summits of mountains (as on Mt. Olympus), have chambers deep below the earth, or are invisibly all around us. (One major deity is rumored to be domiciled entirely off this earth.) The Yana said that Mt. Lassen of northern California—"Waganupa" in Ishi's tongue, a ten-thousand-foot volcano—is home to countless *kukini* who keep a fire going inside. (The smoke passes out through the smoke-hole.) They will enjoy their magical stick-game gambling until the time that human beings reform themselves and become "real people" that spirits might want to associate with once again.

The spirit world goes across and between species. It does not need to concern itself with reproduction, it is not afraid of death, it is not practical. But the spirits do seem to have an ambivalent, selective interest in cross-world communication. Young women in scarlet and white robes dance to call down the gods, to be possessed by them, to speak in their voices. The priests who employ them can only wait for the message. (I think it was D. H. Lawrence who said, "Drink and carouse with Bacchus, or eat dry bread with Jesus, but don't sit down without one of the gods.")

(The *personal* quality of mountain dreaming: I was half asleep on the rocky ground at Tower Lake in the Sierra. There are four horizontal bands of cream-colored rock wavering through the cliff face, and the dream said "those rock bands are your daughters.")

Where Dōgen and the Zen tradition would walk, chant a sutra, or do sitting meditation, the elder vernacular artisans of soul and spirit would play a flute, drum, dance, dream, listen for a song, go without food, and be available to communication with birds, animals, or rocks. There is a story of Coyote watching the yellow autumn cottonwood leaves float and eddy lightly down to the ground. It was so lovely to watch, he asked the cottonwood leaves if he might do it too. They warned him: "Coyote, you are too heavy and you have a body of bones and guts and muscle. We are light, we drift with the wind, but you would fall and be hurt." Coyote would hear none of it and insisted on climbing a cottonwood, edging far out onto a branch, and launching himself off. He fell and was killed. There's a caution here: do not be too hasty in setting out to "become one with." But, as we have heard, Coyote will roll over, reassemble his ribs, locate his paws, find a pebble with a dot of pitch on it to do for an eye, and trot off again.

Narratives are one sort of trace that we leave in the world. All our literatures are leavings—of the same order as the myths of wilderness peoples, who leave behind only stories and a few stone tools. Other orders of beings have their own literatures. Narrative in the deer world is a track of scents that is passed on from deer to deer with an art of interpretation which is instinctive. A literature of bloodstains, a bit of piss, a whiff of estrus, a hit of rut, a scrape on a sapling, and long gone. And there might be a "narrative theory" among these other beings—they might ruminate on "intersexuality" or "decomposition criticism."

I suspect that primary peoples all know that their myths are somehow "made up." They do not take them literally and at the same time they hold the stories very dear. Only upon being invaded by history and whipsawed by alien values do a people begin to declare that their myths are "literally true." This literalness in turn provokes skeptical questioning and the whole critical exercise. What a final refinement of confusion about the role of myths it is to declare that although they are not to be believed, they are nonetheless aesthetic and psychological constructs which bring order to an otherwise chaotic world and to which we should willfully commit ourselves! Dōgen's "You should know that even though all things are liberated and not tied to anything, they abide in their own phenomenal expression" is medicine for that. The "Mountains and Waters Sutra" is called a sutra not to assert that the "mountains and rivers of this moment" are a text, a system of symbols, a referential world of mirrors, but that this world in its actual existence is a complete presentation, an enactment—and that it stands for nothing.

WALKING ON WATER

There's all sorts of walking—from heading out across the desert in a straight line to a sinuous weaving through undergrowth. Descending rocky ridges and talus slopes is a specialty in itself. It is an irregular dancing—always shifting—step of walk on slabs and scree. The breath and eye are always following this uneven rhythm. It is never paced or clocklike, but flexing— little jumps—sidesteps—going for the well-seen place to put a foot on a rock, hit flat, move on—zigzagging along and all deliberate. The alert eye looking ahead, picking the footholds to come, while never missing the step of the moment. The body-mind is so at one with this rough world that it makes these moves effortlessly once it has had a bit of practice. The mountain keeps up with the mountain.

In the year 1225 Dōgen was in his second year in South China. That year he walked out of the mountains and passed through the capital of the Southern Song dynasty, Hang-zhou, on his way north to the Wan-shou monastery at Mt. Jing. The only account of China left by Dōgen is notes on talks by the master Ru-jing (Kodera, 1980). I wonder what Dōgen would have said of city walking. Hang-zhou had level broad straight streets paralleling canals. He must have seen the many-storied houses, clean cobbled streets, theaters, markets, and innumerable restaurants. It had three thousand public baths. Marco Polo (who called it Quinsai) visited it twenty-five years later and estimated that it was probably the largest (at least a million people) and most affluent city in the world at that time (Gernet, 1962). Even today the people of Hang-zhou remember the lofty eleventh-century poet Su Shi, who built the causeway across West Lake when he was governor. At the time of Dōgen's walk North China was under the control of the Mongols, and Hang-zhou would fall to the Mongols in fifty-five more years.

The South China of that era sent landscape painting, calligraphy, both the Sōtō and Rinzai schools of Zen, and the vision of that great southern capital to Japan. The memory of Hang-zhou shaped both Osaka and Tokyo in their Tokugawa-era evolution. These two positions—one the austere Zen practice with its spare, clean halls, the other the possibility of a convivial urban life rich in festivals and theaters and restaurants—are two potent legacies of East Asia to the world. If Zen stands for the Far Eastern love of nature, Hang-zhou stands for the ideal of the city. Both are brimming with energy and life. Because most of the cities of the world are now mired in poverty, overpopulation, and pollution we have all the more reason to recover the dream. To neglect the city (in our hearts and minds for starters) is deadly, as James Hillman (1989, 169) says.

The "Mountains and Waters Sutra" goes on to say:

> All waters appear at the foot of the eastern mountains. Above all waters are all mountains. Walking beyond and walking within are both done on water. All mountains walk with their toes on all waters and splash there.

Dōgen finishes his meditation on mountains and waters with this: "When you investigate mountains thoroughly, this is the work of the mountains. Such mountains and waters of themselves become wise persons and sages"—become sidewalk vendors and noodle-cooks, become marmots, ravens, graylings, carp, rattlesnakes, mosquitoes. *All* beings are "said" by the mountains and waters—even the clanking tread of a Caterpillar tractor, the gleam of the keys of a clarinet.

Ancient Forests of the Far West

*But ye shall destroy their altars,
break their images, and cut down their groves.*
EXODUS 34:13

AFTER THE CLEARCUT

We had a tiny dairy farm between Puget Sound and the north end of Lake Washington, out in the cutover countryside. The bioregionalists call that part of northwestern Washington state "Ish" after the suffix that means "river" in Salish. Rivers flowing into Puget Sound are the Snohomish, Skykomish, Samamish, Duwamish, Stillaguamish.

I remember my father dynamiting stumps and pulling the shards out with a team. He cleared two acres and fenced it for three Guernseys. He built a two-story barn with stalls and storage for the cows below and chickens above. He and my mother planted fruit trees, kept geese, sold milk. Behind the back fence were the woods: a second-growth jungle of alder and cascara trees with native blackberry vines sprawling over the stumps. Some of the stumps were ten feet high and eight or ten feet in diameter at the ground. High up the sides were the notches the fallers had chopped in to support the steel-tipped planks, the springboards, they stood on while felling. This got them above the huge swell of girth at the bottom. Two or three of the old trees had survived—small ones by comparison—and I climbed those, especially one Western Red Cedar (*xelpai'its* in Snohomish) that I fancied became my advisor. Over the years I roamed the second-growth Douglas Fir, Western Hemlock, and cedar forest beyond the cow pasture, across the swamp, up a long slope, and into a droughty stand of pines. The woods were more of a home than home. I had a permanent campsite where I would sometimes cook and spend the night.

When I was older I hiked into the old-growth stands of the foothill valleys of the Cascades and the Olympics where the shade-tolerant skunk cabbage and devil's club underbrush is higher than your head and the moss carpets are a foot thick. Here there is always a deep aroma of crumbled, wet organisms—fungus—and red rotten logs and a few bushes of tart red thimbleberries. At the forest edges are the thickets of salal with their bland seedy berries, the yellow salmonberries, and the tangles of vine-maples. Standing in the shade you look out into the burns and the logged-off land and see the fireweed in bloom.

A bit older, I made it into the high mountains. The snow-peaks were visible from near our place: in particular Mt. Baker and Glacier Peak to the north and Mt. Rainier to the south. To the west, across Puget Sound, the Olympics. Those unearthly glowing floating snowy summits are a promise to the spirit. I first experienced one of those distant peaks up close at fifteen, when I climbed Mt. Saint Helens. Rising at 3 A.M. at timberline and breaking camp so as to be on glacier ice by six; standing in the rosy sunrise at nine thousand feet on a frozen slope to the crisp tinkle of crampon points on ice—these are some of the esoteric delights of mountaineering. To be immersed in ice and rock and cold and upper space is to undergo an eery, rigorous initiation and transformation. Being above all the clouds with only a few other high mountains also in the sunshine, the human world still asleep under its gray dawn cloud blanket, is one of the first small steps toward Aldo Leopold's "think like a mountain." I made my way to most of the summits of the Northwest—Mt. Hood, Mt. Baker, Mt. Rainier, Mt. Adams, Mt. Stuart, and more—in subsequent years.

At the same time, I became more aware of the lowlands. Trucks ceaselessly rolled down the river valleys out of the Cascades loaded with great logs. Walking the low hills around our place near Lake City I realized that I had grown up in the aftermath of a clearcut, and that it had been only thirty-five or forty years since all those hills had been logged. I know now that the area had been home to some of the largest and finest trees the world has ever seen, an ancient forest of hemlock and Douglas Fir, a temperate-zone rainforest since before the glaciers. And I suspect that I was to some extent instructed by the ghosts of those ancient trees as they hovered near their stumps. I joined the Wilderness Society at seventeen, subscribed to *Living*

Wilderness, and wrote letters to Congress about forestry issues in the Olympics.

But I was also instructed by the kind of work done by my uncles, our neighbors, the workers of the whole Pacific Northwest. My father put me on one end of a two-man crosscut saw when I was ten and gave me the classic instruction of "don't ride the saw"—don't push, only pull—and I loved the clean swish and ring of the blade, the rhythm, the comradeship, the white curl of the wood that came out with the rakers, the ritual of setting the handles, and the sprinkle of kerosene (to dissolve pitch) on the blade and into the kerf. We cut rounds out of down logs to split for firewood. (Unemployed men during the Depression felled the tall cedar stumps left from the first round of logging to buck them into blanks and split them with froes for the hand-split cedar shake trade.) We felled trees to clear pasture. We burned huge brush-piles.

People love to do hard work together and to feel that the work is real; that is to say primary, productive, needed. Knowing and enjoying the skills of our hands and our well-made tools is fundamental. It is a tragic dilemma that much of the best work men do together is no longer quite right. The fine information on the techniques of hand-whaling and all the steps of the flensing and rendering described in *Moby Dick* must now, we know, be measured against the terrible specter of the extinction of whales. Even the farmer or the carpenter is uneasy: pesticides, herbicides, creepy subsidies, welfare water, cheap materials, ugly subdivisions, walls that won't last. Who can be proud? And our conservationist-environmentalist-moral outrage is often (in its frustration) aimed at the logger or the rancher, when the real power is in the hands of people who make unimaginably larger sums of money, people impeccably groomed, excellently educated at the best universities—male and female alike—eating fine foods and reading classy literature, while orchestrating the investment and legislation that ruin the world. As I grew into young manhood in the Pacific Northwest, advised by a cedar tree, learning the history of my region, practicing mountaineering, studying the native cultures, and inventing the little rituals that kept my spirit sane, I was often supporting myself by the woodcutting skills I learned on the Depression stump-farm.

AT WORK IN THE WOODS

In 1952 and '53 I worked for the Forest Service as a lookout in the northern Cascades. The following summer, wanting to see new mountains, I applied to a national forest in the Mt. Rainier area. I had already made my way to the Packwood Ranger Station and purchased my summer's supply of lookout groceries when the word came to the district (from Washington, D.C.) that I should be fired. That was the McCarthy era and the Velde Committee hearings were taking place in Portland. Many of my acquaintances were being named on TV. It was the end of my career as a seasonal forestry worker for the government.

I was totally broke, so I decided to go back to the logging industry. I hitched east of the Oregon Cascades to the Warm Springs Indian Reservation and checked in with the Warm Springs Lumber Company. I had scaled timber here the summer of '51, and now they hired me on as a chokersetter. This is the lava plateau country south of the Columbia River and in the drainage of the Deschutes, up to the headwaters of the Warm Springs River. We were cutting old-growth Ponderosa Pine on the middle slopes of the east side, a fragrant open forest of massive straight-trunked trees growing on volcanic soils. The upper edge verged into the alpine life-zone, and the lower edge—farther and farther out into the desert—became sagebrush by degrees. The logging was under contract with the tribal council. The proceeds were to benefit the people as a whole.

11 August '54
Chokersetting today. Madras in the evening for beer. Under the shadow of Mt. Jefferson. Long cinnamon-colored logs. This is "pine" and it belongs to "Indians"—what a curious knotting-up. That these Indians & these trees, that coexisted for centuries, should suddenly be possessor and possessed. Our *concepts to be sure.*

I had no great problem with that job. Unlike the thick-growing Douglas Fir rainforests west of the Cascades, where there are arguments for clearcutting, the drier pine forests are perfect for selective cutting. Here the slopes were gentle and they were taking no more than 40 percent of the canopy. A number of healthy mid-sized seed trees were left standing. The D8 Cats could weave their way through without barking the standing trees.

Chokersetting is part of the skidding operation. First into the woods are the timber cruisers who estimate the standing board feet and mark the trees. Then come the road-building Cats and graders. Right on their heels are the gypo fallers—gypos get paid for quantity produced rather than a set wage—and then comes the skidding crew. West-of-the-mountains skidding is typically a high-lead or skyline cable operation where the logs are yarded in via a cable system strung out of a tall spar tree. In the east-side pine forest the skidding is done with top-size Caterpillar tractors. The Cat pulls a crawler-tread "arch" trailer behind it with a cable running from the Cat's aft winch up and over the pulley-wheel at the top of the arch, and then down where the cable divides into three massive chains that end in heavy steel hooks, the butt-hooks. I was on a team of two that worked behind one Cat. It was a two-Cat show.

Each Cat drags the felled and bucked logs to the landing—where they are loaded on trucks—from its own set of skid trails. While it is dragging a load of logs in, the chokersetters (who stay behind up the skid trails) are studying the next haul. You pick out the logs you'll give the Cat next trip, and determine the sequence in which you'll hook them so they will not cross each other, flip, twist over, snap live trees down, hang up on stumps, or make other dangerous and complicating moves. Chokersetters should be light and wiry. I wore White's caulked logger boots with steel points like tiny weasel-fangs set in the sole. I was thus enabled to run out and along a huge log or up its slope with perfect footing, while looking at the lay and guessing the physics of its mass in motion. The Cat would be coming back up the skid trail dragging the empty choker cables and would swing in where I signaled. I'd pluck two or three chokers off the butt-hooks and drag the sixteen-foot cables behind me into the logs and brush. The Cat would go on out to the other chokersetter who would take off his cables and do the same.

As the Cat swung out and was making its turnaround, the chokersetters would be down in dirt and duff, ramming the knobbed end of the choker under the log, bringing it up and around, and hooking it into the sliding steel catch called a "bell" that would noose up on the log when the choker pulled taut. The Cat would back its arch into where I stood, holding up chokers. I'd hook the first "D"—the ring on the free end of the choker—over the butt-hook and send the Cat to the next log. It could swing ahead and pull alongside while I leaped atop another load and hung the next choker onto the butt-hook. Then the winch on the rear of the Cat would wind in, and the butts of the logs would be lifted clear of the ground, hanging them up in the arch between the two crawler-tread wheels.

> Stood straight
>   holding the choker high
> As the Cat swung back the arch
>   piss-firs falling,
> Limbs snapping on the tin hat
>   bright D caught on
> Swinging butt-hooks
>   ringing against cold steel,
>   (from *Myths and Texts*)

The next question was, how would they fan out? My Cat-skinner was Little Joe, nineteen and just recently married, chewing plug and always joking. I'd give him the highball sign and at the same time run back out the logs, even as he started pulling, to leap off the back end. Never stand between a fan of lying logs, they say. When the tractor hauls out they might swing in and snap together—"Chokersetters lose their legs that way." And don't stand anywhere near a snag when the load goes out. If the load even lightly brushes it, the top of the snag, or the whole thing, might come down. I saw a dead school-marm (a tree with a crotch in its top third) snap off and fall like that, grazing the tin hat of a chokersetter called Stubby. He was lucky.

> The D8 tears through piss-fir
> Scrapes the seed-pine
>   chipmunks flee,
> A black ant carries an egg

>   Aimlessly from the battered ground.
>   Yellowjackets swarm and circle
>   Above the crushed dead log, their home.
>   Pitch oozes from barked
>   trees still standing,
>   Mashed bushes make strange smells.
>   Lodgepole pines are brittle.
>   Camprobbers flutter to watch.

I learned tricks, placements, pulls from the experienced chokersetters—ways to make a choker cable swing a log over, even to make it jump out from under. Ways and sequences of hooking on chokers that when first in place looked like a messy spiderweb, but when the Cat pulled out, the tangle of logs would right itself and the cables mysteriously fan out into a perfect pull with nothing crossed. We were getting an occasional eight-foot-diameter tree and many five and six footers: these were some of the most perfect Ponderosa Pine I have ever seen. We also had White Fir, Douglas Fir, and some larch. I was soon used to the grinding squeaking roar and rattle of the Cat, the dust, and the rich smells that rose from the bruised and stirred-up soil and plant life. At lunchtime, when the machinery was silent, we'd see deer picking their way through the torn-up woods. A Black Bear kept breaking into the crummy truck to get at the lunches until someone shot him and the whole camp ate him for dinner. There was no rancor about the bear, and no sense of conquest about the logging work. The men were stoic, skillful, a bit overworked, and full of terrible (but funny!) jokes and expressions. Many of them were living on the Rez, which was shared by Wasco, Wishram, and Shoshone people. The lumber company gave priority to the Native American locals in hiring.

>   Ray Wells, a big Nisqually, and I
>   each set a choker
>   On the butt-logs of two big Larch
>   In a thornapple thicket and a swamp.
>   waiting for the Cat to come back,
>   "Yesterday we gelded some ponies
>   "My father-in-law cut the skin on the balls

> "He's a Wasco and don't speak English
> "He grabs a handful of tubes and somehow
> >   cuts the right ones.
> "The ball jumps out, the horse screams
> "But he's all tied up.
> The Caterpillar clanked back down.
> In the shadow of that racket
> >   diesel and iron tread
> I thought of Ray Wells' tipi out on the sage flat
> The gelded ponies
> Healing and grazing in the dead white heat.

There were also old white guys who had worked in the lumber industry all their lives: one had been active in the Industrial Workers of the World, the "Wobblies," and had no use for the later unions. I told him about my grandfather, who had soapboxed for the Wobblies in Seattle's Yesler Square, and my Uncle Roy, whose wife Anna was also the chief cook at a huge logging camp at Gray's Harbor around World War I. I told him of the revived interest in anarchosyndicalism among some circles in Portland. He said he hadn't had anyone talk Wobbly talk with him in twenty years, and he relished it. His job, knotbumper, kept him at the landing where the skidding Cats dropped the logs off. Although the buckets cut the limbs off, sometimes they left stubs which would make the logs hard to load and stack. He chopped off stubs with a double-bitted axe. Ed had a circular wear-mark impressed in the rear pocket of his stagged jeans: it was from his round axe-sharpening stone. Between loads he constantly sharpened his axe, and he could shave a paper-thin slice off a Day's Work plug, his chew, with the blade.

> Ed McCullough, a logger for thirty-five years
> Reduced by the advent of chainsaws
> To chopping off knots at the landing:
> "I don't have to take this kind of shit,
> Another twenty years
> >   and I'll tell 'em to shove it"
> >   (he was sixty-five then)
> In 1934 they lived in shanties
> At Hooverville, Sullivan's Gulch.

When the Portland-bound train came through
The trainmen tossed off coal.

"Thousands of boys shot and beat up
For wanting a good bed, good pay,
                decent food, in the woods—"
No one knew what it meant:
"Soldiers of Discontent."

On one occasion a Cat went to the landing pulling only one log, and not the usual 32-foot length but a 16. Even though it was only half-length the Cat could barely drag it. We had to rig two chokers to get around it, and there was not much pigtail left. I know now that the tree had been close to being of record size. The largest Ponderosa Pine in the world, near Mt. Adams, which I went out some miles of dust dirt roads to see, isn't much larger around than was that tree.

How could one not regret seeing such a massive tree go out for lumber? It was an elder, a being of great presence, a witness to the centuries. I saved a few of the tan free-form scales from the bark of that log and placed them on the tiny altar I kept on a box by my bunk at the logging camp. It and the other offerings (a flicker feather, a bit of broken bird's-egg, some obsidian, and a postcard picture of the Bodhisattva of Transcendent Intelligence, Manjusri) were not "my" offerings to the forest, but the forest's offerings to all of us. I guess I was just keeping some small note of it.

All of the trees in the Warm Springs forest were old growth. They were perfect for timber, too, most of them rot-free. I don't doubt that the many seed-trees and smaller trees left standing have flourished, and that the forest came back in good shape. A forester working for the Bureau of Indian Affairs and the tribal council had planned that cut.

Or did it come back in good shape? I don't know if the Warm Springs timber stands have already been logged again. They should not have been, but—

There was a comforting conservationist rhetoric in the world of forestry and lumber from the mid-thirties to the late fifties. The heavy clearcutting that has now devastated the whole Pacific slope from the Kern River to Sitka, Alaska, had not yet begun. In those days forestry professionals still believed in selective logging and actually practiced sustained yield. Those were, in hindsight, the last years of righteous forest management in the United States.

EVERGREEN

The raw dry country of the American West had an odd effect on American politics. It transformed and even radicalized some people. Once the West was closed to homesteading and the unclaimed lands became public domain, a few individuals realized that the future of these lands was open to public discussion. Some went from exploration and appreciation of wilderness to political activism.

Daoist philosophers tell us that surprise and subtle instruction might come forth from the Useless. So it was with the wastelands of the American West—inaccessible, inhospitable, arid, and forbidding to the eyes of most early Euro-Americans. The Useless Lands became the dreaming place of a few nineteenth- and early-twentieth-century men and women (John Wesley Powell on matters of water and public lands, Mary Austin on Native Americans, deserts, women) who went out into the space and loneliness and returned from their quests not only to criticize the policies and assumptions of the expanding United States but, in the name of wilderness and the commons, to hoist the sails that are filling with wind today. Some of the newly established public lands did have potential uses for lumber, grazing, and mining. But in the case of timber and grass, the best lands were already in private hands. What went into the public domain (or occasionally into Indian reservation status) was—by the standards of those days—marginal land. The off-limits bombing ranges and nuclear test sites of the Great Basin are public domain lands, too, borrowed by the military from the BLM.

So the forests that were set aside for the initial Forest Reserves were not at that time considered prime timber land. Early-day lumber interests in the Pacific Northwest went for the dense, low-elevation conifer forests like those around the house I grew up in or those forests right on saltwater or near rivers. This accessible land, once clearcut, became real estate, but the farther reaches were kept by the big companies as commercial forest. Much of the Olympic Peninsula forest land is privately held. Only by luck and chance did an occasional low-elevation stand such as the Hoh River forest in Olympic National Park, or Jedediah Smith redwoods in California, end up in public domain. It is by virtue of these islands of forest survivors that we can still see what the primeval forest of the West Coast—in its densest and most concentrated incarnation—was like. "Virgin forest" it was once called, a telling term. Then it was called "old growth" or in certain cases "climax." Now we begin to call it "ancient forest."

On the rainy Pacific slope there were million-acre stands that had been coevolving for millennia, possibly for over a million years. Such forests are the fullest examples of ecological process, containing as they do huge quantities of dead and decaying matter as well as the new green and preserving the energy pathways of both detritus and growth. An ancient forest will have many truly large old trees—some having craggy, broken-topped, mossy "dirty" crowns with much organic accumulation, most with holes and rot in them. There will be standing snags and tons of dead down logs. These characteristics, although not delightful to lumbermen ("overripe"), are what make an ancient forest more than a stand of timber: it is a palace of organisms, a heaven for many beings, a temple where life deeply investigates the puzzle of itself. Living activity goes right down to and under the "ground"—the litter, the duff. There are termites, larvae, millipedes, mites, earthworms, springtails, pillbugs, and the fine threads of fungus woven through. "There are as many as 5,500 individuals (not counting the earthworms and nematodes) per square foot of soil to a depth of 13 inches. As many as 70 different species have been collected from less than a square foot of rich forest soil. The total animal population of the soil and litter together probably approaches 10,000 animals per square foot" (Robinson, 1988, 87).

The dominant conifers in this forest, Douglas Fir, Western Red Cedar, Western Hemlock, Noble Fir, Sitka Spruce, and Coastal Redwood, are all long-lived and grow to great size. They are often the longest-lived of their genera. The old forests of the western slopes support some of the highest per-acre biomass—total living matter—the world has seen, approached only by some of the Australian eucalyptus forests. An old-growth temperate hardwood forest, and also the tropical forests, average around 153 tons per acre. The west slope forests of the Oregon Cascades averaged 433 tons per acre. At the very top of the scale, the coastal redwood forests have been as high as 1,831 tons per acre (Waring and Franklin, 1979).

Forest ecologists and paleoecologists speculate on how such a massive forest came into existence. It seems the western forest of twenty or so million years ago was largely deciduous hardwoods—ash, maple, beech, oak, chestnut, elm, gingko—with conifers only at the highest elevations. Twelve to eighteen million years ago, the conifers began to occupy larger areas and then made continuous connection with each other along the uplands. By a million and a half years ago, in the early Pleistocene, the conifers had completely taken over and the forest was essentially as it is now. Forests of the type that had prevailed earlier, the hardwoods, survive today in the eastern United States and were also the original vegetation (before agriculture and early logging) of China and Japan. Visiting Great Smoky Mountains National Park today might give you an idea of what the mountain forests outside the old Chinese capital of Xian, known earlier as Ch'ang-an, looked like in the ninth century.

In the other temperate-zone forests of the world, conifers are a secondary and occasional presence. The success of the West Coast conifers can be attributed, it seems, to a combination of conditions: relatively cool and quite dry summers (which do not serve deciduous trees so well) combined with mild wet winters (during which the conifers continue to photosynthesize) and an almost total absence of typhoons. The enormous size of the trunks helps to store moisture and nutrients against drought years. The forests are steady-growing and productive (from a timber standpoint) while young, and these particular species keep growing and accumulating biomass long after most other temperate-zone trees have reached equilibrium.

Here we find the northern Flying Squirrel (which lives on truffles) and its sacred enemy the Spotted Owl. The Douglas Squirrel (or Chickaree) lives here, as does its sacred enemy the treetop-dashing Pine Marten that can run a squirrel down.

Black Bear seeks the grubs in long-dead logs in her steady ambling search. These and hosts of others occupy the deep shady stable halls—less wind, less swing of temperature, steady moisture—of the huge tree groves. There are treetop-dwelling Red-backed Voles who have been two hundred feet high in the canopy for hundreds of generations, some of whom have never descended to the ground (Maser, 1989). In a way the web that holds it all together is the mycelia, the fungus-threads that mediate between root-tips of plants and chemistry of soils, bringing nutrients in. This association is as old as plants with roots. The whole of the forest is supported by this buried network.

The forests of the maritime Pacific Northwest are the last remaining forests of any size left in the temperate zone. Plato's *Critias* passage (¶iii) says: "In the primitive state of the country [Attica] its mountains were high hills covered with soil . . . and there was abundance of wood in the mountains. Of this last the traces still remain, for although some of the mountains now only afford sustenance to bees, not so very long ago there were still to be seen roofs of timber cut from trees growing there . . . and there were many other high trees. . . . Moreover the land reaped the benefit of the annual rainfall, not as now losing the water which flows off the bare earth into the sea." The cautionary history of the Mediterranean forests is well known. Much of this destruction has taken place in recent centuries, but it was already well under way, especially in the lowlands, during the classical period. In neolithic times the whole basin had perhaps 500 million acres of forest. The higher-elevation forests are all that survive, and even they occupy only 30 percent of the mountain zone—about 45 million acres. Some 100 million acres of land once densely covered with pine, oak, ash, laurel, and myrtle now have only traces of vegetation. There is a more sophisticated vocabulary in the Mediterranean for postforest or nonforest plant communities than we have in California (where everything scrubby is called chaparral). *Maquis* is the term for oak, olive, myrtle, and juniper scrub. An assembly of low waxy drought-resistant shrubs is called *garrigue*. *Batha* is open bare rock and eroding ground with scattered low shrubs and annuals.

People who live there today do not even know that their gray rocky hills were once rich in groves and wildlife. The intensified destruction was a function of the *type* of agriculture. The small self-sufficient peasant farms and their commons began to be replaced by the huge slave-run *latifundia* estates owned in absentia and planned according to central markets. What wildlife was left in the commons might then be hunted out by the new owners, the forest sold for cash, and field crops extended for what they were worth. "The cities of the Mediterranean littoral became deeply involved in an intensive region-wide trade, with cheap manufactured products, intensified markets and factory-like industrial production. . . . These developments in planned colonization, economic planning, world currencies and media for exchange had drastic consequences for the natural vegetation from Spain through to India" (Thirgood, 1981, 29).

China's lowland hardwood forests gradually disappeared as agriculture spread and were mostly gone by about thirty-five hundred years ago. (The Chinese philosopher Meng-zi commented on the risks of clearcutting in the fourth century B.C.) The composition of the Japanese forest has been altered by centuries of continuous logging. The Japanese sawmills are now geared down to about eight-inch logs. The original deciduous hardwoods are found only in the most remote mountains. The prized aromatic Hinoki (the Japanese chamaecypress), which is essential to shrine and temple buildings, is now so rare that logs large enough for renovating traditional structures must be imported from the West Coast. Here it is known as Port Orford Cedar, found only in southern Oregon and in the Siskiyou Mountains of northern California. It was used for years to make arrow-shafts. Now Americans cannot afford it. No other softwood on earth commands such prices as the Japanese buyers are willing to pay for this species.

Commercial West Coast logging started around the 1870s. For decades it was all below the four-thousand-foot level. That was the era of the two-man saw, the double-bitted axe-cut undercuts, springboards, the kerosene bottle with a hook wired onto it stuck in the bark. Gypo handloggers felled into the saltwater bays of Puget Sound and rafted their logs to the mills. Then came steam donkey-engine yarders and ox teams, dragging the huge logs down corduroy skidroads or using immense wooden logging wheels that held the butt end aloft as the tail of the log dragged. The ox teams were replaced by narrow-gauge trains, and the steam donkeys by diesel. The lower elevations of the West Coast were effectively totally clear-cut.

Chris Maser (1989, xviii) says: "Every increase in the technology of logging and the utilization of wood fiber has expedited the exploitation of forests; thus from 1935 through 1980 the annual volume of timber cut has increased geometrically by 4.7% per year. . . . By the 1970s, 65% of the timber cut occurred above 4,000 feet in elevation, and because the average tree harvested has become progressively younger and smaller, the increase in annual acreage cut has been five times greater than the increase in volume cut during the last 40 years."

During these years the trains were replaced by trucks, and the high-lead yarders in many cases were replaced by the more mobile crawler-tread tractors we call Cats. From the late forties on, the graceful, musical Royal Chinook two-man falling saws were hung up on the walls of the barns, and the gasoline chainsaw became the faller's tool of choice. By the end of World War II the big logging companies had (with a few notable exceptions) managed to overexploit and mismanage their own timberlands and so they now turned to the federal lands, the people's forests, hoping for a bailout. So much for the virtues of private forest landowners—their history is abysmal—but there are still ill-informed privatization romantics who argue that the public lands should be sold to the highest bidders.

> San Francisco 2 × 4s
>   were the woods around Seattle:
> Someone killed and someone built, a house,
>   a forest, wrecked or raised
> All America hung on a hook
>   & burned by men in their own praise.

Before World War II the U.S. Forest Service played the role of a true conservation agency and spoke against the earlier era of clearcutting. It usually required its contractors to do selective logging to high standards. The allowable cut was much smaller. It went from 3.5 billion board feet in 1950 to 13.5 billion feet in 1970. After 1961 the new Forest Service leadership cosied up to the industry, and the older conservation-oriented personnel were washed out in waves through the sixties and seventies. Through the eighties the USFS had a huge road-building program. The silviculturalists said and thought of "fiber"—to "professionalize" themselves, and marginalize the actuality of "forests," and some claimed to see no difference between a monoculture plantation of even-age seedlings and a wild forest. The public-relations people would continue to recycle the conservation rhetoric of the thirties, as if the Forest Service had never permitted a questionable clearcut or sold old growth timber at a financial loss. For a few years this worked, and the public was held at bay.

The legislative mandate of the Forest Service leaves no doubt about its responsibility to manage the forest lands *as forests*, which means that lumber is only one of the values to be considered. It is clear that the forests must be managed in a way that makes them permanently sustainable. But Congress, the Department of Agriculture, and business combine to find ways around these restraints. *Renewable* is confused with *sustainable* (just because certain organisms keep renewing themselves does not mean they will do so—especially if abused—forever), and *forever*—the length of time a forest should continue to flourish—is changed to mean "about a hundred and fifty years." Despite the overwhelming evidence of mismanagement that environmental groups brought against the Forest Service bureaucracy, it arrogantly and stubbornly resisted what had become a clear public call for change. So much for the icon of "management" with its uncritical acceptance of the economic speed-trip of modern times (generating faster and faster logging rotations in the woods) as against: slow cycles.

The ragtag (and sleek D.C.-based) Forest Activist groups called for slower rotations, genuine streamside protection, fewer roads, no cuts on steep slopes, only occasional shelterwood cuts, and only the most prudent application of the appropriate smaller clearcut. We call for a return to selective logging, and to all-age trees, and to serious heart and mind for the protection of endangered species. (The Spotted Owl, the Fisher, and the Pine Marten are only part of the picture.) They said (and still say) there should be *absolutely no more logging in the remaining ancient forests.* In addition we all seek the establishment of habitat corridors to keep the old-growth stands from becoming impoverished biological islands. Many of the people in the U.S. Forest Service would now agree that such practices are essential to genuine sustainability. They are usually constrained by the tight net of exploitative policies forced on them by Congress, industry and occasional administrations. With good practices North America could maintain a lumber industry and protect a halfway decent amount of wild forest for ten thousand years. That is about the same number of years as the age of the continuously settled village culture of the Wei River valley in China, a span of time which is not excessive for humans to consider and plan by.

The deep woods turn, turn, and turn again. The ancient forests of the West are still around us. All the houses of San Francisco, Eureka, Corvallis, Portland, Seattle, Longview, are built with those old bodies: the 2x4s and siding are from the logging of the 1910s and 1920s. Strip the paint in an old San Francisco apartment and you find prime-quality coastal redwood panels. We live out our daily lives in the shelter of ancient trees. Our great-grandchildren will more likely have to live in the shelter of riverbed-aggregate. Then the forests of the past will be truly entirely gone.

Out in the forest it takes about the same number of years as the tree lived for a fallen tree to totally return to the soil. If societies could learn to live by such a pace there would be no shortages, no extinctions. There would be clear streams, and the salmon would always return to spawn.

> A virgin
> Forest
> Is ancient; many-
> Breasted,
> Stable; at
> Climax.

EXCURSUS: SAILOR MEADOW, SIERRA NEVADA

We were walking in mid-October down to Sailor Meadow (about 5,800 feet), to see an old stand on a broad bench above the north fork of the American River in the northern Sierra Nevada. At first we descended a ridge-crest through chinquapin and manzanita, looking north to the wide dome of Snow Mountain and the cliffs above Royal Gorge. The faint trail leveled out and we left it to go to the stony hills at the north edge of the hanging basin. Sitting beneath a cedar growing at the top of the rocks we ate lunch.

Then we headed southwest over rolls of forested stony formations and eventually more gentle slopes into a world of greater and greater trees. For hours we were in the company of elders.

Sugar Pines predominate. There are properly mature symmetrical trees a hundred and fifty feet high that hold themselves upright and keep their branches neatly arranged. But then *beyond* them, *above* them, loom *the ancient trees*: huge, loopy, trashy, and irregular. Their bark is redder and the plates more spread, they have fewer branches, and those surviving branches are great in girth and curve wildly. Each one is unique and goofy. Mature Incense Cedar. Some large Red Fir. An odd Douglas Fir. A few great Jeffrey Pine. (Some of the cedars have catface burn marks from some far-back fire at their bases—all on the northwest side. None of the other trees show these burn marks.)

And many snags, in all conditions: some just recently expired with red or brown dead needles still clinging, some deader yet with plates of bark hanging from the trunk (where bats nest), some pure white smooth dead ones with hardly any limbs left, but with an occasional neat woodpecker hole; and finally the ancient dead: all soft and rotten while yet standing.

Many have fallen. There are freshly fallen snags (which often take a few trees with them) and the older fallen snags. Firm down logs you must climb over, or sometimes you can walk their length, and logs that crumble as you climb them. Logs of still another age have gotten soft and begun to fade, leaving just the pitchy heartwood core and some pitchy rot-proof limbs as signs. And then there are some long subtle hummocks that are the last trace of an old gone log. The straight line of mushrooms sprouting along a smooth ground surface is the final sign, the last ghost, of a tree that "died" centuries ago.

A carpet of young trees coming in—from six inches tall to twenty feet, all sizes—waiting down here on the forest floor for the big snags standing up there dead to keel over and make more canopy space. Sunny, breezy, warm, open, light—but the great trees are all around us. Their trunks fill the sky and reflect a warm golden light. The whole canopy has that sinewy look of ancient trees. Their needles are distinctive tiny patterns against the sky—the Red Fir most strict and fine.

The forests of the Sierra Nevada, like those farther up the West Coast, date from that time when the earlier deciduous hardwood forests were beginning to fade away before the spreading success of the conifers. It is a million years of "family" here, too, the particular composition of local forest falling and rising in elevation with the ice age temperature fluctuations, advancing or retreating from north and south slope positions, but keeping the several plant communities together even as the boundaries of their zones flowed uphill or down through the centuries. Absorbing fire, adapting to the summer drought, flowing through the beetle-kill years; always a web reweaving. Acorns feeding deer, manzanita feeding robins and raccoons, Madrone feeding Band-tailed Pigeon, porcupine gnawing young cedar bark, bucks thrashing their antlers in the willows.

The middle-elevation Sierra forest is composed of Sugar Pine, Ponderosa Pine, Incense Cedar, Douglas Fir, and at slightly higher elevations Jeffrey Pine, White Fir, and Red Fir. All of these trees are long-lived. The Sugar Pine and Ponderosa are the largest of all pines. Black Oak, Live Oak, Tanbark Oak, and Madrone are the common hardwoods.

The Sierra forest is sunny-shady and dry for fully half the year. The loose litter, the crackliness, the dustiness of the duff, the curl of crisp Madrone leaves on the ground, the little coins of fallen manzanita leaves. The pine-needle floor is crunchy, the air is slightly resinous and aromatic, there is a delicate brushing of spiderwebs everywhere. Summer forest: intense play of sun and the vegetation in still steady presence—not giving up water, not wilting, not stressing, just quietly holding. Shrubs with small, aromatic, waxy, tough leaves. The shrub color is often blue-gray.

The forest was fire-adapted over the millennia and is extremely resistant to wildfire once the larger underbrush has burnt or died away. The early emigrants described driving their wagons through parklike forests of great trees as they descended the west slope of the range. The early logging was followed by devastating fires. Then came the suppression of fires by the forest agencies, and that led to the brushy understory that is so common to the Sierra now. The Sailor Meadow forest is a spacious, open, fireproof forest from the past.

At the south end of the small meadow the area is named for, beyond a thicket of aspen, standing within a grove of flourishing fir, is a remarkably advanced snag. It once was a pine over two hundred feet tall. Now around the base all the sap wood has peeled away, and what's holding the bulky trunk up is a thin column of heartwood which is itself all punky, shedding, and frazzled. The great rotten thing has a lean as well! Any moment it might go.

How curious it would be to die and then remain standing for another century or two. To enjoy "dead verticality." If humans could do it we would hear news like, "Henry David Thoreau finally toppled over." The human community, when healthy, is like an ancient forest. The little ones are in the shade and shelter of the big ones, even rooted in their lost old bodies. All ages, and all together growing and dying. What some silviculturists call for—"even-age management," plantations of trees the same size growing up together—seems like rationalistic utopian totalitarianism. We wouldn't think of letting our children live in regimented institutions with no parental visits and all their thinking shaped by a corps of professionals who just follow official manuals (written by people who never raised kids). Why should we do it to our forests?

"All-age unmanaged"—that's a natural community, human or other. The industry prizes the younger and middle-aged trees that keep their symmetry, keep their branches even of length and angle. But let there also be really old trees who can give up all sense of propriety and begin throwing their limbs out in extravagant gestures, dancelike poses, displaying their insouciance in the face of mortality, holding themselves available to whatever the world and the weather might propose. I look up to them: they are like the Chinese Immortals, they are Han-shan and Shi-de sorts of characters—to have lived that long is to have permission to be eccentric, to be the poets and painters among trees, laughing, ragged, and fearless. They make me almost look forward to old age.

In the fir grove we can smell mushrooms, and then we spot them along the base of rotten logs. A cluster of Elegant Polypores, a Cortinarius, and in the open, pushing up dry needles from below, lots of russula and boletus. Some scooped-out hollows where the deer have dug them out. Deer love mushrooms.

We tried to go straight across the southern end of the meadow but it was squishy wet beneath the dry-looking collapsed dead plants and grasses, so we went all the way around the south end through more aspen and found (and saved) more mushrooms. Clouds started blowing in from the south and the breeze filled the sky with dry pine needles raining down. It was late afternoon, so we angled up steep slopes cross-country following deer-paths for an hour and found the overgrown trail to an abandoned mine, and it led us back to the truck.

US YOKELS

This little account of the great forests of the West Coast can be taken as a model of what has been happening elsewhere on the planet. All the natural communities of the world have been, in their own way, "ancient" and every natural community, like a family, includes the infants, the adolescents, the mature adults, the elders. From the corner of the forest that has had a recent burn, with its fireweed and blackberries, to the elder moist dark groves—this is the range of the integrity of the whole. The old stands of hoary trees (or half-rotten saguaro in the Sonoran Desert or thick-boled well-established old manzanita in the Sierra foothills) are the grandparents and information-holders of their communities. A community needs its elders to continue. Just as you could not grow culture out of a population of kindergarten children, a forest cannot realize its own natural potential without the seed-reservoirs, root-fungus threads, birdcalls, and magical deposits of tiny feces that are the gift from the old to the young. Chris Maser says, "We need ancient forests for the survival of ancient forests."

When the moldboard plows of the early midwestern farmers "cut the grass roots—a sound that reminded one of a zipper being opened or closed—a new way of life opened, which simultaneously closed, probably forever, a long line of ecosystems stretching back thirty million years" (Jackson, 1987, 78). But the oldest continuous ecosystems on earth are the moist tropical forests, which in Southeast Asia are estimated to date back one hundred million years.

> Thin arching buttressing boles of the white-barked tall
> straight trees, Staghorn ferns leaning out from the limbs
> and the crotches up high. Trees they call brushbox,
> coachwood, crabapple, Australian red cedar (names
> brought from Europe)—and Red carrabeen, Yellow
> carrabeen, Stinging-trees, Deep blue openings leaning
> onward.
>
> Light of green arch of leaves far above
> Drinking the water that flows through the roots
> Of the forest, Terania creek, flowing out of Pangaia,
> Down from Gondwanaland,
> Stony soil, sky bottom shade
>
> Long ago stone deep
> Roots from the sky
> Clear water down through the roots
> Of the trees that reach high in the shade
> Birdcalls bring us awake
> Whiplash birdcalls laugh us awake—
>
> Booyong, Carrabeen, Brushbox, Black butt, Wait-a-while
> (Eucalypts dry land thin soil succeeders
> Searching scrabbly ground for seventy million years—)
>
> But these older tribes of trees
> Travel always as a group.
> Looking out from the cliffs
> On the ridge above treetops,

Sitting up in the dust ledge shelter
Where we lived all those lives.

Queensland, 1981

A multitude of corporations are involved in the deforestation of the tropics. Some got their start logging in Michigan or the Pacific Northwest—Georgia Pacific and Scott Paper are now in the Philippines, Southeast Asia, or Latin America with the same bright-colored crawler tractors and the buzzing yellow chainsaws. In the summer of 1987 in Brazil's western territory of Rondonia—as part of the chaotic "conversion" of Amazonia to other uses—an area of forest the size of Oregon was in flames. One sometimes hears the innocent opinion that everyone is a city-dweller now. That time may be coming, but at the moment the largest single population in the world is people of several shades of color farming in the warmer zones. Up until recently a large part of that realm was in trees, and the deep-forest-dwelling cultures had diverse and successful ways to live there. In those times of smaller population, the long-rotation slash-and-burn style of farming mixed with foraging posed no ecological threat. Today a combination of large-scale logging, agribusiness development, and massive dam projects threatens every corner of the backcountry.

In Brazil there is a complex set of adversaries. On one side the national government with its plans for development is allied with multinationals, wealthy cattle interests, and impoverished mainstream peasants. On the other side, resisting deforestation, are the public and private foresters and scientists making cause with the small local lumber firms, the established jungle-edge peasants, environmental organizations, and the forest-dwelling tribes. The Third World governments usually deny "native title" and the validity of communal forest ownership histories, such as the *adat* system of the Penan of Sarawak, a sophisticated multidimensional type of commons. The Penan people must put their bodies in the road to protest logging trucks *in their own homeland* and then go to jail as criminals.

Third World policies in regard to wilderness all too often run a direction set by India in 1938 when it opened the tribal forest lands of Assam to outside settlement saying "indigenous people alone would be unable, without the aid of immigrant settlers, to develop the province's enormous wasteland resources within a reasonable period" (Richards and Tucker, 1988, 107). All too many people in power in the governments and universities of the world seem to carry a prejudice against the natural world—and also against the past, against history. It seems Americans would live by a Chamber-of-Commerce Creationism that declares itself satisfied with a divinely presented Shopping Mall. The integrity and character of our own ancestors is dismissed with "I couldn't live like that" by people who barely know how to live *at all*. An ancient forest is seen as a kind of overripe garbage, not unlike the embarrassing elderly.

> Forestry. "How
> Many people
> Were harvested
> In Viet-nam?"
>
> Clear-cut. "Some
> Were children,
> Some were over-ripe."

The societies that live by the old ways (Snyder, 1977) had some remarkable skills. For those who live by foraging—the original forest botanists and zoologists—the jungle is a rich supply of fibers, poisons, medicines, intoxicants, detoxicants, containers, waterproofing, food, dyes, glues, incense, amusement, companionship, inspiration, and also stings, blows, and bites. These primary societies are like the ancient forests of our human history, with similar depths and diversities (and simultaneously "ancient" and "virgin"). The *lore* of wild nature is being lost along with the inhibitory human cultures. Each has its own humus of custom, myth, and lore that is now being swiftly lost—a tragedy for us all.

Brazil provides incentives for this kind of destructive development. Even as some mitigations are promised, there are policies in place that actively favor large corporations, displace natives, and at the same time do nothing for the mainstream poor. America disempowers Third World farmers by subsidizing overproduction at home. Capitalism plus big government often looks like welfare for the rich, providing breaks to companies that clearcut timber at a financial loss to the public. The largest single importer of tropical hardwoods is Japan (Mazda, Mitsubishi) and the second largest is the USA.

We must hammer on the capitalist economies to be at least capitalist enough to see to it that the corporations which buy timber off our public lands pay a fair market price for it. We must make the hard-boiled point that the world's trees are virtually worth more standing than they would be as lumber, because of such diverse results of deforestation as life-destroying flooding in Bangladesh and Thailand, the extinction of millions of species of animals and plants, and global warming. And, finally, we are not speaking only of forest-dwelling cultures or endangered species like voles or lemurs when we talk of ecological integrity and sustainability. We are looking at the future of our contemporary urban-industrial society as well. Not so long ago the forests were our depth, a sun-dappled underworld, an inexhaustible timeless source. Now they are vanishing. We are all endangered yokels. (*Yokel*: some English dialect, originally meaning "a green woodpecker or yellowhammer.")

On the Path, Off the Trail

WORK IN PLACE OF PLACE

PLACE IS one kind of place. Another field is the work we do, our calling, our path in life. Membership in a place includes membership in a community. Membership in a work association—whether it's a guild or a union or a religious or mercantile order—is membership in a network. Networks cut across communities with their own kind of territoriality, analogous to the long migrations of geese and hawks.

Metaphors of path and trail are from the days when journeys were on foot or by horse with packstock, when our whole human world was a network of paths. There were paths everywhere: convenient, worn, clear, sometimes even set with distance posts or stones to measure *li*, or *versts*, or *yojana*. In the forested mountains north of Kyoto I came on mossy stone measuring posts almost lost in the dense bamboo-grass ground cover. They marked (I learned much later) the dried-herring-by-backpack trade route from the Japan Sea to the old capital. There are famous trails, the John Muir trail on the crest of the High Sierra, the Natchez Trace, the Silk Road.

A path is something that can be followed, it takes you somewhere. "Linear." What would a path stand against? "No path." Off the path, off the trail. So what's *off* the path? In a sense everything *else* is off the path. The relentless complexity of the world is off to the side of the trail. For hunters and herders trails weren't always so useful. For a forager, the path is *not* where you walk for long. Wild herbs, camas bulbs, quail, dye plants, are away from the path. The whole range of items that fulfill our needs is out there. We must wander through it to learn and memorize the field—rolling, crinkled, eroded, gullied, ridged (wrinkled like the brain)—holding the map in mind. This is the economic-visualization-meditation exercise of the Inupiaq and Athapaskans of Alaska of this very day. For the forager, the beaten path shows nothing new, and one may come home empty-handed.

In the imagery of that oldest of agrarian civilizations, China, the path or the road has been given a particularly strong place. From the earliest days of Chinese civilization, natural and practical processes have been described in the language of path or way. Such connections are explicit in the cryptic Chinese text that seems to have gathered all the earlier lore and restated it for later history—the *Dao De Jing*, "The Classic of the Way and the Power." The word *dao* itself means way, road, trail, or to lead/follow. Philosophically it means the nature and way of truth. (The terminology of Daoism was adopted by early Chinese Buddhist translators. To be either a Buddhist or Daoist was to be a "person of the way.") Another extension of the meaning of *dao* is the practice of an art or craft. In Japanese, *dao* is pronounced *dō*—as in *kadō*, "the way of flowers," *bushidō*, "way of the warrior," or *sadō*, "tea ceremony."

In all the traditional arts and crafts there has been customary apprenticeship. Boys or girls of fourteen or so were apprenticed to a potter, or a company of carpenters, or weavers, dyers, vernacular pharmacologists, metallurgists, cooks, and so forth. The youngsters left home to go and sleep in the back of the potting shed and would be given the single task of mixing clay for three years, say, or sharpening chisels for three years for the carpenters. It was often unpleasant. The apprentice had to submit to the idiosyncrasies and downright meanness of the teacher and not complain. It was understood that the teacher would test one's patience and fortitude endlessly. One could not think of turning back, but just take it, go deep, and have no other interests. For an apprentice there was just this one study. Then the apprentice was gradually inducted into some not so obvious moves, standards of craft, and in-house working secrets. They also began to experience—right then, at the beginning—what it was to be "one with your work." The student hopes not only to learn the mechanics of the trade but to absorb some of the teacher's power, the *mana*—a power that goes beyond any ordinary understanding or skill.

In the Zhuang-zi (Chuang-tzu) book, a third-century B.C. witty radical Daoist text, perhaps a century or so after the *Dao De Jing*, there are a number of craft and "knack" passages:

> The Cook Ting cut up an ox for Lord Wenhui with dance-like grace and ease. "I go along with the natural makeup, strike in the big hollows, guide the knife through the big openings, and follow things as they are. So I never touch the smallest ligament or tendon, much less a main joint. . . . I've had this knife of mine for nineteen years and I've cut up thousands of oxen with it, and yet the blade is as good as though it had just come from the grindstone. There are spaces between the joints, and the blade of the knife has really no thickness. If you insert what has no thickness into such spaces, then there's plenty of room. . . . That's why after nineteen years the blade of my knife is still as good as when it first came from the grindstone." "Excellent!" said Lord Wenhui. "I have heard the words of Cook Ting and learned how to care for life!" Watson, 1968, 50–51

These stories not only bridge the spiritual and the practical, but also tease us with an image of how totally accomplished one might become if one gave one's whole life up to a work.

The occidental approach to the arts—since the rise of the bourgeoisie, if we like—is to downplay the aspect of accomplishment and push everyone to be continually doing something new. This puts a considerable burden on the workers of every generation, a double burden since they think they must dismiss the work of the generation before and then do something supposedly better and different. The emphasis on mastering the tools, on repetitive practice and training, has become very slight. In a society that follows tradition, creativity is understood as something that comes almost by accident, is unpredictable, and is a gift to certain individuals only. It cannot be programmed into the curriculum. It is better in small quantities. We should be grateful when it comes along, but don't count on it. Then when it *does* appear it's the real thing. It takes a powerful impulse for a student-apprentice who has been told for eight or ten years to "always do what was done before," as in the production tradition of folk pottery, to turn it a new way. What happens then? The old guys in this tradition look and say, "Ha! You did something new! Good for you!"

When the master artisans reach their mid-forties they begin to take on apprentices themselves and pass their skills along. They might also take up a few other interests (a little calligraphy on the side), go on pilgrimages, broaden themselves. If there is a next step (and strictly speaking there need not be one, for the skill of the accomplished craftsperson and the production of impeccable work that reflects the best of the tradition is certainly enough in one lifetime), it is to "go beyond training" for the final flower, which is not guaranteed by effort alone. There is a point beyond which training and practice cannot take you. Zeami, the superlative fourteenth-century Noh drama playwright and director who was also a Zen priest, spoke of this moment as "surprise." This is the surprise of discovering oneself needing no self, one with the work, moving in disciplined ease and grace. One knows what it is to *be* a spinning ball of clay, a curl of pure white wood off the edge of a chisel—or one of the many hands of Kannon the Bodhisattva of Compassion. At this point one can be free, with the work and from the work.

No matter how humble in social status, the skilled worker has dignity and pride—and his or her skills are needed and respected. This is not to be taken as any sort of justification for feudalism: it is simply a description of one side of how things worked in earlier times. The Far Eastern craft-and-training mystique eventually reached every corner of Japanese culture from noodle-making (the movie *Tampopo*) to big business to the high-culture arts. One of the vectors of this spread was Zen Buddhism.

Zen is the crispest example of the "self-help" (*jiriki*) wing of Mahayana Buddhism. Its community life and discipline is rather like an apprenticeship program in a traditional craft. The arts and crafts have long admired Zen training as a model of hard, clean, worthy schooling. I'll describe my experience as a *koji* (lay adept) at the monastery of Daitoku-ji, a Rinzai Zen sect temple in Kyoto, in the sixties. We sat cross-legged in meditation a minimum of five hours a day. In the breaks everyone did physical work—gardening, pickling, firewood cutting, cleaning the baths, taking turns in the kitchen. There were interviews with the teacher, Oda Sessō Rōshi, at least twice a day. At that moment we were expected to make a presentation of our grasp of the koan that had been assigned us.

We were expected to memorize certain sutras and conduct a number of small rituals. Daily life proceeded by an etiquette and a vocabulary that was truly archaic. A steady schedule of meditation and work was folded into weekly, monthly, and annual cycles of ceremonies and observations which went back to Song-dynasty China and in part clear back to the India of Shakyamuni's time. Sleep was short, the food was meager, the rooms spare and unheated, but this (in the sixties) was as true in the worker's or farmer's world as it was in the monastery.

(Novices were told to leave their pasts behind and to become one-pointed and unexceptional in all ways except the intention to enter this narrow gate of concentration on their koan. *Hone o oru*, as the saying goes — "break your bones," a phrase also used (in Japan) by workingmen, by the martial arts halls, and in modern sports and mountaineering.)

We also worked with lay supporters, often farmers, in downright convivial ways. We would stand out back in the vegetable gardens with locals discussing everything from new seed species to baseball to funerals. There were weekly begging walks down city streets and country lanes chanting and pacing along, our faces hidden under a big basket hat (waterproofed and dyed brown with persimmon juice). In fall the community made special begging trips for radishes or rice to country regions three or four ranges of hills away.

But for all its regularity, the monastic schedule could be broken for special events: on one occasion we all traveled by train to a gathering of hundreds of monks at a small but exquisite country temple for the celebration of its founding exactly five hundred years before. Our group came to be kitchen-workers: we labored for days chopping, cooking, washing, and arranging alongside the farm wives of the district. When the big feast was served we were the servers. That night, after the hundreds of guests had left, the kitchen-workers and laborers had their own feast and party, and old farmers and their wives traded crazy funny dances and songs with the Zen monks.

FREEDOM AT WORK

During one of the long meditation retreats called *sesshin*, the Rōshi lectured on the phrase "The perfect way is without difficulty. Strive hard!" This is the fundamental paradox of the way. One can be called on not to spare one's very bones in the intensity of effort, but at the same time we must be reminded that the path itself offers no hindrance, and there is a suggestion that the effort itself can lead one astray. Mere effort can heap up learning, or power, or formal accomplishment. Native abilities may be nourished by discipline, but discipline alone will not get one into the territory of "free and easy wandering" (a Zhuang-zi term). One must take care not to be victimized by one's penchant for self-discipline and hard work. One's lesser talents may lead to success in craft or business, but then one might never find out what one's more playful capacities might have been. "We study the self to forget the self," said Dōgen. "When you forget the self, you become one with the ten thousand things." Ten thousand things means all of the phenomenal world. When we are open that world can occupy us.

Yet we are still called on to wrestle with the curious phenomenon of the complex human self, needed but excessive, which resists letting the world in. Meditation practice gives us a way to scrape, soften, tan it. The intent of the koan theme is to provide the student with a brick to knock on the gate, to get through and beyond that first barrier. There are many further koans that work deeper into nondualistic seeing and being—enabling the student (as the tradition would like to have it) to ultimately be mindful, graceful, grateful, and skillful in daily life; to go beyond the dichotomy of natural and "worked." In a sense it's a practice of "an art of life."

The *Dao De Jing* itself gives us the most subtle interpretation of what the way might mean. It starts out by saying this: "The way that can be followed ('wayed') is not the constant way." *Dao ke dao fei chang dao.* First line, first chapter. It is saying: "A path that can be followed is not a *spiritual* path." The actuality of things cannot be confined within so linear an image as a road. The intention of training can only be accomplished when the "follower" has been forgotten. The way is without difficulty—it does not itself propose obstacles to us, it is open in all directions. We do, however, get in our own way—so the Old Teacher said "Strive hard!"

There are also teachers who say: "Don't try to prove something hard to yourself, it's a waste of time; your ego and intellect will be getting in your way; let all such fantastic aspirations go." They would say, at this very moment, just *be* the very mind that reads *this* word and effortlessly knows it—and you will have grasped the Great Matter. Such were the instructions of Ramana Maharshi, Krishnamurti, and the Zen Master Bankei. This was Alan Watts' version of Zen. One whole school of Buddhism takes this position—Jodo Shin, or Pure Land Buddhism, which elegant old Morimoto Roshi (who spoke Osaka dialect) said "is the only school of Buddhism that can scold Zen." It can scold it, he said, for trying too hard, for considering itself too special, and for being proud. One must have respect for the nakedness of these teachings and their ultimate correctness. Pure Land Buddhism is the purest. It resolutely resists any and all programs of self-improvement and stands only by *tariki*, which means "other-help." The "other" that might help is mythologically described as "Amida Buddha." Amida is no other than "emptiness"—the mind without conceptions or intentions, the Buddha-mind. In other words: "Give up trying to improve yourself, let the true self be your self." These teachings are frustrating for motivated people in that no real instruction is offered the hapless seeker.

Then there have always been countless unacknowledged Bodhisattvas who did not go through any formal spiritual training or philosophical quest. They were seasoned and shaped in the confusion, suffering, injustice, promise, and contradictions of life. They are the unselfish, big-hearted, brave, compassionate, self-effacing, ordinary people who in fact have always held the human family together.

There are paths that can be followed, and there is a path that cannot—it is not a path, it is the wilderness. There is a "going" but no goer, no destination, only the whole field. I first stumbled a bit off the trail in the mountains of the Pacific Northwest, at twenty-two, while a fire lookout in the North Cascades. I then determined that I would study Zen in Japan. I had a glimpse of it again looking down the aisle of a library in a Zen temple at age thirty and it helped me realize that I should not live as a monk. I moved near the monastery and participated in the meditation, the ceremonies, and the farmwork as a layperson.

I returned to North America in 1969 with my then wife and firstborn son and soon we moved to the Sierra Nevada. In addition to the work with farms, trees, and politics my neighbors and I have tried to keep up some formal Buddhist practice. We have deliberately kept it lay and nonprofessional. The Japanese Zen world of the last few centuries has become so expert and professional in the matter of strict training that it has lost to a great extent the capacity to surprise itself. The entirely dedicated and good-hearted Zen priests of Japan will defend their roles as specialists by pointing out that ordinary people cannot get into the finer points of the teachings because they cannot give enough time to it. This need not be the case for the layperson, who can be as intent on his or her Buddhist practice as any worker, artisan, or artist would be with their work.

The structure of the original Buddhist order was inspired by the tribal governance of the Shakya ("Oak Tree") nation—a tiny republic somewhat like the League of the Iroquois—with democratic rules of voting (Gard, 1949; 1956). Gautama the Buddha was born a Shakya—hence his appellation Shakyamuni, "sage of the Shakyas." The Buddhist sangha is thus modeled on the political forms of a neolithic-derived community.

So our models for practice, training, and dedication need not be limited to monasteries or vocational training, but can also look to original communities with their traditions of work and sharing. There are additional insights that come only from the nonmonastic experience of work, family, loss, love, failure. And there are all the ecological-economical connections of humans with other living beings, which cannot be ignored for long, pushing us toward a profound consideration of planting and harvesting, breeding and slaughtering. All of us are apprenticed to the same teacher that the religious institutions originally worked with: reality.

Reality-insight says get a sense of immediate politics and history, get control of your own time; master the twenty-four hours. Do it well, without self-pity. It is as hard to get the children herded into the car pool and down the road to the bus as it is to chant sutras in the Buddha-hall on a cold morning. One move is not better than the other, each can be quite boring, and they both have the virtuous quality of repetition. Repetition and ritual and their good results come in many forms. Changing the filter, wiping noses, going to meetings, picking up around the house, washing dishes, checking the dipstick—don't let yourself think these are distracting you from your more serious pursuits. Such a round of chores is not a set of difficulties we hope to escape from so that we may do our "practice" which will put us on a "path"—it *is* our path. It can be its own fulfillment, too, for who would want to set enlightenment against non-enlightenment when each is its own full reality, its own complete delusion. Dōgen was fond of saying that "practice *is* the path." It's easier to understand this when we see that the "perfect way" is not a path that leads somewhere easily defined, to some goal that is at the end of a progression. Mountaineers climb peaks for the great view, the cooperation and comradeship, the lively hardship—but mostly because it *puts you out there* where the unknown happens, where you encounter surprise.

The truly experienced person, the refined person, *delights in the ordinary*. Such a person will find the tedious work around the house or office as full of challenge and play as any metaphor of mountaineering might suggest. I would say the real *play* is in the act of going totally off the trail—away from any trace of human or animal regularity aimed at some practical or spiritual purpose. One goes out onto the "trail that cannot be followed" which leads everywhere and nowhere, a limitless fabric of possibilities, elegant variations a millionfold on the same themes, yet each point unique. Every boulder on a talus slope is different, no two needles on a fir tree are identical. How could one part be more central, more important, than any other? One will never come onto the three-foot-high heaped-up nest of a Bushy-tailed Woodrat, made of twigs and stones and leaves, unless one plunges into the manzanita thickets. Strive hard!

We find some ease and comfort in our house, by the hearth, and on the paths nearby. We find there too the tedium of chores and the staleness of repetitive trivial affairs. But the rule of impermanence means that nothing is repeated for long. The ephemerality of all our acts puts us into a kind of wilderness-in-time. We live within the nets of inorganic and biological processes that nourish everything, bumping down underground rivers or glinting as spiderwebs in the sky. Life and matter at play, chilly and rough, hairy and tasty. This is of a larger order than the little enclaves of provisional orderliness that we call ways. It *is* the Way.

Our skills and works are but tiny reflections of the wild world that is innately and loosely orderly. There is nothing like stepping away from the road and heading into a new part of the watershed. Not for the sake of newness, but for the sense of coming home to our whole terrain. "Off the trail" is another name for the Way, and sauntering off the trail is the practice of the wild. That is also where—paradoxically—we do our best work. But we need paths and trails and will always be maintaining them. You first must be on the path, before you can turn and walk into the wild.

Grace

THERE IS a verse chanted by Zen Buddhists called the "Four Great Vows." The first line goes: "Sentient beings are numberless, I vow to save them." *Shujō muhen seigando.* It's a bit daunting to announce this intention—aloud—to the universe daily. This vow stalked me for several years and finally pounced: I realized that I had vowed to let the sentient beings save *me*. In a similar way, the precept against taking life, against causing harm, doesn't stop in the negative. It is urging us to *give* life, to *undo* harm.

Those who attain some ultimate understanding of these things are called "Buddhas," which means "awakened ones." The word is connected to the English verb "to bud." I once wrote a little parable:

> *Who the Buddhas Are*
> All the beings of the universe are already realized. That is, with the exception of one or two beings. In those rare cases the cities, villages, meadows, and forests, with all their birds, flowers, animals, rivers, trees, and humans, that surround such a person, all collaborate to educate, serve, challenge, and instruct such a one, until that person also becomes a New Beginner Enlightened Being. Recently realized beings are enthusiastic to teach and train and start schools and practices. Being able to do this develops their confidence and insight up to the point that they are fully ready to join the seamless world of interdependent play. Such new enlightened beginners are called "Buddhas" and they like to say things like "I am enlightened together with, the whole universe" and so forth.
>
> *Boat in a Storm*, 1987

Good luck! One might say. The test of the pudding is in the *eating*. It narrows down to a look at the conduct that is entwined with food. At mealtime (seated on the floor in lines) the Zen monks chant:

> Porridge is effective in ten ways
> To aid the student of Zen
> No limit to the good result
> Consummating eternal happiness

and

> Oh, all you demons and spirits
> We now offer this food to you
> May all of you everywhere
> Share it with us together

and

> We wash our bowls in this water
> It has the flavor of ambrosial dew
> We offer it to all demons and spirits
> May all be filled and satisfied
> *Om makula sai svaha*

And several other verses. These superstitious-sounding old ritual formulas are never mentioned in lectures, but they are at the heart of the teaching. Their import is older than Buddhism or any of the world religions. They are part of the first and last practice of the wild: *Grace.*

Everyone who ever lived took the lives of other animals, pulled plants, plucked fruit, and ate. Primary people have had their own ways of trying to understand the precept of non-harming. They knew that taking life required gratitude and care. There is no death that is not somebody's food, no life that is not somebody's death. Some would take this as a sign that the universe is fundamentally flawed. This leads to a disgust with self, with humanity, and with nature. Otherworldly philosophies end up doing more damage to the planet (and human psyches) than the pain and suffering that is in the existential conditions they seek to transcend.

The archaic religion is to kill god and eat him. Or her. The shimmering food-chain, the food-web, is the scary, beautiful condition of the biosphere. Subsistence people live without excuses. The blood is on your own hands as you divide the liver from the gallbladder. You have watched the color fade on the glimmer of the trout. A subsistence economy is a sacramental economy because it has faced up to one of the critical problems of life and death: the taking of life for food. Contemporary people do not need to hunt, many cannot even afford meat, and in the developed world the variety of foods available to us makes the avoidance of meat an easy choice. Forests in the tropics are cut to make pasture to raise beef for the American market. Our distance from the source of our food enables us to be superficially more comfortable, and distinctly more ignorant.

Eating is a sacrament. The grace we say clears our hearts and guides the children and welcomes the guest, all at the same time. We look at eggs, apples, and stew. They are evidence of plenitude, excess, a great reproductive exuberance. Millions of grains of grass-seed that will become rice or flour, millions of codfish fry that will never, and *must* never, grow to maturity. Innumerable little seeds are sacrifices to the food-chain. A parsnip in the ground is a marvel of living chemistry, making sugars and flavors from earth, air, water. And if we do eat meat it is the life, the bounce, the swish, of a great alert being with keen ears and lovely eyes, with foursquare feet and a huge beating heart that we eat, let us not deceive ourselves.

We too will be offerings—we are all edible. And if we are not devoured quickly, we are big enough (like the old down trees) to provide a long slow meal to the smaller critters. Whale carcasses that sink several miles deep in the ocean feed organisms in the dark for fifteen years. (It seems to take about two thousand to exhaust the nutrients in a high civilization.)

At our house we say a Buddhist grace—

> We venerate the Three Treasures [teachers, the wild, and friends]
> And are thankful for this meal
> The work of many people
> And the sharing of other forms of life.

Anyone can use a grace from their own tradition (and really give it meaning)—or make up their own. Saying some sort of grace is never inappropriate, and speeches and announcements can be tacked onto it. It is a plain, ordinary, old-fashioned little thing to do that connects us with all our ancestors.

> A monk asked Dong-shan: "Is there a practice for people to follow?" Dong-shan answered: "When you become a real person, there is such a practice."

Sarvamangalam, Good Luck to All.

From
A PLACE IN SPACE
ETHICS, AESTHETICS, AND WATERSHEDS

Smokey the Bear Sutra

ONCE IN the Jurassic, about 150 million years ago, the Great Sun Buddha in this corner of the Infinite Void gave a great Discourse to all the assembled elements and energies: to the standing beings, the walking beings, the flying beings, and the sitting beings—even the grasses, to the number of thirteen billion, each one born from a seed—assembled there: a Discourse concerning Enlightenment on the planet Earth.

"In some future time, there will be a continent called America. It will have great centers of power such as Pyramid Lake, Walden Pond, Mount Rainier, Big Sur, the Everglades, and so forth, and powerful nerves and channels such as the Columbia River, Mississippi River, and Grand Canyon. The human race in that era will get into troubles all over its head and practically wreck everything in spite of its own strong intelligent Buddha-nature.

"The twisting strata of the great mountains and the pulsings of great volcanoes are my love burning deep in the earth. My obstinate compassion is schist and basalt and granite, to be mountains, to bring down the rain. In that future American Era I shall enter a new form, to cure the world of loveless knowledge that seeks with blind hunger, and mindless rage eating food that will not fill it."

And he showed himself in his true form of

SMOKEY THE BEAR.

A handsome smokey-colored brown bear standing on his hind legs, showing that he is aroused and watchful.

Bearing in his right paw the Shovel that digs to the truth beneath appearances, cuts the roots of useless attachments, and flings damp sand on the fires of greed and war;

His left paw in the Mudra of Comradely Display—indicating that all creatures have the full right to live to their limits and that deer, rabbits, chipmunks, snakes, dandelions, and lizards all grow in the realm of the Dharma;

Wearing the blue work overalls symbolic of slaves and laborers, the countless people oppressed by a civilization that claims to save but only destroys;

Wearing the broad-brimmed hat of the West, symbolic of the forces that guard the Wilderness, which is the Natural State of the Dharma and the True Path of beings on earth—all true paths lead through mountains—

With a halo of smoke and flame behind, the forest fires of the kali yuga, fires caused by the stupidity of those who think things can be gained and lost whereas in truth all is contained vast and free in the Blue Sky and Green Earth of One Mind;

Round-bellied to show his kind nature and that the great Earth has food enough for everyone who loves her and trusts her;

Trampling underfoot wasteful freeways and needless suburbs; smashing the worms of capitalism and totalitarianism;

Indicating the Task: his followers, becoming free of cars, houses, canned food, universities, and shoes, master the Three Mysteries of their own Body, Speech, and Mind, and fearlessly chop down the rotten trees and prune out the sick limbs of this country America and then burn the leftover trash.

Wrathful but Calm, Austere but Comic, Smokey the Bear will illuminate those who would help him; but for those who would hinder or slander him,

HE WILL PUT THEM OUT.

Thus his great Mantra:

> Namah samanta vajranam chanda maharoshana
> Sphataya hum traka ham mam
>
> "I DEDICATE MYSELF TO THE UNIVERSAL
> DIAMOND—BE THIS RAGING FURY DESTROYED"

And he will protect those who love woods and rivers, Gods and animals, hoboes and madmen, prisoners and sick people, musicians, playful women, and hopeful children;

And if anyone is threatened by advertising, air pollution, or the police, they should chant SMOKEY THE BEAR'S WAR SPELL:

> DROWN THEIR BUTTS
> CRUSH THEIR BUTTS
> DROWN THEIR BUTTS
> CRUSH THEIR BUTTS

And SMOKEY THE BEAR will surely appear to put the enemy out with his vajra shovel.

> Now those who recite this Sutra and then try to put it in practice will accumulate merit as countless as the sands of Arizona and Nevada,
> Will help save the planet Earth from total oil slick,
> Will enter the age of harmony of humans and nature,
> Will win the tender love and caresses of men, women, and beasts,
> Will always have ripe blackberries to eat and a sunny spot under a pine tree to sit at,
>
> AND IN THE END WILL WIN HIGHEST PERFECT ENLIGHTENMENT.

Thus have we heard.

(may be reproduced free forever)

REGARDING "SMOKEY THE BEAR SUTRA"

It's hard not to have a certain amount of devotional feeling for the Large Brown Ones, even if you don't know much about them. I met the Old Man in the Fur Coat a few times in the North Cascades—once in the central Sierra—and was suitably impressed. There are many stories told about humans marrying the Great Ones. I brought much of that lore together in my poem "this poem is for B__r," which is part of *Myths and Texts*. The Circumpolar B__r cult, we are told, is the surviving religious complex (stretching from Suomi to Utah via Siberia) of what may be the oldest religion on earth. Evidence in certain Austrian caves indicates that our Neanderthal ancestors were practicing a devotional ritual to the Big Fellow about seventy thousand years ago. In the light of meditation once it came to me that the Old One was no other than that Auspicious Being described in Buddhist texts as having taught in the unimaginably distant past, the one called "The Ancient Buddha."

So I came to realize that the U.S. Forest Service's "Smokey the B__r" publicity campaign was the inevitable resurfacing of our ancient benefactor as guide and teacher in the twentieth century, the agency not even knowing that it was serving as a vehicle for this magical reemergence.

During my years in Japan I had kept an eye out for traces of ancient B__r worship in folk religion and within Buddhism, and it came to me that Fudo Myoō, the patron of the Yamabushi (a Shinto-Buddhist society of mountain yogins), whose name means the "Immovable Wisdom King," was possibly one of those traces. I cannot provide an academic proof for this assertion; it's an intuition based on Fudo's usual habitat: deep mountains. Fudo statues and paintings portray a wickedly squinting fellow with one fang down and one fang up, a braid hanging down one side of the head, a funny gleam in his eye, wreathed in rags, holding a vajra sword and a lariat, standing on rough rock and surrounded by flames. The statues are found by waterfalls and deep in the wildest mountains of Japan. He also lurks in caves. Like the Ainu's Kamui Kimun, Lord of the Inner Mountains—clearly a B__r deity—Fudo has surpassing power, the capacity to quell all lesser violence. In the iconography he is seen as an aspect of Avalokiteśvara, the Bodhisattva of Compassion, or the consort of the beautiful Bodhisattva Tārā, She Who Saves.

It might take this sort of Buddha to quell the fires of greed and war and to help us head off the biological holocaust that the twenty-first century may well prove to be. I had such thoughts in mind when I returned to Turtle Island (North America) in December of 1968 from a long stay in Japan. A copy of the *San Francisco Chronicle* announced the Sierra Club Wilderness conference of February 1969; it was to be the following day. I saw my chance, sat down, and the sutra seemed to write itself. It follows the structure of a Mahayana Buddhist sutra fairly faithfully. The power mantra of the Great Brown One is indeed the mantra of Fudo the Immovable.

I got it printed overnight. The next morning I stood in the lobby of the conference hotel in my old campaign hat and handed out the broadsides, saying, "Smokey the B__r literature, sir." Bureau of Land Management and Forest Service officials politely took them. Forest beatniks and conservation fanatics read them with mad glints and giggles. The Underground News Service took it up, and it went to the *Berkeley Barb* and then all over the country. *The New Yorker* queried me about it, and when I told them it was both free and anonymous, they said they couldn't publish it. It soon had a life of its own, as intended.

> [*This commentary was written to accompany the sutra's inclusion in the anthology* Working the Woods, Working the Sea, *edited by Finn Wilcox and Jeremiah Gorsline (Port Townsend, Wash.: Empty Bowl Press, 1986).*]

Four Changes, with a Postscript

I. POPULATION

The Condition
POSITION: Human beings are but a part of the fabric of life—dependent on the whole fabric for their very existence. As the most highly developed tool-using animal, we must recognize that the unknown evolutionary destinies of other life forms are to be respected, and we must act as gentle steward of the earth's community of being.

SITUATION: There are now too many human beings, and the problem is growing rapidly worse. It is potentially disastrous not only for the human race but for most other life forms.

GOAL: The goal should be half of the present world population or less.

Action
SOCIAL/POLITICAL: First, a massive effort to convince the governments and leaders of the world that the problem is severe. And that all talk about raising food production—well intentioned as it is—simply puts off the only real solution: reduce population. Demand immediate participation by all countries in programs to legalize abortion, encourage vasectomy and sterilization (provided by free clinics); try to correct traditional cultural attitudes that tend to force women into childbearing; remove income-tax deductions for more than two children above a specified income level, and scale it so that lower-income families are forced to be careful, too, or pay families to limit their number. Take a vigorous stand against the policy of the right wing in the Catholic hierarchy and any other institutions that exercise an irresponsible social force in regard to this question; oppose and correct simpleminded boosterism that equates population growth with continuing prosperity. Work ceaselessly to have all political questions be seen in the light of this prime problem.

In many cases, the governments are the wrong agents to address. Their most likely use of a problem, or crisis, is as another excuse for extending their own powers. Abortion should be legal and voluntary. Great care should be taken that no one is ever tricked or forced into sterilization. The whole population issue is fraught with contradictions, but the fact stands that by standards of planetary biological welfare there are already too many human beings. The long-range answer is a steady low birthrate. Area by area of the globe, the measure of "optimum population" should be based on what is best for the total ecological health of the region, including its wildlife populations.

THE COMMUNITY: Explore other social structures and marriage forms, such as group marriage and polyandrous marriage, which provide family life but many less children. Share the pleasures of raising children widely, so that all need not directly reproduce in order to enter into this basic human experience. We must hope that no woman would give birth to more than one or two children during this period of crisis. Adopt children. Let reverence for life and reverence for the feminine mean also a reverence for other species and for future human lives, most of which are threatened.

OUR OWN HEADS: "I am a child of all life, and all living beings are my brothers and sisters, my children and grandchildren. And there is a child within me waiting to be born, the baby of a new and wiser self." Love, lovemaking, seen as the vehicle of mutual realization for a couple, where the creation of new selves and a new world of being is as important as reproducing our kind.

II. POLLUTION

The Condition

POSITION: Pollution is of two types. One sort results from an excess of some fairly ordinary substance—smoke, or solid waste—that cannot be absorbed or transmitted rapidly enough to offset its introduction into the environment, thus causing changes the great cycle is not prepared for. (All organisms have wastes and by-products, and these are indeed part of the total biosphere: energy is passed along the line and refracted in various ways. This is cycling, not pollution.) The other sort consists of powerful modern chemicals and poisons, products of recent technology that the biosphere is totally unprepared for. Such are DDT and similar chlorinated hydrocarbons; nuclear testing fallout and nuclear waste; poison gas, germ and virus storage and leakage by the military; and chemicals that are put into food, whose long-range effects on human beings have not been properly tested.

SITUATION: The human race in the last century has allowed its production and scattering of wastes, by-products, and various chemicals to become excessive. Pollution is directly harming life on the planet—which is to say, ruining the environment for humanity itself. We are fouling our air and water and living in noise and filth that no "animal" would tolerate, while advertising and politicians try to tell us we've never had it so good. The dependence of modern governments on this kind of untruth leads to shameful mind pollution, through the mass media and much school education.

GOAL: Clean air, clean clear-running rivers; the presence of pelican and osprey and gray whale in our lives; salmon and trout in our streams; unmuddied language and good dreams.

Action
SOCIAL/POLITICAL: Effective international legislation banning DDT and other poisons—with no fooling around. The collusion of certain scientists with the pesticide industry and agribusiness in trying to block this legislation must be brought out in the open. Strong penalties for water and air pollution by industries: Pollution is somebody's profit. Phase out the internal combustion engine and fossil fuel use in general; do more research into nonpolluting energy sources, such as solar energy, the tides. No more kidding the public about nuclear waste disposal: it's impossible to do it safely, so nuclear-generated electricity cannot be seriously planned for as it now stands. Stop all germ and chemical warfare research and experimentation; work toward a safe disposal of the present stupid and staggering stockpiles of H-bombs, cobalt gunk, germ and poison tanks

and cans. Provide incentives against the wasteful use of paper and so on, which adds to the solid wastes of cities—develop methods of recycling solid urban wastes. Recycling should be the basic principle behind all waste-disposal thinking. Thus, all bottles should be reusable; old cans should make more cans; old newspapers should go back into newsprint again. Establish stronger controls and conduct more research on chemicals in foods. A shift toward a more varied and sensitive type of agriculture (more small-scale and subsistence farming) would eliminate much of the call for the blanket use of pesticides.

THE COMMUNITY: DDT and such: don't use them. Air pollution: use fewer cars. Cars pollute the air, and one or two people riding lonely in a huge car is an insult to intelligence and the earth. Share rides, legalize hitchhiking, and build hitchhiker waiting stations along the highways. Also—a step toward the new world—walk more; look for the best routes through beautiful countryside for long-distance walking trips: San Francisco to Los Angeles down the Coast Range, for example. Learn how to use your own manure as fertilizer if you're in the country, as people in the Far East have done for centuries. There's a way, and it's safe. Solid waste: boycott bulky wasteful Sunday papers, which use up trees. It's all just advertising anyway, which is artificially inducing more energy consumption. Refuse bags at the store and bring your own. Organize park and street cleanup festivals. Don't work in any way for or with an industry that pollutes, and don't be drafted into the military. Don't waste. (A monk and an old master were once walking in the mountains. They noticed a little hut upstream. The monk said, "A wise hermit must live there." The master said, "That's no wise hermit—you see that lettuce leaf floating down the stream? He's a Waster." Just then an old man came running down the hill with his beard flying and caught the floating lettuce leaf.) Carry your own jug to the winery and have it filled from the barrel.

OUR OWN HEADS: Part of the trouble with talking about something like DDT is that the use of it is not just a practical device, it's almost an establishment religion. There is something in Western culture that wants to wipe out creepy-crawlies totally and feels repugnance for toadstools and snakes. This is fear of one's own deepest inner-self wilderness areas, and the answer is to *relax*. Relax around bugs, snakes, and your own hairy dreams. Again, we all should share our crops with a certain percentage of bug life as a way of "paying our dues." Thoreau says, "How then can the harvest fail? Shall I not rejoice also at the abundance of the weeds whose seeds are the granary of the birds? It matters little comparatively whether the fields fill the farmer's barns. The true husbandman will cease from anxiety, as the squirrels manifest no concern whether the woods will bear chestnuts this year or not, and finish his labor with every day, relinquish all claim to the produce of his fields, and sacrificing in his mind not only his first but his last fruits also." In the realm of thought, inner experience, consciousness, as in the outward realm of interconnection, there is a difference between balanced cycle and the excess that cannot be handled. When the balance is right, the mind recycles from highest illuminations to the muddy blinding anger or grabbiness that sometimes seizes us all—the alchemical "transmutation."

III. CONSUMPTION

The Condition
POSITION: Everything that lives eats food and is food in turn. This complicated animal, the human being, rests on a vast and delicate pyramid of energy transformations. To grossly use more than you need, to destroy, is biologically unsound. Much of the production and consumption of modern societies is not necessary or conducive to spiritual and cultural growth, let alone survival, and is behind much greed and envy, age-old causes of social and international discord.

SITUATION: Humanity's careless use of "resources" and its total dependence on certain substances such as fossil fuels (which are being exhausted, slowly but certainly) are having harmful effects on all the other members of the life network. The complexity of modern technology renders whole populations vulnerable to the deadly consequences of the loss of any one key resource. Instead of independence we have overdependence on life-giving substances such as water, which we squander. Many species of animals and birds have become extinct in the service of fashion fads, or fertilizer, or industrial oil. The soil is being used up; in fact, humanity has become a locustlike blight on the planet that will leave a bare cupboard for its own children—all the while living in a kind of addict's dream of affluence, comfort, eternal progress, using the great achievements of science to produce software and swill.

GOAL: Balance, harmony, humility, growth that is a mutual growth with redwood and quail; to be a good member of the great community of living creatures. True affluence is not needing anything.

Action
SOCIAL/POLITICAL: It must be demonstrated ceaselessly that a continually "growing economy" is no longer healthy, but a cancer. And that the criminal waste that is allowed in the name of competition—especially that ultimate in wasteful needless competition, hot wars and cold wars with "communism" (or "capitalism")—must be halted totally with ferocious energy and decision. Economics must be seen as a small subbranch of ecology, and production/distribution/consumption handled by companies or unions or cooperatives with the same elegance and spareness one sees in nature. Soil banks; open spaces; logging to be truly based on sustained yield (the U.S. Forest Service is—sadly—now the lackey of business). Protection for all scarce predators and varmints: "Support your right to arm bears." Damn the International Whaling Commission, which is selling out the last of our precious, wise whales; ban absolutely all further development of roads and concessions in national parks and wilderness areas; build auto campgrounds in the least desirable areas. Initiate consumer boycotts of dishonest and unnecessary products. Establish co-ops. Politically, blast both "communist" and "capitalist" myths of progress and all crude notions of conquering or controlling nature.

THE COMMUNITY: Sharing and creating. The inherent aptness of communal life, where large tools are owned jointly and used efficiently. The power of renunciation: if enough Americans refused to buy a new car for one given year, it would permanently alter the American economy. Recycling clothes and equipment. Support handicrafts, gardening, home skills, midwifery, herbs—all the things that can make us independent, beautiful, and whole. Learn to break the habit of acquiring unnecessary possessions—a monkey on everybody's back—but avoid a self-abnegating antijoyous self-righteousness. Simplicity is light, carefree, neat, and loving—not a self-punishing ascetic trip. (The great Chinese poet Tu Fu said, "The ideas of a poet should be noble and simple.") Don't shoot a deer if you don't know how to use all the meat and preserve what you can't eat, to tan the hide and use the leather—to use it all, with gratitude, right down to the sinew and hooves. Simplicity and mindfulness in diet are the starting point for many people.

OUR OWN HEADS: It is hard even to begin to gauge how much a complication of possessions, the notions of "my and mine," stand between us and a true, clear, liberated way of seeing the world. To live lightly on the earth, to be aware and alive, to be free of egotism, to be in contact with plants and animals, starts with simple concrete acts. The inner principle is the insight that we are interdependent energy fields of great potential wisdom and compassion, expressed in each person as a superb mind, a handsome and complex body, and the almost magical capacity of language. To these potentials and capacities, "owning things" can add nothing of authenticity. "Clad in the sky, with the earth for a pillow."

IV. TRANSFORMATION

The Condition

POSITION: Everyone is the result of four forces: the conditions of this known universe (matter/energy forms and ceaseless change), the biology of one's species, individual genetic heritage, and the culture one is born into. Within this web of forces there are certain spaces and loops that allow to some persons the experience of inner freedom and illumination. The gradual exploration of some of these spaces constitutes "evolution" and, for human cultures, what "history" could increasingly be. We have it within our deepest powers not only to change our "selves" but to change our culture. If humans are to remain on earth, they must transform the five-millennia-long urbanizing civilization tradition into a new ecologically sensitive harmony-oriented wild-minded scientific-spiritual culture. "Wildness is the state of complete awareness. That's why we need it."

SITUATION: Civilization, which has made us so successful a species, has overshot itself and now threatens us with its inertia. There is also some evidence that civilized life isn't good for the human gene pool. To achieve the Changes, we must change the very foundations of our society and our minds.

GOAL: Nothing short of total transformation will do much good. What we envision is a planet on which the human population lives harmoniously and dynamically by employing various sophisticated and unobtrusive technologies in a world environment that is "left natural." Specific points in this vision:

- A healthy and spare population of all races, much less in number than today.
- Cultural and individual pluralism, unified by a type of world tribal council. Division by natural and cultural boundaries rather than arbitrary political boundaries.
- A technology of communication, education, and quiet transportation, land use being sensitive to the properties of each region. Allowing, thus, the bison to return to much of the High Plains. Careful but intensive agriculture in the great alluvial valleys; deserts left wild for those who would live there by skill. Computer technicians who run the plant part of the year and walk along with the elk in their migrations during the rest.
- A basic cultural outlook and social organization that inhibits power and property seeking while encouraging exploration and challenge in things like music, meditation, mathematics, mountaineering, magic, and all other ways of authentic being-in-the-world. Women totally free and equal. A new kind of family—responsible, but more festive and relaxed—is implicit.

Action
SOCIAL/POLITICAL: It seems evident that throughout the world there are certain social and religious forces that have worked through history toward an ecologically and culturally

enlightened state of affairs. Let these be encouraged: Gnostics, hip Marxists, Teilhard de Chardin Catholics, Druids, Taoists, Biologists, Witches, Yogins, Bhikkus, Quakers, Sufis, Tibetans, Zens, Shamans, Bushmen, American Indians, Polynesians, Anarchists, Alchemists—the list is long. Primitive cultures, communal and ashram movements, cooperative ventures. Since it doesn't seem practical or even desirable to think that direct bloody force will achieve much, it would be best to consider this change a continuing "revolution of consciousness," which will be won not by guns but by seizing the key images, myths, archetypes, eschatologies, and ecstasies so that life won't seem worth living unless one's on the side of the transforming energy. We must take over "science and technology" and release its real possibilities and powers in the service of this planet—which, after all, produced us and it.

(More concretely: no transformation without our feet on the ground. Stewardship means, for most of us, find your place on the planet, dig in, and take responsibility from there—the tiresome but tangible work of school boards, county supervisors, local foresters, local politics, even while holding in mind the largest scale of potential change. Get a sense of workable territory, learn about it, and start acting point by point. On all levels, from national to local, the need to move toward steady state economy—equilibrium, dynamic balance, inner growth stressed—must be taught. Maturity/diversity/climax/creativity.)

THE COMMUNITY: New schools, new classes, walking in the woods and cleaning up the streets. Find psychological techniques for creating an awareness of "self" that includes the social and natural environment. Consideration of what specific language forms—symbolic systems—and social institutions constitute obstacles to ecological awareness. Without falling into a facile interpretation of McLuhan, we can hope to use the media. Let no one be ignorant of the facts of biology and related disciplines; bring up our children as part of the wildlife. Some communities can establish themselves in backwater rural areas and flourish, others can maintain themselves in urban centers, and the two types can work together—a two-way flow of experience, people, money, and homegrown vegetables. Ultimately cities may exist only as joyous tribal gatherings and fairs, to dissolve after a few weeks. Investigating new lifestyles is our work, as is the exploration of ways to explore our inner realms—with the known dangers of crashing that go with such. Master the archaic and the primitive as models of basic nature-related cultures—as well as the most imaginative extensions of science—and build a community where these two vectors cross.

OUR OWN HEADS: Are where it starts. Knowing that we are the first human beings in history to have so much of our past culture and previous experience available to our study, and being free enough of the weight of traditional cultures to seek out a larger identity; the first members of a civilized society since the Neolithic to wish to look clearly into the eyes of the wild and see our selfhood, our family, there. We have these advantages to set off the obvious disadvantages of being as screwed up as we are—which gives us a fair chance to penetrate some of the riddles of ourselves and the universe, and to go beyond the idea of "human survival" or "survival of the biosphere" and to draw our strength from the realization that at the heart of things is some kind of serene and ecstatic process that is beyond qualities and beyond birth and death. "No need to survive!" "In the fires that destroy the universe at the end of the kalpa, what survives?" "—The iron tree blooms in the void!"

Knowing that nothing need be done is the place from which we begin to move.

POSTSCRIPT (1995)

Four Changes was written in 1969. Michael McClure, Richard Brautigan, Steve Beckwitt, Keith Lampe, Cliff Humphreys, Alan Watts, Allen Hoffman, Stewart Brand, and Diane di Prima were among those who read it during its formative period and offered suggestions and criticisms. It was widely distributed in several free editions. I added a few more lines and comments in 1974, when it was published together with the poems in *Turtle Island* (New York: New Directions, 1974). Now it's 1995, and a quarter century has elapsed. The apprehension we felt in 1969 has not abated. It would be a fine thing to be able to say,

"We were wrong. The natural world is no longer as threatened as we said then." One can take no pleasure, in this case, in having been on the right track. Many of the larger mammals face extinction, and all manner of species are endangered. Natural habitat ("raw land") is fragmented and then destroyed ("developed"). The world's forests are being relentlessly logged by multinational corporations. Air, water, and soil are all in worse shape. Population continues to climb, and even if it were a world of perfect economic and social justice, I would argue that ecological justice calls for fewer people. The few remaining traditional people with place-based sustainable economies are driven into urban slums and cultural suicide. The quality of life for everyone everywhere has gone down, what with resurgent nationalism, racism, violence both random and organized, and increasing social and economic inequality. There are whole nations for whom daily life is an ongoing disaster. Naive and utopian as some of it sounds now, I still stand by the basics of "Four Changes." As I wrote in 1969,

> My Teacher once said to me,
> —become one with the knot itself,
> till it dissolves away.
> —sweep the garden.
> —any size.

"Energy Is Eternal Delight"

A YOUNG WOMAN at Sir George Williams University in Montreal asked me, "What do you fear most?" I found myself answering "that the diversity and richness of the gene pool will be destroyed," and most people there understood what I meant.

The treasure of life is the richness of stored information in the diverse genes of all living beings. If the human race, following on some set of catastrophes, were to survive at the expense of many plant and animal species, it would be no victory. Diversity provides life with the capacity for a multitude of adaptations and responses to long-range changes on the planet. The possibility remains that at some future time another evolutionary line might carry the development of consciousness to clearer levels than our family of upright primates.

The United States, Europe, the Soviet Union, and Japan have a habit. They are addicted to heavy energy use, great gulps and injections of fossil fuel. As fossil fuel reserves go down, they will take dangerous gambles with the future health of the biosphere (through nuclear power) to keep up their habit.

For several centuries Western civilization has had a priapic drive for material accumulation, continual extensions of political and economic power, termed "progress." In the Judeo-Christian worldview humans are seen as working out their ultimate destinies (paradise? perdition?) with planet earth as the stage for the drama—trees and animals mere props, nature a vast supply depot. Fed by fossil fuel, this religio-economic view has become a cancer: uncontrollable growth. It may finally choke itself and drag much else down with it.

The longing for growth is not wrong. The nub of the problem now is how to flip over, as in jujitsu, the magnificent growth energy of modern civilization into a nonacquisitive search for deeper knowledge of self and nature. Self-nature. Mother Nature. If people come to realize that there are many nonmaterial, nondestructive paths of growth—of the highest and most fascinating order—it would help dampen the common fear that a steady state economy would mean deadly stagnation.

I spent a few years, some time back, in and around a training place. It was a school for monks of the Rinzai branch of Zen Buddhism, in Japan. The whole aim of the community was personal and universal liberation. In this quest for spiritual freedom every man marched strictly to the same drum in matters of hours of work and meditation. In the teacher's room one was pushed across sticky barriers into vast new spaces. The training was traditional and had been handed down for centuries—but the insights are forever fresh and new. The beauty, refinement, and truly civilized quality of that life has no match in modern America. It is supported by hand labor in small fields, gathering brushwood to heat the bath, drinking well water, and making barrels of homemade pickles.

The Buddhists teach respect for all life and for wild systems. A human being's life is totally dependent on an interpenetrating network of wild systems. Eugene Odum, in his useful paper "The Strategy of Ecosystem Development," points out how the United States has the characteristics of a young ecosystem. Some American Indian cultures have "mature" characteristics: protection as against production, stability as against growth, quality as against quantity. In Pueblo societies a kind of ultimate democracy is practiced. Plants and animals are also people and, through certain rituals and dances, are given a place and a voice in the political discussions of the humans. They are "represented." "Power to *all* the people" must be the slogan.

On Hopi and Navajo land, at Black Mesa, the industrial world is eating away at the earth in the form of strip-mining. This to provide electricity for Los Angeles. The defense of Black Mesa is being sustained by traditional Indians, young Indian militants, and longhairs. Black Mesa speaks to us through old stories. She is said to be sacred territory. To hear her voice is to give up the European word *America* and accept the new-old name for the continent, Turtle Island.

The return to marginal farmland on the part of some young people is not some nostalgic replay of the nineteenth century. Here is a generation of white people finally ready to learn from the Elders. How to live on the continent as though our children, and on down, for many ages, will still be here (not on the moon). Loving and protecting this soil, these trees, these wolves. Natives of Turtle Island.

A scaled-down, balanced technology is possible, if cut loose from the cancer of exploitation/heavy industry/perpetual growth. Those who have already sensed these necessities and have begun, whether in the country or the city, to "grow with less" are the only counterculture that counts. Electricity for Los Angeles is not exactly energy. As Blake said, "Energy is eternal delight."

> [*This was first published in the "Plain Talk" section of* Turtle Island *(New York: New Directions, 1974).*]

Unnatural Writing

"Nature writing" has become a matter of increased literary interest in the last few years. The subject matter "nature," and the concern for it (and us humans in it), have come—it is gratifying to note—to engage artists and writers. This interest may be another strand of postmodernism, since the modernist avant-garde was strikingly urban-centered. Many would-be writers approach this territory in a mode of curiosity, respect, and concern, without necessarily seeking personal gain or literary reputation. They are doing it for love—and the eco-warrior's passion, not money. (There is still a wide range of views and notions about what nature writing ought to be. There is an older sort of nature writing that might be seen as largely essays and writing from a human perspective, middle-class, middlebrow Euro-American. It has a rhetoric of beauty, harmony, and sublimity. What makes us uncomfortable sometimes with John Muir's writing is an excess of this. He had contemporaries, now forgotten, who were far worse.)

Natural history writing is another branch. Semiscientific, objective, in the descriptive mode. Both these sorts are "naively realistic" in that they unquestioningly accept the front-mounted bifocal human eye, the poor human sense of smell, and other characteristics of our species, plus the assumption that the mind can, without much self-examination, directly and objectively "know" whatever it looks at. There has also always been a literature of heroic journals and adventure. And there is an old mix of science, nature appreciation, and conservation politics that has been a potent part of the evolution of the conservation movement in the United States. The best of this would be seen in the work of Rachel Carson and Aldo Leopold. All of these writings might be seen by some as mildly anthropocentric, but the work is worthy and good-hearted. We are in its debt.

Nature writing has been a class of literature held in less than full regard by the literary establishment, because it is focused on something other than the major subject matter of mainstream occidental writing, the moral quandaries, heroics, affairs of the heart, and soul searchings of highly gifted and often powerful people, usually male. Tales of the elites. In fact, up until a decade ago nature writing was relegated pretty much to a status like that of nineteenth-century women's writing—it was seen as a writing of sensibility and empathy and observation, but off to the side, not really serious, not important.

But if we look at the larger context of occidental history, educated elites, and literary culture, we see that the natural world is profoundly present in and an inescapable part of the great works of art. The human experience over the larger part of its history has been played out in intimate relationship to the natural world. This is too obvious even to say, yet it is often oddly forgotten. History, philosophy, and literature naturally foreground human affairs, social dynamics, dilemmas of faith, intellectual constructs. But a critical subtheme that runs through it all has to do with defining the human relationship to the rest of nature. In literature, nature not only provides the background, the scene, but also many of the characters. The "classical" world of myth is a world in which animal beings, supernatural figures, and humans are actors and interacters. Bears, bulls, and swans were not abstractions to the people of earlier times but real creatures in very real landscapes. The aurochs—the giant wild cow, *Bos primigenius*, who became Zeus to Europa—survived in pockets of the European forests until medieval times.

In *The Practice of the Wild*, I point out that through most of human history

> populations were relatively small and travel took place on foot, by horse, or by sail. Whether Greece, Germania, or Han China, there were always nearby areas of forest, and wild animals, migratory waterfowl, seas full of fish and whales, and these were part of the experience of every active person. Animals as characters in literature and as universal presences in the imagination and in the archetypes of religion are there because they were *there*. Ideas and images of wastelands, tempests, wildernesses, and mountains are born not of abstraction but of experience: cisalpine, hyperboreal, circumpolar, transpacific, or beyond the pale. [This is the world people lived in up

until the late nineteenth century. Plentiful wildlife, open space, small human population, trails instead of roads—and human lives of individual responsibility and existential intensity. It is not "frontier" that we're considering, but the Holocene era, our *present* era, in all its glory of salmon, bear, elk, deer, and moose.] Where do the sacred salmon of the Celts, the Bjorns and Brauns and Brun-(hilde)-s [bher = bear] of northern European literature, the dolphins of the Mediterranean, the Bear dances of Artemis, the Lion skin of Herakles come from but the wild systems the humans lived near?

> Those images that yet
> Fresh images beget
> That dolphin-torn, that gong-tormented sea.

Many figures in the literary field, the critical establishment, and the academy are not enthralled with the natural world, and indeed some positively doubt its worth when compared to human achievement. Take this quote from Howard Nemerov, a good poet and a decent man:

> Civilization, mirrored in language, is the garden where relations grow; outside the garden is the wild abyss.

The unexamined assumptions here are fascinating. They are, at worst, crystallizations of the erroneous views that enable the developed world to displace Third and Fourth World peoples and overexploit nature globally. Nemerov here proposes that language is somehow implicitly civilized or civilizing, that civilization is orderly, that intrahuman relations are the pinnacle of experience (as though all of us, and all life on the planet, were not interrelated), and that "wild" means "abyssal," disorderly, and chaotic.

First take language. Some theorists have latched onto "language" as that which somehow makes us different. They have the same enthusiasm for the "Logos" as the old Summer Institute of Linguistics had for Bible translation into unwritten languages. In fact, every recent writer who doesn't know what else to say about his or her work—when asked to give a sound bite—has declared, "Well, I'm just fascinated with language." The truth is language is part and parcel of consciousness, and we know virtually nothing about either one. Our study and respect should extend to them both.

On another tack, the European deconstructionists assume, because of their monotheistic background, that the Logos died along with God. Those who wish to decenter occidental metaphysics have begun to try to devalue both language and nature and declare them to be further tools of ruling-class mythology. In the past, the idea that the external world was our own invention came out of some variety of idealist thought. But *this* version leads to a weird philosophical position that, since the proponents are academic "meta-Marxists," might be called "materialist solipsism." But they are just talk.

There is some truly dangerous language in a term heard in some business and government circles: "sustainable development." Development is not compatible with sustainability and biodiversity. We must drop talking about development and concentrate on how to achieve a steady-state condition of real sustainability. Much of what passes for economic development is simply the further extension of the destabilizing, entropic, and disorderly functions of industrial civilization.

So I will argue that consciousness, mind, imagination, *and* language are fundamentally wild. "Wild" as in wild ecosystems—richly interconnected, interdependent, and incredibly complex. Diverse, ancient, and full of information. At root the real question is how we understand the concepts of order, freedom, and chaos. Is art an imposition of order on chaotic nature, or is art (also read "language") a matter of discovering the grain of things, of uncovering the measured chaos that structures the natural world? Observation, reflection, and practice show artistic process to be the latter.

Our school-in-the-mountains here at Squaw Valley is called "Art of the Wild." (I was wondering just what edible root might have been growing so profusely in this wet mountain bottomland to have caused it to be called "Squaw Valley." Any place with the word *squaw* in the name is usually where some early trappers saw numerous Native American women at work gathering wild food; here it might have been *Brodiaea* bulbs. This naming practice is as though some native women coming on a Euro-American farming community had called it White Boy Flats.)

The "art of the wild" is to see art in the context of the process of nature—nature *as* process rather than as product or commodity—because "wild" is a name for the way that phenomena continually actualize themselves. Seeing this also serves to acknowledge the autonomy and integrity of the nonhuman part of the world, an "Other" that we are barely beginning to be able to know. In disclosing, discovering, the wild world with our kind of writing, we may find ourselves breaking into unfamiliar territories that do not seem anything like what was called "nature writing" in the past. The work of the art of the wild can well be irreverent, inharmonious, ugly, frazzled, unpredictable, simple, and clear—or virtually inaccessible. Who will write of the odd barbed, hooked, bent, splayed, and crooked penises of nonhuman male creatures? Of sexism among spiders? Someone will yet come to write with the eye of an insect, write from the undersea world, and in other ways that step outside the human.

In *Practice* it says:

> Life in the wild is not just eating berries in the sunlight. I like to imagine a "depth ecology" that would go to the dark side of nature—the ball of crunched bones in a scat, the feathers in the snow, the tales of insatiable appetite. Wild systems are in one elevated sense above criticism, but they can also be seen as irrational, moldy, cruel, parasitic. Jim Dodge told me how he had watched—with fascinated horror—orcas methodically batter a gray whale to death in the Chukchi Sea. Life is not just diurnal and a property of large interesting vertebrates, it is also nocturnal, anaerobic, cannibalistic, microscopic, digestive, fermentative: cooking away in the warm dark. Life is well maintained at a four mile ocean depth, is waiting and sustained on a frozen rock wall, and clinging and nourished in hundred-degree desert temperatures. And there is a world of nature on the decay side, a world of beings who do rot and decay in the shade. Human beings have made much of purity, and are repelled by blood, pollution, putrefaction. The other side of the "sacred" is the sight of your beloved in the underworld, dripping with maggots. Coyote, Orpheus, and Izanagi cannot help but look, and they lose her. Shame, grief, embarrassment, and fear are the anaerobic fuels of the dark imagination. The less familiar energies of the wild world, and their analogs in the imagination, have given us ecologies of the imagination. . . .

Narratives are one sort of trace that we leave in the world. All our literatures are leavings, of the same order as the myths of wilderness peoples who leave behind only stories and a few stone tools. Other orders of beings have their own literatures. Narrative in the deer world is a track of scents that is passed on from deer to deer, with an art of interpretation which is instinctive. A literature of bloodstains, a bit of piss, a whiff of estrus, a hit of rut, a scrape on a sapling, and long gone. And there might be a "narrative theory" among these other beings—they might ruminate on "intersexuality," or "decomposition criticism."

I propose this to turn us loose to think about "wild writing" without preconception or inhibition, but at the same time with craft. The craft could be seen as the swoop of a hawk, the intricate galleries of burrowing and tunneling under the bark done by western pine bark beetles, the lurking at the bottom by a big old trout—or the kamikaze sting of a yellow jacket, the insouciant waddle of a porcupine, the constant steadiness of a flow of water over a boulder, the chatter of a squirrel, hyenas moaning and excavating the bowels of a dead giraffe under a serene moon. Images of our art. Nature's writing has the potential of becoming the most vital, radical, fluid, transgressive, pansexual, subductive, and morally challenging kind of writing on the scene. In becoming so, it may serve to help halt one of the most terrible things of our time—the destruction of species and their habitats, the elimination of some living beings forever.

Finally, let us not get drawn too far into dichotomous views and arguments about civilization versus nature, the domesticated versus the wild, the garden versus the wild abyss. Creativity draws on wildness, and wildness confers freedom, which is (at bottom) the ability to live in the real physical daily world at each moment, totally and completely.

SOME POINTS FOR A "NEW NATURE POETICS"

- That it be literate—that is, nature literate. Know who's who and what's what in the ecosystem, even if this aspect is barely visible in the writing.
- That it be grounded in a place—thus, place literate: informed about local specifics on both ecological-biotic

and sociopolitical levels. And informed about history (social history and environmental history), even if this is not obvious in the poem.
- That it use Coyote as a totem—the trickster, always open, shape shifting, providing the eye of other beings going in and out of death, laughing with the dark side.
- That it use Bear as a totem—omnivorous, fearless, without anxiety, steady, generous, contemplative, and relentlessly protective of the wild.
- That it find further totems—this is the world of nature, myth, archetype, and ecosystem that we must each investigate. "Depth ecology."
- That it fear not science. Go *beyond* nature literacy into the emergent new territories in science: landscape ecology, conservation biology, charming chaos, complicated systems theory.
- That it go further with science—into awareness of the problematic and contingent aspects of so-called objectivity.
- That it study mind and language—language as wild system, mind as wild habitat, world as a "making" (poem), poem as a creature of the wild mind.
- That it be crafty and get the work *done*.

[*The original version of this essay was given as a talk the first year of the "Art of the Wild" nature-writing conference series, held at Squaw ("Brodiaea Harvesters") Valley in July 1992.*]

The Porous World

CRAWLING

I WAS forging along the crest of a ridge, finding a way between stocky deep red mature manzanita trunks, picking the route and heading briskly on. Crawling.

Not hiking or sauntering or strolling, but *crawling*, steady and determined, through the woods. We usually visualize an excursion into the wild as an exercise of walking upright. We imagine ourselves striding through open alpine terrain—or across the sublime space of a sagebrush basin—or through the somber understory of an ancient sugar-pine grove.

But it's not so easy to walk upright through the late-twentieth-century midelevation Sierra forests. There are always many sectors regenerating from fire or logging, and the fire history of the Sierra would indicate that there have always been some areas of manzanita fields. So people tend to stay on the old logging roads or the trails, and this is their way of experiencing the forest. Manzanita and ceanothus fields, or the brushy ground cover and understory parts of the forest, are left in wild peace.

This crawl was in late December, and although the sky was clear and sunny, the temperature was around freezing. Patches of remnant snow were on the ground. A few of us were out chasing corners and boundary lines on the Bear Tree parcel (number 6) of the 'Inimim Community Forest with a retiring Bureau of Land Management forester, a man who had worked with that land many years before and still remembered the surveys. No way to travel off the trail but to dive in: down on your hands and knees on the crunchy manzanita leaf cover and crawl around between the trunks. Leather work gloves, a tight-fitting hat, long-sleeved denim work jacket, and old Filson tin pants make a proper crawler's outfit. Along the ridge a ways, and then down a steep slope through the brush, belly-sliding on snow and leaves like an otter—you get limber at it. And you see the old stumps from early logging surrounded by thick manzanita, still-tough pitchy limbs from old wolf trees, hardy cones, overgrown drag roads, four-foot butt logs left behind, webs of old limbs and twigs and the periodic prize of a bear scat. So, face right in the snow, I came on the first of many bear tracks.

Later, one of our party called us back a bit: "A bear tree!" And sure enough, there was a cavity in a large old pine that had opened up after a fire had scarred it. A definite black bear hangout, with scratches on the bark. To go where bears, deer, raccoons, foxes—all our other neighbors—go, you have to be willing to crawl.

So we have begun to overcome our hominid pride and learned to take pleasure in turning off the trail and going directly into the brush, to find the contours and creatures of the pathless part of the woods. Not really pathless, for there is the whole world of little animal trails that have their own logic. You go down, crawl swift along, spot an opening, stand and walk a few yards, and go down again. The trick is to have no attachment to standing; find your body at home on the ground, be a quadruped, or if necessary, a snake. You brush cool dew off a young fir with your face. The delicate aroma of leaf molds and mycelium rise from the tumbled humus under your hand, and a half-buried young boletus is disclosed. You can *smell* the fall mushrooms when crawling.

We began to fantasize on the broader possibilities of crawling. We could offer Workshops in Power Crawling! And in self-esteem—no joke! Carole said, "I've learned an important lesson. You can attain your goals, if you're willing to crawl!"

It's not always easy, and you can get lost. Last winter we took a long uphill cross-country transect on some of the land just above the Yuba Gorge; this soon turned into a serious crawl. We got into denser and denser old manzanita that had us doing commando-style lizard crawls to get under the very low limbs. It became an odd and unfamiliar ridge, and I had no idea where we might be. For hundreds of yards, it seemed, we were scuttling along, and then we came on a giant, totally fresh, worm-free *Boletus edulis*, the prize of all the boletes. That went into the little day pack. And a bit farther the manzanita opened and there we were! We were in a gap below an old cabin built half onto BLM land at the edge of the Hindu yoga camp, and soon we found the dirt road that led toward home. One more victorious expedition through the underbrush.

As wide open spaces shrink around us, maybe we need to discover the close-up charms of the brushlands, and their little spiders, snakes, ticks (yikes!), little brown birds, lizards, wood rats, mushrooms, and poison-oak vines. It's not for everyone, this world of little scats and tiny tracks. But for those who are bold, I'd say get some gloves and a jacket and a hat and go out and *explore California*.

LIVING IN THE OPEN

One can choose to live in a place as a sort of visitor, or try to become an inhabitant. My family and I decided from early on to try to be here, in the midelevation forests of the Sierra Nevada, as fully as we could. This brave attempt was backed by lack of resources and a lot of dumb bravado. We figured that simplicity would of itself be beautiful, and we had our own extravagant notions of ecological morality. But necessity was the teacher that finally showed us how to live as part of the natural community.

It comes down to how one thinks about screens, fences, or dogs. These are often used for keeping the wild at bay. ("Keeping the wild at bay" sounds like fending off hawks and bears, but it is more often a matter of holding back carpenter ants and deer mice.) We came to live a permeable, porous life in our house set among the stands of oak and pine. Our buildings are entirely opened up for the long Sierra summer. Mud daubers make their trips back and forth from inside the house to the edge of the pond like tireless little cement trucks, and pour their foundations on beams, in cracks, and (if you're not alert) in rifle-bore holes and backpack fire-pump nozzles. They dribble little spots of mud as they go. For mosquitoes, which are never much of a problem, the house is just another place to enjoy the shade. At night the bats dash around the rooms, in and out of the open skylights, swoop down past your cheek and go out an open sliding door. In the dark of the night the deer can be heard stretching for the lower leaves of the apple trees, and at dawn the wild turkeys are strolling a few yards from the bed.

The price we pay is the extra effort to put all the pantry food into jars or other mouse-proof containers. Winter bedding goes into mouse-proof chests. Then ground squirrels come right inside for fresh fruit on the table, and the deer step into the shade shelter to nibble a neglected salad. You are called to a hopeful steadiness of nerves as you lift a morsel of chicken to the mouth with four meat bees following it every inch of the way. You must sometimes (in late summer) cook and eat with the yellow jackets watching every move. This can make you peevish, but there is a kind of truce that is usually attained when one quits flailing and slapping at the wasps and bees.

It's true, living and cooking in the outdoor shade shelters someone occasionally gets stung. That's one price you might pay for living in the porous world, but it's about the worst that can happen. There's a faint risk of rattlesnake bite as we stride around the little trails, and the ever-present standoffishness of poison oak. But if you can get used to life in the semiopen, it's a great way to enjoy the forest.

It's also a form of conservation. As people increasingly come to inhabit the edges and inholdings of forest lands, they have to think carefully about how they will alter this new-old habitat. The number of people that can be wisely accommodated on the land cannot be determined simply by saying how many acres are required for a single household. This kind of planning is essential right now, and I'm all for it, but we have to remember that the cultural practices of households alone can make huge differences in impact.

Necessary roads should be thoughtfully routed and of modest width, with the occasional fire-truck turnout. Fire protections should be provided by having the roads well brushed along the edges, with plenty of thinning back into the woods, rather than building an excessively wide roadbed. If roads are a bit rough, it will slow cars down, and that's not all bad. If there are no or very few fences, if people are not pumping too heavily from their wells to irrigate pasture or orchards, if the number of dogs is kept modest, if the houses are well insulated and temperatures are held at the low sixties in the winter, if feral cats are not allowed, if an attitude of tolerance is cultivated toward the occasional mischief of critters, we will cause almost no impact on the larger forest ecosystem. But if there are too many people who hate insects and coyotes, who are perpetually annoyed by deer and who get hysterical about bears and cougars, there goes the neighborhood.

It's possible and desirable to take out firewood lightly, to cut some deliberately chosen sawlogs, to gather manzanita berries for the cider, to seek redbud for basketry supplies, and to pursue any of a number of other subtle economic uses of the forest. As we thin saplings, remove underbrush, and move tentatively toward the occasional prescribed burn, we are even helping the forest go its own direction. Maybe we will yet find ways to go past the dichotomy of the wild and the cultivated. Coyotes and screech owls make the night magic; log-truck airhorns are an early morning wakeup.

Permeability, porousness, works both ways. You are allowed to move through the woods with new eyes and ears when you let go of your little annoyances and anxieties. Maybe this is what the great Buddhist philosophy of interconnectedness means when it talks of "things moving about in the midst of each other without bumping."

[*"Living in the Open" (1991) and "Crawling" (1992) appeared in numbers 2 and 3 of* Tree Rings, *the newsletter of the Yuba Watershed Institute.*]

Coming into the Watershed

I HAD BEEN too long in the calm Sierra pine groves and wanted to hear surf and the cries of seabirds. My son Gen and I took off one February day to visit friends on the north coast. We drove out of the Yuba River canyon, and went north from Marysville—entering that soulful winter depth of pearly tule fog—running alongside the Feather River and then crossing the Sacramento River at Red Bluff. From Red Bluff north the fog began to shred, and by Redding we had left it behind. As we crossed the mountains westward from Redding on Highway 299, we paid special attention to the transformations of the landscape and trees, watching to see where the zones would change and the natural boundaries could be roughly determined. From the Great Valley with its tules, grasses, valley oak, and blue oak, we swiftly climbed into the steep and dissected Klamath range with its ponderosa pine, black oak, and manzanita fields. Somewhere past Burnt Ranch we were in the redwood and Douglas fir forests—soon it was the coastal range. Then we were descending past Blue Lake to come out at Arcata.

We drove on north. Just ten or fifteen miles from Arcata, around Trinidad Head, the feel of the landscape subtly changed again—much the same trees, but no open meadows, and a different light. At Crescent City we asked friends just what the change between Arcata and Crescent City was. They both said (to distill a long discussion), "You leave 'California.' Right around Trinidad Head you cross into the maritime Pacific Northwest." But the Oregon border (where we are expected to think "the Northwest" begins) is still many miles farther on.

So we had gone in that one afternoon's drive from the Mediterranean-type Sacramento Valley and its many plant alliances with the Mexican south, over the interior range with its dry pine-forest hills, into a uniquely Californian set of redwood forests, and on into the maritime Pacific Northwest: the edges of four major areas. These boundaries are not hard and clear, though. They are porous, permeable, arguable. They are boundaries of climates, plant communities, soil types, styles of life. They change over the millennia, moving a few hundred miles this way or that. A thin line drawn on a map would not do them justice. Yet these are the markers of the natural nations of our planet, and they establish real territories with real differences to which our economies and our clothing must adapt.

On the way back we stopped at Trinidad Head for a hike and a little birding. Although we knew they wouldn't be there until April, we walked out to take a look at the cliffs on the head, where tufted puffins nest. For tufted puffins, this is virtually the southernmost end of their range. Their more usual nesting ground is from southeastern Alaska through the Bering Sea and down to northern Japan. In winter they are far out in the open seas of the North Pacific. At this spot, Trinidad, we could not help but feel that we touched on the life realm of the whole North Pacific and Alaska. We spent that whole weekend enjoying "liminality," dancing on the brink of the continent.

I have taken to watching the subtle changes of plants and climates as I travel over the West. We can all tell stories, I know, of the drastic changes we have noticed as we raged over this or that freeway. This vast area called "California" is large enough to be beyond any one individual's ability (not to mention time) to travel over and to take it all into the imagination and hold it clearly enough in mind to see the whole picture. Michael Barbour, a botanist and lead author of *California's Changing Landscapes*, writes of the complexity of California: "Of the world's ten major soils, California has all ten. . . . As many as 375 distinctive natural communities have been recognized in the state. . . . California has more than five thousand kinds of native ferns, conifers, and flowering plants. Japan has far fewer species with a similar area. Even with four times California's area, Alaska does not match California's plant diversity, and neither does all of the central and northeastern United States and adjacent Canada combined. Moreover, about 30 percent of California's native plants are found nowhere else in the world."

But all this talk of the diversity of California is a trifle misleading. Of what place are we speaking? What is "California"? It is, after all, a recent human invention with hasty straight-line boundaries that were drawn with a ruler on a map and rushed off to an office in D.C. This is another illustration of Robert Frost's lines, "The land was ours before we were the land's." The political boundaries of the western states were established in haste and ignorance. Landscapes have their own shapes and structures, centers and edges, which must be respected. If a relationship to a place is like a marriage, then the Yankee establishment of a jurisdiction called California was like a shotgun wedding with six sisters taken as one wife.

California is made up of what I take to be about six regions. They are of respectable size and native beauty, each with its own makeup, its own mix of birdcalls and plant smells. Each of these proposes a slightly different lifestyle to the human beings who live there. Each led to different sorts of rural economies, for the regional differences translate into things like raisin grapes, wet rice, timber, cattle pasture, and so forth.

The central coast with its little river valleys, beach dunes and marshes, and oak-grass-pine mountains is one region. The great Central Valley is a second, once dominated by swamps and wide shallow lakes and sweeps of valley oaks following the streams. The long mountain ranges of the Sierra Nevada are a third. From a sort of Sonoran chaparral they rise to arctic tundra. In the middle elevations they have some of the finest mixed conifer forests in the world. The Modoc plateau and volcano country—with its sagebrush and juniper—makes a fourth. Some of the Sacramento waters rise here. The fifth is the northern coast with its deep interior mountains—the Klamath region—reaching (on the coast) as far north as Trinidad Head. The sixth (of these six sisters) consists of the coastal valleys and mountains south of the Tehachapis, with natural connections on into Baja. Although today this region supports a huge population with water drawn from the Colorado River, the Owens Valley, and the great Central Valley, it was originally almost a desert.

One might ask, What about the rest? Where are the White Mountains, the Mojave Desert, the Warner Range? They are splendid places, but they do not belong with California. Their watersheds and biological communities belong to the Great Basin or the lower Colorado drainage, and we should let them return to their own families. Almost all of core California has a summer-dry Mediterranean climate, with (usually) a fairly abundant winter rain. More than anything else, this rather special type of climate is what gives our place its fragrance of oily aromatic herbs, its olive-green drought-resistant shrubs, and its patterns of rolling grass and dark forest.

I am not arguing that we should instantly redraw the boundaries of the social construction called California, although that could happen some far day. But we are becoming aware of certain long-range realities, and this thinking leads toward the next step in the evolution of human citizenship on the North American continent. The usual focus of attention for most Americans is the human society itself with its problems and its successes, its icons and symbols. With the exception of most Native Americans and a few non-natives who have given their hearts to the place, the land we all live on is simply taken for granted—and proper relation to it is not considered a part of "citizenship." But after two centuries of national history, people are beginning to wake up and notice that the United States is located on a landscape with a severe, spectacular, spacy, wildly demanding, and ecstatic narrative to be learned. Its natural communities are each unique, and each of us, whether we like it or not—in the city or countryside—lives in one of them.

Those who work in resource management are accustomed to looking at many different maps of the landscape. Each addresses its own set of meanings. If we look at land ownership categories, we get (in addition to private land) the Bureau of Land Management, national forest, national park, state park, military reserves, and a host of other public holdings. This is the public domain, a practice coming down from the historic institution of the commons in Europe. These lands, particularly in the arid West, hold much of the water, forest, and wildlife that are left in America. Although they are in the care of all the people, they have too often been managed with a bent toward the mining or logging interests and toward short-term profits.

Conservationists have been working since the 1930s for sustainable forestry practices and the preservation of key blocks of public land as wilderness. They have had some splendid success in this effort, and we are all indebted to the single-minded dedication of the people who are behind every present-day wilderness area that we and our children walk into. Our growing understanding of how natural systems work brought us the realization that an exclusive emphasis on disparate parcels of land ignored the insouciant freeness of wild creatures. Although individual islands of wild land serving as biological refuges are invaluable, they cannot by themselves guarantee the maintenance of natural variety. As biologists, public land managers, and the involved public have all agreed, we need to know more about how the larger-scale natural systems work, and we need to find "on-the-ground" ways to connect wild zone to wild zone wherever possible. We have now developed the notion of biological corridors or connectors. The Greater Yellowstone Ecosystem concept came out of this sort of recognition. Our understanding of nature has been radically altered by systems theory as applied to ecology, and in particular to the very cogent subdisciplines called island biogeography theory and landscape ecology.

No single group or agency could keep track of grizzly bears, which do not care about park or ranch boundaries and have necessary, ancient territories of their own that range from late-summer alpine huckleberry fields to lower-elevation grasslands. Habitat flows across both private and public land. We must find a way to work with wild ecosystems that respects both the rights of landowners and the rights of bears. The idea of ecosystem management, all the talk now in land management circles, seems to go in the right direction. Successfully managing for the ecosystem will require as much finesse in dealing with miners, ranchers, and motel owners as it does with wild animals or bark beetles.

A "greater ecosystem" has its own functional and structural coherence. It often might contain or be within a watershed system. It would usually be larger than a county, but smaller than a western U.S. state. One of the names for such a space is "bioregion."

A group of California-based federal and state land managers who are trying to work together on biodiversity problems recently realized that their work could be better accomplished in a framework of natural regions. Their interagency "memorandum of understanding" calls for us to "move beyond existing efforts focused on the conservation of individual sites, species, and resources . . . to also protect and manage ecosystems, biological communities, and landscapes." The memorandum goes on to say that "public agencies and private groups must coordinate resource management and environmental protection activities, emphasizing regional solutions to regional issues and needs."

The group identified eleven or so such working regions within California, making the San Francisco Bay and delta into one, and dividing both the Sierra and the valley into northern and southern portions. (In landscapes as in taxonomy, there are lumpers and splitters.) Since almost 50 percent of California is public domain, it is logical that the chiefs of the BLM, the Forest Service, California Department of Fish and Game, California Department of Forestry, State Parks, the federal Fish and Wildlife Service, and such should take these issues on, but that they came together in so timely a manner and signed onto such a far-reaching plan is admirable.

Hearing of this agreement, some county government people, elected officials, and timber and business interests in the mountain counties went into a severe paranoid spasm, fearing—they said—new regulations and more centralized government. So later in the fall, an anonymous circular made its way around towns and campuses in northern California under the title "Biodiversity or New Paganism?" It says that "California Resource Secretary Doug Wheeler and his self-appointed bioregional soldiers are out to devalue human life by placing greater emphasis on rocks, trees, fish, plants, and wildlife." It quotes me as having written that "those of us who are now promoting a bioregional consciousness would, as an ultimate and long-range goal, like to see this continent more sensitively redefined, and the natural regions of North America—Turtle Island—gradually begin to shape the political entities within which we work. It would be a small step toward the deconstruction of America as a superpower into seven or eight natural nations—none of which have a budget big enough to support missiles." I'm pleased to say I did write that. I'd think it was clear that my statement is not promoting more centralized government, which seems to be a major fear, but these gents want both their small-town autonomy and the military-industrial state at the same time. Many a would-be westerner is a rugged individualist in rhetoric only, and will scream up a storm if taken too far from the government tit. As Marc Reisner makes clear in *Cadillac Desert*, much of the agriculture and ranching of the West exists by virtue of a complicated and very expensive sort of government welfare: big dams and water plans. The real intent of the circular (it urges people to write the state governor) seems to be to resist policies that favor long-range sustainability and the support of biodiversity, and to hold out for maximum resource extraction right now.

As far as I can see, the intelligent but so far toothless California "bioregional proposal" is simply a basis for further thinking and some degree of cooperation among agencies. The most original part is the call for the formation of "bioregional councils" that would have some stake in decision making. Who would be on the bioregional councils is not spelled out. Even closer to the roots, the memorandum that started all this furor suggests that "watershed councils" would be formed, which, being based on stream-by-stream communities, would be truly local bodies that could help design agreements working for the preservation of natural variety. Like, let's say, helping to preserve the spawning grounds for the wild salmon that still come (amazingly) into the lower Yuba River gravel wastelands. This would be an effort that would have to involve a number of groups and agencies, and it would have to include the blessing of the usually development-minded Yuba County Water Agency.

The term *bioregion* was adopted by the signers to the Memorandum on Biological Diversity as a technical term from the field of biogeography. It's not likely that they would have known that there were already groups of people around the United States and Canada who were talking in terms of bioregionally oriented societies. I doubt they would have heard about the first North American Bioregional Congress held in Kansas in the late eighties. They had no idea that for twenty years communitarian ecology-minded dwellers-in-the-land have been living in places they call "Ish" (Puget Sound and lower British Columbia) or "Columbiana" (upper Columbia River) or "Mesechabe" (lower Mississippi), or "Shasta" (northern California), and all of them have produced newsletters, taken field trips, organized gatherings, and at the same time participated in local politics.

That "bioregion" was an idea already in circulation was the bad, or good, luck of the biodiversity agreement people, depending on how you look at it. As it happens, the bioregional people are also finding "watershed councils" to be the building blocks of a long-range strategy for social and environmental sustainability.

A watershed is a marvelous thing to consider: this process of rain falling, streams flowing, and oceans evaporating causes every molecule of water on earth to make the complete trip once every two million years. The surface is carved into watersheds—a kind of familial branching, a chart of relationship, and a definition of place. The watershed is the first and last nation whose boundaries, though subtly shifting, are unarguable. Races of birds, subspecies of trees, and types of hats or rain gear often go by the watershed. For the watershed, cities and dams are ephemeral and of no more account than a boulder that falls in the river or a landslide that temporarily alters the channel. The water will always be there, and it will always find its way down. As constrained and polluted as the Los Angeles River is at the moment, it can also be said that in the larger picture that river is alive and well under the city streets, running in giant culverts. It may be amused by such diversions. But we who live in terms of centuries rather than millions of years must hold the watershed and its communities together, so our children might enjoy the clear water and fresh life of this landscape we have chosen. From the tiniest rivulet at the crest of a ridge to the main trunk of a river approaching the lowlands, the river is all one place and all one land.

The water cycle includes our springs and wells, our Sierra snowpack, our irrigation canals, our car wash, and the spring salmon run. It's the spring peeper in the pond and the acorn woodpecker chattering in a snag. The watershed is beyond the dichotomies of orderly/disorderly, for its forms are free, but somehow inevitable. The life that comes to flourish within it constitutes the first kind of community.

The agenda of a watershed council starts in a modest way: like saying, "Let's try and rehabilitate our river to the point that wild salmon can successfully spawn here again." In pursuit of this local agenda, a community might find itself combating clear-cut timber sales upstream, water-selling grabs downstream, Taiwanese drift-net practices out in the North Pacific, and a host of other national and international threats to the health of salmon.

If a wide range of people will join in on this effort—people from timber and tourism, settled ranchers and farmers, fly-fishing retirees, the businesses and the forest-dwelling new settlers—something might come of it. But if this joint agreement were to be implemented as a top-down prescription, it would go nowhere. Only a grass-roots engagement with long-term land issues can provide the political and social stability it will take to keep the biological richness of California's regions intact.

All public land ownership is ultimately written in sand. The boundaries and the management categories were created by Congress, and Congress can take them away. The only "jurisdiction" that will last in the world of nature is the watershed, and even that changes slightly over time. If public lands come under greater and greater pressure to be opened for exploitation and use in the twenty-first century, it will be the local people, the watershed people, who will prove to be the last and possibly most effective line of defense. Let us hope it never comes to that.

The mandate of the public land managers and the Fish and Wildlife people inevitably directs them to resource concerns. They are proposing to do what could be called "ecological bioregionalism." The other movement, coming out of the local communities, could be called "cultural bioregionalism." I would like to turn my attention now to cultural bioregionalism and to what practical promise these ideas hold for fin-de-millennium America.

Living in a place—the notion has been around for decades and has usually been dismissed as provincial, backward, dull, and possibly reactionary. But new dynamics are at work. The mobility that has characterized American life is coming to a close. As Americans begin to stay put, it may give us the first opening in over a century to give participatory democracy another try.

Daniel Kemmis, the mayor of Missoula, Montana, has written a fine little book called *Community and the Politics of Place*.

Mr. Kemmis points out that in the eighteenth century the word *republican* meant a politics of community engagement. Early republican thought was set against the federalist theories that would govern by balancing competing interests, devise sets of legalistic procedures, maintain checks and balances (leading to hearings held before putative experts) in place of direct discussion between adversarial parties.

Kemmis quotes Rousseau: "Keeping citizens apart has become the first maxim of modern politics." So what organizing principle will get citizens back together? There are many, and each in its way has its use. People have organized themselves by ethnic background, religion, race, class, employment, gender, language, and age. In a highly mobile society where few people stay put, thematic organizing is entirely understandable. But place, that oldest of organizing principles (next to kinship), is a novel development in the United States.

"What holds people together long enough to discover their power as citizens is their common inhabiting of a single place," Kemmis argues. Being so placed, people will volunteer for community projects, join school boards, and accept nominations and appointments. Good minds, which are often forced by company or agency policy to keep moving, will make notable contributions to the neighborhood if allowed to stay put. And since local elections deal with immediate issues, a lot more people will turn out to vote. There will be a return of civic life.

This will not be "nationalism" with all its danger, as long as sense of place is not entirely conflated with the idea of a nation. Bioregional concerns go beyond those of any ephemeral (and often brutal and dangerous) politically designated space. They give us the imagination of "citizenship" in a place called (for example) the great Central Valley, which has valley oaks and migratory waterfowl as well as humans among its members. A place (with a climate, with bugs), as Kemmis says, "develops practices, creates culture."

Another fruit of the enlarged sense of nature that systems ecology and bioregional thought have given us is the realization that cities and suburbs are all part of the system. Unlike the ecological bioregionalists, the cultural bioregionalists absolutely must include the cities in their thinking. The practice of urban bioregionalism ("green cities") has made a good start in

San Francisco. One can learn and live deeply with regard to wild systems in any sort of neighborhood—from the urban to a big sugar-beet farm. The birds are migrating, the wild plants are looking for a way to slip in, the insects in any case live an untrammeled life, the raccoons are padding through the crosswalks at 2:00 A.M., and the nursery trees are trying to figure out who they are. These are exciting, convivial, and somewhat radical knowledges.

An economics of scale can be seen in the watershed/bioregion/city-state model. Imagine a Renaissance-style city-state facing out on the Pacific with its bioregional hinterland reaching to the headwaters of all the streams that flow through its bay. The San Francisco/valley rivers/Shasta headwaters bio-city-region! I take some ideas along these lines from Jane Jacobs's tantalizing book *Cities and the Wealth of Nations*, in which she argues that the city, not the nation-state, is the proper locus of an economy, and then that the city is always to be understood as being one with the hinterland.

Such a non-nationalistic idea of community, in which commitment to pure place is paramount, cannot be ethnic or racist. Here is perhaps the most delicious turn that comes out of thinking about politics from the standpoint of place: anyone of any race, language, religion, or origin is welcome, as long as they live well on the land. The great Central Valley region does not prefer English over Spanish or Japanese or Hmong. If it had any preferences at all, it might best like the languages it heard for thousands of years, such as Maidu or Miwok, simply because it's used to them. Mythically speaking, it will welcome whoever chooses to observe the etiquette, express the gratitude, grasp the tools, and learn the songs that it takes to live there.

This sort of future culture is available to whoever makes the choice, regardless of background. It need not require that a person drop his or her Buddhist, Jewish, Christian, animist, atheist, or Muslim beliefs but simply add to that faith or philosophy a sincere nod in the direction of the deep value of the natural world and the subjecthood of nonhuman beings. A culture of place will be created that will include the "United States," and go beyond that to an affirmation of the continent, the land itself, Turtle Island. We could be showing Southeast

Asian and South American newcomers the patterns of the rivers, the distant hills, saying, "It is not only that you are now living in the United States. You are living in this great landscape. Please get to know these rivers and mountains, and be welcome here." Euro-Americans, Asian Americans, African Americans can—if they wish—become "born-again" natives of Turtle Island. In doing so we also might even (eventually) win some respect from our Native American predecessors, who are still here and still trying to teach us where we are.

Watershed consciousness and bioregionalism is not just environmentalism, not just a means toward resolution of social and economic problems, but a move toward resolving both nature and society with the practice of a profound citizenship in both the natural and the social worlds. If the ground can be our common ground, we can begin to talk to each other (human and nonhuman) once again.

> California is gold-tan grasses, silver-gray tule fog,
> olive-green redwood, blue-gray chaparral,
> silver-hue serpentine hills.
> Blinding white granite,
> blue-black rock sea cliffs.
> —Blue summer sky, chestnut brown slough water,
> steep purple city streets—hot cream towns.
> Many colors of the land, many colors of the skin.

> [*This essay was first given as a talk for the California Studies Center at Sacramento State College, as part of their conference entitled "Dancing at the Edge," on February 6, 1992. It was published in the* San Francisco Examiner *on March 1 and 2, 1992, and was soon reprinted in a number of other periodicals and anthologies in the United States and England.*]

Kitkitdizze: A Node in the Net

JETS HEADING west on the Denver-to-Sacramento run start losing altitude east of Reno, and the engines cool as they cross the snowy Sierra crest. They glide low over the west-tending mountain slopes, passing above the canyon of the north fork of the American River. If you look north out the window you can see the Yuba River country, and if it's really clear you can see the old "diggings"—large areas of white gravel laid bare by nineteenth-century gold mining. On the edge of one of those is a little hill where my family and I live. It's on a forested stretch between the South Yuba canyon and the two thousand treeless acres of old mining gravel, all on a forty-mile ridge that runs from the High Sierra to the valley floor near Marysville, California. You're looking out over the northern quarter of the greater Sierra ecosystem: a vast summer-dry hardwood-conifer forest, with drought-resistant shrubs and bushes in the canyons, clear-cuts, and burns.

In ten minutes the jet is skimming over the levees of the Sacramento River and wheeling down the strip. It then takes two and a half hours to drive out of the valley and up to my place. The last three miles seem to take the longest—we like to joke that it's still the bumpiest road we've found, go where we will.

Back in the mid-sixties I was studying in Japan. Once, while I was on a visit to California, some friends suggested that I join them in buying mountain land. In those days land and gas were both still cheap. We drove into the ridge and canyon country, out to the end of a road. We pushed through manzanita thickets and strolled in open stretches of healthy ponderosa pine. Using a handheld compass, I found a couple of brass caps that mark corners. It was a new part of the Sierra for me. But I knew the assembly of plants—ponderosa pine, black oak, and associates—well enough to know what the rainfall and climate would be, and I knew I liked their company. There was a wild meadow full of native bunchgrass. No regular creek, but a slope with sedges that promised subsurface water. I told my friends to count me in. I put down the money for a twenty-five-acre share of the hundred acres and returned to Japan.

In 1969, back for good in California, we drove out to the land and made a family decision to put our life there. At that time there were virtually no neighbors, and the roads were even worse than they are now. No power lines, no phones, and twenty-five miles—across a canyon—to town. But we had the will and some of the skills as well. I had grown up on a small farm in the Northwest and had spent time in the forests and mountains since childhood. I had worked at carpentry and been a Forest Service seasonal worker, so mountain life (at three thousand feet) seemed do-able. We weren't really "in the wilderness" but rather in a zone of ecological recovery. The Tahoe National Forest stretches for hundreds of square miles in the hills beyond us.

I had also been a logger on an Indian reservation in the ponderosa pine forests of eastern Oregon, where many trees were more than two hundred feet tall and five feet through. That land was drier and a bit higher, so the understory was different, but it grew the same adaptable cinnamon-colored pines. The trees down here topped out at about a hundred feet; they were getting toward being a mature stand, but a long way from old growth. I talked with a ninety-year-old neighbor who had been born in the area. He told me that when he was young he had run cattle over my way and had logged here and there, and that a big fire had gone through about 1920. I trimmed the stump on a black oak that had fallen and counted the rings: more than three hundred years. Lots of standing oaks that big around, so it was clear that the fires had not been total. Besides the pine stands (mixed with incense cedar, madrona, a few Douglas firs), our place was a mosaic of postfire manzanita fields with small pines coming through; stable climax manzanita; an eight-acre stand of pure black oak; and some areas of blue oak, gray pine, and grasses. Also lots of the low ground-cover bush called *kitkitdizze* in the language of the Wintun, a nearby valley people. It was clear from the very old and scattered stumps that this area had been selectively logged once. A neighbor with an increment borer figured that some trees had been cut about 1940. The surrounding lands and the place I was making my home flowed together with unmarked boundaries; to the eye and to the creatures, it was all one.

We had our hands full the first ten years just getting up walls and roofs, bathhouse, small barn, woodshed. A lot of it was done the old way: we dropped all the trees to be used in the frame of the house with a two-man falling saw, and peeled them with drawknives. Young women and men with long hair joined the work camp for comradeship, food, and spending money. (Two later became licensed architects; many of them stayed and are neighbors today.) Light was from kerosene lamps; we heated with wood and cooked with wood and propane. Wood-burning ranges, wood-burning sauna stoves, treadle-operated sewing machines, and propane-using Servel refrigerators from the fifties were the targets of highly selective shopping runs. Many other young settlers found their place in northern California in the early seventies, so eventually there was a whole reinhabitory culture living this way in what we like to call Shasta Nation.

I set up my library and wrote poems and essays by lantern light, then went out periodically, lecturing and teaching around the country. I thought of my home as a well-concealed base camp from which I raided university treasuries. We named our place Kitkitdizze after the aromatic little shrub.

The scattered neighbors and I started meeting once a month to talk about local affairs. We were all nature lovers, and everyone wanted to cause as little impact as possible. Those with well-watered sites with springs and meadows put in small gardens and planted fruit trees. I tried fruit trees, a chicken flock, a kitchen garden, and beehives. The bees went first. They were totally destroyed in one night by a black bear. The kitchen garden did fairly well until the run of dry winters that started in the eighties and may finally be over. And, of course, no matter how you fence a garden, deer find a way to get in. The chickens were constant targets of northern goshawks, red-tailed hawks, raccoons, feral dogs, and bobcats. A bobcat once killed twenty-five in one month. The fruit trees are still with us, especially the apples. They, of all the cultivars, have best made themselves at home. (The grosbeaks and finches always seem to beat us to the cherries.) But in my heart I was never into gardening. I couldn't see myself as a logger again either, and it wasn't the place to grow Christmas trees. Except for cutting fallen oak and pine for firewood, felling an occasional pole for framing, and frequent clearing of the low limbs and underbrush well back from the homestead to reduce fire hazard, I hadn't done much with the forest. I wanted to go lightly, to get a deep sense of it, and thought it was enough to leave it wild, letting it be the wildlife habitat it is.

Living in a place like this is absolutely delicious. Coyote-howl fugues, owl exchanges in the treetops, the almost daily sighting of deer (and the rattle of antlers at rutting season), the frisson of seeing a poky rattlesnake, tracking critters in the snowfall, seeing cougar twice, running across humongous bear scats, sharing all this with the children are more than worth the inconveniences.

My original land partners were increasingly busy elsewhere. It took a number of years, but we bought our old partners out and ended up with the whole hundred acres. That was sobering. Now Kitkitdizze was entirely in our hands. We were cash poor and land rich, and who needs more second-growth pine and manzanita? We needed to rethink our relation to this place with its busy—almost downtown—rush of plants and creatures. Do we leave it alone? Use it, but how? And what responsibility comes with it all?

Now it is two grown sons, two stepdaughters, three cars, two trucks, four buildings, one pond, two well pumps, close to a hundred chickens, seventeen fruit trees, two cats, about ninety cords of firewood, and three chainsaws later. I've learned a lot, but there still is plenty of dark and unknown territory. (There's one boundary to this land down in the chaparral—it borders the BLM—that I *still* haven't located.) Black bear leave pawprints on woodshed refrigerators, and bobcats, coyotes, and foxes are more in evidence than ever, sometimes strolling in broad daylight. Even the diggings, which were stripped of soil by giant nozzles washing out the scattered gold, are colonized by ever-hardy manzanita and bonsai-looking pine. The first major environmental conflict in California was between Sacramento Valley farmers and the hydraulic gold miners of the Yuba. Judge Lorenzo Sawyer's decision of 1884 banned absolutely all release of mining debris into the watershed. That was the end of hydraulic mining here. We now know that the amount of material that was washed out of the Sierra into the valley and onto good farmlands was eight times the amount of dirt removed for the Panama Canal.

The kerosene lights have been replaced by a photovoltaic array powering a mixed AC/DC system. The phone company put in an underground line to our whole area at its own expense. My wife Carole and I are now using computers, the writer's equivalent of a nice little chainsaw. (Chainsaws and computers increase both macho productivity and nerdy stress.) My part-time teaching job at the University of California, Davis, gives me an internet account. We have entered the late twentieth century and are tapping into political and environmental information with a vengeance.

The whole Sierra is a mosaic of ownership—various national forests, Bureau of Land Management, Sierra Pacific Industries, state parks, and private holdings—but to the eye of a hawk it is one great sweep of rocks and woodlands. We, along with most of our neighbors, were involved in the forestry controversies of the last decade, particularly in regard to the long-range plans for the Tahoe National Forest. The county boosters still seem to take more pleasure in the romance of the gold era than in the subsequent processes of restoration. The Sierra foothills are still described as "Gold Country," the highway is called "49," there are businesses called "Nugget" and "Bonanza." I have nothing against gold—I wear it in my teeth and in my ear—but the real wealth here is the great Sierran forest. My neighbors and I have sat in on many hearings and had long and complicated discussions with silviculturalists, district rangers, and other experts from the Forest Service. All these public and private designations seem to come with various "rights." With just "rights" and no land ethic, our summer-dry forests could be irreversibly degraded into chaparral over the coming centuries. We were part of a nationwide campaign to reform forest practices. The upshot was a real and positive upheaval on a national scale in the U.S. Forest Service and the promise of ecosystem management, which if actualized as described would be splendid.

We next turned our focus to the nearby public lands managed by the BLM. It wasn't hard to see that these public lands were a key middle-elevation part of a passageway for deer and other wildlife from the high country to the valleys below.

Our own holdings are part of that corridor. Then we were catapulted into a whole new game: the BLM area manager for central California became aware of our interest, drove up and walked the woods with us, talked with us, consulted with the community, and then said, "Let's cooperate in the long-range planning for these lands. We can share information." We agreed to work with him and launched a biological inventory, first with older volunteers and then with our own wild teenagers jumping in. We studied close to three thousand forested acres. We bushwhacked up and down the canyons to find out just what was there, in what combinations, in what quantity, in what diversity.

Some of it was tallied and mapped (my son Kai learned Geographical Information Systems techniques and put the data into a borrowed Sun Sparc workstation), and the rest of our observations were written up and put into bundles of notes on each small section. We had found some very large trees, located a California spotted owl pair, noted a little wetland with carnivorous sticky sundew, described a unique barren dome with serpentine endemics (plants that grow only in this special chemistry), identified large stands of vivid growing forest, and were struck by the tremendous buildup of fuel. The well-intended but ecologically ignorant fire-exclusion policies of the government agencies over the last century have made the forests of California an incredible tinderbox.

The droughty forests of California have been shaped for millennia by fire. A fire used to sweep through any given area, forest historians are now saying, roughly every twenty-five years, and in doing so kept the undergrowth down and left the big trees standing. The native people also deliberately started fires, so that the California forests of two hundred years ago, we are told, were structured of huge trees in parks that were fire-safe. Of course, there were always some manzanita fields and recovering burns, but overall there was far less fuel. To "leave it be wild" in its present state would be risking a fire that might set the land back to first-phase brush again. The tens of thousands of homes and ranches mixed among the wooded foothills down the whole Sierra front could burn.

The biological inventory resulted in the formation of the Yuba Watershed Institute, a nonprofit organization made up of local people, sponsoring projects and research on forestry, biodiversity, and economic sustainability with an eye to the larger region. One of the conclusions of the joint-management plan, unsurprisingly, was to try to reduce fuel load by every available means. We saw that a certain amount of smart selective logging would not be out of place, could help reduce fuel load, and might pay some of the cost of thinning and prescriptive burning. We named our lands, with the BLM's blessing, the 'Inimim Forest, from the Nisenan word for *pine*, in recognition of the first people here.

The work with fire, wildlife, and people extends through public and (willing) private parcels alike. Realizing that our area plays a critical biological role, we are trying to learn the ground rules by which humans might live together with animals in an "inhabited wildlife corridor." A project for netting and banding migrant songbirds during nest season (providing information for a Western Hemisphere database) is located on some Kitkitdizze brushlands, rather than public land, simply because it's an excellent location. It is managed by my wife, Carole, who is deeply touched by the spirit of the vibrant little birds she bands. Our cooperative efforts here can be seen as part of the rapidly changing outlook on land management in the West, which is talking public-private partnership in a big way. Joint-management agreements between local communities and other local and committed interests, and their neighboring blocks of public lands, are a new and potent possibility in the project of responsibly "recovering the commons" region by region. The need for ecological literacy, the sense of home watershed, and a better understanding of our stake in public lands are beginning to permeate the consciousness of the larger society.

Lessons learned in the landscape apply to our own lands, too. So this is what my family and I are borrowing from the watershed work as our own Three-Hundred-Year Kitkitdizze Plan: We'll do much more understory thinning and then a series of prescribed burns. Some patches will be left untouched by fire, to provide a control. We'll plant a few sugar pines, and incense cedars where they fit (ponderosa pines will mostly take care of themselves), burn the ground under some of the oaks to see what it does for the acorn crop, burn some bunchgrass patches to see if they produce better basketry materials (an idea from the Native basket-weaving revival in California). We'll leave a percentage of dead oak in the forest rather than take it all for firewood. In the time of our seventh-generation granddaughter there will be a large area of fire-safe pine stands that will provide the possibility of the occasional sale of an incredibly valuable huge, clear, old-growth sawlog.

We assume something of the same will be true on surrounding land. The wildlife will still pass through. And visitors from the highly crowded lowlands will come to walk, study, and reflect. A few people will be resident on this land, getting some of their income from forestry work. The rest may come from the information economy of three centuries hence. There might even be a civilization with a culture of cultivating wildness.

You can say that this is outrageously optimistic. It truly is. But the possibility of saving, restoring, and wisely (yes!) using the bounty of wild nature is still with us in North America. My home base, Kitkitdizze, is but one tiny node in an evolving net of bioregional homesteads and camps.

Beyond all this studying and managing and calculating, there's another level to knowing nature. We can go about learning the names of things and doing inventories of trees, bushes, and flowers, but nature as it flits by is not usually seen in a clear light. Our actual experience of many birds and much wildlife is chancy and quick. Wildlife is often simply a call, a cough in the dark, a shadow in the shrubs. You can watch a cougar on a wildlife video for hours, but the real cougar shows herself but once or twice in a lifetime. One must be tuned to hints and nuances.

After twenty years of walking right past it on my way to chores in the meadow, I actually paid attention to a certain gnarly canyon live oak one day. Or maybe it was ready to show itself to me. I felt its oldness, suchness, inwardness, oakness, as if it were my own. Such intimacy makes you totally at home in life and in yourself. But the years spent working around that oak in that meadow and not really noticing it were not wasted. Knowing names and habits, cutting some brush here, getting firewood there, watching for when the fall mushrooms bulge out are skills that are of themselves delightful and essential. And they also prepare one for suddenly meeting the oak.

[1995]

THE PARIS REVIEW INTERVIEW

The Art of Poetry LXXIV

GARY SNYDER is a rarity in the United States: an immensely popular poet whose work is taken seriously by other poets. He is America's primary poet-celebrant of the wilderness, poet-exponent of environmentalism and Zen Buddhism, and poet-citizen of the Pacific Rim—the first American poet to gaze almost exclusively west toward the East, rather than east toward Western civilization. A Snyder poem is instantly recognizable, and often imitated badly: an idiosyncratic combination of the plain speech of Williams, the free-floating, intensely visual images of Pound and the documentary information of both; the West Coast landscape first brought to poetry by Robinson Jeffers and Kenneth Rexroth; the precise and unallegorized observation of everyday life of the classical Chinese poets; and the orality of Snyder's fellow Beats.

He may well be the first American poet since Thoreau to devote a great deal of thought to the way one ought to live, and to make his own life one of the possible models. In person, he is full of humor and surprisingly undogmatic, with the charisma of one who seems to have already considered long and hard whatever one asks him. Snyder is an encyclopedia of things, both natural and artificial; what they are, how they were made, what they are used for, how they work. Then he quickly places that thing into a system that is ecological in its largest sense. Now in his mid-sixties, he would be a likely choice for a personal sage: sharp, wise, enthusiastic and an unexpectedly good listener.

Gary Snyder was born in San Francisco in 1930 and moved shortly after to the Pacific Northwest. Growing up in Washington state, he worked on his parents' farm and seasonally in the woods. He graduated in 1951 from Reed College with a degree in literature and anthropology. After a semester of linguistics study at Indiana University, he transferred to the University of California at Berkeley as a graduate student of Oriental languages, and became actively involved in the burgeoning West Coast poetry scene.

In the summer of 1955, Snyder worked on a trail crew in Yosemite National Park and began to write the first poems that he felt were truly his. That fall, he participated in the famous Six Gallery reading—featuring the first performance of Ginsberg's "Howl"—which launched the Beat movement. (Snyder appears as the character Japhy Ryder in Kerouac's *The Dharma Bums.*)

In 1956, he left the U.S. for what was to become a twelve-year residence abroad, largely in Japan. In Kyoto he pursued an intensive Zen Buddhist practice. During this period he also worked in the engine room of a tanker traveling along the Pacific Rim, and spent six months in India with Ginsberg and several others, where they had a notable discussion of hallucinogens with the Dalai Lama. In 1958, his translation of Han Shan's work, *Cold Mountain Poems*, appeared. His first book of poetry, *Riprap*, was published in Japan in 1959. This was followed by *Myths & Texts* (1960) and the two pamphlets published by the Four Seasons Foundation in 1965 that gained him a wide readership: *Riprap and Cold Mountain Poems* and *Six Sections from Mountains and Rivers Without End*. The first trade edition of his poetry, *The Back Country*, appeared in 1968.

Snyder returned to the United States in 1969 to build a house in the foothills of the northern Sierra Nevada, where he still lives today in a family household that balances modern and archaic technologies. He continues to travel widely, reading poetry and lecturing on Buddhism, the environment and bioregional issues. He works with the local Yuba Watershed Institute, and since 1985 has been teaching at the University of California at Davis, where he helped to form a nature and culture discipline.

His essays have been collected in *Earth House Hold* (1969), *The Practice of the Wild* (1990) and *A Place in Space* (1995). The poetry he has written since his return to the U.S. has been collected in *The Back Country* (1968); *Regarding Wave* (1970); *Turtle Island*, which won the Pulitzer Prize in 1975; *Axe Handles* (1983); *Left Out in the Rain* (1986); and a selected poems, *No Nature* (1992). In 1996, he published the completed version of *Mountains and Rivers Without End*, the long poem he had begun forty years before.

The interview took place before an audience at the Unterberg Poetry Center of the 92nd Street Y in New York City on October 26, 1992 and was later updated. What the transcript doesn't show is how often the conversation was punctuated by laughter. We began with some talk about the imminent presidential election and then turned to the question of poets and political power. Questions were then invited from the audience.

INTERVIEWER

When Jerry Brown of California was running for president, people were kidding you that if he were elected, you would be named Secretary of the Interior. Now, the thing that interests me about this is that you are the only poet in America for whom there is any scenario, no matter how far-fetched, of actually entering into real political power. Is this something you think poets ought to do? Would you do it?

GARY SNYDER

I've never thought seriously about that question. Probably not, although I am foolish enough to think that if I did do it, I'd do it fairly well, because I'm pretty single-minded. But you don't want to be victimized by your lesser talents. One of my lesser talents is that I am a good administrator, so I really have to resist being drawn into straightening things out. The work I see for myself remains on the mythopoetic level of understanding the interface of society, ecology and language, and I think it is valuable to keep doing that.

INTERVIEWER

But it is abnormal for poets not to be involved in the state. The United States remains an exception to most of the rest of the world, where poets commonly have served as diplomats or as bureaucrats in some ministry.

SNYDER

Oh true. The whole history of Chinese poetry is full of great poets who played a role in their society. Indeed, I do too. I am on committees in my county. I have always taken on some roles that were there for me to take in local politics, and I believe deeply in civic life. But I don't think that as a writer I could move on to a state or national scale of politics and remain a writer. My choice is to remain a writer.

INTERVIEWER

Let's get on to the writing and go back forty years or so. One of the amazing things about your work is that you seemed to burst on the scene fully formed with *Riprap* and *Cold Mountain Poems*, which were published in 1959 and 1958 but written earlier in the fifties when you were in your twenties. The poems in both books are unmistakably Snyder poems, and apparently, unlike the rest of us, you are not embarrassed by the work of your youth, for you picked eighteen of the twenty-three poems in *Riprap* for your *Selected Poems*.

SNYDER

Actually the poems in *Riprap* are not the poems of my youth. Those are the poems that I've kept because those were the ones I felt were the beginning of my life as a poet. I started writing poems when I was fifteen. I wrote ten years of poetry before *Riprap*. Phase one: romantic teenage poetry about girls and mountains.

INTERVIEWER

You're still writing that!

SNYDER

I realized I shouldn't have said that as soon as the words were out of my mouth. I would like to think that they are not romantic poems but classical poems about girls and mountains. The first poet that touched me really deeply, as a poet, was D.H. Lawrence, when I was fifteen. I had read *Lady Chatterley's Lover* and I thought that was a nifty book, so I went to the library to see what else he had written, and there was something called *Birds, Beasts and Flowers*. I checked that out. I was disappointed to find out that it wasn't a sexy novel, but read the poems anyway, and it deeply shaped me for that moment in my life.

And then phase two, college. Poems that echoed Yeats, Eliot, Pound, Williams and Stevens. A whole five years of doing finger exercises in the modes of the various twentieth-century masters. All of that I scrapped, only a few traces of that even survive. I threw most of them in a burning barrel when I was about twenty-five.

So when I wrote the first poems in *Riprap* it was after I had given up poetry. I went to work in the mountains in the summer of 1955 for the U.S. Park Service as a trail crew laborer, and had already started classical Chinese study. I thought I had renounced poetry. Then I got out there and started writing these poems about the rocks and blue jays. I looked at them. They didn't look like any poems that I had ever written before. So I said, these must be my own poems. I date my work as a poet from the poems in *Riprap*.

INTERVIEWER

What got you back to poetry at that moment? Was it primarily the landscape?

SNYDER

No, it just happened. What got me back to poetry was that I found myself writing poems that I hadn't even intended to write.

INTERVIEWER

And what poets were important to you then? Who were the masters at this point?

SNYDER

When I was twenty-two or twenty-three, I began working with Chinese and found myself being shaped by what I was learning from Chinese poetry, both in translation and in the original. And I had been reading Native American texts and studying linguistics.

INTERVIEWER

What were you finding in Chinese poetry at that time?

SNYDER

The secular quality, the engagement with history, the avoidance of theology or of elaborate symbolism or metaphor, the spirit of friendship, the openness to work and, of course, the sensibility for nature. For me it was a very useful balancing force to set beside Sidney, *The Faerie Queene,* Renaissance literature, Dante. The occidental tradition is symbolic, theological and mythological, and the Chinese is paradoxically more, shall we say, modern, in that it is secular in its focus on history or nature. That gave me a push.

INTERVIEWER

Were you getting the ideogramic method from Pound or from the Chinese poetry directly?

SNYDER

From the Chinese poetry directly. I could never make sense of that essay by Pound. I already knew enough about Chinese characters to realize that in some ways he was off, and so I never paid much attention to it. What I found in Pound were three or four dozen lines in the *Cantos* that are stunning—unlike anything else in English poetry—which touched me deeply and to which I am still indebted.

INTERVIEWER

Pound as a landscape poet?

SNYDER

No, as an ear. As a way of moving the line.

INTERVIEWER

Since we are talking about Chinese poetry I wanted to ask you about the Han Shan translations, *Cold Mountain Poems.* It is curious because Chinese poetry is so canonical, and Han Shan is not in the canon. I think at the time there were people who thought that you made him up. I wondered how you discovered him?

SNYDER

Well, he is only non-canonical for Europeans and Americans. The Chinese and the Japanese are very fond of Han Shan, and he is widely known in the Far East as an eccentric and as possibly the only Buddhist poet that serious Far Eastern *littérateurs* would take seriously. They don't like the rest of Buddhist poetry—and for good reason, for the most part.

To give you an example: in 1983 I was in China with a party of American writers—Toni Morrison, Allen Ginsberg, Harrison Salisbury, William Gass, Francine du Plessix Grey and others—and we were introduced to some members of the Politburo upstairs in some huge building. The woman who was our simultaneous interpreter introduced me to these bureau members—I am embarrassed to say I don't remember who these impressive Chinese persons were—by saying, "He is the one who translated Han Shan." They instantly started loosening up, smiling and quoting lines from Han Shan in Chinese to me. He is well known. So whose canon are we talking about?

INTERVIEWER

You haven't continued to translate much. Was this just something you felt you should do at the moment but that later there was too much other work to do?

SNYDER

There is a line somewhere—is it Williams who says it?—"You do the translations. I can sing." Rightly or wrongly; I took that somehow, when I ran into it, as a kind of an instruction to myself, not to be drawn too much into doing translation. I love doing Chinese translations, and I have done more that I haven't published, including the longest *shih* in Chinese, the *Ch'ang-hen ko*. "The Long Bitter Song" of Po Chü-i. So I am not just translating these tiny things. I am working right now on finishing up the *P'i-p'a hsing*, the other long Po Chü-i poem about the woman who plays the lute. And I've done a few T'ang poems. Maybe someday I'll get to doing more Chinese translations.

INTERVIEWER

Getting back to the early poems: it's interesting that the American West is essentially invented in literary American poetry by two of your immediate predecessors, Robinson Jeffers and Kenneth Rexroth. Did you feel that they opened it up for you somehow, made it acceptable to write about?

SNYDER

Definitely. Jeffers and Rexroth both, as you say, were the only two poets of any strength who had written about the landscapes of the American West, and it certainly helped give me the courage to start doing the same myself.

INTERVIEWER

What about the community of poets at the time? Philip Whalen, Lew Welch, Allen Ginsberg, Michael McClure, Robert Duncan, among others. One gets the sense that this was the only community of poets in which you were an active participant, that since that time you've been involved in other things. How important is a community of poets to you or to any poet? And what has happened since?

SNYDER

I think that rather than the term *community* it would be more accurate to speak of a *network* of poets. *Community* is more properly applied to diverse people who live in the same place and who are tied together by their inevitable association with each other, and their willingness to engage in that over a long period of time. But that is just a quibble.

When you are in your twenties, in particular, and you are a working, dissenting intellectual and artist, you need nourishment. Up in Portland, where I went to college, there were only a couple of other people you could talk to about poetry—Philip Whalen and Lew Welch and William Dickey. We started hearing little echoes of things in California and ended up there, all of us—for the comradeship, for the exchange of ideas. That was before the Beat generation broke onto the scene. I met Jack Spicer, Robin Blaser, Robert Duncan, Madeline Gleason, Tom Parkinson, Josephine Miles, William Everson, Kenneth Rexroth—that whole wonderful circle of San Francisco Renaissance people, such brilliant minds, such dedication to the art and such unashamed radical politics. Most of them were conscientious objectors in World War II, had rejected Stalinism early on, and with Kenneth Rexroth had formulated an antistatist, neoanarchist political philosophy, anarcho-pacifism, which at that time in American history made great sense. I was proud to be part of that circle at that time.

That group was enlarged when Allen Ginsberg and Jack Kerouac came onto the scene and the phenomenon that we are more commonly aware of as the San Francisco Beat generation poetry emerged. But it came out of that group of Duncan, Spicer, Rexroth and Blaser that was already eight or ten years old—it wasn't just created by Allen and his friends. Through Allen I began to meet people from the East Coast. I met Kenneth Koch, Ed Sanders, Anne Waldman, Jerome Rothenberg, Don Hall, James Laughlin, Robert Creeley, Ed Dorn and many others. I still keep in touch with many of them. A wonderful circle.

INTERVIEWER

Has the Beat thing been a burden for the rest of your life? Are you tired of hearing about the Beats?

SNYDER

I was for a while, but nobody has been beating me on the head with it lately.

INTERVIEWER

I am surprised that very young people now are so fascinated by the Beats, compared to the hippie movement. As an old hippie I think we're much more interesting. What do you think they see in the Beats?

SNYDER

Gee, I don't know if I should say this to you. When I look at the differences, one that emerges is that the political stance of the West Coast Beats was clear. They were openly political and, in terms of the Cold War, it was a kind of a pox-on-both-your-houses position. Clearly our politics were set against the totalitarianism of the Soviet Union and China, and at the same time would have no truck with corporate capitalism. Today you might say, "Okay what else is new? Do you have any solutions to suggest?" I understand that, of course, but at that time the quality of our dissent alone was enough to push things in a slightly new direction. What it led to in the poetry was a populist spirit, a willingness to reach out for an audience and an engagement with the public of the United States. This swell of poetry readings, going to all of the college towns and the big cities, which started around 1956, transformed American poetry. It was a return to orality and the building of something closer to a mass audience.

I do feel that there was a visionary political and intellectual component in the hippie phenomenon, but it is harder to track out what it is. It wasn't so clearly spoken and it was outrageously utopian, whereas the Beat generation's political stance was in retrospect more pragmatic, more hardheaded, easier to communicate, and it didn't rely on so much spiritual rhetoric. So that might be one reason, just as the punks rejected hippie spiritual rhetoric and went for a harder-edged politics, well, the Beat generation had a harder-edged politics.

INTERVIEWER

As long as we're talking about hippies, what about drugs? Obviously in the fifties and sixties you experimented with hallucinogens. Did it help or hurt the writing? Tear down obstacles or erect new ones? Or was it ultimately irrelevant?

SNYDER

That's a whole topic in itself, that deserves its own time. I'll just say that I am grateful that I came to meet with peyote, psilocybin, LSD and other hallucinogens in a respectful and modest frame of mind. I was suitably impressed by their powers, I was scared a few times, I learned a whole lot and I quit when I was ahead.

INTERVIEWER

Going back—you basically left the scene in 1956 to go to Japan.

SNYDER

In May of 1956 I sailed away in an old ship, headed across the Pacific for Japan.

INTERVIEWER

Why did you go? It seems like it was an exciting moment in America when you left.

SNYDER

Well, exciting as the scene was looking in 1956, I was totally ready to go to Japan. I had laid plans to go to the Far East, oh, three years prior to that, and had had several setbacks. The State Department denied me a passport for some of my early political connections.

INTERVIEWER

Would you have gone to China if the political situation had been different at the time?

SNYDER

I certainly would have.

INTERVIEWER

It would have completely changed the course of the rest of your life.

SNYDER

I'm sure it would have changed my life, although I don't know just how much, because my focus in going to the Far East was the study of Buddhism, not to find out if socialism would work, and the only Buddhists I would have found in China would have been in hiding at that time and probably covered with bruises. So it wouldn't have been a good move.

INTERVIEWER

I get the sense that you are much more attracted to Chinese poetry than Japanese poetry.

SNYDER

To some extent that's true. It is a karmic empathy that is inexplicable. I love Japanese literature and Japanese poetry too, but I feel a deep resonance with Chinese poetry.

INTERVIEWER

You stayed in Japan for ten years?

SNYDER

I was resident in Japan for about ten years, and I maintained residence there for twelve. I was away part of the time working on oil tankers and teaching at the University of California–Berkeley for a year.

INTERVIEWER

And how many years were you in the monastery there?

SNYDER

I was in and out of the monastery. That was where my teacher lived, and I was resident in it for *sesshin*—for meditation weeks—and then out, then in again. I had a little house that I rented just five minutes walk from the Daitoku-ji monastery.

INTERVIEWER

Are you still a practicing Buddhist? Do you sit every day?

SNYDER

Almost every day. *Zazen* becomes a part of your life, a very useful and beautiful part of your life—a wonderful way to start the day by sitting for at least twenty, twenty-five minutes every morning with a little bit of devotional spirit. My wife and I are raising a thirteen-year-old adopted daughter. When you have children you become a better Buddhist too, because you have to show them how to put the incense on the altar and how to make bows and how to bow to their food and so forth. That is all part of our culture, so we keep a Buddhist culture going. My grown sons say, when they are asked what they are, because they were raised that way, "Well, we are ethnic Buddhists. We don't know if we really believe it or not, but that is our culture."

INTERVIEWER

What does *zazen* do for the poetry? Do you feel that there is a relation there that helps somehow in the writing?

SNYDER

I was very hesitant to even think about that for many years, out of a kind of gambler's superstition not to want to talk too much or think too much about the things that might work for you or might give you luck. I'm not so superstitious anymore, and to demystify *zazen* Buddhist meditation, it can be said that it is a perfectly simple, ordinary activity to be silent, to pay attention to your own consciousness and your breath, and to temporarily stop listening or looking at things that are coming in from the outside. To let them just pass through you as they happen. There's no question that spending time with your own consciousness is instructive. You learn a lot. You can just watch what goes on in your own mind, and some of the beneficial effects are you get bored with some of your own tapes and quit playing them back to yourself. You also realize—I think anyone who does this comes to realize—that we have a very powerful visual imagination and that it is very easy to go totally into visual realms where you are walking around in a landscape or where any number of things can be happening with great vividness. This taught me something about the nature of thought and it led me to the conclusion—in spite of some linguists and literary theorists of the French ilk—that language is not where we start thinking. We think before language, and thought-images come into language at a certain point. We have fundamental thought processes that are pre-linguistic. Some of my poetry reaches back to that.

INTERVIEWER

You've written that language is wild, and it's interesting that, in your essays and in some of the poems, you track down words as though you're hunting or gathering. But do you believe that language is more a part of nature than a part of culture?

SNYDER

Well, to put it quite simply, I think language is, to a great extent, biological. And this is not a radical point of view. In fact, it is in many ways an angle of thought that has come back into serious consideration in the world of scientific linguistics right now. So, if it's biological, if it's part of our biological nature to be able to learn language, to master complex syntax effortlessly by the age of four, then it's part of nature, just as our digestion is part of nature, our limbs are part of nature. So, yes, in that sense it is. Now of course, language takes an enormous amount of cultural shaping, too, at some point. But the structures of it have the quality of wild systems. Wild systems are highly complex, cannot be intellectually mastered—that is to say they're too complex to master simply in intellectual or mathematical terms—and they are self-managing and self-organizing. Language is a self-organizing phenomenon. Descriptive linguistics come after the fact, an effort to describe what has already happened. So if you define the wild as self-managing, self-organizing and self-propagating, all natural human languages are wild systems. The imagination, we can say, for similar reasons, is wild. But I would also make the argument that there is a pre-linguistic level of thought. Not always, but a lot of the time. And for some people more than other people. I think there are people who think more linguistically, and some who think more visually, or perhaps kinesthetically, in some cases.

INTERVIEWER

Getting back to Buddhism for a second. For many poets, poetry is the religion of the twentieth century. And I'm curious what you get, in that sense, from Buddhism that you don't get from poetry?

SNYDER

I had a funny conversation with Clayton Eshleman, the editor and poet, many years ago while he was still in Kyoto. Clayton was talking, at length and with passion, about poetry. And I said to him, "But Clayton, I already have a religion. I'm a Buddhist." It's like the Pope telling Clare Boothe Luce, "I already am a Catholic." I don't think art makes a religion. I don't think it helps you teach your children how to say thank you to the food, how to view questions of truth and falsehood, or how not to cause pain or harm to others. Art can certainly help you explore your own consciousness and your own mind and your own motives, but it does not have a program to do that, and I don't think it should have a program to do that. I think that art is very close to Buddhism and can be part of Buddhist practice, but there are territories that Buddhist psychology and Buddhist philosophy must explore, and that art would be foolish to try to do.

INTERVIEWER

So you mainly draw that line on ethical grounds?

SNYDER

Well, there's ethics, there is philosophy, there is the spirit of devotion, and there is simply its capacity to become a cultural soil, a territory within which you transmit a way of being, which religion has a very strong role in. And then there is the other end of religious practice and Buddhist practice, which is to leave art behind. Which is to be able to move into the territory of the completeness and beauty of *all* phenomena. You really enter the world, you don't need art because everything is remarkable, fresh and amazing.

INTERVIEWER

So how do you keep writing?

SNYDER

Because you don't want to live in that realm very much of the time. We live in the realm of forms, we should act in the realm of forms. Jim Dodge and I once went to a Morris Graves exhibit in Oakland, where he was arguing with me about this Buddhist position in regard to art. I was saying, "You don't need art in a certain sense, Jim." So he went to the Morris Graves exhibit looking at the Morris Graves paintings, and I went through it looking at the spaces between the paintings with as much attention, and pointing out wonderful little hairline cracks in the plaster, the texture of the light and so forth. There is a point you can make that anything looked at with love and attention becomes very interesting.

INTERVIEWER

So you think people should read the margins of your books?

SNYDER

This is an oral art. They should listen to the unsaid words that resonate around the edge of the poem.

INTERVIEWER

Just as Chinese poetry is full of empty words, deliberately empty words for the *ch'i*, the sort of breath, to circulate through. In 1970 you moved back to the Sierra Nevadas, and you've been there ever since. I think from that moment on, when you finally settle down, you're talking much more about a poetry rooted in place.

SNYDER

Certainly a number of the poems written since 1970 reflect the position of being in a place, a spot in the world to which I always return. A lot of poems, however, do come out of my hunting and gathering trips to other territories. The idea of being a person of place never excludes the possibility of travel. To the contrary, it reminds people of place—everybody else in the world except Canadians, Australians and Americans—that they know where they come from. They have a place to go back to. They have no difficulty answering the question. "Where are you from?" But Americans often can't answer that question. They say, "Well, do you mean where I was born or where I went to high school, or where my parents live now, or where I went to college, or where my job is, or where I'm going to move next year?" That's an American dilemma. So having a place means that you know what a place means. And if somebody asks you, "What folk songs do you sing where you come from?" you have a song you can sing to them. Like in Japan, say, where you're always being asked to sing a song from your native place.

INTERVIEWER

Yes. Ours is "I Love New York in June." Do you think that sense of place is primary for the poetry?

SNYDER

Not in any simple or literal way. More properly I would say it's a sense of what *grounding* means. But place has an infinite scale of expansion or contraction. In fact, if somebody asks me now, "What do you consider to be your place?" my larger scale answer is, "My place on earth is where I know most of the birds and the trees and where I know what the climate will be right now, roughly, what should be going on there on that spot on earth right now, and where I have spent enough time to know it intimately and personally." So that place for me goes from around Big Sur on the California coast all the way up the Pacific coast through British Columbia, through southeast Alaska, out through southwest Alaska, out onto the Aleutian chain, and then comes down into Hokkaido and the Japanese islands, and goes down through Taiwan. Now that's the territory I have moved and lived in and that I sort of know. So that's my place.

INTERVIEWER

Since we're talking about your map of the world, people have wondered about the general absence of European civilization—or at least Europe after the Paleolithic—in your work. To me it's no more shocking than the absence of Asia—not to mention Africa—from everyone else's work. But still the question comes up. Is this a deliberate criticism of Eurocentrism or merely just the track your interest followed?

SNYDER

It's true that I haven't visited Europe much, but it isn't totally absent from my poetry, and there are some key points in my work that connect with occidental cultural insights that are classical, if not Paleolithic. The scholar Robert Torrance even wrote a little paper on the occidental aspect of my work. Much of the value I find in the West is in the pre-Christian, the pagan and the matrifocal aspects, however. And I track things like connections I fancy that I can see from Greek poetics to the Arabic poetry of Spain, in turn to Lorca, in turn to Jack Spicer. And the Bogomils, Waldenses,

Albigenses, shepherds of Montaillou, Anabaptists, Quakers, Luddites, Amish and Wobblies have my gratitude, of course. And now that I'm getting old enough to enjoy hotels as well as camping I think I'll start visiting Europe. I loved Spain—I went there recently.

INTERVIEWER

I want to change gears and talk about the word *work*, which is central to all of your writing. You've written, to take one of many examples, "Changing the filter, wiping noses, going to meetings, picking up around the house, washing dishes, checking the dip stick, don't let yourself think these are distracting you from your more serious pursuits." What does this mean for a writer who would feel that her or his "real work" is the writing, and that all these other things are overwhelming?

SNYDER

If one's real work is the writing and if one is a fiction writer, I guess one's work as a writer really holds one to the literally physical act of writing and visualizing and imagining and researching and following out the threads of one's project. However, if one is a nonfiction prose writer or a poet, one is apt to be much more closely engaged with daily life as part of one's real work, and one's real work actually becomes life. And life comes down to daily life. This is also a very powerful Buddhist point: that what we learn and even hopefully become enlightened by is a thorough acceptance of exactly who we are and exactly what it is we must do, with no evasion, no hiding from any of it, physically or psychologically. And so finding the ceremonial, the almost sacramental quality of the moves of daily life is taught in Buddhism. That's what the Japanese tea ceremony is all about. The Japanese tea ceremony is a model of sacramental tea drinking. Tea drinking is taken as a metaphor for the kitchen and for the dining room. You learn how to drink tea, and if you learn how to drink tea well, you know how to take care of the kitchen and dining room every day. If you learn how to take care of the kitchen and the dining room, you've learned about the household. If you know about the household, you know about the watershed. *Ecology* means house, *oikos*, you know, from the Greek. *Oikos* also gives us economics. *Oikos nomos* means "managing the household." So that's one way of looking at it. I understand that there are other lines and other directions that poets take and I honor them. I certainly don't believe there's only one kind of poetry.

INTERVIEWER

I have a line from Auden here that "the goal of everyone is to live without working." And basically what he's saying in the rest of the passage is that work is something that other people impose on us.

SNYDER

I would agree with Auden. The goal of living is not to consider work work, but to consider it your life and your play. That's another way of looking at it.

INTERVIEWER

But how is that different from Calvinism, in the sense of extolling the virtues of work?

SNYDER

Well, work per se does not bring about salvation, nor is it automatically virtuous. It has more the quality of acknowledgment and recognition and making necessity charming. And it's not always charming, and nothing I've said should lead us to think that an oppressed worker should swallow and accept the conditions of his life without fighting back. It's none of that really. Your question catches me a little bit by surprise because I am so far removed from being a puritan in any way, and so is Buddhism, incidentally. There is a very funny quality in Buddhism, which is enjoying and acknowledging badness. So you can be bad and still be a good Buddhist. So everything

I say has its reverse. "I hate work," you know, let it all go. Or as W.C. Fields once said, "If a thing is worth doing at all, it's worth doing poorly."

INTERVIEWER

Speaking of the doing of things, let me ask you about your mechanics of writing. I gather you have some complicated system of file cards, even for the poems. Can you describe that?

SNYDER

Most writers I know, and certainly prose writers, have a well-organized shop. There are moves in longer poetic projects that are very like the work of researchers. I tell young would-be poets not to fear organization, that it won't stultify their scope. I use some systems I learned from anthropologists and linguists. Now I use a computer too. A friend who's a professional hydrologist gives a good caution. "Write up your field notes at the end of each day!" And then get them into your hard disk fairly soon and always back that up. The main thing though is to give full range to the mind and learn to walk around in memory and imagination smelling and hearing things.

INTERVIEWER

Your poems are notable both for their extreme condensation and their musicality. Do the lines come out in such compact form? Are the poems initially much longer and then chipped away? Do you consciously count syllables or stresses, or do you mainly write by ear?

SNYDER

There is one sort of poem I write that is highly compressed and has a lot of ear in it. As a poem comes to me, in the process of saying and writing it, the lines themselves establish a basic measure, even a sort of musical or rhythmic phrase for the whole poem. I let it settle down for quite a while and do a lot of fine-tuning as part of the revision. Doing new poems at readings brings out subtle flaws in the movement or music to be immediately noted. I don't count syllables or stresses, but I discover after the fact what form the poem has given itself, and then I further that. Of course I write other sorts of poems as well—longer, less lyrical, formal, borrowings or parodies, and so forth. I am experimenting with switching back and forth between a prose voice and a lyric voice in some of the work I'm doing now.

INTERVIEWER

I gather that, unlike many writers, you publish very slowly—allowing things to sit for years before they're brought out in the world. Why is that? And what works are currently hanging up to dry?

SNYDER

Well, I have found that if you let a poem sit around long enough, you come to see and hear it better. Not that a poem in progress doesn't reach a point of being pretty much finished. So I don't rush it—it's a matter of allowing intuition and taste to come into play; you choose to hold onto a piece, waiting for some little turn of insight. This is true of prose writing, too. But letting it wait might be a kind of luxury sometimes because there are often urgent reasons to get things into the world, especially essays dealing with current issues. I recently finished a project I called *Mountains and Rivers Without End*—a series of longish poems that I have been working at for decades. And I'm glad I let it wait that long, it is more tasty.

INTERVIEWER

Why do you think it took so long?

SNYDER

Well of course when I launched myself into this in 1956, having just finished the book-length poem *Myths and*

Texts—which only took three years—I thought it would be wrapped up in five or six years. I started studying *The Lotus Sutra* and some geomorphology and ecology texts as a bit of beginning research, and also I set sail for Japan. It all got more complicated than I had predicted, and the poems were evasive. So I relaxed, and thought, However long it takes. I kept my eye on it, walking, reflecting and researching, but didn't make any big demands on the mountain-goddess muse. So it worked out to about one section a year for forty years.

INTERVIEWER

How does it feel, having completed a forty-year-long project like *Mountains and Rivers Without End*?

SNYDER

How does it feel to finish it? I'm truly grateful. Now I have further work with it though—I'm learning how to read it aloud, and I'm still learning more about its workings.

INTERVIEWER

As with Pound and the *Cantos*, did you find it impossible to tear yourself away from *Mountains and Rivers* to work on other things?

SNYDER

As I say, I was pretty relaxed about results for a long time. But I did keep a really sharp focus going, never neglected it. Through those years I also wrote and published fifteen or sixteen books. Then, between 1992 and 1996, seeing the shape of the whole forming up, I put *Mountains and Rivers* ahead of everything else—stopped all other sorts of writing, neglected the garden, let the pine needles pile up on the road, quit giving poetry readings, didn't answer mail, quit going to parties, my old truck quit running—til it was done.

INTERVIEWER

Working on a book for forty years, do you carry the germ of your next project? What *are* you going to do next?

SNYDER

What I want to do next is restart the garden and the truck, go out with the young people to some deserts and rivers and maybe cities, and reengage with a bunch of old friends. And then back to prose and the thorny problems of our time.

INTERVIEWER

You're one of the few poets whose work is accessible to a non-poetry-reading public. Yet somewhere you say—you're talking about Robert Duncan—that it's the poetry you never fully comprehend that most engages you. I was wondering whether you consciously strike out obscurities, thinking of the general reader, to make the poetry accessible?

SNYDER

Semiconsciously. I've written a number of different sorts of poems and there's a percentage of my poetry—maybe twenty-five percent, maybe forty—that is accessible. I think partly that has been a function of my regard for the audience, my desire to have some poems that I knew that I could share with people I lived and worked with. Certainly a number of the work poems, and poems of travel and poems of place, are works that I could and did share with neighbors or with fellow workers on the job. I've always enjoyed that enormously. At the same time there are territories of mind and challenges that are not easily accessible. I've written a number of rather difficult poems. I just don't read them at poetry readings as a rule.

INTERVIEWER

Let me quickly ask you about your book of selected poems. *No Nature*, as a title, obviously takes many aback. It seems apocalyptic until you realize that it's a kind of Buddhist joke:

the true nature is no nature, the nature of one's self is no nature. Is that correct?

SNYDER

Yes, and it's also a critical-theory joke.

INTERVIEWER

In what sense?

SNYDER

In that some folks hold that everything is a social construction, and I add that society is a natural construction, including the industrial and the toxic.

INTERVIEWER

It's interesting that, for someone involved as much as you are in the environmental movement, your work is surprisingly without disasters. There's very little bad news in the poetry—no Bhopals, no Chernobyls. Are you setting positive examples? Or are you just cheerful?

SNYDER

There are several poems that have some very bad news in them. Going all the way back to a poem written in 1956 called "This Tokyo." And the poem that I wrote as an op-ed piece for *The New York Times* in 1972 called "Mother Earth: Her Whales." However, I feel that the condition of our social and ecological life is so serious that we'd better have a sense of humor. That it's too serious just to be angry and despairing. Also, frankly, the environmental movement in the last twenty years has never done well when it threw out excessive doom scenarios. Doom scenarios, even though they might be true, are not politically or psychologically effective. The first step, I think, and that's why it's in my poetry, is to make us love the world rather than to make us fear for the end of the world.

Make us love the world, which means the nonhuman as well as the human, and then begin to take better care of it.

INTERVIEWER

Many are surprised to discover that you're not a vegetarian and not a Luddite, but rather a carnivore with a Macintosh. This sets you apart from, on the one hand, many Buddhists, and, on the other, from a certain branch of the environmental movement. Any comments?

SNYDER

Come, come, I'm not a carnivore, I'm an omnivore. Carnivores have ridiculously short intestines! I am a very low-key omnivore at that, as are most of the Third World people who eat very little fish or meat, but who certainly wouldn't spurn it. I did a whole discussion of this question—for Buddhists—in a recent issue of *Ten Directions*, from the Zen Center of Los Angeles. The key is still the first precept: "Cause least harm." We have to consider the baleful effects of agribusiness on the global environment, as well as have concern for the poor domestic critters. Ethical behavior is not a matter of following a rule, but examining how a precept might guide one, case by case.

Now, as for environmentalists, my Earth First! and Wild Earth friends are pretty diverse, but one thing they all share is that they are not prigs or puritans. They do ecological politics as a kind of contact sport. I'm all for that.

As for computers: the word processor is not the agent of transformation, it's language that is the agent. The word processor is just a facilitating device. Keep your eye on the ball!

AUDIENCE MEMBER

I was on the phone this afternoon with my teacher, who is a Lakota. I mentioned that I was going to see Gary Snyder. And she said, "Oh, Gary Snyder. He's an Indian. Ask him if he knows it." Do you know that you are an Indian? A Native American.

SNYDER

That was very kind of her to say that. I don't know if I know I'm an Indian or not. However, I do know that I'm a Native American. Here again is a Turtle Island bioregional point. Anyone is, metaphorically speaking, a Native American who is "born again on Turtle Island." Anyone is a Native American who chooses, consciously and deliberately, to live on this continent, this North American continent, with a full spirit for the future, and for how to live on it right, with the consciousness that says, "Yeah, my great-great-grandchildren and all will be here for thousands of years to come. We're not going on to some new frontier, we're here now." In that spirit, African-Americans, Euro-Americans, Asian-Americans, come together as Native Americans. And then you know that those continents that your ancestors came from are great places to visit, but they're not home. Home is here.

INTERVIEWER

But do you think that the myths that come out of here belong to everyone?

SNYDER

They belong to the place, and they will come to belong to those who make themselves members of this place. It's not that easy, however. It takes real practice.

INTERVIEWER

I'm just playing devil's advocate for a moment. I know in the seventies there were Native Americans who were criticizing you—I don't think rightly—essentially saying, "Hey, white boy, keep your hands off our coyote."

SNYDER

You know, coyote—the trickster image—is found all over the globe. In myth and world folklore, it blankets the planet from forty thousand years ago on. It is totally cosmopolitan, and we know this. So, in that sense, mythology and folklore are archaic international world heritages. The question is to understand what to do with them and how to respond to them. The stories about Coyote Old Man are in fact genuinely something that came out of Native American experience, broke through the civilization-history time barrier and are now fully rooted in twentieth-century literature. That's something that has come across. It's quite amazing. And I'm sure that other things will prove in time to have come across like that. You can't be against it. It makes both worlds, the old and new, richer, and it testifies to the openness of the imagination.

AUDIENCE MEMBER

There are a lot of things that are splitting the country apart nowadays. Does this scare you?

SNYDER

Well, along with everyone else, I have very troubled moments about the future of the United States and our society. And it would be foolish to say that I've got any easy answers. For those who can do it, one of the things to do is not to move. To stay put. Now staying put doesn't mean don't travel. But it means have a place and get involved in what can be done in that place. Because without that we're not going to have a representative democracy that works in America. We're in an oligarchy right now, not a democracy. Part of the reason that it slid into oligarchy is that nobody stays anywhere long enough to take responsibility for a local community and for a place.

AUDIENCE MEMBER

In a radio interview several years ago, you were asked about your politics and you responded that you were an anarchist. Can you explain that, and how that really works?

SNYDER

You know I really regretted saying that on the radio. That was on "Fresh Air." I try not to say that on the radio. In fact, I try not to even use the word *anarchist* because it immediately raises the question that you just raised which is, "Can you explain that?" The term shouldn't be used, it has too many confusing associations. Anarchism should refer to the creation of non-statist, natural societies as contrasted with legalistically organized societies, as alternative models for human organization. Not to be taken totally literally, but to be taken poetically as a direction toward the formation of better and more viable communities. Anarchism, in political history, does not mean chaos, it means self-government. So a truly anarchist society is a self-governing society. We all need to learn better how to govern ourselves. And we can do that by practice, and practice means you have to go to meetings, and going to meetings means you'll be bored, and so you better learn how to meditate.

INTERVIEWER

The tao of bureaucracy.

SNYDER

That's right. The tao of bureaucracy. Anybody who meditates knows how to handle boredom so then you can go to meetings. That's how I got into politics.

AUDIENCE MEMBER

You've had to submit to a very rigorous discipline in your religious practice, learning of languages and study of poetry. Do you find your students now willing to submit to that kind of discipline?

SNYDER

You know, I never felt like I was submitting to discipline. Since I was about sixteen or seventeen, I've never done anything

I didn't want to do. It was always my own choice. When I was studying Chinese, it was what I wanted to do. I could have left at any time, nobody was paying me to do it, and I didn't have any parents insisting that I do it. So, I don't know how to answer that. I've always operated from my own free choice. However, I certainly would say that a highly motivated person, willing to engage intensely with something, is not easy to find among the students I've run into. But there are always a few that have some sort of fire under them.

AUDIENCE MEMBER

What would you tell sixteen-year-olds with the world before them, what should they do?

SNYDER

This is one of the occupational hazards of being a poet. You're asked questions that you really don't know an answer for. I'd say the same thing that I say to my eighteen-year-old stepdaughter: you're going to have to get a lot of formal education. And don't think that a four-year education is the end of it. Nowadays you have to go on a little bit farther or it isn't going to mean a whole lot. But even while doing education, don't think it makes you superior to uneducated people or illiterate people, because there's a tremendous amount of cultural wisdom and skill out in the Third World, out in the pre-literate world that is intrinsically every bit as viable as anything that Euro-American society has created. And then the fundamental ethical precept: whatever you do, try not to cause too much harm.

—Eliot Weinberger

From
BACK ON THE FIRE

ESSAYS

The Ark of the Sierra

I'M A longtime forest and mountain person of the West Coast. I grew up on a farm outside Seattle, my father and uncles all worked at various times in logging and fishing, and I started off helping my dad on one end of a two-man saw when I was about eleven. I've worked in the woods from the Canadian border down to Yosemite. I've fought fire, built trails, planted trees, done seasons on lookouts, been a timber-scaler and a choker-setter. And I've considered myself a conservationist since I was seventeen—when I first wrote to Congress in regard to an issue in the Olympic National Forest.

I'm concerned primarily with two things: our new understanding of the ecological role of fire, and something bigger that goes with that, the possibility of a truly sustainable forestry in the Sierra. When I was a self-righteous youth in my twenties I thought that my jobs as fire lookout and firefighter gave me a real moral advantage—I told my city friends, "Look, when I do this kind of work I can really say I'm doing no harm in the world, and am only doing good." Such ironies. Now I get to join in the chorus that says it was all wrong-headed, even if well-intentioned (almost as wrong as when I climbed to the summit of Mount Saint Helens up in Washington at age fifteen and announced "this beautiful mountain will long outlast the cities." Now the mountain is half gone, and the cities are doing fine).

This North Central Sierra area, especially here on the west side, is not quite as charismatic and scenic as the southern Sierra. We have no Yosemite Valley or Kings River Canyon, but we do have exquisite little high country lakes and many meadows rich in summer flowers, high white granite ridges and crisp, bright snowfields. In the mid-elevations we have some of the finest pine forest in the world. The lower foothills are manzanita fields with extensive oak grasslands that have been changing, during the last two decades, from cattle ranches to ranchettes.

In the watersheds of the American, Feather, and Yuba River systems are some of the loveliest streams in California, offering top quality trout fishing. The oak and brush lands are major migratory songbird nesting territory—I know because my wife, Carole, was out early at least one morning every week last spring mist-net-trapping, banding, and collecting sex and age data on the little things. Deer and wild turkeys grace the front yards of people all across the foothills. My wife and I and many of our friends are among those who welcome back the bears and cougars, even while recognizing the risk. We didn't move up here to live the soft, safe, and easy life, and we love having these hairy scary neighbors. We will try to figure out how to be safe and smart even though they're around. One can always buckle on a bear-attack pepper spray canister when going for a lone jaunt. And speaking of lone jaunts, John Muir's famous adventure—that he wrote about in *The Mountains of California* of climbing high up into a sugar pine during a severe windstorm—took place a few ridges over, probably near the town of Challenge.

Our North Central Sierra shares its geological and biological history with the rest of the Greater Sierran ecosystem. There are paleo-Indian sites in this county that indicate human presence from eight thousand years ago. The "pre-contact" forest was apparently a mosaic of various different forest stages, from brush fields to many broad and open ancient-forest stands. Spring and fall, salmon ran up all the rivers. Deer, salmon, waterfowl from the valley, and black oak acorns were the basis of a large and economically comfortable native population, a people who made some of the most skillful and beautiful baskets in the world.

The Yankee newcomers initially came to look for gold. They needed lumber and thought, as newcomers did everywhere else in North America, that the forest was limitless. One can see early photographs taken around the foothill towns, and the hills are denuded. It's a tribute to the resilience of the local forest that, where allowed to, it has come back quite well.

So early on there was the vigorous mining industry and extensive logging. Later much of the mountain land was declared public domain, and it came to be the responsibility of the U.S. Forest Service (USFS) and the Bureau of Land

Management. The USFS from the twenties up until the seventies was a confident and paternalistic organization that thought it always knew best, and for a while maybe it did. During those years it was generally trusted by both the conservation movement and the timber industry. In any case, from the 1950s on there was a lot of heavy industrial logging in the public and private lands of the Sierra.

With the seventies came a renewed rise of environmental concern. Part of that consciousness was connected maybe to better biology education in the schools and a general growth of interest in nature. Curious people got out in the mountains by pickup, on foot, or by bike, and sometimes studied the areas that had been logged. People could see that old-growth habitat was drastically shrinking. We all knew that some species were being lost or endangered (the wolf and grizzly already gone, probably the wolverine) and there were rumors that the national forest logging was sometimes subsidized at an actual financial loss to the taxpayers. The public became aware, as never before, of its stake in the Sierra Nevada.

So we entered an era of reevaluation and reconsideration of past policies. The USFS unfortunately lost much of the respect of the conservation community, and it also got hammered by the timber industry. For a while it looked like the Forest Service couldn't win, *whatever* it did. There *have* been some highly contested issues. For conservationists, extensive clear-cutting became symbolic of how the federal land managers seemed to be hostage to the timber economy; and the spotted owl became symbolic to the timber industry of hated environmental regulations, and money-losing issues involving critters that almost nobody has ever seen. The owl itself is a hapless and innocent bird that never meant to cause so much trouble. The gold rush era left many worthy legacies in this land; it also left some people with a sort of "use it up" attitude. Those who arrived in the seventies and after may have been quick to love nature, but they seemed to have little concern for the economy.

During the hearings that led to the establishment of Redwood National Park on the north coast, a sawmill operator testified, "Why, nobody ever goes in those woods but hippies and their naked girlfriends." Well, some of those girls went on to college and became lawyers.

These wrangles have led some of us to try and figure out where the different parties, those able and willing to argue with sincerity and in good faith, might find areas of agreement. The fairly recent realization that the Sierra Nevada is a fire-adapted ecosystem, and that a certain amount of wildfire has historically been necessary to its health, has given everyone at least one area within which they can agree. Another area of potential agreement is the growing awareness that we will sooner or later have to manage long-range sustainable forestry. In fact, the two absolutely go together. If we don't reduce the fuel load, the really big fires that will inevitably come will make good forestry a moot point. But it will take a little more than new fire policies to achieve good forestry.

I was on a panel in San Francisco several years ago with Jerry Franklin, the eminent forest scientist now based at the University of Washington. So last month I took it on myself to write him the following question:

> Dear Jerry,
> I would like to be able to say that "Long range sustainable forestry practices—such as will support full biodiversity—and be relatively fire-resistant—and also be on some scale economically viable—lasting over centuries—is fully possible. And what we must now do is search out and implement the management program that will do that." Do you think I can say this & that the science will support it?

Jerry Franklin immediately wrote me back:

> What you propose is totally and absolutely feasible for the Sierra Nevada, i.e., long-term sustainability, full biological diversity, relative fire resistance (low probability of catastrophic crown fire), and economic viability. A system which provides for restoration and maintenance of a large diameter tree component (with its derived large snags and down logs) and which provides for moderate to high levels of harvest in the small and medium diameter classes (allowing escapement of enough trees into the large diameter class to provide replacements for mortality in the large diameter group) and prescribed burning in some locations can do this. Other considerations include riparian protection and, perhaps, shaded fuel breaks. Economic and sustainable in perpetuity!

So it's theoretically possible. But science can only suggest—such a marvelous sustainable forestry cannot actually happen unless the culture itself chooses that path. "The culture" means not only the national public but also the working people of the very region where the resource policy decisions are made. It will take local people working together with local land managers to make the serious changes in public lands policies that we need. Just a quarter of a century ago, the idea of active local engagement with public land decision-making would have been thought pretty utopian.

One of the reasons we might trust the people of the Sierra to provide valuable input has to do with how much the local people have learned on their own. In the twenty-five years I've lived in this part of the Sierra we have seen a growing contribution of knowledge from a multitude of fine amateur naturalists. Just here in Nevada County we have seen the formation of a California Native Plant Society chapter, the local production of a hiking guide to the region, a locally written and published bird species checklist, a fine botany of a high country lake region by a person of the area, a similar low-elevation wildflower guide, and detailed forest inventories done by volunteers on San Juan Ridge. There's a sophisticated, locally based research project on pileated woodpecker behavior, family life, and reproduction going on right now. Extensive research has been done on the stream systems and main rivers of the Yuba by another set of volunteers. And many of us are in personal debt to the esteemed Lillian Mott for her generous help in identifying mushrooms.

Also the forestry and biology experts of the Tahoe National Forest, the B.L.M., and our colleges and universities have been generous in sharing their time and expertise with ordinary citizens. Timber operators have visited at least one school I know of, Grizzly Hill, and allowed children to come and observe a logging show. There are a number of significant new organizations in the North Central Sierra. Many are focused on ecological issues, and some are concerned with access to resources. They all have a stake in the health of the Greater Sierran Ecosystem. This process of newcomers becoming a "people of the place," which started in 1849, has been progressing at variable speeds ever since, and has surged ahead in the last two decades.

For new fire and forestry practices to really become national public policy, they must be *local* public choices first.

We locals can help bring this to reality by getting involved with the Bureau of Land Management and USFS in further community forestry projects, in working toward innovative value-added wood-products industries, and in supporting cooperative fire management projects. If we can clarify and express our own choices, our congresspersons just might represent us, and federal policies might begin to reflect local desires. Agencies might facilitate this process by being a lot more willing to take risks with the public than they've been so far, putting more of their people out in the field where they can meet folks, and looking for opportunities to break out and try things with locals.

There has always been fire. The catfaces on the oaks, the multiple stems sprouting from certain old oak centers, and the black cedar stumps that seem to be timeless made it clear to me that there had been a sizeable fire through our land some years back. A neighbor, now passed on, told me of a big burn some sixty years ago. But our local forest has recovered well. This Sierra ecosystem has been fire-adapted for millions of years, and fire can be our ally. The growing recognition of this fact—with the public and with the fire agencies—has been a remarkable change to watch develop during the past ten years. In my own neighborhood a small prescribed burn was done this spring with considerable success. And we have also been trying out the mechanical crunching of brushfields—expensive, but it works.

One word of caution, however. As our enthusiasm for prescribed burns and more sophisticated fire management grows, we need to remember for a moment the fire ideologies and bureaucracies of the past. Steve Pyne, in his book *World Fire*, traces the history of the American wildfire-fighting establishment and the way it demonized fire as an enemy. He points out how the language of forest firefighting for years ran parallel to the language of the Cold War—clearly militaristic, and speaking of forest fires as though they were Godless Communist armies. Firefighting requires organization, courage, and tremendous energy and dedication, to be sure. But we are called now to a more complex moral attitude, where we see fire as an ally in the forest, even while recognizing its power to do damage.

The understanding of fire—its hazards, its use as a tool, and the way it shapes a fire-adapted forest—should help keep our different factions working together. We may disagree as to how important the survival of some species might be or how many acres of land should reasonably be converted to suburbs or what the annual allowed timber cut ought to be, but we surely will agree that we're against tall flames burning timber and houses, and that we should work together for a "fire management" that sees fire as a partner in the ecosystem, not an enemy. This may be a tentative step toward new and more amicable relations between the conservationists, who want to go slow and be careful, and the resource users, who have their businesses to run.

There's another hard fact here that I haven't yet mentioned. It may in the long run be the most important factor of all. The whole west side of the Sierra (the entire *West*) is experiencing an amazing rate of housing growth, which brings suburban homes right up against wildlife habitat, public forests or mineralized zones, a zoning term meaning "areas under which significant mineral resources are known to lie, hence zoned so that mining might still be permitted at some point." These developments may be in conflict with both loggers and environmentalists. Public lands will become all the more precious to us, as ranches and farms give way to development.

Our public lands are lands held in trust for all of us. A certain responsibility goes with that, for the government, for the public at large, and for the people of the region. As for stewardship, or trust, we can see that the whole world is in the trust of humans now, whether we want this responsibility or not. The air and waters, the rivers, the deer and owls, the genetic health of all life are in our trust. We are here discussing Biodiversity—a word that sends shivers of alarm through some hearts—but it only means variety of life, and it means "Right to Life for Nonhuman Others," a moral sentiment I religiously support. If God hadn't wanted all these critters to be around, including rattlesnakes and cougars, he wouldn't have put them on the Ark. The high country and the forests are the twenty-first century Ark of the Sierra, an Ark even for all of California. Let's be sure it's an ark that stays afloat. Let's not try to second-guess God.

Grass Valley/Nevada City, 6.VI.96

Ecology, Literature, and the New World Disorder

Gathered on Okinawa

THE MAIN island of the Ryukyu chain, Okinawa, is an old cultural crossroads. There is a long history of trade in goods and songs with Taiwan and Korea, and a record of highly respectful formal relations with mainland China still well remembered in Okinawa. In prehistoric times Pacific and Southeast Asian coastal cultural influences met and mingled with influences that came across from the Korean peninsula. This is where the oceanic and the continental cultures have long met and where the northern and the southern parts of East Asia came together.

Naha, the largest city on Okinawa and the old capital of the Ryukyu Kingdom, is rich in craft and art. The inscription on the sign at the big gate to Shuri Castle says in Chinese characters, "A Nation That Preserves Ceremony"—which I understand in its ancient spiritual meaning of "good manners toward the whole world."

Old Okinawa had a society that became famous for its hospitality, its music (especially the songs and melodies of the *sanshin*, the Okinawan prototype to the *shamisen*), its dance, its cheerful hardiness, and its self-sufficiency in art and culture. In recent decades in the aftermath of World War II, the Ryukyus have sometimes absorbed influence from the United States. The presence of the huge military airbase has been very difficult for the island—but many Okinawans also feel that Hawai'ian and mainland American cultural movements have had creative and broadening effects on the ongoing culture.

Based on a keynote talk given at the Association for the Study of Literature and the Environment international conference held in Naha, Okinawa, in the Ryukyu Archipelago, March 4–6, 2003.

The whole Ryukyu chain is a place of natural and cultural distinction. Ocean currents, volcanoes, Pacific storms, deep sea orcas, flying fish, and wheeling birds. Here's a salute to the spirits of rice and sweet potato, and as always, the Goddess of Dance and Song.

THIS NEW WORLD DISORDER

We all know that the "post–Cold War" era has suddenly and rudely ended, and we have entered a period in which global relations are defined by new nationalisms, religious fundamentalism, developed world hubris, stepped-up environmental damage, and everywhere expanding problems of health and poverty. What was to have been a "New World Order" is revealed as a greater disorder, much of it flowing from the top down.

Disorder is nothing new in the human world. East Asia, the Indian subcontinent, the Middle East, and Europe have all gone through cycle after cycle of violent change—oppression at home, exploitation abroad, and bloody warfare. Much of it has been driven by various combinations of fanatic ideological beliefs, whipped-up nationalisms, and institutionalized greed. The great civilizations have had moments of peace and marvelous cultural and artistic accomplishments, punctuated by eruptions of hysteria, outbreaks of violence, and war after war after war.

The destruction of the World Trade Towers and the sudden loss of thousands of lives are, realistically, not a historical anomaly. Famines, plagues, huge fires, earthquakes, eruptions, and warfare are registered all through history. There was never a time when a little wisdom, patience, and reflection wouldn't serve to improve decision-making in times of emergency.

The Bush administration that was and is in power in the United States has little sense of history and no patience. With the war on Iraq, we have all been drawn into what Jonathan Schell calls "An American Tragedy." The shredding of international trust, the deceptions practiced on the people of the United States and Britain, and the unresolved chaos in the lives of Iraqis, Israelis, and Palestinians make this a worldwide tragedy.

But perhaps we could focus on considering the natural world as regarded by human society, the natural world as it is found in the literary and other arts. In most of the world now the outlook for the natural environment is not good. Initially the Bush administration's retreat from environmental priorities was presented as being simply "pro business." The aftermath of September 11, 2001, then enabled the Bush/Rumsfeld/Cheney forces to cloak their anti-environmentalism in the rhetoric of patriotism. There are corporations and government agencies that enthusiastically welcome this. The post 9/11 world of research universities is also changing directions. My own school, the University of California at Davis, quickly developed plans to build a "biocontainment laboratory" to study deadly viruses and bacteria, clearly a response to the rise of terrorist fears.

In the Modern Language departments, there are probably Eurocentric scholars who always thought that the new interest in "nature literature" was just a shallow trend and who have begun to hope that things like the recent emergence of ecocriticism, or the study of "the environmental imagination," or concerns for "environmental ethics," "nature literacy," and "the practice of the wild" will now pack up and head back to the hills. But it won't happen.

A huge number of contemporary people realize that we can no longer think that the fate of humanity and that of the nonhuman natural world are independent of each other. A society that treats its natural surroundings in a harsh and exploitative way will do the same to "other" people. Nature and human ethics are not unconnected. The growing expansion of ecological consciousness translates into a deeper understanding of interconnectedness in both nature and history, and we have developed a far more sophisticated grasp of cause and effect relationships. The lively discipline of environmental history is constantly enlarging how we understand both nature and culture. Politically there is a constituency for environmental causes in every nation. Every one of the world religions has examined its own relation to the environment and is hoping to improve it. In a number of societies, a reverence and care for nature has been deep in the culture from the beginning. In the case of Japan we can see how a long-established love of nature can wither in the face of extreme urbanization and aggressive economic expansion. The grassroots public of Japan, however, has a resilient spirit for the defense of nature.

In literature—in North America certainly—nature was long seen as a marginal subject area, with ties to writings of adventure and travel, and mixed into eccentric solitary musings, trappers' journals, farm wife diaries, cowboy and logger narratives, and quasi-religious pantheistic landscape enthusiasms.

However, over the last forty years a body of fresh creative work has been written that remakes the field. A small number of critics and scholars have responded to this with admirable energy, and we are in the midst of the emergence of a distinguished territory of literature that calls for further analysis and for expanded teaching. I am thinking of people who came after Rachel Carson and Aldo Leopold to develop a new form of literary/ecological theory. Consider the critical and social insights in the writings of Tom Lyon, Sherman Paul, John Elder, Stephanie Mills, Lawrence Buell, Cheryl Glotfelty, David Abrams, Scott Slovic, and, most recently, Jed Rasula. Or the creative nonfiction and "natural history" writings of Gary Paul Nabhan, Peter Matthiessen, David Rains Wallace, David Quammen, Douglas Chadwick, Rick Bass, Barry Lopez, Richard Nelson. Then there is the towering oeuvre of John McPhee, who writes out of the magic of sheer information and lately has begun to create a prehuman geological mythos for North America. And I'm not even mentioning the recent advances in the ecological and earth sciences, or the committed and engaging research and writings of environmental activist writers and groups, with their contribution to shaping public policy and a growth of grassroots American connections with the land.

What we refer to as nature or the "environment" or the wild world is our endangered habitat and home, and we are its problem species. Living in it well with each other and with all the other beings is our ancient challenge. In this time of New World Disorder, we need to find the trick of weaving civilized culture and wild nature into the fabric of the future. This will take both art and science. We can take heart, however, from the fact that the actual physical world sets conditions that are some of the strongest guards against ignorant extremism and fanaticism. "Get real! Get a life!" is the daily message of Mother Nature.

Stay the course, my friends.

THE OPENING OF THE FIELD

A poem of this title by Robert Duncan concludes with the lines

> Often I am permitted to return to a meadow
> as if it were a given property of the mind
> that certain bounds hold against chaos

In our field of literature and the environment, we are permitted to return to this meadow, this forest, this desert, as a given property of the deeply natural human mind. Here are the bounds that—in ways too complex for us to grasp—hold against chaos. Remember that chaos is a human invention.

The English word "nature" is from Latin *natura*, "birth, constitution, character, course of things"—initially from *nasci*, to be born. It connects with the root *nat*, which is connected with birth, so we have nation, natal, and native. The Chinese word for nature is *zi-ran* (in Japanese *shizen*), meaning "self-thus." The English word "nature" is commonly used in its practical science sense, referring to the material universe and its rules. In other words, nature means "everything" except perhaps the "supernatural." The rural and the urban are part of the phenomenal world natural.

Wild nature is that part of the physical world that is largely free of human agency. Wild nature is most endangered by human greed or carelessness. "Wild" is a valuable word. It refers to the process or condition of nature on its own, without human intervention. It is a process, a condition, not a place. "The wilds" is a place where wild process dominates.

The word "environment" is functionally equivalent to the term "nature." In English the environment is that which "surrounds"—from the Old French *viron*, encircle. In Japanese the term *kankyo* has much the same set of meanings. The weight of feeling between "nature" and "environment," though, is different. We can relate instantly to a "nature lover," while an "environment lover" sounds slightly odd and clumsy. But the latter term is useful, because it highlights the point that all entities are members of each other's environment. I am part of your surroundings just as you are part of mine. This sort of mutuality is acknowledged in Buddhist philosophy and highly developed in ecological thought.

Before writing was invented there were many literary traditions that flourished entirely in the oral mode. These oral literary traditions, some of which are still alive, contain oceans of stories and huge numbers of riddles, proverbs, myths, rhythmic epic narratives, secular songs, and religious chants. Many deal in great depth with the natural world, and yet they may seem unlike what we might think of as "nature writing" today. They are never distanced from their subject matter. They clearly reflect the bioregion of the society, whether arid lands or moist tropical jungle, and they do not speak of nature in the abstract. They often reflect the mode of subsistence and so may be largely agrarian in their interests, or they might be engaged with hunting and gathering and explore interactions with a wide range of animals. They offer an acute observation of and a deep sense of identification with the nonhuman. The line between the life of the fields and that of the village is not hard and fast. In any case wilderness, in the sense of being the most inaccessible part of a given territory, is seen as a shared space that is both dangerous and magical, a place to visit for spiritual and economic reasons. The body of lore that we are all heir to is constantly enlarging.

Economy and ecology, two key terms, both have the Greek *oikos* as their main root, with the simple meaning of "household." Economics is "rules of the household," and ecology referred originally to the study of biological and metabolic systems. The term literally means something like "household studies." More recently it took on additional meanings, something like "love of and virtuous behavior in regard to nature."

I have already mentioned the "new world disorder." And what is order? The whole phenomenal world, and the mathematics that might be said to underlie it, are all creatively and freely orderly. Art, architecture, philosophy, and agriculture are, from the human standpoint, models of orderliness. There is much that humans find disorderly, but "wild nature" is the ultimate source of order. In the nonhuman universe, not a single leaf that falls from a tree is ever out of place.

EAST ASIA TEACHES US ALL

The remarkably coherent and persistent cultures of East Asia have yielded a literature (in Japan, Korea, Taiwan, and China) that is unmatched in the matter of representing nature in art and writing.

Art and song everywhere begins in folk culture: celebration, dance, music, story, song, poem. In a way the greatest of the original five Chinese classics is the fifth century B.C. *Shih Ching* (*Shikyo* in Japanese), the "Book of Songs." It is, for East Asian poetry, the "mother of poems." It is also, possibly, the "mother of Confucius." It has its roots clearly in a folk song tradition that is easily a thousand years older than the written text. Is it about nature? Not exactly. This is poetry of an agrarian society, so there are few "wild landscapes." There are many poems of people going about their daily life in nature, working in the fields and orchards, loving and courting, and occasionally celebrating and feasting. Many plants are named, wild and domestic. East Asian civilizations have never made the sharp separation between the human and the rest of biological nature that is formalized in the "religions of Abraham"—Judaism, Christianity, and Islam. This Abrahamic dichotomy persists in contemporary monotheisms and is severely with us yet today. Most educated Occidental people who profess to be secularists are still often in thrall to such dualism. In East Asia, from earliest folk religion through Daoism and Confucian teachings, and on into the practices and philosophy of Mahayana Buddhism and its coexistence with surviving folk Shinto in Japan, humans have been seen as part of nature. In all the high schools of Japan, Korea, China, Taiwan, and Vietnam, they teach Darwinian evolution as the model of biological being on earth. They are amazed that school boards in the United States might try to ban this.

Paradoxically, because East Asians so easily feel a part of nature, it has been assumed that whatever humans did was perfectly natural—not a bad assumption in its way—and so deforestation and extinction of species in earlier centuries did not usually alarm people. It was just nature beating up on nature, like elephants I saw smashing and ripping the twigs and limbs off mopane trees, their favorite food, in the forests of Botswana.

The songs of the *Shih Ching* are benign, practical, innocent, and sweet. The founding anthology of Japanese poetry, the *Manyoshu*, has a morning-of-the-world feeling, too. There is love and loneliness, and there are long solitary travels through what were wild landscapes in the early Heian era, the wild grassy fields and reed marshes of lowlands that had not yet been converted to farming. These grassland and wetland poems disappear from later Japanese poetry—the changes in a landscape reflected in poems over centuries could be a study in itself.

Hsieh Ling-yun (Setsu Reiun in Japanese) (385–433 A.D.) is considered the first self-conscious Chinese poet of larger landscapes. He was a bold mountain explorer in the steep hills of south China. He also wrote a very long prose poem on the matter of dwelling in the mountains. English speakers are indebted to the Australian scholar J. D. Frodsham for making these lyric poems available in translation. From the T'ang dynasty onward some of China's finest poets were writing lyrics of nature. David Hinton compiled an anthology of English translations of what he calls "Chinese wilderness poems" that was published as *Mountain Home* (Counterpoint Press, 2002). It contains poems by Wang Wei (Oi), Tu Fu (Toho), Li Po (Rihaku), Po Chu-i (known as Hakurakuten in Japan), Su Shih (Soshi), and many others. These are the prime Chinese poets, and they don't really qualify as "wilderness poets." The Chinese themselves would call some of them "field and garden" poets. I like the term "mind/nature poets," because the "mind/nature" axis reaches deeply into the interior wildness, and so these poets deserve our great regard. Most of these Chinese writers are well known in Korea and Japan, and some have had a profound influence. In Chinese prose writings there are also remarkable travel journals, geographical and geological essays, land-use surveys, and many other sorts of works that deserve closer attention.

The Japanese haiku is truly a "nature tradition" but a sharply focused one. The vocabulary of the seasons and the symbolic implications of different plants is codified—social construction meets poetic landscape! There are thousands of insightful and precious little poems in the tradition. In spite of the haiku's limits, it helps people pay attention to botany, the many facets of the seasons, and countless other tiny details of the natural daily world.*

The Korean poet Ko Un, though very much a contemporary, is also a kind of bridge from the ancient *Book of Songs* (through his knowledge of both Chinese literature and Korean folk song) into twentieth-century modernism, mixed with a strong influence of Zen practice. The poems in his English-language book *The Sound of My Waves* are richly human, often village-based, funny and sweet. Another English-language collection, *Beyond Self* (with an astute foreword by Allen Ginsberg), should be called Zen poems, and they are better than most poems called such, because of their genuine inventiveness and gritty joy. Ko Un is another "mind/nature" poet.

Many of the best-known East Asian poets were touched by, or even deeply engaged with, the teachings of the Zen or Ch'an or Son (Korean) school of Buddhism. A sly Zen influence can be seen everywhere in East Asian art. In terms of environmentalism, the Buddhist ethical teaching that we should "avoid harm to all beings" as far as reasonably possible, which is the Buddhist teaching of *ahimsa* or nonharming/nonviolence or *fusessho*, has had a profound effect. It is not always an easy precept to follow, especially for a modern industrial nation with a developing economy. East Asian industries and expansion have severely damaged the environment, including forests of the Third World countries in recent years.

We study the great writings of the Asian past so that we might surpass them today. We hope to create a deeply grounded contemporary literature of nature that celebrates the wonder of our natural world, that draws on and makes beauty of the incredibly rich knowledge gained from science, and that confronts the terrible damage being done today in the name of progress and the world economy.

---

*Haruo Shimane's *Traces of Dreams: Landscape, Cultural Memory, and the Poetry of Basho* (Stanford, 1998) provides fascinating new details as to the daily social and economic lives of the haiku poets and their interactions with each other.

ECOLOGICAL IMPERATIVES

"Nature" and "environment" are words that basically refer to "that which is." As such, they are bland terms—colorless, or a light shade of green. (The color of the environment could just as well be blood red, or sap-amber, or sky blue.) Nature, and environment, as terms, feel like "places." "Ecology" is a term, like "wild," for *process.*

"Ecology" refers to a dynamic always in flux. It moves us away from the old sense of the world as something created in time that might now be running down and getting worn; away from the idea of the world as a clock or a machine or a computer, to a "world as process," a creation happening constantly in each moment. A close term in East Asian philosophy is the word *Dao*, the Way, *dô* in Japanese.

When we come to the field of ecology we are looking at population dynamics, plant and animal succession, predator–prey relationships, competition and cooperation, feeding levels, food chains, whole ecosystems, and the flow of energy through ecosystems—and this is just the beginning. In my work on western American forest issues over the last few years, I have learned a great deal from forest ecology, with the help of my older son Kai Snyder, who is a professional in the field. Forest ecology calculates the constant dynamism of natural systems, the continuous role of disturbance, and the unremitting effects of climatic fluctuations.

What sort of poem or story can draw from the inner energy of an ecosystem? If this "literature of the environment" were parallel to the history of fiction, I'd say we have now reached the point where we're tired of stock figures and charming plots, and we want to get into the inner lives and psyches of our characters, all their obsessions, kinkiness, and secrets. We will necessarily be exploring the dark side of nature—nocturnal, parasitic energies of decomposition and their human parallels. Also, the term "ecology," which includes energy exchange and interconnection, can be metaphorically extended to other realms. We speak of "the ecology of the imagination" or even of language, with justification: "ecology" is a valuable shorthand term for complexity in motion.

I've enjoyed and learned a lot from Jed Rasula's *This Compost: Ecological Imperatives in American Poetry* (University of Georgia Press, 2002). It picks up from Lawrence Buell's brilliantly learned and instructive book *The Environmental Imagination* (Harvard, 1995) and penetrates the territory of both ecology and the adventurous side of contemporary poetics. Rasula does so without needless nature piety, getting right down to the metaphors of decay and fertility, mulch and nutrition, as singularly critical to language and art—and demonstrates this in Walt Whitman's poem "This Compost," in Emily Dickinson, in George Santayana, and in Thoreau, who wrote in his *Journals*, "Decayed literature makes the richest of all soils." Rasula's forays into Ezra Pound, Charles Olson and the Black Mountain poets, the Beats (in particular Michael McClure), Rothenberg's ethnopoetics, Clayton Eshleman's Deep History, Paul Shepard's "coming home to the Pleistocene," and Gregory Bateson's *Steps to an Ecology of Mind* are supplemented by my own thinking as in "Poetry, Community, and Climax." I will quote a section from it here:

> Detritus cycle energy is liberated by fungi and lots of insects. I would then suggest: as climax forest is to biome, and fungus is to the recycling of energy, so "enlightened mind" is to daily ego mind, and Art to the recycling of neglected inner potential. When we deepen ourselves, looking within, understanding ourselves, we come closer to being like a mature ecosystem. Turning away from grazing on the "immediate biomass" of perception, sensation, and thrill; and reviewing memory ... blocks of stored inner energies, the flux of dreams, the detritus of day-to-day consciousness, liberates the energy of our own mind-compost. Art is an assimilator of unfelt experience, perception, sensation, and memory for the whole society. It comes not as a flower, but—to complete the metaphor—as a mushroom: the fruiting body of the buried threads of mycelia that run widely through the soil, intricately married to the root hairs of all the trees. "Fruiting"—at that point—is the completion of the work of the poet, and the point where the artist reenters the cycle: gives what she or he has re-created through reflection, returning a "thought of enlightenment" to community.

Human history, with its languages and migrations, is like an old forest floor of detritus, old and new mingled together, old resentments recycled, ancient recipes rediscovered, and perennial mythologies strutting shamelessly on the stage of the moment. The "ecological imperative" must be that we try to see whatever current crisis we are in as part of an older larger pattern. But it also is an imperative to honor diversity, whether of species or of languages and customs.

Scholarship continually spades and turns the deep compost of language and memory; and creative writing does much the same but adding more imagination, direct experience, and the ineluctable "present moment" as well. Our work as writers and scholars is not just "about" the environment, not just "speaking for" nature, but manifesting in ourselves and our work the integrity of the wild. The complexity of a working metropolis, with its energy, sewage treatment, transportation, public auditoriums, parks, water, and solid waste systems, is rather like a climax ecosystem. Making these links into song and story is work for an artist—a chance for somebody to write some great super-urban haiku.

PERFORMANCE IS CURRENCY

The name of the peerless traditional Japanese theater called Noh, one of the world's greatest art forms, means "accomplishment." Zeami, the founder of Noh, wrote dozens of essays on what it took to be accomplished: background learning and reading, attention and much attendance at the performances of others, and practice, practice, practice. Further, he suggests the almost-magical capacity to go beyond years of practice into selfless freedom again. The ability to surprise yourself even years later. Poets and artists who are dedicated to their craft know the importance of skill. And there is one more point: Who is this flower for?

A Zen verse says,

> The moon shines on the river,
> The wind blows through the pines—
> Who is this long, beautiful evening for?
> (from the *Cheng Dao Ke*)

Outwardly the Noh plays were for the dedicated aristocrats and warrior-administrators who supported the arts. Inwardly they are for the tender, deep, mind-hearts of everyone.

One time in Alaska a young woman asked me, "If we have made such good use of animals, eating them, singing about them, drawing them, riding them, and dreaming about them, what do they get back from us?" An excellent question, directly on the point of etiquette and propriety, and from the animals' side. I told her, "The Ainu say that the deer, salmon, and bear like our music and are fascinated by our languages. So we sing to the fish or the game, speak words to them, say grace. We do ceremonies and rituals. Performance is currency in the deep world's gift economy." I went on to say I felt that nonhuman nature is basically well inclined toward humanity and only wishes modern people were more reciprocal, not so bloody. The animals are drawn to us, they see us as good musicians, and they think we have cute ears.

The human contribution to the planetary ecology might be our entertaining craziness, our skills as musicians and performers, our awe-inspiring dignity as ritualists and solemn ceremonialists—because that is what seems to delight the watching wild world.

The critic and writer Ronald Grimes took up this aspect of my curious line of thought—he is a performer himself—and developed it into an actual performance that he called "Performance Is Currency in the Deep World's Gift Economy: An Incantatory Riff for a Global Medicine Show" (the text of it was published in *Isle* 9: 1 [Winter 2002]). Grimes's background as teacher, performer, and student of religion gave him outstanding insight into what I had thrown out as a Mahayanistic intuition and gave it solid footing.

The "deep world" is of course the thousand-million-year-old world of rock, soil, water, air, and all living beings, all acting through their roles. "Currency" is what you pay your debt with. We all receive, every day, the gifts of the Deep World, from the air we breathe to the food we eat. How do we repay that gift? Performance. A song for your supper. Gift economy? That might be another perspective on the meaning of ecology. We are living in the midst of a great potluck at which we are all the invited guests. And we are also eventually the meal. The Ainu, when they had venison for dinner, sang songs aloud to the deer spirits who were hanging about waiting for the performance. The deer visit human beings so that they might hear some songs. In Buddhist spiritual ecology, the first thing to give up is your ego. The ancient Vedic philosophers said that the gods like sacrifices, but of all sacrifices that which they most appreciate is your ego. This critical little point is the foundation of yogic and Buddhist *askesis*. Dôgen famously said, "We study the self to forget the self. When you forget the self you become one with the ten thousand things." (There is only one offering that is greater than the ego, and that is "enlightenment" itself.)

The being who has offered up her enlightenment is called a Bodhisattva. In some of the Polynesian societies the Big Person, the most respected and powerful figure in the village, was the one who had nothing—whatever gift came to him or her was promptly given away again. This is the real heart of a gift economy, an economy that would save, not devour, the world. Gandhi once said, "For greed, all of nature is insufficient." Art takes nothing from the world; it is a gift and an exchange. It leaves the world nourished.

> "Ripples on the surface of the water—
> were silver salmon passing under—different
> from the ripples caused by breezes"
>
> A scudding plume on the wave—
> a humpback whale is
> breaking out in air up
> gulping herring
>   —Nature not a book, but a *performance*, a
> high old culture
>
> Ever-fresh events
> scraped out, rubbed out, and used, used, again—
> the braided channels of the rivers
> hidden under fields of grass—
>
> The vast wild
>   the house, alone.
> The little house in the wild,

>   the wild in the house.
> Both forgotten.
>
> >   No nature
>
> > Both together, one big empty house.

Writers and the War Against Nature

THOSE WHO LOVE THE WORLD

I GREW UP in the maritime Pacific Northwest, on a farm north of Seattle, where we kept a hen flock, had a small orchard, and tended dairy cows. My uncles were loggers, merchant seamen, and fishermen.

After college, where I studied anthropology, literature, and East Asian culture, I had no choice but to go back to working in the woods and at sea. In the late fifties I spent nine months working in the engine room on an American-flag oil tanker that hired me out of the port of Yokohama. I was a member of the National Maritime Union, had my seaman's papers, and it wasn't hard to pick up a job in almost any port of the world. That ship kept me at sea for a continuous nine months. Two things touched me deeply on that job: One was the stars, night after night, at every latitude, including way below the equator. With my little star book and red-beam flashlight I mastered the constellations of the southern hemisphere. The other was getting to know the birds of the ocean. I loved watching the albatross—a few of those huge graceful birds would always be cruising along behind our ship, trailing the wake for bits of food. I learned that a Wandering Albatross (of the southern hemisphere) might fly a million miles in one lifetime, and that it takes a pair of them almost a year to raise one chick. Night and day, they always followed us, and if they ever slept it seems it was on the wing.

Just recently a study was released describing the sudden decline of albatross numbers worldwide. It even prompted an editorial in the *New York Times* (January 20, 2005). Their sharp decline is attributed to much death by drowning. The long-line fishing boats lay out lines with bait and hooks that go miles back, dragging just below the surface. An albatross will go for the bait, get hooked, and be pulled down to drown. As many as one hundred thousand a year are estimated to perish in this way, enough to threaten the survival of the species if it keeps up. What have the albatross, "Distinguished strangers who have come down to us from another world," ever done to us? The editorial concludes, "The long-line fishing fleet is over-harvesting the air as well as the sea."

Out on the South Pacific in 1958, watching the soaring albatrosses from the stern of a ship, I could never have guessed that their lives would be threatened by industrial societies, turning them into "collateral damage" of the affluent appetite for *ahi*, and *maguro*. Yet this is just a tiny example of the long reach of the globalized economy and the consumer society into the wild earth's remote places. A recent book on global logging and deforestation is titled *Strangely Like War.* What is happening now to nature worldwide, to plant life and wildlife, in ocean, grassland, forest, savannah, and desert in all spaces and habitat can be likened to a war against nature.

Although human beings have interacted with nature for millennia, and sometimes destructively so, it was never quite like "war." The active defense of nature has been joined by a few artists and writers who have entered the fight on "the wild side" along with subsistence peoples, indigenous spiritual leaders, and many courageous scientists, conservationists, and environmentalists worldwide.

There is a tame, and also a wild, side to the human mind. The tame side, like a farmer's field, has been disciplined and cultivated to produce a desired yield. It is useful but limited. The wild side is larger, deeper, more complex, and though it cannot be fully known, it can be explored. The explorers of the wild mind are often writers and artists. The "poetic imagination" of which William Blake so eloquently spoke is the territory of wild mind. It has landscapes and creatures within it that will surprise us. It can refresh us and scare us. Wild mind reflects the larger truth of our ancient selves, of our ancient animal and spiritual selves.

The French anthropologist Claude Lévi-Strauss once said something like "Art survives within modern civilization rather like little islands of wilderness saved to show us where we came from." Someone else once said that what makes writing good is the wildness in it. The wildness gives heart, courage, love, spirit, danger, compassion, skill, fierceness and sweetness—all at once—to language. From ancient times storytellers, poets, and dramatists have presented the world in all its fullness: plants, animals, men and women, changing shape—speaking multiple languages—inter-marrying—traveling to the sky and under the earth. The great myths and folktales of human magic and nature's power were our education for ten thousand years. Whether they know it or not, even modern writers draw strength from the wild side.

How can artists and writers manage to join in the defense of the planet and wild nature? Writers and artists by their very work "bear witness." They don't wield financial, governmental, or military power. However, at the outset they were given, as in fairy tales, two "magic gifts": One is "The mirror of truth." Whatever they hold this mirror up to is shown in its actual form, and the truth must come out. May we use that mirror well! The second is a "heart of compassion," which is to say the ability to feel and know the pains and delights of other people, and to weave that feeling into their art. For some this compassion can extend to all creatures and to the earth itself. In a way nature even borrows the voices of some writers and artists. Anciently this was a shamanistic role where the singer, dancer, or storyteller embodied a force, appearing as a bear dancer or a crane dancer, and became one with a spirit or creature. Today, such a role is played by the writer who finds herself a spokesperson for nonhuman entities communicating to the human realm through dance or song. This could be called "speaking on behalf of nature" in the ancient way.

Song, story, and dance are fundamental to all later "civilized" culture. In archaic times these were unified in dramatic performance, back when drama and religious ceremony were one. They are reunited today in the highest and greatest of performance arts—the grand scale of European opera and ballet, the spare and disciplined elegance of Japanese Noh theater, the grand and almost timeless dance-and-story of Indonesian Gamelan, the wit and hardiness of Bertolt Brecht's plays, or the fierce and stunningly beautiful intensity of Korean P'ansori performance. Performance is of key importance because this phenomenal world and all life is, of itself, not a book but a performance.

For a writer or artist to become an advocate for nature, he or she must become a lover of that vast world of energies and ecologies. Because I was brought up in a remote rural district, instead of having kids to play with I sometimes had to entertain myself by exploring the forest surrounding our farm, observing the dozens of bird species and occasional deer, fox, or bobcat; sometimes hunting, sometimes gathering plants that I could sell to herb buyers for a few pennies, sometimes camping out alone for several days at a time. Heavy logging was going on in the nearby hills.

At fifteen I got into the higher mountains of the Cascade range in Washington State, starting with the ridges and high meadows around the snow-covered volcano called Mount Saint Helens, or Luwit, a nine-thousand-foot peak just north of the Columbia River. This is what I finally chose to write about in my book *Danger on Peaks*:

THE CLIMB

Walking the nearby ridges and perching on the cliffs of Coldwater Mountain, I memorized the upper volcano. The big and little Lizards (lava ridges with their heads uphill), the Dogshead, with a broad bulge of brown rock and white snowpatches making it look faintly like a St. Bernard. The higher-up icefields with the schrund and wide crevasses, and the approach slopes from timberline. Who wouldn't take the chance to climb a snowpeak and get the long view?

Two years later the chance came. Our guide was an old-time Mazama from Tigard in Oregon. His climbing life went back to World War One. Then he got a big orchard. He wore a tall black felt hunting hat, high corked loggers-boots, stagged-off pants, and carried the old style alpenstock. We put white zinc oxide paste on our noses and foreheads, each got our own alpenstock, and we wore metal-rimmed dark goggles like Sherpas in the thirties. We set out climbing the slidey pumice lower slopes well before dawn.

Step by step, breath by breath—no rush, no pain. Onto the snow on Forsyth Glacier, over the rocks of the Dogshead, getting a lesson in alpenstock self-arrest, a talk on safety and patience, and then on to the next phase: ice. Threading around crevasses, climbing slow, we made our way to the summit just like Issa's

> "Inch by inch
> little snail
> creep up Mt. Fuji"

West Coast snowpeaks are too much! They are too far above the surrounding lands. There is a break between. They are in a different world. If you want to get a view of the world you live in, climb a little rocky mountain with a neat small peak. But the big snowpeaks pierce the realm of clouds and cranes, rest in the zone of five-colored banners and writhing crackling dragons in veils of ragged mist and frost-crystals, into a pure transparency of blue.

St. Helens' summit is smooth and broad, a place to nod, to sit and write, to watch what's higher in the sky and do a little dance. Whatever the numbers say, snowpeaks are always far higher than the highest airplanes ever get. I made my petition to the shapely mountain, "Please help this life." When I tried to look over and down to the world below—*there was nothing there.*

And then we grouped up to descend. The afternoon snow was perfect for glissade and leaning on our stocks we slid and skidded between cracks and thumps into soft snow, dodged lava slabs, got into the open snowfield slopes and almost flew to the soft pumice ridges below. Coming down is so fast! Still high we walked the three-mile dirt road back to the lake.

ATOMIC DAWN

The day I first climbed Mt. Saint Helens was August 13, 1945.

Spirit Lake was far from the cities of the valley, and news came slow. Though the first atomic bomb was dropped on Hiroshima August 6 and the second dropped on Nagasaki August 9, photographs didn't appear in the *Portland Oregonian* until August 12. Those papers must have been driven in to Spirit Lake on the 13th. Early on the morning of the 14th I walked over to the lodge to check the bulletin board. There were whole pages of the paper pinned up: photos of a blasted city from the air, the estimate of 150,000 dead in Hiroshima alone, the American scientist quoted saying "nothing will grow there again for seventy years." The morning sun on my shoulders, the fir forest smell and the big tree shadows; feet in thin moccasins feeling the ground, and my heart still one with the snowpeak mountain at my back. Horrified, blaming scientists and politicians and the governments of the world, I swore a vow to myself, something like, "By the purity and beauty and permanence of Mt. St. Helens, I will fight against this cruel destructive power and those who would seek to use it, for all my life."

The statement in that 1945 newspaper saying that nature would be blighted for decades to come astounded me almost as much as the enormity of the loss of innocent human life. Already a conservationist, I later went on to be active in the anti-nuclear movement as a student and argued and struggled against the use and proliferation of nuclear weapons. Even though it seemed at times that these efforts were naive and hopeless, we persevered.

During my college years I was studying the philosophies and religions of the world. A central teaching of the Buddhist tradition is nonviolence toward all of nature, *ahimsa*. This seemed absolutely right to me. In the Abrahamic religions, "Thou shalt not kill" applies only to human beings. In Socialist thought as well, human beings are all-important, and with the "labor theory of value" it is as though organic nature contributes nothing of worth. Later it came to me, green plants doing photosynthesis are the ultimate working class. Nature creates the first level of value, labor the second.

In the *Lun yü*—the Confucian "Analects"—we can see how the Master called for Etiquette in regard to nature as well as human society (7.27). Almost all of the later "high civilizations" have been the sort of social organizations that alienate humans from their own biological and spiritual heritage.

While I was laboring in the forests, most of my fellow loggers were Native Americans of the Wasco and Wishram tribes of eastern Oregon. From them I learned that it was possible to be a hunter and a fisherman with a spiritual attitude of deep gratitude and nonviolence.

After some work as a graduate student at the University of California at Berkeley, I finally got a chance to go to Asia. I lived for a while in a Zen practice hall in Kyoto, Japan, and studied with a Zen teacher in the Rinzai (Chinese, *Linji*) tradition. I took the precepts under my teacher, who told me that "Of all the precepts, the first precept is most important and contains the others: *ahimsa*, nonharming, 'Cause the least possible harm.'" To live with that precept is a challenge—he once said to me, "How do you not harm a fence? How would you save a ghost?"

I lived in Japan for ten years, partly in the monastery but also in my own little house, and supported myself by teaching English conversation to Japanese salarymen. I asked my adult students, "Why are you so intent on learning English?" They answered, "Because we intend to extend our economic influence worldwide, and English is the international language." I didn't take them seriously.

In my spare time I hiked in the local mountains, learned East Asian plants and birds, and started seriously reading scientific books on ecology and biology. All those essays analyzing food chains and food webs—this was a science, I realized, dealing with energy exchange and the natural hierarchies of various living systems. "When energy passes through a system it tends to organize that system," someone wrote. It finally came to me that this was about "eating each other"—almost as a sacrament. I wrote my first truly ecological poem, which explores the essential qualities of human foods:

Song of the Taste

Eating the living germs of grasses
Eating the ova of large birds

    the fleshy sweetness packed
    around the sperm of swaying trees

The muscles of the flanks and thighs of
        soft-voiced cows
   the bounce in the lamb's leap
   the swish in the ox's tail

Eating roots grown swoll
        inside the soil.

> Drawing on life of living
>   clustered points of light spun
>   out of space
> hidden in the grape.
>
> Eating each other's seed
>   eating
> ah, each other.
>
> Kissing the lover in the mouth of bread:
>   lip to lip.

This innocent celebratory poem went straight to the question of conflict between the ethics of *ahimsa*, nonviolence, "respect for all beings," and the lives of necessity and subsistence of indigenous peoples and Native Americans I had known. They still practiced ceremonies of gratitude and were careful not to present themselves as superior to other life forms. Ahimsa taken too literally leaves out the life of the world and makes the rabbit virtuous but the hawk evil. People who must fish and hunt to live can enter into the process with gratitude and care, and no arrogant assumptions of human privilege. This cannot come from "thinking about" nature; it must come from being *within* nature.

There are plenty of people of influence and authority in the churches, in industry, the universities, and high in government who still like to describe nature as "red in tooth and claw" (a line of Alfred Tennyson's)—a fundamental misunderstanding—and use it as part of the justification for the war against nature.

The organic life of the planet has maintained itself, constantly changing, and has gone through and recovered from several enormous catastrophic events over hundreds of millions of years. Now we are at another potentially disastrous time for the organic world. The overdeveloped world's impact on air, water, soil, wildlife, and plant life causes species extinctions, poisons air and water, leaves mountains with mudslides but no trees, and gives us soil that can't grow food without the continuous subsidy provided by fossil fuels. As we learned over time to positively work for peace to head off the possibilities of war, so now we must work for sustainable biological practices and a faith that embraces wild nature if we are to reverse the prospect of continually dwindling resources and rising human populations.

One can ask what might it take to have an agriculture that does not degrade the soils, a fishery that does not deplete the ocean, a forestry that keeps watersheds and ecosystems intact, population policies that respect human sexuality and personality while holding numbers down, and energy policies that do not set off fierce little wars. These are the key questions worth our lifetimes and more.

Many of our leaders assume that the track we're on will go on forever and nobody will learn much; politics as usual. It's the same old engineering, business, and governmental message with its lank rhetoric of data and management. Or, when the talk turns to "sustainability," the focus is on a limited ecological-engineering model that might guarantee a specific resource for a while longer (like grass, water, or trees) but lacks the vision to imagine the health of the whole planet. An ethical position that would accord intrinsic value to nonhuman nature, and would see human beings as involved in moral as well as practical choices in regard to the natural world, would make all the difference.

"As . . . a dewdrop, a bubble, a cloud, a flash of lightning, view all created things." Thus ends the *Diamond Sutra*, reminding us of irreducible impermanence. Sustainability cannot mean some kind of permanence. A waggish commentary says "Sustainability is a physical impossibility. But it is a very nice sentiment." The quest for permanence has always led us astray—whether in building stone castles, Great Walls, pyramids and tombs for pharaohs, great navies, giant cathedrals to ease us toward heaven, or cold war–scale weapons systems guaranteeing mutually assured destruction. We must live with change, like a bird on the wing, and doing so—let all the other beings live on too. Not permanence, but living in harmony with the Way.

The albatross, all sixteen species of them, are companions with us on earth, sailing on their own way, of no use to us humans, and we should be no use to them. They can be friends at a distance, fellow creatures in the stream of evolution. This is fundamental etiquette. We do not need to crowd in on them, look at them, dream or write about them.

So, back to those key questions, what would it take? We know that science and the arts can be allies. We need far more women in politics. We need a religious view that embraces nature and does not fear science; business leaders who know and accept ecological and spiritual limits; political leaders who have spent time working in schools, factories, or farms, and maybe a few who still write poems. We need intellectual and academic leaders who have studied both history and ecology and who like to dance and cook. We need poets and novelists who pay no attention to literary critics. But what we ultimately need most are human beings who love the world.

Poems, novels, plays, with their great deep minds of story, awaken the Heart of Compassion. And so they confound the economic markets, rattle the empires, and open us up to the actually existing human and non-human world. *Performance* is art in motion; in the moment; both enactment and embodiment. This is exactly what nature herself is.

> Soaring just over the sea-foam
> riding the wind of the endless waves
> albatross, out there, way
>
> away,   a far cry
> down from the sky

Entering the Fiftieth Millennium

LET'S SAY we're about to enter not the twenty-first century but the fiftieth millennium. Since the various cultural calendars (Hindu, Jewish, Islamic, Christian, Japanese) are each within terms of their own stories, we can ask what calendar would be suggested to us by the implicit narrative of Euro-American science—since that provides so much of our contemporary educated worldview. We might come up with a "Homo sapiens calendar" that starts at about 40,000 years before the present (B.P.), in the Gravettian/Aurignacian era when the human tool kit (already long sophisticated) began to be decorated with graphs and emblems and when figurines were produced not for practical use but apparently for magic or beauty.

Rethinking our calendar in this way is made possible by the research and discoveries of the last century in physical anthropology, paleontology, archaeology, and cultural anthropology. The scholars of hominid history are uncovering a constantly larger past in which the earlier members of our species continually appear to be smarter, more accomplished, more adept, and more complex than we had previously believed. We humans are constantly revising the story we tell about ourselves. The main challenge is to keep this unfolding story modestly reliable.

One of my neopagan friends, an ethnobotanist and prehistorian, complains about how the Christians have callously appropriated his sacred solstice ceremonies. "Our fir tree of lights and gifts," he says, "has been swept into an orgy of consumerism, no longer remembered as a sign of the return of the sun," and, "People have totally forgotten that the gifts brought from the north by Santa Claus are spiritual, not material; and his red clothes, white trim, round body, and northern habitat show that he represents the incredibly psychoactive mushroom *Amanita muscaria*."

My friend is one of several poet-scholars I know who study deep history (a term he prefers to "prehistory")—in this case that of Europe—for clues and guides to understanding the creature that we have become and how we got here, the better to steer our way into the future. Such studies are especially useful for artists.

I went to France one summer to further pursue my own interest in the Upper Paleolithic. Southwest Europe has large areas of karst plateau, which allows for caves by the thousands, some of them enormous. Quite a few were decorated by Upper Paleolithic people. With the help of the poet and paleo-art historian Clayton Eshleman, my wife and I visited many sites and saw a major sampling of the cave art of southwest Europe, in the Dordogne and the Pyrenees. Places like Pêche-merle, Cougnac, Niaux, El Portel, Lascaux, and Trois Frères. The cave art, with its finger tracings, engravings, hand stencils, outline drawings, and polychrome paintings, flourished 10,000 to 35,000 years ago. The Paleolithic cave and portable art of Europe thus constitute a 25,000-year continuous artistic and cultural tradition. The people who did this were fully Homo sapiens and, it must be clearly stated, not just ancestors of the people of Europe but in a gene pool so old that it is to some degree ancestor to everyone everywhere. The art they left us is a heritage for people of the whole world.

This tradition is full of puzzles. The artwork is often placed far back in the caves, in places almost inaccessible. The quality fluctuates wildly. Animals can be painted with exquisite attention, but there are relatively few human figures, and they are strangely crude. Almost no plants are represented. Birds and fish are scarce compared to mammals. Some animal paintings, as at Niaux, appear unfinished, with the feet left off.

The theories and explanations from the twentieth-century cave-art specialists—the great Abbe Breuil and the redoubtable André Leroi-Gourhan—don't quite work. The hunting-magic theory, which holds that the paintings of animals were to increase the take in the hunt, is contradicted by the fact that the majority of animal representations are of wild horses, which were not a big food item, and that the animals most commonly consumed, red deer and reindeer, are depicted in very small number. The horse was not yet domesticated, so why this fascination for horses? My wife, Carole, suggests that maybe the artists were a guild of teenage girls. The bison is a close second, however, and was a food source.

The other most commonly represented animals, the huge Pleistocene bison and the aurochs, a huge *bos* (living in the forests of northern Europe until the sixteenth century), were apparently too large and dangerous to be major hunting prey. Ibex, chamois, and panther occasionally show up, but they were not major food items. There are also pictures of animals long extinct now—woolly rhinoceros, mammoth, cave bear, giant elk.

In the art of early civilized times, there was a fascination with large predators—in particular, the charismatic Anatolian lions and the brown bears from which the word *arctic* derives. Big predators were abundant in the Paleolithic, but sketches or paintings of them are scarce in nearly all caves. It was the bears who may have first used the caves and entirely covered the walls of some, like Rouffignac, with long scratches. Seeing this may have given the first impetus to humans to do their own graffiti.

The theory that these works were part of a shamanistic and ceremonial cultural practice, though likely enough, is still just speculation. There have been attempts to read some narratives out of certain graphic combinations, but that too cannot be verified.

After several decades of research and comparison, it came to seem that cave art began with hand stencils and crude engravings around 32,000 B.P. and progressively evolved through time to an artistic climax at the Lascaux cave. This is the most famous of the caves, discovered during World War II. It is generally felt to contain the most remarkable and lovely of all the world's cave art. The polychrome paintings are dated at around 17,000 B.P. In the summer of 1996 I had the rare good fortune to be admitted to *le vraie grotte* of Lascaux (as well as the replica, which is itself excellent and what all but a handful of people now see). I can testify. There's an eighteen-foot-long painting of an aurochs arcing across a ceiling twelve feet above the floor. A sort of Lascaux style is then perceived as coming down in other, later caves, excellent work, up to the Salon Noir in the Niaux cave in the Ariège, dated about 11,500 B.P. After that, cave art stops being made, many caves were closed up from landslides or cave-ins, and they were forgotten.

Until quite recently everyone was pretty comfortable with this theoretical evolutionary chronology, which fits our contemporary wish to believe that things get better through time. But in 1994 some enthusiastic speleologists found a new cave, on the Ardèche, a tributary of the Rhone. Squeezing through narrow cracks and not expecting much, they almost tumbled into a fifty-foot-high hall and a quarter mile of passageways of linked chambers full of magnificent depictions that were the equal of anything at Lascaux. There are a few animals shown here that are totally new to cave art. Images of woolly rhinoceros and the Pleistocene maneless lion, which are rare in other caves, are the most numerous. This site is now known, after one of the lead discoverers, as the Chauvet cave.

The French scientists did their initial carbon dating, and were puzzled, and looked again, and had to conclude that these marvelous paintings were around 32,000 years old, 15,000 years older than those at Lascaux—almost as distant in time from Lascaux as Lascaux is from us. The idea of a progressive history to cave art is seriously in question. A new, and again larger, sense of the Homo sapiens story has opened up for us, and the beginnings of art are pushed even further back in time.

I wrote in my notebook:

> Out of the turning and twisting calcined cave walls, a sea of fissures, calcite concretions, stalactites, old claw-scratchings of cave bears, floors of bear wallows & slides; the human finger-tracings in clay, early scribblings, scratched-in lines and sketchy little engravings of half-done creatures or just abstract signs, lines crossed over lines, images over images; out of this ancient swirl of graffiti rise up the exquisite figures of animals: swimming deer with antler cocked up, a pride of lions with noble profiles, fat wild horses, great bodied bison, huge-horned wild bulls, antlered elk; painted and powerfully outlined creatures alive with the life that art gives: on the long-lost mineraled walls below ground. Crisp, economical, swift, sometimes hasty; fitting into the space, fitting over other paintings, spread across . . . outlined in calligraphic confident curving lines. Not photo-realistic, but true.

To have done this took a mind that could clearly observe and hold within a wealth of sounds, smells, and images and then carry them deep underground and re-create them. The reasons elude our understanding. For sure the effort took organization and planning to bring off: we have found stone lamps and evidence of lighting supplies and traces of ground pigments sometimes obtained from far away. The people must have gathered supplies of food, dried grass for bedding, poles for scaffolding. Someone was doing arts administration.

One important reminder here is, as T. S. Eliot said when writing of Magdalenian art, "Art never improves. There is no progress in art." Art that moves us today can be from anywhere, any time. This is quite true, in certain ways, for the literary arts as well.

The cave paintings had their own roles to play back in the late Pleistocene. Having been protected by the steady temperatures of the underground, they return to human eyes again today, and across the millennia can move us. No master realist painter of the last five hundred years could better those painted critters of the past: they totally do what they do, without room for improvement.

And there may be no "progress" in religion, in Practice, or in the Dharma, either. There was an Ancient Buddha. There were archaic Bodhisattvas. All that we have to study of them is their shards and paintings.

What was the future? One answer might be, "The future was to have been further progress, an improvement over our present condition." This is more in question now. The deep past also confounds the future by suggesting how little we can agree on what is good.

If our ancient rock artists skipped out on painting humans, it just may be that they knew more than enough about themselves and could turn their attention wholeheartedly to the nonhuman other. In any case the range of their art embraces both abstract and unreadable signs and graphs and a richly portrayed world of what today we call "faunal biodiversity." They gave us a picture of their animal environment with as much pride and art as if they were giving us their very selves.

Maybe in some way they speak from a spirit that is in line with Dôgen's comment, "We study the self to forget the self. When you forget the self, you can become one with the ten thousand things."

We have no way of knowing what the verbal arts of 35,000 years ago might have been. It is possible that the languages of that time were in no way inferior in complexity, sophistication, or richness to the languages spoken today. It's not far-fetched to think that if the paintings were so good, the poems and songs must have been of equal quality.

One can imagine myths and tales of people, places, and animals. In poetry or song, I fancy wild horse chants, "salutes" (as are sung in some parts of Africa) to each creature, little lyrics that intensify some element in a narrative, a kind of deep song—*cante jondo*—to go together with deep history; or on the other side, quick "bison haiku."

It was all in the realm of orality, which as we well know can support a rich and intense "literary" culture that is often interacting with dance, song, and story, such as do our prime high arts today, opera and ballet.

Today, then: the Franco-Anglo creole known as English has become the world's second language and as such is a major bearer of diverse literary cultures. English is and will be all the more a future host to a truly multicultural "rainbow" of writings. The rich history of the English language tradition is like a kiva full of lore, to be studied and treasured by writers and scholars wherever they may find themselves on the planet. It will also continue to diversify and to embrace words and pronunciations that will move it farther and farther from London Town. Even as I deliberately take my membership to be North American and feel distant from much of European culture, I count myself fortunate to have been born a native speaker of English. Such flexibility, such variety of vocabulary! Such a fine sound system! And we can look forward to its future changes. Performance and poetry, storytelling and fiction, are still alive and well. Orality and song stay with poetry as long as we are here.

Multiculturalism is generally conceived in synchronic terms: cultures and peoples of this historical time frame, in their differences. I'm suggesting we also be open to a diachronic view and extend our tolerance back in time. It would do no harm to take a sympathetic, open, and respectful attitude toward the peoples of the deep past. We can try to hear their language coming through paintings of lions and bison. This is now part of what our past will be.

Then we can also wonder through what images our voices will carry to the people 10,000 years hence—through the swirls of still-standing freeway off-ramps and on-ramps? Through the ruins of dams? For those future people will surely be there, listening for some faint call from us, when they are entering the sixtieth millennium.

Lifetimes with Fire

In 1968 I packed my books and robes, and with my young family I sailed back to California from ten years in Japan. When I first moved to a piece of Sierra mountain forest land the next summer, I wouldn't let even a tractor drive over it. Except for a couple of faint logging tracks that evolved into an access road, I wouldn't take a truck into the woods. We built a house that summer. We felled trees for posts and beams using an old Royal Chinook two-man falling saw and then barked the logs with large draw-knives. They were not skidded or trucked to the building site, but carried by crews of strong young men and women using rope slings and little oak pole yokes. The three-month job—the workers were mostly just out of college and only a few had architecture and building skills—was done entirely with hand tools. Our ridge had no grid power available and we had no generator. The rocky road ran across a barren mile of ancient rounded riverbed stone laid open by hydraulic mining in the 1870s. Beyond the diggings and three miles from the paved road deep in the pine forest was our building site. Town was twenty-five miles away across a twelve-hundred-foot-deep river canyon.

Twelve years later I took a trip back to Japan to visit Buddhist monk and artist friends. The Zen gardens and temples were lovely to see and smell again. Also I looked at the new farming and forestry. Small gas engines had taken over what oxen or humans had done before: ingenious tillers, small precise rice thrasher-huskers, a variety of weed-whackers, beautiful tiny trucks, brightly colored miniature backhoes and excavators, and everyone using them without the least sign of guilt or stress. I thought, if the two- and four-stroke engine had a place even in the Asian scheme of things, maybe they'd work for me as well.

The roads have not improved yet, and there's still no grid power. Though I have stayed mostly with hand tools, over the years since we have gone from kerosene lamps to solar panels with a backup generator. I take my four-wheel pickup into the woods for firewood, and our homestead is now a hybrid of nineteenth- and twenty-first-century technologies. There's a wood-burning kitchen range and two large wood-burning heating stoves, but we also use laptop computers, have a fax and copying machine, and we buck the big down oak rounds with a large Husqvarna and a small Stihl chain saw.

Every summer season we did a bit more work clearing back the underbrush (ceanothus and manzanita) from under the trees, and every winter we burned the brush piles. California and southern Oregon forests are fire-adapted and are tuned to fairly regular low-level wildfires sweeping through. But then a few summers back it seemed the wildfires got hotter and the roads and houses closer together, and some big plans for firebreaks were designed by the California Division of Forestry.

I'd prefer to clear the understory fuel the natural way, with fire. I stood watch on a prescribed burn a few years back on Bureau of Land Management forest, with the planned burn zone overlapping onto an adjacent private parcel. It torched up a few big trees and burned a lot of underbrush down to ash. It was scary, but the fire chief assured us everything was okay. Bulldozer operators were on alert, ready to come if needed; and so were the CDF pilots at the county airport with their spotter and tanker planes. The burn went well all day. There were some complaints about the smoke. That's one problem with prescribed burns: the air quality goes down, and newcomers don't like it. But the bigger problem is that the site is getting brushy again eight years later. It needs a follow-up burn, and we don't know if we'll ever be able to do it. "The window of safety is too small." So maybe mechanical crunching is another answer.

In 1952 and '53 I worked on fire lookouts in the Skagit District of the Mount Baker forest, northern Washington Cascades. Crater Mountain first and then Sourdough. Those were the first jobs I'd held that I felt had some virtue. Guarding against forest fires, finally I had found Right Occupation. I congratulated myself as I stood up there above the clouds memorizing various peaks and watersheds, for finding a job that didn't contribute to the Cold War and the wasteful modern economy. The joke's on me fifty years later as I learn how much the fire suppression ideology was wrong-headed and how it has contributed to our current problems.

I fought on a few fire-lines back in the fifties too—as I was working alternately in logging camps and on lookouts or trail crews. I'd be carrying the little backpack pump full of water with its trombone-slide pump, and always toting a Duff-hoe, which in California for some reason they call a "McLeod." Nowadays I have the yellow nomex jacket and a forest firefighter helmet. I found them both at the Salvation Army. Maybe a young firefighter just ran away. I am reminded that my roots are in the Pacific Northwest when California forestry people seem never to have heard of Filson tin pants and I'm the only one wearing White's boots from Spokane.

Fire in the very high mountains is most commonly caused by lightning. A lively lightning storm passes over, lasts all night, and hundreds of strikes are visible. Flashes light up the whole sky with their distant forks and prongs. Every once in a while a strike goes to ground, and even from a distance one might see a little fire blossom and bloom where it has started a spot fire, becoming a distant light that usually soon is quenched (storms coming with rains). A dry lightning storm is what's dangerous; you might have hundreds of spot fires going at the same time. A few of those are still going at dawn, and you take a reading on them with the Osborne fire-finder. You radio in the bearing and describe the drainage. Fifty years ago, the crews hiked in with the help of a pack string. Then there were only a few smoke jumpers.

In 1954 I was working as a choker-setter on a logging crew at the Warm Springs Indian Reservation in Oregon. A light plane crashed in the nearby hills and started a fire. They drafted a bunch of us off the crew and we hiked in, along with some Forest Service boys; half of our logging crew was local Wasco and Warm Springs Indians. The fire had spread to about two acres, but the time was slow and the weather overcast and finally drizzly, so it wasn't hard to put it out. The pilot had been killed.

Fifty years later, I have three of those same backpack pumps, all in good condition, under the eaves near the toolshed door. They are filled with water and kept covered with cloth to protect them from the sun. A McLeod hangs on a bracket, and next to that in the woodshed there's a whole section full of hoes, shovels, and a few extra fire rakes. The classic wildfire fighter's tool, a pulaski, hangs in the shop. In the open porch space of the house is a line of wood pegs holding work clothes, and one peg is reserved for firefighting clothes: ragged old Wild Ass logger jeans on a hanger, with the nomex fire coat and yellow helmet, and a full canteen looped on the peg as well. Wild Ass is a fetching label, a brand name from a logger supply company. They also make light blue boxer underwear, which for a while became de rigueur among some West Coast girls studying at Brown University. In one nomex coat pocket are firefighting goggles, and in the big pocket a pair of work gloves.

There are several hundred families living in the pine-oak zone on this Sierra ridge. Higher up is national forest and heavy winter snow; lower down the blue oak, grass, and gray-pine country that once was hot and drouthy ranch land but now is either air-force base or becoming air-conditioned new development. At our higher forest elevation, most of the community seems to feel that we should be prepared to step out the door anytime to help hold the fire line until the Forestry crew trucks (men and women) come. There would be help from air tanker planes and backup bulldozers eventually, too, but if there are big fires going elsewhere in California, thousands of firefighters and all the equipment might be there instead. So then it's us and our small but dedicated volunteer fire department.

In the Yuba country's forested areas, there are plenty of firefighting protocols in place. The San Juan Ridge Volunteer Fire Department, the U.S. Forest Service, the Bureau of Land Management, the California Division of Forestry, and the local citizens with their Yuba Watershed Institute. There have been several little fires that my family and I took care of ourselves. One time a tree only a few hundred feet from the house took a lightning strike, and the lower trunk and forest floor around were quietly burning. I saw the flickering light against the window. Three A.M. we went out and doused it with our backpack pumps, and went back to bed. At dawn we checked it again and doubled the width of the fire line.

Those of us who live in the actual wildland interface know and respect the public land agencies. But in the last decade some sort of white-flight semiretired population of right-wing suburbanites has also moved in to the lower elevations, many of them expecting all their neighbors to be like-minded. This faux-conservative ideology—I say "faux" because true conservatives believe in conservation—includes a habit of nasty attacks on the county land-use planners, animosity in principle against the Forest Service (and especially *biologists*!), and a deep distrust of the California Department of Foresty (CDF) because they require "logging plans" and might want you to clear more brush around your house for fire safety reasons even though it's "PRIVATE PROPERTY!" And some of them have convinced themselves that the Volunteer Fire Department is secretly run by former hippies. All is not bliss in the rural counties.

Back to fires: when there's suspicious smoke, the spotter plane takes off and cruises over, and if it's not just somebody's transgressive brush pile, tanker bombers might go out on it right away. If it looks needed, the bulldozer trailer hauler will start moving in that direction. CDF stations are staffed with crews all summer. They have admirable fire trucks, and they'll be there pronto. Still, in a place maybe twenty-five miles or more from a fire station, if there's a fire started, you're the one to hold it in check and maybe even put it out.

I had an education that pulled together a combination of labor in the woods and on the farm, seasonal U.S. Forest Service work, and a college major in Native North American ethnology, with a good dose of art, philosophy, and world history. My readings on native California cultures, and then doing backcountry trail-crew work for the Yosemite Park, helped me eventually realize that fire was not an enemy but could be a partner. The huge Sierra Nevada range, from the timberline high country down to the oak and grass foothills, is all one big fire-adapted ecosystem, and a century of fire suppression has somewhat messed things up. I wrote the following poem in 1971:

CONTROL BURN

What the Indians
here
used to do, was,
to burn out the brush every year.
in the woods, up the gorges,
keeping the oak and the pine stands

> tall and clear
> with grasses
> and kitkitdizze under them,
> never enough fuel there
> that a fire could crown.
>
> Now, manzanita,
> (a fine bush in its right)
> crowds up under the new trees
> mixed up with logging slash
> and a fire can wipe out all.
>
> Fire is an old story.
> I would like,
> with a sense of helpful order,
> with respect for laws
> of nature,
> to help my land
> with a burn. a hot clean
> burn.
> > (manzanita seeds will only open
> > after a fire passes over
> > or once passed through a bear)
>
> And then
> it would be more
> like,
> when it belonged to the Indians
>
> Before.
> > (from *Turtle Island*, 1974)

—nowadays they would call it a "prescribed burn" instead of "control"—and it's true you can't always control it. The "Indians" in this particular "here" were the Nisenan.

The Tahoe National Forest boundary is just a few miles east of where we live. From there and over the Sierra crest clear to Nevada is a checkerboard of public land and Sierra Pacific Industry lands, section by section. A 28,000-acre fire went through there in early fall 2001. Recovery and salvage logging* arguments have been divisive, and the Washington, D.C., Agriculture brass has been putting pressure on the Forestry Service line officers to cut more timber. Late summer 2002, from July to September, the "Biscuit Fire" in southwest Oregon swept over half a million acres, largely in the drainage of the lower Rogue. It got national coverage. Next came the always-contentious plans for salvage logging. The media fell into line, and much of the public has been sweet-talked into thinking cutting merchantable trees contributes to "forest health."

Three points: First, media reporting on wildfires is usually off the mark. It rarely tells us whether the fire is in brush, grass, or forest, and if in forest, what type. TV reporting might say "ten thousand acres were destroyed," when the truth is that fire intensity is highly variable and islands of green, patches of barely scorched trees, and totally scorched stands create what foresters might well call a healthy mosaic. A good percentage of Oregon's Biscuit fire was probably a good thing.

Two, as for the intensely burned areas, the outstanding forest ecologist Jerry Franklin had this to say in his "Comments" on the "Draft Environmental Impact Statement" for the planned recovery project in the Siskiyou National Forest and Rogue River National Forest's Biscuit Fire area:

> Salvage logging of large snags and down boles does not contribute to recovery of late-successional forest habitat; in fact, the only activity more antithetical to the recovery process would be removal of surviving green trees from burned sites. Large snags and logs of decay resistant species, such as Douglas-fir and cedars, are critical as early and late successional wildlife habitat as well as for sustaining key ecological processes associated with nutrient, hydrologic, and energy cycles.
>
> . . .
>
> Effectively none of the large snags and logs of decay-resistant species can be judged as being in excess of those needed for natural recovery to late-successional forest conditions. . . .
>
> . . .

---

* "Salvage logging" refers to the extraction of trees from stands killed or scorched by wildfire (not always dead), or by dead or dying beetle-kills.

> Slow re-establishment of forest cover is common following natural stand-replacement disturbances in the Pacific Northwest... This circumstance provides valuable habitat for early-successional species, particularly animals that require snags and logs and diverse plant resources, and for many ecosystem processes. Fifty years for natural re-establishment of forest cover is not a particularly long period; many 19th and early 20th century burns are still not fully reforested.
>
> . . .
>
> In fact, naturally disturbed habitat that is undergoing slow natural reforestation—without salvage or planting—is the rarest of the forest habitat conditions in the Pacific Northwest. Yet, it is increasingly evident from research, such as at Mount St. Helens, that such large, slowly reforesting disturbed areas are important hotspots of regional biodiversity.
>
> 20.1.04

This is bold and visionary science and contains the hope that both the Forest Service and the logging industry might learn to slow down and go more at the magisterial pace of the life of a forest. The bottom line for all talk of forest sustainability is holding to an undiminished quality of soil and the maintenance of the entire diverse array of wildlife species in full interaction. In earlier times, no matter what the bug-kills, fires, or blowdowns, the ecosystems slowly and peacefully adapted and recovered. After all, until recently the entire human project itself was a lot more leisurely and measured.

The third point, then, is we shouldn't use a forest fire's aftermath as a cover for further logging. What's called salvage logging should be prudent, honest, and quick. The "quick" part is difficult to achieve though, because the Forest Service has a miserable record of not being clear and aboveboard about its motivations and practices, and the skeptical environmental critics are always planning to sue the Forest Service. Almost any recovery plan tends to end up in court.

Here in the Sierra we live with the threat of fire six months of the year—miles of forest stretching in every direction from our small clearing. Over the last thirty-five years we've taken out the brushiest manzanita for several hundred yards, and thinned out a bit of the pine, oak, and madrone canopy. But any fire with enough wind behind it to crown could still overwhelm our little place—four outbuildings, a small barn converted to a seriously useful library and gear room, and a 1,700-square-foot handmade house—and hundreds of miles beyond.

I saw, and most of my neighbors saw, that our hand-clearing work was too slow, and that prescribed burns are also too slow and chancy. Even so it was a big step to let an excavator with the "brontosaurus" thrasher head go down our ridge through the oak and pine woods, crunching all the old-growth manzanita (leaving the pine and the oak), and spitting out wood shards everywhere, leaving big tracks in the duff. This for a fuel-break to help slow down a wildfire: not just for my place, but for all the forests to the north of me, on both private and public land.

Looking back on it later and recalling travels in the Chobe forest of Botswana in the early nineties, I can see it's not unlike the way the Mopane groves look after a herd of elephants has browsed through, breaking limbs and thrashing the trees to get the leaves. Mother Nature allows for a bit of rough sex, it seems.

Our balance here with this mostly wild ecosystem is the same balance that we would hope for the whole North American West. We'd like to see the forests be a mix of mature and all-age trees cleared out or under-burned enough to be able to take the flames when they do come, and big and diverse enough to quickly recover from all but the very worst fires. This is doable—but it sickens one to see whatever clueless administration that is passing through use fear of fire to warp public policy in favor of more exploitation, more industry, and more restrictive law. It is an exact parallel of the use of "terrorism" to warp American values and circumvent our Constitution to justify aggressive foreign policy and to promote again the sick fantasy of a global American empire.

Fire can be a tool and a friend. I've always cooked on wood, outdoors and in. For several decades we had an open fire pit in the center of the house. The kitchen range was made in Saint Louis in 1910 with curvy floral Art Nouveau motifs. There's an outside kitchen area with a stone fire circle, forked sticks and cross bar, iron cook pots neatly hanging, and a wood-fired sauna bath from the Nippa company of Bruce Crossing, Michigan—last we heard, the only company still making wood-burning sauna stoves in North America. My sons and daughters learned kindling splitting, fire-laying, and feeding the stove as part of daily life.

Now that the fire pit is gone, the main heating stove is an Irish Waterford with a round stone watchtower (for Vikings) as its symbol, cast into a side panel. The other is a Danish Lange. Along one side it has a cast bas-relief of a stag with a crucifix between its antlers. The kitchen range: you start the fire going with some dry pine splits, then slip in dry oak to stabilize it and bring the heat up. If needed you can flash the heat up higher with more pine then slow it down with a chunk of green oak. Those are old kitchen cooking tips I learned orally from elders.

We use a short-handled hatchet, a graceful slender-handled Hudson Bay axe, a full length poll axe, and a double bitted axe for specific tasks. For green wood bucking there is a Swede saw, a two-man saw, a small Stihl chain saw, and the big Husqvarna chain saw. For limbing the trees high up there are two pole-mounted pruning saws. For splitting, use the double-jack with a ten-pound head and a set of wedges. Also a twelve-pound maul. One needs at least five wedges for going at it: two for working a round from the top, and at least two more for opening it on the sides when it gets sticky. I've used hydraulic splitters too, and they are fast, but there's a lot of setup time. Every year we put five or six cords of oak and pine into the woodsheds, all of it from down and dead trees, and no sign of it ever running short. New trees grow, old trees drop, spring after spring.

The firebreak is in. Sixteen acres of forest and brushland were thinned and brushed, in a long skinny swathe, with some watershed improvement and firefighting funds helping pay the bill.

But there will always be brush piles, too. Year after year in the Sierra summer we work with axe and saw taking off limbs and knocking down manzanita, ceanothus, and too-dense pine, fir, or cedar saplings. We drag the limbs and little trees and pile them in an opening. When it gets to be fall, we scythe or Duff-hoe back the weeds around them, and make a mineral-earth fire line to be ready for winter burning. (Bailey's in Laytonville sells wide rolls of tough brown paper to put over your brush piles, and this will keep them dry through the first sprinkles of fall rain so that they'll light more easily. Since it's paper, you won't be burning the quickly shredding, black 4 mil plastic.)

You have to look for proper burning weather, just as with prescribed burns. Not too dry, not too windy, not too wet, not too hot. The very best is when you've had dry weather and can now see the rain clouds definitely coming. It has been a good burn day when the big pile burns to the ground and is still hot enough to keep burning up limb ends from around the edges when you throw them back. Then comes the rain, but still it all burns to ash. No further spreading or underground simmering can take place.

One late November day, standing by a twelve-foot-high burning brush pile, well-dressed for it, gloves and goggles, face hot, sprinkles of rain starting to play on my helmet, old boots that I could risk to singe a bit on the embers. A thermos of coffee on a stump. Clouds darkening up from the west, a breeze, a Pacific storm headed this way. Let the flames finish their work—a few more limb-ends and stubs around the edge to clean up, a few more dumb thoughts and failed ideas to discard—I think—this has gone on for many lives!

> How many times
>   have I thrown you
>   back on the fire

Regarding "Smokey the Bear Sutra"

When the Wild gave the U.S. Forest Service the gift of the Sacred Cub some years back, the Agency failed to understand the depth of its responsibility. It did not seek to comprehend who this little messenger was, and instead the young bear was reduced to a mere anti-forest fire icon and manipulated in its one-sided and foolish campaign against wildfire. Now it is time for the truth to come out. "Smokey Bear" brought a rich and complex teaching of Non-Dualism that proclaimed the power and the truth of the Two Sides of Wildfire. This was the inevitable resurfacing of our ancient Benefactor as Guide and Teacher in the new millennium. The Agency never guessed that it was serving as a vehicle for the magical reemergence of the teachings and ceremonies of the Great Bear.

As one might expect, the Great Bear's true role of teaching and enlightening through the practice and examination of both the creative and destructive sides of Fire was not evident at first. As with so much else in regard to the Forest Service, it was for the ordinary people, trail crew workers and fire line firefighters, to expose the deeper truths. On fire lines and lookouts in the remote mountains, through deep conversations all night among the backcountry men and women workers, it came to be seen that the Great Bear was no other than that Auspicious Being described in Archaic Texts as having taught in the unimaginably distant past, the one referred to as "The Ancient One." This was the Buddha, who only delivered her teachings to mountain and river spirits, wild creatures, storm gods, whale ascetics, bison philosophers, and a few lost human stragglers.

It will take this sort of Teaching to quell the fires of greed and war and to guide us in how to stave off the biological holocaust that the twenty-first century may prove to be. The return of the Ancient Wild Teachings! The little Cub that restored our relationship with that Old Inspirer! What marvels!

We can start enacting these newly rediscovered truths by making fires, storms, and floods our friends rather than our enemies, and by choosing for wise restraint and humorous balance on behalf of all.

A sutra is a talk given by a Buddha-teacher. The Smokey sutra first appeared on Turtle Island, North America. Like all sutras, it is anonymous and free.

SMOKEY THE BEAR SUTRA

Once in the Jurassic, about 150 million years ago,
the Great Sun Buddha in this corner of the Infinite
Void gave a great Discourse to all the assembled elements
and energies: to the standing beings, the walking beings,
the flying beings, and the sitting beings
— even grasses, to the number of thirteen billion, each one born from a
seed, assembled there: a Discourse concerning
Enlightenment on the planet Earth.

"In some future time, there will be a continent called
America. It will have great centers of power called such as
Pyramid Lake, Walden Pond, Mt. Rainier, Big Sur,
Everglades, and so forth; and powerful nerves and channels
such as Columbia River, Mississippi River, and Grand Canyon.
The human race in that era will get into troubles all over
its head, and practically wreck everything in spite of its own
strong intelligent Buddha-nature."

"The twisting strata of the great mountains and the pulsings
of great volcanoes are my love burning deep in the earth.
My obstinate compassion is schist and basalt and
granite, to be mountains, to bring down the rain. In that
future American Era I shall enter a new form: to cure
the world of loveless knowledge that seeks with blind hunger;
and mindless rage eating food that will not fill it."

And he showed himself in his true form of

REGARDING "SMOKEY THE BEAR SUTRA"

SMOKEY THE BEAR.

A handsome smokey-colored brown bear standing on his
hind legs, showing that he is aroused and watchful.

Bearing in his right paw the Shovel that digs to the
truth beneath appearances; cuts the root of useless
  attachments,
and flings damp sand on the fires of greed and war;

His left paw in the Mudra of Comradely Display—
indicating that all creatures have the full right to live to their
  limits
and that deer, rabbits, chipmunks, snakes, dandelions,
and lizards all grow in the realm of the Dharma;

Wearing the blue work overalls symbolic of slaves and
laborers, the countless men oppressed by a civilization
that claims to save but only destroys;

Wearing the broad-brimmed hat of the West, symbolic of
the forces that guard the Wilderness, which is the Natural
State of the Dharma and the True Path of man on earth;
all true paths lead through mountains—

With a halo of smoke and flame behind, the forest fires
of the kali-yuga, fires caused by the stupidity of those
who think things can be gained and lost whereas in truth all is
contained vast and free in the Blue Sky and Green Earth
of One Mind;

Round-bellied to show his kind nature and that the great
Earth has food enough for everyone who loves her and trusts
her;

Trampling underfoot wasteful freeways and needless
suburbs; smashing the worms of capitalism and totalitarianism;

Indicating the Task: his followers, becoming free of cars,
houses, canned food, universities, and shoes, master the

Three Mysteries of their own Body, Speech, and Mind; and fearlessly chop down the rotten trees and prune out the sick limbs of this country America and then burn the leftover trash.

Wrathful but Calm, Austere but Comic, Smokey the Bear will Illuminate those who would help him; but for those who would hinder or slander him,

> HE WILL PUT THEM OUT.

Thus his great Mantra:

> Namah samanta vajranam chanda maharoshana
> Sphataya hum traka ham mam
>
> "I DEDICATE MYSELF TO THE UNIVERSAL DIAMOND
> BE THIS RAGING FURY DESTROYED."

And he will protect those who love woods and rivers, Gods and animals,
hobos and madmen, prisoners and sick people,
musicians, playful women, and hopeful children;

And if anyone is threatened by advertising, air pollution, or the police, they should chant SMOKEY THE BEAR'S WAR SPELL:

> DROWN THEIR BUTTS
> CRUSH THEIR BUTTS
> DROWN THEIR BUTTS
> CRUSH THEIR BUTTS

And SMOKEY THE BEAR will surely appear to put the enemy out with his vajra-shovel.

Now those who recite this Sutra and then try to put it in practice will accumulate merit as countless as the sands of Arizona and Nevada,

Will help save the planet Earth from total oil slick,
Will enter the age of harmony of man and nature,
Will win the tender love and caresses of men, women, and
 beasts,
Will always have ripe blackberries to eat and a sunny spot
 under a pine tree to sit at,

AND IN THE END WILL WIN HIGHEST PERFECT
ENLIGHTENMENT.

> thus have we heard.

(Yuba River redaction.)

From
TAMALPAIS WALKING
POETRY, HISTORY, AND PRINTS

Underfoot Earth Turns

1. Not the True Way / May 11, 1996

*"If a path that can be followed is not the true path,
why do Bears shit right on the trail?"* M.G.

STANDING ON the stream-smooth rocks in the bed of Redwood Creek, the water's not that deep, and I begin to blow the conch, then chant the "Heart of the Perfection of Great Wisdom Sutra" in both Zen-Japanese and Americano, plus some other old magic chants in no known language, while more conch-blowers join in. Those who know the cantos start in chanting. The group circles closer and the last shoes are tied and water bottles packed. It's mid-May, a great day for another walk on Mt. Tamalpais. It must be about seven-thirty in the morning.

Carole and my stepdaughter Robin KJ had driven in to the town of Davis the night before to join me. We ate dinner out and put up in the Ecolodge Motel with a five A.M. wakeup.

Just light, we drove the 80 west to the 37, west to the 101 down to coast highway numero uno, going over and toward the ocean past Green Gulch and back a bit up the valley to Redwood Creek and the lower Muir Woods parking lot. Now we are at the bottom of the watercycle almost at sea level in the endless play of rock and rain.

Friends turn up in cars, and three whole classes of students from Davis. David Robertson (gifted and quirky fellow-teacher) with his Nature & Culture folks, students from my "Long Poem" seminar and the class of young poets I'm teaching via "brief" poems. Also there are a few faculty colleagues who are not ashamed to be walkers. Then some friends who had once befriended me in Homestead Valley (where the eucalyptus are always rustling in the wind) arrive with sunproof hats.

We cross the creek on a rickety temporary bridge, duck through some overgrowth and head up the (famous) Dipsea trail—soon in the open—stretch our legs out along the meadows and live oak groves. It feels like I've been doing this for lifetimes now, just as it felt on Vulture Peak in the dry hills of Bihar once in the sixties.

A stiff coast breeze is blowing. We're on a part-trail, part-dirt fire road, going through meadows. East into the canyon side, out of the wind, it's deep forest. California Native Plant Society volunteers are along the road wearing green Tamalpais Conservation Club T-shirts, rooting out stems and roots. I ask them what, they say "Thoroughwort, an invasive plant from Mexico."

We cut through the woods. Around Pan Toll the State Park campground and Ranger Station is all paved. The Old Mine Trail goes on up toward Rock Springs, also partly paved. Great back views from the grassy openings look out to the City and the Bay, they always look so clean. Dip over and climb again to the flats and old campsite called Rock Springs. There used to be a cement tank here that you could dip your tin cup into for a drink. Or get it out a pipe. Your horse could slurp. But now the Rock Springs spring has been piped down to a storage tank and is all paved over, so we walk a short ways to another site that was first observed by Hopi Elder David Monongye. Matthew Davis says that feng-shui people, and even a Wicca coven, use this little ridge-site for meetings now—it is a four-hundred-foot-long barren streak of serpentine outcropping with a series of greenish four- to six-foot rocks protruding in a row from the ground, like teeth. Serpentine, from deep under the sea. Banged up against the plate and pushed up here (see John McPhee). Our big crowd chats and jokes, mills and strolls, but we all stay in sight of each other. We are on the ridge edge that runs a straight line northwest to Olema and Tomales Bay, looks west to the ocean "with wild surmise" and sends Cataract Creek north into Alpine Lake. Serpentine, the state mineral of California—blue-green, half sterile, shapely. That's the San Andreas fault valley down there west of the ridge. It was once deeply forested.

Go back to the Rock Springs meadow and follow a course that can be described as a short distance on the Simmons trail and then a right on the Benstein trail, which takes you to the Potrero Meadows fire road, and then along the upper edge of Potrero Meadows (famous once for socialists) and around to Rifle Camp. We stop for lunch—very low water in the creek.

We're leaving the redwood and Douglas fir slopes zone, with its wind-shaped trees.

From here the Northside trail climbs right out of the creek bed and goes into the realm of canyon live oak, madrone, the flat needle-spray California nutmeg, several manzanita species, and all the aromatic drouth-adapted ("xeric"—I like that word) bushes of the northern slope. Colier Spring has lost its pipe, but there's a newly developed spring called Tara farther along the trail with a strong flow. A purple flowering shrub, the chaparral pea. Streaks of serpentine, host to Sargent cypress.

The northside walk starts in earnest: contouring around to the north and northeast side of the mountain, with long views out over the Marin Water District lakes and reservoirs, meadows, chaparral, and forest. The trail is narrow and sometimes brushy going in and out of the canyons: a long hike way in, back out again—another canyon—until it finally surfaces up on Inspiration Point. Inspiration Point looks out on miles of hills and brush-land, plus Kentfield, San Anselmo, and the golf course. Then next it's a scratchy scramble up the ridge line. The final section here is on a shrubby little narrow straight-up trail which does however get you to the level path that girds the final summit of the mountain, paved and set with a few benches. How many times I wonder has all this been swept by fire.

We stop at the snack bar in the small parking lot for chilled drinks. Then to the summit, a short steep further trail. Robin KJ tries to blow the conch but too much giggling so she can't. Carole and I are getting the Americano version of the *Hannya Shingyo*, the "Heart of the Perfection of Great Wisdom Sutra," really down—and also chanting the long *dharani* as a duet now. Those folks who know them join in on the summit chants and bring out extra conches for the blowing. We've spiralled around from the valley bottom through the life-zones—meadow and oak trees, fir and redwood clumps by the humid oceanic side, and on to the slopes that face the continent with its dry heat and thunderclouds, and come to the summit. The whole view of the cities of the Bay. Magic mountain, magic cities, swept by sun and fog. Below us three vultures cruising.

Fifty-four people in this group we finally count. One wayfarer leaves, met by friends in the parking lot, to be driven over to Alameda for a barbecue. Most of us go down the Fern Ravine trail, a steep route, now that the previous rocky Hogback trail has been closed to stop the erosion. Gather at Mountain Home parking lot, and again that long delicious descent of Panoramic trail, Ocean View trail, through fir and redwood gradually ever downward to the soft duff floor of Muir Woods. We weave our way through the end-of-day tourists, Germany and Japan, on the long walkways—they may never see such trees again. You could stretch out and sleep in some of their hollows.

And one final circle of chanting again at the bed of Redwood Creek, eleven hours to do this long day's hike (the striking and very common bird song, here and around Kitkitdizze through much of the summer, di di di dididi I learn is a kind of wren-tit). I saw some strict and thoughtful old big trees this time I'd never noticed before—and some mossy twisty Douglas firs of great size; the always lovely complexly standing live oak; and a big set of blow-downs shortly after the first long meadow. Every day is a new day and a different world or as Master K'ung said, "Every day is a good day." This was a somewhat warm day, with a hazy outlook over the Bay.

As the conch echoes fade we begin to break up. Carole, Robin, and I, meeting Mark and David, eat at the Cactus Inn by Miller and Throckmorton down on the flats. Carole and her daughter go on to San Francisco to stay at her sister's (which is just across the street from Grandview Park, which has an outcropping of the same Radiolarian chert as Tam). I get a ride back to Davis and my truck, and head east toward our place on the ridge above the South Yuba River in the northern Sierra.

2. You Make the Path / October 22, 1965

Caminante no hay camino / se hace camino al andar.
Walker, there is no path, you make the path as you walk.
ANTONIO MACHADO

The first "formal" circumambulation of Mount Tamalpais was a long and pleasant one-day walk. With Allen Ginsberg and Philip Whalen, just us three, all of us in good condition then.

As I confessed later, Allen, Philip, and I basically made that ceremony, that ritual, that whole walk, up; based on some

Japanese yamabushi background, a lot of mantra-singing in India, and a long experience of the crisscross of the Tamalpais trails with their many names, testament to volunteers and the admirable fanatics of years gone by.

This walk around the mountain that takes all day.

I don't recall exactly when I became aware of walking in the world, it was certainly formalized for me with the first day of first grade. Close to a mile walk down a straight road past raggedy woods, little farms, and a sizeable truck garden run by a Japanese-American family, the Matsumotos. They plowed with a horse. Their son was just my age and we played together.

Every day with a lunch pail, stout leather shoes and corduroy pants I made the walk, cut across one of the Matsumoto fields by an established path, jumped a creek, went past an older unused wooden school building and crossed the paved road to the new school, all brick. 1936.

Going home from school I figured out an alternative route that was mostly by trail through healthy second-growth woods. It went by some pretty big stumps. The small-size tastier wild blackberries grew around them. I could walk the trail all the way to our back cow pasture, go through a narrow gate past the barn and up to the house.

What with uncles who worked in the woods or at sea, and my father's handy way with tools and cows, it seemed natural enough to get out in the forest and to begin to plan to explore the mountains soon as I could, the Cascades so clear to the east, with snow summits. Mount Rainier, always looming there. Our small dairy farm was north of Seattle, on land reclaimed from the logging era, between Puget Sound and Lake Washington, always with plenty of rain. Dogwood, salmonberries, salal, China pheasants, cowpies, loose friendly dogs, cows and goats in the fenced meadows. Woods beyond the fences.

If you look, you'll find a way. A path, a trail, an old road. I got around the hill and wooded parts on foot and on the roads by a bike. That's not about childhood, it's about discovering mobility, independence, choice, and places to hang out in the underbrush. It's about getting there on your own two legs.

So in the fall of 1965, making plans to return to Japan again after a few months' visit to the West Coast, I felt it was time to take not just another hike on Mt. Tam, the guardian peak for the Bay and for the City—as I had done so many times—but to do it with the intent of circling it, going over it, and doing it with the formality and respect I had seen mountain walks given in Asia—both in Japan and in India. The mountain herself surely didn't need this extra attention, but Allen Ginsberg, Philip Whalen, and I wanted to do it for ourselves and our place. We packed our gear and picked a day in late October to make our trip around the mountain, with food (no water bottles because in those days we always just drank country water, the springs on the hillsides. I still do, I keep forgetting not to).

That first circumambulation is part of a book on "Opening the Mountain"—a dignified and useful text—and also serves as one of the sections in my long poem "Mountains and Rivers Without End." It needn't be recounted right here. But it was the true intersection between rambles and explorations of earlier times pursuing adventure, solitude, love, birds, plants, long views, and big deep breath—and a new way to be on Mount Tamalpais for some of us. A way to see the mountain with gratitude and attention in all seasons; in a steady circuit which is never the same twice. There is no exact repetition. "Not even once," someone said, "can you step in the same river." Landscape with nuance.

Such are the teachings of ritual and ceremony. Every night the drama will have new turns and meanings. One who learns this will never be bored. I think we had come to see the mountain more clearly. No longer just a playground or a getaway, but a temple and a teacher, a helper and a friend. Nature, not in the abstract, but (like anybody) a kind of being actually there to respond to being seen in the moment. Gratitude to the particular is never in vain. Relationship to place is real, not as an idea but as a way. Why Tamalpais? Because it's there, you might say. And it blessedly balances the magic city along the tightrope of the fault line.

3. WALKING BACKWARD / APRIL, 1956

Study the mountains, using numerous worlds as your standards:
Walking backward, and backward walking; walking forward and
backward, has never stopped since the very moment before form arose.

Walking backward does not obstruct walking forward.

A mountain always practices in every place.

DŌGEN, Mountains and Waters Sutra

Once I got admitted to the graduate program in East Asian languages at UC Berkeley I searched around for tiny affordable places. I had few possessions and even less money so it was handy the first year to have a small room in the basement of a full-size apartment building. It was on Ashby. Starting that fall I worked every weekend with my father on a house he was building in Corte Madera, and spent the weekdays in Berkeley attending classes. I had no friends in Marin County that first year so my Saturday evening entertainment was exploring the eastside mountain trails and fire roads in the dusk and dark. I began to learn the mountain, with the trusty orange-covered trail map from the Freese company (finely detailed black-and-white line drawn, and the trails all named)—a map that had served I gather for years, and there is still a version in print. Even after I quit doing carpentry with my father, I made trips to Tam and beyond learning roads and routes. It was fun to drag other students and new friends along, this was a pre-ecology era and they were grateful (it turned out) for the push.

In the fall of 1955 I quit studies in East Asian languages at Berkeley. I had lined up a way to get to Japan, and arranged a berth on a twelve-passenger freighter leaving in early May of '56. I gave up my little place in Berkeley. My good friend Locke McCorkle had offered me the use of an abandoned bungalow up the back end of his property in Mill Valley's Homestead Valley, on a steep trail with no road. It took some work and a few loads of supplies and materials, but I made it livable. It had water and a wood heating stove, and the old dead eucalyptus lying around was fine firewood.

Jack Kerouac, whom I'd met earlier (that's a totally different story), was returning west and he took me up on the offer to share the place. I was putting the final miles on a 1937 Packard and so we got a bit around. Jack and I met with friends and wandered through bars in North Beach and South of Market. He was a sweet and helpful companion. But I was out mostly on foot that early 1956 spring, trying further mountain trails, the orange map and compass in hand. I should have asked more questions, like "how come all these many trails?" and "who indeed were (the old-time) Matt Davis, Benstein, Alice Eastwood, Barth, Simmons, Colier, Schmidt, Verna Dunshee, Williams, and so many others?" My collaborator and friend Tom Killion has studied this history in detail. The Olmsted Rambler's Guide map fills out a lot, defining place names and describing personalities. I camped at Barth's Retreat long before I knew that Emil Barth was a flutist, organist, and composer who arrived from Germany in 1886 and died in the 1920s.

The natural ecosystems—plant zones—life zones—mini floristic provinces—are a great and complicated mosaic, from the ocean-facing foggy and windy side to the different faces on the dryer sides, each with its own logging, ranching, and fire history. A good part of the mountain is chaparral, which has been through several hot wildfires just in historical times. The drainage of Redwood Creek with its amazingly saved redwood groves (so much was lost to sawmills . . . "Corte Madera . . . Mill Valley"). But we can imagine a bit of what was there. It all remains resilient, however, through logging, fires, and tourists. We have the modest and self-effacing William Kent to thank for Muir Woods (and John Muir for much else).

I first learned the name of Alice Eastwood from the group camp of that name established up back in Muir Woods. Then, years later, after eating various safe species of boletes for many seasons, I found what seemed an atypical huge *Boletus* with a bulbous red stalk, a reddish cap eight inches across, and the pore-mouths under the fat cap all red or orange. It turned out to be a *Boletus eastwoodiae*, listed as definitely poisonous. Some books saw a slight difference between the Satan's boletus and the Eastwood boletus, others saw them as the same species. West Coast, rare, under conifers and hardwoods. I never found another one so far, now counting thirty-four years. It was under an incense cedar in the Sierra. I was told that the type-specimen was from Muir Woods.

Alice Eastwood was the Curator of the California Academy of Sciences Department of Botany for fifty-seven years. She gathered, preserved, identified, and named a huge number of species, including the manzanita of Mt. Tamalpais. Someone else, in jest, must have named this sinister poisonous mushroom after one of the brightest, most optimistic, generous, hardy, tireless persons you'll ever know, living on as always Miss Alice Eastwood until 1953, her ninety-third year. She had a house on one ridge of the lower mountain for over a decade. It was lost in the wildfire of 1929. I think now she was the manifest spirit of the guardian mountain who appeared for a while in human form to help point us toward redemption—the redemption of all species, all systems, as one big organic family. It's kind of like a medieval Japanese Noh play (in my imagination) and I keep looking out of the corner of my eye for her ragged skirt walking off through the bright blue ceanothus or the little white bells of manzanita flowers. I am still studying the life and work of Alice Eastwood and hope that someone someday will do a biography that will do her justice.

Many others—individuals, clubs, and associations—volunteered tens of thousands of hours over the decades in a remarkably generous movement for the preservation of a public space open to whoever came. Nobody exactly owned it and few knew where any boundaries or jurisdictions were. This puts the lie to the crabbed idea that if "nobody owns it, everyone abuses it."

John Thomas Howell's research blocked out those ownerships and responsibilities, which are almost as complex as Marin County's ecology. This from the preface to the 2007 edition of *Marin Flora*:

> *In spite of large population increases and spreading subdivisions throughout the Bay Area, the open spaces described by Howell in 1949 are still here, and many more of them are now public land.... About 48.5% of the county is now public land including Federal Park land (Golden Gate National Recreation Area, Point Reyes National Seashore,* Muir Woods National Monument, *State Park lands (Angel Island, China Camp,*

Mount Tamalpais, *Olompali, Samuel P. Taylor, Tomales Bay, and Marconi Conference Center State Parks), County Open Space Preserves, County Parks, and watershed lands* (Marin Municipal and North Marin Water Districts), *plus many smaller city parks and other properties protected by conservation organizations, e.g., the Audubon Society's Tiburon Sanctuary and* Canyon Ranch at Stinson Beach, *as well as 38,000 acres preserved in agriculture by Marin Agricultural Land Trust in west Marin. All of this has been accomplished with a population growth from 15,702 in 1940 . . . to 252,195 in 2005.* [emphasis added]

I knew only a few of these details in 1956 when Jack Kerouac joined me in the Homestead Valley place. He was preparing himself to take a summer job on Desolation Lookout in the North Cascades; I was preparing to say goodbye to North America, and (having done language and culture studies on East Asia) trying to learn more about the mountains, rivers, trails, and railroads of Japan. We cooked on one of those Coleman two-burner camp stoves with white gas. Pumped it up each time. It worked quite well.

In April I took Jack out on a long overnight hike across the south flank and over the shoulder at Rock Springs, to a site in Potrero Meadows. Backpacking camping was still permitted then, not that I had asked. What I remember best is the steep, dark, shadowy descent to the ocean down the Steep Ravine trail, part of it by ladder. Once at the narrow ocean front we went in for a swim in the breakers. It doesn't matter what time of year you swim in the Pacific off northern California, the water's never warm, so you don't have to wonder when's a good time. I wrote "The North Coast" for friends and students that I have tricked into making that shocking dash.

In early May of 1956 I sailed away from San Francisco on the *Arita-maru*, leaving Mount Tamalpais and many dear people behind. I never saw Jack again.

The North Coast

Those picnics covered with sand
No money made them more gay

We crossed over hills in the night
And walked along beaches by day.

Sage in the rain, or the sand
Spattered by new-falling rain.
That ocean was too cold to swim
But we did it again and again

4. A Path with Heart / September, 1948

"All paths lead nowhere, so choose a path with heart."
                                                    Don Juan
inscribed at the top of the bulletin board at the timberline trailhead where climbers park and set out on the mountaineers route to the summit of Mt. Shasta (noted on site, 27 June 2003)

I had hitchhiked to New York City in June of 1948 in the hopes of getting seaman's papers and shipping out. I wanted to earn some money at sea and then resume my studies in college. I made a profitable trip to South America, and was then hitching back west by late August. The luck of the rides took me to Los Angeles. I let myself out at the Greyhound station at six in the morning, and caught a bus to Bakersfield. From there I hitched again.

My ride was a cream-colored convertible with the top down. The driver seemed affluent, middle aged, and claimed to work in Hollywood. As he drove we talked politics. That May the nation of Israel had finally taken form; as a student I had helped on some fundraisers. I asked him what he thought about it all. "I'm Jewish," he said, "but I dislike any and all nationalistic impulses. There should be an alternative to nationalism and the nation-state." And that wasn't the first time I'd heard that said.

In San Francisco I connected with my sweetheart—we'd been exchanging letters during the summer—and made a plan to spend the weekend out in the country. She suggested Mt. Tamalpais. I slept on the floor of her mother's apartment on Lyons Street.

We took a bus bound for Bolinas that let us off (in those days) at the Pan Toll campground. From there we walked over the upper ridges of Mt. Tamalpais with our packs and no map and bushwhacked cross-country downslope till we found water and camped. I guess we were by Alpine Lake. Next day we hiked again, found a road, and caught rides that took us eventually to Tomales Bay. Again, partly cross-country and by luck we descended to a fine sheltered beach and made camp.

The evening was surprisingly windless and warm, not the usual Point Reyes fog and wind. We waded out into the water a ways to look at the seals' heads and eyes, and the stars.

> *Seals in the light-flecked saltwater,*
> *naked, still innocent,*
> *a boy and a girl in the fault zone*
> *under the old hill*
> *holding hands, knee deep in seawater*
> *watching tiny shoots of light*
> *warm night air, Tomales Bay.*

The next day hitching back to San Francisco.

5. Backward Walking / May, 2008

1948: Over the western arm of the mountain we looked down a long gentle slope of what I took to be recovering chaparral. (A fire had passed over in 1944.) Far off, the glint of a lake. If we'd had a map we would have known there was water at Colier Spring, or good camps with water at Barth's Retreat or Laurel Dell, both nearby. Instead, we left the trail and headed downslope for the promise of water below.

We got there, made a fire, cooked, and slept. There are things to be learned, and stories to be found only when you leave the trail. Many of the earlier trails on Tamalpais are growing back in, and some have disappeared. Much of the mountain, of the world itself, can never be seen without leaving the path. Hiking on the trails, circumambulating a mountain, are "practices." Nobody should leave a perfectly good trail unless they want to, like when looking for a certain mushroom, or a hope of seeing big heaped-up woodrat nests. Our foraging ancestors worldwide only used trails to get to other places, but in between, the whole terrain, was where they looked for edible roots, fiber plants, fungi, dye plants, berries, nuts, wild pome or wild stone fruits, leafy leaves, glues, basket-weaving materials, arrow shafts, bow wood, construction poles, workable bark, medicinal barks and herbs, soap, poison, recreational plants, decorations, rock outcroppings of useful minerals, and then all the nests and dens of animals and birds which you can map into your mind and go back to when needed. And much else. All this is mostly "off the trail."

Not to mention, the spiritual discoveries (and frights) that await in the brush, the boonies, the wild, the bush, the back country, waste land, the cave, the dark, the places where "human" presence is minimal. So, the first line of the first chapter in the *Dao De Jing—The Way and Its Spirit-Power*—goes:

A way that can be followed is not the ultimate way.

(That's how I translate it: taking the second occurrence of the term *dao* in line 1 to mean not the usual "speak" but the verb "to follow," i.e., "to *way*.")

But we always need trails. And walking on trails can be plenty hard enough—a good pack on, a switchbacking path with broken rock and dust in the bed of the trail, bigger rocks to step over, step/ step/ step/ one goes—not lightly and swiftly—but slow and deliberate, watching the breath, keeping up a sustainable speed, pegging steps to breath and heartbeat, maybe humming an old tune or some chant that matches the pace, and taking it one step at a time.

> inch by inch, little snail   climb Mt Fuji
>
>   ISSA

And this is how you go to the top of any mountain, or around any mountain, or on any long road—to get to a good camp by dark, and lay this body down for a rest. But that's not exactly the destination. We don't play music to get to the end of it. Or make love to go to sleep (I hope). Or meditate and study to become enlightened. Realization or somesuch might come along, but suppose it doesn't? So what? Basho said, "The journey is home." Before venturing off trail, we need to learn to follow the path.

Back in 1948 off the trail, taking Mount Tamalpais's lessons in grateful blessed ignorance, not really looking at the landscape but totally aware of being beside my (teenage) lady, walking almost in harmony but different, talking, glancing, hoping; taking the easiest way through the chaparral like a pair of little god and goddess critters, our souls as big as the sky; did we make up that great space, or did it make us up?

May we all find the Bay Mountain that gives us a crystal moment of being and a breath of the sky, and only asks us to hold the whole world dear.

Hills of Home

I.

Today is like no day that
came before
I'll walk the roads and trails to Tamalpais.
    one clear day of fall,
    wind from the north
    that cleans the air a hundred
        miles
A little girl in a dark garage:
her home in the redwood shade,
    her father there
    he saws
  a board
(across the hill is
    nothing but sunshine,
liveoak, hardscrabble, hot little
    lizards)
      wet shade
made those huge damp trees.
At my sister's house
at the foot of the trail,
I stop
drink coffee, tell her of my walk.

II.

I know nothing
of planes: I have seen pictures
    of the bomb:
It is beautiful to watch

jets skim by Richmond
         and the prison, pass the
         mountain, out
on a shining endless ocean
lift up on clouds and gleam
         even the noise is
interesting to hear and how it
         echoes across these
         manzanita hills.

III.

Stop the sailing sailboats:
         they are still.
just west of Alcatraz,
beyond them San Francisco town
         bonewhite in blue sea bay
         two major jails
         an oil refinery
sailboats all the way.
I eat my lunch on
sharp rocks at the top.

IV.

to see your own tracks climbing
up the trail that you go down.
the ocean's edge is high
it seems to rise and hang there
halfway up the sky.

V.

sun goes down.
on the dark side of the hill
         through pecker redwood trees
         in gloom and chill
         a small red blossom
         agitates the shade.
                  the pipeline trail.
weave forward
carried on these feet
feel of the body

    & abstract recollection held in time.
    abandoned house at road's end:
            gray and real the
            glassless square holes
    black/the steps all sidewise
    and the wise inside.

    I walk back to my cabin door
    And leave this day behind.

THE GREAT CLOD

NOTES AND MEMOIRS ON NATURE
AND HISTORY IN EAST ASIA

to Burton Watson

The Great Clod burdens me with form, labors me with life, eases me in old age, and rests me in death. So if I think well of my life, for the same reason I must think well of my death.

Chuang-tzu

Summer in Hokkaido

For some years I lived in Japan, in the old capital of Kyoto. I had come to study Buddhism, but I couldn't break myself of walking in the forests and mountains and learning the names and habits of birds, animals, and plants. I also got to know a little about the farmers, the carpenters, and the fishermen; and the way they saw the mountains and rivers of their land. From them I learned there were deep feelings about the land that went below, and from before, the teachings of Buddhism. I was drawn to worship from time to time at Shinto shrines—at the foot of a mountain; by a waterfall; where two rivers come together; at the headwaters of a drainage. Doing this made me feel more at home in Japan, and for the first time I could relate to the forests of sugi and hinoki and pine almost as well as I could to the fir forest of my native Pacific Northwest. In other ways this drawing near to the gods of the earth and waters of Japan only added to my confusion. I was witnessing the accelerating modern Japanese economy, and the incredible transformation of the life of the people, and the landscape, that this brought. I had just begun to absorb the deep sense of place and reverence for the forces of nature this fine old civilization had maintained, to see it then turn and begin to devour itself. My literary peers, the avant-garde poets and artists of Tokyo, had no concern for either nature or the Buddha's teaching; but our minds met when we talked of the exploitation of the People, and sang radical folksongs. The young monks and laymen I meditated with in the temples of Kyoto were marvelous students of Buddhism and true bearers of the fine old manners of earlier Japan, but their sense of nature was restricted to tiny gardens, and they did not wish to speak about the exploitation of the masses at all. When I finally did, by good chance, meet a man I could speak with, about these things, he was neither a monk nor a marxist, but a property-less vagabond Japanese Air Force veteran of World War II who spent his life walking with the mountains and rivers and farmers and working people of Japan.

We soon realized the questions we were raising about nature, human nature, and Far Eastern civilization have ramifications on a planetary scale. Here I have limited myself to working through the Buddhist teachings, the pre-Buddhist almost universal "old ways," the information of history, and my own experience of the natural world. Working in this book, with the question, how did the old civilization of Japan end up becoming so resolutely growth and profit oriented? There will be no answer here, but there will be many angles of vision and something about civilization and ourselves. It was with this question that I found myself, one midsummer, in Sapporo, a city of over a million with wide straight streets—in Hokkaido—the northernmost island of Japan; the one place still considered somewhat wild.

The first time I had set foot in Japan was almost twenty years before, straight off the ship *Arita Maru*; two weeks churning across the Pacific watching the Laysan Albatrosses weave back and forth in its wake. There was a truckload of caged seals on the way through Customs in Kobe, snaking their small heads about. What I saw was the tightness of space: the crowded narrow-gauge commuter train, tens of thousands of tiny tile-roof houses along the track, little patches of vegetable gardens that shake every twenty minutes with the Special Express. Living then in Kyoto, I saw Hokkaido as the picture of cows and silo on a cheese box; I heard it was a sub-arctic wilderness, and my Japanese friends said "it's a lot like America," so for years I never went there. Will Petersen had been stationed as a soldier up north after the war; he loved it, he raved about the beautiful walls of snow the trains ran through, like tunnels, in the dead of winter.

But now it's summer in Hokkaido and really hot and I'm going through the swinging glass doors of the fourteen story Hokkaido circuit-government office building, into the wide lobby with elevators at several ends and sides. Across two walls, taking a right angle bend, is a mural. About eighty feet long, low relief on stone, "Hokkaido's hundred years." It starts, as such murals do, with a native person sailing a little boat through great waves; with woods and deer; and then come the early explorers. It goes on to axe men, toppling trees and stumps; then expert advisors arriving on horses (these happened to be Americans), and soon there's an agricultural experiment station, cows and sheep, a college with a clock tower, a city laid out, a brewery, a pulp mill, a railroad train, and finally—men with air hammers blasting rocks.

One hundred years: since Japan moved in with finality and authority to this island—one fifth the size of all the rest of the country—and decided to leave it no longer to hunters and fisherfolk but to "put it to work" economically.

Through the ground floor lobby, across the back street and down the block is the entrance to the Botanical Gardens, where I am to meet Dr. Misao Tatewaki, a little mustache, big open smile, ponderous walk, suspenders. A large, handsome, friendly, dignified old man. He takes me upstairs in the wood-frame office building of the gardens, a semi-occidental 19th-century house with creaky stairs and fluttering curtains, to an empty meeting-room with an oiled plank floor. At the head of the stairs on the wall is an oil portrait of a Japanese gentleman in the high collar of the Victorian era. Dr. Tatewaki stopped and made a little bow. "Dr. Miyabe, my teacher of Botany," he says, and, "Dr. Miyabe was a disciple of Asa Gray." Lineages. Dr. Tatewaki asks for tea to be sent up. I open out two folding chairs and place them side by side at one end of the large table. I tell him only a little of what I hope to do and he leans back, sighs, looks at me and says, "Japan has a sickness. It is a sightseeing sickness. That means people don't come to see or learn of nature or beauty, but for fad." And he speaks long and sorrowfully of what has already happened to the mountains and forests of the main island of Honshu, and of what little hope he sees for Hokkaido.

So then we go for a stroll in the wild-looking garden, which is in part a swampy remnant of the original plant community in the heart of the city, with towering virgin birch and elm. "Sapporo" from the Ainu, meaning "Large Plain."

Later I meet Dr. Tatewaki at his office in the dark cement corridors of the building of the Faculty of Agriculture at Hokkaido University. Books to the ceiling, books in heaps. Cases of boxes of color slides of plants. Hulten, *Arctic Flora*, Kihara's three volumes on Nepal, the U.S.F.S. *Atlas of U.S.*

Trees, an old Shanghai Commercial Press book on forestry in China . . . Russian books . . . and he shows me the famous study, *Crabs of Sagami Bay* by the Showa Emperor himself, with superb color plates. Dr. Toyama, his former student, shows slides and Dr. Tatewaki names off the bushes and plants in Latin. "Those scholars in Tokyo don't understand the actual state of Hokkaido, they think it's one with maritime Siberia and east Manchuria . . . it's right in between warm-temperate Japan and the Siberian sub-arctic . . ."

Age nineteen, he came north hoping to study the plants of Sakhalin and the Kuriles. He has been here ever since. And browsing about the bookshelves, I find a little book of poems by Dr. Tatewaki, published in the late twenties. They are *waka*, the thirty-one-syllable poetic form one size up from haiku. The collection is called *Oka*, "hill"—and there's one on the Siberian people called Gilyaks who had a settlement in Hokkaido:

> "The misery of the Gilyaks
> and the Gilyaks—not knowing their misery—
> today they laugh"

All He Sees Is Blue: Basic Far East

When the P'eng bird journeys to the southern darkness the waters are roiled for three thousand li. He beats the whirlwind and rises ninety thousand li setting off on the sixth-month gale. Wavering heat, bits of dust, living things blowing each other about—the sky looks very blue. Is that its real color, or is it because it is so far away and has no end? When the bird looks down, all he sees is blue too.

CHUANG-TZU

I GUESS Dr. Tatewaki must have run into Gilyak people in Sakhalin; or perhaps the little colony in Abashiri on Hokkaido; I never asked him. This corner of the world; this place to live. Another human habitat. Eastern Manchuria, Maritime Siberia, North China drainages of the China Sea, Sakhalin, the Kuriles out as far as the end of Kamchatka, all the Japanese islands and the Ryukyus. The whole area, if you go by the grids on maps, roughly between 25 degrees and 50 degrees of latitude, 110 degrees to 160 degrees longitude. All of it more southerly than it *feels*: Hokkaido itself, in latitude, is level with Oregon. The Ryukyus will take you through Mexico and Bombay. Straight through the globe you'd find yourself somewhere around the Rio Grand Rise and the Argentine Basin, on the bottom of the South Atlantic, east of Uruguay and Argentina.

Tenki, the Japanese word for weather, means spirit / breath / energy: of Heaven. You don't see the stars so much in this part of the world, there's a swirl of cloud mist-moisture always going. Before I went to Asia, I had heard that Japan would be like the Pacific Northwest. Northwest Pacific is not like Pacific Northwest, and the difference most obvious is summer rains, warm slow drizzles through June, sharp cooler downpours in July and August with some thunderstorms; windy typhoon-carried rains in September. Summer rains make for wet-rice agriculture, bamboo, and a different forest. It means that grasses have a harder time, with a great scramble of weeds and vines every spring, so that natural pastureland is scarce, only found in northern Japan uplands and in SE Hokkaido.

The coast of Asia and these offshore islands is the playground of ocean and continent forces that spiral and swirl—a *yin* and *yang* dance of cold and warm, wet and dry. Through the winter months the cold polar-continental air masses, "Siberian Air," centered over Lake Baikal, send dry chilly winds toward the oceans, giving the west side of the Japanese islands colder temperatures, clouds, and heavy snows. In late spring, moist air from the Okhotsk Sea brings the "plum rain" month of drizzles, with mould on the books, rust on the sewing needles, and soggy tobacco. Most of the rest of the summer "Ogasawara Air" from the Pacific streams northwest, sliding along tropical continental fronts, and culminating in whiplashes of typhoons in late August and September. Hokkaido gets less "plum rain" and fewer typhoons; much colder air in winter. Though not so far north as most of Europe, on the east side of Eurasia it has a climate like the maritime provinces of Canada, or New England.

Japan as a whole doesn't have as many thunderstorms as the American Southeast, but what it gets is strong—especially the winter storms. Only about 1 percent of all lightning bolts in the world are superbolts, which release 1 trillion watts of visible energy in 1/1000 of a second. Winter storms over Japan get considerably more than their share of globally observed superbolts. Some sort of dragons abound.

From the bottom up, too, energy and tension. The islands rise from a deep ocean—as much as seven miles from the top to bottom. (The average depth of the Pacific is two and a half miles.) The Ramapo Deep to the east is 34,448 feet. Even the Japan Sea, between Japan and the continent, is over 10,000 feet deep in spots. Five hundred volcanoes, with sixty eruptions known to history. Arcs and nodes of mountains: Hokkaido has at its center a rolling mass of mountains called Daisetsu, "Great Snowy Mountains," and this is the node of three arcs: one down from Saghalien, another arc which is the anchor point of the Kurile Islands, and a third arc which connects south with the mountains of Honshu.

Around these islands, and along the Asian coast, a system of currents is also swirling. The warm Kuroshio, Black Current (or "black tide") flowing north from near Taiwan, splits and the west part, Tsushima Current, flows on north through the Japan Sea and east through Tsugaru Strait between Honshu and Hokkaido; both branches meet the cold Oyashio, or Kurile current, moving down from the northeast, and at about latitude 38 degrees it slides below the warm current and weaves its way on south, undersea. The warm current, Kuroshio, is clear and salty, not so nutritious, indigo-blue. Tuna (maguro) and bonito (katsuo) ride with this current—the bonito loves water with 20 m transparency, not below 18 degrees C. The Japanese anchovy (*katakuchi iwashi*) and Pacific sardine (*iwashi*) are also found in the Kuroshio. The Oyashio is rich in phosphates and full of plankton, and greenish-blue. The cold current gives eastern Hokkaido and Honshu coasts their fog and cold summers. Pacific herring (*nishui*), Pacific cod (*tara*), *masu* salmon, and especially the mackerel pike, *sanma*, follow the cold current. The meeting place—interface—current rip—is off the island of Kinka-san on the NE coast of Honshu. It's a rich and famous fishing ground.

For most of Japan rain averages more than sixty inches a year. Hokkaido gets between forty and forty-five, with less in the area northeast of the Daisetsu mountains, the side facing toward the Okhotsk Sea.

Temperatures, and the amounts and patterns of rainfall, watershed by watershed, from sea-level to headwaters, make up the main terms that plants, animals, and finally humans respond to. Establish, first, the conditions of the plant communities: and everything flows from that. Temperature: the cherry comes into bloom when average daytime temperature reaches 50 degrees F. Thus blooming in Kyushu in late March, Tokyo in early April, Hokkaido in mid-May.

The realm of life is this place where air and ground, air and ocean surface meet, and down some depths more into the water. Living beings are down into the soil a yard or so, and into caves or cracks wherever water goes, and up into the sky as high as spiders ride on threads. On snowfields in the highest mountains are populations of mites that feed entirely on wind-blown pollen. A Bar-headed goose was once seen flying over the summit of Mt. Everest.

Great areas of Asia, particularly lowland China, no longer have their original/potential natural vegetation, and are missing much of their original fauna, but *what was* and *what might be* are still the basic terms of even human life in a place. Take away the farmers and the woodcutters and in a few centuries those excellently adapted beings, the life-forms of, say, the Yellow River Basin, will come back, ultimately to a climax forest. Not that in actual fact it will be exactly what it was three thousand years ago for some soils have moved away and some hills eroded bare. But given the chance, the forest will reconstitute.

The hills and valleys of the Pacific drainages of East Asia and the string of islands on the continental shelf were covered with a diverse and extensive forest. It was a direct descendant of Miocene plant communities, having undergone virtually no ice-age disturbance. Thus it had many affinities with the great hardwood forests of eastern North America (Great Smoky National Park). South China and Japan (southwest of Tokyo) were an evergreen broadleaf forest of laurels, evergreen oaks, and other trees with hard glossy leaves. The Yangtze basin, central Japan, and most of Korea were a broadleaf deciduous forest. In the Yellow River lowlands this forest became predominantly oak. The mixed hardwood forest of Northeast Manchuria, north Korea and southwest Hokkaido (maple, tulip-tree, birch, and walnut slightly dominant out of forty or so commonly found species) gave way to conifer forests in the higher elevations and to the north. The Daisetsu mountains of Hokkaido are a rainfall line, and the beginning of a boreal coniferous forest, or taiga that covers the rest of the island. A taiga flourishes where the annual average temperature is below 43 degrees.

At the peak of the Würm glaciation, about 45,000 years ago, sea level was much lower and Hokkaido was simply part of Siberia; the land bridge eastward to Alaska was a thousand miles wide. Southern Japan was connected to China, via what is now the shallow Yellow Sea. Glaciers themselves were not so vast, just a few touches in the highest mountains. Glacial traces can be seen in the Hidaka range of Hokkaido, but ice was mainly in Siberia in the mountains north of the Lena River. The land bridge to the New World was ice-free and relatively level. Taiga and steppe moved south a few hundred miles and East Asia was if anything more hospitable to paleolithic hunters than Europe at the same time. In the final glaciation, about

18,000 years ago, Hokkaido was again connected with Siberia, and southwestern Japan was separated from Korea by about twenty miles of water. Human beings moved in at this time, if not before. The oldest known site in Hokkaido is 20,000 years old; Japan about the same. We don't have more and earlier sites and human remains probably because the people and their homes along the coast and at the mouths of rivers have been buried under risen sea waters since the end of the last ice-age.

Across the plains of Northern Siberia and into the New World came circumpolar hunters; and along the gentler exposed coastal plains of glacial times, from the south, came people of seas and rivers. The Japanese islands are a meeting of maritime south and continental north, and a westernmost meeting-point of techniques and styles that are found around the whole North Pacific. From the European standpoint, Hokkaido was a forgotten corner of the world that finally Captain Cook sailed by; in planetary terms it is a pivot and crossroad of peoples as well as climates, trees, and animals. Here's where the Arctic bear meets the shorter-haired black bear of the south with the white moon bib. And the Gilyak, a paleo-Asiatic people of the Siberian Amur Coast, also called Nivkhi (a Mongoloid people who wore conical birchbark hats and provided Marxist anthropologists with what they thought was one clear case of Group Marriage).

The Gilyaks had a delicious raw-fish-with-wild-garlic-salad; sometimes trading-friends, sometimes enemies, of their neighbors the Ainu.

The whole of Japan today is a population of around 127,000,000. Hokkaido, about the size of Ireland, has 5,255,000 people, of which 25,000 are considered Ainu. Mr. Tawara of the Nature Protection Agency, over tea in his office upstairs in the Hokkaido Circuit Government Building, told me there are still about three thousand *Ursus arctos* in Hokkaido, big as grizzlies, too—not bad, when you consider that wild bears became extinct in Britain in the 12th century AD.

The Great Clod: China and Nature

> You hide your boat in the ravine and your fish net in the swamp and tell yourself that they will be safe. But in the middle of the night a strong man shoulders them and carries them off, and in your stupidity you don't know why it happened. You think you do right to hide little things in big ones, and yet they get away from you. But if you were to hide the world in the world, so that nothing could get away, this would be the final reality of the constancy of things.
>
> CHUANG-TZU

THE CASCADES of Washington, and the Olympics, are wet, rugged, densely forested mountains that are hidden in cloud and mist much of the year. As they say around Puget Sound, "If you can see Mt. Rainier it means it's going to rain. If you can't see Mt. Rainier, that means it's raining." When I was a boy of nine or ten I was taken to the Seattle Art Museum and was struck more by Chinese landscape paintings than anything I'd seen before, and maybe since. I saw first that they looked like real mountains, and mountains of an order close to my heart; second that they were different mountains of another place and true to those mountains as well; and third that they were mountains of the spirit and that these paintings pierced into another reality which both was and was not the same reality as "the mountains."

That seed lodged in my store-house-consciousness to be watered later when I first read Arthur Waley's translations of Chinese poetry and then Ezra Pound's. I thought, here is a high civilization that has managed to keep in tune with nature. The philosophical and religious writings I later read from Chinese seemed to back this up. I even thought for a time that simply because China had not been Christian, and had been spared an ideology which separated humankind from all other living beings (with the two categories of redeemable and unredeemable) that it naturally had an organic, process-oriented view of the world. Japan and China have had indeed a uniquely appropriate view of the natural world, which has registered itself in many small, beautiful ways through history. But we find that large, civilized societies inevitably have a harsh effect on the natural environment, regardless of philosophical or religious values.

OSTRICH EGGS

The late Pleistocene was a rich time for the people of Asia. Great herds of mammals on the tundra and grasslands. The reindeer-herders of present-day Soviet Siberia come down in a direct line from the later ice age when reindeer was the major food of people across Eurasia. A few Tungusic reindeer herders are probably still there in the NW Khingan mountains of Manchuria, within China's present borders.

The early post-glacial warming trend changed tundra to forest. The dry lake beds of Mongolia ("nors" to our North American "playas") were wet then, and people making many microtools lived on their marshy margins. Their quarry was largely ostrich and ostrich eggs. Parts of North China which are barren now were densely forested with oaks, beeches, elms, ash, maple, catalpa, poplar, walnut, chestnut; and pines, firs, larch, cedar, spruce species—and much more.

At Lin-hsi in Jehol, Sha-kang in Hsin-min Hsien, Liaoning, and Ang-ang-hsi in Heilungchiang, cultural deposits were found in a black earth layer, which lies beneath a yellowish sandy layer of recent formation and above the loess deposits of Pleistocene origin. This black earth layer . . . probably represents an ancient forest cover. The existence of a thick forest cover in North China and on the Manchurian plains is further indicated by cultural remains from prehistoric sites, such as the abundance of charcoal and woodworking implements (axe, adze, chisel, etc.) and by the frequency of bones of wild game. Some of these bones are definitely from forest-dwelling animals such as tigers and deer.

A little farther north, at Djailai-nor, in North China, implements of stone, bone, and antler, and willow basketwork have been found in direct association with remains of woolly rhinoceros, bison, and mammoth—an association of tools and animal remains also found in southern Manchurian sites.

At other North Chinese sites animal remains have been found that indicate it was a bit warmer in early recent times; Chang's list of species:

> Bamboo rat
> Elephant
> Rhinoceros
> Bison
> Tapir
> Water Buffalo
> Water deer
> Pere David's deer
> Menzies' deer
> Porcupine
> Squirrel
> Warmth-loving molluscs

Kwang-chih Chang thinks the woodland mesolithic of China is likely the forerunner of Neolithic agricultural settlements, and was in its time related to the Siberian paleolithic, the European mesolithic, and the woodland cultures of Japan and North America. This archaic internationalism has long been lost to China and civilized Japan, but for those who have eyes and ears it is still present in tiny spots in North America. The life of the Ainu on the island of Hokkaido was a continuation of that culture up until less than a century ago.

The mountains of Eastern Manchuria are still a refuge of the old forest. Dudley Stamp said (before World War II) that the forests of oak, ash, walnut, poplar, spruce, fir, and larch were largely untouched except near the railways. George Cressey, also writing in the thirties, says twenty to thirty thousand men were employed every winter logging the forest at the headwaters of the Manchurian Sungari River—floating the logs down to Kirin City—"and the forests are being rapidly destroyed with slight regard for the future."

"MILLET"

Civilized China has its roots in the Neolithic villages along the Huang (Yellow) River Valley, especially at the place where the Huang River takes a sharp turn north, and the Wei and Lo and Fen Rivers join it. Millennia of fishing, gathering, and hunting on the forest-river-marsh margins—and here a slow steady domestication of plants and animals; the emergence of weaving and pottery. Settlements of the Yang-shou type, which are dated as being between four and six thousand years old, present us with an already accomplished painted hand-turned pottery, round and square houses, and differentiated kiln and cemetery sections of town. Yet agrarian life is still interfaced with the wild: leopard, water deer, wild cattle, deer, rhinoceros, bamboo rat, hare, marmot and antelope bones are found in the middens, along with stone and bone points. We find net-weights of pottery or stone and bone harpoons and fish-hooks. Chang lists the characteristics of those autonomous, self-sufficient, flourishing communities:

> cultivated millet and rice; possibly kao-liang and soybean; domesticated pigs, cattle, sheep, dogs, chickens, possibly horses; tamped-earth and wattle-and-daub construction; white plastered walls; domesticated silkworms; weaving silk and hemp; pottery with cord or mat-impressed designs; pottery with three hollow legs; pottery steamers; crescent-shaped stone knives and rectangular cleaver-axe; jade and wood-carving.

These already-sophisticated, stable villages are witness to a way of life, in place, of great attention and care that antedates their archaeological dates by several thousand years. They are already by 4000 BC fine expressions of the possibilities of the Yellow River watershed bio-region; Andersson described burial sites on the Panshan Hills, twelve hundred feet above the village-sites along the T'ao River and a six-mile trip from the houses, where people had been carried and buried for countless decades, "resting places from which they could behold in a wide circle the place where they had grown up, worked, grown grey, and at last found a grave swept by the winds and bathed by sunshine."

To the east and along the coast, another pottery tradition, black and polished, took precedence about five thousand years ago—given the type-name Lung-shan. This culture pioneered and expanded both north and south from Shantung and the mouth of the Huang; and the mix of the several types that resulted is the full Chinese Neolithic. The size and specializations of some of the later sites would seem to set the stage for an urban civilization.

WRITING AND SLAVES

The first civilization is called the "Shang," basically the successful rule of one city-state over a number of other emerging city-states. It is dated from the middle of the second millennium BC. It is distinguished by bronze technology, writing, horse-and-chariot, a ruling class made up of several aristocratic warrior clans of luxurious ways, large numbers of apparent slaves as well as a very poor peasant class. These traits are all discontinuous with the Neolithic.

This is a great change in ways. How a free, untaxed, self-sustaining people can be made into a serf or slave populace, whose hard-earned surplus is taken by force to support a large class of non-producers, is perhaps the major question of history. It is, in fact, where "history" starts—not an auspicious beginning. We have some traces of how the people thought in that free time. There seems to have been bear worship, deer dances, festivals for mountains and rivers, festivals for the spirits of plants and great get-togethers for young lovers and musicians. We even have some songs surviving which may be close to the very songs they sang.

Part of the trick in corralling an energy supply beyond your own labor and skill is organization. Slavery is the fossil fuel of the second millennium; bronze the uranium. The invention of writing (analogous to the computer today) and a class of clerks provide the organizing pathways for re-channeling wealth away from its makers. In primitive society, surpluses are exchanged directly among groups or members of groups; peasants, however, are rural cultivators whose surpluses are transferred to a dominant group of rulers that uses the surpluses both to underwrite its own standard of living and to distribute the remainder to groups in society that do not farm but must be fed for their specific goods and services to turn. From that time, 1500 BC, the balance of man and nature, and the standard of living of the farming people of China, began to go down.

The rulers become persons who are alienated from direct contact with soil, growth, manure, sweat, craft—their own bodies' powers. The peasants become alienated from the very land they used to assume belonged to Mother Earth herself, and not to a Duke or King. Games of social and political intrigue absorb the aristocrats—"getting by" absorbs the farmers. The old religion of gratitude, trust, and exchange with nature is eroded. The state seeks only to maximize its stance, and it begins to seem possible to get away with excessive exploitation of nature itself, as the scene of impact is moved over the hills, into the next watershed, out of sight. Gratitude is channeled toward the Rulers in a state religion, and the Mother-oriented Neolithic religion becomes "low-class" or goes underground. The Shang rulers, in the intoxication of wealth and power, became profligate and turbulent to the point that even later Chinese history frowns.

It may be that the parallel between our own fossil fuel era is apt—energy beyond imagining—"energy slaves" available—throws a whole society off keel into excess, confusion, and addiction.

The Shang made staggering use of its human energy slaves. An estimate has been made of the work it took to build the great earthen wall around the Shang city of Cheng-chou:

The wall was roughly rectangular in shape, with a total perimeter of 7195 meters and an enclosed area of 3.2 square km. The maximum height of the surviving wall is 9.1 meters and the maximum width at the base of the wall, 36 meters. The wall was built in successive compressed layers, each of which has an average thickness of 8 to 10 centimeters. On the surface of each layer are clear depressions made by the pestles used for compressing work, and the soil making up the wall is hard and compact. Chin-huai estimates the original wall to have been 10 meters in average height, with an average width of 20 meters, which, multiplied by the total length of 7195 meters, required no less than 1,439,000 meters cubed of compressed soil or (using a ratio of 1.2) 2,878,000 meters cubed of loose soil. Experiments carried out by archaeologists show that an average worker produced 0.03 meters cubed of earth by means of a bronze pick or 0.02 meters cubed by means of a stone hoe. He concludes that to build the whole city wall of Cheng-chou, including earth digging, transporting, and compressing, required no less than eighteen years, with ten thousand workers working three hundred and thirty days a year.

Civilization came to China, it seems, fifteen hundred years later than it did to the ancient near east. But the evidence shows that a neolithic economy and style begins as early in China as in the Occident. Thus China gets less civilization and more neolithic. Rather than taking that (as most do) as puzzling on the part of China, or a sign of western superiority, I think the opposite: by somehow staving off urbanization and class structure longer, Chinese culture was able to more fully incubate itself in the great strengths of Neolithic-type culture: village self-government networks, an adequate and equal material base, a round of festivals and ceremonies, and a deep grounding in the organic processes and cycles of the natural sphere. This accounts I think for the basic health and resilience of the Chinese people through all the trials of civilization since.

The *Shih Ching*, "Classic of Songs," was gathered up from the oral tradition and put in writing around the fifth century BC. It reflects a much larger and older song-lore. Many songs are clearly from the feudal circles of the Shang and Chou societies; but some are from the fields and hills, and in that way echo the people's archaic culture with its playfulness and sanity. Here's one, a girl's song—

> Gathering fennel
> gathering fennel,
> on top of Sunny Point,
> the stories people tell don't
> believe them at all
> let it be, let it be
> it's not so at all the
> stories people tell,
> what could be gotten from them?
>
> Gathering bitterleaf
> gathering bitterleaf
> under Sunny Point,
> the stories people tell don't
> pay them any mind

let it be, let it be
it's not so at all the
stories people tell,
what could be gotten from them?

Gathering wild carrot
gathering wild carrot
east of Sunny Point,
the stories people tell don't
go along with them
let it be, let it be
it's not so at all the
stories people tell,
what could be gotten from them?

THE WAY

The Shang dynasty dissipated around the beginning of the first millennium BC and was followed by the Chou. For five hundred years the Chou maintained itself as an increasingly divided federation of smaller states and then broke up completely. That next period is called "Warring States."

Civilized China had become two widely separated cultures—a patriarchal, militaristic, pragmatic network of related rulers and ruling families (that crossed the lines of the various Warring States), and a "common people" with a folk-culture rooted in a long healthy past and a strong measure of surviving village customary government. The bronze-age rulers even had a religion of their own (saying "The Rites do not go down to the common people"), which revolved around auguries and sacrifice. Auguries because a ruling house has a stake in the longer future just like a man with money in stocks suddenly starts figuring interest rates and worries about the economic "climate." Sacrifice, a curious perversion of food-chain sacramentalism, was offered largely to the legendary memories of the successful power-seizing clan forebears, fathers of the state, whom they thought of as "Ancestors in Heaven."

The rulers and scholars of fourth century BC China were people obsessed by society and its problems. Out of the literate class of record-keeping scribes, clerks, astrologers, and teachers, individuals emerged with ideas for rectifying the social and political scene—or totally doing away with it.

Some of these people come to us in history as "sages." (Members of the oppressed class who thought similar thoughts might be called "charismatic peasant prophets" or "inflammatory female faith-healers"—or sometimes they just drew back into the mountains to be woodcutter-hermits. Later Chinese sages often aspired to be taken for woodcutter-hermits.)

Actually, one philosophical set, the Legalists, were all in favor of the State and argued only that rulers should be more draconian and purge themselves of any concern for the feelings of the common people.

Confucius and his school tried to mediate between the arrogance of the aristocrats and the people they ruled by teaching a philosophy of humanitarian government conducted by virtuous professionals. Much of Confucianism is charming and sensible, but the tilt toward the State is visible in it from the first.

Followers of Mo-tzu, a school little-known now but strong in its time, seemed allied in form if not in spirit with the common people. They wore coarse clothes, ate coarse food, and labored incessantly, with a doctrine of universal love. Their feelings about the State were ambiguous—they believed in strong defensive warfare and rule by the virtuous.

And that brings us to the most striking world-view in the whole Far East and one of the world's top two or three: Philosophical Daoism. By what standard does one dare criticize a whole society?

One can criticize a society by measuring it against a set of religiously received values—as do say, the Amish or the Jehovah's Witnesses. Or, quite common in the world today, one can subscribe to an analysis of society and history which holds that there are better alternatives of a rational, humanitarian, and utilitarian order. (A truly "scientific" critique of a society would have to draw on the information we are now gathering worldwide from anthropology, ecology, psychology, and whatnot—and that study is still in its infancy.)

The ancient mystics—artisans and thinkers now called "Daoists"—sought a base of value in the observable order of nature and its intuitable analogs in human nature. The size of Mind this gave them, and their irreverent, witty, gentle, accurate insights still crackle in the world today. The key texts are the *Dao-de Jhing*, and the texts called *Chang-tzu* and *Lieh-tzu*.

Dao is translated path, or way, the way things are, the way beyond a "way." They were social visionaries, naturalists, and mystics, living in a China still rich with wildlife and upland forest.

The Daoist social position invokes a pre-civilized, Mother-oriented world which once existed, and could exist again:

> I have heard that in ancient times the birds and beasts were many and the people few . . . people all nested in trees in order to escape danger, during the day gathering acorns and chestnuts, at sundown climbing back up to sleep in their trees. Hence they were called the people of the Nestbuilder. In ancient times the people knew nothing about wearing clothes. In summer they heaped up great piles of firewood, in winter they burned them to keep warm. Hence they were called "the people who know how to stay alive." In the age of Shen Nung, the people lay down peaceful and easy, woke up wide-eyed and blank. They knew their mothers but not their fathers, and lived side by side with the elk and the deer. They plowed for food, wove their clothing, and had no thought in their hearts of harming one another. This was Perfect Virtue at its height!

Following Marcel Granet and other scholars it seems the case that Neolithic Chinese society was indeed matrilineal and matrilocal, with a large share of religious life conducted by the *wu*, shamans—largely female.

Confucianists declined to look closely at nature. Daoists were not only good observers, but rose above human-centered utilitarianism, as in this story from Lieh-tzu:

> Mr. T'ien, of the State of Ch'i, was holding an ancestral banquet in his hall, to which a thousand guests had been invited. As he sat in their midst, many came up to him with presents of fish and game. Eyeing them approvingly, he exclaimed with unction, "How generous is Heaven to man! Heaven makes the five kinds of grain to grow, and brings forth the finny, and the feathered tribes, especially for our benefit." All Mr. T'ien's guests applauded this sentiment to the echo, except the twelve-year-old son of a Mr. Pao, who, regardless of seniority,

came forward and said, "It is not as my Lord says. The ten thousand creatures in the universe and we ourselves belong to the same category, that of living things, and in this category there is nothing noble or nothing mean. It is only by reason of size, strength, or cunning, that one particular species gains the mastery over another, or that one feeds upon another. None of them are produced in order to subserve the uses of others. Man catches and eats those that are fit for his food, but how could it be said that Heaven produced them just for him? Mosquitoes and gnats suck blood through human skin, tigers and wolves devour human flesh but we do not thereby assert that Heaven produced man for the benefit of mosquitoes and gnats, or to provide food for tigers and wolves."

In pursuing their study of nature ("nature" in Chinese is tzu-jan, self-so, self-thus, that which is self-maintaining and spontaneous) into human nature and the dark interior of phenomena, the Daoist writers stress softness, ignorance, the flow, a wise receptivity; silence. They bring forward a critical paradox; namely, thermal physical energy flows into unavailability and is lost apparently forever: entropy. Life appears to be an intricate strategy to delay and make use of this flow. But what might be called "spiritual" energy often grows in strength only when you "let go"— give up—"cast off body and mind"—become one with the process. The Lao Tzu text says,

> The Valley Spirit never dies.
> It is called the Mysterious Female.
> The gate of the Mysterious Female
> Is the beginning of Heaven and Earth.
> It's always there—
> No matter how much you draw on it—
> It will never be exhausted.
> *Dao-de Jhing*, Chapter 6

This principle is the key to understanding Daoism. Do nothing against the flow, and all things are accomplished. Daoists taught that human affairs as well as the systems and sub-systems move smoothly of their own accord; and that all order comes from within, all the parts, and that the notion of a need for a centralized ruler, Divine or Political, is a snare.

How then did mankind lose the way? The Daoists can only answer, through meddling, through doubt, through some error. And, it can't really be lost. The Ch'an (Zen) Buddhists centuries later addressed this with typical paradoxical energy: "The Perfect Way is without difficulty: strive hard!" China has been striving all these centuries.

THE HOUSE OF LIFE

Another way of seeing nature, out of the south (the old pre-Han state of Ch'u), is in a body of poems that echoes a culture open to vision and communication with the non-human realms, using a rich language of Yangtze valley vegetation. These poems—Ch'u Tz'u, "Words of Ch'u"—include the elegant "Nine Songs" of young girl—or young man—dance and spirit-calling trance. They are in Chinese official history almost by accident. Literate persons, Ch'u Yüan himself perhaps, rewrote songs heard at folk festivals and they entered the canon as political allegories. The "Mountain Goddess" is described as

> Driving tawny leopards, leading the striped lynxes;
> > A carriage of lily-magnolia with banner of
> > woven cassia;
> Her cloak of stone-orchids, her belt of asarum:
> She gathers sweet scents to give to the one she loves.

The shrines or temples or glades used for this worship were called "House of Life."

SALT AND IRON

Government monopolies on salt and iron and alcohol for revenue; huge public works projects; the draining of marshes and thousands of miles of canals built by conscript labor. Though Daoism was granted a certain prestige that rose and fell with different periods of history, the work of an expanding civilization and its dedicated, orderly administrators, was the real line of force.

Ssu-ma Ch'ien, the great historian, writes on canals, second century BC, early Han dynasty—

> ... the emperor Wu Ti ordered Hsi Po, a water engineer from Ch'i, to plot the course of the transport canal, and called up a force of twenty or thirty thousand laborers to do the digging. After three years of labor it was opened for use in hauling grain and proved to be extremely beneficial. From this time on grain transport to the capital gradually increased, while people living along the canal were able to make considerable use of the water to irrigate their fields.

Emperor Wu's regime employed Legalist Party advisors: the People were stretched close to breaking. Even Confucian critics, though heard, were ridiculed.

81 BC, a high official answered their debates—

> See them now present us with nothingness and consider it substance, with emptiness and call it plenty! In their coarse gowns and cheap sandals they walk gravely along sunk in meditation as though they had lost something. These are not men who can do great deeds and win fame. They do not even rise above the vulgar masses!

The Han dynasty had succeeded the Ch'in—3rd century BC—brutal and short-lived—which unified the Warring States. For four hundred years Han rulers maintained a centralized, imperial nation that at its farthest reach made trading contact with Rome. It broke apart, like the Chou, into competing smaller powers and states.

"Wild" in China

HSIEH'S SHOES

THE PEOPLE of mainstream China call themselves "*Han*" people, even today. The term is contrasted with any and all "ethnic" groupings—such as the people of the south known as the *Yüeh* (modern *Viet* of Vietnam), who "cut their hair short and tattooed themselves."

Even in the fourth century AD we can assume that the forests and agriculturally marginal areas of greater China were inhabited, even if thinly, by either backwoods Han people or tribal people.

The post-Han "Six Dynasties" period witnessed a flourishing back-to-nature movement from within the ruling gentry class, a "nature" that extended from the fields and gardens of the suburbs to the really deep hills. Many people who might in less turbulent times have exercised their class prerogative of administrative employment turned away toward an idea of purity and simplicity. Not all were wealthy or self-indulgent. The poet T'ao Yuan-ming (T'ao Ch'ien) (365–427) was a very minor official, whose early retirement to a small farm was his own choice. His poems are still the classic standard of a certain quietness, openness, emptiness, and also human frankness and frailty in the confusions of farm, family, and wine, that much later Chinese poetry aspires to. The Daoist idea of being nobody in the world, "behind instead of in front" gave strength to those who often must have missed the social life of their urban *literati* friends, as they sat up late reading and drinking alone in their estates or in homesteads out amongst the peasants.

Some of the Han dynasty poems picture wild mountain scenery as scary and horrible. As Burton Watson points out, a gradual shift in the mode of *seeing* nature is taking place. In the songs of the *Classic of Songs*, reflecting so much of the life of the people, plants are named specifically; the scene is the ground and brush right before one—where one dances or harvests. By the Six Dynasties, the view has moved back and become more panoramic. A case in point is the work of the poet Hsieh Ling-yün (385–433)—who has only a few rare poetic ancestors in earlier China. His aristocratic family had moved south, and he grew up in a biome that would have been considered exotic and barbarous by Confucius.

Hsieh was a mountain-lover, whose fascination with the densely-wooded steep hills of South China (peaking between 4,000 and 6,000 feet) took him on long climbs and rambles, including one month-long trail-cutting exploration. He combined in himself the would-be Daoist recluse and the vigorous wilderness adventurer. He was also an early follower of Buddhism (a new thing at that time, limited to upper-class circles) and wrote an essay expounding "instant enlightenment."

His ambivalent pursuit of success in politics ended when he was banished to a minor position in a remote south coast town; he soon resigned totally from the administration and moved to a run-down family estate in the hills southeast of present-day Hangchow. The place and life there is detailed in his long *fu* ("rhyme-prose") called "Living in the Mountains." The farther and nearer landscapes are described quarter by quarter. The fish, birds, plants, and mammals are listed. The whole is seen as an ideal place for pursuing Daoist and Buddhist meditations. Thus,

> I cast no lines for fish.
> I spread no nets for hare.
> I have no use for barbed shafts.
> Who would set out rabbit snares or fish traps?

and he says he has "awoke to the complete propriety of loving what lives." Yet, a bit further on in the poetical essay he describes his workers, ". . . felling trees; they clear the thorns and cut bamboo," and sundry bark and reed and rush gathering activities; and charcoal-making. This faint contradiction, intensified later in history, can become a major problem: individual animals' lives are carefully spared, while the habitat that actually sustains them is heedlessly destroyed.

Hsieh is a puzzle. Arrogant and overbearing at court, he made enemies. Intensely intellectual as a Buddhist, and careless of the needs or feelings of local people, he managed to get intrigued into a charge of rebellion, and was beheaded in the marketplace. Hsieh was probably already out of place in China—he should have joined the Rocky Mountain Fur Company and gone out to be a trapper. He was "wild," and as an aristocrat that took some contradictory and nasty turns. But he opened up the landscape—"mountains and waters"—to the poetic consciousness for all time, and he was a fine poet.

Mountains are always foci of spirit power in China, early perhaps as habitat for the shaman who gains "power" in the hills, a "*hsien*." Later they become a place of retreat for the Daoist practitioner of "harmonizing with the Way" and again as sites for Buddhist monasteries. Hsieh Ling-yün plunged into the watercourses and thickets, camped in the heights alone, walked all night in the moonlight. These years and energies are what lies behind what we now take to be the Chinese sense of nature as reflected in art. Hsieh is also remembered as the inventor of a unique mountaineering shoe or clog—no one is quite sure how it looked.

OXHEAD MOUNTAIN

Buddhism began and remains (at center) a set of ethical observances and meditation disciplines by means of which hardworking human beings can win through to self-realization and understanding the way of existence. This effort is instructed by the content of Shakyamuni's enlightenment experience: a realization that all things are co-arising, mutually causing and being caused, "empty" and without "self."

In the time of the historical Buddha Gautama Shakyamuni, the community or Sangha of Buddhists was an order of monks and nuns who had renounced the world. It was held that one could not really achieve enlightenment as a householder. Laypersons might build up a store of good merit by helping the Buddhist Order, and living virtuous lives, but the deeper experiences were not for them.

The expansion of the concept of Sangha, or Community, is a key theme in the history of Buddhism. In the Mahayana, or "Great Vehicle" branch, laymen and women are also considered worthy aspirants and almost equal practicers with monks, or, at the very least, theoretically capable of achieving enlightenment while living the householder's life. The inherent capacity to achieve enlightenment is called "Buddha-nature." At one stage in Buddhist thought (second century AD India roughly), it was held that not quite all human beings had the capacity. Those excluded, called *icchantikas*, were (to judge by description) tribal and aboriginal people who lived by hunting.

Some early Chinese Buddhist thinkers were troubled by this. In another century or so, other Indian Buddhist texts were brought to China that taught that salvation was accessible not only to all human beings but to all *sentient* beings, vindicating the Chinese thinkers. This was commonly understood to mean that animals and even plants are part of the Mahayana drama, working out their karma through countless existences, up to the point of being born into a human body. It was popularly assumed that a human body was a pre-requisite to Buddhist practice.

The eighth-century monk Chan-jan, of the T'ien T'ai sect, was one of the first to argue the final step. He concluded that non-sentient beings also have the Buddha-nature. "Therefore we may know that the single mind of a single particle of dust comprises the mind-nature of all sentient beings and Buddhas" and "The person who is of all-round perfection, knows from beginning to end that Truth is not dual and that no objects exist apart from Mind. Who then, is 'animate' and who 'inanimate'? Within the Assembly of the Lotus, all are present without division."

The Chinese philosophical appreciation of the natural world as the visible manifestation of the Dao made a happy match with Indian Mahayana eschatology. Chinese Buddhists could say, these beautiful rivers and mountains are Nirvana in the here and now. Buddhists located themselves on famous old numinous mountains, or opened up wilderness for new monasteries. In Ch'an (Zen) the masters were commonly known by the name of the mountain they lived and taught on. An early line of Ch'an, which died out in the eighth century, was called the "Oxhead Mountain" sect. These monks did more than just admire the scenery—they were on intimate terms with the local wildlife, including tigers. The Oxhead Master Dao Lin built a nest in a tree for his meditation. Sitting up in it, he once had a conversation with the poet Po Chü-i: "Isn't it dangerous up there?" Po asked, in his Government Official's robes. "Where you are is far more dangerous" was Dao-Lin's response. In this branch of Ch'an when monks died, their bodies were left out in the forest for the animals to consume. It's also said, they had a great sense of humor.

THE CHASE IN THE PARK

In Shang dynasty times hunting had already become an upper-class sport. The old hunters' gratitude for the food received, or concern for the spirits of the dead game, had evaporated. This hunting was actually "the chase"—an expensive group activity requiring beaters who drove the game toward the waiting aristocrats who then pursued and shot with bows from chariots or horseback. Large-scale exercises of this sort were considered good training for warfare. They were followed by feasts with musicians, and slender dancers wearing diaphanous gowns. Warfare and hunting are popularly thought to be similar in spirit, and in post-civilized times this has often been the case. In hunting and gathering cultures the delicacy of preparation, and the care surrounding the act of taking life, puts hunting on a different level.

Chinese culture is strikingly free from food taboos and the upper-class cuisine is the most adventurous in the world. Even so, from Shang times on, meat was a luxury that the common people could seldom afford. Furs and feathers of animals were vastly used in the costuming of officials. Idealized instructions can be found in the *Li Chi* or "Collected Rituals" which was put together in the Han dynasty.

> When a ruler wore the robe of white fox fur, he wore one of embroidered silk over it to display it. When the guards on the right of the ruler wore tigers' fur, those on the left wore wolves' fur. An ordinary officer did not wear the fur of the white fox. Great officers wore the fur of the blue fox, with sleeves of leopard fur, and over it a jacket of dark-colored silk to display it; with fawn's fur they used cuffs of the black wild dog, with a jacket of bluish yellow silk, to display it . . .

Han dynasty ritualism has an oddly alienated quality. The nature philosophy and the plant and mineral experimentation of the Daoists, or the direct knowledge of the natural world necessary to the life of working people, is far from the highly ordered ceremoniousness that surrounded government bureaus and the court. The Han upper class did admire those who were skilled and bold in gambling for power, but it was played against a background of strict propriety. Beheading, or being boiled alive, was the fate of those who lost in the game of power.

Taking animal lives is even easier for those accustomed to taking human lives. Respect for nature comes with knowledge and contact, but attention to the observable order of nature is rarely practiced by those who think that wealth is purely a creation of human organization, labor, or ingenuity.

Still, the Emperor continued to offer sacrifices to the Earth, to Heaven, and to the great mountains and rivers of the land, all through history. Calamitous floods, or prolonged drought, would bring the State up short, and the Emperor himself would have to ask if he had somehow offended heaven. Whatever these offenses might be, it doesn't seem that destruction of wildlife habitat or waste of animal or human lives, or deforestation, was perceived as a possible offense against the un-earthly power of *T'ien*, Sky, or Heaven. The Wealthy Governors and Emperors thus maintained large hunting parks. Edward Schafer's study of "Hunting Parks in China" (the source for all this information) suggests that they evolved from Bronze age preserves established originally to continue supplying certain wild species for the periodic state sacrifices; species whose use had been established when their numbers were far greater. By the Chou dynasty such preserves were a place for sport and recreation that might contain exotic species as well as native animals, with artificial lakes and ponds, stables, hunting lodges, and pleasure pavilions. They were an ideal place to lodge and entertain visiting heads of state. The park of the Han Emperor Wu Ti, "The Supreme Forest," was about forty by twenty miles in size and contained thirty-six detached palaces and lodges. Within its varied terrain it contained both native and exotic species of fish, birds, amphibians, and mammals. Rivers were stocked with giant softshell turtle and alligator as well as sturgeon and other fish. Caribous, sambar, rhinoceros and elephants were symbolically (and perhaps practically) located in the "south" of the preserve, and wild horses and yaks in the "north." "The ground of the Supreme Forest was prepared for the great winter hunt by the royal foresters. They burned clear a large open space and cut away brambles. Beaters, hunters and athletes readied themselves for the onslaughts of wild beasts and forest demons with spells and periapts. When the royal party arrived, the birds and beasts were driven into the cleared areas, and the slaughter began:

> A wind of feathers, a rain of blood,
> Sprinkled the countryside, covered the sky."

Parks were openly criticized by some advisors as wasteful and politically inexpedient. In Ssu-ma Hsiang-ju's *Fu* on the "Supreme Forest" the Emperor is urged to terminate the park and open it to the people for cultivation and firewood and fishing. It's interesting to note that no middle course is considered, such as keeping a wildlife preserve for its own natural, noumenal, or scientific interest. The virtuous alternative is to turn it over entirely to human use.

(No comparison could be made between Chinese hunting park wantonness and the destruction of animal, not to mention human, life that took place in the Roman Arena. Thousands of animals were destroyed sometimes in a few days. The constant supplying of animals to the Arena actually extinguished numerous species throughout the Mediterranean basin.)

Hunting parks survived into T'ang times and later, but new ideas from Buddhism or old ideas revived from Daoism stressing compassion for all creatures, enveloped them in a mist of moral doubt. T'ang was the high point of much poetry, and of Ch'an Buddhist creativity—but it must be remembered that it was not peopled by effete scholars in flowing robes who detested violence. It was a time of hardy Northern-derived gentry who were skilled horsepersons and archers and falconers, hard drinkers and fighters. Women were much freer then, and the custom of bound feet was yet to come. These aristocrats backed Buddhism, in part from a cosmopolitan interest in the cultural and trade exchanges possible with the little nations of Central Asia, but they kept their robust habits. An aristocratic maiden was once sought out by a suitor who was told by her parents she'd gone out hunting on horseback. That probably never happened again after T'ang.

EMPTY MOUNTAIN

China is wide. Travel was mostly on foot, maybe with a packhorse, sometimes also a riding horse. In the lowlands a network of canals provided channels for slow-moving passenger boats as well as the freight barges. Travellers moved by boat on the big rivers—slowly and laboriously upstream, pulled by men on shore, and swiftly and boisterously back down. Boats sailed across the lakes and slow-moving lower river reaches. Horse and ox carts moved men and materials in the alluvial plains and rolling hills. In the mountains and deserts, long caravans of pack animals moved the goods of empire.

Government officials were accustomed to travelling weeks or even months to a new appointment, with their whole family. Buddhist monks and Daoist wanderers had a tradition of freely walking for months or years on end. In times of turmoil whole populations of provinces, and contending armies, might be tangled in frenzied travel on the paths and waterways. It was said, "If a man has his heart set on great things 10,000 *li* are like his front yard." So the people of the watersheds of the Yang and Huang Rivers came to know the shape of their territory.

The officials and monks (and most poets were one or the other) were an especially mobile group of literate people. Travellers' prose or rhymed-prose descriptions of landscapes were ingenious in evoking the complexity of gorges and mountains. Regional geographies with detailed accounts of local biomes were encouraged. Hsieh Ling-yun's *fu* on his mountain place is descriptive and didactic—but his poems in the *shih* (lyric) form already manifest the quiet intensity that becomes the definitive quality of Chinese *shih* poetry in its greatest creative T'ang and Sung dynasty phases.

The Chinese and Japanese traditions carry within them the most sensitive, mind-deepening poetry of the natural world ever written by civilized people. Because these poets were men and women who dealt with budgets, taxes, penal systems, and the overthrow of governments, they had a heart-wrenching grasp of the contradictions that confront those who love the natural world and are yet tied to the civilized. This must be one reason why Chinese poetry is so widely appreciated by contemporary Occidentals.

Yet it's hard to pin down what a "Chinese nature poem" might be, and why so effective. They are not really about landscapes or scenery. Space of distant hills becomes space in life; a condition the poet-critic Lu Chi called "calm transparency." Mountains and rivers were seen to be the visible expression of cosmic principles; the cosmic principles go back into silence, non-being, emptiness; a Nothing that can produce the ten thousand things, and the ten thousand things will have that marvelous emptiness still at the center. So the poems are also "silent." Much is left unsaid, and the reverberation or mirroring—a flight of birds across the mind of the sky—leaves an afterimage to be savoured, and finally leaves no trace. The Chinese poetic tradition is also where human emotions are revealed; where an official can be vulnerable and frail. Lu Chi says poetry starts with a lament for fleeting life, and regard for the myriad growing things—taking thought of the great virtuous deeds of people past, and the necessity of making "maps" for the future. Chinese poetry steps out of narrow human-centered affairs into a big-spirited world of long time, long views, and natural processes; and comes back to a brief moment in a small house by a fence.

The strain of nostalgia for the self-contained hard-working but satisfying life of the farmer goes along somehow with delight in jumbled gorges. Nature is finally not a "wilderness" but a habitat, the best of habitats, a place where you not only practice meditation or strive for a vision, but grow vegetables, play games with the children, and drink wine with friends. In this there is a politics of a special order—the Chinese nature poet is harking back to the Neolithic village, never forgotten and constantly returned to mind by the Daoist classics—as a model for a better way of life. Sectarian Daoism and its secret societies fomented a number of armed peasant uprisings through history that unwittingly had "neolithic" on their standards. "Playing with your grandchildren"—"growing chrysanthemums"—"watching the white clouds"—are phrases from a dream of pre-feudal or post-revolutionary society.

Chinese poets of these centuries were not biologists or primitive hunters, though, and their poetics did not lead them to certain precisions. What they found were landscapes to match inner moods—and a deep sense of reverence for this obvious actual mystery of a real world. In his analysis of nature imagery in T'ang poems, Burton Watson finds more references to non-living phenomena than living, and over half of those looking upward to sky, weather, wind, clouds, and moon. Downward: rivers, waters and mountains predominate. Among living things willow and pine are the most-mentioned trees, but the specific names of herbaceous plants and flowers are few—with "flowers" usually meaning the blossoms of trees like cherry or peach. Wild goose is the most common bird, associated with being separated from a friend; and monkey the most common mammal—because of its mournful cry. Cicada and moth are the most common insect. The point is made that many natural references are used for their symbolic or customary human associations, and not for intrinsic natural qualities. No doubt the oral poetry of a pre-literate people will have more acquaintance with the actual living creatures as numinous intelligences in furry or scaly bodies. But this does not detract from what the Chinese poems are, highly disciplined and formal poems that open us to the dilemma of having "regard for the myriad growing things" while being literate monks or administrators or wives of officials in the world's first "great society." The reign of the Emperor Hsuan Tsung (712–756) is considered one of the high points of Chinese cultural history: the poets Wang Wei, Li Po, and Tu Fu were at the height of their powers during those years, and so were the brilliant and influential Ch'an Masters Shen-hui, Nan-yüeh, Ma-tsu, and Po-chang. The national population may have been as high as 60 million.

I first came onto Chinese poems in translation at nineteen, when my ideal of nature was a 45 degree ice slope on a volcano, or an absolutely virgin rain forest. They helped me to "see" fields, farms, tangles of brush, the azaleas in the back of an old brick apartment. They freed me from excessive attachment to wild mountains, with their almost subliminal way of presenting even the wildest hills as a place where people, also, live.

Empty mountains:
>   no one to be seen,
Yet—hear—
>   human sounds and echoes.
>   Returning sunlight
>   enters the dark woods;
Again shining
>   on green moss, above.

WANG WEI

Ink and Charcoal

ONE OF THE earliest descriptions of the vegetation of China is by Li Tao-yuan, fifth century AD. He travelled the whole region from Vietnam to the far deserts of Sinkiang:

> ... In the Hwang-Ho valley, he noted thickets of *Corylus* and other shrubs; pasture; plains covered with miles of *Ephedra*; forests of elms; pines; *Juniperus* growing on cliffs and on the peaks of distant mountains; and mixed hardwood forests.
>
> Farther south, in the upper Yangtze Valley, he noted bamboo thickets; *Cupressus* on rocky cliffs; and in the gorges, tall forests with numerous monkeys. In the lower Yangtze Valley he found oak forests, evergreen forests . . . in northern Viet-nam he found dense forests and immense swamps that swarmed with herds of elephants and rhinoceros.[1]

Early T'ang dynasty China (618–906 AD) with its 50 million people had a very energetic economy. The balance was already clearly shifting away from a "world of human beings winning a living from a vast wild landscape," to a condition of wild habitats shrinking before a relentlessly expanding agricultural society.

The grounds of temples became the last refuges of huge old trees; in fact the present-day reconstruction of original forest cover in north China is done to a great extent by plotting the distribution of relict stands on temple grounds. In the higher elevations and in the remoter regions some forest remains to this day, but other than temples, the grounds of the tombs of emperors and royal hunting preserves were about the only areas firmly set aside and protected. The importance of watershed protection was understood and sometimes enforced by policy; the emperor Hsüan Tsung forbade wood cutting on Mount Lim, near the capital. But the forests were slowly nibbled away,

---

[1] C.W. Wang. *The Forests of China*, Marla Moors Cabot Foundation Publications Series #5 (Cambridge: Harvard University Press, 1961) p. 19

without any national forest policy ever coming into being. The history of environment in China can be understood in terms of the frog in hot water. A frog tossed into a pan of boiling water, it is said, will jump right out. A frog placed in a pan of cold water over a slow flame will not leap out, and soon it's too late.

That tool of the poet and painter, the inkstick (even more essential to the Chinese administration), was responsible for much deforestation.

> The best source of black ink for the clerks and scholars of the nation was soot, made by burning pine. Even before T'ang times, the ancient pines of the mountains of Shantung had been reduced to carbon, and now the busy brushes of the vast T'ang bureaucracy were rapidly bringing baldness to the T'ai-hang mountains between Shansi and Hopei.[2]

The original climax forest of China south of the Huai River was an evergreen broadleaf forest. These were trees of the laurel family such as cinnamon and sassafras, plus chinquapins and liquidambars. Most of the wooded landscape to be seen in south China today is secondary growth. Pines and brush replace deciduous hardwoods after logging or fire. Writing of the lower Yangtze, C.W. Wang notes:

> The lower elevations, especially the alluvial plains, have long been under cultivation, and the natural vegetation has been altered almost beyond recognition. The existing vegetation outside of cultivated areas consists mostly of pine and hardwood mixed stands, *Pinus massoniana* and *Cunninghamia* plantations and scrubby vegetation.[3]

The great plain that reaches from the lower Yangtze River north almost to Manchuria has no original plant life left except salt-adapted plants on the coast. It was once a dense forest abundant with beeches, maples, catalpa, chestnut, walnut, elm, and ash.

Planted farm woodlots are common, however:

---

[2] Edward Schafer. "The Conservation of Nature Under the T'ang Dynasty," *Journal of the Economic and Social History of the Orient* 5. (1962) p. 300
[3] Wang, p. 103

> Contrary to general belief, the Plain, except for the large cities, is not only self-sufficient in its wood supply, but it produces poplar logs for match factories, and exports Paulownia wood to Japan.[4]

The forests of northeast Manchuria are, or were, the last large-scale virgin timberlands in China. In 1913 Arthur Sowerby wrote:

> But the forest! Time and again it riveted one's attention as its millions and millions of trees appeared, clothing the hills, ridges upon ridges, to the horizon. There was no break in the sea of green; there was no gap visible.[5]

It is thought that tigers were originally a northern animal, and that some of them moved south, ultimately as far as what is now Bali. The Siberian tiger, with its whiter stripes and longer fur, is the largest. It was considered the Master of the Wild by many Siberian tribal people. There are stories of mountain shaman types, "immortals" and priests who were on friendly terms with tigers. Shih K'o's whimsical tenth-century painting shows a Ch'an monk napping over the back of a tiger that is also asleep.

Ranging from the subarctic to the tropics, the fauna of China was varied and rich. An east-west line can be drawn following the Tsin-ling mountains and the Huai River that serves as a rough boundary between northern-Asian animals and the animals that range up from the south. The Siberian roe deer comes as far south as these mountains as do the yak, wild horse, and wapiti.

Elephants were widespread in China in early civilized times, and wandered from the south as far north as the plains of the Yellow River. Macaque monkeys are now pretty much in the south, but must have ranged north because they are still found wild in Japan in all the islands except Hokkaido. The Indian Muntjac never goes north of central Yunnan. Cats, lynxes,

[4] Wang, p. 85
[5] Wang, p. 35

wolves, martens, bears, weasels, wild pigs, antelopes, sika deer, goral, serow, goats, and many other small mammals mingle through both zones. Bird life can be broken into regions too, but there is obviously more mingling than with mammals. Ducks which winter in India or Vietnam may be summering in Siberia.

One guide to environmental practice in China was a kind of farmers' annual schedule, called the *Yüeh Ling* ("Monthly Ordinances"). In describing the timing of appropriate tasks and preparations through the cycle of the year, it takes a conservationist tone, with "warning against gathering eggs, destroying nests, and hunting young or pregnant animals."[6] It allows an autumn hunting season. The teachings of Buddhism were never accepted by the Chinese to the point that total prohibition of taking life could be made law, although Emperor Hsuan Tsung actually tried. At one time he even issued an edict banning the killing of dogs and chickens:

> Dogs, as guardians and defenders, and chickens, which watch for daybreak, have utility for mankind comparable to that of other domestic animals. We may rightly make the virtue of loving life extend everywhere, and, from now on, the slaughter and killing of these will in no case be allowed.[7]

Such an edict was unenforceable. So with the shrinking forests, animal and bird life also declined. The pressure on certain species was intensified by their real or supposed use for medicine. All parts of the tiger were considered of medical value. The horn of the rhinoceros was prized as material for a beautiful wine cup, and the powdered horn greatly valued as an antidote to poison. So the rhinoceros is no longer found in China, and illegal poaching today on rhinoceros preserves in India is for the Chinese market. Wild elephants "trampled the cultivated fields of Honan and Hupeh in the fifth Christian century"[8] and the tribal *Man* people of the south domesti-

---

[6] Schafer 1962, p. 289
[7] Schafer 1962, p. 303
[8] Edward H. Schafer. *The Vermilion Bird: T'ang Images of the South* (Berkeley: UC Press, 1967) p. 224

cated them, training them even to perform at parties for Chinese envoys. Elephants also are gone now. A more widespread animal, the Sika deer, has almost been exterminated for the trade in antlers-in-velvet, also of value as medicine. "Economic interest also prevented the protection of kingfishers, whose feathers were used in jewelry, of muskdeer, which provided a popular scent for ladies of fashion, of martens, whose furs gave style to martial hats, and of alligators, whose tough hides were used to cover drums."[9]

Dr. Edward Schafer's paper on "The Conservation of Nature under the T'ang Dynasty" sums it up:

> All of the psychological conditions necessary to produce sound policy for the protection of nature, both as an economic and esthetic resource, were present in T'ang times. But though enlightened monarchs issued edicts, conformable to the best morality of their times, these were ignored by their successors. In short, there was no permanent embodiment of these advanced ideas in constitutional forms. And so they were ultimately ineffective.[10]

Moreover, the common sense of farmers embodied in the *Yüeh Ling* (of which Schafer says, "It appears that the *Yüeh Ling* was a more important source of moral conservationism in that period than the doctrines of either the Buddhists or the Daoists"[11]) was often directly contradicted by the official class:

> Sometimes even city parks and avenues suffered because of the demand for fuel. For example, certain officials in the capital city devised a scheme to finance donatives for the imperial troops, at a time when firewood was dear and silk was cheap, by cutting down the trees which embellished the city, and exchanging the wood for textiles at great profit.[12]

The environmental good sense of the people was not unrelated to their ongoing folk religion and the power of countryside

[9] Schafer 1962, pp. 301–2
[10] Schafer 1962, p. 308
[11] Schafer 1962, p. 289
[12] Schafer 1962, p. 299

shamanesses. Just as wild habitat was being steadily cut back, the ancient local shrines of the people were being gradually demolished by Confucian officials:

> A notable example is that of Ti Jen-chieh—in our own century transformed in the sagacious Judge Dee of van Gulik's detective novels—who after an inspection tour immediately south of the Yangtze in the seventh century, was gratified to report that he had destroyed seventeen hundred unauthorized shrines in that region.[13]

And in the eleventh century, the brilliant scientist-humanist-official Shen Kua experimented with making ink out of naturally-occurring petroleum, called "stone oil," saying:

> The black color was as bright as lacquer and could not be matched by pinewood resin ink . . . I think this invention of mine will be widely adopted. The petroleum is abundant and more will be formed in the earth while supplies of pine-wood may be exhausted. Pine forests in Ch'i and Lu have already become sparse. This is now happening in the Tai Hang mountains. All the woods south of the Yangtze and west of the capital are going to disappear in time if this goes on, yet the ink-makers do not yet know the benefit of petroleum smoke.[14]

He was one thousand years ahead of his time.

---

[13] Edward H. Schafer. *The Divine Woman: Dragon Ladies and Rain Maidens in T'ang Literature* (Berkeley: UC Press, 1973) pp. 10–11
[14] Sir Joseph Needham. *Science and Civilization in China*, Vol. III (Cambridge, UK: Cambridge University Press, 1959) p. 609

Walls Within Walls

High population, deforestation, a cash economy, and tribal nomad horsemen bring a partial end to one of the peak urban cultures: Sung Dynasty China.

CITY WALLS

DWELLING WITHIN walls-within-walls was normal for the Chinese people of the plains and valleys. In the Former-Han dynasty there were an estimated 37,844 walled settlements of various sizes, with perhaps 60 million people living behind them.[1] Walls are a striking part of the Chinese landscape even today, the gently slanted stone walls of a provincial capital, broken by occasional towers that project two or three stories higher yet, rising through the mist fronting a river or lake, or mirrored in half-flooded fields.

The early Neolithic settlements of the Yang-shao type had no walls. Instead they were surrounded by ditches or moats about 15 feet wide and deep. These were probably to keep out animals; deer are notorious nibblers on orchards and vegetable gardens. Digs of Yang-shao settlements have turned up few, if any, fighting weapons. Lung-shan type settlements of the later Neolithic have tamped-earth fortifications and weapons.[2]

Around the fifth century BC, as the Eastern Chou dynasty slipped toward the era of "Warring States," the basic style of walled city began to take shape.

> The type consisted of at least three contrasting spatial units: a small enclosure which was the aristocratic and administrative centre, mixed (in early times) with dependent tradesmen and artisans; industrial and commercial quarters, with residences, in a large enclosure; farmlands immediately beyond the city walls. In the warring states period sometimes three successive

---

[1] Yi-fu Tuan. *China* (Chicago: Aldine, 1970)
[2] Kwang-chih Chang. *The Archeology of Ancient China* (New Haven: Yale University Press, 1977) p. 152

ramparts were built, suggesting a need to extend protection to increasingly large areas of commercial activity. Another change lay in the strengthening of the outer walls at the expense of the walls of the inner citadel, which were allowed to go into decay.[3]

The city of Hsia-tu, in the state of Yen, is estimated to have been ten square miles within the walls. There were also the "great walls" to keep out the northern nomad tribesmen, the walls originally built by the states of Ch'in, Yen, and Chao. When Ch'in became the first all-China empire, 221 BC, it joined together previous sections to make a more continuous barrier.

The dominant element of the Han dynasty townscape was the wall. It separated a settlement from the outlying fields, and by creating an enclosure facilitated the regimentation of life within . . . it had the character of a succession of walled-in rectangles. There was the town wall with gates on the four sides. Within the wall the settlement was partitioned into a number of wards. Ch'ang-an itself had as many as 160 wards. Streets separated the wards, which were in turn surrounded by walls. Each ward had only one gate opening to the street during Han times and contained up to one hundred households, each of which was again surrounded by a wall. The inhabitants, to get out of town, would thus have to pass through three sets of gates: that of their house, that of their ward, and that of their town. Moreover, all the gates were guarded and closed up at night.[4]

Climbing over these walls after dark is a staple in Chinese storytelling: lovers, criminals, and spies.

T'ang dynasty cities had a little more night life than those of the Han, and larger, looser markets, with special quarters for the Persian, Turkish, and Arab traders. The plan of the capital city of Ch'ang-an followed in good part the old ritual ideal— "The Polar star and the celestial meridian writ small became the royal palace and the main north-south streets through the city."[5] The north-south streets were 450 feet wide. The upper

[3] Tuan, p. 67
[4] Tuan, p. 104
[5] Tuan, p. 106

classes were in the eastern sector and the working people in the west. Each wing had its own market area. There were also vacant lots with vegetable gardens and pasture within the walls. The great city was spacious and open.

Such city planning seemed to work, but no one could have foreseen the relentless (if fluctuating) rise of population, especially after the year 1100, when the national number first exceeded 100 million. Part of the later rise reflects an increase in the size of the Chinese territory and the inclusion of people considered non-Chinese in earlier times. After 1100 there were five urban centers with over a million people each south of the Huai River.

FLYING MONEY

Between the ninth and the thirteenth centuries China became what it basically was to be into modern times. During the three centuries of the Sung dynasty not only people but wealth and high culture moved south and in towards towns. In the early twelfth century only six percent of the population was urban, but by the fourteenth an estimated 33 percent were living in or around large cities.[6]

In the second phase of the T'ang dynasty, after An Lu-shan's rebellion, the tax base was changed from per capita to a straight land tax. This meant that wealthy manors which had long been exempt began to pay taxes. It was the first of a series of shifts or tendencies with profound effects. Some of the changes were:

- from a people's corvée army to an army of mercenaries
- manor-owning country gentlemen often became absentee landlords
- cumbersome metal coin was replaced by paper money
- from a rustic naïveté to a street-wise hedonism
- from an interest in cultural diversity to a China-centered cultural chauvinism
- from regional agricultural self-sufficiency to cash-crop specialization

[6] Mark Elvin. *The Pattern of the Chinese Past* (Stanford: Stanford University Press, 1973) p. 175

- from status determined by family connections to a greater emphasis on status derived from high ranks in government examinations
- from hiking through the mountains to tending an artificially wild-looking backyard garden

The society that began to emerge we can recognize at many points as analogous to what we now consider "modern"—but more convivial and peaceful. It was the best society one could hope to see in a world of high population and dwindling resources. It was a kind of human cultural climax, from which the contemporary world may still have much to learn. The sophistication of social devices was remarkable:

> Local tax collectors developed the corollary function of wholesalers or brokers, gathering the local surplus of agricultural or manufactured goods for sale to transport merchants. The latter ranged from itinerant peddlers to large-scale, monopolistic operators. An extensive network of inns that developed to accommodate these traveling merchants became the inn system that was to continue with little change until recent times.[7]

Old and already effective farming skills were enhanced by new tools, seeds, plants, and a broad exchange of information via the exhaustive agricultural encyclopaedias and treatises now made available by mass woodblock printing. The poet and administrator Su Shih wrote a prose piece on a unique new rice-transplanting device that looked like a wooden hobbyhorse. In rice seed alone a revolution took place: a drought-resistant seed from central Vietnam came to be used widely. It could be grown on poorer soil, and so expanded available rice acreage. "By Sung times almost all of the types in use before the middle of Tang had disappeared . . . a southern Sung gazetteer for the county of Ch'ang-shu in the lower Yangtze delta lists twenty-one kinds of moderate gluten rice, eight of high gluten rice, four of low gluten rice and ten miscellaneous varieties as being cultivated there."[8] Mark Elvin says that by the thirteenth cen-

---

[7] Edwin O. Reischauer and John K. Fairbank. *East Asia: The Great Tradition* (New York: Houghton Mifflin, 1960) p. 213
[8] Elvin, p. 121

tury China had the most sophisticated agriculture in the world, with India the only possible rival.[9]

> Increased contact with the market made the Chinese peasantry into a class of adaptable, rational, profit-oriented, petty entrepreneurs. A wide range of new occupations opened up in the countryside. In the hills, timber was grown for the booming boatbuilding industry and for the construction of houses in the expanding cities. Vegetables and fruit were produced for urban consumption. All sorts of oils were pressed for cooking, lighting, waterproofing, and to go into haircreams and medicines. Sugar was refined, crystallized, used as a preservative.
>
> Fish were raised in ponds and reservoirs to the point where the rearing of newly-hatched young fish for stock became a major business.[10]

Trade and commerce weren't new to China, though. In the first century BC Ssu-ma Ch'ien wrote:

> ... from the age of Emperor Shun and the Hsia dynasty down to the present, ears and eyes have always longed for the ultimate in beautiful sounds and forms, mouths have desired to taste the best in grass-fed and grain-fed animals, bodies have delighted in ease and comfort, and hearts have swelled with pride at the glories of powers and ability. So long have these habits been allowed to permeate the lives of the people that, though one were to go from door to door preaching the subtle arguments of the Daoists, he could never succeed in changing them.[11]

Ssu-ma did short biographies of famous commoners who made fortunes by buying low and selling high, gambling on surplus and dearth. The merchant Chi-jan of the fifth century BC said, "When an article has become extremely expensive, it will surely fall in price, and when it has become extremely cheap then the price will begin to rise. Dispose of expensive goods as though they were so much filth and dirt; buy up cheap goods

---

[9] Elvin, p. 129
[10] Elvin, p. 167
[11] Ssu-ma Ch'ien, translated by Burton Watson. *Records of the Grand Historian*, Vol. II (New York: Columbia University Press, 1961) pp. 476-7

as though they were pearls and jade. Wealth and currency should be allowed to flow as freely as water!"[12]

This trade was conducted with rolls of silk, bales of rice, salt, or copper cash as the media of exchange. Cash was often scarce, and by mid-Tang it was noted that mining the copper and minting and transporting new coin cost twice as much as its face value as money. All sorts of "flying money"—promissory notes, letters of credit, and private-issue proto-money—were succeeded by government-issue paper money in the eleventh century. During the thirteenth century, and under the Mongols in the early fourteenth, the government even accepted paper money for the payment of taxes! Marco Polo was astonished to see paper used just as though it were metal. If the flow of currency began to falter, the government instantly offered silver or gold as payment for paper. "For 17 or 18 years the value of paper money did not fluctuate."[13]

THE SOUTHERN CAPITAL

In the coastal province of Chekiang, south of Shanghai, there are still some upland areas of Miao population. In the fifth century AD, when Hsieh Ling-yun walked the hills and worked on his rural estate, the greater part of the province was considered barbarian. It is named for the Che River, which reaches into the southern slopes of the Huang mountains, and the 3,000-foot hills on the Kiangsi-Anhwei border. The river is famous for the tidal bore that plays in its mouth at Hangchou bay. A decade after the fall of the Northern Sung capital K'ai-feng to the Juchen (Chin), the town of Lin-an, at the rivermouth, was declared the new capital. The emigre emperor, his court, and crowds of refugees of the northern ruling class settled in. The name was changed to Hang-chou.

In earlier times the Lin-an area had been a marsh. The main river was channelized and subsidiary streams dammed in the fifth century AD. The original town grew then on land between the lake thus formed, "West Lake," and the main Che River. It has come to be considered one of the most scenic places

[12] Ssu-ma, p. 48
[13] Elvin, p. 160

in China. Great care has been taken to keep the shallow lake clean. It was a true public park, with laws against planting water-chestnut (which would rapidly spread) or dumping trash in the water. Public pavilions, docks, and shade areas were built. Zoning restrictions designated acceptable architectural styles. Buddhist temples were looked on with favor; one of the most famous structures overlooking the lake was the pagoda at Thunder Point. Built of blue glazed brick, it was 170 feet high.

Po Chu-i had served as prefect here in the ninth century, and Su Shih did major maintenance and improvement on the lake when he was briefly prefect in the late eleventh century. The causeway on the lake is named after him.[14]

In 1136 Hang-chou had a population of around 200,000. In 1170 this had become half a million, and in 1275 it was well over a million and perhaps the largest single concentration of human beings in the world at that time.[15] It may also have been the richest. The capital fell to the Mongols in 1279, after a siege of several years. Marco Polo was in the city soon after it surrendered (he worked for Kublai Khan for 17 years) and has left eloquent description:

> On one side is a lake of fresh water, very clear. On the other is a huge river, which entering by many channels, diffused throughout the city, carries away all its filth and then flows into the lake, from which it flows out towards the Ocean. This makes the air very wholesome. And through every part of the city it is possible to travel either by land or by these streams. The streets and watercourses alike are very wide, so that carts and boats can readily pass along them to carry provisions for the inhabitants.
>
> There are ten principal marketplaces, not to speak of innumerable local ones. These are square, being a half a mile each way. In front of them lies a main thoroughfare, 40 paces wide, which runs straight from one end of the city to the other. It is crossed by many bridges . . . and every four miles, there is one of these squares. . . . And in each of these squares, three days in the week, there is a gathering of 40 to 50 thousand people,

---

[14] Jacques Gernet. *Daily Life in China on the Eve of the Mongol Invasion* (Stanford: Stanford University Press, 1962) pp. 51–52
[15] Gernet, p. 28

who come to market bringing everything that could be desired to sustain life. There is always abundance of victuals, both wild game, such as roebuck, stags, harts, hares, and rabbits, and of fowls, such as partridges, pheasants, francolins, quails, hens, capons, and as many ducks and geese as can be told. . . . Then there are the shambles, where they slaughter the bigger animals, such as calves, oxen, kid, and lambs, whose flesh is eaten by the rich and upper classes. The others, the lower orders, do not scruple to eat all sorts of unclean flesh.

All the ten squares are surrounded by high buildings, and below these are shops in which every sort of craft is practiced and every sort of luxury is on sale, including spices, gems, and pearls. In some shops nothing is sold but spiced rice wine, which is being made all the time, fresh and very cheap.[16]

Hang-chou was kept spotless. The authorities had the streets cleaned and refuse piled at key points where it was loaded into boats. The boats in turn converged and took it out to the country in convoys. Nightsoil (human waste) was collected by corporations each with their own gathering territory who sold it to the intensive truck gardens of the eastern suburbs.[17] (Contrary to common opinion in the West, the use of nightsoil does not pose a health problem if it is aged properly before applying—as it usually is. I poured and gardened with it myself as a Zen student in Japan.) Marco Polo's account of what he and the Mongols called *Kinsai* (from *Hsing-ts'ai*, "temporary residence of the emperor") describes 3,000 public baths. "I assure you they are the finest baths and the best and biggest in the world—indeed they are big enough to accommodate a hundred men or women at once."[18]

The rich, bustling life of thirteenth-century southern China set the tone for seventeenth- and eighteenth-century Osaka and Tokyo. (In reading Jacques Gernet and Marco Polo on Hang-chou, I find myself reliving moments in the Kyoto of the 1950s and '60s. A coffee shop on Kawaramachi full of chic

---

[16] Marco Polo. *The Travels*, translated by R.E. Latham (New York: Penguin, 1958) p. 187
[17] Gernet, p. 43
[18] Polo, p. 143

western-dressed youth, called "Den-en" after T'ao Ch'ien's poetry of "fields and gardens." A public bath in the Gion proud of its tradition of extra-hot bathwater, to please the ladies of the quarter and the late-night drinkers and gamblers. A small modern-style bar called Tesu—where when asked what the name meant, the modish lady who owned it said, "Why of course, from *Tess of the D'Urbervilles*.") Such cities, though crowded, are not dangerous. Our American image of a city as a faceless network of commercial canyons, bordered by suburbs where no one ever goes on foot, reflects little of the conditions of city life in pre-modern cultures. Like a huge village, Hang-chou had about 15 major festivals a year. In one of these the emperor opened up part of the palace grounds for the street entertainers to put on a street-life show for the people of the court.

Marco Polo:

> The natives of Kinsia are men of peace . . . they have no skills in handling arms and do not keep any in their houses. There is prevalent among them a dislike and distaste for strife or any sort of disagreement. They pursue their trades and handicrafts with great diligence and honesty. They love one another so devotedly that a whole district might seem, from the friendly and neighborly spirit that rules among men and women, to be a single household.
>
> If they come across some poor man by day, who is unable to work on account of illness, they have him taken to one of the hospitals, of which there are great numbers throughout the city, built by the ancient kings and lavishly endowed. And when he is cured, he is compelled to practice some trade.[19]

Life in the city went on virtually without cease; the bars and brothels closed around two A.M. and the *abattoirs* started up at three. Till late at night, illuminated pleasure boats drifted on the lake with clan or guild or fraternity parties singing and drinking and eating. Boats of all sizes and styles were available for hire.

---

[19] Polo, pp. 191–2

They are roofed over with decks on which stand men with poles which they thrust into the bottom of the lake.... The deck is painted inside with various colours and designs and so is the whole barge, and all around it are windows that can be opened or shut so that the banqueters ranged along the sides can look this way and that and feast their eyes on the diversity and beauty of the scenes through which they are passing.... On one side it skirts the city, so that the barge commands a distant view of all its grandeur and loveliness, its temples, palaces, monasteries, and gardens with their towering trees, running down to the water's edge. On the lake itself is the endless procession of barges thronged with pleasure-seekers. For the people of this city think of nothing else, once they have done the work of their craft or their trade, but to spend a part of the day with their womenfolk or with hired women in enjoying themselves whether in these barges or in riding about the city in carriages.[20]

Produce and firewood came into the city by boat, the latter some distance from the hills of the interior. At the very least 70 tons of rice a day were consumed. Shoppers at the market discriminated between "new-milled rice, husked winter rice, first quality white rice, rice with lotus-pink grains, yellow-eared rice, rice on the stalk, ordinary rice, glutinous rice"[21] and many others. There were some great places to eat:

Formerly ... the best-known specialties were the sweet soya soup at the Mixed-wares Market, pig cooked in ashes in front of Longevity-and-Compassion Palace, the fish-soup of Mother Sung outside the Cash-reserve Gate, and rice served with mutton. Later, around the years 1241–1252, there were, among other things, the boiled pork from Wei-the-Big-Knife at the Cat Bridge, and the honey fritters from Chou-number-five in front of the Five-span Pavilion.[22]

By the tenth century, woodblock printing was in common use. Literacy and learning spread, so that the earlier, simpler division of society into an illiterate mass and a literate Confucian

---

[20] Polo, p. 190
[21] Gernet, p. 86
[22] Gernet, p. 137

elite no longer applied. Merchants, wandering monks, peasant-entrepreneurs, daughters of substantial merchants—all read books. "Catalogs, encyclopedias, and treatises appeared which dealt with a wide variety of topics: monographs on curious rocks, on jades, on coins, on inks, on bamboos, on plum-trees . . . treatises on painting and calligraphy; geographical works. The first general and unofficial histories of China made their appearance."[23] The West Lake, already famous from its association with two of China's most highly regarded poets, gave its name to the "Poetry Society of the Western Lake" which counted both natives of the city and visiting literati among its members. It held picnics, banquets, and competitions, and the winning poems were circulated through the society. Hangchou was a world of soft-handed scholars, dainty-stepping maidens raised behind closed doors, hustling town dandies, urban laborers, just-arrived country girls whose looks would determine if they'd work in a back kitchen or a teahouse.

> The best rhinoceros skins are to be found
>   at Ch'ien's, as you go down from
>   the canal to the little Ch'ing-hu lake.
> The finest turbans at K'ang-number-three's
>   in the street of the Worn Cash-coin;
> The best place for used books at the bookstalls
>   under the big trees near the summer-house of the
>   Orange Tree Garden;
> Wicker cages in Ironwire Lane,
> Ivory combs at Fei's
> Folding fans at Coal Bridge.[24]

Most people rose early, finished work early, and left time in the afternoon for shopping and social calls. About three A.M. in the summer, and four in the winter, the bells of the Buddhist temples on the outskirts would begin to boom. At four or five in the morning, Buddhist and Daoist monks were walking down the lanes, beating a rhythm on the hand-held "wooden fish" and calling out the morning's weather—"a light snow just

---

[23] Gernet, pp. 229–30
[24] Gernet, p. 85

starting"—and announcing the day's events, whether preparations for a festival, a court reception, or a building-code hearing. "Imperial audiences were held at five or six o'clock in the morning. Seven o'clock was considered to be already late in the day."[25]

HATS AND BUCKLES

At the time of the Mongol conquest poor people still had some meat to eat, a little pork or fish. In recent centuries meat has been a once- or twice-a-year treat. The wealthy could also afford wild game. There were no sanctions, apparently, against market hunting, though shoppers were warned to beware of donkey or horsemeat being sold as venison.[26] The deforestation that had been predicted by Shen Kua two centuries earlier (he was almost exactly contemporary with Su Shih) was well underway. Sung economic expansion stimulated remarkable industrial development—"comparable to that which took place during the earlier phases of England's industrial revolution." The quantity of iron produced during the Northern Sung period was not matched again until the nineteenth century. Tuan Yi-fu summarizes:

> The rapid growth of ironworks exerted pressure on timber resources, which were already heavily pressed to meet the needs of large city populations and of shipbuilding. Many hundreds of thousands of tons of charcoal were swallowed up by the metal industries. In addition, there was the demand for charcoal in the manufacture of salt, alum, bricks, tiles and liquor. The Northern Sung period must be seen as a time of rapid deforestation. North China suffered first. . . . Firewood and charcoal for the cities and the industries had to be transported from the South. There was an acute shortage which was partially met by the effective substitution of coal for charcoal in the eleventh century.[27]

Wetlands were drained. It seems the expansion of ricefields into "wastelands" or marshes often went against the interests and

[25] Gernet, p. 182
[26] Gernet, p. 137
[27] Tuan, pp. 130–1

desires of the local people, who relied on ponds and estuaries for fishing and gathering edible water plants. Large landowners or the government itself undertook these projects, looking for profits or taxes. (The chain of events that led to the execution of Hsieh Ling-yun started with his plan to drain the Hui-chung lake, near the modern town of Shao-hsing. This lake was on public land, but a landowner of Hsieh's stature could usually have expected to get away with it. The governor of the province, however, was an old rival, and his enmity combined with the reports of clashes between local peasants and Hsieh's armed retainers opened the way to a charge of rebellion.) In the late Sung the government encouraged small farmers, by granting tax exemptions, to go into marshy grounds on the Yangtze delta. The loss was not only wild food previously gathered by the poor, but habitat for water-fowl and other members of the marshy ecosystems.

Along with wetlands and forests, the people as a whole were losing accurate knowledge of nature. For the last few centuries it has been believed in China that tortoises were female to the male of snakes; a bronze statuette shows a tortoise and snake copulating. The correct information of sunburned naked boys or old fishermen who knew better became no account. The harmless gecko (wall lizard) and the toad came to be considered poisonous. The big-shouldered wild boar, *Sus scrofa*, which appears in Han hunting scenes, and is still the type of pig in T'ang art, is replaced in the art of later dynasties by the sway-backed droop-eared domestic pig type.[28]

From Shang to Ch'in times animals and insects appear in Chinese art in the conventionalized forms sometimes associated with the "Scythian" art of ancient central Asia. None of the designs are floral, and those which seem so are actually loops and spirals of insects and reptiles.[29] Realistic animals appear from the Han dynasty onward—deer being chased by hounds, a tiger with a collar. Later representation of animals tends more and more to cleave to symbolic and legendary significance. "Everything in their painting, carved panels, lacquered

---

[28] Arthur de Carle Sowerby. *Nature in Chinese Art* (New York: John Day, 1940) pp. 65, 99
[29] Sowerby, p. 129

screens, pieces of tapestry or embroidery, stone bas-reliefs, or the decorations on furniture and buildings means something. It is this fact that helps to explain why certain animals appear with great frequency, while others equally well known occur but seldom, or are altogether absent."[30]

Thus leopards were far more common in China than tigers, yet are rarely seen in art. Other animals that seldom appear are the hedgehog, shrews and moles, the common muskshrew of the southeast, the scaly anteater, the civets, and many rodents including the porcupine. Insects are often represented in many media. In Han times carved jade cicada were placed in the mouth of the dead. Entirely lifelike hairy-clawed crabs were constructed in bronze. In Sowerby's study on "nature in Chinese art" we find included a glass snuff bottle with a butterfly in low relief on black glass; an unidentified fish in jade; a marble seal with a toad carved on the top; realistic scroll paintings of carp, minnows, knife-fish, mandarin fish, catfish, and bitterlings; a split bamboo with a wasp inside all carved in ivory; an unglazed statue of a Bactrian camel; a lifelike elephant with a harness from the Six Dynasties period; and a bronze buckle inlaid in silver, in the form of a rhinoceros.

The poor rhinoceros. A hat of some sort, and a girdle or belt with a buckle, were essential to male dress. Gernet says:

> These were the two things which distinguished the Chinese from the barbarian . . . the finest girdles had plaques or buckles in jade, in gold, or in rhinoceros horn. The horn was imported from India, and in particular Bengal, which was supposed to have the best horn. . . . "The Chinese," says an Arab account of the ninth century, "makes from this horn girdles which fetch a price of two or three thousand dinars or more. . . ." The astonishing prices fetched by these horns and the intense delight taken by Chinese in ornaments made from them can hardly be explained by their rarity value alone: superstition as well as artistic taste must lie at the root of this passion. And indeed we find that "sometimes the horn is in the image of a man, or a peacock, or a fish or some other thing."[31]

---

[30] Sowerby, p. 44
[31] Gernet, pp. 131–2

DISTANT HILLS

For those men who passed the civil service examinations and accepted official posts, travel from place to place became a way of life. They were commonly transferred every three years. Su Shih was born in Szechwan near the foot of Mount Omei in 1037. Like many who rose to political and literary eminence in the Sung, he came from relatively humble people, "connected with the local weaving industry." His grandfather had been illiterate. He and his younger brother were locally tutored by a Daoist priest. Together with their father they travelled the thousand-mile journey down the Yangtze and north to the capital of Kai-feng, where both boys passed the examinations the first try, a striking feat. In his early poem "On the Yangtze Watching the Hills"—travelling by boat with his father and brother through the San-hsia Gorge—Su Shih opens some of that space for us:

> From the boat watching hills—swift horses:
> a hundred herds race by in a flash.
> Ragged peaks before us suddenly change shape,
> Ranges behind us start and rush away.
> I look up: a narrow trail angles back and forth,
> A man walking it, high in the distance.
> I wave from the deck, trying to call,
> But the sail takes us south like a soaring bird.[32]

All three were given employment. In 1066 the father died and the two sons returned to bury him in Szechwan. It was the last time Su Shih saw his native village. He was 29.

This mobility contributes to the impression we get from Su and his cohorts that they no longer cared about particular landscapes. Indeed, for many of them there was no place in China they called home enough to know the smells and the wild plants, but during their interminable journeys on river boats and canal barges the scenery slowly unrolled for them like a great scroll. At the same time there was a cheerful recognition

---

[32] Su Tung-P'o. *Selections from a Sung Dynasty Poet*, translated by Burton Watson (New York: Columbia University Press, 1965) p. 23

and acceptance of the fact that "we live in society." The clear, dry funny poems of daily life with family and neighbors that came of this are marvelous. Daoist ideas of living in mountain isolation, or breaking conventions, came to be seen as romantic and irresponsible. Yoshikawa comments on the optimism of Sung poetry, and suggests that it echoes the optimism of the ancient *Book of Songs* (*Shih Ching*), with its care for daily tasks and the busy space within the farmyard. The dominant emotion expressed in T'ang dynasty writing is sorrow and grief: humankind is all too impermanent, only mountains and rivers will remain.[33] Sung poets like Mei Yao-ch'en might write in rough plain language, or a low-key style, of things the elegantly intense T'ang poets would never touch. Such is Yang Wan-li's poem on a fly:

> Noted outside the window: a fly, the sun on his back,
> rubbing his legs together, relishing the
>   morning brightness.
> Sun and shadow about to shift—already he
>   knows it,
> Suddenly flies off, to hum by a
>   different window.[34]

Su Shih, lying on his back in a boat, takes detachment a step further:

> I greet the breeze that happens along
> And lift a cup to offer to the vastness:
> How pleasant—that we have no thought of each
>   other![35]

Kojiro Yoshikawa's quick analysis of nature images in Sung poetry notes that "sunset" is a common reference in the T'ang

---

[33] Kojiro Yoshikawa. *An Introduction to Sung Poetry*, translated by Burton Watson (Cambridge, MA: Harvard University Press, 1967) p. 25
[34] Burton Watson. *Chinese Lyricism* (New York: Columbia University Press, 1971) p. 202
[35] Yoshikawa, p. 23

with a strong overtone of sadness. Su Shih, writing on a sunset
seen from a Buddhist temple, is able to freshly say

> Faint wind: on the broad water,
>   wrinkles like creases in a shoe;
> Broken clouds: over half the sky,
>   a red the color of fish tails.[36]

Rain, Yoshikawa observes, is a frequent Sung reference
—rain to listen to at night while talking with a bedmate, rain
to burn incense and study by.

> Shall I tell you the way to become a god
>   in this humdrum world?
> Burn some incense and sit listening to the rain.
>   LU YU[37]

In a society of such mobility, complexity, and size, it is to be
expected that a "sense of place" would be hard to maintain.
Humanistic concerns can be cultivated anywhere, but certain
kinds of understanding and information about the natural
world are only available to those who stay put and keep look‑
ing. There is another kind of "staying put" which flourished in
some circles during the Sung, namely the meditation practice
of Ch'an Buddhism, *zazen*. What some Sung poets and think‑
ers may have lost in terms of sense of natural place was balanced
perhaps by a better understanding of natural self. A different
sort of grounding occurred.

Much of the distinctive quality of Sung poetry can be
attributed to the influence of the relentless and original Su
Shih. Su was also an advanced Ch'an practicer, which is evi‑
dent in his resolute, penetrating, sensitive body of work. The
Ch'an influence is not at its best in the poems about monks
or temples; we find it in plainer places. But when Su says of
the sky, "How pleasant—that we have no thought of each
other" it is not to be taken as an expression of the heartless‑
ness or remoteness of nature. Within the mutual mindlessness:

[36] Yoshikawa, p. 47
[37] Yoshikawa, p. 48

of sky and self the Ch'an practicer enacts the vivid energy and form of each blade of grass, each pebble. The obsession that T'ang poets had with impermanence was a sentimental response to the commonly perceived stress of Mahayana Buddhism on transiency and evanescence. Ch'an teachers never bothered with self-pity, and brought a playful and courageous style of give-and-take to the study of impermanent phenomena. I suspect that Sung poets were more dyed with the true spirit of Ch'an than those of the T'ang. From the standpoint of the natural environment, the T'ang view can almost be reversed—it seems the mountains and rivers, or at least their forests and creatures, soils and beds, are more fragile than we thought. Human beings grimly endure.

THE BORE

The rulers and courtiers of Hang-chou never fully grasped the seriousness of the Mongol threat. Dallying in the parks, challenging each other's connoisseurship, they carried aestheticism to impressive levels. Mongka Khan, who ravaged Tibet, and his brother Khubla left Southern Sung on the back burner for a decade or so while they consolidated their northern and western borders.

In Hang-chou every September the people of the city thronged out to the banks of the Che River to witness a spectacle belonging to a scale even larger—their own unwitting point of contact with the dragons of the whole planetary water cycle. This was the annual high-point of the tidal bore which came in from the bay, up the river, and right by the town. Viewing platforms were erected for the emperor and his family. One year when the huge wall of water came rushing up, a surprise wind rose behind it, and the eagre went over the barriers and drowned hundreds of people.[38]

MOUNT BURKHAN KHALDUN

Sung dynasty China was a high-water mark of civilization. Joseph Needham and Mark Elvin take thirteenth-century

[38] Gernet, p. 195

China to have been on the verge of a western-style technological revolution; at least many of the preconditions were there. (Yet it would be foolish to assume that such an evolution is necessarily desirable.) The Mongol conquest was a blow to the culture, but without it, China would probably have gone through a similar process—a stabilization, fading of innovation and experiment, and a long slow retreat of both economy and creativity. Having granted this decline, it must be pointed out that no Occidental culture can approach the time-scale of stability and relative prosperity this decline encompassed. Reischauer's comment that "there are few historic parallels except among primitive peoples"[39] strikes far.

Lively though it was, the Sung had severe problems. Half the people of the Northern Sung were tenant farmers paying half their farm income as rent to the landlords. Declining natural resources and growing population ended experimental ventures into labor-saving devices: materials grew expensive as labor became cheap. Smaller farms, over-worked soil, and more people brought tax revenue and personal income down. The frontier territories of the south and southwest were saturated. In spite of all the (almost self-congratulatory) social concern of the Neo-Confucian philosophers, no analysis went deep enough. Millions of people who worked in the salt marshes of the Huai River valleys were virtual slaves.

Far north of the sinicized Juchen and their captured realm, across the Ordos and the Gobi, lived the Mongol tribes. Some Mongol groups associated Mount Burkhan Khaldun, near the head of the Onon River (a tributary of the Amur) and south-southeast of Lake Baikal, with their legendary ancestors the Blue Wolf and his wife the Fallow Deer. About 1185 an 18-year-old youth named Temujin fled for his life to the slopes of this mountain, pursued by rival Mongol horsemen of the Merkit tribe. For days they pursued him through the willow thickets and swamps of the densely forested upland. They could follow his horse's tracks but they could not catch up with him. Eventually the Merkit contented themselves with taking some women from the camps below, and left. *The Secret History of the Mongols* has Temujin saying, as he descends the mountain,

---

[39] Reischauer and Fairbank, p. 241

> "Though it seemed I'd be crushed like a louse,
> I escaped to Mount Burkhan Khaldun.
> The mountain has saved my life and my horse.
> Leading my horse down the elk-paths,
> making my tent from the willow branches,
> I went up Mount Burkhan.
> Though I was frightened and ran like an insect,
> I was shielded by Mount Burkhan Khaldun.
> Every morning I'll offer a sacrifice to Mount Burkhan.
> Every day I'll pray to the mountain. . . .
> Then striking his breast with his hand,
> he knelt nine times to the sun
> sprinkling offerings of mare's milk in the air,
> and he prayed."[40]

This survivor, who had lived for years with his abandoned mother and brothers by trapping ground squirrels and marmots, snaring ducks, and fishing, went on to be chosen the supreme leader of all the Turko-Mongol tribes. At the gathering or *quriltai* of 1206 he was given the title "Jenghiz Khan." After that, he began his first campaign in northern China, attacking the cities of the Tungusic Chin. Many campaigns and victories later the Buddhist monk Li Chih-ch'ang visited him at his headquarters in Karakorum. Jenghiz Khan is reported as saying,

> Heaven is weary of the inordinate luxury of China. I remain in the wild region of the north, I return to simplicity and seek moderation once more. As for the garments that I wear and the meals that I eat, I have the same rags and the same food as cowherds and grooms, and I treat the soldiers as my brothers.[41]

Jenghiz Khan did not exactly live a simple life, but he was determined and very tough. He was also a brilliant military strategist. Many grassland nomad warriors before him had won

---

[40] Yuan Ch'ai Pi Shih. *Secret History of the Mongols*, translated by Paul Kahn (Berkeley: North Point Press, 1983)

[41] Rene Grousset. *The Empire of the Steppes* (New Brunswick, NJ: Rutgers University Press, 1970) p. 249

victories from the Chinese or Turko-Iranians, but none left behind an empire and the beginnings of an administration. This was partly because he paid close attention to the engineers and architects among his prisoners of war, and they taught him how to besiege a city and how to breach the walls.

Beyond Cathay: The Hill Tribes of China

The lands south of the Kiang (Yangtze) are broad and sparsely populated, and the people live on rice and fish soups. They burn off the fields and flood them to kill the weeds, and are able to gather all the fruit, berries, and univalve and bivalve shellfish they want without waiting for merchants to come around selling them. Since the land is so rich in edible products, there is no fear of famine, and therefore the people are content to live along from day to day: they do not lay away stores of goods, and many of them are poor. As a result, in the region south of the Yangtze and Huai rivers no one ever freezes or starves to death, but on the other hand there are no very wealthy families.

SSU-MA CHIEN, the grand historian
(d. 90 BC)

THESE PEOPLE of the south, though the same race as the northern Chinese, were once considered barbarians, "monkeys with caps on." Now they are thoroughly assimilated, and most are fully accounted as civilized. Only in remote enclaves in the hills does some trace of the vast civilized southern Chinese world survive.

The source of the wealth of the Chinese state was the labor of the masses applied to cultivation of millet and rice. To the northeast of the northern Chinese heartlands (the lowlands along the Yellow River) the land climbs and the rainfall drops off. It is a high grassland and semidesert unsuited for agriculture. The south, difficult though it seemed, was convertible to agriculture up all the valleys and branches, so China expanded south. By 605 AD a grain transport canal system from the Yangtze north to the capital was completed, and southern China gradually began to become the most productive part of the empire. Over the centuries the lowland-dwelling natives were converted to Chinese ways, their Chinese names put on the tax lists, and the ethnic past forgotten, or Hua (the old term for heartland Chinese) immigrants simply overwhelmed them with their numbers. However, the specialized agricultural system that was so appropriate in the lowlands had less economic use for the hills. Hundreds of upland islands of non-Hua culture survived as scattered forest communities in which hunting and gathering was combined with slash-and-burn farming. They did not give up easily; within the area of Hupei-Shensi-Honan-Anhwei, the very center, there were over forty insurrections of tribal peoples between 404 AD and 561 AD. South of the Kiang, or Yangtze, watershed and west in Kweichow and Yunnan there are some very large populations that are mostly non-Chinese, known nowadays by such names as Yi, Pai, Tai, Miao, Yao, and Lisu.

Much of this southern landscape is over three thousand feet high and rises in western Yunnan and Szechwan as high as fifteen thousand feet. The southeastern part has the heaviest rainfall in all China—as much as ninety inches a year on the hills. In Kweichow, the main home of the Miao people, the protected forest of Wumong Mountain gives us a sample of what the southwestern forest was all once like: walnuts, alders, dogwoods, tulip trees, liquidambar, beech, evergreen, oak, chinquapins, and members of the laurel family such as cinnamon and sassafras. Outside such protected areas the later successional pines are now dominant.

In Tang and Sung times the non-Hua peoples of the south were collectively called the Man, the "Man" of Marco Polo's "Manzi," the area in his travels south of what he calls "Cathay." *Man* is the word translated into English as "barbarian." The oldest name for the area, in Medieval Chinese pronunciation, is Nam-Ywat, which in modern Mandarin is Nan-Yueh— "South Yueh"—and in another modern pronunciation (the "south" reversed) "Vietnam." In the politics of Tang times this southern region included the whole southern Chinese coast, and the major city was Canton; the territorial boundary was south of the delta of the Red River, south of Hanoi, where Chinese cultural influence was finally brought up against the cultural influence of India—the Cham empire. *Ywat* probably means "ax"; the southerners were people of the "stone ax." In Vietnam the surviving hill tribes, essentially of the same lineages as those farther north, are now called "montagnards." These many peoples speak languages of the Sino-Tibetan family: Tibetan, Burman,

Tai, Yao, and Miao. The tribes were called Huang, Nung, Mak, La, Ning, Lao. On the southwestern border of Yunnan a few peoples spoke a Mon-Khmer language.

Travelling through the south in the thirteenth century, Marco Polo writes of the freedom of the women and constant rumors of violence and brigandage. Some of this may have been heard from prudish and patriarchal Chinese. He describes a rich life: "The traveller enters a country of great mountains and valleys and forests, through which he makes his way for twenty days towards the west. . . . The people are idolators, living on the fruits of the earth, on wild game and domestic animals. There are lions, bears, and lynxes, harts, stags, and roebuck, besides great numbers of the little deer that produce musk." (It seems unlikely he saw lions.)

The Hua people regarded the tribal Man as semi-animals, whose speech resembled the chatter of monkeys. There was a totemic legend of a dog ancestor among the Miao, the Nosu, or Lolo, now called Yi by the People's Republic that had a "pine tree ancestor." Such legends only confirmed this view for the conquerors. Yet the Hua found the Man women beautiful. There was a regular trade in girls of the southern tribes who were sold as concubine-slaves to wealthy Chinese of the north. The fighting courage of the men was also acknowledged—"They love swords, and treat death lightly." The Chinese scorned them for their occasional cannibalism and head-hunting and then sent against them the sadistic general Yang Szu-hsu, who built a pyramid of the bodies of natives he killed in 722 AD and reputedly took scalps and peeled the skin from the faces of prisoners.

In spite of uprisings and struggle there were also periods of peaceful trade between the tribesmen and the Chinese. The government policy of "controlling barbarians with barbarians" meant sanctioning the authority of some chiefs over others, and in return receiving tribute: kingfisher feathers, elephant tusks, and rhinoceros horn. In China, as in North America and Siberia, when natural peoples get caught in a trade relationship with a civilization, it is the wildlife which suffers first.

Liu Yu-hsi was exiled in Kwangtung in the ninth century. Edward Schafer translates his "Song of the Man":

> The speech of the Man is a *kou-chou* sound.
> The dress of the Man is a *pan-lan* linen.
> Their odorous raccoons dig out the sand rats;
> At seasonal periods they sacrifice to P'an-hu.
> Should they meet a stranger riding a horse,
> They are flustered, and glance round like startled muntjacs.
> With axes at their waists they ascend the high mountains,
> Proposing to go where no old road exists.[1]

Assimilated Man individuals were scarcely distinguishable from Hua Chinese, and some rose to local power as merchants or administrators. Perhaps the most famous aboriginal half-breed in Chinese history is the sixth patriarch of the Ch'an sect, Hui-nêng. Hui-nêng's father was Hua, but his mother was an aboriginal—possibly a Lao. His biography apologetically says, "Although he was soaked and dyed with the airs of the Man and the customs of the Lao, they were not deep in him." According to one legend, Bodhidharma himself came into China by way of the southern port of Canton. (In the territory of the Miao nation, now called Kweichow, early Buddhists carved images on the cliffs in the southern style of Javanese and South Indian art.) The "Southern School" of Ch'an, which may have started with Hui-nêng, is notorious for its vivid rejection of received forms and ideas and its demand that we look directly into the ground of Mind without preconceptions. Perhaps the earthy and independent lives of the indigenous peoples, through Hui-nêng, contributed to the force and flavor of this still flourishing school of Ch'an/Zen.

The most prized of all incenses used in the temples of the Far Eastern Buddhist world is from resinous aloe wood, called *jinko* in Japanese. Its smoke pervades the high-ceilinged head temples at Founders Day ceremonies in Kyoto even today. It was obtained in trade with the isolated aboriginal Li people of Hainan, who got steel axes, cereals, silks, and hatchets in return.

---

[1] Edward H. Schafer. *The Vermilion Bird* (Berkeley: University of California Press, 1967) p. 54

Today, the People's Republic of China had made almost half of Kweichow province, where three million Miao are living, into an autonomous district. The whole province of Kwangsi, home of seven million Tai-speaking Chuang, is also autonomous. Yunnan has a number of autonomous districts for the Tibet-Burman hill people. Mainstream Chinese and Christian missionaries alike have been jolted by the Miao. An American traveler of the twenties wrote: "Every village had its club-house where the girls gathered nightly to sing and dance, and where the youths not of their own but from neighboring villages came to try them out as possible wives." The women wore brilliant multicolored blouses, jackets, and skirts—"red perhaps predominating in the intricate patterns, but no conceivable combination of colors barred. Evidently there was nothing worn beneath the short, pleated skirts that swung so saucily as the girls walked . . . cut so conveniently for hoeing corn on a steep hillside."[2] The Miao distilled their own alcohol and had a supposedly spectacular orgiastic festival, called "Fifth of the Fifth," up until recently.

It is significant that the mountain forests, much altered in the past few centuries, were protected and replanted more by the local mountain people than by the economically dominant Chinese, at least before the PRC took over. The way the tribes saw their wild hills as home, and the wildlife as fellow beings, is apparent in their magical folklore term for the tiger: in myths and tales he is called "Streaked Lad."

---

[2] Harry A. Franck. *Roving Through Southern China* (New York: Century, 1925) p. 494

Wolf-Hair Brush

THE ELITES of premodern China's high civilization were urbane, bookish, secular, arty, and supremely confident. The Imperial Government rested in a ritualized relationship with Great Nature, and the seasonal exchanges between Heaven and Earth—sun, rains, and soils—were national sacraments conducted at elaborate Earth and Heaven shrines. (The most powerful of rituals were conducted in solitude by the Emperor himself.)

Nature and its landscapes were seen as realms of purity and selfless beauty and order, in vivid contrast to the corrupt and often brutal entanglements of politics that no active Chinese official could avoid. The price an intellectual paid for the prestige and affluence that came with being a member of the elite was the sure knowledge of the gap between humane Confucian theory and the actual practices of administering a county or a province—with multiple levels of graft, well-cooked books, and subtle techniques of coercion. And the higher one rose in the ranks, the more one's neck was exposed to the deadly intrigues of enemies.

The mountain horizons were a reminder of the vivid world of clear water, patient rocks, intensely focused trees, lively coiling clouds and mists—all the spontaneous processes that seemed to soar above human fickleness. The fu (prose-poem) poet Sun Ch'o said of these processes, "When the Dao dissolves, it becomes rivers, when it coagulates it becomes mountains." Tsung Ping, an early fifth-century painter whose work does not survive, is described as having done mountain landscapes when ill and no longer able to ramble the hills he loved. He wrote the perfect program for a recluse:

> Thus by living leisurely, by controlling the vital breath, by wiping the goblet, by playing the *ch'in*, by contemplating pictures in silence, by meditating on the four quarters of space, by never resisting the influence of Heaven and by responding to the call

of the wilderness where the cliffs and peaks rise to dazzling heights and the cloudy forests are dense and vast, the wise and virtuous men of ancient times found innumerable pleasures which they assimilated by their souls and minds.[1]

He also stated a philosophy of landscape painting that stood for centuries to come: "Landscapes exist in the material world yet soar in the realms of the spirit . . . the Saint interprets the Way as Law through his spiritual insight, and so the wise man comes to an understanding of it. Landscape pays homage to the Way through Form, and so the virtuous man comes to delight in it."[2] Half a century later Hsieh Ho declared the First Principle of landscape painting to be "Spirit resonance and living moment"—meaning, a good painting is one in which the very rocks come alive, and one yearns to go walking in it. The basic aesthetics of the tradition had been articulated, but it was almost a thousand years before the implications of these statements were fully realized in painterly terms. The art of painting "mountains and waters" slowly unfolded through the centuries.

The concept of *ch'i*—a term that translates as indwelling energy, breath, and spirit—is a rich sophistication of archaic East Asian animism. Joseph Needham calls it "matter-energy" and treats it as a proto-scientific term. Contemporary people everywhere tend to see matter as lifeless. The notion of a rock participating in life and spirit—even as metaphor—is beneath adult consideration. Yet for those who work for long amid the forms of nature, the resonating presence of a river-system or prairie expanse or range of hills becomes faintly perceptible. It's odd but true that if too much human impact has hit the scene, this presence doesn't easily rise.

Archaic art worldwide is often abstract and geometrical. The spiral motif is widely found—from tattoos on the cheek to petroglyphs on a canyon wall. This representation of the *ch'i* of things becomes a design of volutes in very early Chinese

---

[1] Quoted in Oswald Siren. *The Chinese on the Art of Painting* (New York: Schocken, 1963) p. 16
[2] Quoted in J.L. Frodsham. *The Murmuring Stream*, Vol I (Kuala Lumpur: U. of Malaya, 1976) p. 103

decorative art. Artists started tracing the lines of energy flow as observed in the clouds, running water, mist and rising smoke, plant growth—tendrils, rock formations, and various effects of light, in their patterns. They went on, according to Michael Sullivan, to draw images of fantastically-formed animal/ energy-bodied nature spirits, and this provided a main bridge from archetypal being to archetypal landform. The lines finally twisted themselves into ranges of mountains.[3]

The word for civilization in Chinese is *wên-ming*, literally, "understanding writing." In the time of Confucius people wrote on slats of bamboo with a stylus. When paper and the soft-haired brush came into use, the fluidity of calligraphy became possible. In China calligraphy is considered the highest of the graphic arts. The painter uses the same equipment as a writer—the "four treasures" of brush, ink, inkstone, and paper. The brush usually has a bamboo handle with rabbit, badger, goat, deer, wolf, sable, fox, and other hairs for the tip. Even mouse-whiskers have been tried. Everything from a broken roof-tile to rare and unusual stones have been used for grinding the ink. Paper, which is said to have been invented in the first century AD, is commonly made from mulberry, hemp, and bamboo. The paper preferred by Sung and Yuan dynasty painters was called "Pure Heart Hall" paper. It was smooth, white, and thin. Paintings were also done on silk, but paper lasts longer. Ink was made by burning dry pine logs in a kind of soot-collecting kiln. The soot was mixed with glue, one famous glue being made of donkey skin boiled in water from the Tung River. Fragrance was added, and the whole pressed into an inscribed stick.[4] Grinding the ink with a slow steady back-and-forth stroke, softening the brush, spreading the paper—amounts to a meditation on the qualities of rock, water, trees, air, and shrubs.

The earliest surviving landscape paintings (early T'ang, the seventh century) are more like perspective maps. Wang Wei's *Wang Chuan Villa* is a visual guide to a real place, with little

---

[3] Michael Sullivan. "On the Origins of Landscape Representation in Chinese Art." *Archives of the Chinese Art Society of America* VII, 1953, pp. 61–62
[4] Sze Mai Mai. *The Way of Chinese Landscape Painting* (New York: Vintage, 1959)

labels on the notable locations. These first painted mountains are stark and centered, and the trees look stuck on. The painting might be a guidebook scene of a famous temple on a famous mountain. They are still half-tied to accounts of journeys, land-use records, or poems.

Then, with the Sung dynasty, the eleventh century, paintings open out to great space. The rock formations, plants and trees, river and stream systems, flow through magically realistic spatial transitions. The painter-essayist Kuo Hsi reminded us that the mountains change their appearance at every step you take. For those interested in bio-geographic provinces the paintings can be seen to be distinguishing the wider drier mountains of the north from the tighter, wetter, mistier valleys of the south. These vast scenes, with a few small fishing boats, little huts—cottages—travellers with pack stock—become visionary timeless lands of mountain-rocks and air-mist-breath and far calm vistas. People are small but are lovingly rendered, doing righteous tasks or reclining and enjoying their world.

In terms of technique painters moved between extremes of wet ink-dripping brushes and drier sparser ink on the brush. From hard-boned fine-detailed meticulous workmanship leaf by leaf and pebble by pebble it went to wet flung washes of lights and darks that capture a close hill, a distant range, a bank of trees with an effect that can be called impressionistic.

The Sung dynasty painters of large scale, including the horizontal handscrolls of a type sometimes called "Streams and Mountains Without End," didn't always walk the hills they portrayed. With an established vocabulary of forms and the freedom of the brush they could summon up mountains that totally defied gravity and geomorphology, and seemed to float in mist. But these invented landscapes were somehow true to organic life and the energy-cycles of the biosphere. The paintings show us the earth surface as part of a living being, on which water, cloud, rock, and plant growth all stream through each other—the rocks under water, waterfalls coming down from above clouds, trees flourishing in air. I overstate to make the point: the cycles of biosphere process do just this, stream vertically through each other. The swirls and spirals of micro- and macroclimate ("the tropical heat engine" for example) are all creations of living organisms; the whole atmosphere is a breath of plants, writhing over the planet in elegant feedback coils instructed by thermodynamics and whatever it is that guides complexity. "Nature by self-entanglement produces beauty."[5]

The mountains and rivers of the Sung dynasty paintings are numinous and remote. Yet they could be walked. Climbers take pleasure in gazing on ranges from a near distance and visualizing the ways to approach and ascend. Faces that seem perpendicular from afar are in fact not, and impossible-looking foreshortened spur-ridges or gullies have slopes, notches, ledges, that one can negotiate—a trained eye can see them. Studying Fan K'uan's "Travellers Among Streams and Mountains" (about 1000 AD)—a hanging scroll seven feet tall— one can discern a possible climbing route up the chimneys to the left of the waterfall. The travellers and their packstock are safe below on the trail. They could be coming into the Yosemite Valley in the 1870s.[6] Southern Sung and Yuan dynasty landscape painting (especially with the horizontal handscroll format) tends to soften the hills. In the time of the evolution of the paintings, the mountains become easier, and finally can be easily rambled from one end to the other. As Sherman Lee says the landscapes are no longer "mountain-and-water" but "rock-and-tree-and-water."[7]

The cities of the lower Yangtze became a haven for refugee artists and scholars during the Southern Sung dynasty, twelfth century, when the northern half of the country fell to the Khitans, a forest-dwelling Mongol tribe from Manchuria. The long-established southern intelligentsia had always been closer to Daoism than the northerners. At that time Ch'an Buddhism and painting both were popularly divided into a northern and southern school. In both cases, the southern school was taken to be more immediate and intuitive. This large community of artists in the south launched new styles of painting. Lighter,

---

[5] Otto Rössler, quoted in Gleick. *Chaos* (Penguin, 1987) p. 142

[6] Fan K'uan's painting can be seen in plate 11 in Wen Fong. *Summer Mountains* (New York Metropolitan Museum of Art, 1975). Original is in the National Palace Museum, Taipei. Also in Lee and Fong [see next footnote for full citation], plate 8.

[7] Sherman E. Lee and Wen Fong. *Streams and Mountains Without End* (Ascona, Switzerland: Artibus Asiae, 1976) p. 19

more intimate, suggestive, swift, and also more realistic. Some of the painters—Hsia Kuei, Mu Ch'i, Liang K'ai—were much admired by the Japanese Zen monks and merchants, so many of their works were bought by the Japanese, traded for the exquisite Japanese swords that the Chinese needed to fight off the northern invaders. Many of the paintings ended up in the Zen Honzans ("Main Mountains"—headquarters temples) of Kyoto, where they are kept today.

The fact that some scrolls were landscapes of the imagination should not be allowed to obscure the achievement of Chinese artists in rendering actual landscapes. The most fantastic-looking peaks of the scrolls have models in the karst limestone pinnacles of Kuangsi; misty cliffs and clinging pines are characteristic of the ranges of southern Anhwei province. The painting manual *Chieh-tzu Yuan Hua Chuan*, "Mustard-seed Garden Guide to Painting" (about 1679) distinguishes numerous types of mountain formations, and provides a traditional menu of appropriate brushstroke-types for evoking them. Geological identifications of the forms indicated by different brushstrokes are described in Needham:

> Glaciated or maturely eroded slopes, sometimes steep, are shown by the technique called "spread-out hemp fibers," and mountain slopes furrowed by water into gullies are drawn in the *ho yeh ts'un* manner ("veins of a lotus-leaf hung up to dry"). "Unraveled rope" indicates igneous intrusions and granite peaks; "rolling clouds" suggest fantastically contorted eroded schists. The smooth roundness of exfoliated igneous rocks is seen in the "bullock hair" method, irregularly jointed and slightly weathered granite appears in "broken nets," and extreme erosion gives "devil face" or "skull" forms . . . cleavages across strata, with vertical jointed up-right angular rocks, looking somewhat like crystals, are depicted in the "horse teeth" (*ma ya ts'un*) technique.[8]

The *Ta Ch'ing I Tung Chih* is an eighteenth-century geographical encyclopedia with an illustrated chapter on "mountains and rivers." These woodblocks, based on the painting tradition, not only give a fair rendering of specific scenes, but

---

[8] Joseph Needham. *Science and Civilization in China III*, p. 597

do so with geological precision. Needham notes how one can identify water-rounded boulder deposits, the Permian basalt cliffs of Omei-shan, the dipping strata of the Hsiang mountains near Po tomb, U-shaped valleys and rejuvenated valleys.[9]

Huang Kung-wang (born in 1269) was raised in the south. After a short spell with the civil service he became a Daoist teacher, poet, musician, and painter. He is said to have recommended that one should "carry around a sketching brush in a leather bag" and called out to his students "look at the clouds—they have the appearance of mountain tops!"[10] His handscroll "Dwelling in the Fu-ch'un Mountains"[11] came to be one of the most famous paintings within China. He started it one summer afternoon in 1347, looking out from his house, and doing the whole basic composition on that one day. It took another three years to finish it. It's a clean, graceful painting that breathes a spirit of unmystified naturalness. The scene is not particularly wild or glamorous; it has the plain power of simply being its own quite recognizable place. This is in tune with the Ch'an demand for "nothing special" and its tenderness for every entity, however humble.

From around the Ming dynasty (1368 on) China had more and more people living in the cities. Painting helped keep a love of wild nature alive, but it gradually came to be that many paintings were done by people who had never much walked the hills, for clients who would never get a chance to see such places. There were also later painters like Wang Hui, who was a master of all historical styles, but also an acute observer of nature. His "Landscape in the Style of Chü-jan and Yen Wen-Kuei" (1713) carries the hills and slopes on out to sea as the painting fades away, by a portrayal of sea-fog twisting into scrolls and curls of water-vapor / wind-current / energy-flow that faintly reminds us of the origins of Chinese paintings, and takes us back to the mineral- and water-cycle sources. Chinese painting never strays far from its grounding in energy, life, and process.

[9] Ibid., pp. 593–7
[10] James Cahill. *Hills Beyond a River* (New York: Weatherhill, 1976)
[11] Ibid. Plates 41–44; Color Plate 5. Original is in the National Palace Museum in Taipei.

The space goes on.
But the wet black brush
tip drawn to a point,
      lifts away.

UNCOLLECTED ESSAYS

Walking the Great Ridge Ōmine on the Womb-Diamond Trail

I STARTED CLIMBING snowpeaks in the Pacific Northwest when I was fifteen. My first ascent was on Mt. St. Helens, a mountain I honestly thought would last forever. After I turned eighteen I worked on ships, trail crews, fire lookouts, or in logging camps for a number of seasons. I got into the habit of hiking up a local hill when I first arrived in a new place, to scan the scene. For the Bay Area, that meant a walk up Mt. Tamalpais.

I first arrived in Kyoto in May, 1956. Because the map showed Mt. Atago to be the highest mountain on the edge of the Kitano River watershed, I set out to climb it within two or three days of my arrival. I aimed for the highest point on the western horizon, a dark forested ridge. It took several trains and buses to get me to a complex of *ryokan* in a gorge right by a rushing little river. The map had a shrine icon on the summit, so I knew there had to be a trail going up there, and I found it. Dense *sugi* groves, and only one other person the whole way, who was live-trapping small songbirds. Up the last slope, wide stone steps, and a bark-roofed shrine on top. Through an opening in the sugi trees, a long view north over hills and villages, the Tamba country. A few weeks later I described this hike to a Buddhist priest-scholar at Daitoku-ji, who was amused ("I've never been up there") and mischievous enough to set me up with a friend who had Yamabushi connections. I was eventually invited to join a ritual climb of the northern summit of Ōmine, the "Great Ridge." As it turned out I was inducted as a novice Yamabushi (*sentachi*) and introduced to the deity of the range, Zaō Gogen, and to Fudō Myō-ō.

After that experience on Mt. Ōmine I took up informal mountain walking meditations as a complement to my Zen practice at Daitoku-ji. I spent what little free time I had walking up, across, and down Hieizan or out the ridge to Yokkawa, or on other trails in the hills north of Kyoto. I did several backpacking trips in the Northern Japan Alps. I investigated Kyoto on foot or by bike and found an occasional Fudō Myō-ō—with his gathered intensity—in temples both tiny and huge, both old and new. (Fierce as he looks, he's somehow comforting. There is clearly a deep affection for this fellow from a wide range of Japanese people.) I studied what I could on the Yamabushi tradition. What follows, by way of prelude to a description of a pilgrimage down the length of the Great Ridge, barely touches the complexity and richness of this rich and deeply indigenous teaching. My own knowledge of it is, needless to say, rudimentary.

It must have started as prehistoric mountain-spirit folk religion. The Yamabushi ("those who stay in the mountains") are back country Shaman-Buddhists with strong Shinto connections, who make walking and climbing in deep mountain ranges a large part of their practice. The tradition was founded in the 7th or 8th centuries A.D. by En-no-Gyōja, "En the ascetic," who was the son of a Shinto priest from Shikoku. The tradition is also known as Shugendō, "the way of hard practice." The Yamabushi do not constitute a sect, but rather a society with special initiations and rites whose members may be lay or priesthood, of any Buddhist sect, or also of Shinto affiliation. The main Buddhist affinity is with the Shingon sect, which is the Sino-Japanese version of Vajrayana, esoteric Buddhism, the Buddhism we often call "Tibetan." My mountain friends told me that the Yamabushi have for centuries "borrowed" certain temples from the Shingon sect to use as temporary headquarters. In theory they own nothing and feel that the whole universe is their temple, the mountain ranges their worship halls and zendos, the mountain valleys their guest-rooms, and the great mountain peaks are each seen as bodhisattvas, allies, and teachers.

The original Yamabushi were of folk origin, uneducated but highly spiritually motivated people. Shugendō is one of the few [quasi] Buddhist groups other than Zen that make praxis primary. Zen, with its virtual requirement of literacy and its upper class patrons, has had little crossover with the Yamabushi. The wandering Zen monk and the travelling Yamabushi are two common and essential figures in *Nō* dramas, appearing as bearers of plot and resolvers of karma. Both types have become Japanese folk figures, with the Yamabushi the more fearful for they have a reputation as sorcerers. Except that the

Zen people have always had a fondness for Fudō, and like to draw mountains even if they don't climb them.

Yamabushi outfits make even Japanese people stop and stare. They wear a medieval combination of straw *waraji* sandals, a kind of knicker, the deer or *kamoshika* (a serow or "goat-antelope" that is now endangered) pelt hanging down in back over the seat, an underkimono, a hemp cloth over-robe, and a conch shell in a net bag across the shoulder. They carry the *shakujo* staff with its loose jangling bronze rings on top, a type of sistrum. A small black lacquered cap is tied onto the head. (I have a hemp over-robe with the complete text of the Hannya Shingyo brush-written on it, as well as black block-printed images of Fudō Myō-ō, En-no-Gyōja, some little imps, and other characters. The large faint red seals randomly impressed on it are proof of pilgrimages completed. The robe was a gift from an elder Yamabushi who had done these trips over his lifetime. He had received it from someone else and thought it might be at least a century old.) Yamabushi will sometimes be seen flitting through downtown Kyoto begging and chanting sutras, or standing in inward-facing circles jangling their sistrum-staffs in rhythm at the train station while staging for a climb. They prefer the cheap, raw Golden Bat cigarettes. Yamabushi have a number of mountain centers, especially in the Dewa Sanzan region of Tohoku. Then there's Mt. Ontake, where many women climb, and shamanesses work in association with Yamabushi priests who help them call down gods and spirits of the dead. At one time the men and women practitioners of mountain religion in its semi-Buddhist form provided the major religious leadership for the rural communities, with hundreds of mountain centers.

The "Yamabushi" aspect of mountain religion apparently started at Ōmine, in eastern Wakayama Prefecture, the seat of En-no-Gyōja's lifelong practice. The whole forty-mile-long ridge with its forests and streams was En's original zendo. Two main routes lead the seven or eight miles up, with wayside shrines all along the route. Although the whole ascent can be done by trail, for those intent on practice the direct route is taken—cliffs scaled while chanting the Hannya Shingyo. Near the top there is an impressive face over which the novices are dangled upside down. There are two temples on the main summit in the shade of big conifers. When you step in it is cooler, and heady with that incense redolence that only really old temples have.

> A jangling of shakujo staffs and the blowing of
> conches in the courtyard between buildings.
> A fire-circle for the *goma* or fire ceremony—mudras
> hid under the sleeves—and the vajra-handled sword
> brought forth. Oil lanterns and a hard-packed
> earthen floor, the *uguisu* echoing in the dark
> woods. A Fudō statue in the shadows,
> focussed and steadfast on his rock,
> > backed by carved flames,
> > > holding the vajra-sword and a noose.

He is a great Spell-holder and protector of the Yamabushi brotherhood. His name means "Immovable Wisdom-king." Fudō is also widely known and seen in the larger Buddhist world, especially around Tendai and Shingon temples. Some of the greatest treasures of Japanese Buddhist art are Fudō paintings and statues. His faintly humorous glaring look (and blind or cast eye) touches something in the psyche. There are also crude little Fudō images on mountains and beside waterfalls throughout central Japan. They were often placed there by early Yamabushi explorers.

A great part of the Shingon teaching is encoded onto two large mandala-paintings. One is the "Vajra-realm" (Kongō-kai) and the other the "Garbha-realm" (Taizō-kai). They are each marvelously detailed. In Sanskrit "Vajra" means diamond (as drill tip, or cutter), and "Garbha" means womb. These terms are descriptive of two complementary but not exactly dichotomous ways of seeing the world, and representative of such pairs as: mind/environment, evolutionary drama/ecological stage, mountains/waters, compassion/wisdom, the Buddha as enlightened being/the world as enlightened habitat, etc.

For the Yamabushi these meanings are projected onto the Ōmine landscape. The peak Sanjo-ga-dake at the north is the Vajra Realm center. The Kumano Hongu shrine at the south end is at the center of the Garbha Realm. There was a time when—after holding ceremonies in the Buddha-halls at the summit—the Yamabushi ceremonists would then walk the many miles along the ridge—with symbolic and ritual stations the whole way—and down to the Kumano River for another service at the shrine. Pilgrims from all over Japan, by the tens of thousands, were led by Yamabushi teachers through this strict and elaborate symbolic journey culminating in a kind of rebirth. A large number of pilgrims now make a one-day hike up from the north end, a few do a one-day hike up at the south end, but it's rare to walk the whole Great Ridge.

In early June of 1968 three friends and I decided to see what we could find of the route. My companions were Yamao Sansei, artist and fellow worker from Suwa-no-se Island; Saka, also an island communard and spear fisherman; and Royall Tyler, who was a graduate student at that time. He is now an authority on Japanese religion.

MY NOTES: FIRST DAY

Early morning out of town. From Sanjo *eki* in Kyoto take the train to Uji. Then hitchhike along thru Asuka, by a green mounded *kofun* ancient emperor's tomb shaped like a keyhole, as big as a high school. Standing by quiet two-lane paved roads through the lush fields, picked up by a red tradesman's van, a schoolteacher's sedan—reflecting on long-gone emperors of the days when they hunted pheasants in the reedy plains. All ricefields now.

As we get into the old Yamato area it's more lush—deeper green and more broad-leaf trees. Arrive in Yoshino about noon—meet up with Royall & Saka (we split up into two groups for quicker hitching—they beat us) at the Zaō Dō, an enormous temple roofed old-style with *sugi* bark. A ridge rises directly behind the village slanting up and back to the massive mountains, partly in light cloud. Yoshino village of sakura-blooming hills, cherries planted by En-no-Gyōja ("ascetic" but it would work to translate it "mountaineer") as offerings to Zaō the Mountain King. In a sense the whole of Yoshino town stands as a *butsudan*/altar. So the thousands of cherry trees make a perennial vase of flowers—(and the electric lights of the village the candle?)—offerings to the mountain looming above. Here in the Zaō Dō is the large dark image, the mountain spirit presented in a human form, Zaō Gongen—"King of the Womb Realm." ("Manifestation [*gongen*] of the King [ō] of the Womb [*za*]."

I think he was seen in a flash of lightning, in a burst of mountain thunder, glimpsed in an instant by En the Mountaineer as he walked or was sitting. Gleaming black, Zaō dances, one leg lifted, fierce-faced, hair on end. We four bow to this wild dancing energy, silently ask to be welcome, before entering the forest. Down at the end of the vast hall two new Yamabushi are being initiated in a lonely noon ceremony by the chief priest.

Zaō is not found in India or China, nor is he part of an older Shinto mythology. He is no place else because this mountain range is the place. This mountain deity is always here, a shapeshifter who could appear in any form. En the Mountaineer happened to see but one of his possible incarnations. Where Fudō is an archetype, a single form which can be found in many places, Zaō is always one place, holding thousands of shapes.

We adjust our packs and start up the road. Pass a small shrine and the Sakuramoto-bo—a hall to En the Mountaineer. Walk past another little hall to Kanki-ten, the seldom-seen deity of sexual pleasure. Climb onward past hillsides of cherry trees, now past bloom. (Saigyō, the monk-poet, by writing about them so much, gave these Yoshino cherry blossoms to the whole world.) The narrow road turns to trail, and we walk uphill til dusk. It steepens and follows a ridge-edge, fringe of conifers, to a run-down old *koya*—mountain hut—full of hiker trash. With our uptight Euro-American conservationist ethic we can't keep ourselves from cleaning it up and so we work an hour and then camp in the yard. No place else level enough to lay a bag down.

I think of the old farmers who followed the mountain path, and their sacraments of Shamanist/Buddhist/Shinto style—gods and Buddha-figures of the entranceway, little god of the kitchen fire, of the outhouse, gods of the bath house, the woodshed, the well. A procession of stations, of work-dharma-life. A sacramental world of homes and farms, protected and nourished by the high, remote, rainy, transcendent symbolic mountains.

SECOND DAY

Early morning, as the water is bubbling on the mountain stove, a robust Yamabushi in full gear appeared before the hut. He had been up since before dawn and already walked up from Yoshino, on his way to the temples at the top. He is the priest of Sakuramoto-bo, the little temple to En the Mountaineer. Says he's doing a 200-day climbing and descending practice. And he is grateful that we cleaned up the mess. The racket of a *kakesu*: Japanese Jay.

The Ōmine range as headwaters sets the ancient boundaries between the countries of Kii, Yamato, and Ise. These mountains get intense rainfall, in from the warm Pacific. It is a warm temperate rainforest, with streams and waterfalls cascading out of it. Its lower elevations once supported dense beech and oak forests, and the ridges are still thick with fir, pine, hemlock, and fields of wild azalea and camellia. The slopes are logged right up to the ridge edge here & there, even though this is in the supposed Yoshino-Kumano "National Park." (National Park does not mean protected land wholly owned by the public, as in the U.S. In Japan and many other countries the term is more like a zoning designation. Private or village-owned land may be all through the area, but it is subject to management plans and conservation restrictions.)

On the summit, center of the Diamond Realm, we visit the two temple halls, one to En the founder, and the other to Zaō. He makes me think of underground twists and dips of strata, the deep earth thrust brought to light and seen as a slightly crazed dance. And like Fudō, he is an incarnation of deep and playful forces. In Buddhist iconography, sexual ecstasy is seen as an almost ferocious energy, an ecstatic grimace that might be taken for pain.

We blow our conch, ring our shakujo, chant our sutras and dharanis, while standing at the edge of the five-hundred-foot cliff over which I was once suspended by three ascetics who then menacingly interrogated me on personal and Dharma points. In the old days, some stories say, they would just let a candidate drop if he lied or boasted. From the seventh century on no women have been allowed on this mountain. [Several college women who loved hiking changed that in 1969.] Elevation 5675 feet.

We descend from the summit plateau and are onto the branch trail that follows the ridge south. It is rocky, brushy, and narrow—no wide pilgrim paths now. We go clambering up the narrow winding trail, steps made by tree-roots, muddy in parts, past outcroppings and tiny stone shrines buried in *kumazasa*, the mountain "bear bamboo-grass" with its springy thriving erect bunches and sharp-edged leaves. We arrive at the Adirondack-type (open on one side) shelter called "Little *Sasa*" hut and make our second camp.

THIRD DAY

> Rhododendron blossoms, mossy rocks,
>   fine-thread grasses—
> running ridges—wind and mist—it had
>   rained in the night.
> A full live blooming little tree of white
>   bell flowers its
> limbs embracing a dead tree standing—
> moss & a tuft of grass on the trunk.
> The dead tree twisting—wood grain
>   rising laid bare white—
> sheen in the misty brightness. When a tree dies
> its life goes on, the house of moss
>   and countless bugs.
> Birds echoing up from both steep
>   slopes of the ridge.

And now we are in the old world, the old life. The Japan of gridlock cities, cheerful little bars, uniformed schoolkids standing in lines at castles, and rapid rattling trains, has retreated into dreamlike ephemerality. This is the perennial reality of vines and flowers, great trees, flitting birds. The mist and light rain blowing in gusts uphill into your wet face, the glimmer of mountains and clouds at play. Each step picked over mossy rock, wet slab, muddy pockets between vines. Long views into blue-sky openings, streaks of sunlight, arcs of hawks.

A place called Gyôja-gaeri—"Where the ascetics turn back." For a rice-ball-lunch stop. These trails so densely overgrown they're almost gone.

Now at Mi-san peak, the highest point along the Great Ridge, 6283 feet. Another place to stop and sit in zazen for a while, and to chant another round of sutras and dharanis. A little mountain hut a bit below the summit. White fir and spruce-mist blowing afternoon. Yellow-and-black eye of a snake. A fine polish and center line on each scale.

Here for the night. Tending the fire in the hut kitchen—open firepit on the dirt floor—weeping smoky eyes sometimes but blinking and cooking—sitting pretty warm, the wind outside is chilly. Lost somehow our can of *sencha*, good green tea. We have run onto our first hikers, the universal college student backpackers with white towels around their necks and Himalayan-style heavy boots. They had come up a lateral trail, and were shivering in the higher altitude cool. Hovering over the cook-fire, stirring, I mused on my family at home, and my two-month-old baby son. Another sort of moment for mountain travellers.

FOURTH DAY

Oyama renge—a very rare flowering tree, *Magnolia sieboldii*, found here.

A *darshan*, the gift of a clear view of, a Japanese Shika Deer's white rump. Deep water—deep woods—wide. Green leaves—jagged and curved ones, a line-energy to play in. White-flowering low trees with red-rimmed glossy leaves.

We angle up an open flowery ridge and leafy forest to Shaka-dake, Shakyamuni Peak, and have lunch. Chant here the Sanskrit mantra of Shakyamuni learned in Nepal—"Muni muni mahamuni Shakyamuni ye svaha"—"Sage, sage, great sage, sage of the Shakyas, ye svaha." Shakya means "oak." Gautama's people were known as the "Oak Nation."

All this trip we have stayed over 5000 feet. Then stroll down a slope to the west into a high basin of massive broadleafed trees, without a hint of any path, open and park-like. An old forest. A light wind rustling leaves, and a dappled golden light. Thick soft fine grass—Tibetan cat's eye green—between patches of exposed rock. A rest, sitting on the leaves: sighing with the trees. Then a sudden chatter shocks us—a rhesus monkey utters little complaints and gives us the eye.

> (Old men and women who live alone
>   in the woods.
> in a house with no trail or sign—characters of
>   folktale or drama—)
>
> To hear the monkey or the deer
> leave the path.

And I realize that this is the stillest place I had ever been—or would ever be—in Japan. This forgotten little corner of a range, headwaters of what drainage? Totsugawa River? Is it striking because it seems so pristine and pure? Or that it is anciently wise, a storehouse of experience, hip? A place that is full, serene, needing nothing, accomplished, and—in the most creative sense—half rotten. Finished, so on the verge of giving and changing.

Maybe this is what the *Za* of Zaō's name suggests—za (or zō—Chinese *tsang*) means a storehouse, an abundance, a gathering, or in esoteric Buddhism, "womb." Sanskrit *alaya*, as in "storehouse of consciousness" (*alaya-vijñana*) or Storehouse of Snow: Himalaya. The three divisions of Buddhist literature are called zō. *Pitaka* in Sanskrit, "basket." Baskets full of the wealth of teachings. Could it be analogous to the idea of climax in natural systems? (Translating "Zaō" as "King of the Womb Realm" is the Imperial Chinese reading of his name. "Chief of Storage Baskets" would be the Neolithic translation. "Master of the Wilds" is the Paleolithic version.)

We walk back up to our packs. Down the east ridge, loggers are visible and audible high on the slope. Load up and push through sasa on down the trail. A view of a large hawk: some white by the head. Likely a *hayabusa*—falcon—to judge by its flight and dive.

(I find myself thinking we in America must do a Ghost Dance: for *all* the spirits, humans, animals, that were thrown aside.)

—And come on a small Buddha-hall below Shaka-peak. We slip into it, for halls and temples are never locked. It is clean swept, decked out, completely equipped, for a simple *goma* service, with a central fire pit, an altar tray with vajra-tools, all fenced off with a five-colored cord, and a mediation seat before the fire spot. We know thus that there are villages below from which ascetics climb to meditate here. We are nearing the south end of the Great Ridge.

Another hour or so later, the trail that was following the top of the ridge has totally disappeared into the *kumazasa* and brush. It has started raining again. We stop, unload, study the maps, confer, and finally decide to leave the ridge at this point. We take the lateral trail east, swiftly steep and endlessly descending, stepping and sliding ever downward. Go past a seven-layer dragon-like waterfall in the steady rain. Sloshing on down the overgrown trail, find leeches, *hiru* on our ankles, deduced from the visible threads of blood. They come right off—no big deal. And still descending, until dark, we arrive at a place called Zenki, "Front Devil." (Zenki is one of Fudō's two boy imp helpers. Somewhere there's a place called "Back Devil.") We camp in another damp wooden hut along the trail. Someone has kindly left dry wood, so we cook by smoky firelight, and I reflect on the whole Ōmine route as we cook.

We are not far now from the Kitayama River, and the grade from here will be gentle. The Kitayama flows to the Kumano, and goes on out to the seacoast, ancient site of fishing villages and Paleolithic salmon runs. It would seem likely that from very early times, Neolithic or before, anyone wishing to travel between the pleasant reed-plains of Yamato and this southern coast would have followed the Great Ridge. No other route so direct, for the surrounding hills are complex beyond measure, and the Great Ridge leads above it all, headwaters of everything, and sinuous though it be, clear to follow. The mountain religion is not a religion of recluses and hermits (as it would look to contemporary people, for whom the mountains are not the direct path) but a faith of those who move simultaneously between different human cultures, forest ecosystems, and various spiritual realms. The mountains are the way to go! And Yamabushi were preceded, by a mix of vision-questing mountain healers and sturdy folk who were trading dried fish for grains. In a world where everyone walks, the "roadless areas" are perfectly accessible.

The humans were preceded by wildlife, who doubtless made the first trails. The great ridge a shortcut for bears between seacoast fish and inland berries? All these centuries Ōmine has also been a wildlife corridor and a natural refuge, a core zone, protecting and sustaining beings. A Womb of Genetic Diversity.

FIFTH DAY

Next morning find the start of a dirt road going on down to the river. A pilgrims/hikers register on a post there, where we write "Sansei, Saka, Royall, Gary—followed the old Yamabushi route down the Ōmine ridge 5000 above the valleys walking 4 days from Yoshino and off the ridge at Zenki. June 11 to 16, 1968."

By bus and hitchhiking we make it to the coast and camp a night by the Pacific. Hitching again, parting with Saka who must head back to Kyoto, we make our way to the Kumano "new shrine," Shingu. Dark red fancy shrine boat in the museum and an old painting of whaling. A coffeeshop has a little slogan on the wall, "chiisa no, heibon na shiawase de ii—" "A small, ordinary happiness is enough."

Travelling on, riding the back of a truck. Up the Kumano river valley running parallel to cascades of cool sheets of jade riverwater strained through the boulders. Houses on the far side tucked among wet sugi and hinoki, we are let off directly in front of Kumano Hongu at dusk. Found a nook to make a camp in, cook in, sleep the night. Riverbed smooth-washed granite stones now serve as the floor of the god's part of the shrine. Grown with moss, now that no floods wash over.

Then dreamed that night of a "Fudō Mountain" that was a new second peak to Mt. Tamalpais in Northern California. A Buddhist Picnic was being held there. I walked between the two peaks—past the "Fudō Basketball Court"—and some *kami* shrines (God's House is like the house the Ainu kept their Bear in?) and got over to the familiar parking-lot summit of Mt. Tamalpais. I was wondering how come the Americans on the regular peak of Tam didn't seem to know or care about Fudō Mountain, which was so close. Then I went into a room where a woman was seated crosslegged, told she was a "Vajra-woman"—*Vajrakanha*—a tanned Asian woman on a mat, smiling, who showed me her earrings—like the rings of a shakujo. Smiled & smiled.

6:30 A.M. the next morning we enter the center of the Garbhadhātu at Kumano Hongu, "The Main Shrine at Bear-fields." On a wood post is carved: "The most sacred spot in Japan, the main holy ground of the Womb Realm."

And it goes on to say that on April 15 every year a major fire ceremony is conducted here. Shinto, way of the spirits, outer; Buddha, way of the sentient beings, inner. It's always like this when you walk in to the shrine and up to the god's house. It is empty; or way back within, in the heart of the shrine, is a mirror: *you* are the outside world.

> They say—Kannon is water—Fudō is uplift—Dainichi is
> energy.
> Mountain and Water practice. Outer pilgrimages & inner
> meditations.
> They are all interwoven: headwaters and drainages,
>
> The whole range threatens & dances,
> The subsiding
> Mountain of the past
> The high hill of the present
> The rising peak that will come.
>
> Bear   Field.

And poking around there, in back, we come on a carpentry shed, mats on the ground, and workers planing hinoki beams. With that great smell. We have run onto a *miya daiku*, a shrine builder, Yokota Shin'ichi. We chat at length on carpentry tools, and forestry, and the ancient routes of supply for perfect sugi and hinoki logs to be used in the repair of temples, and the making of sacred halls and their maintenance. I ask him how would one build a sacred hall in America? He says, "know your trees. Have the tools. Everyone should be pure when you start. Have a party when you end." And he says "go walking on the mountain." He gives us fresh fish, he was just given so much.

> deep in the
> older hills
> one side rice plains

                    Yamato
one side black pebble
whale-spearing beach.
who built such shrine?
such god my face?
planing the beam
shaping the eave
blue sky
Keeps its shape.

Thinking,
"symbols" do not stand for things,
but for the states of mind that engage those things.
    / Tree / = tree intensity of mind.

We hitchhike up on the Totsugawa gorge, cross the pass, and in some hours are out in the Nara prairies and ricefields. With *ayu* ("sweetfish") and *funa* (a silver carp, a gibel; *Lyrinus auratus*) given us by Shin'ichi-san—tucked into a cookpot along with shredded ice to keep it cool, arrive in Kyoto by train and bus by 9 P.M. We hello and hug and all cook up the fish— and brown rice for our meal. And I hold the baby, crosslegged on the tatami, back from the Great Ridge, linking the home hearth and the deep wilds.

That was 1968. It is doubtless drastically changed by now. The Yamabushi have much given way to hikers and tourists. Roads, logging, and commercial tourist enterprises spread throughout the Japanese countryside. Japan has extended its baleful forest-product extraction habits to the world. We in North America have nothing to be proud of, however. In the twenty-some years since I returned to Turtle Island we have worked steadily to reform the US Forest Service and private logging practices. We are finally beginning to see a few changes. Nonetheless, in these years since 1968 Northern California, Oregon, Washington, British Columbia, and Southeast Alaska have been subjected to some of the heaviest logging and destruction of habitat in the twentieth century. As Nanao Sakaki ruefully suggests, "Perhaps we shall have to change Tu Fu's line to read 'The State remains, but the mountains and rivers are destroyed.'"

Turn Off the Calculating Mind!

Life is not just a diurnal property of large interesting vertebrates; it is also nocturnal, anaerobic, cannibalistic, microscopic, digestive, fermentative: cooking away in the warm dark.
—GARY SNYDER, *The Practice of the Wild*

THE MOST difficult question of all is, what is the nature of art in relationship to the wild? It's interesting and complicated. But what you have to go after is, what is it that is not *wild*? And start at that end.

People often think of art as being the most highly cultured, the most disciplined, the most organized of human productions, but at the same time that it requires a lot of training, it doesn't happen unless you let the wild in.

I'm reminded of what Robert Duncan said: "To be poetry it has to have both music and magic." And magic is the entry of the wild.

Turn off the calculating mind!

The little series of poems that I wrote with the title "How Poetry Comes to Me," I wrote them thinking about the ways that I perceive poetry as being *there*, or being accessible, and one particular poem, I think, was "It stays frightened outside the circle of our campfire. I go to meet it at the edge of the light."

That came to me, actually, camping one night in the Northern Sierra. It happened the night that I went up that peak on the boundary line—the Matterhorn.

I started getting my woods training when I was only six or seven years old, and I was going into the thickets and finding ways through the swamps in Washington, and then finding my own campsites, and fixing them up a little bit, and then I would go back to it in order to learn to see where I was and to get around.

That is like enlightenment.

I was hiking in the Sierra high country on scree and talus fields one time, you know, looking at my feet. And I noticed then every rock was different—no two little rocks the same. Maybe there is no identity in the whole universe. No two things are actually totally alike.

Nature is what we are in. Then "the wild" really refers to process—a process that has been going on for eons or however long. And finally, "wilderness" is simply topos—it is areas where the process is dominant. So one of the terms I find myself using more now is the term "working landscapes," to be distinguished from the idea of totally pristine wilderness landscapes. And that's what we have here along the California coast—a lot of working landscapes. The wild works on all scales.

The point is, "nature" always happens in a place, and generally, what you see and learn, you do so in a small place. You learn the mushroom, you learn the flower, you learn a bird, a slope, a canyon, a gulch, a grove of trees—*as place*. And we all live in a place. So why not look around and see where you are?

I have a falconer friend who catches and releases different kinds of raptors. He released a young male goshawk about three years ago, and after a little bit of training the hawk settled into the territory, which is a pine forest. And every morning, when he goes for a walk, the goshawk comes out and flies above him.

Fooling around has great survival value, really. Evolution's fueled by fooling around. So don't call all of it intelligent design—some of it's goofy design.

So how do we put that into a poem?

CHRONOLOGY

NOTE ON THE TEXTS

NOTES

INDEX

Chronology

1930–32 Born Gary Sherman Snyder in San Francisco, California, on May 8, 1930, the first child of Harold Alton Snyder, twenty-nine, and Ethel Lois Wilkie Snyder, twenty-four. Father, a native of Seattle whose parents, Henry W. Snyder and Missouri L. Snyder, came to Washington as homesteaders, is employed as a telephone salesman. After enlisting in the Marines in 1918 and serving at the Mare Island Naval Shipyard, he worked until about 1925 as a purser on the West Coast passenger ship *H.F. Alexander*. Mother, born in Palestine, Texas, to Rob Wilkey and Lula Callicotte Wilkey, moved to Seattle with her mother around 1919. She graduated from Queen Anne High School in 1922 (her yearbook motto "What man dares, I dare"), afterwards working as a clerk before enrolling at the University of Washington in 1925. They married at St. James Presbyterian Church in Bellingham, Washington, on July 11, 1929. On October 13, 1932, having settled just north of Seattle in rural Lake City, Washington, they have a daughter, Anthea Corinne Snyder. The family lives on a subsistence farm where they tend a small orchard and a few dairy cows, keep chickens, and make cedarwood shingles.

1933–38 Without regular work for much of the Great Depression, father takes whatever odd jobs he can find. Mother reads poetry aloud before bedtime, including Edgar Allan Poe's "The Raven" and Robert Louis Stevenson's anthology *A Child's Garden of Verses*. At seven, walking accidentally over some hot ash, burns his feet and is unable to walk for several months; reads voraciously while he recuperates, his parents borrowing books from the Seattle Public Library.

1939–40 Spends the summer of 1939 with an aunt in Richmond, California, travelling there alone by train; they visit the Golden Gate International Exposition, Muir Woods, Muir Beach, and Mt. Tamalpais. Father finds work as an interviewer for Washington state Employment Security Service.

1941–42 At age eleven or twelve, is impressed by Chinese landscape paintings at the Seattle Art Museum: "It looks just like the Cascades." Makes frequent visits to the University of Washington's Anthropology Museum. Moves with mother and sister to Portland, Oregon, father now a housing administrator in San Francisco; parents soon divorce. Later recalls: "At that time I was intensely concerned with American Indians. I was sewing my own moccasins and spending as much time as possible out in the woods around the Columbia River, or south of Portland, camping and hiking."

1943–44 Attends nearby St. John's High School, but soon transfers to the more academically demanding Lincoln High in downtown Portland. Joins staff of the school paper, *The Cardinal*, and gets a job as a copyboy on the graveyard shift for the Portland *Oregonian*, where his mother, an aspiring journalist, works in the circulation department. Spends summers at a YMCA camp in Spirit Lake, Washington, working on the trail crew.

1945 Climbs Mount St. Helens in August, starting from Spirit Lake.

1946 Earns membership in the Mazamas, a Portland mountaineering club, after climbing Mt. Hood; publishes "A Young Mazama's Idea of a Mount Hood Climb" in *Mazama*, the club's annual journal, and frequents the clubhouse library.

1947 Graduates from Lincoln High. Joins an informal group of young mountain climbers, the Youngsteigers; climbs Mt. Rainier and other peaks. Attends Reed College beginning in the fall, with a grant-in-aid; unable to afford board and too far from home to commute regularly, sometimes camps out in the dorm rooms of friends. In December, publishes essay "The Youngsteigers" in *Mazama*.

1948 Mother marries Douglas Hennessy in Portland on January 24. In May, appears in the Reed student revue "Nobody Else Has Frances." Over the summer, hitchhikes to New York City, obtains his seaman's papers, and, as a member of the Marine Cooks and Stewards Union, ships out to the Caribbean, visiting Colombia and Venezuela. Hitchhikes back to Portland by way of Los Angeles and San Francisco; in September, hikes and camps on Mt. Tamalpais with Reed girlfriend Robin Collins. Moves into a basement room in an off-campus apartment building at 1414 Lambert Street in Portland, working as a part-time custodian in exchange for reduced rent; meets several lifelong friends among the building's student tenants and visitors, including poets Lew Welch and Philip Whalen.

1949 Teaches himself sitting meditation. Over the summer, works on a trail crew for the U.S. Forest Service in the Columbia National Forest (now the Gifford Pinchot Forest).

1950 Publishes poems in Reed student magazine *Janus*. On June 5 marries Alison Gass, a fellow student, but they separate six months later. During the summer, works for the U.S. Park Service excavating the archaeological site of old Fort Vancouver in Washington state. Meets William Carlos Williams, who visits Reed in November; Williams reads his poems and offers encouragement.

1951 Graduates from Reed with a BA in Anthropology and Literature, completing a senior thesis on "The Dimensions of a Haida Myth." Over the summer works as a timber scaler on the Warm Springs Indian Reservation; attends Warm Springs berry feast. Backpacks in the Olympic Mountains. In the fall, with the aid of a scholarship, begins graduate study in anthropology and linguistics at the University of Indiana; reads D. T. Suzuki's *Essays in Zen Buddhism* while hitchhiking to Bloomington, where he shares an apartment with Reed friend Dell Hymes.

1952 Decides against a career in anthropology, leaving Indiana after one semester and moving to San Francisco in March. Moves in with Philip Whalen. Works as an installer of burglar alarms and in a film-processing lab. Attends study sessions at the Berkeley Buddhist Church, where he meets visiting speaker Alan Watts, and at the American Academy of Asian Studies in San Francisco. Over the summer months works as a U.S. Forest Service lookout on inaccessible Crater Mountain, in Mt. Baker National Forest. Divorce from Alison Gass is finalized. In the fall, applies for U.S. Customs Service and Coast Guard jobs in San Francisco.

1953 Father, in the wake of son's job applications, is questioned by government agents who claim Snyder was "closely associated with members or supporters of the Communist Party during the past several years." Corresponds with Ruth Fuller Sasaki of the First Zen Institute of America in June about how he might begin Zen Buddhist study in Japan. In the summer, works once more as a Forest Service lookout, this time on Sourdough Mountain in Mt. Baker National Forest. Moves to Berkeley in the fall, enrolling as a graduate student in the Oriental Languages Department at the University of California; studies Chinese and Japanese language, literature, and art. Meets poet Kenneth Rexroth in November and begins attending his Friday evening workshops.

1954   In February, learns that he has been blacklisted from U.S. Forest Service jobs because of his membership in the Communist-linked Marine Cooks and Stewards Union. Finds another summer job as a choker-setter for the Warm Springs Lumber Company, returning to Berkeley in mid-October.

1955   Tries peyote for the first time on January 1: "An astonishing experience," he writes Philip Whalen. In April, with the help of Alan Watts, meets Ruth Fuller Sasaki; she offers him a yearlong scholarship to study Zen in Kyoto. Unable to obtain a passport because of alleged Communist ties, even after submitting an affidavit and signing a loyalty oath, loses his Zen Institute scholarship; Sasaki promises legal help and a job in Kyoto as her assistant. (A later ACLU case resolves his and others' passport problems.) Despite his blacklisting, obtains a National Park Service job at Yosemite, working on a trail crew beginning in July. At UC–Berkeley in the fall, studies Chinese poetry with Chen Shih-hsiang; translates the "Cold Mountain" poems of Han-Shan. In October, at Kenneth Rexroth's suggestion, is invited by Allen Ginsberg to read at the Six Gallery in San Francisco, along with Philip Lamantia, Michael McClure, and Philip Whalen; follows Ginsberg's "Howl" with "A Berry Feast." Is introduced by Ginsberg to Jack Kerouac, with whom he climbs Yosemite's Matterhorn Peak later that month. Moves into a Mill Valley cabin he names "Marin-an."

1956   At the beginning of the year, hitchhikes with Ginsberg through the Pacific Northwest, mountaineering and giving poetry readings along the way. In April, while conversing over tea with visiting artist Saburo Hasegawa, is inspired to begin *Mountains and Rivers Without End*. Hikes Mt. Tamalpais with Jack Kerouac, who lives at

Marin-an during the spring. About to depart for Kyoto, entrusts his only manuscript of *Myths & Texts* to Robert Creeley, who promises to find it a publisher. On May 6, after a three-day farewell party, sails for Japan aboard the freighter *Arita Maru*. Awaiting the arrival of his teacher, Miura Isshu Roshi, climbs Mt. Atago and Mt. Hiei; attends first Noh performances; assists Ruth Fuller Sasaki with Japanese translations, joining her staff of a half dozen at Daitoku-ji. Begins formal Zen training in July at Shokoku-ji temple complex.

1957   Leaves Kyoto in August, taking a job in the engine room of the S.S. *Sappa Creek*; over the next eight months travels through the Persian Gulf, the Red Sea, the Suez Canal, the Mediterranean, the Bay of Bengal, and the Pacific.

1958   Returns to the United States in April, staying briefly with friend Locke McCorkle in San Francisco and with his father in Corte Madera before settling in Marin-an. Meets Joanne Kyger, a bookstore clerk and poet, at a San Francisco poetry reading in June, and they become a couple. Essay "Spring *Sesshin* at Sokoku-ji" is published in a special summer Zen issue of the *Chicago Review*, and his "Cold Mountain" translations in the fall *Evergreen Review*. Backpacks in the Sierras with Locke McCorkle. Appears as "Japhy Ryder" in Jack Kerouac's semifictional novel *The Dharma Bums*, published in October; one of Kerouac's early titles for the book was "Visions of Gary." Camps out with Philip Whalen on the Olympic Peninsula in Oregon; hikes in Sequoia National Park with other friends. Toward the end of the year, improvises a tiny zendo at Marin-an, hosting and teaching meditation.

1959   In January, after a farewell poetry reading at Bread & Wine Mission in San Francisco, returns to Kyoto, renting a house in suburban Yase. Begins studies under Oda Sesso Roshi, abbot at Daitoku-ji. Attends Noh performances with Cid Corman and Will Petersen, the former a poet and publisher of the magazine *Origin*, the latter an artist. In August, travels along the coast of the Sea of Japan. *Riprap* is published by Corman's Origin Press and printed in Kyoto; Lawrence Ferlinghetti of San Francisco's City Lights Bookstore underwrites the publication, and the first printing quickly sells out.

1960   Marries Joanne Kyger on February 23 at the American Consulate in Kobe, a few days after her arrival in Japan. (Ruth Fuller Sasaki objects to her employee and his girlfriend living together out of wedlock.) In June they move into a larger house in Kyoto; she works as an English tutor, learns flower arranging, and writes poetry (her journals of 1960–64 later published as *Strange Big Moon*). With British potter John Chappell and his wife Anya, they spend two weeks at the beach near Kurayoshi and visit the island of Nishijima. In September, *Myths & Texts* is published in New York by LeRoi Jones's Totem Press in association with Corinth Books.

1961   In May, after a fight between Ruth Fuller Sasaki and his fellow translator Philip Yampolsky, resigns from the First Zen Institute; takes English-teaching jobs to pay rent. Climbs Mt. Omine the following month with *yamabushi* mountain monks and becomes an honorary initiate; acquires a *yamabushi* conch horn. Works on Japanese translation of *Riprap*. Sketches Japanese farmhouses, imagining he might build one in America. With Joanne, sails from Yokohama on December 12 heading for India by way of Hong Kong, Saigon, and Sri Lanka, where they arrive two weeks later. On the last day of the year, in Kandy, rides an elephant.

1962   Travels with Joanne throughout India, and to Nepal, from January through April, later publishing an account of their journey as *Passage Through India*. They visit the Sri Aurobindo and Sri Ramana Maharishi Ashrams; temples at Konarak; Bodh Gaya, where the Buddha achieved enlightenment; the ruins at Nalanda; Kathmandu; and the Taj Mahal. At the end of February, they connect with Allen Ginsberg and Peter Orlovsky, continuing to Almora in the Himalayas, where they meet Lama Govinda, author of *The Foundations of Tibetan Mysticism*. On March 31 they have an audience with the Dalai Lama at Dharamshala; Ginsberg and Orlovsky ask about drugs and meditation (offering to send psilocybin), Kyger asks about meditation practices for Westerners, and the Dalai Lama asks Snyder about Zen practices in Japan. Returning to Kyoto in May, resumes English teaching and Zen training; receives his dharma name, "Chofu" ("Listen to the Wind"). Gives a dinner party for a group of Daitoku-ji monks in July, serving spaghetti, jello, and ice cream; socializes with John and Anya Chappell, Will and Ami Petersen, Philip Yampolsky, Burton Watson, and others. Blows his *yamabushi* horn at a party ringing in the new year.

1963 With Joanne, travels to Kyushu in March, visiting Nagasaki and Kagoshima. They host Allen Ginsberg, who arrives in mid-June for a monthlong stay. Tibald, one of five cats in the house (the others Fudo, Henry, Nansen, and Theadora), has kittens. Meets poet Nanao Sakaki. Spends time with Alan Watts and his girlfriend Mary Jane King, attending Noh performances, drinking sake, and taking LSD.

1964 Returns to the United States in April, renting an apartment in San Francisco; wife Joanne, who left Japan in January, lives separately. Reads with Lew Welch and Philip Whalen at the Pacific Longshoremen's Memorial Hall in San Francisco; in the same month, tours Native American sites in the Southwest with Donald Allen (founder of the Four Seasons Foundation and Grey Fox Press) and visits Robert Creeley in Texas. Hikes in Kings Canyon National Park, up the Bubbs Creek Trail. Teaches freshman composition and poetry writing at UC–Berkeley during the fall. Wins *Poetry* magazine's annual Bess Hokin Prize for poems from the sequence "Six Years." Reads with Robert Duncan at UCLA, and lectures on "Buddhist Practices" at the Berkeley Buddhist Temple.

1965 Continues teaching at Berkeley during the spring. Leads weekend meditation seminar in March at the Esalen Institute in Big Sur. On June 22, with Philip Whalen and a half dozen others, sits in meditation outside the Oakland Army Terminal, departure point to Southeast Asia for many U.S. troops, as part of a larger protest against the war in Vietnam. Reads at the Berkeley Poetry Conference in July. The Four Seasons Foundation publishes *Riprap and Cold Mountain Poems* and *Six Sections from Rivers and Mountains Without End*. Hikes with Drum Hadley and Philip Whalen to States Lake Basin in Kings Canyon National Park, and in September, with Martine Algier and Allen Ginsberg, hikes up Glacier Peak in the North Cascades. On October 2, circumambulates Mt. Tamalpais with Ginsberg and Whalen, chanting at points from

Hindu and Buddhist texts. Returns to Kyoto at the end of October for another year of Buddhist study, this time with a grant from the Bollingen Foundation. Divorce from Joanne Kyger is finalized.

1966 While living in Kyoto, *A Range of Poems* is published in London by Fulcrum Press, and the documentary *USA: Poetry*, featuring Snyder and Whalen, airs on American television. Meets Masa Uehara, a recent graduate of Kobe University, at a dinner party; they begin to see each other frequently. Hosts writer Pupul Jayakar—an acquaintance from Bombay, now cultural adviser to Indira Gandhi—introducing her to Oda Sesso Roshi, abbot of Daitoku-ji, and touring Nara. Oda dies in September. Reads with Franco Beltrametti, Nanao Sakaki, Tetsuo Nagasawa, and Sansei Yamao at a "Bum Academy Festival" in Tokyo. Back in the United States in October, settles in Mill Valley. Hikes through Sequoia National Park; spends time in San Francisco ("the dance-joy-costume-love-acid scene is too beautiful," he writes Ginsberg). Visits a 160-acre property near Nevada City, California, which he purchases with Ginsberg, Richard Baker Roshi, and J. Donald Waters (Swami Kriyananda), envisioning a future home. Reads widely: at UC–Berkeley, the Houston Poetry Festival, New Mexico State, the Guggenheim in New York (with David Ignatow), and elsewhere. Travels with Drum Hadley in the Pinacate Desert in Sonora, Mexico.

1967 Reads at the January 8 opening of the Unicorn Bookshop, co-owned by future publisher Jack Shoemaker, in Isla Vista, California. Blowing a *yamabushi* conch-shell trumpet, opens the Human Be-In, a "Gathering of the Tribes" held in San Francisco's Golden Gate Park on January 14 with approximately 20,000 in attendance; performs a ritual circumambulation of the event with Allen Ginsberg. Joins Ginsberg, Timothy Leary, and Alan Watts in a conversation published in February in the counterculture newspaper the *City of San Francisco Oracle*. Departs for Kyoto on March 23. Kenneth Rexroth and Nanao Sakaki visit for much of May. The following month, with girlfriend Masa Uehara, helps Sakaki build one of two ashrams Sakaki has planned for his "Bum Academy" (later *Buzoku*, "the Tribe"). Hitchhikes with Masa to Tokyo, where he reads for the Bum Academy magazine *Psyche*. In July they sail to Suwanosejima, a volcanic island in the Ryukyus that is home to Sakaki's Banyan Ashram. Marries Masa there on August 6. *The Back Country* is published in London by Fulcrum Press. Wins *Poetry* magazine's Frank O'Hara prize for "Three Worlds, Three Realms, Six Roads." During the winter months, studies with Nakamura Sojun Roshi at Daitoku-ji.

1968 *The Back Country* is published in the United States in March by New Directions. Wins a Guggenheim Fellowship for poetry the following month; hopes to complete *Mountains and Rivers Without End* "in the next two years." Son Kai is born in Kyoto on April 17. ("Fatherhood is like having a Zen Master in the house all the time," he writes Ginsberg. "Talk about dignity, demands, non-verbal communication; and a mirror held up to yourself.") In June joins *yamabushi* mountain pilgrims on five-day ritual hike. Presents essay "Poetry and the Primitive" at Kanto Gakuin University in Yokohama. Beginning in August spends six weeks at Banyan Ashram, Masa and Kai remaining in Kyoto. In November wins *Poetry* magazine's Levinson Prize for his sequence "Eight Songs of Cloud and Water." Father dies on December 23 in Palma de Mallorca, Spain. Returning to the U.S. after a long trip at sea, the family stays with sister Thea in San Anselmo.

1969 At the end of January, leaving Kai with Thea, drives to Tucson with Masa in their new Volkswagen camper van to join Drum and Diana Hadley for a three-week trip through Baja California. Attends the Sierra Club Wilderness Conference in San Francisco in March, distributing copies of his "Smokey the Bear Sutra" and giving interviews: "Ecology radicals should call for Green Studies programs at universities—teaching emergency planet information and the non-negotiable demands of nature if the biosphere is to remain intact." *Earth House Hold*, a collection of essays and journal entries, is published by New Directions the next month, followed in June by *Regarding Wave*, in a limited edition from Windhover Press. Rents a house in Mill Valley, near Muir Woods, while planning a move to "Kitkitdizze" (the family's land in Nevada County, California—its name taken from the Miwok word for Bear Clover, a native shrub). Hikes in the High Sierra with Nanao Sakaki ("one of my most important teachers," he writes Ginsberg), who stays with the family. Alan Watts visits. Gen, his second son, is born early on November 1, his father in Minnesota for a reading.

1970 Reads and lectures across Canada in March and gives an Earth Day speech at Colorado State. Moves with family to Kitkitdizze where, with the aid of many friends, they begin building a home, borrowing features from Native American earth lodges and Japanese farmhouses. *Six Sections from Mountains and Rivers Without End Plus One* is published by Four Seasons Press in June and an expanded *Regarding Wave* by New Directions in October. By the end of the year, the house at Kitkitdizze is inhabited and almost done; a group of those who helped to build it join together to buy an adjacent property.

1971 Teaches at the University of California–Riverside from January to early March, and travels for readings throughout the year: to the University of California at Santa Cruz, Washington University, Iowa State University, Goucher College, Sonoma State College, Boston College, and elsewhere. Reads "The Wilderness" at the Center for the Study of Democratic Institutions in Santa Barbara. In May, Lew Welch, camping near Kitkitdizze during a bout of depression, disappears, leaving his car and a suicide note behind. Despite a five-day community search, his body is never found. Helps fight a forest fire on a neighbor's land. At sunrise on the day of the fall equinox, as part of a multimedia "ecological service" at San Francisco's Grace Cathedral, presents "Prayer for the Great Family" with Masa and children.

1972 Along with Theodosius Dobzhansky and Loren Eiseley, serves as writer-in-residence at the University of Redlands in March. In June, with the support of the *Whole Earth Catalog*, attends United Nations Conference on the Human Environment in Stockholm ("full of groups of people who came to argue over the spoils, not to quit spoiling," he writes Ginsberg). Travels to Hokkaido, climbing in the Daisetsuzan mountains; studies Ainu culture and the local Ussuri brown bear. *Manzanita*, a chapbook, is published by Four Seasons.

1973 Spends three weeks in Montana in April as guest lecturer for the Round River Experiment in Environmental

Studies, a University of Montana program; Masa attends, teaching Asian dance. Visits Wendell Berry and his wife Tanya at their farm, Lanes Landing, in Port Royal, Kentucky, amid end-of-year readings in the Midwest. Shaman Drum publishes his chapbook *The Fudo Trilogy*.

1974 Lectures on "The Incredible Survival of Coyote" at Utah State College, and on "The Yogin and the Philosopher" at the Conference on the Rights of the Nonhuman in Claremont, California; reads poetry at the University of North Carolina and the University of Utah. In May the "Ring of Bone" zendo, a Mahayana Buddhist *sangha*, is formally declared at Kitkitdizze, its meetings held in a small barn (the "barndo"). In November, New Directions publishes *Turtle Island*, the title an "old/new name" for North America, "based on many creation myths of the people who have been living here for millennia." Reads with Allen Ginsberg, Michael McClure, and Nanao Sakaki at a Berkeley benefit for the Banyan Ashram.

1975 In February, is appointed to the California Arts Council by newly elected governor Jerry Brown, an admirer of *Turtle Island*. Wins the Pulitzer Prize in Poetry for *Turtle Island* in May, donating his $1,000 prize money toward the completion of Oak Tree School, a new elementary school and community project on San Juan Ridge. Mother moves to nearby Grass Valley, California.

1976 Reads at a Berkeley benefit for Balasaraswati Music and Dance Company, of which his wife is a member. Bob Steuding's *Gary Snyder*, the first book-length study of the poet's work, is published in Twayne's United States Authors Series. Writes to the editor of the *Sacramento Bee* on August 1, defending the work of the California Arts Council amid criticism of its nontraditional and multicultural funding priorities. Joins Governor Brown, Joni Mitchell and other musicians, conservationists, and whale researchers at a "California Celebrates the Whale" event at the Sacramento Memorial Auditorium.

1977 Reads poems with Wendell Berry at the San Francisco Museum of Modern Art in March; attends symposium on "Chinese Poetry and the American Imagination" in New York the following month. *The Old Ways*—"six brief approaches to the old ways via poetry, myth, and sense of place"—is published by City Lights. In the fall, goes backpacking with his sons in the Olympic Mountains; joins Olga Broumas, Carolyn Kizer, and others at a poetry-teaching symposium in Port Townsend, Washington, and lectures at the Church of the Holy Communion in New York, home of the Lindisfarne Association.

1978   With Nelson Foster, Robert Aitken Roshi, Anne Aitken, Joanna Macy, Jack Kornfield, Al Bloom, and others, becomes a member of the newly formed Buddhist Peace Fellowship. Visits with Tanya and Wendell Berry on their Kentucky farm in March, amid many readings and speaking engagements, one of them a San Francisco benefit for Greenpeace. Receives the ongoing support of Governor Brown as critics of the California Arts Council introduce legislation to abolish it; Brown is an occasional guest at Kitkitdizze and considers buying a nearby property. Begins an annual Ring of Bone zendo summer tradition, the "Mountains and Rivers" sesshin, combining hiking and meditation; later describes it as the zendo's singular "contribution to Zen practice." Backpacks with friends in the high country of Yosemite in August. Co-edits and writes an introductory statement for the *Journal for the Protection of All Beings*, a special issue of *CoEvolution Quarterly*.

1979   *Songs for Gaia*, a chapbook illustrated with Michael Corr's woodblock prints, is published by Copper Canyon, and *He Who Hunted Birds in His Father's Village: The Dimensions of a Haida Myth*, based on his Reed College thesis, by Grey Fox Press. In July, with Masa, participates in a symposium on "Poetry and Dance of Life and Place" at the University of Hawaii; meets W. S. Merwin, reading with him at a Honolulu benefit for Robert Aitken Roshi's Diamond Sangha. Joins Wendell Berry at a Menninger Foundation conference in Topeka, Kansas, reading essay "Poetry, Community, and Climax." Discusses "Zen and Contemporary Poetry" with Robert Bly, Richard Brautigan, Lucien Stryk, and Philip Whalen at a Modern Language Association meeting in San Francisco.

1980   Reads from his poems in Sitka, Alaska; at Berkeley; at a San Francisco benefit for Fay Stender, an activist lawyer paralyzed after a shooting; and on Earth Day at Purdue. *The Real Work: Interviews & Talks, 1964–1979* is published in August by New Directions. In October, Robert Aitken Roshi leads a sesshin at Kitkitdizze.

1981 Reads in Newport, Brookings, and Astoria, Oregon, telling one audience: "First thing I do here when I get up into the Northwest is get out of the car and go a few yards off into the woods and just sniff that distinctive moldy underbrush. Nothing like it anywhere else." Takes a rafting trip down the Stanislaus River. Travels to Japan with Masa, Kai, and Gen over the summer, visiting Masa's extended family. In September and October spends six weeks in Australia with Nanao Sakaki, reading poems in cities and outback Aboriginal communities throughout the country; meets Aboriginal poet Kath Walker on North Stradbroke Island in Queensland and in Tasmania reconnects with potter Les Blakebrough, a friend from his years in Kyoto. Installs solar panels at Kitkitdizze.

1982 Gives talk "Sacred Land: A Cross-Cultural Perspective" in Wyoming in February; speaks at the University of Montana with Native American activist Russell Means. Spends the summer at Kitkitdizze helping to build a community hall for the Ring of Bone zendo. In a friendly letter published in *Earth First!* in August, urges environmental activist Dave Foreman to reconsider his advocacy of violent "monkey-wrenching" (the destruction of machines or property in defense of wild nature). Hosts a Nevada City benefit for Gene Covert, a candidate for Nevada County supervisor running on an environmental platform. In October travels to Sweden where *The Old Ways* has recently been translated. Meets up with Wendell Berry in Edinburgh; they read together in London and address the Schumacher Society in Bristol (Snyder on "Good, Wild, and Sacred Land"). Attends the annual meeting of the Lindisfarne Association in Crestone, Colorado. Reads with poet-anthropologist Stanley Diamond at the New School in New York and at the annual meeting of the American Anthropological Association in Washington, D.C.

1983 Appears at a San Francisco benefit for the new Rainforest Action Network in March with activists Dave Foreman and John Seed; the following month, reads from his poetry with Drummond Hadley at the University of Kentucky and the University of Louisville. Lectures at the Naropa

Institute in Boulder over the summer. Tanya and Wendell Berry visit Kitkitdizze. In October, publishes a new collection of poems, *Axe Handles*, from North Point Press.

1984 In March, *A Passage Through India*, an edition of his journals and travel writings of 1961–62, is published by Grey Fox Press. Reads throughout Alaska in April and May—in Sitka, Kenai, Unalaska, Anchorage, Haines, Shungnak, Kobuk, and elsewhere—in association with the Alaska Humanities Forum. Attends community meetings on San Juan Ridge to protest the proposed development of a local mine. Visits Oregon's Willamette National Forest, speaking at the Cathedral Forest Rendezvous. In October, sponsored by the Chinese Writers Association and the University of California–Los Angeles, travels with Ginsberg, Maxine Hong Kingston, Toni Morrison, and others to Beijing for a conference on "The Sources of Creativity"; visits Hanshan Temple in Suzhou, giving the head priest a copy of his "Cold Mountain" translations. Wins an American Book Award for *Axe Handles*.

1985 Reads from his poems at UCLA, the California Institute of the Arts, and the Herbst Theater in San Francisco. In Kansas in June for the Kansas Prairie Festival, tracks down and visits the grave of his great-grandmother, Harriet Callicotte. In August, sponsored by the University of Alaska–Fairbanks, teaches a course on "Nature Literature: Gates of the Arctic National Park" at Summit Lake and Chimney Lake in central Brooks Range. Travels to Hawaii in October as a guest of the Hawaii Literary Arts Council. Joins Wendell Berry at the University of Montana for "On Common Ground," a conference on the relationship between wilderness and agriculture.

1986 Teaches "The Literature of the Wilderness" at the University of California–Davis in the spring, joining the English Department there. Rafts down the Tatshenshini River in British Columbia with Gen in July; later Kai joins them for a trip exploring the headwaters basin of the Noatak River in northern Alaska. Receives the Poetry Society of America's Shelley Memorial Award. Publishes poetry collection *Left Out in the Rain* with North Point Press.

1987 Gives talk "Recollections of Early Zen" at Green Gulch Farm Zen Center in Muir Beach, California, in April; the following month, is inducted into the American Academy of Arts and Letters. Visits Sitka, Alaska, with son Gen and Nanao Sakaki, staying with anthropologist Richard Nelson; reads at the Sitka Summer Writers Symposium. Climbs and hikes on Baranof Island, Alaska, in the Yukon ranges, and, back in California, in the Sierra Nevada. In the fall, reads in Vermont with novelist Jim Dodge. Celebrates the centennial of Robinson Jeffers's birth with William Everson, Czesław Miłosz, Diane Wakoski, and others. Kai, recovering from a serious car accident, resumes his studies at the University of California–Santa Cruz.

1988   Writes to friends in March: "Masa and I are realigning our lives," she beginning a relationship with Zen teacher Nelson Foster while remaining at Kitkitdizze, he a relationship with Carole Koda, a physician's assistant and avid hiker and climber. Arranges for Allen Ginsberg to speak at UC–Davis and the North Columbia Cultural Center. Joins Ginsberg, Joanne Kyger, Michael McClure, and Nanao Sakaki at an August "Eco Poetry Round Up" in San Francisco to benefit conservation of the Shiraho reef in the Ryukyu Islands; over 1,000 attend. In September, with friend David Padwa and others, travels across Tibet.

1989   Divorce from Masa Uehara is finalized; in June, Carole Koda moves to Kitkitdizze with her daughters Mika (b. 1978) and Kyung-jin Robin (b. 1983). Travels with Carole in southeast Alaska in July, following the route of John Muir; they take sea-kayaks to the base of Muir Glacier. Back home, suffers from apparent asthma or bronchitis, later diagnosed as pneumonia; an x-ray reveals a lesion on his lung. Returning from a speaking engagement at the University of the Ryukyus in Okinawa, undergoes surgery to remove the growth, which on biopsy proves benign.

1990   Recovering slowly from surgery, drives with Carole to Arizona in February, where they visit with Dave Foreman and Drum Hadley. Gives an Earth Day lecture at Bridgeport, on the South Yuba River; in May, circumambulates Mt. Tamalpais. Works with Nanao Sakaki at Kitkitdizze on a new Japanese translation of *Turtle Island*. In July travels with Carole to the Naropa Institute where they meet with Ginsberg. *The Practice of the Wild*, an essay collection, is published in September by North Point Press. With Nevada County neighbors, helps to establish the Yuba Watershed Institute; they reach an agreement with the Bureau of Land Management, taking cooperative responsibility for over 2,000 local forest acres. In October gives talk on "Meditation, (Chan), and Poetry" at a conference on literature and religion at Fu Jen University in Taipei.

1991 Marries Carole Lynn Koda in Kitkitdizze Meadow on April 18; they travel widely in Alaska in July, climb in the Palisades region of the Sierras with Kai in August, and in October hike in Japan with Nanao Sakaki. Reads with Sakaki in Kyoto and, as part of a protest against nuclear energy, in Obama, a city in Fukui Prefecture with many nuclear power stations. Is described as the "poet laureate of Deep Ecology" in Max Oelschlaeger's influential book *The Idea of Wilderness*. Toward the end of the year, Carole is diagnosed with a rare cancer, pseudomyxoma.

1992 Buys Bedrock Mortar, Allen Ginsberg's cabin adjoining Kitkitdizze. Helps to establish an annual "Art of the Wild" writers' conference at UC–Davis. In September travels to Leh in the Indian territory of Ladakh, presenting essay "A Village Council of All Beings." *No Nature: New and Selected Poems* is published by Pantheon the same month; it is a National Book Award finalist. Joins Sue Halpern, William Kittredge, Bill McKibben, and Terry Tempest Williams for a November "Evening with Nature Writers" at Miami-Dade Community College. Reads in Spain in December.

1993 Cofounds the Nature and Culture Program at UC–Davis, supporting an undergraduate major for students of society and the environment. In June, quietly resigns from the board of advisors of *Tricycle: The Buddhist Review*, explaining to its editor Helen Tworkov: "So much time has elapsed and nothing has yet been done to address the question of the role of Asian-Americans in the evolution of American Buddhism, and how they are feeling about Caucasian Buddhist assumptions."

1994 Reads from his poems at Butler University in Indianapolis. In April, with Gen, flies to Botswana to meet with Kai, who is working there; they travel through Tanzania,

Kenya, and Zimbabwe. Tanya and Wendell Berry visit Kitkitdizze in May; with Carole, they camp out in the Black Rock Desert of Nevada. Attends a tribute to Allen Ginsberg at the Naropa Institute in Boulder, and the Geraldine R. Dodge Poetry Festival in Bryam Township, New Jersey.

1995 Speaks on "Rediscovering Turtle Island" at the University of Arizona in April; reads with Stanley Kunitz and Denise Levertov at the National Poetry Festival in Des Moines, Iowa. Is featured on the PBS television program *The Language of Life with Bill Moyers*, which premieres in July, and at a September benefit for the Sonoma Land Trust. In the fall, travels to Nepal with Carole; they trek to Sagarmatha (Mt. Everest) Base Camp. Essay collection *A Place in Space: Ethics, Aesthetics, and Watersheds* is published by Counterpoint in October.

1996 Teaches "The Making of the Long Poem" at UC–Davis in the spring. Joins other noted writers in Washington, D.C., for conference "Watershed: Writers, Nature and Community," organized by poet laureate Robert Hass and the Orion Society. With Carole, travels to France in June and July to study cave art, visiting Peche-merle, Cougnac, Niaus, El Portel, Lascaux, and Trois-Frères. In September, *Mountains and Rivers Without End* is published by Counterpoint Press, representing the culmination of four decades of writing and revision. Reads selections from the book at the Library of Congress the following month. Carole undergoes surgery and chemotherapy.

1997 Wins the Bollingen Prize in Poetry from Yale University Library in January, and in April both the John Hay Award for Nature Writing, presented by the Orion Society, and the 1996 Robert Kirsch Award for lifetime achievement, from the *Los Angeles Times*. Allen Ginsberg dies on April 5. Is diagnosed with prostate cancer and begins treatment. Travels to Japan over the summer, reading at the Tokyo Summer Festival. With the aid of his $50,000 Bollingen award, builds a 600-square-foot addition onto the house at Kitkitdizze, including its first indoor toilet.

1998 Travels to Japan in March to receive the thirty-second Bunka-Sho (Buddhism Transmission Award) from the Bukkyo Dendo Kyokai (Society for the Propagation of

Buddhism), the first American to be thus honored. Also wins a Lila Wallace–Reader's Digest Fund award, supporting both his own writing and a program of readings at the nearby North Columbia Schoolhouse Cultural Center. Reads in Hawaii, Greece, and the Czech Republic. In October, amid controversy over a state ballot measure that would ban forest clearcutting and pesticide use, and an attempt to prevent him from speaking on campus, addresses an audience of over 1,000 at Oregon State University on "Gratitude to Trees: Buddhist Resource Management in Asia and California." Visits new granddaughter, Kiyomi, and son Kai, a graduate student in forestry at Oregon State. Lectures at Westminster College in Salt Lake City and at the Connecticut Museum of Natural History in Hartford; reads with Mexican poet Alberto Blanco at the Art Institute of Chicago.

1999 Appears with cultural historian Mike Davis and state senator Tom Hayden in April in a program to benefit the Friends of the Los Angeles River. *The Gary Snyder Reader: Prose, Poetry, and Translations, 1952–1998* is published by Counterpoint in June. Reads with Wendell Berry in Santa Fe, hosted by the Lannan Foundation; the two are interviewed onstage by their publisher, Jack Shoemaker.

2000 Visits Hawaii in February; appears with Nanao Sakaki and Albert Saijo at the Volcano Arts Center. Is named Faculty Research Lecturer at UC–Davis, the university's highest peer honor; receives an honorary degree at Colby College commencement. As cohost, joins environmental leaders traveling through the Tongass region of southeast Alaska aboard the *Catalyst*, a restored 1930s wooden ship. In August, accompanied by San Juan Ridge musicians Ludi Hinrichs and Daniel Flanigan, reads from *Mountains and Rivers Without End* for an audience of over 500 in the amphitheater of the North Columbia Schoolhouse Cultural Center. In September, attends "Writing Across Boundaries" symposium in Seoul, South Korea. Presents lecture "Zen and Ecology" at Komazawa University in Tokyo.

2001 Receives the California State Library Gold Medal for Excellence in the Humanities and Social Sciences.

2002 In January, sister Thea is killed after being struck by a car in Novato, California. Formally retires as Professor Emeritus from UC–Davis; donates his papers to the university library. Philip Whalen dies in June. Reads from *Mountains and Rivers Without End* at the Tokyo Summer Festival, accompanied by San Juan Ridge musicians. Prepares a short selection of his writings, *Look Out*, published by New Directions in November. Heyday Books publishes *The High Sierra of California*, with selections from his journals and woodblock prints by Tom Killion. Reads from *Mountains and Rivers Without End* in December at the Maison de la Culture du Japon in Paris, accompanied by Noh musicians.

2003 Gives keynote speech—"Ecology, Literature, and the New World Disorder"—at a "Literature and the Environment" conference at the University of the Ryukyus in April, and reads poetry in Tokyo. Is elected a chancellor of the Academy of American Poets.

2004 Receives the Masaoka Shiki International Haiku Awards Grand Prize from the Ehime Cultural Foundation in Matsuyama City, Japan; in his acceptance speech, highlights "the influence from haiku and from the Chinese" on his poetry. Mother dies in Grass Valley on August 13, at ninety-eight. Visits Italy with Carole in the fall, but she returns home early, in declining health. *Danger on Peaks*, a new poetry collection, is published by Shoemaker & Hoard in September.

2005 *Danger on Peaks* is named a National Book Critics Circle award finalist. Reads from the book at Iowa State University, and in May speaks on "Lessons from Mount St. Helens" in Portland alongside ecologist Jerry Franklin. The same month, with Carole, visits Death Valley, where the wildflowers are blooming. Attends "Writing for Peace" conference in Seoul as a guest of the Daesan Foundation, and reads at a year-end exhibition celebrating the Black Rock Desert at the Nevada Museum of Art.

2006 On June 29, Carole Koda dies at home from cancer.

2007 *Back on the Fire*, a collection of essays, is published by Shoemaker & Hoard in February; reads from the book, and from *Danger on Peaks*, in Santa Fe, Charlotte, and Chicago. Attends the Prague Writers Festival in June.

2008 Wins the Ruth Lilly Poetry Prize from the Poetry Foundation, and $100,000. In June, in San Francisco, introduces a program of his poems set to music by Fred Frith, Allaudin Mathieu, Robert Morris, and Roy Whelden, and performed by contralto Karen Clark and the Galax Quartet.

2009 Counterpoint publishes *The Selected Letters of Allen Ginsberg and Gary Snyder, 1956–1991*, edited by Bill Morgan, and a fiftieth-anniversary edition of *Riprap and Cold Mountain Poems*; Heyday Books publishes *Tamalpais Walking: Poetry, History, and Prints*, a collaboration with artist Tom Killion.

2010 *The Practice of the Wild*, a documentary about Snyder directed by John J. Healey and produced by Jim Harrison and Will Hearst, premieres at the San Francisco Film Festival on May 3. A companion book—*The Etiquette of Freedom: Gary Snyder, Jim Harrison, and "The Practice of the Wild,"* edited by Paul Ebenkamp—is published by Counterpoint later in the year. Reads with Ursula K. Le Guin in Portland, on the thirtieth anniversary of the Mount St. Helens eruption.

2011 Contributes a foreword to the anthology *The Nature of This Place: Investigations and Adventures in the Yuba Watershed*, and discusses the book with environmental journalist David Lukas at UC–Davis.

2012 Wins the Wallace Stevens Award for lifetime achievement from the Academy of American Poets, and a $100,000 stipend. In April, receives the Henry David Thoreau Prize for Literary Excellence in Nature Writing from PEN New England. Reads at the Folger Shakespeare Library. On August 30, writes to Wendell Berry: "I'm beset, as I'm sure you are, by numerous requests, but I try to hold the line so that I can finish up a couple more writing projects before I get too close to (as Gore Vidal put it) the exit."

2013 Reads with Kashaya Pomo poet Martina Morgan at Fort Ross State Historic Park in Sonoma County, to benefit the Fort Ross Conservatory, and at the twelfth annual Quivira Coalition Conference, "Inspiring Adaptation," in Albuquerque.

2014 *Distant Neighbors: The Selected Letters of Wendell Berry and Gary Snyder*, edited by Chad Wriglesworth, is published by Counterpoint in June, and in November *Nobody*

Home: Writing, Buddhism, and Living in Places by Trinity University Press, the latter gathering Snyder's conversations and correspondence with South African scholar Julia Martin.

2015 Publishes *This Present Moment* with Counterpoint, and a third collaboration with artist Tom Killion, *California's Wild Edge: The Coast in Prints, Poetry, and History.* The Center for Gary Snyder Studies at Hunan University in Changsha, China, hosts an "International Symposium on Ecopoetics, Ekphrasis, and Gary Snyder Studies."

2016 Lectures on "Scholars, Hermits, and People of the Land" at Cornell University. Counterpoint publishes *The Great Clod: Notes and Memoirs on Nature and History in East Asia* in March—a collection of environmental essays—and in November *Dooby Lane: Also Known as Guru Road, a Testament Inscribed in Stone Tablets by DeWayne Williams*, a celebration of the Nevada folk artist DeWayne Williams, with photographs by Peter Goin.

2017 Travels to Santa Fe in May, giving a keynote address as part of the New Mexico History Museum's exhibit "Voices of Counterculture in the Southwest." At the end of the year is inducted into the California Hall of Fame by Governor Jerry Brown.

2018 Talks with students and reads from his poems at Macalester College in October, and at the University of California–Santa Cruz the following month.

2019 Contributes a foreword to *Karst Mountains Will Bloom* by Hmong American poet Pos Moua, a former student.

2020 Joins poet Jane Hirshfield for a reading at Mill Valley Public Library.

2021 Hikes in the High Sierra with Kim Stanley Robinson, the novelist, and David Robertson, the photographer. Visits northern California's Giant Sequoia groves with Tom Killion; they meet with foresters and ecologists.

Note on the Texts

This volume gathers selections from eight of Gary Snyder's prose books—*Earth House Hold* (1969), *He Who Hunted Birds in His Father's Village* (1979), *The Real Work* (1980), *Passage Through India* ([1984]), *The Practice of the Wild* (1990), *A Place in Space* (1995), *Back on the Fire* (2007), and *Tamalpais Walking* (2009)—along with an interview published in *The Paris Review* in 1996, the entirety of *The Great Clod* (2016), and two uncollected essays.

The texts of Snyder's books have been taken from their most recent American trade editions, in the most recent printings known to be available: for *Earth House Hold* and *The Real Work*, from New Directions in New York; for *Tamalpais Walking* from Heyday Books in Berkeley; and for the remainder from Counterpoint Press in Berkeley. Snyder has often corrected and revised his prose works in later printings of these editions. Some of his prose has also appeared in small press and overseas editions, as well as in a variety of periodicals and anthologies, but these editions and printings do not consistently reflect his latest intentions.

Snyder has approved the contents of the present volume and its choices of texts, and he has guided their arrangement. For further information about the publication history of individual works in periodicals and elsewhere, see Katherine McNeil's *Gary Snyder: A Bibliography* (New York: Phoenix Bookshop, 1983) and the 2010 second edition of John Sherlock's "Bibliography of the Works of Gary Snyder," available online at library.ucdavis.edu/wp-content/uploads/2022/07/bib-garysnyder-2ed.pdf.

From *Earth House Hold: Technical Notes & Queries to Fellow Dharma Revolutionaries*. The book was first published by New Directions in New York on April 25, 1969, in an edition that has since appeared in at least fourteen printings. A British edition, from Jonathan Cape in London, followed in 1970. Of the seven items in the book selected for inclusion here, six are known to have been published in earlier forms, as listed below:

Lookout's Journal. *Caterpillar*, April–July 1968.
Spring Sesshin at Shokoku-ji. *Chicago Review*, Summer 1958.
Buddhism and the Coming Revolution. *Journal for the Protection of All Beings*
    #1, 1961 (as "Buddhist Anarchism"); *San Francisco Oracle*, November 1966.

Passage to More Than India. *Fire*, March 1968.

Poetry and the Primitive. *Poetry and the Primitive: Berkeley Poetry Conference* (Berkeley: University of California Language Laboratory, 1965), an audio publication, on cassette tape, of Snyder's July 16, 1965, lecture at the Second Berkeley Poetry Conference.

Suwa-no-se Island and the Banyan Ashram. *San Francisco Oracle*, December 1967.

The text of *Earth House Hold* in the present volume is that of the undated fourteenth printing of the original New Directions edition.

From *He Who Hunted Birds in His Father's Village: Dimensions of a Haida Myth*. *He Who Hunted Bird in His Father's Village* was Snyder's undergraduate thesis at Reed College, from which he graduated in June 1951. The thesis was first published as a book in 1979, in an edition from Grey Fox Press of Bolinas, California; a second edition, with a new foreword and afterword, followed in 2007 from Shoemaker & Hoard and has subsequently appeared in additional printings from Counterpoint Press. Snyder's source for the first selection that appears herein, "The Myth," was Henry Moody's retelling of the original Haida narrative, published by John R. Swanton in *Haida Myths and Texts: Skidegate Dialect* (*Bureau of American Ethnology, Bulletin 29*, 1905); "I have changed Indian names throughout this study, from phonetic spelling to their nearest English equivalents," Snyder notes. Snyder's endnotes have been included among the present volume's regular Notes. The text of *He Who Hunted Birds in His Father's Village* in the present volume is that of the most recent Counterpoint printing, supplied in electronic form in July 2023.

From *The Real Work: Interviews & Talks, 1964–1979*. The book was first published by New Directions on July 30, 1980; it gathered Snyder's significantly revised versions of his interviews and talks of the previous fifteen years, with additional commentary by Wm. Scott McLean. Three items from the book are included here: "The Real Work," first published as "An Interview With Gary Snyder" (*Ohio Review*, Fall 1977); "The East West Interview," first published, in three parts, as "The Original Mind of Gary Snyder" (*East West Journal*, June, July, and August 1977); and "Poetry, Community, & Climax," first published under the same title (*Field*, Spring 1979). McLean's additional commentary has been omitted. The text of these selections from *The Real Work* in the present volume is that of the undated latest printing of the original New Directions edition of 1980.

From *Passage Through India*. *Passage Through India* recounts a journey Snyder made with his wife, Joanne Kyger, from Japan to India and back, from December 1961 to May 1962; it began as an extended letter to Snyder's sister, Thea Snyder Lowry, and bears a dedication to her. First published by Grey Fox Press in San Francisco on March 1, 1984—with a 1983 copyright date—the book contains a corrected, revised, and extended text of "Now India," which appeared in the Spring 1972 issue of *Caterpillar*.

A second edition of the work, expanded with a new preface and illustrated with Snyder's original photographs, was published by Shoemaker & Hoard in June 2007 and subsequently printed by Counterpoint Press. The text of the selections from *Passage Through India* included in the present volume is that of the most recent Counterpoint printing, supplied in electronic form in July 2023.

From *The Practice of the Wild: Essays*. The book was first published by North Point Press in San Francisco in September 1990 and has subsequently appeared in two new editions from Counterpoint Press, in 2010 and 2020. Of the eight items from the book that have been selected for inclusion here, four are known to have been printed before September 1990, as described below:

The Etiquette of Freedom. *Sierra*, September/October 1989.
Good, Wild, Sacred. *Resurgence*, May–June 1983 (as "Wild, Sacred, Good Land"); *CoEvolution Quarterly*, Fall 1983; *The Schumacher Lectures, Volume Two* (London: Anthony Blond, 1984); *Good, Wild, Sacred* (Hereford: Five Seasons Press, 1984); *Ten Years of CoEvolution Quarterly*, Art Kleiner & Stewart Brand, eds. (San Francisco: North Point Press, 1986). Originally presented in Bristol, England, in October 1982, as the 1982 E. F. Schumacher Lecture.
On the Path, Off the Trail. *Antaeus*, Autumn 1989.
Grace. *CoEvolution Quarterly*, Fall 1984.

The essay "Grace," originally published separately, became a section of the longer essay "Survival and Sacrament" in *The Practice of the Wild*; it appears separately in the present volume, without the rest of "Survival and Sacrament." The text of all selections from *The Practice of the Wild* is that of the Counterpoint edition of 2020 in its most recent printing, supplied in electronic form in July 2023.

From *A Place in Space: Ethics, Aesthetics, Watersheds (New and Selected Prose)*. The book was first published by Counterpoint Press in September 1995 and has since appeared in further printings. Of the seven items in the book selected for inclusion here, five are known to have been published in earlier form, as listed below:

Smokey the Bear Sutra. *Smokey the Bear Sutra* (San Francisco: The Author, 1969); commentary from *Working the Woods, Working the Sea*, Finn Wilcox and Jeremiah Gorsline, eds. (Port Townsend, WA: Empty Bowl Press, 1986).

Four Changes, with a Postscript. *Turtle Island* (New York: New Directions, 1974); postscript first published in *A Place in Space*.

"Energy Is Eternal Delight." *Turtle Island* (New York: New Directions, 1974).

The Porous World. Combines "Crawling" (*Tree Rings*, Summer 1992) and "Living in the Open" (*Tree Rings*, Winter 1992).

Coming into the Watershed. *San Francisco Examiner*, March 1–2, 1992; *Coming into the Watershed* (Sacramento: Center for California Studies, CSU Sacramento, [c. 1992]); *Wild Earth*, Special Issue, 1993; *Wild California*, Winter 1993; *Chicago Review*, Winter 1993.

The texts of these items from *A Place in Space* have been taken from the most recent Counterpoint printing of the 1995 first edition, supplied in electronic form in July 2023.

The Paris Review Interview. On October 26, 1992, Snyder appeared in conversation with Eliot Weinberger at the Unterberg Poetry Center of the 92nd Street Y in New York. A revised version of this conversation was later published in the Winter 1996 *Paris Review*, as No. 74 in their "Art of Poetry" series. The text of "*The Paris Review* Interview" in the present volume is that of the Winter 1996 *Paris Review*.

From *Back on the Fire: Essays*. The book was first published by Shoemaker & Hoard in Washington, D.C., on February 20, 2007, and has since appeared in additional printings from Counterpoint Press. The following is a list of the original periodical and book appearances of those items from *Back on the Fire* selected for inclusion here:

The Ark of the Sierra. *Tree Rings*, Spring 1997.

Ecology, Literature and the New World Disorder. *ISLE: Interdisciplinary Studies in Literature and the Environment*, Winter 2004.

Writers and the War Against Nature. *Kyoto Journal*, Winter 2006.

Entering the Fiftieth Millennium. *The Gary Snyder Reader: Prose, Poetry, and Translations, 1952–1998* (Washington, D.C.: Counterpoint, 1999).

Lifetimes with Fire. *The Wildfire Reader: A Century of Failed Forest Policy*, ed. George Wuerthner, (Washington, D.C.: Island Press, 2006).

Regarding "Smokey the Bear Sutra." *Smokey the Bear Sutra* (San Francisco: The Author, 1969); prefatory text first published in *Back on the Fire*.

The text of these selections from *Back on the Fire* in the present volume is that of the most recent Counterpoint printing, supplied in electronic form in July 2023.

From *Tamalpais Walking: Poetry, History, and Prints*. The book was first published by Heyday Books in Berkeley in April 2009, in an edition illustrated with Tom Killion's multiblock color prints. The text of "Underfoot Earth Turns" in the present volume, selected from the book, has been taken from the most recent printing of the first edition, supplied by Heyday Books in electronic form in April 2024. One parenthetical cross-reference in the original text—"(see pp. 28–31 of this volume)," referring to a passage from Snyder's poem "Mountains and Rivers Without End" not included here—has been cut from the present text, at page 504, line 18.

The Great Clod: Notes and Memoirs on Nature and History in East Asia. First published by Counterpoint Press on May 10, 2016, *The Great Clod* had an unusually long gestation. By the late 1970s or thereabouts, Snyder began to envision and work on what he referred to as "The China Book." His essays "'Wild' in China," "Ink and Charcoal," and "Walls Within Walls"—three of the eight chapters ultimately included in *The Great Clod*—all appeared in *CoEvolution Quarterly* (in Fall 1978, Winter 1981, and Spring 1983, respectively). Even earlier, in 1972, he had tried unsuccessfully to write about environmental issues on Hokkaido for David Brower of the Earth Island Institute, who had sent him to Japan with a photographer for that purpose; "Summer in Hokkaido," first published in *The Great Clod*, belatedly fulfills this original assignment. Another chapter in the book, "Wolf-Hair Brush," was first published in *The Gary Snyder Reader* in 1999, where it appears as a selection from "*The Great Clod* Project" under the title "The Brush." The remaining sections of the book are believed to have been published for the first time in 2016.

The text of *The Great Clod* in the present volume is that of the Counterpoint first edition of 2016 in its most recent printing, supplied in electronic form in July 2023.

Uncollected Essays. This volume concludes with two items not included in Snyder's individual prose books. "Walking the Great Ridge Ōmine on the Womb-Diamond Trail" was first published on December 24, 1993, in the *Kyoto Journal*, and subsequently in *The Gary Snyder Reader: Prose, Poetry, and Translations, 1952–1998* (Washington, D.C.: Counterpoint, 1999); the latter collection, in its most recent Counterpoint printing, has provided the text in the present volume. "Turn Off the Calculating Mind!", which adapts and revises parts of *The Etiquette of Freedom: Gary Snyder, Jim Harrison, and the Practice of the Wild*, edited by Paul Ebenkamp (Counterpoint, 2010), first appeared in the March 25, 2024, *Alta Journal*, from which the text in the present volume has been taken.

This volume presents the texts of the original printings chosen for inclusion here, but it does not attempt to reproduce features of their typographic design. The texts are reprinted without change, except for the emendations noted above and the correction of typographical errors. Spelling, punctuation, and capitalization are often expressive features, and they are not altered, even when inconsistent or irregular. The following is a list of typographical errors corrected, cited by page and line number: 26.25, fall; 45.7, is being; 193.4, Osesshin; 194.34, *Time-Picayune*; 195.30, Peoples'; 246.31, or Bellingham; 259.39, *Osytropus*; 290.40, has long; 295.8, quagg; 301.31, three to; 305.15, is a; 442.5, Carole was; 453.4, you part; 454.22, the "the; 483.11, are a several; 492.20, Colombia; 506.10, others? My; 511.16, "to way"; 528.16, Kwan-chih; 529.27, Anderson; 541.3, Rock; 544.7, were the; 547.16–17, alterimage; 547.37, fermented; 551.18, liquidambers; 553.16, Hstian; 576.5, broach; 578.16, Keichow; 578.19, liquidamber; 579.2, Yunan; 579.18–19, Peoples'; 582.28, has having; 592.29, boddhisattvas; 593.23, Diatokuji; 597.2, summit, the.

Notes

In the notes below, the reference numbers denote page and line of this volume (the line count includes headings but not blank lines). For further information on Snyder's life and works, and references to other studies, see Bert Almon, *Gary Snyder* (Boise: Boise State University Press, 1979); David Stephen Calonne, ed., *Conversations with Gary Snyder* (Jackson: University Press of Mississippi, 2017); Mark Gonnerman, ed., *A Sense of the Whole: Reading Gary Snyder's "Mountains and Rivers Without End"* (Berkeley: Counterpoint, 2015); Timothy Gray, *Gary Snyder and the Pacific Rim: Creating Countercultural Community* (Iowa City: University of Iowa Press, 2006); Jon Halper, ed., *Gary Snyder: Dimensions of a Life* (San Francisco: Sierra Club, 1991); Anthony Hunt, *Genesis, Structure, and Meaning in Gary Snyder's "Mountains and Rivers Without End"* (Reno: University of Nevada Press, 2004); Howard McCord, *Some Notes to Gary Snyder's "Myths & Texts"* (Berkeley: Sand Dollar, 1971); Katherine McNeil, comp., *Gary Snyder: A Bibliography* (New York: Phoenix Bookshop, 1983); Bill Morgan, ed., *The Selected Letters of Allen Ginsberg and Gary Snyder* (Berkeley: Counterpoint, 2009); Patrick D. Murphy, ed., *Critical Essays on Gary Snyder* (Boston: G. K. Hall, 1991); Patrick D. Murphy, *A Place for Wayfaring: The Poetry and Prose of Gary Snyder* (Corvallis: Oregon State University Press, 2000); Bob Steuding, *Gary Snyder* (Boston: Twayne, 1976); John Suiter, *Poets on the Peaks: Gary Snyder, Philip Whalen, & Jack Kerouac in the North Cascades* (Washington, D.C.: Counterpoint, 2002); Chad Wriglesworth, ed., *Distant Neighbors: Selected Letters of Wendell Berry and Gary Snyder* (Berkeley: Counterpoint, 2014).

From EARTH HOUSE HOLD

4.9 Hui Nêng] Also known as Dajian Huineng (638–713), author of the *Platform Sutra of the Sixth Patriarch*.

5.14 shoji] In traditional Japanese architecture, doors or windows made of translucent paper over a frame.

5.16 yoga-system of Patanjali] See the Sanskrit *Yoga Sutras of Patañjali* (c. 400 CE?), a foundational compilation of writings on the philosophy and practice of yoga.

6.6 Jeffers] American poet Robinson Jeffers (1887–1962).

6.12–13 *"Were it not for Kuan Chung . . . left side"*] From the *Analects* of Confucius (c. 551–c. 479 BCE); Kuan Chung (Guan Zhong, c. 720–645 BCE), chancellor of the state of Qi, is credited with holding off barbarian invasion.

6.14–17 A man should stir . . . Lun Yü] From the *Analects* (*Lun Yü*) of Confucius.

6.21–22 "By God . . . worth a tord."] From the prologue to "The Tale of Melibee" in Chaucer's *Canterbury Tales* (c. 1387–1400).

7.3 zoris] Traditional Japanese sandals, akin to flip-flops.

8.2–5 "Is this real . . . Haida song] See the "Pawnee War-Song" collected by Daniel Garrison Brinton in *Essays of an Americanist* (1890).

9.11 a haiga] A traditional Japanese style of painting, often accompanied by haiku poems.

9.12 Om Mani Padme Hum] A common Sanskrit mantra, often written on prayer flags.

9.13 zenga] A Zen Buddhist painting or calligraphic work, in ink.

9.18 SCREE] Small, loose stones covering a mountain slope.

10.19 yuga] In Hinduism, an era or age of time.

11.12 Cratershan] Crater Mountain, in the North Cascades of Washington state (borrowing *shan*, Chinese for *mountain*).

11.27–28 "If a Bodhisattva retains . . . Bodhisattva."] From the *Diamond Sutra*, a Mahayana Buddhist sutra written sometime in the second to fifth centuries.

12.1 Bosatsu] Japanese form of Bodhisattva, a person on the path to enlightenment.

12.7 *sabi*] Japanese: old and faded, having a weathered patina.

12.26 Diablo Dam] Hydroelectric dam on the Skagit River in Whatcom County, Washington.

13.10 Koma Kulshan] Native American name for Mt. Baker, in the northwest of Washington state.

13.17–18 Mr. Pulaski . . . the Pulaski Tool] Ed Pulaski (1866–1931), a ranger in the U.S. Forest Service, invented what is known as the Pulaski tool, combining features of axe and adze, around 1911.

13.19–20 "It is . . . sane enough."] The first line of Ezra Pound's poem "Sub Mare," first collected in *Ripostes* (1912).

NOTES 641

15.11–12 the water of Hokusai] Katsushika Hokusai (1760–1849), famous for his woodblock print *The Great Wave Off Kanagawa* (1831).

15.25 Phil Whalen] Whalen (1923–2002), like Snyder, graduated from Reed College in 1951 and presented his poetry at the 1955 Six Gallery reading, a major event of the San Francisco Renaissance. In 1973 he was ordained as a priest at the San Francisco Zen Center, eventually adopting the dharma name Zenshin Ryufu. His *Collected Poems* was published posthumously in 2007.

16.19–20 "because there are no . . . mountains"] From a poem by the Tang dynasty "Ancient Recluse," T'ai-Shang ying-che: "Somehow I ended up beneath pines / sleeping in comfort on boulders / there aren't any calendars in the mountains / winter ends but who counts the years."

16.27 SX aerial] A simplex antenna used for two-way radio communication.

17.12 LINGAMS] Pillar-like or phallic symbols of the Hindu god Shiva, representing his generative and destructive power.

17.25 the Huang Po doctrine of Universal Mind] See the *Ch'uan-hsin Fa-yao* (*Essentials of Mind Transmission*) by Huangbo Xiyun (Huang Po, d. 850).

19.6–9 Blake . . . his caverns.] See *The Marriage of Heaven and Hell* (1793).

21.11–12 Legalistic rule . . . Wang An-shih] The emergence of Legalism or the *Fajia* during the Qin dynasty, 221–206 BCE, is believed to have fostered the development of Chinese empire. Wang Anshi (1021–1086), a Song dynasty politician and poet, was influenced by these earlier reforms.

21.19–22 "For in this period . . . the artery."] From William Blake's epic *Milton* (1804–10), plate 28.

21.25–26 Prajña girl statue from Java] The Prajñāpāramitā of Java, a thirteenth-century depiction of the bodhisattva known as the "Great Mother," now in the National Museum of Indonesia.

24.13 tokonomas] In Japanese domestic architecture, reception-room alcoves in which items for aesthetic contemplation, such as flower arrangements or picture scrolls, are displayed.

25.4–21 Lawrence . . . Only that."] All of these quotations are from D. H. Lawrence's novel, first published in 1922.

25.27 Awaji Isle—jokes about Genji] Genji, the principal character in Murasaki Shikibu's early eleventh-century novel *The Tale of Genji*, composes a poem about Awaji as he passes by the island.

26.13 Fêng Kuan] Also known as Bukan (fl. ninth century), head priest at Kokusei-ji (Guoqing Temple, in what is now Zhejiang Province, China) and teacher of the poet Hanshan.

26.16 Dengyo Daishi] Posthumous honorary name of Saichō (767–822), a Japanese Buddhist monk credited with bringing Tiantai Buddhism to Japan; he founded a temple on Mt. Hiei near Kyoto, and is buried there.

26.20 Kwannon] Also known as Kannon or Guanyin, a bodhisattva of compassion and mercy revered throughout East Asia.

26.25 Cryptomeria] A genus including the single species *Cryptomeria japonica*, also known as Japanese cedar or sugi.

26.28 Uguisu] *Horonis diphone*, the Japanese bush warbler.

28.12 Chao-chou] Also known as Zhaoxhou Congshen (778–897), a long-lived Zen Buddhist master.

28.18 Manjusri] In Mahāyāna Buddhism, the bodhisattva of transcendent wisdom.

28.28 bindles] Bags or sacks tied to a stick, for carrying.

28.30 Han Shan] Also spelled Hanshan, a Chinese Buddhist monk and poet of the ninth century.

29.15–20 "wisdom and berries . . . freedom."] See Emerson's journal *G* for September 12, 1841, published posthumously in his *Journals & Miscellaneous Notebooks*, vol. 8 (1970).

30.17 Indra's net] In Hinduism, a weapon belonging to the king of divine beings; used in Buddhist philosophy as a metaphor for the interconnectedness of all phenomena.

31.16 Daitoku-ji] A Rinzai Zen Buddhist temple in Kyoto, Japan, where Snyder studied in 1959–60.

31.27 Oda Rōshi] Oda Sessō Rōshi (1901–1966), Snyder's Zen teacher at Daitoku-ji.

32.5 jikatabi] Traditional Japanese two-toed, bootlike footwear.

32.12 geta clogs] Traditional Japanese sandal-like clogs, with flat wooden bases.

33.9 MU] A reference to the first koan in the *Gateless Barrier* or *Gateless Gate*, an early thirteenth-century collection of Zen koans compiled by Wumen Huikai (1183–1260).

33.11 Tōdai-ji's "Water-gathering" ceremony] An annual spring festival at Tōdai-ji temple in Nara, Japan.

34.10 Hideyoshi's tomb] Toyotomi Hideyoshi (1537–1598), a feudal lord and imperial advisor considered one of the unifiers of Japan, is buried in the Higashimaya section of Kyoto.

34.21 Miura Rōshi] Miura Isshu (1903–1978), Snyder's first teacher at Rinko-in.

37.21–22 *Prajña-paramita-hridaya Sutra*] The *Heart Sutra*, the earliest text of which has been dated to 661 CE.

42.3–4 *Mumonkan* or *Hekiganroku*] Collections of koans: *The Gateless Barrier* (see note 33.9) and *The Blue Cliff Record*, the latter expanded by Yuanwu Kequin (1063–1135) from an original compilation of 1125.

42.17 hinoki] *Chamaecyparis obtuse* or Japanese cypress, a tree known for its rot-resistant timber.

48.2–4 "It will be a revival . . . MORGAN] See Morgan's *Ancient Society, or, Researches in the Lines of Human Progress from Savagery, through Barbarism to Civilization* (1877).

48.8 Shaivite] A branch of Hinduism organized around the worship of Shiva.

49.16 kalpa] An immense measure of time, spanning a complete cosmic cycle.

49.27 Lao-tzu . . . Yellow Turban revolt] The semilegendary Lao-tzu, also spelled *Laozi* (fl. sixth–seventh centuries BCE), was the author of the foundational *Tao Te Ching*. Leaders of the Yellow Turban revolt, a peasant uprising that began in 184 CE, were associated with Taoist secret societies.

52.33 D. T. Suzuki's books] Suzuki (1870–1966) was the author of *Essays in Zen Buddhism: First Series* (1927), *Essays in Zen Buddhism: Second Series* (1933), *Essays in Zen Buddhism: Third Series* (1934), *Zen and Japanese Culture* (1959), and other books, including translations of Buddhist texts.

53.2 Vajrayana] Also known as tantric or esoteric Buddhism, a branch of Buddhism most commonly practiced in Bhutan, Mongolia, Nepal, and Tibet.

53.17–18 "When Adam . . . gentleman?"] A medieval couplet sometimes attributed to John Ball (c. 1338–1381), an English priest who was imprisoned for his sermons during the peasant revolt of 1381.

54.5–9 They "confounded . . . time and place."] See Norman Cohn, *The Pursuit of the Millennium* (1957), chapter 8 ("An Elite of Amoral Supermen, 2").

56.13–14 The chorus . . . live again."] See "Songs of the Comanche" in James Mooney's *The Ghost-Dance Religion and the Sioux Outbreak of 1890* (1896), where the song is described as a Comanche adaptation of an Arapaho song.

56.15–17 "Passage to more . . . like those?"] From the opening of section 9 of Walt Whitman's "Passage to India," first collected in *Passage to India* (1871).

60.12–14 Breuil . . . to be fertile."] Henri Breuil (1877–1961), French archaeologist and anthropologist, as quoted in S. Giedion, *The Eternal Present*, vol. 1: *The Beginnings of Art* (1962).

60.14–20 A Haida . . . thinking of it.] See John R. Swanton, "Haida Texts and Myths," *Bureau of American Ethnology, Bulletin 29* (1905).

60.29–61.9 Lévi-Strauss quotes . . . dugouts underground."] See Lévi-Strauss, *The Savage Mind* (1966; originally published in 1962 as *La Pensée Sauvage*), and J. R. Swanton, "Social and Religious Beliefs of the Chickasaw Indians," *44th Annual Report, Bureau of American Ethnology, 1926–27* (1928).

61.22 queynt] Middle English: vulva.

61.33–34 A recent article by Lynn White] See Lynn White Jr., "The Historic Roots of Our Ecologic Crisis," *Science*, March 10, 1967.

61.38–62.4 "The Deivill . . . dealing with us."] See Robert Pitcairn's *Criminal Trials and Other Proceedings before the High Court of Justiciary in Scotland*, vol. 3 (1833), in which the quotation is attributed to Jonet Watson of Dalkeith, Scotland, in 1661.

62.11–17 An Arapaho dancer . . . as I fly."] See "Songs of the Arapaho" in James Mooney's *Ghost-Dance Religion and the Sioux Outbreak of 1890* (1896).

63.36 vīna] Also spelled *veena*, an ancient stringed musical instrument.

63.37–64.3 "She is again . . . Supreme Power."] See chapter 1 ("Vâk or the Word") of *The Garden of Letters: Studies in the Mantra-shâstra* (1922) by Sir John Woodroffe.

64.7 BusTon] Butön Rinchen Drub (1290–1364), Tibetan Buddhist leader and author of *History of Buddhism in India and Tibet* (1322), translated into English beginning in 1931.

64.16–18 Koptos . . . god Min] Koptos, now known as Qift, was a city in upper Egypt, and Min an Egyptian fertility god of the predynastic era, c. 4000–3000 BCE.

64.19 Magdalenian] Of the last part of the Paleolithic era, c. 15,000–10,000 BCE.

64.24–34 James Mooney . . . perpetuated."] See *The Ghost-Dance Religion and the Sioux Outbreak of 1890* (1896).

64.39–65.2 "Reverence to Her . . . Candī says."] See note 63.37–64.3.

65.4–6 *The clouds . . . Haida*] See John R. Swanton, "Haida Texts and Myths," *Bureau of American Ethnology, Bulletin 29* (1905).

65.17–18 "on beauty bare,"] See Edna St. Vincent Millay's 1913 sonnet "Euclid alone has looked on Beauty bare."

65.22–24 Stanley Diamond . . . limits of the primitive."] See Diamond's essay "The Search for the Primitive" in Ashley Montagu, ed., *The Concept of the Primitive* (1968).

NOTES 645

66.3–6 A poem . . . I cannot measure."] For a translation of the complete poem by Tsangyang Gyatso (1683–c. 1706), see chapter 11 ("Christian Missionaries in Lhasa") of *The Religion of Tibet* (1931), by Sir Charles Bell.

66.17–19 Isobel Gowdie's . . . well-water"] The case of Isobel Gowdie (1632–1662), who confessed to witchcraft, is recorded in Robert Pitcairn's *Ancient Criminal Trials in Scotland* (1833).

66.28–29 H. C. Conklin's . . . plant-knowledge] Conklin (1926–2016) was the author of *The Relation of Hanunoo Culture to the Plant World* (1955), a pioneering ethnobotanical study.

67.16 Arjuna] A warrior prince in the *Mahābhārata* (c. third century BCE– fourth century CE), friend and companion of the god Krishna.

67.18 Tsong-kha-pa] Also known as Losang Drakpa (c. 1357–1419), a Tibetan monk and author of numerous philosophical works.

68.7–14 "We see that the successive . . . D'Arcy Thompson] See Thompson's *On Growth and Form* (1917), chapter 6 ("The Equiangular Spiral").

70.39–71.1 snake-head "jabisen" . . . "shamisen."] Traditional three-stringed musical instruments, akin to the banjo.

71.12 *Tabu*] *Machilus thunbergia*, also known as the Japanese bay tree.

73.39 sawara] The mature form of a type of mackerel, *Scomberomorus niphonius*.

74.12 shochu] A Japanese alcoholic beverage, usually distilled from barley, rice, or sweet potatoes.

74.38 tai] *Pagarus major*, Red Seabream.

75.36 Harijan] Literally "children of God," a term used by Narsinh Mehta (1409–1488) to describe worshippers of Krishna; much later applied to the Dalits or "untouchable" caste in India.

76.5–6 *Eighth Moon . . . paintings*)] In some of his early works, Snyder marked time on a 40,000-year scale, "reckoning roughly from the earliest cave paintings." *Eighth Moon, 40067,* is August 1967.

From HE WHO HUNTED BIRDS IN HIS FATHER'S VILLAGE

79.2 HE WHO HUNTED BIRDS] Snyder reprints the text of the myth from John Swanton and Henry Moody, "Haida Texts and Myths," *Bureau of American Ethnology 29* (1905).

79.4–5 He wore two . . . the other.] As was once customary with the sons of chiefs. (Swanton's note.)

79.7 geese] Canada geese. (Swanton's note.)

79.30 *tcal*] Plants with edible roots growing around the mouths of creeks. (Swanton's note.)

80.40 bones] Such as were used to make awls and gimlets out of. (Swanton's note.)

81.11 "Now brave man . . . looking at me] Supernatural beings are often said to be tickled by having someone merely look at them. (Swanton's note.)

82.12–13 something red] This is undoubtedly the pole held on the breast of supernatural-being-standing-and-moving, which rose in the middle of the Haida country and extended to the sky. (Swanton's note.)

82.26 a half-man] Master Hopper (*Lkienqa-ixon*), referred to in many other places throughout these stories. He was a one-legged supernatural being having one leg shorter than the other. Here he is represented as only a halfman. (Swanton's note.)

83.27 as a seagull.] That is, the man became a seagull. (Swanton's note.)

85.15 to Andrew Lang's . . . dismay] See Lang's *Myth, Ritual, and Religion* (1887).

85.21 as studied by Abram Kardiner] See *The Individual and His Society* (1939) and *The Psychological Frontiers of Society* (1945).

86.16–27 Mark Shorer . . . culture."] See Shorer's *William Blake* (1949). Snyder notes, "Perhaps Shorer's 'indispensable ingredient of all culture' is misquoting Malinowski's 'vital ingredient of all human civilization.'"

86.32–36 Robert Lowie . . . mystic aura.] See Lowie's *History of Ethnological Theory* (1937).

87.1–29 C. Kerenyi . . . in the germ.] See C. G. Jung and C. Kerenyi, *Essays on a Science of Mythology* (1949).

87.31–88.3 I. A. Richards . . . without aim.] See Richards's *Coleridge on the Imagination* (1934).

88.27–89.8 Kardiner's analysis . . . desertion by parents] See *The Psychological Frontiers of Society* (1945).

90.31–91.5 A magic-flight story . . . prematurely independent.] "Thus one might see the Haida Swan-Maiden myth," Snyder adds in a note, "as a projection of a male sense of inferiority to women, coupled with a distrust of the mother. Woman is portrayed as having supernatural attributes and the power to come and go at will. The hero's loss of the maiden is a projection of the childhood loss of mother; the reunion in the sky is a wish-fulfillment projection which proves unsatisfactory—leaving the hero no recourse but to become a seagull (infantile regression). Since there is no way of checking this against Haida child training, such interpretation is idle."

93.22–36   Campbell writes . . . nature's season.] See *The Hero with a Thousand Faces* (1949).

94.6–14   Frazer's description . . . part of his person.] See *The Golden Bough* (1890). Snyder notes, "Frazer's patronizing attitude toward preliterate peoples, which has annoyed many anthropologists, may be seen here."

94.15–24   Malinowski . . . verbal magic.] See Malinowski's essay "The Problem of Meaning in Primitive Languages," collected in C. K. Ogden and I. A. Richards, eds., *The Meaning of Meaning: A Study of the Influence of Language upon Thought and the Science of Symbolism* (1923).

94.27–31   Ernst Cassirer . . . *metaphorical thinking.*] See *Language and Myth* (1946).

95.3–17   A. L. Kroeber . . . only through speech.] See Kroeber's *Anthropology* (revised edition, 1949).

96.4–10   George Santayana . . . science and philosophy.] See *The Sense of Beauty* (1896).

97.3–16   T. S. Eliot's discussion . . . mythical method.] See Eliot's "'Ulysses,' Order and Myth," first published in *The Dial* in November 1923.

97.18–25   that of Philip Wheelwright . . . everything else.] See Wheelwright's essay "Poetry, Myth, and Reality," collected in Allen Tate, ed., *The Language of Poetry* (1942).

97.28–98.2   Viereck . . . poetry and verse.] See Viereck's essay "My Kind of Poetry" in the August 27, 1949, *Saturday Review*.

98.4–12   Graves claims . . . blood! blood!"] See *The White Goddess* (1948).

98.25–32   Campbell . . . personal despair] See *The Hero with a Thousand Faces* (1949).

100.19   "There digge!"] Ezra Pound uses this archaic phrasing on several occasions, as in his *Guide to Kulchur* (1938): "Hence the yarn that Frobenius looked at the two African pots and, observing their shapes and proportions, said: if you will go to a certain place and there digge you will find traces of a civilization with such and such characteristics."

From THE REAL WORK

104.24   *From Ritual to Romance*] A 1920 account by folklorist Jessie Weston (1850–1928) of the origins of Arthurian legends, cited by Eliot in his notes to *The Waste Land* (1922).

104.36 *Ding an sich*] The thing-in-itself.

105.12 *The Mabinogion*] A collection of Welsh prose narratives assembled in the twelfth to thirteenth centuries from prior oral traditions.

105.15 Olson] Charles Olson (1910–1970), American poet.

111.32 kiva] Among the Pueblo peoples of the American Southwest, a large, circular, underground room used for ceremonial purposes.

114.13 Wallace Stevens . . . parasite.] See Stevens's "Adagia," first collected in his 1957 *Opus Posthumous*: "The writer who is content to destroy is on a plane with the writer who is content to translate. Both are parasites."

118.24–25 Marshall McLuhan . . . campfire.] See McLuhan's books *The Gutenberg Galaxy* (1962), *Understanding Media* (1964), and *The Medium Is the Massage* (1967).

119.1–2 W. H. Auden . . . anything.] See Auden's elegy "In Memory of W. B. Yeats," first published in 1939: "For poetry makes nothing happen."

119.3–4 Ezra Pound . . . race.] See Pound's essay "Henry James," first published in the August 1918 *Little Review*.

119.15 batholith] Large igneous rock formations, originally part of Earth's crust.

119.31–33 Christopher Stone . . . Have Standing?"] See Christopher D. Stone, "Should Trees Have Standing?—Toward Legal Rights for Natural Objects," *Southern California Law Review* 45 (1972): 450–501.

122.4–5 Rosebud and Pine Ridge] Lakota Indian reservations in South Dakota.

122.27 CETA] The Comprehensive Employment and Training Act, a federal employment program through which many artists obtained work, signed into law in 1973 and repealed in 1981.

123.13 *The Four Quartets*] A collection of four long poems by T. S. Eliot (1888–1965), first published together in 1943.

123.17 "tender and junior Buddha."] From Whitman's poem "Passage to India," first collected in *Passage to India* in 1871.

125.20–21 What Allen Ginsberg has in Boulder] In 1974, with poet Anne Waldman, Ginsberg founded the Jack Kerouac School of Disembodied Poetics, a part of the Naropa Institute, now Naropa University.

127.6 Borges, for example, told me] See Paul Geneson, "Interview with Jorge Luis Borges," *Michigan Quarterly Review* 16 (1977): 243–55.

129.15 your poem, "The Real Work,"] First collected in *Turtle Island* (1974).

130.3–4 the poem . . . Maverick Bar,"] First collected in *Turtle Island* (1974).

131.13–14 You have said . . . interesting to me."] See "LSD and All That," a conversation between Snyder and Aelred Graham that took place on September 4, 1967, and subsequently appeared in Graham's *Conversations, Christian and Buddhist: Encounters in Japan* (1968).

131.20 sadhana] Spiritual practice aimed at achieving transcendence.

132.15 *Peter Orlovsky*] Orlovsky (1933–2010), an actor and poet, was Allen Ginsberg's partner; Snyder and his wife Joanne Kyger traveled with the couple in India in 1962.

136.8 satori] Sudden enlightenment.

137.4 *teisho*] A Zen master's formal talk about a koan or other Zen text; literally, "presentation of the shout."

137.15–17 As William Butler Yeats . . . my veins] From Yeats's poem "The Fascination of What's Difficult," first collected in *The Green Helmet and Other Poems* (1912).

139.22 *bhakta*] One who practices *bhakti*, or religious devotion.

139.23 *nirmanakaya*] The physically or historically manifest body of the Buddha.

141.14 *sangha*] Community, association.

141.29 a book . . . Kline and Jonas] See David Jonas and Doris Kline, *Man-Child: A Study of the Infantilization of Man* (1970).

145.24 samadhi] Meditative absorption.

145.29–30 William Laughlin . . . children.] See William S. Laughlin, "Hunting: An Integrating Biobehavior System and Its Evolutionary Importance," in *Man the Hunter* (1968), edited by Richard B. Lee and Irven DeVore.

150.38–151.1 Some time ago you said . . . someplace else."] From a 1965 interview with Snyder on the National Education Television program *Poetry U.S.A.*

153.5–6 In *Earth House Hold* . . . over."] See page 51, lines 36–38, in the present volume.

153.35 Eugene Odum] Odum (1913–2002) was the author of *Fundamentals of Ecology* (1953) and pioneering works on ecosystems and energy.

155.6–7 An essay in *Turtle Island* . . . dig in."] See page 368, lines 17–18, in the present volume.

156.14 "Front Lines"] First collected in *Turtle Island* (1974).

159.5 "California Water Plan"] First published in *Clear Creek* in November 1971.

160.12–16 In *Earth House Hold* . . . enlightened return."] See the journal "Japan First Time Around" on page 31 in the present volume.

161.34–35 Robert Sund . . . one book out] Sund (1929–2001) published *Bunch Grass* in 1969.

162.19–21 Lillian Robinson . . . a little magazine] Robinson (1941–2006) published "In the Night Kitchen" in the May 1976 *Beefsteak Bigonia*.

163.33–34 the Trilateral Commission] An international NGO founded in 1973 with the goal of fostering good relations among Europe, Japan, and North America; often claimed by conspiracy theorists as an agent of clandestine world government.

173.7 fellaheen] A peasant or agricultural worker, particularly in Arab countries.

179.27–28 *Howl* became . . . Pocket Poets series] *Howl and Other Poems*, published in the fall of 1956, was the fourth title in the affordable, paperback Pocket Poets series from City Lights Books, inaugurated by Lawrence Ferlinghetti in August 1955 with his own book *Pictures of the Gone World*.

186.5 Lilith Abye] In folk etymology, *lullaby* comes from the Hebrew "Lilith Abi," meaning "Lilith, begone."

188.30–31 Peach blossoms . . . nature white.] These lines, generally attributed to an unknown Zen master, respond to one of the koans in the *Mumonkan* or *Gateless Gate*, in which Zhaozhou Congshen (778–897) meets a hermit, and then later another, responding in different ways to their identical greetings.

From PASSAGE THROUGH INDIA

193.4 Rohatsu Sesshin] A meditation retreat on the occasion of Bodhi Day or Rohatsu, the anniversary of Siddhartha Gautama's enlightenment.

194.25 Krishnamurti] Jiddu Krishnamurti (1895–1986), Indian writer, philosopher, and public speaker.

195.36 Kowloon (nine dragons)] The name Kowloon refers to nine dragons—the eight large peaks around the city, and the child emperor Zhao Bing (1272–1279).

198.24 Chiang Kai-shek] Chiang (1887–1975) led the Republic of China from 1928 to 1949; after his defeat by Communist forces, he resumed this position in exile, on Taiwan.

200.20 Frederick Spiegelberg] Spiegelberg (1897–1994) was a professor of religion at Stanford from 1941 to 1962; with Haridas Chaudhuri, he edited

The Integral Philosophy of Sri Aurobindo: A Commemorative Symposium (1960).

200.27 Nestorian Xtianity] Christian belief influenced by the teachings of Nestorius (d. c. 450 CE), patriarch of Constantinople, who argued heretically that Jesus Christ the man and Jesus Christ the son of God were not completely identical.

200.28 Catharites] Heretical, dualist Christian sect active in southern Europe until 1350, when it was destroyed by the Inquisition.

202.11 godown] Warehouse.

204.19 *puri*] Also spelled *poori*, deep-fried wheat bread.

204.25–26 Thuggee] An Indian organized crime fraternity, known for highway robbery and murder.

205.20 gendarmes] In mountaineering, rock pinnacles on a ridge.

210.6 *tankas*] Also spelled *thangkas*, temple banners or hanging scrolls.

From THE PRACTICE OF THE WILD

217.21–24 Thoreau says . . . preservation of the world,"] See "Walking," first presented as a lecture on April 23, 1851, and published posthumously in the *Atlantic Monthly* in June 1862.

218.27 Jim Kari (1982; 1985)] Kari, James. *Dena'ina Elnena, Tanaina Country*. Fairbanks: University of Alaska Native Languages Center, 1982; *Native Place Names in Alaska: Trends in Policy and Research*. Montreal: McGill University Symposium on Indigenous Names in the North, 1985.

220.12 Thoreau's "awful ferity"] See note 217.21–24.

220.22 "Wild and wanton . . . 1614] See Daniel Duke, *The Mystery of Selfedeceiuing; or, a Discourse and Discouery of the Deceitfulnesse of Mans Heart* (1614).

220.24–25 "Warble his native . . . Milton] See Milton's "L'Allegro," first collected in his 1645 *Poems*.

222.9–10 John Milton . . . sweets."] See *Paradise Lost*, V.294.

224.2 (Todorov, 1985, 134)] Todorov, Tzvetan. *The Conquest of America*. New York: Harper & Row, 1985.

224.11–12 Ishi the Yahi] Ishi (c. 1861–1961), last of the Yahi people of what is now California, whose life is recounted in Theodora Kroeber's *Ishi in Two Worlds* (1961).

226.1–2 "What's that dark . . . otter?"] Adapted from "Das Valdez," a comic song written by Snyder's friend Greg Keeler, a Montana poet and professor, following the 1989 *Exxon Valdez* environmental disaster.

228.34–35 "nasty, brutish, and short"] See Thomas Hobbes's *Leviathan* (1651).

229.11 "nature red in tooth and claw"] See *In Memoriam A.H.H.* (1850) by Alfred, Lord Tennyson (1809–1892).

229.38 Dōgen] Dōgen Zenji (1200–1253), Japanese Buddhist monk, philosopher, and poet.

231.18–25 Xie Lingyun . . . Hsieh's time] Hsieh Ling-yun or Xie Lingyun (385–433), Chinese "mountain and stream" landscape poet.

232.16–17 "To have nothing . . . Lord Buckley says] From Buckley's monologue "Cabenza de Gasca—The Gasser," included on his 1956 album *Euphoria, Volume II*.

233.16–20 Florence Edenshan . . . stay home."] See Margaret B. Blackman, *During My Time: Florence Edenshaw Davidson, a Haida Woman* (1982).

236.22–23 "ceremonial time" . . . phrase] See John Hanson Mitchell's *Ceremonial Time: Fifteen Thousand Years on One Square Mile* (1984).

237.25 (See Jim Dodge, 1981).] Dodge, Jim. "Living by Life." *CoEvolution Quarterly*, Winter 1981.

240.12 (Netting, 1976)] Netting, R. "What Alpine Peasants Have in Common: Observations on Communal Tenure in a Swiss Village." *Human Ecology*, 1976.

241.13 Karl Polanyi (1975)] Polanyi, Karl. *The Great Transformation*. New York Octagon Books, 1975.

241.29 *tanbo*] Japanese: rice field.

242.37 "sagebrush rebellion"] A political movement in the western United States that emerged in the wake of the 1976 Federal Land Policy and Management Act; its proponents sought greater local control over federal lands, particularly for purposes of mining, ranching, and timber harvesting.

243.11–12 (Thirgood, 1981)] Thirgood, J. V. *Man and the Mediterranean Forest: A History of Resource Depletion*. New York: Academic Press, 1981.

243.33–34 Ivan Illich . . . against subsistence."] See Illich's *Shadow Work* (1981).

244.4–5 (Hardin and Baden, 1977)] Hardin, Garrett, and John Baden. *Managing the Commons*. San Francisco: W. H. Freeman, 1977.

244.10 (Cox, 1985)] Cox, Susan Jane Buck. "No Tragedy in the Commons." *Environmental Ethics*, Spring 1995.

245.24 *The Region . . .* CAFARD] See "The Surre(gion)alist Manifesto," *Mesechabe*, Autumn 1989.

245.29 (Kroeber, 1947)] Kroeber, A. L. *Cultural and Natural Areas of Native North America*. Berkeley: University of California Press, 1947.

246.9 (Cafard, 1989)] See note 245.24.

246.40 Gary Holthaus] Holthaus (1932–2022), longtime director of the Alaska Humanities Forum, was the author of *Circling Back* (1984), *Wide Skies: Finding a Home in the West* (1997), *Learning Native Wisdom: What Traditional Culture Teaches Us about Subsistence, Sustainability, and Spirituality* (2008), and other books.

248.35 (Snyder, 1974)] Snyder, Gary. *Turtle Island*. New York: New Directions, 1974.

248.38–39 "The State . . . rivers remain."] From a poem by Du Fu (Tu Fu, 712–770) written in 755, sometimes translated as "Spring View."

251.8 (Berg and others, 1989)] Berg, Peter, et al. *A Green City Program for San Francisco Bay Area Cities and Towns*. San Francisco: Planet Drum, 1989.

251.11 (*Raise the Stakes*, 1987)] *raise the Stakes*. Journal of the Planet Drum Foundation. San Francisco, CA, 94131.

251.21–24 As Jim Dodge says . . . it's successful."] See "Living by Life," *CoEvolution Quarterly*, Winter 1981.

251.34 (Cafard, 1989)] See note 245.24.

252.9 *nors*] Old English: northern parts.

252.31 cirque] A craterlike depression formed by glacial erosion, in mountainous regions.

253.10 EIR] Environmental Impact Report.

253.33–254.1 a mural . . . Lou Silva] Silva (b. 1951) painted the mural, titled *Cross Section*, in 1979; it was destroyed around 2017 to make way for new Berkeley student housing.

257.4 "Acres of Clams."] Also titled "Old Settler's Song," a folk song with lyrics by Francis D. Henry (1842–1893), written around 1874 and subsequently performed and recorded by Bing Crosby, Pete Seeger, and others.

267.32 *gatha*] Sanskrit: song, verse.

271.5 (Friedrich, 1970)] Friedrich, Paul. *Proto-Indo-European Trees*. Chicago: University of Chicago Press, 1970.

272.38 "proper study of mankind"] See the second epistle of *An Essay on Man* (1732–34), by Alexander Pope (1688–1744).

274.7–9 Wilhelm von Humboldt . . . brother Alexander] German philosopher Wilhelm von Humboldt (1767–1835) and his younger brother Alexander (1769–1859), a naturalist.

275.7 Whorfian] Associated with the ideas of American linguist Benjamin Lee Whorf (1897–1941) about the relationship between language and the world.

276.11–24 John Gumperz . . . p. 420).] Gumperz, John J. "Speech Variation and the Study of Indian Civilization." In *Language in Culture and Society*, ed. Dell Hymes. New York: Harper & Row, 1964.

279.38–280.7 Thoreau wrote . . . I have referred."] See note 217.21–24.

280.17 cosms] Worlds or universes.

287.18 Geoffrey Blainey (1976, 202)] Blainey, Geoffrey. *The Triumph of the Nomads*. Melbourne: Sun Books, 1976.

291.19 Thoreau . . . say beans"] See *Walden* (1854), chapter 7 ("The Bean-Field").

291.30 kitkitdizze] Miwok term for mountain misery (*Chamaebatia foliolosa*), an evergreen shrub endemic to the mountainous parts of California; Snyder borrowed the term for the name of his house.

292.38–39 Charles Doughty . . . Arabia Deserta] Doughty (1843–1926), an English poet and explorer, published *Travels in Arabia Deserta* (1888) about his time living with the Bedouins in the 1870s.

293.8 Zhuang-zi] Also spelled Zhuang Zhou (c. 369–c. 266 BCE), author of the *Zhuangzi*, a foundational work of Taoism.

294.23 kami . . . kukini] In Shintoism, *kami* include a wide variety of spirits, deities, and natural phenomena; Maidu *kukini* are guardian spirits inhabiting lakes, mountains, waterfalls, and sometimes animals.

296.4 Bodhi Day] Buddhist holiday, marked on December 8, celebrating Gautama Buddha's enlightenment, around 528 BCE.

299.5 (Grapard, 1982)] Grapard, Allan. "Flying Mountains and Walkers of Emptiness: Toward a Definition of Sacred Space in Japanese Religions." *History of Religions*, February 1982.

303.3 (Watson, 1971, 82)] Watson, Burton. *Chinese Lyricism: Shih Poetry from the Second to the Twelfth Century*. New York: Columbia University Press, 1971.

304.12–14 Blue mountains . . . walking.] From the *Sansui kyō* (*Mountains and Waters Sutra*, 1240) of Dōgen Zenji (1200–1253).

306.7–12 All beings . . . only on water.] See note 304.12–14.

306.24 "cliff-edge of life and death."] See *The Gateless Barrier* or *Gateless Gate* by Wumen Huikai (1183–1260).

306.30–307.5 Green mountain walks . . . some tea.] From Snyder's "Arctic Midnight Twilight," first collected in *Mountains and Rivers Without End* (1996).

308.26 "Hungry ghosts . . . blood] See note 304.12–14.

309.8 Izanagi] A creator deity in Japanese mythology.

309.31–33 D. H. Lawrence . . . one of the gods."] See chapter 2 of Lawrence's *Studies in Classic American Literature* (1923), in which he imitates the style of Benjamin Franklin.

311.24 (Kodera, 1980)] Kodera, Takashi James. *Dogen's Formative Years in China*. Boulder: Prajna Press, 1980.

311.31–32 (Gernet, 1962)] Gernet, Jacques. *Daily Life in China: On the Eve of the Mongol Invasion*. Stanford: Stanford University Press, 1962.

312.2 Tokugawa-era] Also known as the Edo period, spanning from 1603 to 1868.

312.12 James Hillman (1989, 169)] Hillman, James. *Blue Fire*. New York: Harper & Row, 1989.

314.24–25 Aldo Leopold's "think like a mountain"] See Leopold's essay "Thinking Like a Mountain" from *A Sand County Almanac* (1949).

315.14 froes] Also known as paling knives or shake axes, tools for splitting wood.

316.9 the Velde Committee hearings] Hearings held in Portland, Oregon, in June 1954 to investigate the political activities of three Reed College professors, Leonard Marsak, Stanley Moore, and Lloyd Reynolds; they were led by Illinois Republican Harold H. Velde, chairman of the House Un-American Activities Committee.

322.32 BLM] Bureau of Land Management.

323.34–35 (Robinson, 1988, 87)] Robinson, Gordon. *The Forest and the Trees: A Guide to Excellent Forestry*. Covelo, CA: Island Press, 1988.

324.7–8 (Waring and Franklin, 1979).] Waring, R. H., and Jerry Franklin. "Evergreen Coniferous Forests of the Pacific Northwest." *Science* 29, June 1979.

325.7 (Maser, 1989).] Maser, Chris. *Primeval Forest*. San Francisco: Sierra Club, 1989.

326.5 *latifundia*] Large, landed estates producing agricultural commodities for sale.

326.16 (Thirgood, 1981, 29)] Thirgood, J. V. *Man and the Mediterranean Forest: A History of Resource Depletion*. New York: Academic Press, 1981.

327.8 Chris Maser (1989, xviii)] Maser, Chris. *Primeval Forest*. San Francisco: Sierra Club, 1989.

327.30–35 San Francisco . . . own praise.] From Snyder's poem "Logging," first collected in *Myths & Texts* (1960).

329.33–38 A virgin . . . Climax.] From Snyder's poem "Toward Climax," first collected in *Turtle Island* (1974).

333.4 Han-shan and Shi-de] Also spelled *Hanshan* and *Shide*, Buddhist poets of the Tang dynasty, active in the ninth century.

334.1–2 Chris Maser . . . ancient forests."] See Maser's August 24, 1987, National Audubon Society convention speech, "Ancient Forests, Priceless Treasures," later collected in Michael Pilarski, ed., *Restoration Forestry: An International Guide to Sustainable Forestry Practices* (1994).

334.7 (Jackson, 1987, 78).] Jackson, Wes. *Altars of Unhewn Stone: Science and the Earth*. San Francisco: North Point, 1987.

336.2 (Richards and Tucker, 1988, 107).] Richards, John F., and Richard P. Tucker. *World Deforestation in the Twentieth Century*. Durham, NC: Duke University Press, 1988.

336.12–18 Forestry . . . over-ripe."] See note 329.33–38.

336.19 (Snyder, 1977)] Snyder, Gary. *The Old Ways*. San Francisco: City Lights, 1977.

338.14 *li*, or *versts*, or *yojana*] Ancient or traditional Chinese, Russian, and Southeast Asian units of distance.

340.14 Watson, 1968, 50–51] Watson, Burton (trans.). *The Complete Works of Chuang Tzu*. New York: Columbia University Press, 1968.

341.22 the movie *Tampopo*] A 1985 comedy written and directed by Juzo Hami (1933–1997) about the owner of a ramen shop.

342.4 Shakyuamuni's time] The Buddha, Siddhartha Gautama—also known as Shakyamuni or "sage of the Shakya clan"—is traditionally said to have lived from 563 to 483 BCE, but other dates in the sixth and fifth centuries BCE have been proposed.

345.16 (Gard, 1949; 1956)] Gard, Richard. *Buddhist Influences on the Political Thought and Institutions of India and Japan.* Phoenix Papers, no. 1. Claremont, 1949; *Buddhist Political Thought.* Bangkok: Mahamukta University, 1956.

348.29 *Boat in a Storm*, 1987] A booklet published to accompany an exhibition of Buddhist art at the Ring of Bone Zendo, near Snyder's home.

From A PLACE IN SPACE

356.11 the kali yuga] In Hindu cosmology, one of the four world ages, full of conflict; the present fallen age.

357.8 vajra] An Indo-Tibetan ritual tool believed to have the force of lightning and the hardness of diamond.

364.4–12 Thoreau says . . . last fruits also."] See Thoreau's *Walden; or, Life in the Woods* (1854), chapter 7 ("The Bean-Field").

368.32 McLuhan] See note 118.24–25.

376.11–13 Those images . . . gong-tormented sea.] The concluding lines of "Byzantium" by William Butler Yeats (1865–1939), first collected in *Words for Music Perhaps, and Other Poems* (1932).

376.17–20 Howard Nemerov . . . the wild abyss.] See Nemerov's 1959 lecture, "The Swaying Form: A Problem in Poetry," collected in *Poetry and Fiction: Essays* (1963).

376.32–33 the old Summer Institute of Linguistics] Founded in 1934 and now known as SIL International, an organization devoted to the study of little-known languages, for the purpose of Bible translation.

382.26 Carole] Carole Koda (1947–2006), Snyder's wife; they married in 1991.

388.2–3 Robert Frost's . . . the land's."] From Frost's poem "The Gift Outright," first published in the Spring 1942 *Virginia Quarterly Review.*

391.27–36 It quotes me . . . I did write that.] From an interview with Snyder published in the September 1984 *Mother Earth News.*

395.8–9 Kemmis quotes Rousseau . . . modern politics."] The quotation is from Michael Ignatieff's book *The Needs of Strangers* (1985), which paraphrases Rousseau's arguments.

THE PARIS REVIEW INTERVIEW

409.10 Williams] American poet William Carlos Williams (1883–1963).

414.6 Sidney, *The Faerie Queene*] English poet Sir Philip Sidney (1554–1586), and Edmund Spenser's epic poem, first published in its entirety in 1596.

415.26–27 There is a line . . . I can sing."] See "The Slop Barrel: Slices of the Paideuma for All Sentient Beings," in *Like I Say* (1960), by Philip Whalen (1923–2002).

415.31 *shih*] Chinese: poem.

426.30–32 Robert Torrance . . . my work] See Robert M. Torrance, "Gary Snyder and the Western Poetic Tradition," in John Halper, ed., *Gary Snyder: Dimensions of a Life* (1991).

427.9–12 "Changing the filter . . . pursuits."] See lines 345.39–346.2 in the present volume.

428.10–11 a line from Auden . . . without working."] See "Romantic or Free?", Auden's June 17, 1940, Smith College commencement address, first published in the August 1940 *Smith Alumnae Quarterly*.

433.20 "This Tokyo"] First collected in *The Back Country* (1967).

434.14–15 I did a whole discussion . . . *Ten Directions*] See "Indra's Net as Our Own," first published in *The Ten Directions* in 1991 and subsequently collected in Thich Nhat Hanh, ed., *For a Future to Be Possible: Commentaries on the Five Wonderful Precepts* (1993).

From BACK ON THE FIRE

448.22 *shamisen*] A traditional Japanese three-stringed musical instrument.

449.33–34 what Jonathan Schell . . . Tragedy."] See "An American Tragedy," *The Nation*, March 20, 2003.

452.4–8 THE OPENING . . . chaos] First collected in Duncan's book *The Opening of the Field* (1960).

455.19–20 J. D. Frodsham . . . translation] See Frodsham's *Anthology of Chinese Verse: Han Wei Chin and the Northern and Southern Dynasties* (1967), translated with Ch'eng Hsi.

459.33 *Cheng Dao Ke*] Sometimes translated as the *Song of Enlightenment* or *Song of Freedom*, a Chinese Buddhist work usually attributed to Yongjia Xuanjue (665–713).

461.20–462.4 "Ripples on the surface . . . empty house."] From Snyder's poem "Ripples on the Surface," first collected in *No Nature* (1992).

463.29 an editorial . . . 2005).] See "At the Limits of Ocean and Air," *New York Times*, January 20, 2005.

464.9 *ahi*, and *maguro*] Yellowfin and Bigeye Tuna (*Thunnus albacares* and *Thunnus obesus*), and Pacific Bluefin Tuna (*Thunnus orientalis*).

464.12–13 A recent book . . . *Strangely Like War*] See Derrick Jensen and George Draffan, *Strangely Like War: The Global Assault on Forests* (2003).

464.29–30 The "poetic imagination" of which William Blake so eloquently spoke] Possibly a reference to Blake's letter to John Trusler of August 23, 1799: "to the Eyes of the Man of Imagination, Nature is Imagination Itself."

466.23 schrund] From the German *bergschrund*, a crevasse formed when flowing glacier ice separates from immobile ice; often dangerous to mountaineers.

466.27 Mazama] Founded in 1894, the Mazamas are a Pacific Northwest mountaineering club with headquarters in Portland; Snyder earned membership as a teenager.

466.37 alpenstock] A wooden staff capped at one end with a metal spike, used in mountaineering.

467.2 Issa's] Known for his haiku poems and journals, Kobayashi Issa (1763–1828), more often known simply as Issa (a pen name meaning "Cup-of-tea"), was a Japanese poet and lay Buddhist priest of the Pure Land sect.

467.11 five-colored banners] Tibetan prayer flags come in sets of five, traditionally arranged from left to right in a specific order: blue (sky-space), white (air-wind), red (fire), green (water), and yellow (earth).

468.28–30 In the *Lun yü* . . . (7.27).] See *Analects* 7.27: "When the Master fished he did not use a net; when he hunted, he did not shoot at nesting birds."

469.25 SONG OF THE TASTE] First collected in Snyder's book *Regarding Wave* (1970).

478.11 *cante jondo*] Spanish, *deep song*, a type of Andalusian folk music.

From TAMALPAIS WALKING

500.2 Vulture Peak] Snyder visited Vulture Peak, site of many of the Buddha's discourses, near present-day Rajgir, Bihar, in January 1962.

500.21 Matthew Davis] Davis has organized walks around Mt. Tamalpais since 1971; in 2006, with Michael Farrell Scott, he published *Opening the Mountain: Circumambulating Mount Tamalpais, a Ritual Walk*.

500.30 "with wild surmise"] From John Keats's sonnet "On First Looking into Chapman's Homer," first collected in his 1817 *Poems*.

501.30 *dharani*] Buddhist chants or recitations believed to have healing or protective power.

502.19 Master K'ung] Another name for the Chinese philosopher Confucius (c. 551–c. 479 BCE).

502.30–32 *Caminante* . . . MACHADO] See Machado's "Proverbios y Cantares," XXVIII, collected in *Campos de Castilla* (1912).

503.1 yamabushi] Japanese mountain ascetics; see also Snyder's essay "Walking the Great Ridge Ōmine" on pages 591–604 of the present volume.

506.27 William Kent] Kent (1864–1928), a California congressman from 1911 to 1917, helped to establish the National Park Service and to protect what is now the Muir Woods National Monument.

507.29–35 John Thomas Howell's . . . *1949*] See *Marin Flora: Manual of the Flowering Plants and Ferns of Marin County, California* (1949), by John Thomas Howell (1903–1994).

508.30 "The North Coast"] First collected in Snyder's *Left Out in the Rain* (2005).

509.8–9 *"All paths* . . . DON JUAN] A paraphrase of Carlos Castaneda's *The Teachings of Don Juan: A Yaqui Way of Knowledge* (1968).

THE GREAT CLOD

519.22 Asa Gray] Gray (1810–1888) was a longtime professor of botany at Harvard.

521.9 CHUANG-TZU] Also spelled Zhuang Zhou or Zhuangzi, a Chinese philosopher of the fourth century BCE, and also the name of his principal work.

528.3–15 Chang's list of species . . . molluscs] See Kwang-chih Chang, *The Archaeology of Ancient China* (1963).

528.26 Dudley Stamp . . . World War II)] See Stamp's *Asia: A Regional and Economic Geography* (1929).

528.28–33 George Cressey . . . the future."] See Cressey's book *China's Geographic Foundations* (1934), chapter 11 ("The Mountains of Eastern Manchuria").

529.16 kao-liang] A Chinese alcoholic liquor distilled from sorghum.

529.27–34 Andersson . . . bathed by sunshine."] See J. G. Andersson, "Researches into the Prehistory of the Chinese," *Bulletin of the Museum of Far Eastern Antiquities, Stockholm*, 1943.

531.32 Chin-huai estimates] See An Chin-huai, "The Shang City at Chengchou and Related Problems," in K. C. Chang, ed., *Studies in Shang Archaeology: Selected Papers from the International Conference on Shang Civilization* (1986).

533.26–27 "The Rites . . . common people"] From *The Book of Rites*, one of the Five Classics of Confucianism, probably compiled c. 475 BCE–220 CE.

535.9–22 I have heard . . . at its height!] From the *Zhuangzi* (also spelled *Chang-tzu*) of Zhuang Zhou, a foundational text of Taoism. Shen Nung, also spelled *Shennong*, "The Divine Husbandman," was a mythological ruler of ancient China.

537.21 asarum] A plant genus containing several species of wild ginger, including Chinese wild ginger, *Asarum splendens.*

538.13–18 See them now . . . masses!] From the *Yen T'ieh Lun* ("Dispute on Salt and Iron"), c. 81 BCE.

541.3–4 the Rocky Mountain Fur Company] Fur-trading firm founded in 1822 by William Henry Ashley (c. 1778–1838) and Andrew Henry (c. 1775–1832); the mountain men originally employed by the company were known as "Ashley's Hundred."

544.22–23 Edward Schafer's study . . . China"] See "Hunting Parks and Animal Enclosure in Ancient China," *Journal of Economic and Social History of the Orient*, October 1968.

548.25–26 "regard for the myriad growing things"] From Lu Chi's third-century *Essay on Literature*, in Shih-Hsiang Chen's 1952 translation.

555.5–6 Judge Dee . . . detective novels] In 1949, the Dutch writer Robert van Gulik (1910–1967) published *Celebrated Cases of Judge Dee*, a translation of the eighteenth-century Chinese detective novel *Dee Goong An*; he subsequently wrote a series of original "Judge Dee" novels, including *The Chinese Maze Murders* (1956), *The Chinese Bell Murders* (1958), *The Chinese Gold Murders* (1959), *The Chinese Lake Murders* (1960), and *Poets and Murder* (1968), the last retitled *Fox-magic Murders* when it appeared in the United States.

564.7 *Tess of the D'Urbervilles*] Novel by Thomas Hardy (1840–1928), first published in 1891.

581.7–11 an American traveler . . . possible wives."] See *Roving Through Southern China* (1925) by Harry A. Franck (1881–1962).

UNCOLLECTED ESSAYS

591.15 *ryokan*] Traditional Japanese inns.

595.9 *shakujo*] A staff topped with metal rings, carried by Buddhist monks.

595.10 sistrum] A rattlelike percussion instrument, originally from ancient Egypt.

595.38 the Hannya Shingyo] The *Heart Sutra*, a Mahayana Buddhist sutra dated to the seventh to eighth centuries CE.

596.7 mudras] In Buddhism and Hinduism, a symbolic or ritual pose or gesture, often made with hands and fingers.

596.10 *uguisu*] See note 26.28.

596.11 Fudō] The wrathful Buddhist deity Acala or Achala is known as Fudō Myō-ō in Japan, where he has been invoked as a defender of the nation.

597.18 *eki*] Train station.

597.33 En-no-Gyōja] Also known as En no Ozuno or Otsuno (634–c. 700), ascetic founder of the Shugendō disciplines followed among *yamabushi*.

599.35 dharanis] See note 501.30.

602.36 *goma*] A fire ritual performed in some Buddhist sects.

604.29 *kami*] Deities, spirits, or natural phenomena venerated in Shintoism.

606.1 Yamato] An ancient region of Japan; the historical period (c. 250–710) in which Japan was ruled from Yamato; the dynastic name of the reigning imperial family of Japan; a name for all of mainland Japan.

607.2–5 *Life is not . . . Wild*] See page 308, lines 34–37, in the present volume.

607.18–23 The little series . . . edge of the light."] Snyder first collected "How Poetry Comes to Me" in *No Nature: New and Selected Poems* (1992).

Index

Aboriginal Arts Board, 284
Abraham, 454, 468
Abrams, David, 451
Aesop, 30
Agriculture Department, U.S., 328, 486
Ahimsa, 456, 470
Ainu, 181, 241, 278, 288–89, 306, 358, 460–61, 519, 525
Alaska, 156, 218, 238, 244, 247, 257, 259–61, 264–79, 306–7, 321, 338, 387, 426, 460, 606
Alaska Humanities Forum, 278
Alaska Native Languages Center, 275
Alcheringa, 185
Aleutian Islands, 426
Alice Springs, Australia, 284, 288
Altamira cave paintings, 60
Amami Islands, 69–76
Amazonia, 163, 335–36
American Academy of Poets, 131
American Indian Movement, 283
Amish, 148, 427, 534
Amsterdam, Netherlands, 48
Anaguta, 67
Anarchist Circle, 51, 178
Anchorage, AK, 273, 278
Angulo, Jaime de, 52
An Lushan, 121, 558
Arabic poetry, 426
Arabs, 557
Arapaho, 62
Arctic National Wildlife Refuge, 277
Arikawa (Amami islander), 72
Arita Maru (Japanese freighter), 24–25, 508, 518
Arjuna, 67

Assam, 335
Association for the Study of Literature and the Environment, 448
Athapaskan, 218, 231, 268, 274, 276, 338
Auden, W. H., 119, 130, 428
Aurobindo Ashram, 199–203
Austin, Mary, 322
Australia, 242, 249, 275, 284–88, 425
Australian aboriginal peoples, 67, 284–88
Avatamsaka Buddhism, 27, 36
Avatamsaka Sutra, 287
Axe Handles (Snyder), 410

Back Country, The (Snyder), 164, 410
Bai Juyi (Po Chui), 455, 542–43; *Chang Hen Ge*, 415; *Pipa Hsing*, 415–16
Balasaraswati, Padma, 256–59
Bangladesh, 337
Bankei, 344
Banyan Ashram, 69–76, 164, 303–4, 597
Barbour, Michael: *California's Changing Landscapes*, 387
Barker, Sam, 19–20
Barth, Emil, 506, 510
Bartolomé de las Casas, 267
Basho, 115, 456, 511
Basques, 252
Bass, Rick, 451
Bateson, Gregory: *Steps to an Ecology of Mind*, 458
Baudelaire, Charles, 160
Beats, 168, 409–10, 417–18, 458
Beaver Creek, 17–18, 22

Beckwitt, Steve, 369
Bedouins, 292
Beebe, Frank, 4
Bellingham, WA, 14, 246
Benares, India, 117
Berg, Peter, 185
Berkeley, CA, 23, 34, 48, 110, 134, 179, 253, 505
Berkeley Barb, 359
Berry, Wendell, 161–62
Beyond Self (anthology), 456
Bhagavad-Gita, 53, 133
Bharat Natyam, 256–59
Bhave, Vinoba, 200
Bhopal disaster, 433
Bible, 85, 262, 313, 376
Big Sur, 48, 52, 355, 426
Black Hills, 283
Black Mesa, 372
Black Mountain poets, 458
Blainey, Geoffrey, 287
Blake, William, 19, 21, 111, 161, 187, 373, 464
Blaser, Robin, 417
Bly, Robert, 120, 141, 161, 169, 181
Boat in a Storm (Snyder), 348
Bodhisattva, 11–12, 27, 33, 45, 145, 172, 339, 300, 321, 341, 344, 358, 461, 477, 594
Boenish, Hans and Bonnie, 260–61, 267, 275
Borges, Jorge Luis, 127
Bosch, Hieronymus, 53–54
Botswana, 488
Boulder, CO, 103, 125
Bozeman, MT, 247
Brahma, 63–64, 258
Brahmacharin, 201
Brahminism, 143, 153, 173
Brand, Stewart, 185, 369
Brautigan, Richard, 369
Brazil, 335–36
Brecht, Bertolt, 465
Breuil, Henri-Édouard, 60, 474
Brihadaranyaka Upanishad, 66

Britain, 240–42, 293, 449, 525, 567
British Columbia, 156, 246, 392, 426
Bronze Age, 105, 272
Brooks Range, 218, 259, 306–7
Brotherhood of the Free Spirit, 53–54
Brower, David, 150
Brown, Jerry, 150, 168–69, 283, 411
Brown University, 176
Buckley, Richard, 232
Buddha, 27, 33, 35, 37–38, 46, 64, 67, 123, 142, 148, 229, 297, 344–45, 348, 355, 358, 477, 492, 541–42, 596–98, 602, 605
Buddhadharma, 46, 139–40, 174, 580
Buddhism, 45–47, 61, 64, 66, 129, 131, 147, 152, 166, 171, 195, 230, 232, 262–63, 266, 273, 293, 298–300, 302, 339, 372, 396, 415, 420–24, 427, 432, 434, 453, 461, 517–18, 540, 543, 546, 553–54, 562, 566, 575, 593, 598–99, 602; Avatamsaka, 27, 36; Chan, 143–44, 301, 305, 456, 537, 542, 545, 548, 572–73, 580, 586, 588; Mahayana, 44, 58, 133–34, 145, 173, 341, 358, 454, 460, 541–42, 573; Son, 456; Tantra, 27, 49, 55, 209; Theravadin, 142–43, 173; Tibetan, 209–11, 592; Vajrayana, 49, 53, 299, 594, 596, 604. *See also* Zen Buddhism
"Buddhism and the Coming Revolution" (Snyder), 139, 145
Buell, Lawrence, 451; *The Environmental Imagination*, 458
Bunyan, John: *The Pilgrim's Progress*, 222
Bureau of Aboriginal Affairs, Australia, 287
Bureau of American Ethnology, U.S., 106

Bureau of Land Management, U.S., 224–25, 242, 322, 359, 381–82, 389, 391, 401–4, 442–43, 445–46, 481, 483
Burns, Blackie, 3, 15–16, 18, 22
Bush, George W., 449–50
Bushmen, 68, 368
Bu Ston, 64

Cabeza de Vaca, Alvar Núñez, 218, 224, 232
Cafard, Max, 245–46, 251
California, 61, 107, 122, 149, 155–58, 163, 170, 174, 215, 231, 236, 246–47, 252, 265, 281, 283, 294–95, 309, 323, 325, 344, 383, 386–405, 417, 426, 443, 447, 480–90, 499–514, 606
California Academy of Sciences, 507
California Arts Council, 168–71
California Department of Forestry, 391, 481, 483–84
California Native Plant Society, 445, 500
"California Water Plan" (Snyder), 159
Callahan, Bob, 185
Calvinism, 428
Cambodge (French passenger ship), 193–98
Cambodia, 202
Campbell, Joseph, 93, 98
Canada, 22, 156, 218, 227, 238, 240, 242, 246, 248, 387, 392, 425–26, 606
Carson, Rachel, 374, 451
Cassirer, Ernst, 94
Catholicism, 105, 195, 198, 360, 368, 423
Cave paintings, 60–61, 104, 474–77
Celts, 53, 277
Central Intelligence Agency, 55
Central Valley, 294, 388, 395–96

Chadwick, Douglas, 451
Chan Buddhism, 143–44, 301, 305, 456, 537, 542–43, 545, 548, 572–73, 580, 586, 588
Chang, Kwang-chih, 528–29
Chang'an, China, 557–58
Chang-tzu, 535
Chan-jan, 542
Chaucer, Geoffrey, 7
Chehalis, 250
Cheney, Dick, 450
Cheng Dao Ke, 459
Che River, 561, 573
Chernobyl disaster, 433
Cheyenne, 56
Chiang Kai-shek, 198
Chicago, IL, 52
Chickasaw, 60
Chi-jan, 560
China/Chinese culture, 32–33, 36, 50–51, 58, 71, 121, 124, 134, 139, 143–44, 164, 195–99, 209, 242, 250, 270, 277, 297, 300, 302–3, 305–6, 311–12, 324, 326, 329, 333, 340, 342, 418–19, 448, 523–24, 526–88; Confucianism in, 21, 454, 534–36, 538, 555, 565, 574; Daoism in, 9, 49, 133, 140, 165–66, 217, 293, 298, 339, 368, 454, 534–37, 539–42, 544–47, 554, 560, 566, 570–71, 586, 588; landscape painting, 132, 136, 301, 305, 311, 526, 552, 582–88; language, 7, 35–37, 40, 106, 114–15, 217, 221, 271, 301, 413, 437, 452, 526, 536; poetry, 21, 24, 35, 59, 106, 115, 123, 131, 133, 136, 160, 167, 231, 278, 366, 409, 411, 413–16, 420, 425, 454–56, 526, 532–33, 536–37, 539–42, 545–49, 566, 570–73, 580, 582
"Chinese Poetry and the American Imagination" (Snyder), 131, 167
Chobe Forest, 488
Chowka, Peter Barry, 131–75

Christianity, 35, 46, 49, 53–54, 61, 85–86, 139–40, 147, 173, 200, 223, 250, 265, 268, 282–83, 371, 396, 426, 454, 468, 473, 526, 581
Chugach Mountains, 278
Chu Tzu, 537
Cicero, 279
Coburn, Rod, 109
CoEvolution Quarterly, 185
Colombo, Sri Lanka, 198
Columbia River, 146, 255, 316, 355, 392, 466
Comanche, 90
Concow, 215
Confucianism, 21, 454, 534–36, 538, 555, 565, 574
Confucius, 133, 144, 534, 540, 584; *Analects*, 6, 468
Congress, U.S., 315–16, 328–29, 394, 441
Congress of World Religions, 52
Conklin, H. C., 66
Constitution, U.S., 488
"Control Burn" (Snyder), 484–85
Conversations: Christians and Buddhists, 138
Cook, James, 525
Cooper, John, 269–70
Cortés, Hernán, 224
Coyote's Journal, 52
Craig, Jack and Ginko, 194
Crater Mountain, 3–16
Creeley, Robert, 417
Cressey, George, 528
Cro-Magnons, 151
Crow, 114, 247

Daisetsu Mountains, 522–24
Daitoku-ji monastery, 31, 136, 138, 147, 193, 297, 341, 420–21, 593
Dalai Lama (Fourteenth), 206–11, 410
Dalai Lama (Sixth), 66
Danger on Peaks (Snyder), 466–68
Dante Alighieri, 187, 414

Daoism, 9, 49, 133, 140, 165–66, 217, 293, 298, 339, 368, 454, 534–37, 539–42, 544–47, 554, 560, 566, 570–71, 586, 588
Dao Lin, 542–43
Darrington, WA, 14, 20
Darwinism, 167, 274, 292, 454
Dauenhauer, Richard and Nora, 275
Davis, CA, 499, 502
Davis, Matthew, 500, 506
Deloria, Vine, Jr., 185
Dengyo Daishi (Saicho), 26
Descartes, René, 228, 266
Desolation ranger station, 3–23, 508
Dharamshala, India, 206–8, 211
Dharma, 26, 30–31, 33, 36, 45–46, 131, 137, 139, 148, 150–51, 211, 221, 273, 356, 477
Dhaulagiri Mountain, 208
Dialectical Anthropology, 185
Diamond, Stanley, 65, 152–53, 185; *Anaguta Cosmography*, 67
Diamond Sutra, 471
Dickey, William, 417
Dickinson, Emily, 458
Di Prima, Diane, 369
Djailai-nor, 527
Dodge, Jim, 237, 251, 308, 424
Dogen, 113, 235, 273, 280, 343, 461, 477; *Sansuikyo*, 297–302, 306–7, 309–12, 505
Dong-shan, 351
Dorn, Ed, 417
Doughty, Charles, 292
Draffan, George: *Strangely Like War*, 464
Druids, 368
Duncan, Robert, 161, 416–17, 432, 605; "The Opening of the Field," 452
Dunshee, Verna, 506

Earth First!, 238, 434
Earth House Hold (Snyder), 137, 139, 141, 153, 160, 410

East West Journal, 131, 141, 148
Eastwood, Alice, 506–7
Edenshaw, Florence, 233
Egypt, ancient, 31
Elder, John, 451
Eliot, T. S., 97, 412, 477; *Four Quartets*, 104–5
Elvin, Mark, 559–60, 573
Emerson, Ralph Waldo: Journals, 29
Engaku-ji temple, 52
Engels, Friedrich, 50–51, 55
English ballads, 181
English language, 274
En-no-Gyoja, 594–95, 597–99
Epping Forest, 241
Eshleman, Clayton, 193, 423, 458, 474
Evans, Patricia: *Hopscotch*, 68
Evans-Wentz, Walker: *The Tibetan Book of the Dead*, 52–53, 209; *The Tibetan Book of the Great Liberation*, 209
Everglades, 355
Everson, William, 417
Exodus (biblical book), 313

Fairbanks, AK, 259, 270–71, 273
Fan Kuan, 586
Farallones Institute, 185
Feng Kuan, 26
Ferlinghetti, Lawrence, 179
Field, 176
Fields, W. C., 428
Fish and Wildlife Service, U.S., 391
Foreman, David, 238
Forest Service, U.S., 3, 13, 22, 134, 224, 242, 283, 316, 327–29, 358–59, 391, 399, 402, 442–43, 446, 482–84, 487, 491, 606
Four Seasons Foundation, 410
France, 151, 279, 422, 474–77
Franklin, Jerry, 444, 486
Frazer, James George: *The Golden Bough*, 93–94, 98

Fresh Air (radio program), 436
Freud, Sigmund, 88, 92
Friedrich, Paul: *Proto-Indo-European Trees*, 270–71
Friends of the Earth, 150
Frodsham, J. D., 455
"Front Lines" (Snyder), 156
Frost, Robert, 388
Fudo, 300, 358, 595–96, 598, 603–4
Furong, 301

Gaddis, 207
Galápagos Islands, 307
Gamelan, 465
Gandhi, Mohandas K., 200–201, 461
García Lorca, Federico, 426
Gass, William, 415
"Gathering of Tribes, A" (be-in), 48
Gautama (Buddha), 541
Geneson, Paul, 103–30
Genghis Khan, 250, 574–76
George, Tom, 259
Georgia-Pacific, 335
Germany, 54, 277
Gernet, Jacques, 563, 569
Ghose, Aurobindo, 200, 203; *The Life Divine*, 200
Ghost Dance, 51, 56, 62, 64, 602
Gilyaks, 520–21, 525
Ginsberg, Allen, 111, 125, 131, 167–68, 179, 206–7, 210–11, 238, 410, 415–17, 456, 502–4; *Howl*, 168, 179, 410
Glacier Peak, 238, 314
Gleason, Madelin, 417
Glotfelty, Cheryl, 451
Gnosticism, 49, 200, 368
Goethe, Johann Wolfgang von, 187
Golden Gate National Recreation Area, 507
Gowdie, Isobel, 66
Graham, Aelred, 139, 148–49
Grand Canyon, 355
Granet, Marcel, 535

Granite Creek, 4, 12–13
Granquist, Erik, 271–72
Graves, Morris, 424
Graves, Robert, 97–98
Gray, Francine du Plessix, 415
Great Basin, 238, 248, 252, 322, 388
Great Depression, 315
Greater Sierran Ecosystem, 445
Greater Yellowstone Ecosystem, 390
Great Smoky Mountains National Park, 324
Greece, ancient, 32, 262–63, 265, 268, 272, 277–79, 426
Greek language, 87, 219, 240, 273, 428, 453
Gregorian chants, 123
Grimes, Ronald, 460
Grossinger, Richard, 185
Grubis, Steve, 259–60, 264, 275
Guangzhou, China, 578
Guan Zhong, 6
Guatemala, 293
Gumperz, John, 276
Guo Xi, 585
Gurdip (Sikh guide), 207
Gurdjieff, George, 141
Gwich'in, 279

Hadley, Drummond, 163
Haida, 8, 60, 65, 79–84, 98–99, 106, 233
Hall, Donald, 417
Hammond, Austin, 247
Han dynasty, 537–39, 543–45, 556–57, 568–69
Hangzhou, China, 311–12, 540, 561–67, 573
Hannya Shingyo, 501, 595
Hanshan, 28, 303, 333; *Cold Mountain Poems*, 410, 414–15
Hardin, Garrett, 243–44
Hardy, Thomas: *Tess of the D'Urbervilles*, 564

Harijan, 69, 74–75
Harrison, Jane Ellen: *Prolegomena to the Study of Greek Religion*, 104
Harvard University, 210
Hawaii, 257, 267, 448
Haydn, Josef, 29
Hayward, CA, 52
Heian period, 455
Hekiganroku, 42
Hemingway, Ernest, 194
Hesiod, 279
Hevajra Tantra, 53
Hideyoshi, Toyotomi, 34
Hillman, James, 312
"Hills of Home" (Snyder), 512–14
Himalayas, 206, 208, 211
Hindi, 276
Hinduism, 53, 61, 63–64, 66–67, 133, 139–40, 147, 173–74, 200, 205, 229, 258, 473
Hinton, David, 455
Hiroshima, atomic bombing of, 467–68
Hobbes, Thomas, 228
Hoffman, Allen, 369
Hokkaido, 181, 426, 517–25, 528
Hokusai, 15
Hold, John, 253
Holocene Epoch, 225, 277
Holthaus, Gary, 246–47, 275, 278–79
Homer, 187, 265, 272; *Iliad*, 279; *Odyssey*, 97, 279
Hong Kong, 194–96, 198
Hopi, 133, 147, 153, 174, 237, 372, 500
Hopkins, Gerard Manley, 106
Hough, Lindy, 185
House Committee on Un-American Activities, 316
Howell, John Thomas, 507
"How Poetry Comes to Me" (Snyder), 607
Hozomeen Mountain, 17–18
Hsiatu, China, 557

Hsi Po, 538
Hua, 577–81
Huai River, 551–52, 558, 574, 577
Huangbo Xiyun, 17
Huang Gongwang, 588
Hudson Review, 178
Huineng, 4, 580
Humboldt, Wilhelm von, 274
Humphreys, Cliff, 369
Hunt, Hilda, 194
Hunter, Neale, 195
Hybart, Burt, 251–52
Hymes, Dell, 135
Hypatia, 279

Iditarod dogsled race, 267
India/Indian culture, 32–33, 49, 55, 116–17, 134, 144, 166, 182, 194–96, 199, 201–4, 206–11, 259, 263, 269–70, 276, 305, 335, 410, 503–4, 540, 553, 560, 569, 578, 580; Brahminism in, 143, 153, 173; Hinduism in, 53, 61, 63–64, 66–67, 133, 139–40, 147, 173–74, 200, 205, 229, 258, 473
Indiana University, 134–35, 409
Indonesia, 465
Industrial Revolution, 141, 567
Industrial Workers of the World, 46, 51, 320, 427
Inquisition, 54
Integral Yoga, 200
International Whaling Commission, 365
Inupiaq, 230, 257, 259–62, 266, 269–70, 272, 275–76, 278–79, 338
Iraq, 449
Iroquois, 50, 345
Islam, 49, 140, 201, 250, 276, 396, 454, 468, 473
Israel, 449
Israelites, ancient, 282, 313
Issa, 467, 511
Italy, 157

Jackson, Wes, 291–92, 334; *New Roots for Agriculture*, 292
Jacobs, Jane: *Cities and the Wealth of Nations*, 396
Jaipur, India, 258
Japan/Japanese culture, 4, 24–43, 59, 64, 69–76, 108, 113, 116, 133–34, 139–40, 144, 147, 149, 179, 181, 193–96, 229, 242, 288, 290, 304, 312, 324, 326, 337, 344–45, 371, 387, 410, 415, 419, 421, 425–26, 449–50, 460–61, 463, 473, 480, 503–4, 517–26, 528, 546, 552, 563–64, 587, 593–606; landscape painting, 15; language, 35, 114, 136, 217, 302, 339, 342, 452–53, 455, 521, 580, 602; poetry, 115, 123, 127, 163, 420, 455–56, 467, 511; Rinzai sect in, 35, 52–53, 136–38, 143, 311, 341, 372, 469; Shingon sect in, 299, 594, 596; Shintoism in, 289, 298, 305, 358, 454, 517, 594, 598, 605; Soto sect in, 53, 136–37, 143, 311, 339; tea ceremony, 427; Tendai sect in, 241, 297, 542, 596; theater, 29, 34, 224, 341, 459, 465, 594
Java, 21, 580
Jeffers, Robinson, 104, 409, 416
Jehovah's Witnesses, 534
Jensen, Derrick: *Strangely Like War*, 464
Jerusalem, 117
Je Tsongkhapa, 67
Jodoshin, 344
Journal of Backcountry Writing, 185
Joyce, James, 105, 187; *Ulysses*, 97
Judaism, 46, 61, 174, 250, 268, 371, 396, 454, 468, 473
Jung, Carl, 52; *Psychology of the Unconscious*, 86–87, 98
Juran, 588

Kagoshima, Japan, 69, 75
Kaifeng, China, 570

Kamo River, 32, 297
Kannon, 26, 33, 300, 341
Karakorum, 266, 575
Kardiner, Abram: *The Individual and His Society*, 85, 88–92, 95
Kari, Jim, 218, 275
Kashyapa, 38–41
Kemmis, Daniel: *Community and the Politics of Place*, 394–95
Kent, William, 506
Kent State University, 125
Kentucky, 162
Kenyon Review, 178
Kerenyi, Carl, 87–88
Kerouac, Jack, 179, 417, 505–6, 508; *The Dharma Bums*, 410; *Mexico City Blues*, 110
Khajuraho, India, 204–5
Khitans, 586
Killion, Tom, 506
Kitayama River, 603
Kitkitdizze, 398–405, 502
Klyce, Al, 194
Knossos, Crete, 56
Kobe, Japan, 25, 289–90, 518
Kobuk, AK, 259–61, 265, 267–69
Kobuk River, 259–60, 264–69, 273
Koch, Kenneth, 417
Koptos, Egypt, 64
Korea, 448, 454–55, 465, 524–25
Korean poetry, 456
Ko Un: *The Sound of My Waves*, 456
Koyukuk River, 218, 306
Krauss, Michael, 275
Krishna, 67, 258, 276
Krishnamurti, Jiddu, 194, 344
Kroeber, A. L., 95, 245
Kublai Khan, 562, 573
Kugl, Helmut, 194
Kuksu, 185
Kumano, Japan, 299, 597, 604–5
Kurile Islands, 520–22
Kuuvangmiut, 260–61, 272, 278
Kwakiutl, 106

Kyoto, Japan, 26, 29, 32–43, 59, 75, 136–39, 147, 149, 193–94, 242, 297, 341, 410, 423, 469, 517–18, 563–64, 580, 587–93, 595, 597, 604, 606

Lake Washington, 313, 503
Lakota, 283, 434
Lamantia, Philip, 179
Lampe, Keith, 369
Lang, Andrew, 85
Langer, Susanne: *Philosophy in a New Key*, 96
Lankavatara Sutra, 53
Lao, 580
Laozi, 49, 143; *Dao De Jing*, 133, 270, 339, 343, 511, 535–36, 539
Lascaux cave paintings, 474–76
Latin language, 219–20, 240, 452
Laughlin, James, 417
Laughlin, William, 145
Lawrence, D. H., 104, 309; *Aaron's Rod*, 25; *Birds, Beasts and Flowers*, 412; *Lady Chatterley's Lover*, 412
Leary, Timothy, 210
Lee, Sherman, 586
Left Out in the Rain (Snyder), 410
Legalists, 21, 534, 538
Leopold, Aldo, 239, 374, 451
Leroi-Gourhan, André, 474
Lévi-Strauss, Claude, 170, 464; *The Savage Mind*, 58, 60
Lhasa, Tibet, 70, 209
Li, 580
Liang Kai, 587
Library of Congress, 185
Li Chihchang, 575
Liehzi, 534–35
Liji, 543
Lindisfarne Association, 185
Li Po, 455, 548
Li Taoyuan, 550
Liu Yuxi, 579–80
Living Wilderness, 314–15
London, England, 48

Longmoor, Jud, 18
Lopez, Barry, 451
Los Angeles, CA, 48, 261, 363, 372, 509
Los Angeles River, 393
Los Angeles Zen Center, 434
Lotus Sutra, 430, 542
Lowie, Robert, 86
Luce, Clare Boothe, 423
Lu Chi, 547
Luddites, 427, 434
Lummi, 14
Lu Yu, 572
Lu Yuan, 305
Lyon, Tom, 451

Mabinogion, The, 105
Machado, Antonio, 502
Madhyamika, 263
Magdalenian stone carvings, 152
Mahanirvana Sutra, 53
Maharshi, Ramana, 344
Mahayana Buddhism, 44, 58, 133–34, 145, 173, 341, 358, 454, 460, 541–42, 573
Maidu, 250, 281, 294, 396
Malinowski, Bronislaw: "Myth in Primitive Psychology," 85–88, 94, 98
Manchuria, 520–21, 524, 527–28, 552, 586
Manichaeism, 200
Manjushri, 28, 229
Manyoshu, 455
Marblemount ranger station, 3–4, 13–14, 19–20
Marcus Aurelius, 279
Marcuse, Herbert: *One Dimensional Man*, 149–50
Margalef, Ramon: *Perspectives in Ecological Theory*, 153–54
Margolis, Malcolm, 231
Marx, Karl, 266
Marxism, 45–46, 50–51, 133, 168, 368, 377, 525

Maser, Chris, 327, 334
Masters, Edgar Lee, 104
Mather, Elsie, 275
Matsumoto family, 503
Matthiessen, Peter, 451
Mazu, 548
McCarthy, Joseph, 316
McClure, Michael, 161, 179, 185, 369, 416, 458
McCorkle, Locke, 505
McCullough, Ed, 320
McGregor, Walter, 79
McGuire, Bob and Cora, 267–68
McLuhan, Marshall, 118, 368
McPhee, John, 451, 500
Means, Russell, 283
Mediterranean forests, 243, 290, 325–26
Meeker, Joe, 185
Mei Yaochen, 571
Melanesians, 263
Melville, Herman, 111; *Moby-Dick*, 315
Mencius, 143, 326
Merkits, 574
Mexico, 218, 223–24, 232, 247–48, 386
Miao, 578–81
Michigan, 335
Micronesians, 68
Middle Ages, 223
Miles, Josephine, 417
Mills, Stephanie, 451
Milton, John, 187; "L'Allegro," 220; *Paradise Lost*, 222
Min, 64
Ming dynasty, 588
Minneapolis, MN, 180
Mississippi River, 355, 392
Missoula, MT, 394
Mitchell, John Hanson, 236
Miura Isshu Roshi, 136
Miwok, 250, 396
Miyazaki, Japan, 70, 75
Mojave Desert, 52, 237, 253, 388

Mongke Khan, 573
Mongolia, 527
Mongols, 311, 561–63, 567, 573–75, 586
Monongye, David, 500, 502
Montreal, Canada, 371
Mooney, James, 64
Morgan, Lewis Henry, 48, 50, 55; *Ancient Society*, 50
Morimoto Roshi, 344
Morrison, Toni, 415
"Mother Earth: Her Whales" (Snyder), 433
Mott, Lillian, 445
Mount Adams, 314, 321
Mountain Home (anthology), 455
Mountains and Rivers Without End (Snyder), 410, 430–31, 504
Mount Atago, 593
Mount Baker, 8, 17–18, 314, 481
Mount Baker National Forest, 3
Mount Everest, 523
Mount Fuji, 289, 511
Mount Hiei, 26–27, 241, 297
Mount Hood, 314
Mount Jefferson, 316
Mount Jing, 311
Mount Lassen, 309
Mount Omine, 299, 593–606
Mount Ontake, 595
Mount Rainier, 132, 314, 316, 355, 503, 526
Mount St. Helens, 314, 441, 466–68, 593
Mount Shasta, 252–53, 392, 396
Mount Stuart, 314
Mount Tamalpais, 499–514, 593, 604
Mount Terror, 8, 18
Moyers, Guy, 264–65
Mozi, 534
Muir, John, 239, 374, 506; *The Mountains of California*, 442
Muir Woods National Monument, 499, 502, 506–7

Mumonkan, 42
Muqi, 587
Murasaki, Shikbu: *The Tale of Genji*, 25
Myths & Texts (Snyder), 318–21, 327, 329, 334–36, 357, 410, 430

Nabhan, Gary Paul, 451
Nagano, Japan, 69, 75
Nagasaki, atomic bombing of, 467
Naha, Japan, 448
Nanyue, 548
National Endowment for the Arts, 182
National Maritime Union, 463
National Park Service, 242, 413, 507
Native American Heritage Commission, 283
Native Americans, 48, 52, 55, 59, 61, 115–17, 145, 223–24, 243, 248, 291, 309, 316, 322, 368, 389, 397, 413, 435–36, 470; Arapaho, 62; Athapaskan, 218, 231, 268, 274, 276, 338; Cheyenne, 56; Chickasaw, 60; Comanche, 90; Crow, 114, 247; Ghost Dance, 51, 56, 62, 64, 602; Gwich'in, 279; Haida, 8, 60, 65, 79–84, 98–99, 106, 233; Hopi, 133, 147, 153, 174, 237, 372, 500; Inupiaq, 230, 257, 259–62, 266, 269–70, 272, 275–76, 278–79, 338; Iroquois, 50, 345; Kwakiutl, 106; Lakota, 283, 434; Lummi, 14; Maidu, 250, 281, 294, 396; Miwok, 250, 396; Navajo, 28, 122, 372; Nisenan, 215, 254, 281, 404; Nisqually, 319; Paiute, 134; Pueblo, 51, 153, 372; Salish, 132, 313; Shawnee, 107; Shoshone, 28, 134, 147, 319; Sioux, 114, 283, 434; Tlingit, 8, 244, 247; Wasco, 250, 319–20, 468, 482; Washoe, 250; Wintun, 399; Wishram, 146, 319, 468; Yupik, 257, 276, 279

Nature Conservancy, The, 225
Nature Protection Agency, Japan, 525
Navajo, 28, 122, 372
Neanderthals, 151, 357
Needham, Joseph, 573, 583, 587–88; *Science and Civilization in China*, 165–66
Nelson, Richard, 231, 275, 451
Nemerov, Howard, 376
Neolithic Age, 105, 146, 151–52, 165, 173, 177, 299, 528–30, 532, 535, 547, 556, 602–3
Neoplatonism, 200
Nepal, 601
Neruda, Pablo, 114
Netherlands, 54
Nevada, 254
New Alchemy, 185
New Guinea, 65, 74, 163
New Orleans, LA, 194
News from Native California, 231
Newton, Isaac, 228, 266
New Wilderness Newsletter, 185
New York City, 48, 50, 118, 125, 131, 180, 219, 222, 410, 425, 509
New Yorker, The, 359
New York Review of Books, 185
New York Times, The, 433, 463
Niaux cave paintings, 474–75
Nietzsche, Friedrich, 97
Nigeria, 67
92nd Street Y, 410
Nisenan, 215, 254, 281, 404
Nisqually, 319
Nivkhi, 525
Noh drama, 29, 34, 224, 341, 459, 465, 594
No Nature (Snyder), 410, 432
Normans, 240, 274
North American Bioregional Congress, 392
North Cascades, 14, 20, 22, 132, 313–14, 316, 344, 357, 466, 481, 503, 508, 526

"North Coast, The" (Snyder), 508–9
North San Juan Fire Hall, 185
Nuño de Guzmán, 223–24

Oakland, CA, 424
Oberlin College, 176
Oda Sesso Roshi, 31, 34, 136–38, 156, 341
Odum, Eugene, 153; "The Strategy of Ecosystem Development," 372
Oedipus myth, 85
Ohara, Japan, 241
Ohio Review, 103
Okinawa, 70, 73, 448–49
Old English, 221
Olson, Charles, 105, 458
Olympic Mountains, 132, 238, 313–15, 526
Olympic National Forest, 441
Olympic National Park, 323
Omine Yamabushi, 299, 358, 503, 593–98, 600, 603–4, 606
Oregon, 107, 122, 163, 246, 250, 252, 255, 316–22, 324, 326, 386, 399, 466, 468, 481–82, 486, 521, 606
Oregon Cascades, 316, 324
Organic Gardening, 185
Orlovsky, Peter, 132, 134–35, 139, 166, 206, 210–11
Osaka, Japan, 312, 344, 563
Osborne, Dan, 157
Oxford University, 53, 117

Packwood ranger station, 316
Paiute, 134
Paleolithic Age, 49, 60, 73, 104–5, 151, 177, 299, 426, 474–77, 527–28, 602–3
Palestinians, 449
P'ansori, 465
Paris Review, 407
Parkinson, Thomas, 149, 417
Partisan Review, 178
Patanjali, 5

Patterson, Ray, 18
Paul, Sherman, 451
Penan, 335
Pericles, 272
Peters, Katherine, 275
Persians, 557, 559
Petersen, Will, 518
Petrarch, Francesco, 279
Philippines, 335
Pintubi, 284–85
Place in Space, A (Snyder), 410
Planet Drum Foundation, 185, 251
Plato, 265, 287; *Critias*, 325
Pleistocene Epoch, 105, 259, 277, 324, 475–77, 527
Pochang, 144, 548
"Poetry, Community, and Climax" (Snyder), 458
"Poetry and the Primitive" (Snyder), 176
Point Reyes National Seashore, 507, 510
Polanyi, Karl, 241
Polo, Marco, 311, 561–65, 578–79
Polynesians, 25, 368, 461
Pon (ashram resident), 69, 71, 75
Pondicherry, India, 199–203
Portland, OR, 54–55, 246, 255, 316, 320, 329, 416
Portland Oregonian, 467
Pound, Ezra, 105–6, 119–20, 133, 409, 412, 458, 526; *Cantos*, 414, 431
Powell, John Wesley, 239, 322
Practice of the Wild, The (Snyder), 375–76, 378–79, 410, 607
Prajna Paramita Sutra, 37, 39
Protestantism, 265, 268
Pueblo, 51, 153, 372
Puget Sound, 14, 52, 122, 132, 238, 246, 248, 255, 257, 313–14, 327, 392, 503, 526
Pulitzer Prize, 125, 158, 410
Pyne, Stephen J.: *World Fire*, 446
Pyramid Lake, 355

Qin dynasty, 21, 538, 557, 568
Qing dynasty, 305
Quakers, 180, 368, 427
Quammen, David, 451
Qu Yuan, 537

Ramakrishna, 52
RAND Corporation, 55
Ranters, 55
Rasula, Jed, 451; *This Compost*, 457–58
Raymond, Roy, 21–22
"Real Work, The" (Snyder), 129–30
Redwood Creek, 499, 502, 506
Redwood National Park, 443
Reed College, 112, 133, 409, 412, 416, 463
Regarding War (Snyder), 410
Reisner, Marc: *The Cadillac Desert*, 392
Renaissance, 140, 268, 272, 396, 414
Rexroth, Kenneth, 178, 409, 416–17
Richards, I. A., 87–88, 92
Rimbaud, Arthur, 160
Rimpoche, Dudjon, 209
Rinko-in temple, 29, 32–33
Rinzai sect, 35, 52–53, 136–38, 143, 311, 341, 372, 469
"Ripples on the Surface" (Snyder), 461–62
Riprap (Snyder), 173, 410, 412–13
Riprap and Cold Mountain Poems (Snyder), 410, 412
Rnin ma-pa sect, 209
Robertson, David, 499, 502
Robinson, Lillian: "In the Night Kitchen," 162
Rodale Press, 185
Roethke, Theodore, 179, 181
Rogue River National Forest, 486
Romanticism, 282
Rome, ancient, 249, 272, 279, 298, 538, 545

Ross Lake, 5, 22
Rothenberg, Jerome, 185, 417, 458
Rouffignac cave paintings, 475
Rousseau, Jean-Jacques, 59, 395
Ruby Creek, 15, 20
Rujing, 311
Rumsfeld, Donald, 450
Ryukyu Islands, 70, 448–49, 521

Sacramento State College, 397
Sacramento Valley, 386, 388, 401
Sahlins, Marshall: *Stone Age Economics*, 151–52
Saicho (Dengyo Daishi), 26
Saigon, South Vietnam, 196–97
Sailor Meadow, 330–33
St. Elias Range, 156
Saka (hiker), 597, 604
Sakaki, Nanao, 69–70, 75, 127, 163, 284, 606
Sakhalin, 520–21
Salisbury, Harrison, 415
Salish, 132, 313
Samantabhadra, 229
Sandburg, Carl, 104
Sanders, Ed, 417
San Francisco, CA, 10, 13, 26, 48, 51–52, 130, 178–80, 196, 329, 363, 396, 409, 417, 444, 502, 506–7, 509
San Francisco Chronicle, 358
San Francisco Examiner, 397
San Francisco Poetry Center, 179
San Francisco Zen Center, 142–43, 155
Sangha, 46, 148, 541
San Juan Islands, 14
San Juan Ridge, 254, 265, 281, 445, 483–84
Sansei, Yamao, 597, 604
Sanskrit, 66, 153, 159, 219, 276, 596, 601–2
Santayana, George, 96, 458
Sapper Creek (oil tanker), 225, 463
Sapporo, Japan, 518–19

Sarasvati (Vak), 63–64, 159, 229, 258
Sarawak, 335
Sartre, Jean-Paul, 30, 115
Sasaki, Shigetsu (Sokei-an), 52
Sauk Mountain, 15, 20
Sawyer, Lorenzo, 401
Schafer, Edward H., 579; "The Conservation of Nature under the T'ang Dynasty," 551, 553–55
Schell, Jonathan, 449
Schorer, Mark, 86, 88
Scollon, Ron and Suzanne, 273–75, 278
Scott Paper Company, 335
Scythians, 568
Sealaska Corporation, 244
Seattle, WA, 132, 179, 320, 329, 441, 463, 503
Seattle Art Museum, 132, 526
Secret History of the Mongols, 574–75
Sedro-Woolley, WA, 13–14
Selected Poems (Snyder), 410, 412
September 11 terrorist attacks, 449–50
Serpent Power, The, 53
Set, 31
Shakespeare, William, 207, 265; *Titus Andronicus*, 222
Shakya, 345
Shakyamuni Mantra, 601
Shamanism, 28, 61–62, 368
Shang dynasty, 530–33, 543, 568
Shanghai, China, 198
Shawnee, 107
Shenhui, 548
Shen Kuo, 555, 567
Shepard, Paul, 458
Shide, 333
Shih K'o, 552
Shijing, 231, 454–56, 532, 571
Shimane, Haruo: *Traces of Dreams*, 456
Shingon sect, 299, 594, 596
Shinkai (ashram resident), 69–70, 75

Shintoism, 289, 298, 305, 358, 454, 517, 594, 598, 605
Shiva, 61, 205, 208, 229, 258–59
Shokoku-ji monastery, 35–43, 136–38
Shoshone, 28, 134, 147, 319
Shugendo, 594
Shun, Emperor, 560
Shungnak, AK, 259–60, 264–70
Siberia, 249, 259, 520–21, 524–25, 527–28, 552–53
Sidney, Philip, 414
Siegerman, Beverly, 202
Sierra Club, 358
Sierra Nevada, 52, 174, 215, 246–50, 252–54, 281, 295, 309, 330–33, 338, 344, 357, 381, 383, 386, 388, 391, 393, 398, 402–3, 410, 425, 441–47, 480–90, 502, 507, 607–8
Sierra Pacific Industries, 402, 485
Sikhs, 198, 207
Sikkim, 53, 209–10
Silva, Lou, 254
Sima Qian, 537–38, 545, 560, 577
Singapore, 198
Sioux, 114, 283, 434
Siskiyou Mountains, 326
Siskiyou National Forest, 486
Siskon Gold, 253
Six Dynasties period, 539–43, 569
Six Gallery, 410
Skagit River, 3, 13, 17, 20
Skykomish, WA, 23
Slovic, Scott, 451
"Smokey the Bear Sutra" (Snyder), 355–59, 491–95
Snyder, Carole Koda (wife), 382, 402, 404, 421, 442, 474, 499, 501–2
Snyder, Ethel Wilkie (mother), 409
Snyder, Gen (son), 386, 421, 488
Snyder, Harold (father), 131–32, 313, 315, 409, 441
Snyder, Henry and Missouri (grandparents), 131, 266

Snyder, Joanne Kyger (wife), 193–98, 199–201
Snyder, Kai (son), 403, 421, 488
Snyder, Masa Uehara (wife), 69, 74–76
Snyder, Robin KJ (stepdaughter), 488, 499, 501–2
Snyder, Roy and Anna (uncle and aunt), 320
Socrates, 263–64
Sokatsu Shaku, 52
Sokei-an (Shigetsu Sasaki), 52
Son Buddhism, 456
Song dynasty, 36, 49, 59, 136, 297, 305, 311, 342, 546, 556, 558–59, 561, 567, 571–74, 578, 585–86
"Song of the Taste" (Snyder), 469–70
Sonoran Desert, 333, 388
Sophists, 279
Soto sect, 53, 136–37, 143, 229, 311
Sourdough Mountain ranger station, 8, 10, 15–16, 18–20
Southern Review, 149
South Vietnam, 196–98
Soviet Union, 50–51, 371, 418
Sowerby, Arthur, 552, 569
Soyen Shaku, 52
Spain, 60, 280, 426–27
Spenser, Edmund: *The Faerie Queene*, 414
Spicer, Jack, 114, 126, 417, 426
Spiegelberg, Frederick, 200
Spinoza, Baruch, 267
Squaw Valley, CA, 377
Sri Lanka, 143, 198
Stampe, Dudley, 528
State Department, U.S., 419
Statute of Merton, 240
Stevens, Wallace, 104–5, 114, 412
Stewart, Zach, 157
Stokes, John, 284
Stone, Christopher: "Should Trees Have Standing," 119, 122
Sufism, 49, 368

Sullivan, Michael, 584
Sun Chuo, 582
Sund, Robert, 161
Surre(gion)alist Manifesto, 251
Su Shi, 311, 455, 559, 567, 570–72; "On the Yangtze Watching the Hills," 570
Suwa-no-se Island, 69–76, 164, 303, 597
Suzuki, Teitaro, 52
Swan-Maiden myth, 84, 98–99
Swanton, John R., 60
Sweden, 241
Switzerland, 52, 240

Ta Ching I Tang Chih, 587–88
Tahoe National Forest, 399, 402, 445, 485
Taiwan, 70, 394, 426, 448, 454
Taku-chan, 74
Tampopo (film), 341
Tang dynasty, 35, 59, 133, 144, 303, 416, 545–46, 548, 550–51, 557–59, 568, 571, 573, 578
Tantra Buddhism, 27, 49, 55, 209
Tantra Hinduism, 205
Taoism. *See* Daoism
Tao Yuanming, 539
Tatewaki, Misao, 519–21
Tedlock, Dennis, 185
Teilhard de Chardin, Pierre, 105, 292, 368
Telugu, 259
Ten Commandments, 262
Tendai sect, 241, 297, 542, 596
Ten Directions, 434
Tennyson, Alfred, 470
Teutonic languages, 220
Texas, 218, 232
Thailand, 143, 337
Theravadin Buddhism, 142–43, 173
"This Tokyo" (Snyder), 433
Thomas, Dylan, 179
Thompson, D'Arcy, 68

Thompson, Ken, 18
Thoreau, Henry David, 267, 332, 409; Journals, 458; *Walden*, 21, 291; "Walking," 217, 220, 237, 279–80
Thunder Creek, 17–18, 20
Tibetan Buddhism, 209–11, 594
Tibet/Tibetan culture, 53, 116, 135, 139, 144, 166, 206, 209–11, 233, 305, 368, 573
Ting (cook), 340
Tiruttani temple, 258
Tjungurrayi, Jimmy, 284–85
Tlingit, 8, 244, 247
Todai-ji temple, 33
Tokugawa shogunate, 312
Tokyo, Japan, 28, 69, 193, 222, 312, 517, 520, 563
Tongass National Forest, 277
Topsay, Sonam, 209
Torrance, Robert, 426
Toshima Maru (Japanese freighter), 69–70, 75
"To the Chinese Comrades" (Snyder), 164
Tower Lake, 309
Tree Rings, 385
Trikaya, 30
Trilateral Commission, 163
Trinidad Head, 386–88
Trobriand Islands, 85
Trois Frères cave paintings, 61, 104, 474
Trust for Public Land, 225
Tuan Yifu, 567
Tu Fu, 115, 121, 366, 455, 548, 606
Turks, 557, 575–76
Turtle Island, 116–17, 163, 224, 248, 251, 298, 358, 372–73, 391, 396–97, 492, 606
Turtle Island (Snyder), 115–17, 147, 155, 158, 164, 369, 373, 410
Turtle Island Foundation, 185
Tyler, Royall, 597, 604

Uaji (Amami islander), 73
University of Alaska, 260, 272
University of California, Berkeley, 110, 134, 409, 420, 468, 505
University of California, Davis, 402, 410, 450, 499
University of Chicago, 151
University of Montana, 283
University of Washington, 444
Unterberg Poetry Center, 410
Upanishads, 53, 66, 133
Urdu, 276

Vajrasattva, 64
Vajrayana Buddhism, 49, 53, 299, 594, 596, 604
Vak (Sarasvati), 63–64, 159, 229, 258
Vallejo, César, 114
Vedanta, 52, 200
Vedas, 63, 66, 133, 173
Vierek, Peter, 97–98
Vietnam, 196–98, 336, 454, 539, 553, 559, 578
Vietnam War, 49, 56
Vikings, 489
Virgil, 187
Vimalakirti, 232
Vivekananda, 52

Wakayama, Japan, 25
Walden Pond, 355
Waldman, Anne, 417
Waley, Arthur, 133, 526
Wallace, David Rains, 451
Wang, C. W.: *The Forests of China*, 550–52
Wang Anshi, 21
Wang Hui, 588
Wang Wei, 455, 548–49; *Wang Chuan Villa*, 584–85
Wanshou monastery, 311
Warm Springs Lumber Company, 24, 316–22
Warner Range, 252–53

Warren, Austin: *Theory of Literature*, 96
Warring States period, 533, 538, 556
Wasco, 250, 319–20, 468, 482
Washington, 3–23, 107, 124, 238, 246, 313–15, 323, 344, 409, 441, 466–68, 481, 526, 606–7
Washington, DC, 158, 251, 316, 486
Washoe, 250
Watson, Burton, 340, 539, 548
Watts, Alan, 344, 369
Weinberger, Eliot, 438
Wei River, 329, 529
Welch, Lew, 126–27, 416–17
Wellek, René: *Theory of Literature*, 96
Wells, Ray, 319–20
Wenhui, 340
Wenzi, 300
Weston, Jessie: *From Ritual to Romance*, 104–5
Whalen, Philip, 15, 20, 110, 179, 416–17, 502–4
Wheeler, Doug, 391
Wheelwright, Philip, 97
White, Lynn, 61
Whitman, Walt, 104, 121–23; "By Blue Ontario's Shore," 123; "Passage to India," 56, 123; "Song of the Open Road," 123; "This Compost," 458
Wild Earth, 434
Wilderness Society, 314–15
Williams, William Carlos, 104–5, 409, 412, 415
Wintun, 399
Wishram, 146, 319, 468
Working the Woods, Working the Sea (anthology), 359
World War I, 52, 200, 320
World War II, 55, 140, 182, 289, 327, 417, 448, 475, 517, 528
Wovoka, 51
Wudi, Emperor, 538, 544–45

Xia dynasty, 560
Xia Gui, 587
Xian, China, 324
Xiaojing, 21
Xie He, 583
Xie Lingyun (Hsieh Ling-yun), 231, 455, 540–41, 546, 561, 568
Xuanzong, Emperor, 548, 550, 553

Yakamochi, Otomo no, 30
Yamabushi, 299, 358, 503, 593–98, 600, 603–4, 606
Yana, 309
Yang Szuhsu, 579
Yangtze River, 537, 546, 550–51, 555, 559, 568, 570, 577–78, 586
Yang Wanli, 571
Yeats, William Butler, 49, 105–6, 137, 412
Yellow (Huang) River, 524, 528–30, 546, 550, 552, 577
Yellow Turban revolt, 49
Yen Wen-kuei, 588
Yokohama, Japan, 193–94, 463
Yokokawa temples, 241
Yosemite National Park, 164, 409, 413, 441, 484
Yoshikawa, Kojuro, 571–72
Yoshino, Japan, 299, 597–99
Yoshino-Kumano National Park, 599
Yuan dynasty, 586

Yuba River, 249, 254, 382, 386, 392, 398, 401, 442, 445, 495, 502
Yuba Watershed Institute, 385, 403, 410, 483
Yueh Ling, 553–54
Yugoslavia, 181
Yukon, 218, 227
Yupik, 257, 276, 279

Zao the Mountain King, 597–99, 602
Zeami, 341, 459
Zen Buddhism, 26, 29, 37–43, 49, 116, 133, 139–40, 142, 144, 156, 160, 164, 174, 194, 209–10, 267, 309, 312, 342, 345, 348–51, 368, 409–10, 456, 459, 480, 499, 537, 563, 580, 587, 594–95; Rinzai sect, 35, 52–53, 136–38, 143, 311, 341, 372, 469; Soto sect, 53, 136–37, 143, 229, 311; Tendai sect, 241, 297, 542, 596; Zen Master, 27–28, 35–36, 52, 113, 136, 344
Zenki, 603
Zhang Yan, 302–3
Zhaozhou Congshen, 28
Zhengzhou, China, 531–32
Zhou dynasty, 532–33, 538, 556
Zhuang Zhou (Chuang-tzu), 143, 293, 339–40, 343, 521, 526
Zong Bing, 588

*This book is set in 10 point ITC Galliard, a face designed
for digital composition by Matthew Carter and based
on the sixteenth-century face Granjon. The paper is acid-free
lightweight opaque that will not turn yellow or brittle with age.
The binding is sewn, which allows the book to open easily and lie flat.
The binding board is covered in Brillianta, a woven rayon cloth
made by Van Heek–Scholco Textielfabrieken, Holland.
Composition by Westchester Publishing Services.
Printing by Sheridan, Grand Rapids, MI.
Binding by Dekker Bookbinding, Wyoming, MI.
Designed by Bruce Campbell.*